THE SOUL OF

A SYMPATHETIC STUDY
RELIGIOUS PRACTICES
THE BANTU TRIBE

By

W. C. WILLOUGHBY

PROFESSOR OF MISSIONS IN AFRICA, KENNEDY SCHOOL OF MISSIONS,
HARTFORD SEMINARY FOUNDATION

"No man can know religion who approaches it from its earth-
ward side; to be readily understood, it must be read in the light
of its celestial source."
(From Principal A. M. Fairbairn's Introduction
[p. ix] to Jordan's *Comparative Religion*.)

"Like plants in mines which never saw the sun,
But dream of him, and guess where he may be,
And do their best to climb and get to him."
BROWNING'S *Paracelsus*.

GARDEN CITY, NEW YORK
DOUBLEDAY, DORAN & COMPANY, INC.
1928

PREFACE

WHEN Ananias, the moth, wrote his slashing attack *On Caterpillars*, he produced one of the "best sellers" of the season; and Sapphira, the caterpillar, ran him close when she dipped her pen in gall and told the world what she felt about *The High-fliers*; for both writers were fluent of speech, touched with a fine frenzy that spurned inconvenient evidence, and wedded, moreover, to their own opinions. Entomologists poured contempt on both books, it is true; but the crowd, finding its fancy tickled by caterpillars squirming and moths airing their self-complacency, sneered at the spoil-sports for mooning about in out-of-the-way places, treating bugs as bosom friends, and never coming to market. So both books went off like hot-cross buns on Good Friday morning, and nobody cared for digestion.

This book is written in another temper, and looks for no such high reward. In the belief that the law of the upward urge (the attractive force of the Divine) is as universal in its application to humanity as the law of gravitation, it examines Bantu ancestor-worship, hoping to find some particle of good therein that can be used for the moral and social betterment of the men who hold it dear, and especially for reconciling them to the most uplifting influence that has ever played upon humanity—the religion of Jesus. From its pages the prosaic fact stands forth clear, I think, that the Bantu are neither more nor less than people who differ from us in nothing that is essential to humanity, being strange only in this, that they are but now passing through a phase of civilisation that our fathers outgrew ages ago and their children have forgotten.

The book that I have tried to write is really overdue. A great change has come over Africa during the last two or three decades: Government officials, professional men, publicists, merchants, and missionaries, are alike facing the human problem in Africa as never before; and facing it as practical men, not as dilettanti. They have come to see that he who does not deal justly with a tribesman, can never help him to fit himself for an honourable place in the world, and that if we are to do him justice we must look out on life through his eyes; and so they have made it their business to study the life of the tribe or group of tribes around them, and to assess afresh the ethical values of Bantu social tradition. Some have written books on the subject, or articles for the Journals of learned Societies; but many plod on with their chosen task, content to know without publishing their knowledge. One or two African governments, sure of their need of an intimate knowledge of people whom they rule, have set apart officers for the study of social anthropology in their territories, and others, with slenderer purses, encourage their Native Affairs officials to give time and thought to this subject. Regional studies in social anthropology were never so popular in Africa as they are to-day; and yet no one who knows the Bantu at first hand has tried to gather up and compare all that has been discovered concerning their religion, though all admit that their religion holds the key to their mentality and that without understanding it we cannot get at the heart of their thought on the ordinary affairs of life. Macdonald's *Africana* and Rowley's *Religion of the Africans,* both useful books, were written nearly half a century ago, before much was known about Bantu religion. Le Roy's *Religion of the Primitives,* a much more recent book, hardly comes in this category; for he ran in blinkers and dealt in *ex cathedra* deliverances and fulminations rather than carefully sifted evidence. No other book in the English tongue, so far as I know, attempts the task. Whether I have succeeded in filling the gap, others must judge; but I am sure that students of comparative religion in our home colleges and people who are doing actual field-work in Africa are calling for a comparative conspectus of what has been written concerning Bantu ancestor-worship; and if my book provokes an abler man to write a better, that will be recompense enough for my labour.

A word or two of explanation may prevent misunderstanding. Some people say it is wrong to speak of "the Bantu race": that there is a Bantu *family of languages,* but no Bantu *race.* They base their opinion upon the exploded notion that "race" can be precisely and scientifically defined in terms of biology; but I hold that it is a convenient descriptive term—like "nationality," only vaguer—for a great group of communities which share the same culture and tradition, and that the Bantu-speaking tribes have a common culture and tradition that is as distinctive as their common speech,—though both, being human, share many things with other branches of humanity.

This volume deals only with ancestor-worship, and neglects many "magico-religious practices and beliefs of the Bantu tribes." It is complete in itself, however, and if it pays the cost of production, I hope to issue a second volume (much of which is already written) on Nature-worship, High Gods, the Supreme Being, Taboo, and Magic; and then the sub-title of the book will be fully justified.

Much space might have been saved by giving the gist of what writers have said and the page on which they said it, instead of quoting them verbatim; by omitting footnotes that men versed in the classics and comparative religion can well do without; and by severely pruning the General Index. But the book is intended to help busy field-workers in Africa who cannot give much time to the classics and comparative religion nor come within a hundred miles of a library, as well as students at home; and these people are not content with a ready-to-wear judgment, however shapely its pattern; they want to ponder the evidence and form their own opinion. Many facts specified in the text illustrate other aspects of belief than those which caused me to cite them; and yet it was out of the question to quote them again in other connections. I have therefore tried to supply what is needed by rearranging the facts in a very copious General Index, which has the additional advantage of making the book more useful as a source-book in Bantu ancestor-worship for students of comparative religion and social anthropology.

Readers have a right to know what my qualification is for the task that I have undertaken. While I was working as a missionary among the Bamangwato, Khama, then chief of that tribe (better known as "King Khama"), seeking my advice in a boundary dispute, made it easy for me to gain insight into the customary land-laws of his people; and I became deeply interested in their views of land-rights. After judgment had been given in favour of the tribe, I told Khama of my desire to make a thorough study of the tribal conception of life—law, religion,

custom, folklore: and he made my path easy by publicly appoint-
ing one or two of his wise old men to instruct me in these subjects.
For a quarter of a century after that I diligently studied the life
and thought of tribes between the Vaal and the Zambesi, and read
widely in relevant literature.   The more I knew, the more ready
were my native neighbours to correct my mistakes and provide
what was lacking in my knowledge.   My duties brought me into
close touch with old native men and women all over the country
who were steeped in the collective impressions of their own communities, and I had hundreds of enlightening conversations with
them; but it was my habit to set apart definite periods every week
for being tutored in native law and custom by wise old men of
the tribe with which I happened to be living, and to use the type-
writer freely when they talked and when I was reading what
other observers have written on this theme.   In this way my files
became well stocked with information that had been closely scrutinised and carefully sifted.   In 1919, having to retire from
Africa, I was called to the Chair of Missions in Africa in the
Kennedy School of Missions, which is one of the three constituent
schools of the Hartford Seminary Foundation—an "interdenomi-
national university of religion," as it is called in its charter, with
a staff of thirty professors and twenty-five lecturers, and a library
of over a hundred and twenty-six thousand books.   Here I have
had leisure to think through the mass of notes that I had written
in Africa and keep abreast of current literature on Bantu life, and
the rare privilege of turning when in doubt to colleagues who are
acknowledged authorities in their own fields of sacred learning.
And another godsend has been given me: missionaries on fur-
lough, many of them from Africa, come to Hartford for post-
graduate study, and I owe them much for their criticisms and
suggestions.

It is an axiom among astronomers, I am told, that no observer's
work is reliable till his personal equation is known—the allowance that must be made in all his observations for his personal
peculiarity of vision; and unfortunately there is no known scientific method of accurately measuring the personal equation of
an observer of Bantu religion.   I have tried to put truth always
in the place of pre-eminence, and am not conscious of having any
other end in view; but I am aware that when a white man writes

on African religion, he is providing, not knowledge, but enlightened opinion, or else unenlightened opinion; and every student who uses this book must test my judgments for himself. I do not claim to have given a final interpretation of Bantu ancestor-worship; I have but tried to do a little intensive cultivation in a field that has hitherto had only its surface scratched. Throughout a long and active life I have worked in the faith that God has never ceased striving to clear the vision and nerve the will to righteousness of even the most backward races; that for them as for us it is the Divine within that is the hope of glory; and every year of labour has given me a firmer grip upon this inspiring belief. Whatever else I doubt, I am sure of this: that he who regards the religious ideas with which this book teems as the incoherent babblings of disordered fancy, will miss whatever of value they contain, and that he who regards them as responses of the human spirit to the Eternal Spirit that broods over humanity, can never willingly lie idle in a world where they exist.

CONTENTS

Having obtained a general idea of what the Bantu mean by
the souls of the living and the spirits of the dead, we proceed to
examine their conception of the relation between living men and
the worshipful dead. The first step in this inquiry is to discover
the ways in which the spirits of the dead are thought to reveal
their will to the living.

The second step in our inquiry is to ascertain what events
move the Bantu to seek the help of these divinities; for the nature of these events is indicative of the character and extent of
the influence of the gods upon the everyday life of the people.

CONTENTS

INTRODUCTION

RELATION OF THE MISSIONARY TO BANTU RELIGION

A CRAFTSMAN MUST KNOW HIS MATERIALS AS WELL AS HIS TOOLS

INTELLIGENT amateur missionaries have found interesting and useful employment in Africa; but the needs of Africa can never be met without a liberal supply of men and women trained in missionary craftsmanship. Now three things are necessary for skilled craftsmanship: a knowledge of the tools and how to use them, a knowledge of the materials and how they will behave under the tools, and a constructional plan of the finished article. Most missionaries gain a knowledge of their tools in the Divinity School before appointment, and also some knowledge of the materials that they would have worked on had they remained in the old land; but until lately there has been no serious and systematic attempt to familiarise them with the peculiar qualities of the very different materials which they will have to handle in Africa. That has been left to chance and a missionary's own predilections. And here it is not impertinent to remark that the most helpless man in our caravan when a wheel [1] broke down in what afterwards became German East Africa, was a wheelwright without his tools or the materials with which he had been accustomed to work—though there were fifty miles of timber around the scene of the disaster and all the tools that a sailor used to remedy the defect.

It would be easy and perhaps not unprofitable to push our analogy a little further. In comparison with a carpenter or a mason, an architect has a more profound and scientific knowledge of the behaviour of his materials under stress, strain, torsion, weather, etc., and, inspired by a vision which eye hath not seen, he is able to combine his materials in forms of beauty and stability

---

[1] We were taking up heavy sections of a steel lifeboat, each mounted on a pair of wheels.

by bringing the component parts of the design down to the compass of the man at the bench. But this is not the place to discuss the need for architectural planning in Missions, or the loss that is entailed when an architect is compelled to do what an artisan could do better, or when an artisan is set to do architect's work. Here, the emphasis must be laid on only one point in the analogy—the need for knowledge of the materials with which we have to work. An African missionary may be master of exegesis, dogmatic and pastoral theology, homiletics, and all the other beautiful tools in his kit, but he is not a craftsman in Missions till he has made a profound and sympathetic study of the tribesman. And in this, as in other fields of investigation, the more scientific the method, the more accurate is the finding.

The psychical unity of the human race is more evident than even the physiological. In every variety of humanity the same elemental passions, emotions, and instincts are displayed; and men who have not yet acknowledged the sovereignty of reason, everywhere arm themselves with similar weapons against both their physical and spiritual foes. The African may be primitive in his ideas,—if only we knew what the word "primitive" means: he is certainly un-European; but he does not stand alone; he belongs to the genus *homo sapiens*, and can never be understood till he is studied in conjunction with other varieties of man. Hence it is that the ritual of his old religion must be compared with that of his congeners in other parts of the world, if we are to discover what it was meant to express, or even what those who now use it are really feeling after,—a discovery that missionaries *must* make whatever else they neglect.

MISSIONARIES MUST STUDY AFRICAN RELIGION

In the introductory chapter to his *Religion of the Semites* Robertson Smith says:[1] "No positive religion that has moved men has been able to start with a *tabula rasa*, and express itself as if religion were beginning for the first time; in form, if not in substance, the new system must be in contact all along the line with the older ideas and practices which it finds in possession. A new scheme of faith can find a hearing only by appealing to

[1] RS. 2.

religious instincts and susceptibilities that already exist in its audience, and it cannot reach these without taking account of the traditional forms in which all religious feeling is embodied, and without speaking a language which men accustomed to these old forms can understand." From this generalisation our author proceeds to draw the conclusion that we must know the traditional religion that preceded a positive religion before we can thoroughly comprehend the latter. This is clear thinking. Physiologists dare not limit their investigation to the primates, for they know that an adequate understanding of these complex structures is unattainable by the man who has ignored the simpler forms of life; and Christianity can never tell its own tale to a theologian who has never paid any attention to the lowlier religions of the world. But there is another deduction that may be logically drawn from Robertson Smith's generalisation—a deduction, moreover, that is of profound interest to African missionaries: teachers of a new scheme of faith must be familiar with the traditional forms in which the religious feeling of their pupils has hitherto embodied itself. To cut a man completely away from the heritage that his ancestors left him, the mental and spiritual environment of his earlier years, would be to sever him from all that he has hitherto held sacred. Such an operation would probably involve the irreparable damage of cutting the nerve of reverence, but is providentially unachievable even by missionaries of impetuous temper,—pocket editions of Napoleon rather than of Jesus. The new must be embodied in the old if it is to replace the old weakness with a new strength. Or, to jump from the metaphor of dietetics to that of arboriculture, if the True Vine is to branch and fruit in Africa, it must enter into vital relationship with all that it is able to assimilate of the African soil. The doctrine of the Incarnation carries with it the corollary that an African need not become a European before Christ can dwell in him, any more than a European need become a Jew. Missionaries must meet the African where he is if they wish to lead him up to where he ought to be. We cannot teach him to fill out his old forms with a fuller meaning, nor show him a more excellent way of expressing or of satisfying his aspirations, until we so master his forms and expressions as to become sure of the nature of his cravings and discontents.

Even those who regard Christian Missions as an attack upon false religions must admit that an invading army is likely to meet with some very unpleasant surprises if it is unacquainted with the nature and disposition of the forces that are arrayed against it. But one hardly likes to use a military metaphor in speaking of the relation of Christianity to another religion. Such metaphors are appropriate to warfare with evil; but though there is evil in the old religion of Africa, we may be sure that all that is best in African life will also find expression there. Terms of evolution are preferable to terms of conquest in speaking of the progress of Christianity in heathen lands.

JESUS CAME TO FULFIL, NOT TO DESTROY

Jesus came to fulfil, not to destroy, the best in every religion; and his ambassadors must ascertain by sympathetic study what these best elements are. We shall discover elements in African religion that we cannot encourage, though truth will compel us to confess that even some of these have been historically useful in saving the African from greater evils than those which have befallen him. We shall find others that we can retain and ennoble, when once we recognise them for what they are—efforts of the soul to respond, in spite of darkness and difficulty, to that homing instinct which God has implanted in it—signs that God did not leave the Africans without a witness, and that in their lives, too, religion is the deepest thing.

Man emerges slowly from the mists of the valley of error, escaping the distortion of its false lights only by tedious and toilsome climbing. In spite of the teaching of Jesus and all that Paul said at Lystra and Athens, orthodox Christians believed for many centuries that every religion but their own was a devilish delusion. It was thought, or at any rate believed, that the spirit of God had been sensitising the moral faculties and clearing the spiritual vision of the Jews till they made the Great Refusal, and afterwards of those Europeans whose ability or fortune enabled them to discern the mistake that the Jews had made, but that God had left the mass of mankind to their own unaided devices—a belief not one whit more reasonable than the notion that tribes unable to formulate the law of gravitation are *ipso facto* beyond its influence. It is true that the vast majority of men attribute their inspiration and restraint to other sources, just as they give another explanation of the phenomenon of gravitation, when they trouble themselves about it at all; but that proves nothing more than their need of a liberal education. When Cyrus, sweeping down from the north with his victorious bands, was hailed as liberator by the priests and nobles of Babylon, he authorised the inscription of a cylinder, now in the British Museum, whereon he states definitely that he had been inspired and helped by the gods of Babylon to become liberator of oppressed people. Now, a certain literary prophet, who was at that time captive in Mesopotamia, has left us a remarkable paragraph in which he declares that though Cyrus never knew it, it was really God who inspired him.[1] The prophet was altogether too sanguine as to the results of Cyrus's victory; but in this assertion he was not mistaken; for, as he phrases it, putting his words into the mouth of God: "I am the Lord, and there is none else; beside me there is no God." In their failure to recognise the origin of the light that plays upon them, men often attribute their inspiration to wrong sources. When the true light which lighteth every man was in the world that was made by him, the world knew him not, so the writer of the Fourth Gospel asserts; and the Synoptists agree that the Pharisees thought the power of Jesus flowed forth from a devilish fount [2]—all of which is too human to be astonishing. We marvel more when Paul sounds the unfathomed depths of human thought and feeling, and tells the Athenians that God has so framed the races of mankind that they should all search for him and feel after him, in the hope of finding him who is always near them. As for people of primitive culture, they are unable to explain any but the simplest facts of human experience, and these, often, in a superficial manner; but, whether they know it or not, the spirit of God plays upon their souls, also, seeking to mould their thoughts and actions. If that be untrue, there is no hope for the missionary, and less than none for the people.

[1] Isa. xliv. 28-xlv. 7.
[2] Mt. xii. 24, Mk. iii. 22, Lk. xi. 15.

SUPERCILIOUS EUROPEANS

Many European residents in Africa are intolerant of native custom, irritated by native religion, and contemptuous of native law; and since their superciliousness is born of mere dislike for the unlike, not of enthusiasm for something better, they rapidly destroy the growths of tribal morality, leaving the ground, not only bare, but blighted. Let me confess at once that there is nothing in Bantu religion that appeals to the æsthetic tastes of Europeans: no domes and cupolas that flit dreamlike in the shimmering sunlight; no canopies or robes of broidered gold; no music rising with voluptuous swell. Its uncouthness and immaturity tempts one to be glib of censure, rather than to sympathise and understand. It is the easiest thing in the world for a European to sum up disdainfully all the sanctions of African religion and morality in the vague word, "superstition," [1] a term that is used freely by those who cannot define it, and very sparingly by those who can; but tribesmen, though neither philosophers nor statisticians, see plainly enough that youths who were controlled by these crude old tribal sanctions before they went to great labour centres, like the Witwatersrand, are almost impossible of restraint after their old notions have been merely laughed out of them. Happily, better days are dawning. In the last decades an increasing number of administrators, legislators, missionaries, professional men, merchants, and journalists have studied the native in a scientific temper, or, if you prefer to phrase it in terms of mercy rather than justice, in a Christian spirit, seeking to understand his mentality, so as to deal with him according to the Golden Rule; and, although it takes time for the thoughts of leading thinkers to soak down into the minds of the multitude, echoes of their well-grounded opinions are already heard in the street, the mine, and the camp.

CHRISTIANITY, NOT A FOREIGN RELIGION

One of the dangers that threaten Africa is that Africans may come to regard Christianity as a white-man's religion. It is of paramount importance, therefore, that the religion of Jesus

[1] "Superstition" is the husk of religion without the kernel.

should be presented to them as the full expression of that for which their fathers groped. We must take pains so to preach the truth to the African that he may not mistake it for something foreign to his own life; which means that we must link it on to the best of his aspirations. Africans are not free from race prejudice: it would be astonishing if they were. Seeing that that primitive passion is still strong among nations whose methods of thought were profoundly influenced for centuries by the strong thinkers of Greece and Rome, and later by the logical methods of what is termed science by some and common sense by others, it would be folly to expect that it should be less pronounced in the little parochial communities of Africa, however much their weakness may have taught them to hide their thoughts from the strong. Now the Enemy (whoever or whatever the Enemy may be) will certainly use this prejudice to close the hearts of the people against the Gospel; and it is a grand thing so to present the Gospel as to lift it clear above the distortion of this miasmatic fog.

INSIGHT INTO HEATHENISM HELPFUL IN CHURCH DISCIPLINE

A convert from heathenism cannot suddenly divest himself of what a hundred generations have woven into every strand of his mental and moral nature. Or, to speak in terms of another metaphor which has come to be almost a part of Christianity, the seed sown may be of the very best quality, and the soil may be suited to the new crop; but old hopes, fears, ideas, and impulses spring up—stray seeds of former crops that the field carried. One's past does not lie behind, but within. Of all the hours of pain and anxiety that fall to the lot of an African missionary, none are more burdensome than those in which he has to deal with cases of discipline in the Church. Torn between sympathy for the frailties of a frail people and the duty of keeping the Church's ideal untarnished, he realises then that it is his task to relate the spirit of Christ to the problems that African converts have to face, and that for this purpose close association with the spirit of Christ is not enough, but that there must be intimate acquaintance, also, with the heathenism of the convert's past life and present surroundings. If he would secure anything like the sure touch of a skilful surgeon in handling his spiritual patients, he must ascertain what it is that pulls at their heart-strings and plays upon their passions. Hence his need for social anthropology. For, as Professor Marett has beautifully phrased it: "The ultimate aim of folklore and of its ally, social anthropology, is to illustrate and explain the workings of the human soul."[1]

SPIRITUAL PATHOLOGY

Some people say that though psychological or anthropological investigation may be an interesting and permissible recreation for an African missionary, yet it can have no useful meaning for his converts. This idea, born of misapprehension, is often related to that mistaken attitude towards science that was in vogue among Christians fifty years ago, before they came to see that all truth is of God and that all its parts must harmonise if only they can be seen without astigmatism. A missionary who neglects the field of psychological and anthropological enquiry is sure to make unnecessary and preventable blunders, unless he is guided by some colleague who is better informed. The ideal missionary must be a spiritual pathologist.

Now, modern pathology works back from evident symptoms towards unseen pathogenic fiends that trouble the patient. Mosquitoes, ticks, tsetse flies, rat fleas, filaria and trypanosomes never bothered the brains of the kindly old family doctor of a century ago; but the modern medical practitioner (especially in a tropical country) knows that thorough understanding of these creatures may add more to his professional proficiency than knowledge of drugs, diagnosis, and diet. If he were to discuss the theories and deductions of entomologists and bacteriologists with any but the instructed few among his patients, he would be sadly lacking in discretion; but he would be still more undiscerning if he did not silently base his practice upon the best work that the experts have done. It is true that the discoveries of bacteriologists are incomprehensible to many diphtheria and lock-jaw patients; but in the hands of a capable man these theories of the laboratory have a helpful meaning even for them: they mean the easy and inexpensive control of diseases that used to defy the ablest and

[1] *Psychology and Folk-lore.* London: Methuen, 1920, p. 4.

richest; they mean, in short, the difference between recovery and the grave.

Up-to-date and fully qualified medical men who accept appointment in tropical countries are wont to take a post-graduate course in tropical medicine. Is there any inherent reason why the man who has the cure of souls should be less scientific in temper and method than his brother of the scalpel and phial? Without an analogous discipline, it is no more easy for a fully qualified spiritual practitioner to deal with the tropical diseases of the soul, or to detect the causes of that low spiritual vitality that he will discover among his converts. And a missionary's mistakes are much more serious than those of a doctor. The old saw has it that "A doctor's mistakes are buried"; most of them are, though some outlive the doctor; but a missionary's mistakes are all sent forth to propagate their species among a people who are just entering into the real world of life and thought.

RITUAL IS A VARIETY OF THE VERNACULAR

One word more. "Savage religion is something not so much thought out as danced out," if I may use one of Professor Marett's [1] finely chiseled aphorisms; "it develops under conditions, psychological and sociological, which favour emotional and motor processes, whereas ideation remains relatively in abeyance." The Bantu have made little effort to think out the religion that gives them what hope and confidence they possess; their religion is, indeed, so nearly inarticulate that it habitually seeks expression in gesture-language. John Oxenham says [2] that writers are at times "worried by some thought which dances within them and stubbornly refuses to be satisfied with the sober dress of prose. For their own satisfaction and relief in such a case, if they be not fools, they endeavour to garb it more to its liking, and so find peace." This is true not only of the wizards of words who catch the best thoughts that hover tantalisingly before a cultured people, but also of backward races who have not acquired the faculty of writing, and whose prose, poetry, art, and ritual are alike uncouth. When tribesmen strive to kiss the

[1] *Threshold of Religion*, p. xxxi.
[2] Preface to *Bees in Amber*.

hem of the garment of the unseen, unspeakable thoughts clamour within them for the garb of ritual, and will not be denied; hence it is that every tribe in Africa has a ritual of politeness, as well as of worship, and a ritual of affection, of respect, of authority, of hospitality, of medicine, of war, and of social organisation; all of which, like art, try to express what words are too small to utter,—not the trifles of the soul, but its immensities.   Speech has been called broken light upon the depth of the unspoken; and ritual, even more than speech, is liable to veil what it tries to reveal.   Nevertheless, Bantu ritual is an important form of Bantu utterance, and a clear understanding of it would conduce to the discovery of the Bantu soul.   We spend much time with Grammar and Dictionary, because we know that our success depends upon familiarity with the vernacular, and we do not allow the uncouthness or uncleanness of verbal expressions to alienate us from our task.   Why are we offended at what seems the frippery of a barbarous ritual and disinclined to master this form of utterance?   If we are to penetrate the Bantu soul, we must be willing to travel with unshod feet by any avenue that is open to us, compelled at times to withhold approval, but always ready to show an appreciation that is born of sympathetic understanding.

CHAPTER I

ANCESTOR-SPIRITS

RELIGION, THE BASIS OF BANTU LIFE

BANTU life is essentially religious. The relation of the individual to the family, the clan, and the tribe,—politics, ethics,
law, war, status, social amenities, festivals,—all that is good and
much that is bad in Bantu life is grounded in Bantu religion.
Religion so pervades the life of the people that it regulates their
doings and governs their leisure to an extent that it is hard for
Europeans to imagine. Materialistic influences from Europe are
playing upon Africa at a thousand points and may break up Bantu
life; but the Bantu are hardly likely to be secularised, for they
will never be content without a religion that is able to touch
every phase of life and to interpret the divine in terms of
humanity.

·Bantu religion consists of animism [1] and ancestor-worship.
Animism everywhere obtrudes itself upon the African traveller.
Ancestor-worship is almost as conspicuous in Central Africa; but
casual observers have spent a year or two with tribes south of the
Zambesi and with some tribes in West Africa without suspecting
its existence. Nevertheless, it is everywhere present in Bantu
Africa and always normative to Bantu thought. It is the basis of
their political institutions, the pre-supposition of their law and
ethics, and the key to an understanding of their social life. "Until

[1] Animism is a term that has different meanings with different writers. In its
older sense, it stands for the attribution of a living soul to inanimate objects and
natural phenomena. And it is in that older sense that the term is consistently used
throughout this book. Later, as Murray's Oxford Dictionary points out, it came
to be extended polemically to belief in the existence of the soul as apart from the
body. This double use of the term tends to confusion of thought. In its later
use it makes ancestor-worship a mere phase of animism,—which may or may not be
true. Ancestor-worship and animism certainly have much in common; but the difference between them is so great that we cannot do without a term to denote the
one as distinct from the other. At any rate, we can hardly tie up our parcel till
we have done our shopping.

this point has been thoroughly grasped," as Hobley says,[1] "we are bound to be perpetually brought face to face with absolute enigmas." He naturally adds, "It is therefore maintained that the study of these questions is not merely academic but one of the greatest practical value to the administrator, the missionary, and the colonist, as well as the student."

SURVIVAL AFTER DEATH

To the Bantu, survival after death is not a matter for argument or speculation; it is an axiom of life. Those of them who have not been directly or indirectly influenced by the White-man have never doubted it, or even asked why they should believe it; just as they have never doubted the evidence of their senses or thought of asking why they should trust themselves to its leading. And the belief is general. What Budge says of the ancient Egyptians is equally true of the modern Bantu: "The Egyptian might be more or less religious according to his nature and temperament, but, judging from the writings of his priests and teachers which are now in our hands, the man who was without religion and God in some form or other was most rare, if not unknown."[2] The champion scamp in a Bantu tribe believes in survival after death as thoroughly as the most trustworthy and respected of his neighbours. Neither of them, when they bury their dead, hesitates for a moment to express the hope of seeing them again; and "when souls are passing over, those who remain send greetings to those who have gone before."[3] So far are they from regarding death as extinction that the euphemism o *ipolokile* ("he has saved himself") is an everyday Becwana expression for "he is dead," and so is the use of the verb "to go" as an equivalent of "to die." The embryonic posture of the corpse, which is so common among the Bantu, is usually thought to indicate belief that death is merely birth into another life. Ask the younger generation of tribesmen their reason for placing the body in this attitude, and the reply is, "Our custom,"—than which nothing can be more final; but if you sympathetically discuss the matter with old men

[1] BBM. 281, 283.
[2] EM. 234.
[3] WBT. 293.

who trust you, you will be told that a man can rise up quicker from a sitting than a recumbent posture. The evidence in favour of a general Bantu belief in survival after death is, in fact, so overwhelming that it is unnecessary to labour this point.

ORIGIN OF THE IDEA

If, pushing out enquiries further, we ask what it was that first gave them the notion that death is not the end of life, we open up a fine field for the imagination. The belief appears to be as old as the human race; the funerary rites of the cave-men of the Upper Paleolithic Age prove that they, at any rate, thought it necessary to provide for the future well-being of those whom they buried. Bantu legends attribute man's immortality, and his knowledge of it, to a message from God.[1] After God had made man, so runs the tale that is told with many variations by the grey-heads of many tribes, he sent one of his slower creatures, some say a chameleon, to tell man that he was not to die, or, as others have it, that dying he was to rise again. Later he sent another messenger, as chiefs are sometimes known to do, with a confirmatory message. The second runner, with nimbler feet and slacker brain, or, as other versions suggest, a love of trickery, arrived first with a garbled message: "God says you are to die, and dying leave the world for good." When the correct message came, it was too late, for death had already set in.[2]

Such are their guesses; ours, though less quaint, are none the less conjectural. Homer pictured sleep and death as twin-brothers; and Tylor's theory [3] that the idea of soul and spirit has

[1] One wonders whether the Bantu have not borrowed this story from the Hottentots; the Hottentot story has at any rate more point to it, especially if we remember that they look upon the moon as a minor deity. "They relate that the moon wished one day to send a message to men. The hare offered to carry it. 'Go tell men that they shall rise again, just as I die and rise again,' said he. But the hare attempted to deceive men, and said to them, 'You shall die as I myself die.' To punish him, the moon cursed him. Behold why, among the Namaqua, men must abstain from eating the flesh of the hare." Quatrefages: *The Pygmies* (Appleton & Co., New York), pp. 217-18.

[2] For other versions of this legend and other legends on the same theme, see ABN. 163, AK. 107, HB. 49, IPNR. ii. 101, LSAT. ii. 328, WN. i. 106, 117, 133, 173, 177, 192, 195.

[3] *Primitive Culture*, London, 1871, i. 428 ff., and ii. 143 ff.; *Early History of Mankind*, London: Murray, 1878, pp. 5 ff.; *Anthropology*, London: Macmillan, 1881, pp. 343 ff.

been woven out of the vaporous "dream-figures" of normal sleep and abnormal hallucination, is, perhaps, as good as any other. "The soul can leave the body," says a writer from the lower Congo, ". . . operate independently of it, and return to it at will. It is the explanation of a dream. The soul slips out of the body and talks, sees, hears, travels, and capers entirely on its own account. When out of the body, which it leaves snug under its blanket, it knows neither time nor space. It hunts in distant jungles, interviews dead acquaintances, enjoys the most delightful excursions, performs sensational feats, and gets back to its old clay tenement before the cocks begin to crow in the morning. What better evidence of the existence of a soul does a negro want than that? He has known his own soul stand and look at its own habitat lying as though stark dead on its sleeping-mat before it has got into it in time to rouse it up at break of day. He has even dreamt of his own funeral when his soul has played him the trick of pretending to lead him off to the burial ground. Whilst *nitu* (body) sleeps; *mwanda* (soul) enjoys itself." [1] How much of the gleam of sarcasm is due to the gay impressionism of this writer's style, I cannot undertake to say; but so far as I can see, a truth revealed to man by such a method may be as well worth while as if traced by an occult hand upon the walls of a king's palace, or written by a super-human finger upon tablets of stone, or uttered by an angel visitant from the realms of light, or penned by an inspired seer. God must talk in baby-talk if he is to talk understandingly to babies at all, and his methods of revelation are not limited to the supernatural. Indeed, a truth woven into the fibre of the human soul would be independent of that extrinsic evidence that we rightly demand in support of a theophany.

INATTENTION TO THE NATURE OF THE SOUL AND ITS AFTER-LIFE

All the information that we can gain from Bantu sources concerning the nature of the soul, is of an incidental variety. We have no written literature to aid us, not even such epitaphs as those that illuminate the eschatological beliefs of ancient Mediter-

[1] WBT. 289.

ranean paganism; but we have a great body of ritual, if only we can master its meaning; and we may safely assume, I think, that ritual and belief are correlated, whether belief gave birth to ritual or ritual bred belief. From both the spoken and acted utterances of the people we gather that there is a close connection between the soul, the shadow, the breath, the blood, and the contents of the chest cavity, these last being loosely and generally mentioned in the vernaculars as the "heart," though every Native can give a distinct name to each chest organ if he stays to think about it.

There is, however, very little speculation concerning the nature of the soul and its after-life. The Bantu are keen observers of nature, with an extensive knowledge of their tribal domain and its productions, a name for almost every animal or vegetable in the veld, and an intimate acquaintance with its habits, its uses, and its dangers. Their magical notions of nature often blind them to what would be fairly obvious to a naturalist; but it would take a bulky volume to contain all that they know of their environment. In all fields of inquiry, however, their interest has been strictly utilitarian: scenery does not appeal to them, but fertility does; and they have no use for theoretical speculation. Their thoughts and traditions concerning the origin of things consist largely of bizarre legends, most of which are witty sarcasms on the habits and peculiarities of animals, rather than serious attempts to account for them. God made the world and all that it contains. That is enough. Their thirst for knowledge is soon quenched. Nor have they bestowed more thought upon the nature and destiny of man; with them the individual is almost lost in the crowd, and crowds are animated by emotions rather than ideas. When they talk about the soul, they utter feelings rather than mental conceptions; and unsolved problems of the after-life do not worry them at all. A tribesman finds life peopled with a great number of beings analogous to himself— beings whom he has never tried to understand except in a utilitarian way (he has always been alert to the need for that); and it seems natural to him to conclude that life beyond the grave is much the same. He sees no earthly use in contemplating the personality of the spirits and prying into questions of their omnipotence, omnipresence, and the like.

NATIVE RETICENCE

One of the difficulties confronting an investigator into Bantu beliefs is the absence of written Native literature to which I have referred; but the reluctance of the Bantu to talk to Europeans about the intimacies of their own religion is a still greater difficulty. Rowley was not far wrong when he said that Africans would rather be considered fools, or utterly ignorant of any sort of religion, than divulge their belief to strangers or those who have not gained their confidence.[1] What travellers have written on this subject is, therefore, seldom of much value; and many missionaries, officials, and traders who have won the confidence of the elders by prolonged residence among them, have been uninterested or untrained in the comparative method of studying religion, or have been too busy with a multiplicity of duties at understaffed centres to enrich the world with the result of their ripe experience, or have been deterred by lack of funds from writing what they thought no publisher would care to issue at his own risk. There is an immense amount of work to be done yet in the study of Bantu religion, and every year removes, to our irreparable loss, human records that ought to be carefully examined before they pass away. Still, something has been accomplished, as the many footnotes to this volume show.

IMMORTALITY

In private families worship is rendered only to the three immediate ancestors—father, grandfather, and great-grandfather; that is, to those who are something more than a name to the living members of the family group. But it is evident that more distant forbears are thought of as still existing, for the spirits invoked are always invited to call their ancestors to the sacrificial feast, and in tribal worship the spirits of chiefs of renown who have been dead for many generations are often thought more powerful than the spirits of those who succeeded them in the chieftainship. As far as we can make out, however, the Bantu have not considered the idea of immortality, in the sense of imperishability;

[1] RA. 9.

the fact of survival after death has contented them, and they have not followed the trail farther.

NATURE OF THE SOUL

Nor does it seem possible to discover a Bantu dogma concerning the nature of the soul. Some writers have credited the Bantu with the belief that each individual has two, three, or even four souls, and have tried to distinguish between the personal soul, the ancestral soul, the external soul, and the genius or guardian spirit. For example, Miss Kingsley credits the Calabar Negroes with the belief that every man has four souls: the soul that survives death, the shadow on the path, the dream-soul, and the bush-soul. The bush-soul is always in the form of an animal— never of a plant; and the bush-souls of a family are usually the same for a man and his sons, and for the mother and her daughters, though in some cases all the children take the mother's, and in others all take the father's.[1] What she calls the bush-soul seems rather to be a peculiar relation of the individual to the totem; and the belief that she formulates is a later philosophic refinement than one expects to find in Bantu thinking.

Of the Akamba, Hobley writes: "Some believe that every person has many *Aiimu* in his body, others believe that ordinary people have only one but admit that a big chief may have several. The *Aiimu* are not supposed to reside in any particular part of a man's body but to pervade the whole."[2]

Rattray mentions two important words in the Ashanti vocabulary—*abusua* and *ntoro*. *Abusua* is evidently something which a child receives from its mother, and *ntoro* is something which he receives from his father; and, status and inheritance being matrilineal among these people, *abusua* is of greater sociological importance than *ntoro*. Rattray maintains, unsuccessfully I think, that *abusua* is the equivalent of "blood," not merely in a sociological but in a physiological sense. He says: "The Ashanti believes that it is the male-transmitted *ntoro*, mingling with the blood in the female, which accounts for the physiological mysteries of conception. I have stated that *ntoro* may perhaps be

[1] TWA. 313.
[2] AK. 85.

translated 'spirit.' · Indeed, it appears to be used at times
synonymously with *sunsum*, that spiritual element in a man or
woman upon which depends—not life, *i.e.* breath, for that is the
okra or *'kra*—but that force, personal magnetism, character, personality, power, soul, call it what you will, upon which depend
health, wealth, worldly power, success in any venture, in fact
everything that makes life at all worth living."[1] The problem is
further complicated by this author's statement[2] that "When a
person dies, his or her *ntoro* does not accompany the ghost
(*saman*) to the *samando*, spirit world. It is thought to remain
behind and look after those persons of a similar *ntoro* who remain
alive."

If Rattray is correct in his interpretation of these terms, the
Ashanti seem to believe that each person has both a principle of
animal life and also a spiritual something which endows him with
characteristic human abilities—perhaps it is permissible to say, in
brief, both an animal soul and a human soul; and that the latter
consists of two elements, one of which goes to the underworld
after death, while the other remains in the community. But if
we patiently await the result of further investigation, we shall
probably get more light on this obscure question.

The Herero theory that a small worm which lives in the spinal
cord and becomes the ghost of a deceased person is killed by
fracturing the backbone, has been taken to indicate that this tribe
thinks of the ghost as an entity quite distinct from the discarnate
spirit, inasmuch as they fracture the backbone of all those whom
they bury and yet worship their spirits. The belief that the soul
emerges from the body in the shape of a maggot is widespread
among the Bantu,[3] and the custom of fracturing the backbone of
a corpse prevailed in many tribes. The aim of this operation,
however, was not to kill the maggot or ghost, but to facilitate
the binding of the corpse in the pre-natal posture. This is clearly
shown by the fact that the Becwana fracture the backbone if
rigor-mortis has set in before the corpse has been bound up in
the embryonic posture, but not otherwise.[4] Customs persist ages

[1] AS. 46.
[2] AS. 53.
[3] Cf. MLC. 45, and see pp. 162, 163, 167.
[4] See MLC. 43 for corresponding Mashona custom.

after the theory that gave rise to them has been forgotten; and the probability is that this peculiar Herero notion is due to a belated attempt to explain a persistent custom which had long lost its original significance. All Bantu tribes would expect the ghost of a person to trouble relatives who failed to see that the mortuary rites were fully performed for his body, and the binding of the corpse in the pre-natal posture was of old time regarded as very important. That a Bantu tribe should be illogical enough to accept a theory which kills the ghost and at the same time continue to worship it, will surprise no one who is familiar with their mentality.

Attempts to prove that Bantu religion is polypsychic, like that of ancient Egypt, are not convincing. Theories of soul and "soul-substance," or of a number of souls, in the same body, are sophisticated attempts to explain a quasi-sacred logical incongruity that never troubled the unsophisticated folk who first uttered it. According to an ancient magical interpretation of the world, a person, whether in or out of the body, may be present in more than one place or form at the same time; and when the slowly amassing thought and experience of many minds made this notion a strain upon the imagination, some astute exegete among the faithful tried to harmonise the ancestral aphorisms with the newer conception of life, and thus bring peace to those who were peacefully inclined. But often the gloss is due to European investigators, whose ordered thinking is incapable of the acrobatic feats in which Native mentality excels. If we are to keep close to the truth, we must accept Smith's suggestion,[1] that the Bantu have done no systematic thinking concerning the nature of the soul and are content to express in vague and various terms their inchoate and sometimes incompatible ideas concerning that mysterious, self-evident something which possesses them; or we must fall in with Le Roy's finding:[2] "In reality, the Blacks know nothing at all about it. They have no consistent theory on the subject; their psychological ideas do not retreat in the presence of grave incoherencies. . . . Whether the human soul has several distinct forms or several manners of manifesting itself, it is the soul that beats in the heart and arteries, that breathes, that shines

[1] IPNR. ii. 100-163.
[2] RP. 94.

in the eye: It is the soul that is the principle of life and, as such, disappears momentarily when a man falls into a swoon or lethargy and definitely when he dies. Thus it is a sort of ethereal substance which, during the sleep of the body, is visited by other spirits; it sees them, talks with them, it 'dreams.' It is an interior voice speaking to us, inspiring us with good or wicked feelings, urging us to do good or evil, causing us joy or remorse. Lastly it is represented by that materialisation of our person, which is called a shadow, more striking and more living in sunny countries than in ours."

DISTINCTION BETWEEN "SOUL" AND "SPIRIT"

The cessation of breathing is a noticeable sign of death; hence the close association between breath and life in primitive thought, as in Genesis (ii. 7), for instance, where it is recorded that God breathed into Adam's nostrils "the breath of life, and man became a living soul." Now breath as it rapidly condenses on a cool day becomes visible, and both souls and ghosts were thought to be of this ethereal substance. But most Bantu tribes—perhaps all—use one word for the soul of the living and another for the spirit of the dead.[1] In Kafir and Zulu tongues, *umoya* means both "wind" and "the spirit of a living man,"[2] but a discarnate spirit is called *idhlozi, itongo,* or *isituta.* "In Fernando Po a distinction is made between a demon or spirit (*morimo*) and a man's soul (*mwe*)."[3] The Becwana, almost as far from Fernando Po as the Kafirs and Zulus are, use the same words as the Fernandians do to denote the same distinction: for the soul of the living they use *moea,*[4] which means primarily "breath," like the Sanskrit *âtmán,* the Greek *pneuma,* the Latin *anima,* and the *dusii* of the Celts of Gaul;[5] but for the spirit of the dead they use *-dimo.* It is clear, however, that the *moea* of the living becomes *-dimo* when (as we should say) it leaves the body. Certain mortuary rites are of tremendous importance to the discarnate spirit; but since

[1] Cf. RP. 97.
[2] See RP. 93 for examples in other vernaculars.
[3] GGC. 636.
[4] Cf. also LSAT. ii. 339.
[5] The Greek $v\chi\acute{\eta}$ is connected with $v\chi\omega$, "to blow," and the Semitic words *nephesh* and *ruah* have a similar meaning.

there is a -*dimo* of an unburied person for whom no mortuary rites have been performed, it cannot be that the -*dimo* is made by the mortuary rites, as ancient Egyptians apparently thought of the *ba;* but rather that just as a body becomes a corpse in the act of dying, so in that same act a *moea* becomes a -*dimo*. So also in Uganda, "every one has *mwoyo* (spirit) which at death leaves the body and is called the *muzimu* (ghost)."[1]

The Boloki (or Bangala) who live on the right bank of the Congo, about two degrees north of the equator, have three words for the immaterial part of man. "The first, *elimo*, is the embodied soul that is able to leave the body during sleep, it visits people and places in dreams, travels about, and performs actions. . . . This, I believe, is the only word they have for soul. There is then the *elilingi*, a shadow, shade, reflection that a dead man, or dead thing, does not possess, and a living man can lose and have restored by a witch-doctor, and this word is used in a restricted sense as being synonymous with *elimo*. And, lastly, there is *mongoli*, a disembodied soul, a spirit, a ghost of the bush, forest, and water that sends evil upon the living."[2] The same writer remarks on another page[3] that the two words *elimo* and *elilingi* were frequently employed when speaking of the soul, and also of the shadow of a person; but the word for soul (*elimo*) was never used for the shadow of a tree, house, animal, etc., though these things are said to have no shadow when they have perished.

The Alunda also use three words: *wumi, mwevulu,* and *mukishi*. "All living things and creatures have *wumi* (life) in them. All *wumi* comes from *Nzambi*, and in man (and some animals) *wumi* is conceived as a shadow (*mwevulu*); *mwevulu* is also a shadow in the ordinary sense. The *mwevulu* is separate from, and can exist independently of, the body, which is an envelope for the *mwevulu* or *wumi*. The *mwevulu* after death leaves the body and becomes a *mukishi* (family spirit)."[4] The author quoted remarks that it is very difficult to understand the Alunda conception of *wumi;* it appears to be essential to an animal body, and yet it can be hidden in a convenient external object, so as to

[1] Roscoe in JRAI., vol. xxxii., p. 73.
[2] ACC. 269; see also 250, 261, 263.
[3] ACC. 262.
[4] WBA. 165.

be kept secure; [1] and he suggests that "perhaps *mwevulu* and *wumi* are separate: the latter depending on the former." According to the Bakaonde, neighbours of the Alunda, "In a man's lifetime he has *chimvule*: everything has a *chimvule*: the trees, rocks, hills, everything—it is a shadow. When a man dies his corpse is buried, but not the shadow. The shadow remains in the village where he lived—his soul, his spirit: it is called *chimvule* (it is also then called *mufu*).[2] These shades of the departed are the 'higher power' of the natives' religion; it is on them that they have the habitual all-pervading sense of dependence." [3] But the following pages of the same book show clearly that these "shades of the departed" who are accessible to supplication are called *wakishi* (sing. *mukishi*), the same word that is used by the Alunda. One wonders whether the clue to this mental labyrinth is still awaiting discovery by some resident in that district who is trained in Linguistics and Primitive Religion.

Johnstone writes [4] that "the Bahuana of the great Kwilu River believe that a man is composed of three principles: body, soul, (*bun*, which also means 'heart') and a spirit or phantom—*doshi*—which is a kind of 'double.' " It would seem likely, therefore, that they use *bun* of the soul of the living, and *doshi* of the discarnate human spirit, especially as *doshi* seems to be akin to a word which denotes "smoke," "steam," or "vapour" in some other Bantu vernaculars.[5] But Johnstone proceeds forthwith to quote Torday and Joyce: "The *bun* or soul of a dead man 'who has had no fetishes' can appear to other men; such an apparition, called *fakulu*, occurs at night only, and the *bun* is seen in human form and appears to be composed of a white misty substance. . . . The *doshi* is a shadowy second self, corresponding to the *kra* of the *tshi*-speaking tribes of the Gold Coast and the *ka* of the Ancient Egyptians. It leaves the body in sleep and visits other people in dreams; the *doshi* of the dead appear to the living in the same manner. All people have *doshi*, but only the adult have *bun*. . . . At death the *bun* disappears, no one knows whither, but the

---

[1] See pp. 153, 156.
[2] From the same root as *lufu*, "death," and *kufwa*, "to die."
[3] WBA. 132.
[4] GGC. 641.
[5] In Secwana, *e.g.*, *mosi* = "smoke," cf. the Native name of Victoria Falls, *Mosi-wa-tunya*; and their word *go shwa*, "to die," may be related.

doshi lingers about in the air, visits its friends and haunts its enemies; it will persecute the relations if the body has not received proper burial. . . . In the case of a man who has been the possessor of many fetishes, the *bun* enters the body of some large animal—elephant, hippo, buffalo, or leopard; animals so possessed are recognised by their ferocity." This leaves us wondering what the distinction can be between *bun* and *doshi*, and wishing that some one who has spent years in a sympathetic exploration of the Bahuana soul would unravel the skein; a traveller, no matter how skilled an anthropologist he may be, cannot hope to penetrate far enough into the inner life of an African community for this purpose.

IS THE SOUL BORN WITH THE BODY?

The above-quoted remark that all people have *doshi*, but only the adult have *bun*, opens an interesting question: Is the soul born with the body? Dr. Wilder asserts that an Ndau (Eastern Mashona) mother performs a ceremony after the birth of her child for introducing into the child a spirit called *rombo*, which leaves the body at death and becomes a *dzimu*.[1] Smith mentions that "a child who dies before its teeth are cut is buried outside the hut and no mourning takes place. Only its mother weeps for it."[2] He states also that "among the Bambala it is the custom not to bury a child who dies before cutting its teeth but to throw it out into the bush."[3] Junod says[4] that the Thonga perform no religious act at the burial of a child. "The father digs the grave but does nothing else. He says: 'We, holders of the assegai, do not bury such little ones. They are but water, they are but a womb, they are but a *ntelu*.'" But when speaking of the twin who was formally strangled and buried in a broken pot, he mentions[5] that a hole was left for the air to enter, "so that the spirit (*moya*) may go out." "If they die in infancy," he writes again on another page,[6] "no religious ceremony is performed over the grave, nor are any

---

[1] *Hartford Seminary Record*, April, 1907, p. 161.
[2] IPNR. ii. 106.
[3] IPNR. ii. 114.
[4] LSAT. i. 166.
[5] LSAT. ii. 394.
[6] LSAT. ii. 348.

prayers offered to them. . . . Infants are, however, seen in the sacred woods amongst the adult gods. This is one of the points about which there is no very clear explanation; doubtless the matter did not seem worthy of an enquiry." Ellenberger says: [1] "When a new-born child dies, the spirits of the mother's relations are supposed to have taken it. The mother must therefore be purified by the sacrifice of a black sheep." Macdonald records [2] that among the people around Blantyre, who observe a puerperium of from three to six days, if the child dies before the puerperium is ended, there is no mourning for it, and no offerings to its spirit; but there is mourning if it dies soon after it has been brought out. Miss Werner says [3] that if a Yao baby dies during this period, "no mourning is held for it; it has not been formally introduced into the world, and its spirit is not supposed to count, or require propitiating. Perhaps they think that it has not really attained a separate existence of its own." Miss Mabel Shaw tells us [4] that the women of Mbereshi think that very little children who have no sense pass right out of existence after death; but they are evidently wailed for, according to her article, and Bantu laments are vehement addresses to the dead,[5] not mere soliloquies of unrestrained grief at the loss sustained by the speakers. Le Roy is of opinion [6] that the souls of infants are thought too weak to survive the dissolution of the body, and those of children and slaves and people of no account, not strong enough to persist long after death. On the other hand, Miss Kingsley mentions [7] "wanderer souls" that keep turning up in West Coast babies who all die young; and Rattray observed [8] that among the Ashanti, "the

[1] HB. 248.
[2] A. i. 115.
[3] NBCA. 103.
[4] *Chronicle of the London Missionary Society*, Dec., 1919.
[5] Casalis gives a good sample of the customary lament as he knew it among the Basuto: "The matrons of the place assemble near the hut where the tyrant has entered, and indulge in the most heart-rending lamentations. 'Yo! Yo! Yo! Alas! Alas! my father, where art thou now? Why hast thou left us? What will become of us without thee? Who will defend us from our enemies? Who will supply us with food and clothing? Thou art gone! Thou hast left us! We remain behind in sorrow and bitterness! Yo! Yo! Yo! Alas! Alas!' Such are generally the lamentations that are heard, with those variations required by the age and sex of deceased." (Bs. 202.)
[6] RP. 107.
[7] TWA. 330.
[8] AS. 54.

infant for the first eight days after birth is scarcely considered a human being, being looked upon as possibly merely a 'ghost child' that has come from the spirit world, intending immediately to return. If it die before the eighth day, 'it certainly was such.' " In Uganda, according to Roscoe,[1] infants and still-born babes are buried at four cross roads, and "every woman who passes by throws a few blades of grass upon the grave to prevent the ghost from entering into her womb and the child being reborn." Such cases show that Le Roy's assumption is unwarranted; all these fickle souls are believed to exist both before and after they occupy the little bodies, and people try to prevent them from coming back. The theory that ancestor-spirits are reborn in their descendants points to the same belief. Smith has again and again heard men say,[2] "I am my grandfather, I entered my mother's womb to be born"; but he states that "there is some difference of opinion as to the precise time when the ancestral spirit becomes the child."

Kidd,[3] differing from others who have studied the Kafir-Zulu group, regards the *idhlozi* as the individual and personal soul and the *itongo* as the individual's portion of the corporate ancestral spirit; and he asserts that the people believe that the *itongo* is imparted to the child by the fumigation ceremony to which babies are exposed soon after birth. Fumigation rites are intended, however, to drive away evil influences, not to impart something new.

The fact that the Bantu practised infanticide without scruple has led people to infer that they thought infants had no souls. That inference cannot be legitimately drawn from the premise. Ancient Greek and Roman pagans exposed newly born infants often enough, while believing that the souls of these little waifs of humanity were doomed to eke out the normal span of human life in wandering on the earth in unquiet and pain. In an interesting passage concerning the fate of souls despatched before their time, Cumont quotes [4] Virgil's celebrated lines describing Æneas's descent into Hades: "Ever were heard on the outermost threshold, voices, a great wailing, the weeping souls of infants bereft

---

[1] JRAI., vol. xxxii., p. 30.
[2] IPNR. ii. 153.
[3] SC. 12-13.
[4] ALRP. 28 f.

of sweet life and torn from the breast, whom the ill-omened days swept off and whelmed in bitter death"; and he adds: "In an eschatological myth of Plutarch, the traveller beyond the grave also sees a deep abyss, in which moan the plaintive voices of a multitude of children who had died at the moment of their birth and were unable to rise to heaven."

To sum up, I should say that the evidence, though not conclusive, seems to point to a belief that the soul enters the womb some time before the child is born.

THE SOUL A COUNTERPART OF THE BODY

Roscoe mentions [1] a Baganda belief that if the body is mutilated during life, the ghost goes maimed into the spirit-world. "Hence the idea of amputation was so dreaded by men, that a person preferred to die with a limb, rather than live without it and so lose the chance of possessing full powers in the ghost-world." I have found this notion in all the tribes that I have touched, whether in Unyamwezi or south of the Zambesi, and it is reported from practically all parts of Bantu Africa.[2] There is also a sporadic belief that the body-marks of a man are found on the snake in which his spirit reincarnates itself for the purpose of revisiting the family home.[3]

It seems abundantly evident that Bantu believe the spirit to be an exact counterpart of the deceased.[4] When it visits them in the visions of the night, it comes with the same face, the same figure, the same gait, and even the same dress; and since absent friends and foes enter their dream-pictures in similar guise, it may be permissible to conjecture that they think of the soul as the simulacrum or ethereal "double" of the living person. "The witch-doctor can see the disembodied spirits," writes Weeks,[5] "and those persons who have the occult power (called *likundu*) can also see them. The natives tell me that these spirits are like people in appearance—they come into view, pass, and are

[1] Bg. 281.
[2] Cf., p. 170.
[3] See p. 159 f.
[4] See RAC. 336-37 for somewhat similar notions.
[5] ACC. 267.

lost to sight like ordinary beings. They have quiet voices, and eat monkey-peppers (*amomum*), and drink sugar-cane wine."

THE SOUL, A MINIATURE OF THE MAN

But if the disembodied soul is the "double" of the man, it is evidently a miniature "double." In every Central African village one notices tiny huts which are built for the use of spirits of departed relatives. Miss Werner says:[1] "Whether or not they consciously think of the dead as little shadowy figures, a few inches high (like the representation of the soul as it issues from the body on Greek vases), such was evidently the thought that suggested the erection of these miniature dwellings." In a picture from the Papyrus of Ani,[2] the soul is portrayed outside the tomb in the shape of a human-headed bird; a figure which reminds us of the Harpies, Sirens and Erinyes, of the souls of wrecked mariners that appear as gulls, and of those Celtic souls which flit about as birds,—song-birds, according to old Irish folklore.[3] In the reign of Mikado Kei-ko (A.D. 71-130), according to the *Ko-ji-ki* (*Records of Ancient Matters*), the dead prince Yamato-take appeared as a white plover to his wives and children, who were lamenting round the "august mausoleum" which they had just built for him; but this was an enormous bird—eight fathoms long![4] The idea of the *Ba*-bird is not altogether absent from Bantu folklore. In his version of the story of Masilo, who murdered his younger brother for the sake of the latter's beautiful cattle, Casalis says[5] that the little bird which revives again and again and accuses the murderer afresh after it has been killed and pulverised, declares in its final song, as it perches upon the horns of the stolen beasts, "I am the heart of Masilonyane." The story as I have frequently heard it from Native lips has always lacked this last touch; but the embellishment is quite in accord with annotations given me by Native narrators.

[1] NBCA. 49.
[2] EM. 115 (pl. 18).
[3] SCD. 95.
[4] *Transactions of the Asiatic Society of Japan.* Yokohama: Meiklejohn & Co., vol. x., 1882, p. 221.
[5] Bs. 343.

The point which interests us more particularly at the moment is, however, the size of the discarnate soul. In the above-mentioned picture Ani himself is also portrayed, but the human-headed bird which represents his soul is not more than one-quarter of the size of Ani. One cannot forget that Egypt is in Africa, and that the Hamitic strain in the Bantu breed is closely allied to the Egyptian, while the Negro element is the same as that which associated with the builders of the ancient monuments. In the folktale which Macdonald entitles *The Chief that Hoed at the Graves*[1] the spirit that came from the graves to steal the child appeared as a little man.

According to the Rev. G. Viehe[2] who had spent twelve years among the Herero, these people believe that when a person who was buried in the ground rises again, he is of the stature of a little dog, with skin the colour of the hide in which he was wrapped, and eyes in the hinder part of his head, but with the same capacities and passions that he had before he died. Some Hereros, however, are left, at their own desire, either in the house, which is well secured, or in the stockaded cattle-kraal, and these people rise in the stature of human beings, though their eyes, also, are in the back of the head. Perhaps it is as well to remember in this connection that before burial a Herero corpse has its backbone broken and is wrapped up in the embryonic posture, while a corpse that is left in the house or cattle-pen is laid out at full length.

Fortunately we can dispense with inferences and reported beliefs and fall back upon evidence which is the more valuable because undesigned. All Bantu chiefs have used the religious beliefs of their people for their own political purposes; but not all have had the astuteness which Chaka displayed, when, building up his notorious despotism in Zululand, he found it necessary to buttress his new edifice with a declaration of approval from the old chiefs in the spirit-world. Shooter tells[3] how Chaka secured the help of a prophet who was said to have been devoured by a lion and sent back from the underworld with a message to the people. Of course, the prophet had to describe

[1] A. ii. 324.
[2] *Folk-Lore Journal.* Cape Town, May, 1879, pp. 56 and 65.
[3] KNZC. 271.

the land that he had visited; and he described it as a fine country, in which he found all the old people who had been killed in war or died at home. "They are much smaller than we," he said; "they have plenty of cattle, but all very small. The girls are handsome," etc. One smiles at the trick, but is grateful for the authentic Bantu picture of the underworld—a picture that could substantiate the prophet's crafty claims only by chiming in with the notions of the people. The prophet's picture harmonises perfectly with Miss Werner's suggestion: not only are the spirits diminutive, but even the cattle are small.

SPIRITS OF CATTLE

One would like more information about these cattle. Are they the cattle that have been sacrificed, or do all cattle go to the underworld at death? What is the, inner significance of the prominent use of cattle in the obsequies of the semi-pastoral Bantu? Many of these tribes wrap the master of the herd in the hide of one of his choicest beasts, which is slaughtered for the funeral feast; and some of them bury him in his cattle-pen [1] while others build a new cattle-pen over the grave for the protection of selected cattle which become sacred to the departed spirit.[2] "In every herd," belonging to the Baila, "will be found some oxen, conspicuous for their size. These are the 'funeral oxen.' They await their master's death, and are intended to provide the feast for his relations and mourners. Their hides form the grave-bed. Great efforts are made, and high prices paid, to obtain them, and once secured they are never parted with. As many as a hundred head are killed at the funeral of a big chief."[3] Do these cattle accompany the spirit into the World of Shades?

Junod incidentally remarks [4] that "no one seriously believes in the continued existence of animals after death." Le Roy is still more explicit: "All the 'souls' that give things their 'manner' which specifically distinguishes them and makes them what they are, all these souls 'die' with them—souls of minerals, plants,

[1] Bs. 203.
[2] ECSA. 222.
[3] IPNR. i. 130.
[4] LSAT. ii. 343.

and animals."·¹　But in the ceremony that Nassau was permitted
to witness on the Ogowe² the hunter, kneeling inside the carcase
of the hippopotamus that he had killed the night before, prayed
to "the life-spirit of the, hippo that it would bear him no ill-will
for having killed it, and thus cut it off from future maternity;
and not to incense other hippopotami that they should attack
his canoe in revenge."　And Roscoe states³ that in Uganda
ghosts of sheep and buffalo are feared, and that certain hills
in Uganda are haunted by lion and leopard spirits.　These latter
may turn out, upon strict inquiry, to be reincarnated human
spirits.⁴　Smith writes⁵ that the Bambala think "the spirits of
cattle and wild animals as well as the ghosts of men" are collected in the underworld; and Torday asserts that the Bahuana
believe that the animals have *doshi* but not *bun*.⁶　Hobley gives
us a striking passage that bears upon this point.　"For some
years after the cattle disease (rinderpest) swept off nearly all
the cattle, of an evening high up on the mountain the people
used to hear the lowing of large herds of cattle but could not
see them.　One day the grass on the mountain caught fire and
spread up to an important *Ithembo* or shrine which was under
a large sacred Mumbo tree and when the fire reached the tree
loud shrieks of human beings, bellowing of cattle and bleating
of sheep and goats was heard but nothing was visible to the
human eye.　This throws rather important light on the animistic
beliefs of these people as it shows that the Akamba believe that
the domestic animals possess souls as well as mankind."⁷　Fraser
says: "The lion is supposed to hide the tail and ears of the
animals it kills under the *msoro* tree, so that it may creep up to
its victims unobserved.　Some say that in doing this the lion
is worshipping his own *chibanda* (ancestral spirit), who resides
beneath the tree, but apart from this instance I have found no

¹ RP. 56.
² FWA. 204.
³ Bg. 289, 319.
⁴ Uganda is, however, a marginal area in which Bantu, Hamitic, and Nilotic
people have affected one another's beliefs and practices; and Driberg writes (*The
Lango*, p. 229) that the Nilotic people of Lango, immediately north of Mengo,
consider the ghosts of elephants, rhinos, and warthogs to be vengeful.
⁵ IPNR. ii. 119.
⁶ GGC. 641. See also my pp. 11 f., 58 f.
⁷ AK. 86-87.

belief that animals also have souls."[1]   We shall see presently that in the underworld the herdboy still herds his beautiful beasts, and the hunter still enjoys his favourite sport; which presupposes, one would think, that the animals wend their way thither at death.   Some of the ritual of the chase can hardly be understood, except upon the assumption that the spirit of a beast is still potent after it has been slain.   But here again we must be careful not to assume that the other world of Bantu eschatology is constructed according to the principles of Western logic.

RESURRECTION OF THE BODY

A few facts have been taken to indicate that the Bantu believe in the resurrection of the body.   The strongest evidence that I know in favour of this theory is that strange power of calling forth the dead from their graves, which is attributed to the spells of Bantu witches; but such spells are unavailing, apparently, after the mortuary rites are complete; and this evidence is outweighed by the Becwana belief that discarnate spirits become more efficient as the body decays,—a belief that may suggest spiritualisation of the body, but hardly its resurrection.

Then there is the widespread custom of preserving the corpse. The Mashona smoke and dry the corpse of a chief and place it in the cleft of a rock, or in a cave.[2]   The Bemba make an attempt at mummifying such a corpse by repeatedly rubbing it all over with boiled maize till the skin becomes dry and shrivelled.[3]   The Kaonde seek to ward off decomposition by applying a porridge of the small red millet.[4]   Johnston describes[5] the funeral of a favourite slave of the chief, which he saw at Itimba (a little higher up the Congo than Kwamouth): "The body of the dead man had been previously smoked and dried over a slow fire, so that the flesh, except upon the hands, was shrunken and reduced to a leathery covering round the gaunt bones."   "In the water-shed of the Lopori, Aruwimi and Maringa rivers towards

[1] WPP. 128.
[2] MLC. 43.
[3] NBCA. 163.
[4] WBA. 90, 246.
[5] *The River Congo*, &c., London: Sampson Low, 1884, 3rd Ed., p. 248.

the Egyptian and Uganda borders," says another writer,[1] "the corpse is frequently hung for weeks over a fire and thoroughly smokedried. A similar custom prevails in certain parts of the middle and lower Congo. . . . Amongst the Bakwala tribe, the custom prevails of smoking the body of a deceased wife who may be the daughter of a distant tribe, in order that she may be sent home and find burial amongst her own people."

Rowley quotes [2] the Abbé Froyart as stating in his *History of Loango, Kakongo,* etc. (published in 1776) that the tribes which he knew in that part of Africa were accustomed to place the corpse on a scaffold, and underneath it to light a fire which throws up a thick smoke. After the corpse was sufficiently smoked, they exposed it for a few days in the open air, placing a person to keep the flies away. Monteiro describes a similar custom between Loanda and Ambriz: [3] "The burial of kings, or head men, and their wives in this part of Angola is very singular. When a person dies, a shallow pit is dug in the floor of the hut in which he or she died, just deep enough to contain the body. This, which is seldom more than skin and bone, is placed naked in the trench on its back, and then covered with a thin layer of earth. On this three fires are lighted and kept burning for a whole moon or month, the hot ashes being constantly spread over the whole grave. At the end of this time the body is usually sufficiently baked or dried: it is then taken out and placed on its back on an open framework of sticks, and fires kept burning under it till the whole body is thoroughly smoke-dried. During the whole time the body is being dried, the hut in which the operation is being performed is always full of people, the women keeping up a dismal crying day and night, particularly the latter. . . . When the body is completely desiccated it is wrapped in cloth and stuck upright in a corner of the hut, where it remains until it is buried, sometimes two years after. . . . The natives have great veneration for their dead, and I found it impossible to obtain a dried body as a specimen, although I offered a high price for one." Somewhat similar treatment is given to corpses in San Salvador and in Tungwa

---

[1] DDA. 40. See also ACC. 316-17.
[2] RA. 95-6.
[3] ARC. i. 274-6.

(half-way between that place and the Congo), except that in these districts, when the corpse is dry enough to be wrapped in cotton cloths it is laid on a shelf in the house to await the elaborate preparations for the funeral. "To insinuate that your enemy buried his uncle 'wet,'" says Bentley,[1] "is the worst abuse that can be dealt out to him; a resort to knives is the only sequel left to a man of any self-respect thus 'cursed.'"

Such customs are widespread, though far from general, and it would be interesting to discover the motive that inspires them. They are probably actuated, not by a belief in the resurrection of the body, but by ideas akin to those that prevailed among the builders of the pyramids. "The Egyptian believed that he was immortal, and believed that he would enjoy eternal life in a spiritual body: yet he attempted by the performance of magical ceremonies and the recital of words of power to make his corruptible body to endure for ever."[2] Available evidence does not support the theory that any Bantu tribe believes in the resurrection of the body. On the contrary, my experience is that they ridicule the suggestion that such an occurrence is even thinkable.

The resurrection of the body in the "Death and Resurrection Society," of which Claridge gives an impressionist sketch[3] instead of the serious study that might have been expected from one who knows the Society "from the inside and not merely from observation," appears to be merely a symbolical ceremony.

DESTRUCTION OF THE BODY

The Chinese believe that without a grave the dead have no home.[4] There is evidently a similar idea in the minds of the Bantu. While the corpse remains unburied and deprived of fitting mortuary rites, the relatives who should have furnished the ritual are thought to be in great danger from the anger of the spirit: and in such cases the Bantu, like the Babylonians,[5] dread the ghosts of the unburied. But most Bantu tribes appear to

[1] PC. i. 174-8, ii. 367.
[2] EM. 184.
[3] WBT., chap. xvii.
[4] SCD. 36.
[5] SCD. 206.

believe that if the body be utterly destroyed, the spirit is deprived of power, or perhaps even of existence.

Smith says:[1] "If a person after death is suspected of harassing people or bringing other misfortune upon them, the corpse is taken up and burnt. Or in some instances, where through ill-treatment or sheer malice, a person has expressed an intention on his deathbed of returning to haunt the living, then no actual burial takes place; the corpse is simply thrown out into the bush or burnt." A medicine-man cut up the body of an old woman who had made such a threat, he tells us on the same page, and threw it bit by bit upon a huge fire, chanting his spells meanwhile; and then, to make assurance doubly sure, the very ashes were scattered to the winds. Doke says that among the Lambas, who dwell in North-west Rhodesia and the Katanga district of the Belgian Congo, the punishment for witchcraft "is not only invariably death, but the body is afterwards burnt to ashes and the ashes scattered, so that, in addition to the body, the spirit, according to their beliefs, is also annihilated."[2] Campbell, speaking of dead men who return in vengeance as lions, leopards, snakes, etc., says:[3] "The only cure was to dig up the bones of the dead witch or wizard, and burn them publicly."[4] In the case which he describes, some of the ashes were compounded with occult substances known to the magician, and thus rendered prophylactic against further trouble from the spirit. Members of Transkeian tribes who are killed by lightning or other accident are not buried.[5] The tribes with which Rowley was acquainted in East Central Africa, did not bury those who died of accident or of any cause that was considered natural, but slung them up

---

[1] IPNR. ii. 115.

[2] BNT., Aug., 1923, p. 39.

[3] IHB. 44.

[4] Speaking of the odium which attached to those who had committed suicide or been executed, Cumont remarks (ALRP. 146): "The Greeks believe even to-day that such as perish by a sudden and violent death became *vrykolakes*. Their bodies can again be reanimated, can leave the grave, and can travel through space with extreme rapidity as vampires and become so maleficent that mere contact with them causes loss of life. Suicides and victims of unavenged murders are particularly fearful. It was the custom as late as the eighteenth century to open the grave of a dead man suspected of being a *vrykolakas*, and if his body had escaped corruption, thus proving his supposed character, it was cut into pieces or burnt in order to prevent it from doing further harm."

[5] LA. 167.

in trees to be devoured by birds; he could, however, learn nothing of the hereafter of such persons, simply because the people were afraid to speak of them.[1]   In the early days of European settlement in Nyasaland, persons who died from the poison-cup ordeal were denied sepulture.[2]   The Boloki or Bangala of the Congo refuse burial to those who succumb to the ordeal upon charge of witchcraft.[3]   Witches and other malefactors who are supposed to be possessed by malignant spirits were burnt by many Bantu tribes.   On Likoma Island, in Lake Nyasa, there were several burning places that were used for this purpose, the site of the present cathedral being the most famous of them.[4]   In that district it was usual to burn the carcase of a lion, for a similar reason.   Archdeacon Johnson writes:[5]   "A common idea is, that a spirit takes up his abode in the body of the lion, and if his dwelling-place is destroyed, he can come no more."   The Bantu of the South Central Plateau did not burn those who were guilty of witchcraft; they threw them over precipices; but such victims were denied burial and left for the vultures and hyenas to devour.   When the Akamba have executed a person guilty of witchcraft, they sometimes bury the body very deep, and sometimes they burn it.[6]   In the Kaonde country the bodies of persons executed for witchcraft are burned;[7] and when a vampirelike ghost is causing the illness of some villager, and a diviner identifies the grave from which it emerges, the corpse is exhumed from that grave and burned.[8]   In spite of some difference of local belief, it seems to be the standard opinion of Kaonde "doctors" that the spirit of such a corpse is thoroughly killed, not merely laid.

Miss Kingsley mentions a widely diffused custom in West Africa, which is practised upon "wanderer souls," that is, souls which keep on turning up in successive babies in the same family. "A child dies. . . . A third arrives, and if that dies . . . the

[1] RA. 99.
[2] A. 104-5.
[3] ACC. 283.
[4] NGW. 99.
[5] Op. cit., p. 152; cf. MTR. 11-13.
[6] AK. 96.
[7] WBA. 207, 212, 223.
[8] WBA. 145-48; cf. SRK. 295-96.

father breaks one of the legs of the body before throwing it into the bush. . . . If a fourth child arrives in the family, 'it usually limps,' and if it dies, the justly irritated parent cuts its body up carefully into very small pieces, and scatters them, doing away with the soul altogether."[1]

It appears that other than malignant spirits may lose their power if their remains are scattered. The senior branch of the Bakwena tribe holds the memory of a certain old chief in the highest veneration. Tradition regards him as the King Arthur of their dynasty. I asked some of their experts one day why certain sacrifices for rain had been offered at the grave of a more recent chief, who, for his iniquities, was slain by his people. I expected to be told that the diviner had discovered that the spirit of the murdered chief was troubling them with drought; but he said that inasmuch as the grave of the famous old chief was in a strip of territory that had been wrested from them by another tribe, it may have been robbed of its remains, or otherwise desecrated. And yet the Bakwena, like other Becwana tribes, believe that the power of the spirit increases as the body decays in the grave, and that not much help can be expected from a spirit for a decade after the burial of the corpse. Evidently, decay is one thing; wilful destruction or desecration is another.[2]

All these practices appear to be grounded in the belief that if the corpse be utterly destroyed, the malefactor is truly excommunicated, as Le Roy phrases it,[3] or that the discarnate spirit becomes inert, if it does not utterly perish; but there are facts which forbid the hasty acceptance of this generalisation. Tribes of the Zulu group honoured their chiefs with cremation,[4] and it is risky to approach the dust and unconsumed debris of suicides

---

[1] TWA. 330.

[2] Petrie, referring to the ancient Egyptian custom of eating the flesh of certain sacrificial victims and giving honourable burial to their bones, remarks: "It may seem strange that the bones of sacred animals should be preserved, while the flesh might be burnt or eaten. This is akin to the prehistorical idea that the flesh of a man might be removed, or eaten, or thrown away, while the importance lay in the bones, which were cleaned and reconstituted in the form of the body. In the IIIrd or IVth dynasty, at Meydum, the bones of nobles were entirely stripped, each wrapped separately in muslin, and then reconstituted as a skeleton (with some mistakes in arrangement) for an honoured burial." (RLAE. 188.)

[3] RP. 98.

[4] See p. 47 f.

and witches who were cremated for their social obliquity, unless one does something to compensate for the burial that was denied them. We have yet to find a formula that will reconcile these conflicting customs; and the quest is not facilitated by the suspicion that the unsophisticated Bantu mind is not intolerant of antithetic ideas.

IMPORTANCE OF MORTUARY RITES

It is believed that the earliest Indo-European method of disposing of the dead was to place them where they would be devoured by birds and beasts, and that burial took the place of exposure when the Aryans abandoned their nomadic life.[1] A similar course of events is traceable in Bantu history. When I lived in Unyamwezi (1882-3), men of mark were buried, but people of no importance were laid at some little distance from the village for hyenas to devour. It is well known that the old practice of tribes now living in South-east Africa was to bury the chiefs and expose the common people.[2] The Becwana have buried their dead for so many generations that they deny that they ever disposed of them in any other manner, but I noticed that when little children asked where their missing relatives had gone, older folk, not wishing to discuss death and the grave with little children, were wont to reply: "Oh, he has gone on a journey with Mr. Hyena." The Tumbuka people call gravediggers *bachimbwe* ("hyenas").[3] In the more settled parts of Africa, as in Uganda, burial is such a well-established practice that even slaves are buried.[4]

One of the motives that led to the substitution of burial for exposure, appears in a current Akamba belief. "When an ordinary person dies it is customary for the relatives to throw the body out in the open, and if another relative were to die some time afterwards the same thing would be done, but if a second relative were to die very shortly after the first the second would be buried as it would be considered that the second had died as it had been unlucky to throw out the first. If a third relative were

---

[1] SCD. 122, 124.
[2] LA. 167, ECSA. 222, Bs. 203. See also my p. 116.
[3] WPP. 158.
[4] Bg. 127.

to die shortly he would also be buried, but a fourth relation dying shortly would be thrown out and they would go on ringing the changes till the deaths stopped."[1]   According to the old Wachagga custom the only corpses which might be buried were those of married people who had offspring.   It was absolutely unlawful to bury children, unmarried persons, or sterile men and women; the latter were laid in the bush with their personal belongings, youths and girls being wrapped in banana leaves and laid in the banana grove, and little children, plastered with cowdung and laid in the same place.   Such bodies were eaten by hyenas and jackals, and if dragged away, the parents would always look for the skulls and replace them among the Dracæna stems in the banana groves.   Nowadays all corpses are buried, and Dundas gives an interesting story of what led to the change of custom within the last thirty years.[2]

The tribes of the Gabun district in French Equatorial Africa, especially those of the Interior, "differ very much as to burial customs.   Some bury only their chiefs and other prominent men, casting away corpses of slaves or of the poor into the rivers, or out on the open ground, perhaps covering them with a bundle of sticks; even when graves are dug they are shallow.   Some tribes fearlessly bury their dead under the clay floors of their houses, or a few yards distant in the kitchen-garden generally adjoining.   But, by most tribes who do bury at all, there are chosen as cemeteries dark, tangled stretches of forest, along river banks on ground that is apt to be inundated or whose soil is not good for plantation purposes."[3]   The Boloki, on the northern bend of the Congo, bury free men and women in their houses, but a slave is buried on the edge of the bush, or in any convenient place.[4]   "It is the great desire of a Congo man," says Bentley,[5] "to be buried in a great quantity of cotton cloth, and to have a great funeral.   For *this* he trades, and spins, sparing no pains, not that he may wear fine cloths, and have a comfortable home.   He shivers with cold in the dry season, but will not put on his back the coat or blanket which is reserved for his

[1] AK. 67.
[2] K. 181.
[3] FWA. 61, cf. 235.
[4] ACC. 318.
[5] PC. 174-75.

shroud. . . . A great man is often buried in hundreds of yards of cloths. . . . The expense of a funeral is so great in the case of an important man, that his own accumulations are never sufficient. . . . During this period of mourning the nephews, sons and male relatives of the deceased will have been busy trading, and doing their utmost to raise money for the funeral; junior members of the family may be pawned to raise more, and when the funeral is over they not infrequently forget to redeem them. So every one does his best to give an honourable funeral." The Waguha on the west coast of Tanganyika generally keep the corpse in the house for ten days or more, and never bury it till long after decomposition has set in. Friends are sent for, and sometimes they are so long in arriving that little remains but the bones. Ordinary freemen are buried in a grave with mats over them. A chief is buried with all his finery on, and in a sitting posture. The interval between death and burial of a chief depends partly upon the appearance of deceased to his successor or one of his nearest relatives in a dream; and after the burial the successor builds a spirit-hut for the deceased.[1]

Though the ritual of interment differs in different Bantu tribes, it is always precise, even where none but notables are buried, and stress is laid upon the need for its exact performance. Much of this ceremonial suggests that the soul is still within the body.[2]

FICTIONAL FUNERALS

Perhaps the most remarkable sepulchral usage is that which is observed when there is no corpse that can be buried. According to an old custom, now well-nigh extinct, if a man of standing among the Makalaka disappeared in the wilderness, leaving no trace behind him, and if sickness soon after invaded the village, people said: "We are disturbed by the person who died in the wilderness." Then they sacrificed an ox. Inasmuch as the corpse was presumed to be lying somewhere in the wilderness, a herdsman was directed to spear an ox in the wilderness, but not to wound it so badly that it could not walk home; and upon reaching home it was slaughtered and eaten as a funeral feast,

[1] LMS., *Chronicle*, Feb., 1881.
[2] This was the belief of the ancient Celts; see RAC. 339, 344.

and its bones were wrapped in its hide and solemnly buried in the village. The burial of the ox served as a substitute for the burial of the missing corpse, and people said with confidence, "We shall no longer be troubled by the disease." Or if there was no general sickness in the village and a friend of the lost man fell ill, this illness was attributed to the spirit of the missing man, and they went out and collected the bones of cattle or goats that had died in the wilderness, and buried them,[1] saying, "Now we have seen you, god, let this person get better." And a libation of water was poured over the grave where the bones were buried, as a prayer for him who was sick.

The Thonga have a similar custom. "Should a man have died far away from home, in Johannesburg for instance, no ceremony will take place before the news is thoroughly confirmed. Then all the relatives assemble. A grave is dug and all his mats and clothing are buried in it. The objects which he was using every day, which have been soiled by the exudations from his body, are *himself*. A sacrifice will be made over the grave. . . . The widow will eat with her hands till the burial, though death took place long before and was publicly known; she will begin to use a spoon only after the burial has taken place."[2]

The Baila bury some of a person's belongings and go through the sepulchral rites at his village when his body cannot be buried.[3]

Strange as these customs appear to us, they are not peculiar to the Bantu, nor even to Africa. It was believed by all the nations of antiquity, so Professor Franz Cumont tells us,[4] that those who lacked burial according to the traditional rites, could find no rest in the other life, that their unquiet spirits fluttered near the corpse and wandered over the surface of the earth, taking vengeance on those who had inflicted such ills upon them. In the Greek cities, as in Rome, the law often denied burial to those who had committed suicide or been executed, hoping that fear of a wretched hereafter would deter desperate men from their fatal design; and, on the other hand, the bodies of soldiers and travellers who died abroad were brought home where pos-

[1] Cf. MLC. 46-7.
[2] LSAT. i. 165.
[3] IPNR. ii. 116.
[4] ALRP. 64-67.

sible, "or, if this could not be done, a cenotaph was raised to him, and his soul was summoned aloud to come and inhabit the dwelling prepared for it. When cremation became general in Rome, the old Pontifical law invented another subterfuge which allowed the ancient rites to be accomplished: a finger was cut from the body before it was carried to the pyre, and earth was thrown three times on this 'resected bone.'" "A doctrine to which Plato alludes," says he, "taught that souls which had not been appeased by funeral rites, had to wander for a hundred years, the normal term of human life. Confined in the air near the earth, they remained subject to the power of magicians. Especially if the wizards had been able to obtain possession of some portion of the corpse, whence the soul could not entirely detach itself, they gained influence over it and could constrain its obedience." "The rules of the *cultores* of Diana and Antinoüs of Lanuvium stipulate," he continues, "that when a slave dies and his master maliciously refuses to deliver his body for burial, a '*funus imaginarium*' be made for him, that is, that the ceremony be celebrated over a figure representing the dead man and wearing his mask. From this 'imaginary' burial effects were expected as beneficent as those results are maleficent which a wizard anticipated when he fettered and pierced a waxen doll to work a charm." A somewhat similar proceeding may still be witnessed in India. "When a person has died away from home, or when for any reason a body has disappeared, an effigy is prepared which is cremated in place of the real corpse." [1] In Ashanti when a person dies away from home and it is not possible to bring the body back for burial, some nail-parings and hair are brought home, for it is supposed that the *sunsum* (soul) will accompany them. "It is a custom observed among the Yorubas —a custom observed to this day—to pare the nails and shave the head of any one who dies at a considerable distance from the place where they would have him buried. These relics are taken to the place of interment, and there decently buried, the funeral obsequies being scrupulously observed as if the corpse were buried there." [2] In the Northern Territories of the Gold Coast,

[1] SCD. 126.
[2] Johnson, *History of the Yorubas*, p. 12,

according to Cardinall,[1] if a man dies away from home, it is common to bring earth from his grave, or better a piece of his clothes, so that the returning spirit will know that it has not been neglected.

AFFINITY OF SPIRIT AND CORPSE

The association of the spirit with the grave in which its remains lie, is, however, much closer than the last remark would suggest. In the district of which Cardinall writes, graves are finished as little truncated pyramids with cap-stones on which sacrifices to ancestral spirits are placed; and if a family removes to another locality, it takes earth from its old altars, embodies it in a similar erection at the new place of abode, and there offers its sacrifices.[2] When the *tindana* (who seems to be the representative of the old lords of the land) adjudicated in a case of serious crime between members of the same community, he put accused and accuser on oath by causing them to drink a concoction in which the main ingredient was earth from the *tiangani*, as these little pyramids are called.[3] By a process that is essentially similar, the saintly dead may be brought into a transaction for quite other purposes. Pious pilgrims buy dust from the grave of Muhammad and regard it as a cure for all diseases. "A cake composed of dust from the Prophet's tomb is sometimes sewed up in a leathern case, and worn as an amulet. It is also formed into lumps of the shape and size of a small pear, and hung to the railing or screen which surrounds the monument over the grave of a saint, or to the monument itself, or to the windows or door of the apartment which contains it."[4] Ntindi was a Konde prophet of renown: no word of his ever fell to the ground. Snakes cleared from his path; bees would not sting him, nor driver ants bite him. And to this day Konde people protect their houses from biting ants by sprinkling earth from his grave all around.[5]

That the spirit is very closely associated with the corpse is

[1] NTG. 105.
[2] NTG. 44 f.
[3] NTG. 55.
[4] MCME. 262; cf. my p. 287.
[5] SRK. 309.

put beyond question by many Bantu mortuary customs. Smith cites [1] a curious instance in which the body of a man who had shot himself was buried in the village and the funeral rites performed at the place in the veld where the deed was done; and he adds this comment: "We are told that the ghost is where the blood is, hence this practice."

"The Bateke, who live to the north of Stanley Pool, often bury a man in the floor of his own house. The shroud is cut over the mouth, and in filling up the grave, after the interment, a pole is placed with one end on the mouth of the corpse, and the other end sticking out from the grave. When the earth is properly filled in and trodden down, the pole is withdrawn, and so a clear hole is left to the mouth of the corpse. Into this hole, from time to time, palm wine is poured, that the deceased may not lack the liquor which used to gladden his heart when living." [2] From the mouth of a Tumbuka chief a hollow reed was led to the top of the grave-mound, and down this reed beer was poured for the refreshment of his spirit. [3]

Miss Kingsley says [4] that in the Calabar district, "the heads of important chiefs are usually cut off from the body on burial and kept secretly for fear the head, and thereby the spirit, of the dead chief should be stolen from the town." [5]   In an attempted classification of West Coast spirits which Dr. Nassau gave Miss Kingsley, we read: "There seems to be another class of spirits somewhat akin to the ancient Lares and Penates, who especially

[1] IPNR. ii. 116.
[2] PC. i. 253. There was a similar device in Roman tombs. "Often there is in the tombstone a circular cavity, the bottom of which is pierced with holes; the liquid poured into it went through the perforated slab and was led by a tube to the urn which held the calcinated bones. It is comprehensible that an unbeliever protested against this practice in his epitaph: 'By wetting my ashes with wine thou wilt make mud,' he says, 'and I shall not drink when I am dead.' But how many other texts there are which show the persistence of the ancient ideas! 'Passer-by,' says a Roman inscription, 'the bones of a man pray thee not to soil the monument which covers them; but if thou be benevolent pour wine into the cup, drink and give me thereof.' " (ALRP. 50.)   In the mastabas of early Egyptian dynasties, "the access of the soul to the chamber of provision was sometimes arranged by a narrow tube in the rock, from the tomb pit out to the false door." (RLAE. 125.)
[3] AI. 164.
[4] TWA. 305.
[5] "The Egyptian in prehistoric times often kept the head, or in later times kept the whole mummy in the court of the house." (RLAE. 114, 126-28.)

belong to the household, and descend by inheritance with the family.   In their honour are secretly kept a bundle of finger, and other bones, nail-clippings, eyes, brains, skulls, particularly the lower jaws, called in Mpongwe *oginga,* accumulated from deceased members of successive generations."   Miss Kingsley objects to Nassau's use of the word "secretly," for she saw bundles of this nature among the cannibal Fans, and among the non-cannibal Adooma, openly hanging in the thatch of the sleeping-apartment.[1]

"Among the Bandali," who live on the uplands above the north-west corner of Lake Nyasa, "all bodies are dug up after the flesh has rotted away, and the bones are taken into the forest, where they are placed in a sitting position against a tree and left there.   A much more gruesome custom, which prevails among the Bandali, is that of keeping the bones on the verandah of the heir's house, done up in banana leaves, which are renewed as required, the bones being occasionally anointed with oil."[2] Whether these bones have any religious function or significance, we are not told.

In Uganda, Roscoe says,[3] ghosts hang about the place where their bodies are buried and will not go far away, unless the lower jawbone is removed, when they remove with it.[4]   He mentions that there are jawbones which have been preserved by clans for a thousand years.   The heart is the centre of feeling, will, and understanding, according to Bantu thought;[5] and one

[1] TWA. 300-301; see my p. 330.

[2] SRK. 296.

[3] Bg. 282; see also my p. 281.

[4] Barbot, writing of his travels on the Guinea Coast in the decades preceding A.D. 1700, mentions that it was the custom of some nations on this coast—he cites Commendo in particular, because a native of that district confessed that he had done it—to remove the lower jaws of slain foes before leaving the corpse on the battle-field and to take these relics home as trophies. (C. v. 296.)   A somewhat similar notion appears in the Pacific: On the Marshall Bennets the jawbone of the dead man is worn by his widow, and in some Australian tribes it was sometimes carried as a memento by the father or mother. (JRAI., 1925, p. 109.)

[5] "The representation upon the walls of the Magdalenian Salon Noir de Niaux of a bison with four arrows stuck in its flank, pointing towards the heart, proves that the early hunters recognised that the flank was a peculiarly vital spot in the Bison's anatomy.   But it was not merely the flank as a whole, but the heart in particular, that was regarded as the centre of vitality.   This is shown by the still earlier Aurignacian picture of an elephant from the cave of Pindal in Asturias. The survival of this remarkable manner of depicting the vital node of wild animals

expects, therefore, that it should be regarded as the organ of the soul; but there seems to be no attempt to preserve it.

The Bagesu of Mt. Elgon, "one of the most primitive of the negro tribes of Africa," according to Roscoe, observe a custom which is unusual in Africa, though practised in Australia. After the corpse has been deposited at sunset on the nearest waste land, clansmen hidden in the surrounding bush imitate the cry of jackals, as the darkness deepens, and elderly women relatives of the deceased cut it up under cover of the night and take back portions for the mourners to cook and eat during the next three or four days. The skull is kept in the house or set upon a stone outside, for it is thought to be the relic to which the ghost attaches itself; but parts of the corpse which were not brought for the mourners are left for the beasts to devour, and the bones which the mourners leave are burned. These people believe, so Roscoe tells us, that unless the body of the dead is thus destroyed and eaten, the ghost will be angry and haunt them; and that if they allowed the body to decay, the ghost would be detained in the vicinity of the place of death and would revenge itself by causing illness to the children of the family.[1] Remarkable as these rites are, they embody the doctrine with which we have already become familiar; that ghosts cannot find release from the trammels of the flesh till full mortuary rites are completed, and that if these are denied or unduly delayed, ghosts become vindictive. ·

CANONISATION OF THE DEAD

Whether the Becwana believe that the -*dimo* of an unburied corpse (like the *edimmu* of the Assyrians) finds no place in the

among the Ojibwa Indians of North America, and the aboriginal Australians still further emphasises its significance. The heart thus came to be regarded as a centre of life, feeling, volition, and knowledge. There are also indications that the contents of the heart were regarded as sharing these attributes." (Prof. G. Elliot Smith: *Essays on the Evolution of Man*, pp. 122-23.) Alcmæon of Crotona (B.C. 500) was the first to discover that man thinks with the brain; but Aristotle (B.C. 384-322), misled by experiments that he had made on the brains of animals, reverted to the old view that thinking and feeling were centred in the heart. Among the Egyptians, Budge tells us (EM. 29), "the heart was not only the seat of the power of life, but also the source of both good and evil thought, and it sometimes typified the conscience."

[1] GS. 9, 23, 38, 40; cf. SCD. 260.

land of Shades, is doubtful, though probable; but they do believe that the spirit lingers about the grave till sacrifice is offered, a month after burial, for the repose of the departed,[1] or, as they express it, for sending the spirit home to the abode of the gods.

This final funerary function is common to many Bantu tribes, though the period between burial and the culmination of the ritual varies considerably. Almost immediately after burial, the favourite cattle of some rich Hereros are slaughtered near their graves. These cattle are stabbed with assegais and hurriedly decapitated, though suffocation is the usual Herero method of killing stock for food or sacrifice; their horns are then carried to the tree near which deceased was buried, and their carcases, hastily cut to pieces without being flayed, are thrown away. Such beasts are said to *yondyoza* the deceased. Concerning the meaning of the verb *okuyondyoza* there has been much discussion, but the likeliest definition is that given by the Rev. G. Viehe.[2] He thinks it is the causative form of the verb *okuyondya*, which means "to go on," "to lead the way," and that the cattle are slaughtered to make the deceased go on, or to accompany him after death.

According to Casalis,[3] who wrote in 1861, the Basuto had much the same notion: "As soon as a person is dead he takes his

---

[1] Pliny the younger, nephew of Pliny the Naturalist, tells a story in one of his letters (Bk. vii., chap. 27) of a philosopher named Athenodorus. Two Stoic philosophers of that name came from the neighbourhood of Tarsus: one, surnamed Cordylion, came to Rome in 70 B.C., when already aged, at the invitation of Cato; and the other, son of Sandon, lived for a long time in Rome as the teacher and friend of Augustus. It is impossible to ascertain which of these Pliny refers to. The story runs to this effect: Athenodorus rented a haunted house in Athens, and at night saw a phantom of an old man, thin and stooped, with a long white beard, carrying upon his feet and hands heavy chains which he shook horribly. The spectre motioned him to follow, and seizing a torch he pursued it into the courtyard, where it disappeared. Next day he had the courtyard dug up at that spot, and found a skeleton in chains, relic of an ancient crime. After they had taken the chains from the skeleton and favoured it with the customary honours for the dead, which it had lacked before, it never again troubled the house. Now if we assume that the story owes more to the imagination of the raconteur than to the historicity of the event, we are still driven to the conclusion that the idea that the dead haunted their remains till the customary burial rites were rendered, was not unfamiliar to Athenodorus, or, at any rate, to Pliny. Lucian, the Greek satirist, makes the Pythagorean Arignotus tell a similar tale (if it is not the same) of his own experience in a haunted house at Corinth.

[2] See *Journal of the South African Folklore Society*, May, 1879.

[3] Bs. 250.

place among the family gods. An ox is immolated over his grave: this is the first oblation made to the new divinity, and at the same time an act of intercession in his favour, serving to ensure his happy reception in the subterranean regions. All those present aid in sprinkling the grave, and repeat the following prayer: 'Repose in peace with the gods; give us tranquil nights.'"

I learn from a correspondent who is familiar with the customs of the Zulu that no worship is rendered to a departed spirit till a year has elapsed after burial; then there is a *buyisa* ceremony, to bring back home the departed spirit. At this ceremony a white goat is killed and then a beast, the *umswani* ("contents of the stomach") being burned, together with the inward fat and incense, at the back of the hut.

Mashona chiefs are not canonised till a year after death, and in the interval are proclaimed as living. After the year has passed, the new chief is chosen, and one of his first official acts is to offer sacrifice to the spirits of all past chiefs of the tribe, mentioning in order each name that is known, and concluding with a request that his immediate predecessor will now join the galaxy in the spirit-world. In families of lesser note the procedure is practically identical. Some months (it may be a year) after the head of a Mashona family has been interred, when the time has come for the distribution of his estate, the man who acted as undertaker at his funeral leads forth the mourners, chaunting their dirges, and sprinkles the grave with the blood of a goat which is slaughtered for the purpose. Then a libation of beer is placed upon the grave; and the deceased is informed that his meat and drink are given him, and that he has stayed long in the bush and should now join the spirits of his fathers and look after his people remaining at the kraal.[1]

Wilder tells us [2] that the Ndau people of Mt. Selinda, after keeping up the mourning for a month, offer beer, a goat, a fowl, or a cloth (one or all) to the spirit; and the head of the kraal, standing in the hut, calls the dead by name and thus addresses him: "We call you back from the wilds to your home. We introduce you to our dead ancestors. And we say to you, our ances-

[1] MLC. 53-4.
[2] *Hartford Seminary Record*, April, 1907.

tors, take this your child. Here is the feast prepared for you."
Then he dips up the beer with a ladle, letting a few drops fall
on the ground so that the spirits under the ground may see it;
and the company reverently clap their hands (the royal salutation) and proceed to drink the beer.

The Konde belief is not quite so clear from Mackenzie's account.[1] "At death, or rather at burial, the head of the family,
calling for silence from the wailing women, addresses the spirits
by name, praying them to receive their friend. Then addressing
the dead man direct, he says: 'And you, my friend, go to the land
of spirits. Go in peace. Go to meet all whom we have named.
They will recognise you. Salute them all.'" But he tells us
on another page [2] that at a feast, about a month after the funeral,
a small quantity of beer is taken to the grave, and the dead
man is again bidden to go to his ancestors: "Take this beer as
an offering to them. The ox that we have killed is also for
them." This looks like a sacrificial feast for the opening of the
gates of the nether world. He writes, further, that this tribe
used to bury six or eight slaves with a great chief,[3] four going
into the grave to hold the dead body of their master in their
arms, two at the head and two at the feet, the others being placed
on top and the soil filled in on the living and the dead.

The Tumbuka people seem to lay stress upon the return of the
spirit to the home, rather than upon its being given the road to
the land of the dead. At the end of the long mourning, which
lasts for nearly a year, there is great feasting and dancing, and
the heads of the mourners are shaved. "A procession was made
to the grave with food stuffs, and one of the number taking a
pot of beer in his hand poured it on the grave and prayed to the
spirit of the dead thus: 'We have come to bring you, our friend,
back to the village. Come and visit your family. See, I give
you this food that you may drink.' And then they returned to
the village spilling meal on the path as they went, and placing
a pot of beer in the hut of their dead relative."[4]

Monteiro was an alien to Bantu thought, but he had an eye

[1] SRK. 192.
[2] SRK. 299.
[3] SRK. 70, and cf. my pp. 44 ff.
[4] WPP. 160.

for customs. After describing the process of mummification in Angola,[1] he explains that their reason for keeping the mummy in the hut for a year or more is "that all the relations of deceased may be present at the final ceremony, when the body is wrapped in as many yards of cloth as they can possibly afford. . . . On the occasion of the funeral a 'wake' or feast consisting of 'batuco' or dancing, with firing of guns and consumption of drink, roast pig, and other food, is held for the whole night. It is believed that the spirit of the dead person will haunt the town where he died, and commit mischief if the 'wake' is not held."

What Miss Kingsley inaptly calls "the burying of the spirit," —a practice which she observed among West Coast Negroes and Bantu—is evidently their ritual for sending the spirit forward to the abode of the gods. She says: "The period of the duration of mourning is, I believe, in all the West Coast tribes, that which elapses between the death and the burial of the soul."[2]

The Bantu believe, as did our Aryan forefathers,[3] and as Russian peasants still do, that the spirits of the dead linger for some weeks after the burial before proceeding to the world of Shades. Hence some Bantu customs which are intelligible only in the light of this belief. Funeral feasts and games, for example, are inspired by the thought that the dead are present and share the festivities with their friends. "Some affirm," writes Claridge,[4] "that the soul remains in the body until after the funeral to see that it gets no less attention than the best ritual provides for it,"—an unintelligent phrasing of fact. "I noticed that the mouths and nostrils of the recently dead were always plugged and tied," says Weeks, in writing of the Boloki people,[5] "and to my questions on the subject I always received the same reply: 'The soul of a dying man escapes by his mouth and nose,

[1] See pp. 22 ff.

[2] TWA. 329, 333, 339.

[3] SCD. 142 *et seq.* It was customary in England before the Reformation, and still is in Ireland among Roman Catholics, to observe what was known as "Month's mind." On a day one month after the date of a person's death, a mass was celebrated for the repose of his soul; and elaborate bequests and instructions in "the last will and testament" of some well-to-do people, show how beneficial to the soul this sacrifice was thought to be.

[4] WBT. 291.

[5] ACC. 262.

so we always tie them in that fashion to keep the spirit, as long as possible, in the body.' "

When Becwana tribesmen were prepared for burial, it was customary to show them an ox-bone (or else the hoof of an ox), a *kao* ("thong for fastening a cow's legs before milking"), a *mogala-secho* ("nose-cord for a pack-ox"), and a milk-bowl, and then to imitate the herd-boy's peculiar whistle, and when the corpse was laid in the grave a little dry cow-dung was laid beside it and the ox-bone or hoof was placed at its head. Women of these tribes have nothing to do with oxen, but are specially concerned with growing and preparing cereals. At the burial of a woman, therefore, the corpse was shown a pestle from the corn-mortar, a winnowing-fan, a cook-pot, a *lohétlhó* ("pronged stick used for stirring porridge"), a spoon, a plate, and a cracked pot, such as women use to carry live coals from place to place; and a little Kafir-corn was scattered upon the corpse before the grave was filled.

At the cross-roads on the way to the burial-ground, a Bakaonde funeral-party sits down to wait till late-comers have arrived. "They then address the corpse, saying something as follows: 'Some one has been responsible for your death—you must now revenge yourself on him.'[1] Nothing is more impressive in Smith & Dale's description of a funeral which one of them witnessed,[2] than the fact that the Natives concerned acted as if the deceased were present and knew all that was said or done.

The grave of a Wachagga man is dug inside his senior wife's hut and the corpse is wrapped in the hide of a bull slaughtered for the occasion. A day or two later "the ceremony called *Ngowoe* is performed to bless the grave. A bull is slaughtered in the banana grove and the following prayer said: 'You, great grandfather, our father, he who guards this village, receive this bull that you may eat it with your fathers. Take this man, open to him the door to the ancestors, show him their village, stay with him that you may protect him and he be not troubled by the spirits. Now receive this man for we have given you bulls and goats, and we knew not what had become of your strength. This man of yours was robbed out of your hands, now then

[1] WBA. 91.
[2] IPNR. ii. 105.

stay with him and guard him well for ever.' " [1]   The author cited explains in a footnote that the underlying assumption of the last sentences in the prayer is that the ancestor-spirits were somehow unable to save the deceased from death.

The Wawanga of Elgon district place a leaf of a tree called *mutoto* "underneath the ear, on the side on which the corpse is lying, and two leaves on the other ear," perforating the leaves, "so that deceased may hear what is being said." [2]

The Bangata of Equatorial Congoland,[3] "take care to put the dead body into communication with the world of the living by means of a tube, just like the inhabitants of the Cataract region of the Lower Congo,"—a practice which, strange as it may seem to us, is found in Greek and Roman tombs of ancient days.[4]

"The Baluba of South-central Congoland believe that death is in no way a separation of soul and body: it is a simple stoppage of the heart, produced either by a fatal accident, or by the power of a sorcerer, or still more likely by an act of the spirit of a deceased relative. . . . After death has taken place the Baluba believe that the soul continues to reside unimpaired in the corpse, with the possibility of detaching itself, not freely and untrammelled, but in association with a vague, impalpable something, a kind of phantom or spectre which has the exact appearance of the dead body, but has not its real substance. It is under this shadowy form, which is, in short, the dematerialised body, that the soul will henceforth live in the realm of the dead." [5]   Among these same people, "when a man has breathed his last, his relatives place over his eyes a thick bandage; his gaze would bring misfortune upon them; for through those eyes, glazed by death, his surviving soul sees everything." [6]

The Bakonjo (Mount Ruwenzori) period of mourning lasts two months, or even six if deceased is an important member of

---

[1] K. 182, 185.
[2] JRAI., 1913, p. 35.
[3] GGC. 649, and cf. WBT. 292 and my p. 33.
[4] SCD. 140.   This primitive belief is ingrained in the thought of modern Egyptians, persisting in spite of Christianity and Islam and all the other changes of peoples and faiths. "To this day, we may see a woman go out to the cemetery, and sit talking down through a hole in the roof of the tomb-chamber, to her husband buried below." (RLAE. 113.)
[5] GGC. 642.
[6] GGC. 643.

the clan, and is brought to an end with a sacrificial feast at the grave.[1] The Bambwa mourn for a month in the hut in which deceased is buried, and then feast upon a sacrificial goat, the head of which is placed upon the grave.[2] The people of Busoga believe that the ghost remains among the plantains near the place where the body lies, to watch what is done, for the treatment of the body affects the future of the ghost.[3]

A very similar notion seems to have been taken up into Islam. Lane tells us that the Muslims of Egypt believe that the soul remains in the body during the first night after burial, and that it is visited on this night by two angels, who examine the soul, and perhaps torture the body. Then it departs to the place appointed for the residence of good souls until the last day, or to the appointed prison in which wicked souls await their final doom. In his synopsis of Sale's statements concerning the opinions of Muslims respecting the state of souls in the interval between death and the judgment, he mentions that some Muslims believe that the soul stays near the sepulchre, with liberty of going wherever it pleases, and that others say that it stays near the grave for seven days.[4] The teaching of Zoroastrianism that three days elapse after death before the souls of the departed are conducted into the presence of the judges of the dead, is probably based upon the same idea.

According to Chagga imagination, the inaugural adventures of a discarnate spirit are of a much more strenuous variety. "The way to spirit land is long and terrifying, traversing an immense desert in which there is neither vegetation nor water. The sun beats fiercely on this desert while the bare baked soil scorches the feet. The name of this desert is *Murongo*, and the soul takes eight days to traverse it, arriving on the ninth day. To ease the sufferings of the journey, the corpse of the departed is shrouded in a hide to serve for protection against the grilling sun's rays, and the body is anointed with fat, while milk and fat are poured into the mouth for sustenance on the road. The ninth day after burial is called *Mfiri o funio mengengi*, signifying that on this

[1] GS. 145.
[2] GS. 155.
[3] GS. 105.
[4] MCME. 530-31.

day the soul reaches the Spirit Chief's residence. Here the Chief's warriors bar the new-comer from entering until he has paid a bull for admission, just as a chief among men demands a similar fee from the new-comer who seeks admission to his country. Now the grandfather of the new-comer comes to the gateway with his relatives, and after inquiring as to how he fared on the road, they tell him the reason why he had to die. They then leave the spirit outside until the bull for admission has been received. I conjecture that this is the animal which is sacrificed on the day following the interment and which would consequently be a day behind the spirit. The bull is in fact sacrificed to the grandfather with petition for his protection for the new-comer. The fee having been received, the grandfather returns to the gateway and directs the warriors to admit the stranger." [1]

One wonders whether this notion has come into the tribe with the Swahili-Arab (Wa-kilindini) blood that runs in the veins of some of its ruling families,[2] or been imported from other foreign sources,—possibly Masai, Wangasa, or even the elusive Wakon-yingo.[3] But there is a likelier explanation. Stories of a long and perilous journey for the soul are seldom reported from Bantu communities, but in other parts of the world,[4] where they are a prominent feature of eschatological belief among immigrant peoples, they represent the journey back to the old tribal home whither the soul betakes itself at death that it may find its place in the assembly of its fathers; and this Chagga belief may be genetically related to the terrors of a desert journey that their forefathers made to reach the southern slopes of Kilimanjaro. So, also, with the Baganda belief that ghosts go to Tanda, pay their respects to Walumba, the god of the dead, account to him for their doings in the flesh, and are then free to return to their burial-grounds.[5] It may be surmised that a knowledge of the locality of Tanda and of the earthly career of Walumba would

[1] K. 124.
[2] CSBSL. ii. 35.
[3] K. 41-42.
[4] *The Life After Death in Oceania and the Malay Archipelago*, by Rosalind Moss, B. Sc. Oxon (Oxford: Clarendon Press), 1925, provides an instructive résumé of Polynesian, Melanesian and Indonesian beliefs and practices.
[5] Bg. 286.

throw light on the migrations of patriarchs who taught their children to hold fast by the eternal hope of gathering again with the heroes of their past in sacred soil.

SERVITORS OF THE DEAD

The belief that the spirit makes the corpse its home till the gates of the nether world are opened to it by acts of ritual efficacy, makes it easier to understand the ancient Bantu practice of burying slaves and wives of the dead with their lord and master. Although this appears to us to be the culmination of useless cruelty, it was once approved by mankind from China to Britain.

On the death of a king of the Ist dynasty in Egypt, it was customary to kill the courtiers and high officials and bury them in rows of small graves around the royal tomb. Certain peculiarities of these graves and their occupants suggest that the victims were stunned, stripped, and hastily thrown in, a few of them being slightly conscious at the time of burial. Over five hundred people were killed in the earlier period, but by the end of the dynasty the number was nearer fifty, and in the next dynasty the practice ceased. It was observed in Ethiopia, however, in the second reign of the XIIth dynasty (about 2758-2714 B.C.), the great viceroy, Hepzefa, being buried at Kerma in the far Sudan with three hundred slaughtered Nubians to serve him in the next life.[1]

According to the archives of the Celestial Empire, one hundred and twenty-seven persons were buried with the prince of Ts'in in B.C. 619; a certain Wei Wu-tsu gave orders before his death (about B.C. 600) that a favourite concubine should be buried alive with him; several living persons were interred with Wen, the ruler of Sung, in B.C. 587; and the practice survived till a comparatively recent date.[2]

[1] RLAE. 35, 135, 145 f., 165. Budge writes, in the British Museum monograph on *The Book of the Dead* (1922 ed., p. 36): "The text of Chapter VI was cut on figures made of stone, wood, etc. (*ushabtiu*), which were placed in the tomb, and when deceased recited it these figures became alive and did everything he wished. The *shabti* figure took the place of the human funerary sacrifice which was common all over Egypt before the general adoption of the cult of Osiris under the XIIth dynasty."

[2] S.C.D. 47.

In Japan it is said to have been customary to bury retainers, standing and alive, round the sepulchre of a prince, till Mikado Sun-nin (who reigned, according to the "Accepted Chronology" from B.C. 29 to A.D. 70!) directed that clay images of men should henceforth be substituted for living victims.[1]

The ancient Celts, unlike the Chinese, were ignorant of writing; but in Celtic burial-places "some of the interments undoubtedly point to the sacrifice of wife, children or slaves at the grave. Male and female skeletons are found in close proximity, in one case the arm of the male encircling the neck of the female. In other cases the remains of children are found with them. Or, while the lower interment is richly provided with grave-goods, above it lie irregularly several skeletons, without grave-goods, and often with the head separated from the body, pointing to decapitation, while in one case the arms had been tied behind the back."[2]

Coming down to more recent centuries, Callaway quotes[3] an extract from the Sire de Joinville's *Saint Louis, King of France*. "While he was in their camp a knight of much means died, and they dug for him a broad and deep trench in the earth; and they seated him, very nobly attired, on a chair, and placed by his side the best horse and the best sergeant he had, both alive. The sergeant, before he was placed in the grave with his lord, went round to the King of the Comans, and the other men of quality, and while he was taking leave of them they threw into his scarf a large quantity of silver and gold, and said to him, 'When I come to the other world thou shalt return to me what I now entrust to thee.' And he replied, 'I will gladly do so.' The great King of the Comans confided to him a letter addressed to their first king,[4] in which he informed him that this worthy man had led a good life and had served him faithfully, and begged him to reward him for his services. When this was done they placed him in the grave with his lord and the horse, both alive; then they threw over the trench boards closely fitted together, and the whole army ran to pick up stones and earth, so that

[1] *Transactions of the Asiatic Society of Japan*. Yokohama: Meiklejohn & Co., vol. x., 1882, p. 200 (Note 4).
[2] RAC. 337 (Students should read all Chap. XXII).
[3] RSZ. 101.
[4] Cf. my p. 381.

before they slept they had erected a great mound over it, in remembrance of those who were interred." Tylor says: [1] "In Europe long after the wives and slaves ceased thus to follow their master, the warrior's horse was still solemnly killed at his grave and buried with him. This was done as lately as 1781 at Treves, when a general named Friedrich Kasimir was buried according to the rites of the Teutonic Order; and in England the pathetic ceremony of leading the horse to a soldier's funeral is the last remnant of the ancient sacrifice."

Of the prevalence of this custom in Africa, there is abundant evidence, but a few examples must suffice.

Andrew Battell, the first Englishman to penetrate the interior of what is now called Angola and leave an account of his experiences, spent about eighteen months between A.D. 1590 and 1608 with a horde of "Jagas" who were ravaging the country. "When they bury their dead," he says, referring to the "Jagas," "they make a vault in the ground, and a seat for him to sit. The dead hath his head newly embroidered, his body washed and anointed with sweet powders. He hath all his best robes put on, and is brought between two men to his grave, and set in a seat as though he were alive. He hath two of his wives set with him, with their arms broken, and then they cover over the vault on the top." [2]

Dapper, in his *Travels*, published in Amsterdam in A.D. 1670, states [3] that it was the custom to bury twelve virgins with the earlier kings of Kongo. "To show themselves kind to the dead," writes Father Merolla, in his *Voyage to Congo*, etc., [4] "they are commonly very cruel to the living, shutting up both together in a tomb with meat and drink, [5] to the end (say they) that the

[1] *Anthropology:* London (Macmillan), 1881, p. 347.
[2] SAAB. 34-35.
[3] SAAB. 102-105.
[4] C. i. 605.
[5] What was the motive for burying people *alive* with the dead? Bloodless human sacrifices are attributed, in some parts of the world where they occur, to a belief that people slain by violence have a separate after-life from those who die a natural death; but the slaughter of servitors that marked the burial of many Bantu notables, makes that explanation inapplicable to these tribes. It was the denial of mortuary rites to such impious wretches as suicides, witches, and people killed by lightning or the ordeal that excluded them from spiritland, not the violence of their death; and servitors slain at the grave were thought to pass into the spirit-world in the train of their lord.

dead lord may want for nothing in his grave." He does not tell us whether it was wives, children, retainers, or slaves who were buried alive with their dead lord; but he adds that "the wickedness of these people sometimes goes further; for at the death of any of their friends they have been accustomed to kill one of their slaves, to the end that he may go and serve them in the other world." Barbot gives a more detailed account of similar practices at Benin, stating that when the king's body has been lowered into a huge pit which is dug to receive it, "his most beloved domesticks of both sexes earnestly beg to be allowed the favour of going into it, to wait and attend on their master in the other life"; and that "when a woman dies . . . if she was a person of distinction, they massacre thirty or forty slaves on the day of her burial; and one has been known to have had seventy-eight slaves sacrificed on her account, which were all her own; and to complete the even number of eighty, as she had ordered before her death, they murdered two young children, a boy and a girl, whom she loved extremely." [1] In his description of Loango and Angola—"Lower Æthiopia," as he calls it—he makes no mention of such practices.

Shooter, writing in A.D. 1857, says that when Chaka's mother died, a number of men were executed, ten young girls buried alive with the corpse, and some thousands of people massacred before the mourning ceremonies were ended. [2] "It was especially the case with us at first," said a Zulu to Callaway, [3] "when a chief died, he did not die alone; for at first the bodies of the dead were burnt, [4] and when a chief died, and they went from their homes to dispose of the remains, they took shields and adorned themselves with their military ornaments; and when they came to the place where the remains were to be burnt, they cut much firewood; and as there were oxen there too, the chief ox with which he made royal festivals was killed with him, that it might

[1] C., v. 371 and 366.
[2] KNZC. 242.
[3] RSZ. 213.
[4] The Bantu were wont to burn the bodies of evil-doers (witches, for example) who had been sentenced to *post mortem* outlawry, but not to cremate the bodies of the honoured dead; and honorific cremation, though another instance is reported from Zulu immigrants into Central Africa, seems to have no connection with Zulu or other Bantu beliefs. This group of tribes may have imported the rite from some foreign source at no very distant date.

die with him. When the fire was kindled, the chief was put in; and then his servants were chosen, and put into the fire after the chief; the great men followed, they were taken one by one. They said, 'So-and-so is fit to go with the chief.' When the fire began to sink down, they said, 'Put the fire together, So-and-so.' And when he was putting the firewood together, they cast him in; they went and took all the great men one by one from the chief houses of the chief's brothers, and from those who were not his brothers. Many people were killed on that day." Tyler, who lived on the border of Zululand from 1849, wrote:[1] "It has been the custom in Zululand, . . . when a king dies, to bury with him some of his servants, cupbearers, milkmen, etc., that the saying may be fulfilled, 'The king must not go to the place of the dead alone.' The unfortunate individuals selected were generally strangled, and their bodies placed at the bottom of the grave, the royal corpse being laid upon them. It is reported that some have entered the grave alive and died with perfect submission." He mentions, also, that a missionary whom he knew saved a group of nine or ten people who had been set apart to grace a chief's funeral in this manner.

A social usage upon which Kafir tribes insisted in 1826, shocking as it may seem to us, probably owes its origin to a sweetening of manners that made these Natives evade the cruel custom of burying wives with their deceased husband. "If the deceased was a married man," wrote William Shaw,[2] "his wives fly to the bush or to the mountains immediately on his death being announced, and there remain for several days, only coming to the kraal after dark, to obtain food and sleep, and then going off again to the mountains with the first dawn of day. Sometimes, however, they remain altogether in the mountains, night as well as day." He quotes, also, from a colleague's account of funeral ceremonies for Chief Dhlambi:[3] "All the wives of Dhlambi (ten in number) are now gone into the bush, where they will remain for some time. Their karosses, caps, etc., are buried,[4] and their

---

[1] *Forty Years Among the Zulus,* by the Rev. Josiah Tyler (Boston: Congregational Publishing Society), pp. 208 ff.

[2] *The Story of My Mission in South-Eastern Africa,* by William Shaw. London: Hamilton, Adams & Co., 1860, p. 428.

[3] *Op. cit.,* p. 431.

[4] Cf. my pp. 30 and 32.

beads, buttons, and other trinkets are given away; so that when
the time has expired for their leaving the bush, they have to get
new karosses and ornaments. This custom is also attended to by
the common people, an instance of which I witnessed a few weeks
ago. When the husband died, his wife with an infant was driven
into the large bush near Mount Coke, where she continued five
days and nights without food, excepting a few roots which she
pulled up, which just kept her alive."

Livingstone mentions [1] that it was customary among the Ba-
lunda and the Barotse to slaughter a number of chief's servants
to accompany their deceased lord into the other world.

Rowley gives an instance in which the people of a village a
few miles from Chibisa's on the Shire River had arranged to cut
the throat of one of the slave-wives of their deceased chief and
bury her with the corpse of her husband, pleading that it was
the custom of the country. [2]

Macdonald affirms [3] that if a man of the Abanda or Amilansi
families of the Wayao dies, many of his slaves are at once confined in slave-sticks to be put in the grave with him: sometimes
as many as ten for an important chief, and fewer for one who is
not so rich. And on a subsequent page [4] he says that if slaves
were buried with a corpse, an enormous hole is dug, and those
caught are thrown in, either alive or with their throats cut, and
the body of their master or mistress is laid upon theirs.

A number of women were killed and laid at the bottom of
the grave of a Tumbuka chief, to make a couch for their dead
master. [5]

When the Wemba chief, Chitimukulu, died, "after examining
the king's body they seized all his personal attendants and servants that could be found. Three were straightway killed, the
first slave's lifeless body being put under the king's head as his
pillow, the second slave under his feet as his footstool, while
the third was slain at the gate of the harem stockade, so that his
spirit should act as guardian and ward off evil spirits and thieves
whilst the king slept." After the body, rubbed with preserva-

[1] MTR. 318.
[2] UMCA. 272-75.
[3] A. i. 101, cf. NBCA. 160.
[4] A. i. 106-108.
[5] AI. 163.

tives, had lain in state for almost a year, it was carried in state
to the royal burial-ground, one of the king's servants being slain
at the principal gate of the village and the corpse of the king
passed over his quivering body. The royal burial-place was some
days distant, and any one found travelling on the path was seized
as a victim, and one victim was slain at each of several points
in the journey. At the sacred grove two more slaves were sacrificed. A hut was built over the grave, and furnished with the
usual native furniture and the dead king's bows and arrows and
spears; and tusks of ivory were placed leaning against the walls.
"The head wife was finally dragged into this hut, and the natives say, dispatched (by strangling) by Mwaruli himself and
buried, in cases where she was not instantly killed on the king's
death." [1]

Masters relates [2] that in the days before British rule, Walumba
chiefs were buried in a very large grave, in the bottom of which
their wives were placed alive, the two favourites supporting the
corpse in their arms, while a slave knelt at the dead man's feet
presenting his pipe and spear; and that all the remaining slaves
were then beheaded and thrown in, the living and the dead being
buried together. He mentions, also, that a message was sometimes shouted into the ear of a slave before his head was struck off.

In a future chapter we shall have occasion to mention the burial
of wives with a king of Bunyoro.[3] In some parts of Busoga
widows and slaves were buried with a chief, but as a rule the body
was buried alone.[4] The Bakyiga of Kigezi (south of Ruwenzori)
usually punished a murderer who was caught redhanded by burying him alive beneath the corpse of his victim.[5]

A Belgian missionary describes the funeral of a chieftain of the
Nsakara, on the northern Mubangi.[6] "On a bed, in an immense
circular ditch, his head resting on the arm of his favourite wife, is
laid the body of the deceased, dressed in his richest attire; around
him, attached to stakes, the strangled bodies of the wives who
have been unwilling to survive their husband; thrown pell-mell

---

[1] GPNR. 185-87. See also my p. 165.
[2] WR. 154-56.
[3] See pp. 282 f.
[4] GS. 131.
[5] GS. 180-81.
[6] GGC. 657.

in the ditch, the bodies of slaves and servants who have worked
for the dead man; such is the hideous spectacle presented to a
crowd, craving for pain and slaughter.   The ditch is filled up,
and on the newly piled earth begins the sacrifice destined for the
feasts celebrated in memory of him whom they are lamenting.
. . . These repasts of human flesh last many days." Father
Allaire, who founded the Liranga mission at the confluence of
the Ubangi and the Congo in 1889, wrote: "I recently learned of
the death of a very influential woman chief named Komba-Keka,
whom I knew quite well.   Do you know how many slaves were
slain to accompany her to the grave?   Seventy."[1]   "It must be
remembered," says Johnston,[2] "that in the interior Congo basin
north of about 6° S. Latitude and south of the Muhammadan
regions, no free man or woman of importance could be buried
without the accompanying sacrifice of one or many adult men or
women.   Believing in a life after the grave, these grimly logical
people argued that the dead notability could not be ushered into
the spirit world alone.   There must be a servant or a wife—in the
case of a chief or chieftainess multitudes of retainers—to accompany the dead woman or man and to carry on the spirit life as
nearly as possible on the lines of the terrestrial existence.   Implements, utensils, pottery, cloth, beads, tobacco were similarly interred—usually after being broken, torn, bent, or 'killed.'   As
the slaves or wives of the deceased were by no means willing to
die in the prime of life—and often by cruel means—they were
perpetually seeking to evade this last duty to master or husband
by running away."   Then follow extracts from Grenfell's diary
in which he records sacrifices that he witnessed among the Bolobo:
a man was decapitated and a woman beaten to death with sticks,
to accompany the dead wife of a chief, and next day a man and a
woman were placed alive in the grave under the corpse and buried
with it (July, 1889).   Next year Grenfell mentions that when
the Belgian Commissaire tried to prevent burial-murder and stood
by and saw the corpse buried, the people dug up the corpse during
the following night and put the bodies of five victims in the
grave with the corpse.   Those killed to accompany the dead are
not always buried with the corpse, however; Grenfell mentions

[1] RP. 233.
[2] GGC. 375-76, 382, 386, 388-89.

an instance in which nine slaves were killed at the obsequies of a wife, five of whom were buried and four thrown into the river.

Again the same author writes:[1] "A personage of consequence, still more a great chief, must not go to the spirit-world without wives or attendant slaves. Husbands, it is true, are not obliged to accompany their wives, but it is evident that (at one time) nearly all over Negro Africa *widows* had to die in the graves of their deceased husbands." He quotes a Belgian missionary's description of the obsequies of a Luban chief: soon after death the neck of a young slave is broken with a heavy blow and he is laid by the corpse for two days. He is the chief's boy attendant. The burial takes place several days later, after certain fragments have been removed as relics, their removal being announced by the slaughter of another slave. At the time of the burial two men are beaten to death with clubs and thrown across the public way by which the funeral proceeds. The grave is dug in a marsh, and when ready two female slaves decked in their finest attire, lie face to face in the bottom of the grave, each stretching out the arm nearest the ground and embracing the corpse of their master. If they shrink from the ordeal their skulls are broken or they are bound. Then six slaves are butchered and placed in the hollowed walls of the grave. Two other slaves are sacrificed on the grave, at intervals afterwards.

Among the Boloki of the Congo, it was customary to kill two slaves, and to place one under the head of the corpse, and the other under its feet. The number of wives buried with a man was in proportion to his wealth and social standing; but in every family of importance there was at least one young slave-wife who was known as *mwila ndako*—a name which indicated that she was destined to be buried alive with her dead husband. If she bore her husband a child before his decease, he took another *mwila ndako*, so as to be sure of having one wife to take into *longa* ("the nether world").[2] Another custom mentioned by the same writer,[3] is pertinent to the question before us. The skulls of those slain in war by a Boloki warrior were arranged in front

[1] GGC. 655-56. See also GGC. 111, 139 and 649 for other instances of burial-murder; and PC. i. 253.

[2] ACC. 103, 320.

[3] ACC. 105, 225.

of his house; and at his burial, men came forward, and taking a spear, summoned the spirits of these slain foes to attend their conqueror in the spirit-world.

Smith publishes an account which he had received from old men,[1] of the violence which characterised funerals of important persons at Nanzela in the old times, a custom which has now happily died out, and which seems never to have existed among the Baila proper. When a chief died, a great pit was dug and a mat spread at the bottom, upon which were laid the bodies of several slaves, who had been knocked on the head for the purpose. The chief's corpse was laid on the bodies of these slaves, with wives on either side and children at his head and feet. Over all these, other corpses were placed, and the grave filled in. If a stranger happened to pass, he was promptly killed and added to the pile. Women would voluntarily jump into the grave and suffer themselves to be buried alive with their husbands.

When Bunu, chief of the Amaswazi, died (1898?), a great fire was lit the same evening in front of his hut; his body was brought out and placed on a mat in front of the hut; and after his impis had honoured it with the military salute and war-dance, ten indunas approached in full costume of their rank, and gave the royal salute, beating their shields with their knobkerries in steady rhythmic strokes. Then the head witch-doctor made a speech, announcing that these ten indunas had been chosen of all the people to die with their king; and each of the ten advanced in turn, threw his shield and arms into the fire, stood by the side of the dead king, and received the fatal thrust of the medicine-man's knife.[2]

Seeing that many hours elapsed between the death of the notable and the killing of the victims, it looks like crazy thinking to imagine that they can accompany him into the spirit-world; but the notion becomes intelligible when once we grasp the belief that bodies are still habitats, or at least haunts, of those who are lost to sight, till the final rites for their apotheosis are accomplished.[3]

[1] IPNR. ii. 114.

[2] O'Neil's *Adventures in Swaziland*. London: Allen & Unwin, 1921, pp. 111-15. See my p. 48 for another instance of Zulu practice.

[3] This belief rests, no doubt, upon a psychological basis. At first deceased shows himself frequently in the dreams of survivors; and then after a while he seldom

The funeral of a Boloki man usually takes place within three days of his decease, unless the body is smoke-dried and kept for a more convenient occasion. At the funeral, says Weeks,[1] "there is more or less firing of guns, according to the importance of deceased. This they say is to ensure for him a good entrance into the nether world. The departed spirits in the nether world, hearing the firing, gather about the entrance to welcome the new arrival. Some say that the spirit of the deceased 'hovers near the entrance' (others say 'near to the body'), while they decorate the body, dig the grave, kill the slaves, prepare the wife who is to accompany him; then comes the firing, the entrance into the nether world, and the welcome."

In the last decade of last century, a missionary to the Bailunda of Angola wrote a graphic description of joint rites for the funeral of a chief and installation of his successor, which he had witnessed.[2] The corpse, wrapped in an ox-skin and tied to a palm-pole, was borne by aged counsellors to the rude altar of a hunter-spirit, a few hundred yards beyond the outer gate, where, after the sacrifice of a dog and a fowl, five thousand people danced and sang as they circumambulated the corpse for a couple of hours. Then the incoming chief emerged from his seclusion in the Ombala ("chief's village"), and prepared to receive the insignia of office from the dead chief and his counsellors. He took his stand facing the corpse, which was still carried on the shoulders of two men and flanked on either side by lines of some half-a-dozen leaders of the tribe; and the crowd closed round, gazing in wonderment. After a short speech, declaring that he had not merited the honour awarded him, the incipient chief commenced an interlocution with the corpse. The corpse, so the narrator affirms, is supposed to have the power to move its bearers backward or forward in answer to questions put to it; forward meaning "Yes," and backward, "No." "The interrogations are on this wise: 'You, my father, our chief! I have been chosen chief by the people in your place. I am not worthy of that

appears except when his protection, help, advice or comfort is sadly missed, or when the dreamer is conscious of having done something that he would have condemned.

[1] ACC. 321-22.
[2] *The Story of Chisamba.* Toronto: Canada Congregational Foreign Missionary Society, 1904, pp. 33-39.

position. . . . You know me who I am. I was one of your family when you were here upon earth. Is there anything to prevent my acceptance of the rulership of this people? Have I done evil that discredits me? Is there anything that I have done that may prevent me from being chief in your stead? Speak, I pray you, and let the people know if I am unworthy, or if you have any personal dislike for me.' There is a pause, and the suppressed excitement is felt by all the people surrounding the corpse. The chief's strong commanding voice quavers, and the eyes of the old men are rivetted on the bier in expectation of the answer. The two bearers after standing motionless for some seconds, still amid perfect silence over the crowd, . . . begin to sway slightly under their load; they incline a little to one side, then to the other; they move back a little; and finally and distinctly they lunge forward. The answer is propitious, and the chest of the new chief heaves as he draws a deep breath. The old men exchange wise nods of approval, and a murmur passes from the centre to the edge of the crowd. The interrogation is continued in the same manner and answered in the same way, until it is fully ascertained that the choice of the people entirely meets the wishes of the dead chief." It would be supererogatory to inquire whether the aged councillors that bore the corpse were privy to their late master's will: it is the prevalence of the doctrine, not its validity, that concerns us; [1] and I submit that such a scene would have been impossible if the crowd had not been dominated

[1] A curious example of this belief is reported from the other side of the world. On pp. 19-20 of a book entitled *The Native Tribes of South Australia* (published in 1879 by E. S. Wigg & Son of Adelaide), the Rev. G. Taplin states that the Narrinyeri tribes on the lower reaches of the Murray River always attributed death to sorcery, and continues: "The first night after a man has died his nearest relative sleeps with his head on the corpse, in order that he may be led to dream who is the sorcerer that caused his death. The next day the corpse is elevated on men's shoulders on a sort of bier called ngarratta. The friends of the deceased then gather round, and several names are called out to try if the mention of them produces any effect on the corpse. At last the nearest relative calls out the name of the person of whom he has dreamed, and then an impulse towards him on the part of the dead body is said to be felt by the bearers, which they pretend they cannot resist, and consequently they walk towards him. This impulse is the sign by which it is known that the right name has been called out." On p. 274 of the same book, Police Trooper Samuel Gason mentions that the Dieyerie tribe (630 miles north of Adelaide) used to ask the corpse about the cause of its death and the name of the man who killed him; but he does not describe the method of inquiry.

by a belief that the corpse was still controlled by the spirit that (as we should say) formerly tenanted it.

This belief provides, also, a probable explanation of three other Bantu burial customs: the wake, the burying of the corpse so that earth does not touch it, and the burying of some notabilities with the head above ground. One reason for watching by the corpse before and after burial, is fear lest witches should meddle with it; but the conviviality of these social gatherings points to another fear in the hearts of the bereaved—fear that he who has not yet passed into the spirit-world may feel lonely and take one of them for company. Some tribes place the body in a cavity scooped out in the side of the grave, and close the cavity with a bamboo door,[1] a plastered board,[2] or some other contrivance [3] before the soil is filled in. When Shooter wrote,[4] the practice of burying Zulu chiefs with their heads above ground had been abandoned, but not forgotten. A deceased member of the Lunda Hunters' Guild "must always be buried with his head above ground, and two holes must be left in the mound to enable him to see the surrounding country. A dead bird is placed in each hand prior to burial. Also before burial, one of his canine teeth is taken out and handed to his successor, who uses it as a hunting fetish and must also feed the tooth on blood." [5] In the Elgon district of Kenya Colony, the Wawanga (and apparently most of the Kavirondo tribes) wrap the corpse of their king in the hide of a newly slaughtered bull, and bury him in a sitting posture in his chief wife's hut, with his head above ground, and a tube leading from a beer-pot to his mouth. An inverted bowl is placed over his head, and his chief wife keeps guard in the hut for twenty days, after which the roof is broken down. As soon as the head commences to decay, it is covered over with earth; and a year later the bones are dug up, washed in water, anointed with butter, wrapped in the hide of a bull, and escorted by a great procession to the burial-place of the kings, where they are finally deposited in a grave which the new king visits periodically for purposes of sacrifice.[6] The canonisa-

[1] SRK. 394.
[2] See my p. 70, note 2.
[3] A. i. 106.
[4] KNZC. 241.
[5] WBA. 267.
[6] JRAI., 1913, pp. 28-29.

tion rites are probably performed at the time of final interment, but nothing is said about that in the paper cited.

Among the Bawenda of the Northern Transvaal, "if a boy dies before having married, a girl is sent after him into Hades to be his wife there. Formerly, it may be, the girl was buried with him, either alive or dead. Nowadays the girl is only sent metaphorically into Hades by the art of the witch-doctor." [1] The Wachagga of Kilimanjaro secure the same result by a different device. "A youth who dies unmarried is believed to be unhappy in spirit land and demands a wife of his family. In such a case the father will agree with some one whose daughter died unmarried to give her in marriage to his son. The deceased girl's father then gives a goat's head to the youth's father, and this is buried in his son's grave and marked with three stones—the woman's symbol—as though she were his wife." [2]

LOCALITY OF THE SPIRIT-WORLD

In the minds of the Bantu there is the same confusion between the grave and the underworld as in ancient Babylonia and the Old Testament. The Becwana say that they bury the patriarch just inside his cattle-pen, "so that he may hear the tramp of his cattle as they go out to graze in the morning and return for safety at sundown," and his "great wife" under the threshing-floor "that she may hear the thud of the flails, threshing out each new crop"; and yet when one asks them for tidings of some mutual acquaintance, unaware that he is dead, they are not unlikely to reply that "he is talking with spirits in the bowels of the earth." [3] The Akikuyu also believe that ancestral spirits live underground; [4] so do the Bambala; [5] and the Tumbuka. [6] The Boloki, on the northern bend of the Congo, believe that the spirits of good and bad men (according to the Native's code of morals) go to a nether world, where "the conditions of existence appear to be similar to those in the villages and towns, with this exception, that a man

[1] R. BAAS., 1905, iii. 214.
[2] K. 249, cf. my pp. 73 f.
[3] See also p. 137.
[4] BBM. 28.
[5] IPNR. ii. 119.
[6] WPP. 126.

may be too high in the social scale to be punished on earth, but he cannot escape punishment in the nether regions for the disagreeable qualities he has exhibited on earth." The punishment meted out to "bad" men is that they are expelled from the nether world, and compelled to wander restlessly upon earth, where they do much mischief.[1]

"The gods of the Africans," says Arbousset, thinking of the many tribes in and around Basutoland, "are supposed to enjoy eternal youth, and to be endowed with a wisdom very superior to that of mortals, amongst whom it is easy for them to come when they wish, without being seen, excepting by the so-called diviners. They live and move about freely in large caverns under the ground, the happy possessors of herds of oxen without horns, of a blue colour, mixed with red and white spots."[2]

Junod, the famous student of Thonga lore, has kindly sent me a translation of a prayer-chant which is sometimes sung in a very monotonous melody by Thonga sacrificers, and which contains a phrase (italicised below) indicative of the locality of the spirit-world:

"They (the oxen) are coming, they see me as I mourn for thee, father and mother, my gods.
I have remained outside (on the earth). I am wretched; but I received life from *you who are in the earth, down.*
I slaughter oxen, here they are; I mourn over thee!
Let us eat in peace together, father and mother; give me life, me and my children, that we may live without cough, here, at home."

Again, in his book, after telling a number of stories to show the awe with which the Thonga regard the sacred woods in which their ancient chiefs lie buried, Junod remarks:[3] "According to all these stories, it is evident that for the Thonga the ancestor-gods dwell in the sacred woods, and lead a life there in the earth, and occasionally outside, very similar to the terrestrial one. . . . I never heard it said that the gods are in heaven, notwithstanding the Suto term badimo, those who are above."

Zulu folk-tales tell of two men who dared to explore the under-

[1] ACC. 249, 263.
[2] NET. 341.
[3] LSAT. ii. 358.

world. One was a hunter, Umkachana by name, whose dogs drove a buck into a cave and followed it. He followed his dogs, nothing daunted, and went on and on till he came to a place where the *Abapanzi* ("Underground Folk") were dwelling. Fortunately he found some of his old friends among the *Abapanzi*, and they bade him return home,—which he did, I suppose, else we should never have had his story! The other man, if he was another, chased a porcupine which had been spoiling his garden; the porcupine scuttled into a hole, and in he went after it in hot pursuit. He found it dark in there till his eyes became used to the gloom; but he pressed forward. He reached a pool that stretched from one side of the tunnel to the other, except for a narrow ledge; but he was not to be balked: he crept cautiously along its brink and still pursued his way. When night came he slept upon his track, and pushed on in the morning. After crossing a river, he perceived that it was growing lighter on ahead, and soon he heard dogs barking and children crying, and came upon a village. It was now time to be discreet, and he retraced his steps, walking backward, wily man, so as to mislead any vagrant dweller in the underworld who should happen upon his spoor. At last he emerged through the hole by which he had entered.

This notion of the Underworld of the Dead has been cherished by people at a low stage of civilisation all over the world. "In Rome the idea that the spirits of the dead inhabit a common dwelling in the nether world existed from the time when the city had its beginnings. It kept in religion a coarsely naïve form which proves how archaic it was." [1] The idea once prevailed in Britain. According to Miss Weston, [2] the story of *St. Patrick's Purgatory*, which was exceedingly popular in the Middle Ages, "relates the adventure of a knight of King Stephen's court, who, after leading a reckless and dissipated life, made atonement for his sins by braving the dangers of a descent into Purgatory, the opening to which had been revealed in a vision to Saint Patrick. Owain, the knight in question, after fasting strictly for fifteen days, was led by the abbot and monks of the church wherein the entrance to Purgatory was found, to the cave, and entering, disappeared from their ken for three days. During this time he traversed the different

[1] ALRP. 70.
[2] *The Quest of the Holy Grail.* London: G. Bell & Sons Ltd., 1913, pp. 106-107.

regions of punishment, and, though in grave danger from the fiends who ruled in this nether world, passed in safety to the Terrestrial Paradise, where he was granted a foretaste of the joys of the Blessed. After the expiration of three days, he came forth from the cave, attended by a glory of celestial light, a transformed and regenerated character." So deeply had this pagan notion penetrated into British thought, that it coloured the imaginative literature of the people long after Christianity had made some headway among them.

Belief in an underworld of the dead is very far from being peculiar to the Bantu; but Junod's last remark alludes to the fact that some tribes hold at the same time two apparently contradictory theories of the locality of this obscure domain. Casalis (in substantial agreement with his colleague, Arbousset) writes of the Basuto: [1] "All the natives believe the world of the spirits to be in the bowels of the earth. They call the mysterious region *mosima* (the abyss), *mosima o sa thlaleng* [2] (the abyss which is never filled)." Yet he gives us one of their wailing-songs, which seems to speak of the sky as the abode of the dead:

"We are left outside, we are left for trouble, we are left for tears;
Oh, if there were in heaven a place for me!
Why have I not wings to fly there!
If a strong cord hung down from the sky
I would cling to it; I would go up;
I would go and dwell there." [3]

"Remember us from the heights to which you are going," was a prayer that the Basuto used to offer to those recently dead; and one of their most sacred oaths was, "By my father up above, where he has gone."

Not only are these seemingly antagonistic opinions concerning the whereabouts of the afterworld found in all Basuto and Becwana tribes, but they appear in the Kafir-Zulu group, too. Kidd's Kafirs say that the dead live below the ground near the cattle-

---

[1] Bs. 247.

[2] The Becwana say that their phrase, *molete motlhaélathupa* ("the unfathomable abyss"), refers to the *nethermost* regions of the underworld.

[3] Bs. 243.

kraal,[1] and speak of the Amadhlozi in the underworld;[2] and he dramatically describes a divineress who pretended to be *en rapport* with ancestral spirits and paused in her weird dance as if listening for some voice beneath the ground;[3] yet he makes a village headman invoke ancestor-spirits with the phrase: *"Ye who are above,*[4] see this ox which we are offering to you,"* etc.[5]

Also, some Bantu legends point to a world in the sky. *Mulungu* dwelt on earth, so the Yao say,[6] till men learnt to make fire by friction and set the prairies alight; then, in self-protection, he got a spider to show him how to climb up on high, and ordered that men should come there to him after death and be his slaves. *Leza*, who is now a sky-god, formerly dwelt on earth, according to Barotse tradition; but he climbed up to heaven one day by means of a spider's web.[7]

Fraser tells the tale of *Libanza*,[8] from Lindeman's *Les Upotos*.

Upoto, it should be premised, is on the northern bend of the Congo, in a borderland of Bantu culture that has been exposed to the influence of Sudanic cults and crafts. *Libanza* once roamed the earth, married wives, and had many adventures. His quarrelsome and sanguinary temper estranged the affections of his mother and sister; and one day, lashed by his sister's tongue and told to his face that he had killed his elder brother and nearly killed his father, he climbed a palm-tree in his chagrin and ascended to the sky, where he was surprised to find his aunt whom he had fought and his brother whom he had murdered. Pugnacious as ever, he fought *Lombo*, the King of the Air, and enslaved him and his people. He is now a sky-god: storms are the turmoil of his fighting; mist is the smoke from his pipe; wind is caused by his sneezing; the moon is a huge boat which sails across the whole earth picking up souls of the dead and conveying them to him. He and his relations still retain their human shape, but their skins are bleached white.[9]

[1] EK. 80.
[2] EK. 128.
[3] EK. 171.
[4] Italics are mine.
[5] EK. 169.
[6] NBCA. 74.
[7] LSAT. ii. 393.
[8] WN. i. 146.
[9] For the colour of ghosts cf. pp. 10, 63 note, 100 f.

Weeks mentions a similar inconsistency of belief among Natives of the lower Congo.[1] These people believe "that all the souls of the departed go to a great spirit-town in the forest"; and the reason they give for burying their dead at sunset is that the spirits, like themselves, are away at their different employments during the day,[2] and if the deceased were buried earlier, there would be no one in the spirit-town to welcome him; [3] and yet they believe, with naïve disregard of incompatibilities, that the souls of the dead have their residence in the skies. "When there is a halo round the moon [4] it is a sign that the Supreme Being is there confirming the residence in that cool place—hence state of happiness of some spirits which have just arrived; and when the halo is round the sun, then those who recently lost relatives and friends by death will tremble and wail, because that halo round the sun is an indication to them that the Supreme Being (*Nzambi*) is there confirming the punishment that has consigned the late departed to the hot place—hence state of unhappiness." And our author adds: "There is a proverb that shows the lastingness of this punishment: 'The bad people are tortured like a locust on the burning grass; it wants to die, but is kept alive.' "[5]

At a hasty glance it may look as if these jarring beliefs can never be harmonised, but the history of religion in Europe shows that they can. Although original Roman paganism attached no idea of retribution to the descent of the dead into the infernal regions, where status was more important than character and the inequalities of human society were perpetuated, the spread of Hellenic civilisation modified the old belief, and it came to be popularly held that the dead descend from the tombs to some deep place where they receive rewards and punishments. Then, in course of time, it became intellectually fashionable to believe, under the influence of a new philosophy from the Orient, that the

[1] ACC. 248-49. He does not mention the tribe, but he lived at San Salvador and Matadi for nine years.

[2] Cf. p. 73.

[3] Cf. p. 38.

[4] According to Konde lore, if the moon is red, with a red circle around it, plague is coming, and a halo around the sun is a sign that some woman is about to give birth to twins. (SRK. 246.)

[5] Claridge affirms that the future world of the Old Kongo Kingdom people is in two compartments, one for the good and one for the bad (WBT. 292); but the lenses of his theological spectacles were not corrected for astigmatism.

soul is of celestial origin, akin to the ether and the stars that shine in the sky, and that its home is in the heavens. Now since it is not the way of humanity to scrap an effete but time-honoured religion, nor of its European variety to hold two unreconciled opinions for long together, the old was made companionable to the new by means of an explanation that when the soul is released from the entanglements of its coarse earthly body, it must be purged of its earth-born passions and instincts before it can soar to its abode above, and that the term of its detention in the abyss is a purgatorial prelude, longer or shorter according to the grossness of its clogging passions, to its ascent to the skies. The common Bantu theory of the underworld of the dead could be reconciled with their sporadic notions of a soul-home in the sky by means of some such afterthought; but if tribesmen have ever attempted the task, their efforts have escaped the notice of European writers.

In the more primitive religions, it is comparatively rare for souls to ascend to the sky after death, and students usually attribute belief in two apparently inconsistent afterworlds to a fusion of cults, if not of races; it must be recognised, however, that heavenly bodies are not unrelated to the nether regions. Spirit-land, according to common Bantu cosmography, is underfoot, and its inhabitants pass in and out through graves and burial-caves; but it appears to be coextensive with this great flat upper world, and may be reached by going over the rim of our upper stratum. When European ships emerged from the horizon, West Coast tribes thought they were coming up out of spirit-land, and were confirmed in their opinion by the pale skins of the mariners and their almost incredible wealth and magical knowledge.[1] Now sun and moon enter the underworld by the over-the-edge route, and leave it in the same way; comets travel by that track, too; and some stars do, though most of them are permanently fixed, and now and then an odd one hurries back at night by a short cut. "The sun in its course has only two paths," said a Zulu to Callaway; "by day it travels by a path in the heaven; at night it enters

[1] Cf. GGC. 643; IHB. 17; and *Congo Life and Folklore*, by Rev. John H. Weeks. (London: R. T. S., 1901), pp. 17, 108. The Konde of North Nyasa hold that white people "are water spirits in origin, a belief no doubt due to the widespread story that we came from the sea itself, rather than from some place beyond it." (SRK. 102.)

by a path which goes into the sea, into the water; it passes through the water, until it again comes out at the place where it rises in the morning." [1]

The fact that the sun spends the other half of its time in the underworld, led some of the so-called primitive peoples to elaborate a theory that the abode of departed spirits is an upside-down sort of world, with everything the wrong way round, their night being our day, their left our right, their front our back; [2] and of this theory there are traces in Bantu belief. A few other facts may have had some bearing upon the theory of a sky-home for the soul. The breath, which is sometimes seen to rise and mingle with the air, is a Bantu metaphor for the soul; [3] spirits of paramount chiefs can secure control of the rain-clouds; [4] a comet is associated with the passing of a great chief; [5] and a figure of speech with which some tribes describe a halo round the moon is sometimes taken literally as a Tribal Assembly of Departed Spirits. [6] It would be a hazardous experiment to infer from these precarious premises that the theory of a sky-home for the soul is indigenous to Bantu thought; but it is safe to admit that these ideas might provide a nexus for the doctrine if once it were imported.

The doctrine that the soul is of celestial origin is found in the Upanishads of India, the Zend-Avesta of Persia, the Manichean literature of Mesopotamia, and, as we saw above, in the speculations of various philosophical cults in the ancient Roman world; and according to Egyptian eschatology, the bodies, souls, shad-

---

[1] RSZ. 395. In the *Book of Am Duat* and in the *Book of the Gates*, ancient Egyptian scribes portrayed the Sun sailing through the underworld from west to east on a subterranean river, after the manner of a royal procession on the Nile. (See Wiedemann's *Religion of the Ancient Egyptians*. London: H. Grevel & Co., 1897, pp. 83-102.) According to a quaint conceit of ancient Greek poetry, the sun floats in a golden goblet over the subterranean ocean, from the western land of the Hesperides to the eastern land of the Ethiopians. Bantu tribesmen, most of whom have never seen the ocean, watch the sun sinking every evening beyond the western rim of the forest or the savannah and arriving every morning at the point whence it starts on the next day's journey, and infer that it traversed the underworld throughout the night at its accustomed pace.

[2] Cf. p. 18.

[3] See p. 10.

[4] See pp. 208, 211.

[5] See p. 122.

[6] Perhaps it may not be amiss to add that most Bantu who have ever seen a ghost, probably saw it in the wan light of a failing moon.

ows and hearts of the wicked were doomed to utter destruction (not perpetual torment) by Rā, the Sun-god, who held his court as soon as he got up in the morning, or were treated after the same fashion by Osiris, Lord of the Underworld, at his midnight assizes.[1] Wonder may have played a larger part than veracity in the tales that Herodotus told of five young men who crossed the Sahara, a Persian nobleman who sailed south for many months from the Pillars of Hercules, and Phœnicians who circumnavigated Africa by command of Pharaoh Necho II; and Hanno may not have sailed beyond Sierra Leone on the expedition that he commemorated with a tablet in the temple of Moloch at Carthage;[2] but mariners and merchants from the Persian Gulf, the Red Sea, and India have been in touch with East Coast ports for a very long time, and gossip has always travelled in Africa with greater freedom than explorers had. Rumours of doctrines mentioned above may have soaked through from Carthage, Egypt, or Persia; but the lower Congo notion of endless burnings for the bad and cool bliss for the good, looks more like a whelp from the nightmare of hell and the devil that lay upon the chest of Europe for a thousand years, never more oppressive than when the West Coast was being explored. Whether the notion was imported into the Kongo Kingdom by priests who baptised its fifth Ntotela in 1491, giving him the grandiose title of "King John I" is, however, another matter. Priests from Southern Europe may have known of the schools of lunar philosophy to which I have referred, and of the later teaching of these schools—that the soul, before it can find peace and rest in the ether round the moon, has to be purged of earthly contaminations by being buffeted by the winds of heaven, drenched by the waters of the upper ocean, and scorched in the burning air of the topmost zone from which the lightnings flash; and priests rather like to play with purgatory. But the Kongo notion is said to be that of a hell in the sun and a heaven in the moon, rather than a purgatory in the skies, and Roman priests are not the only people who have been quite at home with hell. Besides, the records seem to show that these priests did much baptising and very

[1] See Budge's British Museum monograph on *The Book of the Dead*, 1922 edition, p. 21.
[2] See my *Race Problems in the New Africa* (Oxford Univ. Press), pp. 140 ff.

little teaching; and there is no sign that they left the people any other legacy than that of a few images of saints and one or two symbols and phrases. How has it come about that this, of all their doctrines (if it was one), has left an indelible mark upon the minds of the tribesmen? Was there something indigenous in Bantu thought to which the notion of a sky-home for the soul could readily cling? At any rate, it must be admitted that if the Kongo notion sprang from any foreign eschatology that we know of, it must have been tinctured by the soil through which it seeped.

But even if this throws light upon the Kongo notion—and the light is admittedly dim—it leaves the Basuto phrases still unexplained. What can we do with them? Junod's translation of *badimo*, "those who are above," [1] and Casalis' rendering of *molimo*, "he who is in the sky," [2] are without justification; but the curious facial resemblance, suggestive of kinship, between *molimo* ("disembodied spirit") and *moholimo* ("above") or *leholimo* ("the sky") has not yet been elucidated; [3] for Casalis' suggestion that *molimo* is an abbreviation of *moholimo* [4] is untenable in the light of modern scholarship.

When Weeks was investigating the Boloki (Upper Congo) doctrine of spirits, the people told him of a race of Cloud-folk, and his remarks are worth quoting in this connection. [5] "There is a race of folk who live somewhere above, as the word indicates (*ba* = people, and *likolo* = above), but up-river and all the country east of them is also called *likolo*; and it is most probable that the word *likolo* in the above phrase had originally that meaning, but as the natives pushed their journeys higher and higher up the river and heard of peoples like themselves still higher up, they removed the *balikolo* from a locality beyond their district to a place *above them* in the sky. These Cloud-folk are said to have tails, and are very fond of ripe plantains,

[1] LSAT. ii. 358.
[2] Bs. 248.
[3] Bleek, "the father of Bantu philology," gave it as his opinion (*Comparative Grammar*, 1862, p. 91), that "whatever may be the origin of the words *h-olimo* and *leh-olimo*," (the scission is his, not mine) "their similarity with *Molimo* seems to be almost accidental."
[4] Bs. 248.
[5] ACC. 273-74.

and in the folk-lore stories they descend on the banana farms solely to eat and carry off the ripe fruit.   There is a legend that the Boloki people bought their first fire from the Cloud-folk in exchange for a young woman.   Previously to that 'we cooked our food in the sun, or ate it quite raw.'   The Cloud-folk are not regarded as spirits, but the natives always speak of them as a great nuisance, and as something uncanny and in possession of supernatural power."

Tribes of the Bechuanaland Protectorate, cousins to the Basuto, use *godimo* [1] in the same way that the Boloki use *likolo*. *Godimo* means "above," "high," and *legodimo* is their word for "sky": not the open space in which clouds float, and lightnings flash, and birds fly—that is *loapi* (they say *maru a a mo loapiñ* = "clouds which are in the sky"), but the firmament, the blue vault of sky in which the heavenly bodies move (they say *legodimo le le bududu* = "the sky which is blue").   But *godimo* has other meanings.   *Godimo* and *bophirimatsatsi* are convertible terms for "west" in the Protectorate, and the former, denoting the quarter from which their streams flow, is oftener heard than the latter, which points to the place of the setting sun.   Further, these tribes lay great stress upon precedence (not priority) of birth, as most Bantu tribes do, and the houses of a chief's sons are located according to their standing in the family, that of the heir being on his father's right hand, west of the chief's dwelling and consequently described by this word *godimo*, though it may not be on higher land.   Nowadays (some people say it was not so in the old times), the configuration of the site is allowed to modify the actual orientation of a chief's dwelling, so that it does not always look south, and the house of his great son, though on his right hand, is therefore not always on the west; the same term, *godimo*, is nevertheless used to indicate its location.   Again, the orientation of a Place of Public Assembly is always determined by wind-screens which turn their curved backs to the prevailing cold winds; but when the Assembly is in session, the

---

[1] *Godimo* is the Secwana form of the Sesuto word *holimo*.   The first consonant of the stem hovers between "d," "l," and "r," never quite taking the English value of any one of these letters, but approximating to one in some communities and to another in others, and passing easily into "z" or "zh" in some other tribal vernaculars.   The Sesuto *molimo* is pronounced more like *modimo* (see pp. 10 f.) by the Becwana tribes.

heir to the chieftainship sits on his father's right hand, and his location is still described as *godimo*, regardless of the points of the compass or the altitude of the ground upon which he places his stool. To sum up in a sentence, the meaning of this very wide term, *godimo*, may be "overhead," or "higher up," or "West," or "on the right-hand of the chief"—this last being a synonym for "superior status." Now, may it not be that this term was first used in some other sense than that of "overhead" to denote the locality of the underworld, and that its very ambiguity lent itself to the poetic imagination from which legends spring? Such phrases as "the heights to which you are going," and even "my father up above, where he has gone," would suggest a burial-cave in the hills, rather than a dwelling in the skies. Or take its meaning of "West"; some Bantu tribes think (as Egyptian worshippers of Osiris, the great Judge of the quick and the dead, used to do) that the underworld is in the West [1]— still under, but west; or if one substitutes the Bechuana term of direction,—still under, but *godimo*. Even the use of the term to indicate superior status is not precluded from the possibilities that we have to consider, for we have it on good authority [2] that the Basuto consider ancient divinities superior (though less accessible) to those who have recently joined the galaxy of the gods. But the whole problem is bewildering, and I suppose we must allow its solution to stand over till the original meaning of important Bantu root-words has been more definitely ascertained —a discovery that is likely to be facilitated by the new science of tonetics.

TRYSTING-PLACE FOR WORSHIPPER AND SPIRIT

Wherever the spirit-world may be, the grave is undoubtedly regarded as the portal by which the dead pass into it, and as the trysting-place where worshippers may have dealings with discarnate spirits. The Ndau people of the Melsetter District in South Rhodesia carefully guard their graves from wild animals, keep them free from grass, and protect them from the weather by

[1] IHB. 17. WBA. 245. The Baila, on the contrary, say that it is somewhere in the east. "When a man dies they often say to him: 'Do not enter into people's houses, go to the east, go to the Creator.'" (IPNR. ii. 119.)
[2] Bs. 249.

erecting a little hut which is constantly renewed.[1] Proceeding
northwards from South Rhodesia, one finds grave-huts or spirit
shrines everywhere till the confines of Bantu Africa are passed [2]
—and, indeed, much farther afield.

Nevertheless, graves are not the only places at which spirits
may be worshipped.[3] The hunter worships under any big tree
that he may find in the hunting-veld, and when he has killed a
buck, he lays there a portion of game for the spirit that gave
him the success that he craved. Tumbuka elephant-hunters remove an ear from the beast that has fallen to their spears, and
take it to the nearest *msoro* tree, where they offer it in worship
to some ancestral spirit.[4]

Furthermore, the spirits are closely associated with the home.
When a woman dies in a Becwana tribe, her side of the conjugal
hut must be left for the use of her spirit; and these tribes associate the threshold and the eaves over the door with the spirit
in ceremonies connected with the purification of widows, notwithstanding the fact that the corpse is not taken out through the
door but through a hole made for the purpose in the back wall
of the hut. Also, as in Chinese homes, many tribes have a little
platform inside the hut and adjacent to the back wall, which is
sacred to the ancestral spirits. A sick man of the Nyasa tribes
places an offering of flour for the spirits at the side of his pillow.[5]
The Lumbu place their offerings to ancestral spirits on the
threshold of the hut, upon certain occasions; and in some tribes
the threshold figures in the ritual of affiliation, at which the presence of ancestral spirits is naturally desired. The Konde associate
the doorway of the hut with the spirits of their ancestors.[6] Smith
says: [7] "On moving his village to a new site, a chief will often
move the temples of his fathers and rebuild them near his huts
in the village. One chief that we know has no fewer than six
of these outside his principal hut. In this way the ghosts are
brought to the new habitation of the living." And again: [8] "An-

[1] Dr. Wilder: *The Hartford Seminary Record*, April, 1907.
[2] See pp. 266-284.
[3] See p. 288.
[4] WPP. 137.
[5] A. i. 87.
[6] SRK. 99, 106.
[7] IPNR. ii. 120.
[8] IPNR. ii. 120.

other idea among the Baila is that the ghosts of the dead continue to hover about the place they used to inhabit; either near the grave or actually in the houses of the living."

This close association of the spirit with the home of his descendants is probably connected with a widespread Bantu practice, still in vogue in remote parts of the country and not long perished in others, of burying the dead either in the hut or just outside the threshold,[1] sometimes the males on one side and the females on the other. Ngoni commoners were buried before the doors of their dwellings,[2] and headmen beside their cattle-kraals;[3] Chipatula was buried *in* his cattle-kraal.[4] The Wawanga of Elgon district, Kenya Colony, bury a married man in his chief wife's hut, with his feet towards the centre-pole and his head towards the wall on the right as one stands at the centre-pole and looks out through the doorway. Women, children and unmarried males are buried under the front verandah on either side of the door, males to the right as one enters and females to the left, all with their feet towards the door. Since males lie on their right side in the grave and females on their left, it is evident that all, whether within the hut or under the verandah, look towards the threshold. Persons killed by lightning, suicides, and those who have come by a violent death are not buried at home—probably because their spirits are dreaded rather than revered.[5] The Bambwa, who live on the western slopes of Mt. Ruwenzori, still bury a man in his own hut, leaving his widow there for a month to guard the grave and the mourners to carry

---

[1] See p. 28. Ellis states in *Negro Culture in West Africa*, p. 70, that the Vai tribes of Liberia and Sierra Leone, bury important men and women in the yard before the house. Johnson states in *History of the Yorubas*, p. 137, that the graves of aged Yorubas are dug generally in the piazza or in one of the sleeping-rooms. "In case of the wealthy dead, after the ground has been dug to a depth of about six feet in the piazza it is then carried on horizontally towards one of the bed-rooms, so that the corpse is literally buried in the bedroom. It is then shut up in this horizontal hole with a piece of board plastered over with mud; the whole grave is then filled up and the floor of the piazza levelled and polished." Mr. O. G. S. Crawford, writing of the upland Celtic villages (R. G. S. Jrnl. May, 1923, p. 351) states: "The villages were well-drained, but even the Roman influence could not break the Britons of the unpleasant habit of burying their relations in their huts and courtyards." Cf. also 1 Sam. xxv. 1, and 1 Kings ii. 34.

[2] AA. 169.

[3] AA. 170.

[4] AA. 23.

[5] JRAI., 1913, p. 33.

out a daily programme of grief; and then, after the sacrifice to
the dead has been offered, the posts of the hut are cut, and it
falls in ruins upon the grave.[1]   "The remains of a young child
in most parts of the Congo are wrapped in a rush mat and buried
in a corner of the mother's hut."[2]   Bayanzi people of wealth
are wrapped after death in the richest cloths they have left, and
then buried in a hole dug in the entrance to their house.[3]   "In
the Aruwimi country people are buried in their own house in
shallow graves."[4]   It was the custom at Bolobo on the Congo
to bury a man under the floor of his house; but in the case of
a man who had repeatedly threatened to haunt his relatives if
they failed to bury his wife with him, and whose wife had escaped, they feared to have the man buried in the village and
found him a grave in the bush.[5]   In view of all this, it is likely
that the close association of the spirit with the home is due to
the belief that spirits are closely linked with the remains of their
earthly tabernacles.

Perhaps we shall not be far wrong if we say that the Bantu
believe that ancestral spirits are where their descendants are, especially at the home of the head of the family; but whether they
live in the ground in that neighbourhood, as some say, or come
there from the grave through which they passed into the spirit-
world, as others assert, is far from clear.   Distance does not ham-
per their movements as it used to do before they discarded their
tenement of flesh; but whether distance exists in the spirit-world
is a question that has never occurred to the Bantu.   It seems certain, however, that spirits find no difficulty in being present at
two or three places at the same time.   Fraser tells us that "the
movements of the dead are not circumscribed.   They wander
over the world, wherever their relatives go, helping or hindering them.   When a man is walking through the wood, he may
hear a twig snap, and concludes that some ancestral spirit (*chibanda*) is there, so he breaks another twig and throws it in the
direction of the sound, and when he gets home puts some of-

[1] GS. 154-55.
[2] GGC. 644.
[3] GGC. 649.
[4] GGC. 649.
[5] GGC. 251.

fering in the little temple." [1]   A careful observer, writing on
"Some Aspects of Religion Among the Azande," [2] notes that the
activity of discarnate spirits is not confined to the vicinity of the
grave or even to their own tribal domain.   He has more than
once heard his porters attributing misfortunes experienced abroad
to the direct intervention of the offended spirits of kinsfolk buried at home as much as a month's trek from their line of march;
and a Tanganyika Native, who was with him in Spain some years
ago and was overtaken by a small but unexpected misfortune of
the kind which is attributed solely to the malevolence of disembodied spirits, repeatedly expressed astonishment that this kind
of thing could occur in Europe—so far away from the land of
his divinities.

THE SPIRIT-WORLD, A COUNTERPART OF THIS WORLD

Tribesmen who have bestowed much thought upon the spirit-
world and its inhabitants, usually belong to families that have
produced long lines of chiefs or medicine-men; and in these
families the use of both speech and silence as a veil for thought
is a traditional accomplishment.   But if these men take you into
their confidence and talk freely on subjects that they have pondered, you will find that they have modelled their spirit-world
after the pattern of their tribal abodes.

Other nations have done the same.   Literary prophets of the
Old Testament people Sheol with weak, forgetful, silent shades; [3]
but Valhalla seems full of roisterers, and the Celtic Underworld
was a place of exuberant life. [4]   "Virgil, taking his inspiration from
Pindar, shows us the blessed occupied by the contests of the pales-
tra, by song and poetry and by chariot races; for, he tells us, the
passion which the dead had in life for arms and horses still pur-
sues them when they have been buried in the earth.   Ovid
sketches with rapid touches an analogous picture.   'The shades,'
he says, 'wander bloodless, bodiless, boneless; some gather in

---

[1] WPP. 126.

[2] JRAI., 1926, p. 180.   The Azande, though Sudanese, share many Bantu beliefs.
We are more familiar with the nickname, Niam-niam, which their Dinka neighbours gave them; because we first heard of them from Arab slavers who reached
them through Dinka-land.   The Tanganyika native would be Bantu, of course.

[3] Cf. SCD. 289 ff.

[4] See RAC. 60, 341, 344.

the forum, others follow their trades, imitating their former way of life.' " [1] In mediæval mythology the exact correspondence of earth and heaven was a leading principle. Ancient Egyptians, if they passed the "Great Reckoning," went to a kind of glorified Egypt after death—the flat country, with fields intersected by canals of running water, that is sketched in the large vignette to the CXth Chapter of the so-called *Book of the Dead;* and, in the larger of these funerary texts and pictures cut in the alabaster sarcophagus of Seti I, they are seen tending the wheat plants as they grow, reaping the ripe grain, and driving the oxen that are treading out the corn.[2]

The world of which the Bantu dream is not so highly idealised as that of ancient Egypt; but there, also, the herd-boy still herds his cattle,[3] the women hoe their gardens, reap their crops, and pound their corn, the hunter hunts,[4] the patriarch delights his eyes with the sleek coats of his beautiful black-and-white cattle, the villagers gather for gossip in the evening hours, the drums are beaten and the dance proceeds. Fraser, speaking of the Tumbuka belief, says: "The land of the dead is a good land where no hunger or sorrow touches them. But they live as young men and women, and grind their heavenly corn, and dance together, and have beautiful domestic fowls. Sometimes in the quiet of the night a sound will be heard in the wood like the beating of a distant drum, and the people say, 'The spirits are dancing in their village.' " [5]

Miss Kingsley contends, however, that marriage is the one thing that does not happen in the nether-world.[6] "The ideas connected with the underworld to which the ghost goes are exceedingly interesting," she says. "The Negroes and Bantu are at one on this subject in one particular only, and that is that no marriages take place there. The Tschwis say that this under-

[1] ALRP. 73.
[2] See Budge's British Museum monograph on the *Book of the Dead* (1922 edition), pp. 30-31.
[3] HB. 247.
[4] If the Bantu are as much afraid of work as their traducers allege, why did they take the tasks of common toil into their idealised continuance beyond the grave, instead of making it a paradise in which the blessed do nothing, sweet nothing, for ever and ever!
[5] WPP. 126.
[6] And see p. 57.

world, Srahmandazi, is just the same as this world in all other
particulars, save that it is dimmer, a veritable shadow-land where
men have not the joys of life, but only the shadow of the joy.[1]
Hence says the Tschwi proverb, 'One day in this world is worth
a year in Srahmandazi.' The Tschwis, with their usual definite-
ness in this sort of detail, know all about their Srahmandazi. Its
entrance is just past the middle Volta, and the way down is difficult to follow, and when the sun sets on this world it rises on
Srahmandazi. The Bantus are vague on this important point.
The Benga, for example, although holding the absence of marriage there, do not take steps to meet the case as the Tschwis do,
and kill a supply of wives to take down with them." [2]

Another point of resemblance between this world and the next
is that the community there is under its paramount chief, like the
community here. But apparently there is only one "there," [3] not
a "there" for each tribe; and consequently only one Supreme
Chief. All their old chiefs are there; and so are the chiefs of
other tribes. But if you ask how these chiefs of various tribes
are related to one another, you get no satisfactory reply; they
have not thought out that problem. You have no difficulty, however, in finding that they are all subjects of the Great Chief, and
may approach him on behalf of their children, just as earthly
patriarchs approach their own chief. In conformity with tribal
usage, too, men of birth may ask greater favours at his hands
than common people could presume to do; only the spirit of a
paramount chief, for instance, could venture to ask the Great
Chief to send down rain upon his old tribal lands.

In the Bantu spirit-world, there is no division of the dead on
the basis of character.[4] The good and the bad alike are there;
and they are all free to intermingle as they please; but just as
like is drawn to like in the village, so there, probably, the scamps

[1] Rattray says the same of the Ashanti underworld. (AS. 80.)
[2] TWA. 339-340.
[3] But compare p. 43.
[4] Good and bad alike descended to Sheol, Hades or Hell, the old underworld
of the dead in ancient Hebrew and European religion. "Originally no idea of
retribution was attached to this descent of the dead into the infernal regions; it
was neither their merits nor their demerits which determined their condition. On
the contrary, the inequalities of human society were perpetuated: a nobleman kept
a higher rank than that of his servants." (ALRP. 72.)

find the scamps and men of probity associate with one another. "We don't know," they say, "it is so here; why not there?"

The statements in the preceding paragraph were first made to me forty years ago by Kisosera, a diviner of the Wanyamwezi tribe in what is now called Tanganyika Territory; but modern literature provides a curious parallel. According to Sir Oliver Lodge,[1] Raymond, speaking to his mother from "the other side," said: "You gravitate here to the ones you're fond of. Those you are not fond of, if you meet them in the street, you don't bother to say 'how-do-you-do.'"

Here and there in the world, where descendants of earlier settlers and of dominant intruders constitute one community, the dead are sometimes supposed to be divided according to lineage; and, time and again, the spirit-land of a subjugated or a hidebound people has been transformed by their enterprising neighbours into a mean abode for base, knavish, villainous souls—adjectives, be it said, in which rank and status have given place to moral qualities.[2] Communities of composite lineage are not uncommon in Africa; but old lords of the land and conquering immigrants are alike Bantu, and it is their way to emphasise social distinctions, both among the living and the dead, not by providing the great with places apart from the common herd, but by according them honour and power. Status, being born with a man, clings to him in the other world;[3] but there is no hint that noble and ignoble are assigned to separate infernal regions.

Vocation, so the Bantu think, is less rigid than status. It depends to a limited extent—much more limited than a son of the West can easily imagine—upon the predilection of the individual; but even a man's vocation goes with him into the other world: the hunter hunts, the minstrel thrums his strings and chants his lays, the potter moulds her clay, and the furrier still makes lovely karosses. That is why weapons, tools, utensils, clothes, etc., are buried with their owners,[4] and why men of mark take wives and retainers into the underworld with them.

Such, they say, is the world to which we are all wending our

[1] *Raymond*, p. 229.
[2] Cf. p. 410 f.
[3] Cf. BBM. 22.
[4] See SCD. 131-35.

way. No single individual that I ever met could give such a complete picture of the after-life; but every part of my composite picture has been provided by my Bantu friends, mostly of Bechuana and Makalaka descent; and in the writings of those familiar with other tribes I find no indication that my picture is inaccurate or incomplete. Inasmuch as each Bantu tribe has lived its own life through the long centuries since their dispersion, considerable variations have crept into usages that they all consider authoritative and profess to have kept unchanged; and the theology behind the ritual, being endowed with no authority of its own, and possessing but little interest for the Bantu type of mind, has naturally become a thing of shreds and patches. In fact, the few rags that still cling to some communities are scarcely sufficient to show what the original garment was like. It is plain, however, that death is regarded in all these tribes as a calamity, which, like other inevitabilities, is met with fortitude, rather than lit with hope. The only hint of hope that I can discover, lies in the readiness of some liegemen and some wives to share the fortunes of their lord even in death; and I suspect that these "willing sacrifices" owe more than a little to the dread of flouting public opinion and the glory of meeting inescapable fate with audacity.

EARTHLY CONCERNS OF ANCESTRAL SPIRITS

Though Indo-Europeans classed the dead with the gods and invited both to partake of the sacrifices, they carefully distinguished between the two varieties of divinity. If we may anticipate a discussion which must be more thorough in a subsequent volume, it may be said at once that Bantu are not much concerned with personifications of Nature, but that they distinguish between spirits of the wild and spirits of the home and the tribe; and that the aspect of religion which has gripped their interest most firmly is that ancestral spirits are active in the affairs of men, especially as protectors of tribal morality, and are persons with whom men can deal. Hence Bantu, probably owing to the Hamitic strain in their breed, lay the stress where it was laid in Semitic, rather than in Aryan, religion.[1]

---

[1] Persians, Greeks, and Romans worshipped ancestral spirits (Fravashis, Genii, Manes, etc.) with sacrifice, regarding them as protective and beneficent beings;

The basis of Bantu ancestor-worship is a belief that discarnate human spirits do not lose interest in their people and things when they pass into the unseen world. It is not thought that they care at all for other people's affairs, and other people pay them no homage; [1] but they are as much interested in their family and tribal affairs as they used to be,—which is saying much! If the family herds are squandered, the ancestors of the family will resent it and punish the waster; if the tribal herds are perishing through drought, the old chiefs in the spirit-world can be moved to pity; and the ancestors of both family and tribe are, like the "divine shades" of ancient Rome, guardians of the traditions of the elders. Later on we shall have occasion to discuss this latter point more fully.

Speaking broadly, the ancestral gods are assigned by the law which regulates inheritance in the family and clan. That is to say, if the community is matrilineal, the children worship the spirits of the mother's ancestors; and if it is patrilineal, they worship the spirits of the father's ancestors. There are not a few Bantu tribes, however, which are in some stage of transition from the ancient matrilineal succession to the newer patrilineal; and for these tribes it is difficult to formulate a common rule. It appears that the ancestral gods are changed from the maternal to the paternal line before the totem is changed; for tribes may be found (like the Baila) in which the children belong to the father's family,[2] but to their mother's totem-group,[3] though they regard the ancestral spirits of their father's family as their divinities.[4]

KNOWLEDGE AND POWER OF THE SPIRITS

The group-consciousness of a Bantu tribesman is strong and his individual-consciousness weak; moreover, he has no leanings towards abstract questions of personality. What one would like to find is a clear and authoritative definition of the knowledge,

but their great gods (Ahura Mazda, Zeus, Uranus, Tellus, etc.), like those of their Aryan ancestors (Dyaus, Varuna, Ushas, Prithivi, etc.) were personifications of natural phenomena.

[1] See, however, pp. 80 ff.
[2] IPNR. i. 284.
[3] IPNR. i. 287, 294.
[4] IPNR. i. 293 and ii. 166.

power, and character of the spirits; but in Africa one looks in vain for clear definitions. Judging by his actions, however, there seems to be at the back of the tribesman's mind, a notion that in knowledge and character the spirits are very much like himself, and that their power, like his own, depends upon the status which they acquired by birth into the clan, not upon ethical or spiritual enrichment of character.[1]

Claridge quotes a strange prayer that people in the old Kongo kingdom offer to their ancestors: *Ampembi y' Amvumbi, toyo! nwafwa kia meso ke nwafwa kia matu ko;* which he translates as, "O innocent dead, hear us, you are blind but you are not deaf."[2] No tribesman that I ever met would admit for a moment that the spirits are blind, though all would agree that they have to be reminded of their children's needs and can often be hoodwinked. In Becwana tribes, a mother who has lost her boys in infancy but reared her girls, often dresses her new baby-boy in girl's things and calls it by a girl's name in order that she may deceive the ancestral spirit who has called back the boys that she so much wanted to keep; or if she has lost babies of both sexes, she will call the new baby by an opprobrious name, such as "Excrement," "Dog's-dung," "Castaway" or even an obscene name, such as *Nywe,* or possibly she will give it to a Mokgala-gadi serf to suckle; all of which is intended to delude the spirit into thinking that she does not care for the new gift. Or she may give the spirit the slip by going off secretly to some remote place where she happens to have relatives living, and being confined there. Or, stranger still, if her babies have died before she has emerged from her seclusion, she will sometimes even dare to violate her *puerperium* and come forth from her hut a month or two too soon, so that the spirits may be deceived into thinking that the time is past; in which case the child is not properly named, but is referred to as *Sooseng* ("What thing?"). A woman of the Bakwena tribe had six sons and six daughters. All the sons died young, and all the daughters proved healthy. She had a seventh son; and in order that she might deceive the spirit who had called back all her boys and left her girls unnoticed, she named this son *Mmagautlwe* ("Mother-of heedlessness"),

[1] Cf. BBM. 22.
[2] WBT. 284.

which is not only a girl's name but an opprobrious one at that, and therefore well calculated to show the spirits that she had no love for the new baby. This one grew to manhood; and as he was one of my neighbours, my Native friends sometimes held him up as a proof that there is something after all in a trick that I called mean. This bit of spiritual chicanery, one may remark, is practised in India and in China[1] as commonly as in Africa. Casalis, speaking of the ancestral spirits of a dynasty that has long dominated a country, says:[2] "If a marauding expedition is made into the country under their protection, no one has any scruple in seeking to deceive them; and for this purpose, on crossing the flats and watercourses, the special haunts of the shades, the marauder gives utterance to those cries and hisses in which cattle-drivers indulge when they drive a herd before them, thinking in this manner to persuade the poor divinities that he is bringing cattle to their worshippers instead of coming to take them from them." Weeks tells[3] of a Boloki invalid, who was advised by his witch-doctor to go right out of the district, where the bad spirit that was causing his illness could not get at him, and to remain away till he was better. "The man had no friends to whom he might have safely gone, so he left his house at dead of night, taking only two of his wives with him, and telling no one of his destination lest the spirit should hear it. He went as far as he safely could from his own town and donned a woman's dress, and assuming a woman's voice he pretended to be other than he was, in order to deceive the spirit should it search for him. This also failed to cure him, and in time he returned to his town, but continued to dress and speak as a woman." In the Chaga country (Kilimanjaro), when death robs a man of children borne to him by a foreign wife, whom he has perhaps captured or stolen, the diviner sometimes discovers that the woman's ancestors are thus demanding an offering. Now a sacrifice to her ancestors should be offered at her home[4]—which is obviously inconvenient to such a husband; and the wily man arranges to outwit her ancestors with a little make-believe. Providing her with

<hr/>

[1] *Researches into Chinese Superstition.* By Henry Doré, S.J. Shanghai: Tusevei Printing Press. 1914. First Part, vol. i., p. 11.

[2] Bs. 253.

[3] ACC. 267.

[4] That is, by her elders.

two goats, he sends her home to offer them to her gods, but admonishes her to return if she meets with danger on the road. So she sets off homewards, accompanied by one or two companions. Meanwhile he arranges with some of his relatives to waylay her and make pretence of attacking her. She turns back to her husband's home and relates what has befallen her; and thereupon the senior elder calls all to witness that this woman was willing to offer sacrifice to her ancestors but was prevented from doing so; and the sacrifice is forthwith offered to the wife's ancestors at the husband's home.[1]   I have met with no hint anywhere in Africa that ancestor-spirits are able to read the heart; but it is commonly held that the veil which hides them from the eyes of their children does not hide their children from them, and that they know most, perhaps all, that their children *do, say* and *suffer.*

The power of the ancestors has not been lessened by death; but it undoubtedly has its limits; there is no claim that they are omnipotent. Even the spirits of famous chiefs, although credited with enormous power, cannot send rain for the salvation of their tribal herds and lands; the utmost they can do in such an important matter is to intercede with the Great Chief of the spirit-world, with whom they are supposed to be as influential as clan-heads are with their political superior. It is the superhuman quality of their power, not its omnipotence, that makes it so valuable, and sometimes so dreadful, to their descendants in any extremity.

Although the help of spirits is generally available to none but their descendants, there are notable departures from this usage.[2]

"Travellers on arriving at the frontier of a foreign country," says Casalis,[3] "seek to propitiate the gods of that country, by rubbing their own foreheads with some dust that they pick up from the road, or by making themselves a girdle of grass."

Bantu tribes have been shattered into innumerable fragments

---

[1] K. 147-48. It may be mentioned that the Burmese bury the image of a sick man in a coffin, so that the afflicting spirit may go away satisfied that its victim is dead.

[2] Cf. LSAT. ii. 344. Spirits of other lineage are often greatly feared, especially spirits of people to whom one has done any harm or owed any obligation. See WBA. 141-42 for Kaonde ideas on this subject; and ACC. 267 for Boloki.

[3] Bs. 253.

and scattered over a vast area; and some of these fragments, whether from courage, cleverness or chance, have managed to establish themselves in desirable domains and afford political shelter to sections of other tribes which have been broken in their fight with fate, thus forming new political confederations. In such communities—and they are the rule rather than the exception in Bantu tribes—though the members of each clan in the coalition claim kinship, real or fictional, with their own clan-head, many clans can claim no kinship with the paramount chief. And yet, notwithstanding this lack of kinship, the worship of the spirits of the ruling dynasty is of value to the whole community in matters of common concern, such as war, epidemic and drought.

Another and still more remarkable exception is this: When a dynasty has held a certain territory for many generations, the spirits of its old chiefs are thought to retain their interest and power in the country long after their descendants have been reduced to serfdom by a powerful invader. The Chagga people speak of ancestors more remote than a father's great-great-grandfather's father as "the forgotten ones." "The still more ancient spirits are known as *Walenge*, meaning the disintegrated. No sacrifices are offered to these excepting they be the founders of clans, Chief's family, or the first to settle in the land—the 'Lord of the Land,' as he is termed." [1] But the spirits of vanquished Chiefs claim to be lords of the land; and when a whole community suffers from some common affliction, which cannot be attributed to the anger of spirits of the reigning dynasty, these spirits have to be appeased with a sacrifice, in the offering of which their earthly representatives join with those of their conquerors. [2] The same writer mentions that when a man occupies a new hut which he has built, he offers a sacrifice to the spirit of one who first built there; [3] whether this means the spirit of the founder of that village, or the spirit of some more aboriginal family that may have occupied the site before, is not clear. In many parts of Africa, fishermen make small offerings to the spirits of the ancient lords of the rivers, and hunters pay the same respect to the old masters of the hunting-veld, [4] sometimes

[1] K. 126.
[2] K. 151-52.
[3] K. 257.
[4] See p. 256.

through the legal representative of the dispossessed house, but sometimes (probably when there are no legal representatives) without sacerdotal intervention.   Except in such small matters, however, Chiefs of the conquering line have no standing with spirits of the ancient dynasty, and if they wish to secure the aid of such divinities in war, epidemic, or drought, they must present their offerings and requests through the senior surviving descendant of the old family, who is the natural priest of the spirits of his fathers.   It is not uncommon, therefore, for a paramount chief to request one of his serfs to invoke the spiritual patronage of a dynasty that he or his forbears have shorn of its temporal powers and possessions.   In the Chagga instance quoted above, these old lords of the land are thought to be resentful of the old wrong done them and are mollified when they hear from their descendants that the latter are content with their changed condition; but often, apparently, such spirits do not resent the fate that has befallen their children, nor turn a deaf ear to requests which their earthly representatives present on behalf of their spoilers; perhaps subjugation is regarded as merited punishment from the spirit-world.

In some parts (along the westerly lines of Bantu migration?) hunters are wont to put up prayers at the grave or shrine of some famous fellow-craftsman whose skill was acknowledged in the neighbouring hunting-grounds, even if they are not of his lineage.[1]

CHARACTER OF THE SPIRITS

The head of a Zulu village, as he addresses the spirits from his cattle-pen before the sacrifice is slaughtered, expostulates with them for always coming in the form of sickness, instead of asking properly for what they want and knowing that they will get it.   "There then is your food," he says.   "All ye spirits of our tribe, summon one another.   I am not going to say, 'So-and-so, there is your food,' for you are jealous.   But thou, So-and-so, who art making the man ill, call all the spirits; come all of you to eat the food.   If it is you, I shall see by the recovery of this man whom it is said that you have made ill. . . . Let the man get well.   Come together, all of you of such-and-such people,

---

[1] See pp. 56, 261.

who did so-and-so." And he glides forthwith into a repetition of their praise-songs. Then he tells them that he greatly wonders that people who used to do such brave things should now come stealthily; let them come openly; the cattle are theirs, and they can have what they want. Then the bullock is stabbed.[1]

Two features of this narrative deserve special attention: the spirits are jealous, and their worshippers scold them.

Bantu worshippers sometimes level accusations of jealousy against the spirits. When a sacrifice has proved unavailing, diviners now and then discover that some neglected member of the family in the other world has looked upon it with a jealous eye and must be propitiated before it can achieve its purpose. Spirits are frequently remonstrated with, or even rebuked, for their lack of consideration, or for allowing themselves to be unduly influenced in favour of other worshippers who are more lavish in their gifts. "The spirits are given to quarrel and seek to gain advantage each for himself," says an exponent of Chagga customs.[2] "Sometimes a spirit will try to exact something secretly—then the grandfather's spirit will demand restitution and will maintain his rights. The luckless mortals on earth suffer from such jealousies among the spirits, but there is a simple device for their avoidance. To each spirit belongs the meat of animals of particular colour or peculiarity." This device does not appear to be in vogue among most Bantu tribes, though there are occasional hints of some such notion. The Baganda belief that the spirit of a man's sister is likely to be malicious towards his children,[3] has probably come down from the time when the patrilineal method of succession was superseding the matrilineal and the sister was naturally jealous of her brother's children, who were supplanting her offspring as inheritors of status and its concomitant possessions in the family. I have known a few instances among the Becwana in which the spirit of a deceased wife was thought to be jealous of her successors and to have sent them sickness and death.

The Bantu insist that members of a family should enter the Puberty Rites and contract marriage in strict order of seniority;

[1] RSZ. 171-79.
[2] K. 129.
[3] Bg. 315.

the senior would regard a junior who preceded him in such matters as a supplanter. Now the Wachagga hold that the spirit of a girl who died before she had undergone the operation of clitoridectomy is likely to be annoyed if her younger surviving sister precedes her in this rite, and have a strange way of obviating the wrath of the spirit-maiden. They pretend to perform the operation upon a banana that is made to resemble a girl, and even go the length of dramatically secluding the banana in a miniature hut for the prescribed period of recovery. "They then solemnly address the dead girl, telling of how they have performed the rite on her and asking her favour that her sister may be neither injured nor fearful of the ordeal." [1] Next day the operation is performed on the younger sister. We are not told why a banana is chosen for the purpose, but we have already learnt [2] that such a corpse would be wrapped in banana leaves and laid in the banana grove.

Anthropologists sometimes refer to the scolding of the spirits [3] as an "insulting of the gods"; but that phrase is much too strong. In the private intercourse of tribesmen who approximate to one another in status, expression is freely given to that contempt for other people's convictions which is characteristic of parochial thinking; and, though courtesy is overdone in some ways, it is regarded as controversy rather than insult to tell an opponent that you despise him, or that he is lying. Wherever the military autocrat has come into power, a man who looses his tongue towards his superiors is likely to lose his head; but in communities of the older and simpler pattern, public speeches and debates are marked by great freedom of speech even towards the paramount chief. To rate the seemingly irreverent expressions of Bantu ancestor-worshippers at their true worth, the peculiarities of Bantu dialectics must be taken into account, and then it will be manifest that a worshipper addresses a discarnate spirit in much the same terms that he would use if he were speaking to the same person in the flesh. [4]

Junod gives a good example of these scolding prayers as he

[1] K. 212.
[2] See p. 28.
[3] See p. 277.
[4] Cf. IPNR. ii. 168 and see my p. 205.

knows them among the Thonga.[1] It is a prayer offered by the maternal uncle of a boy who was ill: "You, our gods, you—so and so . . . here is our offering. Bless this child and make him live and grow. Make him rich, so that when we visit him, he may be able to kill an ox for us. . . . You are useless, you gods! You only give us trouble! For although we give you offerings you do not listen to us! We are deprived of everything! You, so and so (naming the god to which the offering must be addressed in accordance with the decree given by the bones) you are full of hatred! You do not enrich us! All who succeed do so by the help of their gods. Now we have made you this gift. Call your ancestors—so and so; call also the gods of the sick boy's father, because his father's people did not steal his mother. These people, of such and such clan, came in the daylight (to buy the mother). So come to the altar! Eat and distribute among yourselves our ox (it is only a hen) according to your wisdom." Now this is very much what he would have said if, meeting his respected kinsman in the flesh at a family council, he had strongly disapproved of his line of conduct.

The assertion, often made, that spirits are dreaded because of their vindictiveness and caprice needs considerable modification. The spirit of a murdered man is so dreadful to the murderer that even a warrior who has slain a foe in fair fight upon the field of battle may not mingle with his own family again till he has been ceremonially purified. In such a case, the vengefulness of the spirit appears to be due to its untimely release; for the anger of spirits whose bodies have been deprived of full sepulchral honours is thought to be directed solely against those relatives who have neglected this duty; [2] hence strangers and slaves were often left unburied, without fear of untoward spiritual consequences to the community in which they happened to die. The fact that a son who will pay homage at his father's grave may be most unfilial during the old man's lifetime, and that the aged and the sick are often sadly neglected, would seem to indicate that spirits are not thought likely to take vengeance upon those who neglected them while they were in the flesh.[3]

[1] IRM., Oct., 1922.
[2] This does not apply to criminals.
[3] SRK. 292 and cf. my p. 381.

The curse of the dying is, however, much dreaded. It is believed that the children of one who rouses the anger of his patriarch or elder brother are likely to fall ill, even though the irate man does not consciously vent his wrath upon them; that the deliberate curse of any person, especially of a relative, is pregnant with evil towards its object; and that when a man is preparing to throw off mortality and clothe himself with spirit-power, his curse or blessing is peculiarly potent.

In a chapter on "The Curse and Its Manifestations" as observed among the Akikuyu and Akamba, Hobley deals particularly with the curse of the dying.[1] The chapter is unfortunately marred by the author's failure to distinguish between curse and taboo; for, as Sir James Frazer points out in his Introduction to this book,[2] "a curse implies a personal agent, human or divine, who has called down some evil on the sufferer; whereas in many, indeed in most, of the cases enumerated by Mr. Hobley there is no suggestion of such an agent, and the evil which befalls the sufferer is the consequence of his own action or of a simple accident." In spite of this blemish, however, the chapter is of great value to all students of this subject. These tribes hold that a dying person can lay a curse upon property or persons belonging to him, and that, however it may be with people of junior status in the family, it now and then happens that an elder lays a curse upon any one of his descendants who allows a certain plot of ground to pass out of the family, or who disregards his wishes about his herds. In their relation to land, these tribes have evidently departed from the Bantu usage; but all Bantu share their belief in the power of the curse of a dying man; for the dying man will soon be able to fulfil his own malediction.

Grenfell mentioned in his diary in 1894 [3] that a man who had recently died at Bolobo had repeatedly threatened to haunt his relatives if they failed to bury his wife with him when he died. "Many a threat of a return to earth in vengeance was pronounced by a condemned subject of Msidi," says Campbell.[4] "Many a divination test, too, proved that the threat had been fulfilled, and

[1] BBM. 145-153.
[2] BBM. 10.
[3] GGC. 251. Cf. also my p. 71.
[4] IHB. 43.

that the avenger was at work devastating in some direction or another as lion, or leopard, or in snake form, and killing without mercy." This, however, is but one of the methods which the dead may use in wreaking vengeance upon those who trample upon their wishes; they are more likely to vent their wrath by sending disease or disaster.

Bantu ancestor-spirits, like those revealed in the Vedas of ancient India, are malignant when exasperated by the neglect or disobedience of their descendants, but helpful and protective while honoured and obeyed. The Bahuma of Ankole look upon the ghost as a guardian and member of the family, who comes twice daily to partake of the milk which is placed before its shrine in the home after each milking; though they dread the trouble that may be caused by hostile ghosts of other clans.[1] The Bahuma are Hamites; but there is a strong Hamitic strain in the breed and culture of the Bantu. The Bagesu of Mount Elgon, like other Bantu, do not fear an ancestral spirit as long as it is pleased, but regard it as a desirable inmate of the home; hence they keep the skulls of ancestors in the home and honour them with daily offerings of food and drink.[2] This keeping of ancestral skulls is not general in Bantu Africa; but its underlying idea is everywhere entertained.

Death works no change in character, so the Bantu think. What the ancestors were in the days of their flesh, that the ancestor-spirits continue to be; having no higher ethical interests than they used to have; just as liable to take umbrage when their self-esteem is wounded, or to be jealous when others are preferred before them; just as helpful to their mindful and obedient "children," and just as nasty to those who neglect them or flout their will—nastier, in fact, for now they birch offenders with unseen terrors. The one thing that must never be forgotten, however, is that they are vigilant defenders of clan morality and decorum, sure to vent their wrath upon those who waste the patrimony which they conserved, or fail to honour the law and customs which they held as a sacred trust from their earliest forbears.[3]

[1] SCA. 85-86.
[2] SCA. 261.
[3] Students should read WBA. 168 on this point.

SUMMARY OF THIS CHAPTER

Before passing to the next branch of our inquiry, let us summarise very briefly the main conclusions at which we have arrived concerning Bantu belief in ancestor-spirits.

The Bantu believe that death is not the end of life; that those who sleep their last sleep, like those whose bodies are wrapped in healthy slumber, move freely amid distant scenes and old haunts. The Bantu, with no bent towards philosophic investigation and no craving for logical consistency, are content with unhewn and mismatched notions concerning the soul and its after-life. They have not cared to inquire whether life *ever* comes to an end, or just how many souls a person has, or whether souls are born at the same time as bodies, though they have preserved some distinction in terminology between incarnate souls and discarnate spirits. They make no doubt, however, that the soul is a miniature facsimile of the body; that after death it lingers with the body till sent forward to the abode of the gods, by means of appropriate sacrifices and words of power; and that subsequent to this canonisation, it is still in some sense linked with the relics of its earthly tabernacle. In spite of certain phrases which refer to the spirits as being on high—probably reminiscent of an ancient practice of burying important people in mountain caves—they undoubtedly hold that the spirit-world is below the earth, the grave being its portal and the great trysting-place for the spirit and its worshipper. Unlike the Hades of the Greeks and the Sheol of Hebrew literary prophets, the Bantu underworld is inhabited, not by mere shades, but by people who betake themselves to their old pursuits, amuse themselves with their old frolics, and beguile the time with the gossip and good fellowship of such kindred spirits as they find in the motley crowd of good and bad that dwell there together. These spirits of the dead, although they have found enlargement of power through release from the restraints of the body, are not omnipotent; nor can they read the secrets of the human heart, though they know all that their children do, say, or suffer. They are as interested as ever in their descendants who remain "outside on the earth," but indifferent to members of other communities, unless they owe them some grudge or have to hinder them from hurting their protégés. Their characters have not been changed by death; they are as prone to jealousy as they ever were, and as rancorous towards descendants who wound their vanity, flout their wishes, squander their bequests, or infringe the ancient laws and customs of their clans; but they are also as willing as ever to help those of their lineage who treat them with becoming respect and obedience. Patriarchal status is as persistent as life itself; Chiefs are still chiefs in the underworld, and patriarchs, patriarchs; cadets retain their old standing in the family; while serfs continue to be serfs, and slaves remain in slavery. In a word, the underworld is modelled after the pattern of a Bantu tribe, and its inhabitants are Bantu tribesmen armed with subtle spirit-powers.

CHAPTER II

REVELATION BY ANCESTOR-SPIRITS

THE individual is only now beginning to appear in Bantu society: the community has been everything hitherto, and people of junior status had but to obey and serve their seniors, looking to them for guidance, protection, aid, and restraint. The community consists of the quick and the dead: authoritative souls who have been gathered to their fathers are still in touch with the community, and heed must be paid to their admonitions.

REVELATION IN DREAMS

Dreams are regarded as common channels of divine communication, as they have been among people all over the world who have reached no great degree of civilisation, and often among people who have made considerable advance along the pathway of progress. Elihu formulates the belief in his argument with Job:

"God has one mode of speech;
    yes, and if man heeds it not, another.

In dreams, in visions of the night,
    when men fall into trances,
    slumbering on their beds,
he reveals things to them,
    and sends them awful warnings,
to draw them back from evil,
    and make them give up pride,
to save their souls from death,
    their lives from rushing on their doom." [1]

The Bible records many examples of this way of thinking. It was in a dream that Abimelech found the guidance of the unseen

[1] Job xxxiii. 14 ff. (Moffatt's translation).

when both Abraham and Sarah had deceived him.[1] Jacob interpreted his dream at Bethel [2] as a revelation from God; and it was in a dream that God confirmed him in his purpose to flee from Laban.[3] Laban, also, was warned in a similar manner not to treat Jacob harshly.[4] Joseph's dreams of the sheaves [5] and of the sun, moon and eleven stars; [6] and the dreams of Pharaoh's butler and baker,[7] and later of Pharaoh himself,[8] are among the thrilling stories of our childhood. So is Nebuchadnezzar's dream.[9] The dream of the Midianite,[10] with its premonition of defeat for Midian and victory for Gideon, is almost as familiar.

Nor is the belief confined to the Old Testament period. Joseph was guided in a dream to take Mary to wife,[11] and later to take the child Jesus into Egypt.[12] The Magi were warned by God in a dream that they should not return to Herod.[13] And Pilate's wife was inspired by a remarkable dream to plead with her husband on behalf of Jesus.[14]

It is true, no doubt, that dreams do not play that preponderant part in the religion of Israel which they played among some other peoples, and that the comparatively small number of dreams recorded in the Bible cluster in a curious way around a few people who were in close contact with other nations; but it cannot be disputed that the Israelites recognised dreams as a mode of communicating the divine will.

In ancient Egypt it was universally believed that dreams were sent to men by the gods, and men slept in temples of oracular deities in order that they might be favoured with such divine hints for future conduct. An Egyptian prince, weary with hunting, fell asleep at noonday under the shadow of the Sphinx at

[1] Gen. xx. 3 ff.
[2] Gen. xxviii. 11 ff.
[3] Gen. xxxi. 10 ff.
[4] Gen. xxxi. 24.
[5] Gen. xxxvii. 7 ff.
[6] Gen. xxxvii. 9.
[7] Gen. xl.
[8] Gen. xli.
[9] Dan. ii.
[10] Judg. vii. 13 ff.
[11] Mt. i. 20.
[12] Mt. ii. 13.
[13] Mt. ii. 12.
[14] Mt. xxvii. 19.

Gizeh, which is the emblem of the god Rā-Harmachis; and while he slumbered the god came to him and promised him the future sovereignty of Egypt if he would clear away the drift-sand which then, as now, threatened to bury the colossal symbol. The task was performed and the promise redeemed; and in the first year of his reign, as Thothmes IV, he had an account of his interview with the god inscribed upon a stele and set up before the breast of the Sphinx.[1] As a rule, Egyptian dreamers could interpret their own dreams; but there were professional interpreters, mostly priests and officials, some of whom, like Joseph, rose to places of high honour.

Modern Egyptians cherish a similar belief. Lane states[2] that one of the most learned Muslim professors in Cairo placed more reliance upon what had been revealed in a dream to one of his pupils than upon his own previous historic investigations, and justified himself by appealing to the tradition that Mohammed had said, "Whoso seeth me in his sleep, seeth me truly; for Satan cannot assume the similitude of my form."[3]

Similar notions prevailed among Chinese, Greeks, Italians, Celts, and, indeed, all the nations of antiquity.[4] "Both among the continental and Irish Celts those who sought hidden knowledge slept on graves, hoping to be inspired by the spirits of the dead."[5] "It was to the grave of Fergus that two bards resorted in order to obtain from him the lost story of the Tain."[6]

Whether those subliminal uprushes which we call dreams may be counted upon to bring us messages from a spiritual environment to which our waking consciousness is closed, the sleeping state being more plastic than the waking; or whether dreams are merely the disguised children of our fears and anxieties and the strangely transformed apparitions of thoughts which in our waking hours we had beaten down into the lower level of consciousness, deeming them impossible or incompatible with our ideals, we must leave psychologists to discover; but Bantu beliefs de-

---

[1] EM. 214. RLAE. 208.
[2] MCME. 219.
[3] For the Muslim conception of intercourse with the unseen world in sleep, see Macdonald: *The Religious Attitude and Life in Islam*, Lecture III.
[4] SCD. 3, 17, 31, 76, 80, 81.
[5] RAC. 250.
[6] RAC. 340.

mand a much less sophisticated elucidation. Sleep, so the Bantu think, is due to the temporary absence of the soul from the body; hence their fear to wake a sleeper suddenly, lest his spirit should not have time to return to its corporeal abode. On its nocturnal excursions, the soul of the sleeper walks and talks with the dead in the midst of their earthly haunts or, maybe, interviews the spirits in their infernal abode; and subjective dream-consciousness is not sharply differentiated from the objective impressions of one's waking hours.[1]

The old Bantu habit of famishing till sunset and then eating their fill, tends to make them great dreamers, even though hours of dancing or gossip come between the meal and the mat; and their dream-pictures seem very real. Friends swap dreams round the morning fire, and debate the significance of the soul's sensations in its nightly wandering from the body. "All their dreams are construed into visits from the spirits of their deceased friends," says Wilson,[2] writing of West Coast tribes. "The cautions, hints, and warnings which come to them through this source, are received with the most serious and deferential attention, and are always acted upon in their waking hours. The habit of relating their dreams, which is universal, greatly promotes the habit of dreaming itself, and hence their sleeping hours are characterised by almost as much intercourse with the dead as their waking are with the living. This is, no doubt, one of the reasons of their excessive superstitiousness. Their imaginations become so lively that they can scarcely distinguish between their dreams and their waking thoughts, between the real and the ideal, and they consequently utter falsehood without intending, and profess to see things which never existed."

In interpreting dreams, their method is sometimes simple and direct,[3] while at other times it goes by contraries. If a Mwila tells his friends that he dreamt he was flying through the air, over the treetops, they reply, "You live very well. It is life. That is a great dream."[4] If a Zulu dreams that a professed friend is injuring him, he keeps away from him, and if the friend

1 See IPNR. 134 ff and RAA. Chap. xxi.
2 WA. 395.
3 RSZ. 228-30.
4 IPNR. ii. 136.

notices it, he lies about it and denies it.[1]   To dream of a great assembly where there is dancing, is an omen of death; but to dream of the funeral of some sick man, is a sign that he will recover; and to dream that you have killed a man, is an omen of your own death.[2]   The Bakaonde say that to dream of wealth means poverty for the dreamer, and *vice versa;* that when one is absent from home and dreams that he is at home, it signifies that he will never go to his home again; that it is bad to dream of dancing, drum-beating, or of people gathered together for a beer-drink, since these things indicate that there is going to be a funeral; that it is good to dream that one is washing himself, but bad to dream that one is being washed, because corpses are washed; but that to dream that one is killed by a lion means great success in the chase.[3]

Not all dreams are regarded as influential, however; the disordered phantasmagoria of the night are dismissed with scant attention.   Winter dreams are often confused and unintelligible, so the Zulus say, but summer dreams do not usually miss the mark.[4]   Coherent and consequent dreams, especially those in which some dead relative or friend figures, or those which have to do with current affairs,[5] are taken as real revelations from the spirit-world, and are frequently followed by consultation with a diviner.

When a Mosuto dreams of his dead father, he thinks it a supernatural visitation caused by his own neglect; and, upon the diviner's advice, an ox or a sheep of a certain colour is sacrificed, both the dreamer and his father's grave are sprinkled with its gall, and prayer is offered: "Oh, let us now sleep in peace, and trouble us no more."[6]   If one of the dead appears in a dream to a Zulu, and claims that he was embodied in a snake which was recently killed in his village, it is taken as a fact;[7] and, of course, the insult is fittingly expiated.

The Baila say: "It may be that when a person is lying asleep

[1] RSZ. 164.
[2] RSZ. 232-41, 242-46.
[3] WBA. 246.
[4] RSZ. 232-41.
[5] Bg. 18, WPP. 124.
[6] HB. 248.
[7] RSZ. 229-31.

a ghost comes to him and says, 'Go and pluck such-and-such leaves and use them as medicine for such-and-such a disease.' He gets up and in the morning he goes just where the ghost told him, he goes and plucks that medicine and uses it just as he was ordered. To others the ghost comes in sleep and on arrival says, 'To-morrow go to such-and-such a place and you will find such-and-such a thing.' So in the morning he goes and finds it. To another, who has a case in court, a ghost comes in sleep and says, 'As for this affair, you must speak in such a manner.' He does just so, he speaks and all believe what they are told, and say, 'He does not speak of himself, it comes from dreaming.' That is how they are convinced at the court. Or a hunter when he is lying asleep, a ghost comes and tells him, 'In the morning take your gun and go to hunt in such-and-such a place.' So next morning he goes and finds game; just where the ghost told him."[1]

If a Thonga "dreams of one of his dead relatives, he is very much frightened and consults the bones, in order to know exactly what the god desires of him. . . . If the god has come as an enemy fighting, the dreamer, when awake, will take some tobacco or a small piece of cloth, and put it somewhere in the reeds of the wall near the door, as an offering. Or possibly the god has ordered him to give him something to drink."[2]

There are various methods of "closing up the way," as the Zulus phrase it, against the visitation of a troublesome spirit in dreams. If the dreams are good, the Bechuana spit on the floor so that the memory of them may remain; but if they are unpleasant the memory of them may be banished by inducing artificial sneezing. When the Zulu wish to banish a bad dream, they chew up medicine with the spittle which is in their mouth when they wake in the morning, spit it on a stone or piece of firewood and throw it behind the back without looking.[3] Or, if that fails,

[1] IPNR. ii. 134-35.

[2] LSAT. ii. 359.

[3] Lane says that modern "Egyptians place great faith in dreams, which often direct them in some of the most important actions of life. They have two large and celebrated works on the interpretation of dreams, by Ibn-Sháheen and Ibn-Seereen; the latter of whom was pupil of the former. These books are consulted, even by many of the learned, with implicit confidence. . . . When a person has had an evil dream, it is customary for him to say, 'O God, bless our Lord Mohammad'; and to spit over his left shoulder three times to prevent an evil result." (MCME. 268.)

a doctor can conjure a spirit into an ant-heap by means of appropriate "medicines." Women who have been taken to wife by the brother of their deceased husband, or who have left their children and gone to live with another man after the death of their husband, are often troubled with unpleasant visits from the spirit-world. Their remedy is to chew "medicine" with the spittle which is in their mouth when they wake from the dream; spit it out on some more "medicine"; and hire a doctor to brew black *ubulawo* [1] for them and to bury the "medicine" and the spittle in a hole made in a bulb, which he forthwith plants so that it may grow. [2]

Oftener than not, however, the visits of dream-spirits are unobjectionable, and the guidance of the dead is often sought. In Nyasaland, Macdonald noticed that offerings were frequently presented by a man at the top of his bed, close to his head, so that the god might come and whisper into his ear as he slept. [3] Analogous methods are in vogue in all Bantu tribes.

REVELATION BY CALAMITY

Another way in which spirits of the dead reveal themselves, is by calamity. [4] When the Bantu do not attribute death to violence or to witchcraft, they always interpret it as a call from the spirit-world. Zulu diviners often declare of a deceased patient: "He was called by the *amatongo* (spirits); a diviner cannot conquer the *amatongo*." [5] Anything out of the usual run of things, whether personal illness or tribal disaster, [6] indicates that some ancestral spirit is provoked to assert himself in unpleasant ways. Sickness in the family is often believed to be due to the infidelity of a wife; which means, upon the last analysis, that the wife's disregard of ancestral law has roused the ire of the ancestral spirits of the family. "Your gods are not pleased; your ancestors have turned their backs upon you," is the popular interpre-

---

[1] For further particulars about *ubulawo*, a "medicine" in great demand among the Zulus, see pp. 146, 159, 344.

[2] RSZ. 160-61, 317.

[3] A. i. 60. Cf. my p. 363.

[4] K. 125.

[5] RSZ. 312.

[6] Cf. 1 Kings viii. 33 *et seq.*

tation of drought,[1] epidemic among people or cattle, and even ordinary disease.[2] In such supernatural visitations, no remedy can avail till the wrathful spirit has been pacified. It is a common practice to anoint the sick with the bile and fat of a sacrificed animal; but this is not medicine in our sense of the term; [3] it is salve for the soul,—a kind of sacrament of unction, the core of which is prayer to the offended spirit. The first step to be taken in illness, is to discover, through a diviner, what discarnate relative is thus showing his resentment; and the second, is to mollify the spirit with a congenial sacrifice. The Kafir usage is typical of Bantu procedure upon such occasions. When a beast is sacrificed to the ancestors for the recovery of a patient, they place the flesh in a hut for a whole night, so that the spirits may feast upon its essence; and next day, when the relatives have gathered to partake of the sacramental meat, the family priest burns the bones and some special portions of the fat, and intones his invocation to the spirits.[4] The invalid is anointed with bile and fat of the sacrifice, and in some tribes a strip of its hide is fastened around his wrist.[5] The aim of the ritual is to restore friendly relations between the invalid and his forebears. After that is done, the simples of the Bantu herbalist or the drugs of the European physician may bring the patient relief and healing; but without that, all human aid is ineffectual. When a whole community is involved, as in drought or epidemic, the ritual of reconciliation is more elaborate and complicated, but it embodies the same principle.

Miss Werner records an incident which illustrates both of the foregoing methods of revelation—in dreams and by calamity. There was a plague of locusts in the Shire Highlands, and the cause of this visitation was freely canvassed in the Place of Public Assembly. "Chesinka, an old headman on Mlanje moun-

---

[1] See also pp. 207, 211, 214.

[2] Elihu enunciates a similar doctrine when he maintains, in Job xxxiii. 19 et seq., that sickness, like night visions, is a warning of divine displeasure. The Assyrians thought that all diseases were caused by demons, and employed diviners to identify the troubling spirits.

[3] African "medicine" is, in the main, a magical concoction, and there can be no doubt that Bantu think of European drugs as acting in the same way.

[4] LA. 203.

[5] Cf. GS. 153-54 for kindred practice among the Bambwa on the western slopes of the Ruwenzori range.

tain, had a dream, one night in October, which, at any rate, suggested a solution. His old friend, Chipoka, dead some four years, appeared to him, and told him that it was he himself who had sent the locusts, as a hint to his people that they were not treating him properly; it was a long time since they had given him any beer, and he was very thirsty in the spirit-world. So Chesinka sent word to Chipoka's son, who at once took steps to repair the omission. Chipoka had been a person of importance in his way; he was the principal chief on Mlanje in Livingstone's time." [1]

Mishaps much too trivial to be termed calamities are sometimes ranked as admonitions from the spirit-world. [2]

REVELATION BY ECSTASY AND TRANCE

We have already observed that the Bantu, heedless of the distinction between subjective and objective, regard dreams as temporary excursions of the soul, apart from the body, in delightful independence of the hampering restrictions to which flesh and blood must submit. They are familiar, also, with an experience which supervenes upon religious, amative, and other forms of excitement, rather than upon physical fatigue, and is often concomitant with disease of the nervous system, especially hysteria; an experience which they think akin to sleep and death, because it sets the soul free to see and hear things not present to the waking consciousness. This abnormality takes two forms. In its milder form, it is of short duration, and frequently followed by a period of frenzy, like that which seized Saul. [3] Though marked by temporary mental alienation, it falls short of insanity, and appears to be contagious. *Ecstasy* is probably our most appropriate designation of this dervishlike condition, and the word has the additional advantage of fitting in well with the Bantu interpretation of the aberration—a *standing apart* from one's body or mind. In its severer form, the disorder lasts longer, sometimes much longer, and is marked by greater insensibility to external impressions, or even, occasionally, by catalepsy. *Trance* is per-

---

[1] NBCA. 46-47.
[2] See p. 259.
[3] 1 Sam. x. 5-13; xix. 22-24.

haps the best appellation that we can bestow upon this morbid sleep. Now hallucinations of the ecstatic and of the entranced are taken as revelations from the spirit-world.

"If a person is ill and delirious," remarked one of my old Native instructors, "he says, 'The dead crowd around me, as in a dream. The cattle in our family kraal will jump over my grave.'" But sometimes these phantom visitors from the other world give the frenzied new hope.

In 1916 we had a "house-boy" whose mental capacity was certainly not below the average level. He belonged, however, to a family that had produced intelligent eccentricities, and he himself suffered, about once a month, a curious attack of stupidity and absentmindedness, which lasted for a couple of days. The sudden death of his elder brother, whom he unwarrantably believed to have been poisoned, cast a gloom over his life. Week after week he remained disconsolate, till he fell ill and was confined to his hut for about a month. He seemed marked for the grave, though his disease was of a variety, familiar to all missionaries among backward races, in which imagination counts for everything and drugs are of no greater value than anything else which will induce the patient to believe that he will recover. One day he sent me a brief note, which I translate: "I tell you that I have hope of living. On Friday I was very ill indeed; and about three o'clock in the afternoon I went away and saw my father, my elder brother and my uncle" (all of whom were dead). "My uncle alone spoke to me, saying, 'Go back and do not leave your mother; we have five of your seniors here; you go back into yonder sorrow again; although we are absent we are with you in spirit.' And they sent me back with peace. I shall recover. The sickness is still great." The belief, aroused by this vision, that his elders in the spirit-world willed his recovery, gave him new life, and he rapidly regained his normal vigour.

Early in 1902 a man of about thirty years of age, living in one of Khama's outlying villages, had what he called a vision. He told me that having seen a very bright light and felt the wind burning with a very great heat, he fell faint upon the ground. Within the next few weeks, this experience was repeated three times. He was not ill, so he said, except for these brief happenings; but it seemed to me that his eyes betokened mental trouble. It was his conviction that the vision was sent for some purpose, but as he saw no forms and heard no voices he was at a loss to know what the purpose was.

A month or two later, a somewhat younger man of the same village, heard a voice, saying, "You have bought many books, but they have done you no good; you had better burn them all and just do what is written in Matthew alone." Then he felt as if it were a fire burning in his body, and all his joints were loosed. By questioning him, I discovered that the "many books" were four spelling-books, all alike, which he had bought but had not learnt to read. He had not burnt them, but had given them away; and, though he professed to be a catechumen, he had not taken the first step toward learning to read what was written in Matthew.

In 1901, a Mongwato of about sixty years of age, whose friendship I valued, told me of a vision that he had seen upon two occasions. The first time was when he was a boy, too young to enter the Puberty Rites. After a severe illness, his relatives thought him dead, and called the medicine-man to throw the divining-tablets and ascertain whether his spirit would return again to the body. The medicine-man pronounced him dead, and the grave was partly dug for him. While lying as if dead, he went away and visited a very lovely city, full of strange people, white [1] and glistening. The town, also, was radiant with splendour, and there was not a stump in it, nor anything that could cause stumbling or disaster. A superb man whom he met there told him to arise and depart, and so he returned to earth. Upon regaining consciousness and finding that he had lost the power of speech, he crawled to the door of the hut in which he lay; but his mother was so astonished that she cried, "Don't touch him; we don't know who has raised him up!" Many years afterwards, he had another severe illness while travelling on the Botetle River, and his friends, thinking him dead, had come with poles to carry him forth to his burial. During this second period

---

[1] Lest a wrong inference should be drawn from my old friend's imagery, it may be well to state that though the Bechuana politely accept the term "White-man" as it falls from the lips of a European, they themselves think of Europeans as "Red-men."

of unconsciousness he had an experience similar to the first. He was of opinion that he had not been delirious on either occasion.

I suggested to him that the imagery of his vision may have been influenced by reading or hearing of "The Revelation of St. John the Divine." He said that was impossible; that though the first missionary had come to his tribe a short time before his first vision and he had been herding the missionary's goats, he thought (he was not sure) that he had never heard him preach. He declared, moreover, that in every generation there had always been a number of people who were thought to be dead but had recovered before burial, and that many of them had seen what he saw, though they knew nothing whatever of Christianity. The Bechuana, he said, always knew about the town in which the spirits dwell; and as for the radiance of the town and its inhabitants, when he was a child it was common for his playmates to exclaim, upon seeing a beetle or butterfly with iridescent and brilliant colours, "Look, there is a child of the spirits!" And the children would shun the company of a playmate who dared to kill one of these godlike creatures. He maintained, also, that it was not a rare thing for a sick person to say, "I saw a beautiful man who told me to arise and depart"; that the friends of such an invalid usually reply, "You have seen your grandfather, and now by his words you will recover"; and that thereupon word is always passed round to the neighbours that the patient has returned from the town in which the spirits dwell.

In 1915 a Mokwena woman, who had formerly been a member of the Church but now held aloof from us (except that she occasionally came to church on Sunday morning), fell ill of double pneumonia. As I happened to be absent from home, she sent for one of my deacons and dictated a message for me. She had died, she said (her relatives said that she had been unconscious for an hour or two); and while in the spirit-world she felt a flame of fire burning in her breast, and causing her such distress as she had never experienced on earth. She saw her mother's younger sister (who was dead) standing some distance away, and cried to her for water, but got none. Then she saw the Lord Jesus Christ standing before her; and when she looked upon him the flame was quenched within her. He said to her: "Do you know what is happening? The flame that burns within you is

Kafir-beer. Those who drink Kafir-beer are burning up the temple of God with Kafir-beer. Drinkers of Kafir-beer have no escape except by this punishment; because they have driven away the Holy Spirit by Kafir-beer." On her way back to earth, she saw on her right hand a smooth rock with four colours on it: two were yellow, one was black, and one was white, and the white was uppermost; but the meaning of this was not shown to her. She strictly charged us to warn the Church against drinking Kafir-beer, and to enforce our warning by telling the people what had been revealed to her in the spirit-world. She had been told in the spirit-world that she would die before sunset; and she did.

The imagery of this woman's vision, or dream, or whatever it was, appears to spring from intolerable inflammation of the lungs; and its significance for her seems to be due to two facts: (1) She had been secretly struggling against her better self in the matter of beer-drinking; and (2) She had applied to her own peculiar circumstances what I had said when preaching from 1 Cor. vi. 19 and 20, on a Sunday morning about six weeks before.

Callaway, a doctor of medicine as well as a canon of the Anglican Church, describes ecstasy as a state in which a man becomes slightly insensible, but is awake, and sees things which he would not see if he were not in ecstasy. He tells [1] of a Zulu ecstatic whose dreams came true, and who could see people coming on the other side of the hill; and he remarks that this clairvoyant liked to sit alone, and used to yawn and sneeze continually, as Zulu diviners do. He mentions, also, the case of a Zulu convert,[2] who, having heard that men who go into the bush to pray at daybreak (before the people are about) sometimes have to withstand Satan in the form of a savage beast or a venomous snake, had one morning a realistic and gruesome encounter with this infernal foe. Callaway remarks with justice that "the reader will see repeated in this narrative the experiences of St. Anthony, Hilarion, and other early saints"; but the fact that the traditions or experiences of primitive "saints" sprang from a like mentality, does not mitigate one's regret that the Bantu, prone as they are to mistake the children of their fertile fancy for extrinsic sub-

[1] RSZ. 242 *et seq.*
[2] RSZ. 251-52.

stantialities, should add foreign and grotesque images of a personal devil to their superabundant repertory of ghostly terrors.

Hobley [1] "interviewed and cross-examined" an elder of the Akikuyu tribe, who "stated that at intervals, about twice a year, during the night, he falls into a deeper sleep than usual, a trance in fact, and that while in this condition he is taken out of bed and statements are made to him by a voice, but he cannot see who gives the message. The trance always occurs at night, and he is generally taken out of his hut while in the cataleptic condition, but says that he never remembers being able to distinguish the huts or any familiar objects in the village. The interior of the hut appears to be lighted up, and the message comes with a booming sound which he understands. He stated that one day when visiting an elder named Kibutu, he was seized during the night and taken bodily through the thatch of the roof, and was found on the top of the hut next morning. . . . He does not sleep in an ordinary hut with his wife, but in a bachelor hut with another elder. When he is seized with one of his trances the other elder will wake up and find that he has gone, but does not see him go or return. The day following one of his seizures he collects the elders and delivers his message. He states that after one of these seizures he is very exhausted, and for three days cannot rise from his bed. . . . He believed the gift came from God [2] and not from the *ngoma* or ancestral spirits, and that if he did not deliver to the people the messages he received he would be stricken with sickness. . . . He gave examples of the kind of messages he received. On one occasion some time before the advent of Europeans, he was told that the Masai would be severely stricken with small-pox, and that subsequently many would settle among the Kikuyu, and shortly afterwards it happened accordingly. On another occasion he was told that a white race would enter the country, and that they and the Kikuyu would live side by side in the country, and now it has come to pass. He was seized before the great famine of 1900 and foretold its arrival." He was told afterwards to tell the Kikuyu to offer certain sacrifices at the sacred fig-trees; "the orders were obeyed, and the famine and small-pox were lifted from the land."

[1] BBM. 36-38.
[2] The word used was probably *Engai*.

This man's account of how he came by his uncanny powers is significant. His father and paternal grandfather had the gift before him, and he was invested with it when he was a stripling, shortly after his circumcision. He woke one morning with his hands tightly clasped, and "passed blood and urine" for nine days. After a goat had been sacrificed and strips of its skin tied to his wrists, the hematuria stopped and his hands relaxed; and when he was able to open his hands, fifteen white stones, like those used by diviners of his tribe, were found in each.

Cases like those that I have cited provide the psychologist with a problem that he cannot solve without more information than we can give.[1] Our present concern, however, is to note that the Bantu are familiar with these phenomena, and that when a person sees or hears something that nobody else can perceive, they credit him with a peculiar power that they lack. We call it hallucination; they count it inspiration, and regard his visions and auditions as real revelations from the spirit-world.

We shall speak later of the tendency of Christian converts to give these abnormal experiences a quasi-Christian colouring.

REVELATION BY "POSSESSION"

Great ancestor-spirits are thought to enter into individuals occasionally and use them as mediums of communication with men.

---

[1] But such cases are not confined to Africa. My evening paper (*The Hartford Times*, January 11, 1924) gave an account of a man who was to appear that day before an Extraordinary Grand Jury appointed by the State of Connecticut to inquire into the right of certain people to practise medicine. Since 1895 a man, formerly a grocery clerk, had been practising as "healer by and teacher of divine power," and running a factory for the manufacture of "Sun and Moon Sacred Ointment and Oil." He had gathered a large clientele, which included many wealthy people from this city and district. In various books that he had written as an explanation of his healing power, he relates how he was called in 1895 to be a healer. "He had been aware," says the journalist, "of a healing power since boyhood in his hands, voice and mind, but its source had not been recognised. . . . As a result of an injury he had been obliged to undergo a severe operation, after which his soul left the body (apparently death) and he travelled to the very presence of God. He relates the trip to the Divine Presence, the presentation to him of the key of knowledge, and the realisation that this knowledge was to be used by him on earth through the spiritual magnetic electrical power which would be conferred upon him on his return to earth." In that same year he dreamed one night of many herbs, and in the morning saw the names of them written in electricity on the wall; this was the origin of his Sacred Oils and Ointments. "He relates how, as he was travelling from Hartford to Springfield, he saw the rays

These "possessed" people, to quote the words of an intelligent Mosuto correspondent, "say they are able to talk with heavenly[1] spirits; and they call themselves no longer of this world, though still in it." The possessing spirit is occasionally that of an ancestor of the "possessed"; but, oftener a spirit of note, such as that of a celebrated chief or a famous medicine-man. It is said that the possessing spirit is sometimes thought to be that of an animal, but no such case has ever come my way, and I doubt the accuracy of the observation. The medium claims that she (women are much more liable to "possession" than men) is "possessed" by the spirit of So-and-so, and proceeds to deliver his message. The message is not infrequently accompanied with threats, and invariably contains a demand for something that the possessing spirit wants to receive through his medium. The people see that "she is not herself," and when she declares that some defunct notability has taken possession of her body, they adopt a reverent attitude towards her mystic message.

Every tribe is replete with stories of remarkable cases of possession that have occurred in its history; but these stories have gained so much in wonder by constant repetition that it is well-nigh impossible to winnow out the fact from the fiction. In the Bamangwato calendar, the year 1864 is known as "The Year of Mmaborola."[2] Mmaborola was a woman who claimed to be

of the sun shining on a particular part of the Connecticut river, and there then flashed to him the realisation that he should be baptised in that spot. He made arrangements for the baptism but without making it known where he was to be baptised, but one of the attendants led the baptismal party to the very spot. He was immersed three times, and after the third immersion he heard the most wonderful heavenly music."

Underwood (*Conversion: Christian and Non-Christian*. Allen & Unwin, p. 168), after quoting many instances of visions, auditions and photisms in connection with conversion, makes this remark: "Psychology no longer attributes to these visions, voices and photisms an objective reality, but regards them as sensorial automatisms, psychically caused and conditioned. They are by no means confined to the conversion-crisis, but occur at any period of the religious life, as the lives of Paul, St. Teresa, George Fox, Blake, Evan Roberts, Rabi 'a, Nichiren, and Honen (to mention only a few names) show. As is well known, parallel phenomena occur in secular life. A libertine and murderer like Benvenuto Cellini saw visions of angels when he was imprisoned at St. Angelo. The appearance of these automatisms is not due to the Spirit of God, but to the subject's physical and mental condition."

[1] Stress must not be laid on this use of the word "heavenly" (see pp. 66 ff.), the Christian Native is simply using it as a synonym for "discarnate."

[2] It is customary in Bantu tribes to name each year after its most conspicuous event.

possessed by an ancestral spirit of one of the old lords of the land, who kept her informed of approaching rain and abundant harvests. She separated from people, and spent night and day under a shady tree by the Leshosho stream that flowed through Shoshong (when it flowed at all). She told the people that if they would bring her a black ewe, they would have plenty of rain and corn. When they brought the sheep, she tied it up to the tree and pointed at it with her big toe, saying, "Let it die!" Some say that the sheep thereupon fell dead; others that it was found dead in the morning, but without a wound upon its body.[1] The ewe was flayed, and she clad herself in its wet skin, threw herself upon the ground, and lay as dead.[2] When she woke, she staggered and said, "Abundance!" Many people gathered around her and joined her in her song; and they feasted on the sacrificed sheep and danced and sang songs in her honour. Some say that this happened only once; others that it was repeated again and again, and that crowds hung around her for weeks. After that there was a tremendous rain and a harvest so abundant that people had not where to bestow their corn. People humbled themselves before her, believing that if she prayed to the god who possessed her he would give them life, whereas if they despised her she might bring a curse upon them. Some called her a god; but others said, "No, she is not a god, but the servant of the god within her." Such is the story as it came to me some thirty years after it is supposed to have happened.

In April, 1901, I attended a Tribal Assembly of the Bamangwato, which enquired into five cases of "possession" that had been causing excitement in outlying parts of the country, among clans akin to that to which Mmaborola belonged. They were all alike. An old woman met a man carrying a wild guinea-fowl which he had caught, and rated him soundly for having killed one of the birds that are sacred to the spirit whose "mouth" she declared herself to be. The man was so frightened that he

---

[1] It seems that their medicine-men practise a trick of this kind, the success of which, so the knowing ones say, is probably due to poison.

[2] In the *taghairm* of the Highlanders, the seer was usually bound in a cow's hide and left in a desolate place, and while he slept spirits inspired his dreams. Mac-Culloch suggests that the cow's hide was probably the skin of a sacrificial animal in earlier times; and this black sheep suggests the same conclusion. (See RAC. 249-250.)

meekly handed over the bird to the "mouth" of the god that claimed it. Another man, abnormally obsequious toward the chief, stated that he was "possessed" by an ancestral spirit and had commanded the people to worship him. Another man was the "mouth" of an ancestral spirit who had become reincarnate in a snake that he was able to point out. There was a woman, also, who was the "mouth" of a snake-possessing spirit; but she had been more unfortunate than the others. A Christian Native chanced to visit her village, and, wishful to see the god, was shown a puff-adder in a courtyard. "Do you mean to say that there is a god in that puff-adder?" he asked. "Yes!" was the unhesitating reply. Then his stick came down, whack, upon the sacred snake, and he quietly remarked, "Well, there is not much god in it now." All these "possessed" people were evidently touched in the upper storey, and touched also with a kind of cunning that often accompanies mental alienation. Although they lived in different parts of the country, the epidemic was no doubt due to the rapidity, exaggeration and excitement with which news of the first case of "possession" spread from village to village. In some villages it produced no small flutter; people gathered around the poor unfortunate, bringing guinea-fowls to the "mouth" of the spirit who was so mindful of these toothsome birds, or sacrificing goats or sheep to the god who possessed one of the others, and supplementing the gift with libations of home-brewed beer. And since the worshippers always eat and drink with the gods, the feasting, dancing and revelry lasted far into the night. Khama thought it would be wrong to punish these poor daft people; so he dismissed them with a scolding, warning their relatives to keep them out of trouble in the future; but he fined each worshipper double the amount of the sacrifice that he had offered.

As far as we can discover, such cases of "possession" have occasionally occurred, time out of mind, in every Bantu community of any size.[1] They are mentioned by most writers on Bantu life, and both Junod[2] and Smith[3] have valuable pages concerning them.

[1] See p. 146. Cf. also SCD. 27-32.
[2] LSAT. ii. 435-460.
[3] IPNR. ii. 136-140.

Sheane describes the "possession" of men and women by spirits of dead Awemba chiefs.[1] "The possessed person, while the spirit is in him, will prophesy as to future wars, and warn the people of approaching visitations by lions. During the period of possession he eats nothing cooked by fire, but only unfermented dough. The functions of *mfumu ya mipashi* (chiefs of the spirits) are usually performed by women. These women assert that they are possessed by the soul of some dead chief, and when they feel the 'divine afflatus,' whiten their faces to attract attention, and anoint themselves with flour, which has a religious and sanctifying potency. One of their number beats a drum, and the others dance, singing at the same time a weird song, with curious intervals. Finally when they have arrived at the requisite stage of religious exaltation, the possessed woman falls to the ground, and bursts forth into a low and almost inarticulate chant, which has a most uncanny effect. All are silent at once, and the *bashing'anga* (medicine men) gather round to interpret the voice of the spirit. In the old time many men and women were denounced as *waloshi* (sorcerers) by these possessed women, whereupon the accused, unless protected by the king, or willing to undergo the ordeal, were instantly killed or mutilated."

Every Konde chief has an expert hierolatrist, whom he sends daily with an offering to the grave of the last chief, and who accompanies him when he goes thither to pray. When the chief dies, this man "is in great danger, for the spirits take possession of his person, a danger which can only be averted by a powerful medicine supplied by the doctor, and taken as soon as the chief has died. If this is not done, he becomes mad, lives in the bush, gibbering and naming all the dead chiefs of the past, including names known to no living person, but supposed to be those of long-dead chiefs, uttered by themselves through him."[2] These tribesmen think there are other spirits that sometimes take possession of people. "If the possessed makes for water, it is known that a water spirit has entered into him; if he goes to the hills, it is a mountain spirit. In either case the patient is taken by the medicine man to a waterfall, 'where God dwells,' and given medicine to drink. . . . A bell is rung; the doctor speaks, 'We have

[1] GPNR. 83.
[2] SRK. 196.

found you. Come out of the man.' Then he takes water in his mouth and squirts it on the breast and back of the afflicted person, striking him at the same time with the calabash with which he took the water, and holding it for a little over the patient's head." [1]

Hobley states [2] that at a private sacrifice in a Kamba village, in Kenya Colony, "sometimes a woman who goes into a cataleptic condition, which is known as being seized by *aiimu*" (ancestral spirits) "will say that to obtain rain a beast of a particular colour must be sacrificed." And again, [3] "It often happens that during a ceremony at an *ithembo*" (shrine of an ancestor-spirit in a Kamba village) "a woman is seized or possessed, and passes into a condition of semi-trance in which she will prophesy either that the rains are coming or that they will fail, or, in former days, that a Masai raid was imminent. I was told that the message came from the *imu* or spirit of the person of olden time to whom the *ithembo* was dedicated, but quite clearly, that the spirit was only an intermediary, the message really coming from the high god *Engai* or *Mulungu*." The same writer says that there was an epidemic of infectious mania or possession among the Akamba in 1906, and another in 1911. Speaking of the latter, he says: [4] "The spirit of a girl who was said to have died mysteriously was supposed to enter into people in various parts of the district— generally old women—and speak. The whole district rapidly became disturbed; the spirit, through its oracles, demanded that bullocks should be slaughtered; the order was implicitly obeyed, for any one who refused was supposed to be doomed. As a result, several thousand bullocks were slaughtered and consumed in a week or two. Great dances, at which meat was eaten, were held. Very soon the oracles became seditious, and plans were being made for the abolition of European government and attack on the Government station. The whole thing was kept secret at first, but eventually it all came out and a company of troops had to be sent to the district to calm the excited people; the elders, who felt sore at the loss of so many cattle, rallied to

[1] SRK. 224.
[2] BBM. 58.
[3] BBM. 59-60. Cf. AK. 85.
[4] BBM. 255.

the support of law and order and the country gradually regained a normal state."

What is the explanation of these phenomena? The Bantu explanation is simple enough, and convincing to people who know nothing of modern medicine. It is based upon the testimony of the patient, who asserts that he has a *dimo* within him, and upon the ocular evidence of neighbours to whom it is obvious that the man is not himself. Everything is of course viewed through the mystical atmosphere in which both the patient and his neighbours live, and always have lived; but all these cases, however multiform they may be, must unquestionably be classed with insanity, epilepsy, monomania, melancholia, and other forms of neurotic and mental disorder. The "possession" is temporary in some cases, and periodic in others, particularly with women; and wild dancing and music, still more a peculiar drumbeat, induce fresh outbreaks of frenzy in some who seemed to be on the mend.[1] There is often a history of previous eccentricity in the patient; and the attack is not infrequently ushered in with loss of consciousness, or convulsions, or other epileptic symptoms. "A sign that a man or woman has this *motheketheke*,"[2] says a Mosuto correspondent, "is when he or she has crying fits, and running away, and often falling down when running away." "To be possessed" is a literal translation of the commonest Secwana phrase for "to be insane" (*go tsénwa*). All insane people are held in awe,[3] unless they are harmless simpletons of the milder sort; but not all of them claim to be "possessed" by a particular spirit. Among the Bantu, insane people often take to the hills, refusing to return to the community except when pressed by hunger, and spending much of their time, night and day, shouting and talking to some imaginary companion. The insanity with which we are familiar in the homeland, varies considerably in intensity, from simple hysteria to the fixed

[1] IPNR. ii. 138-39.

[2] Mabille's *Sesuto Vocabulary* defines *motheketheke* as "extraordinary (devilish) possession."

[3] Lane tells us that the Muslims of Egypt hold the insane in similar reverence: "Lunatics who are dangerous to society are kept in confinement; but those who are harmless are generally regarded as saints. Most of the reputed saints of Egypt are either lunatics or idiots, or impostors." (MCME. 234.) He gives, also, an interesting description of the artificial production of epilepsy by wild Islamic rites. (MCME. 451 *et seq.*)

idea that one is King of England; and there is corresponding variety among the Bantu. I take these cases of "possession" to be the African equivalent of what is known at home as religious mania. Even insanity depends for the form of its expression upon the thoughts and habits of the patient's saner years; and, like their neighbours, these poor demented people have been nurtured in the belief that the spirit-world is real and near, and that great spirits have a way of entering into a man or woman and using him as their medium when they wish to communicate important tidings to the living.

The cure for "possession" falls in with what the exorcists conceive to be the source of the trouble. The Mosuto correspondent to whom I have more than once referred, disdainfully depicts exorcism as a crowd, daubed with red ochre and garbed grotesquely, dancing and singing around the "possessed." A missionary among the Lumbu gives a more detailed description, in which the drums figure largely and weird rites, lasting from evening to daylight, are performed by the chief exorcist, including in one case, the spearing of the spirits who had been lured forth by the smell of the feast. Among a variety of ceremonies, eminently calculated to excite the imagination of the sufferer, which Junod describes,[1] mention is made of "songs of exorcism, performed with accompaniment of rattles, big tins and drums, close to the ears of the pretended possessed, in order to induce the spirit to reveal its name and to 'come out.'" Discovering the name of the spirit is always important to the exorcist. Le Roy's experience of tribes that must have imbibed not a little Arab folklore during centuries of residence within the orbit of Zanzibar, led him to conclude that a "possessing" spirit is sometimes thought to be a malevolent and perverse being of non-human origin, whose only feeling for man is jealousy, bitterness and hatred. But whether of human or non-human origin, "possessing" spirits generally have names, and always need sacrifices; and so the first business of an exorcist is to discover the spirit's name, why it entered into that body, and what sacrifice will satisfy its demands. This is done by interrogating the patient; and when the sacrifice is slaughtered, it is she ("usually

[1] LSAT. ii. 190, 439 ff.

they are women," he says) who drinks its warm, steaming blood.[1]

It has been noticed that the cured become exorcists, and that they are liable to a recurrence of the trouble. Junod affirms that famous exorcists have been permanently cured by surrender to Christ; which means, I suppose, that in an interval of sanity they got a new interest in life, a new hope, a new faith in One stronger than all the spirits which had troubled them, and that henceforth they were benefited, not only by the expulsive power of a new affection, but by the self-conquest of Christian discipline. Joy in escape from the tyranny of demons was a characteristic note of early Christianity.

Much of the talk about cases of "possession" among backward races must be set down to fondness for the exotic and the unexamined, and much to our failure to see that the doctrine of the Incarnation implies that the Lord's knowledge was limited by the scientific and historical horizons of the age and nation in which he dwelt. Instead of blindly asserting that no human personality can be overmastered by a discarnate spirit, let us keep an open eye for every fact; but if there is a fact of demonic possession at the back of any form of insanity, it is not so likely to be discovered in Africa as in Europe or America, where (notwithstanding our backwardness in mental pathology, especially in relation to criminology, which is still a reproach to us) Asylums and Retreats for the insane are staffed by diligent students of mental disease, trained and alert to discover any fact that lies behind such phenomena. All cases of "possession" that have come in my way may be put down, I think, to mental alienation, often of a mild and temporary nature that yield to a judicious use of cathartics.

REVELATION BY "PROPHETS"

The topical headings in this chapter are nothing more than indications of types that may be distinguished when they occur in well-marked forms; classification is crippled by the shading off of one type into another. It is often doubtful whether a Native is narrating the dream of a healthy sleeper or the vision

[1] RP. 210, 228.

or audition of a psychopath,[1] and lunacy, inspiration, and divination overlap one another.[2]

No exact definition of the African term "prophet" is to be had. The term is applied to people who are thought to be so in touch with the unseen world that they can sometimes discern approaching events or even wield superhuman power; but these people trust to a diversity of gifts: some, to ability to read the signals which controlling spirits give with the tools of divination; some, to what spirits reveal in dreams, or in visions of ecstasy or trance;[3] some, to spirits that take temporary or permanent possession of them;[4] some, to a capacity for hearing voices that others cannot hear, or seeing what is invisible to other eyes; some, to their standing as ministers of gods in caves,[5] hills or groves, though the manner in which these priests receive oracles from their divinities is still shrouded in mystery.

"Prophet" appears to be a new name for an ancient African abnormality. In conformity with a widespread pagan practice of calling a priest by the name of the god whom he serves, a "prophet" was known as a *modimo* (god)[6] in Bechuanaland before Europeans came; or, when his thick-coming fancies were believed to emanate from the spirit of a man of mark, he was called by the name of the old notability. In Basutoland, prior to the advent of the White-man, he was known as a "diviner" (*senoke* or *noge*[7]), though he was a person of much greater political importance than those who merely manipulated the oddments of a diviner's kit. *Bashinshimi*, the Baila name for "prophets," refers primarily to the low muttering tone in which such persons speak.[8] Under a variety of names in various Bantu tribes, these foretellers of coming events seem to have existed, as the Natives say, "from the beginning"; but nowadays, wherever European influence has been at all dominant, they have come to be known by Natives and Europeans alike as "prophets,"

[1] Cf. pp. 99 f., 103, 124 and SRK. 217.
[2] Cf. pp. 106, 108 f., 138, 145, 146 f. and RSZ. 265.
[3] SRK. 216, 219-220.
[4] SRK. 222-23.
[5] SRK. 185.
[6] A "possessed" person was also called *modimo*.
[7] Bs. 283-88. This word, coming from the same root as the word for "snake," is reminiscent of the Pythoness of Delphi.
[8] IPNR. ii. 140.

though I have failed to discover how or when this name first came into vogue.[1] Chibisa, who had made himself famous and powerful on the Shire before Livingstone first ascended that river in the *Ma-Robert*, founded his reputation upon the claim that he was inspired by the spirit of a "prophetess" of that name, who in the days of her flesh had lived among the Nungwi (a tribe dwelling around Tete and between the Zambesi and the Shire). He was a fugitive slave from Tete, so the Portuguese said; but the Nungwi acknowledged his inspiration, and he, taking the name of his spirit-control, traded upon it with considerable ability and secured much power. Rowley speaks[2] of this man as a "prophet" and of the original Chibisa as a "prophetess"; but it is likely that this use of the term came up from the South,[3] either with Livingstone, who brought Rowley to Chibisa's, or with Bishop Mackenzie, who had been Archdeacon of Natal.

Famous Bantu "prophets" date their awareness of their prophetic vocation from a time when, after a crisis of some sort (often delirium followed by a comatose condition), they saw a divine person of majestic mien, or were transported to the spirit-world and sent back whence they came with messages of tremendous importance,[4] or, exceptionally, heard the commanding voice of an invisible speaker. Although a man or woman needs no previous training to become a "prophet," it appears therefore that a predisposition to ecstasy, day-dreams, and visions, is a necessary qualification. They all aspire to the exercise of transcendental and peculiar authority; and their success depends in the main upon the intensity of their convictions, though it is often promoted by their own cleverness, by the support of some

[1] Barbot used it in a vague way in 1746. See my p. 309.
[2] UMCA. 113-16. See my p. 164.
[3] Callaway quotes (RSZ. 82) Pringle as using this term in his description of Makana's incitement of the Amaxosa clans, on p. 299 of his *Narrative of a Residence in South Africa*.
[4] PP. 255. Methuen mentions a man who was giving Livingstone some trouble in 1844 at the Bakgatla town of Mabotsa. He says (*Life in the Wilderness.* London: Richard Bentley, 1848, p. 267): "The rain-maker calls himself *Morimo*, or God, affirming that, during a solitary sojourn in the desert, he had seen the Supreme Being, who authorised him to speak and act as God, so that nobody ought to dispute his words. He has, by every method, been endeavouring to render the missionaries suspected by the people, representing them as the causes of the rain not falling." Methuen's phrase, "the Supreme Being" should be "a divine being."

chief who makes them his political tools, or by the chance fulfilment of one of their predictions.[1]

A point of distinction between the "possessed" and the
"prophet" consists in the quality of the message delivered.
"Possessed" people deliver messages of local importance; but
the "prophet" comes charged with a demand for a new (shall
we say) national movement. He calls people to action, to sacrifice, to return to old loyalties. His ideal age is in the past;
present troubles can only be healed by sweeping away new customs and returning to the ancient manner.[2] The impressive
feature of the "prophet" is that he uses no argument and appeals
to no authority but that of the spirit which inspires him. It is
the Bantu equivalent of "Thus saith the Lord," or "The spirit
of the Lord is upon me." However natural that may be to a
race trained to act on intuition rather than logic, it distinctly
claims a supernatural character for the "prophet's" message. In
form, this message is a kind of Bantu apocalyptic: full of symbolism,[3] visions of coming tribulation, and fantastic happenings.
For instance, a prophet in Northern Rhodesia used the symbolism
of a woman going to and fro in the earth, carrying a calabash
of blood, which, if it should be broken and the blood spilt,
would bring great trouble on the land, such as the dying of
people and cattle. The predictive element is never lacking from
the "prophet's" message; but there is never anything in it that
we should call ethical, and no good result follows it. The
result, indeed, is often disastrous. Most Native risings in South
Africa have been inspired by Native "prophets," who have been
able to play upon the credulity, cupidity, and grievances (real
and imaginary) of their contemporaries till the sane among

[1] There is a good example of this fortuitous expansion of a "prophet's" fame
in IPNR. i. 345-46. A "prophet" had delivered a message from Leza commanding the people to cease scattering inconvenient clouds by waving the *kamwaya*
bush, and immediately afterwards a man, who had just flouted the expostulation
of his more pious companion, was killed by lightning while frantically waving
kamwaya twigs above his head; which was, of course, popularly accepted as a
supernatural confirmation of the "prophet's" message, and enhanced his reputation
accordingly.

[2] A "prophet" who caused some trouble in Bechuanaland not many years ago
demanded that his followers should cease wearing trousers and using things made
by the White-man.

[3] The Bantu have a natural aptitude for symbolism, as witness the killing of
white pigs and white fowls in Natal before the 1906 rebellion against the Whites.

them were willing to take insane risks. Their promises are always material: harvests, rain, sleek and fertile herds, even locusts in time of great hunger; and their penalties for disobedience are of a like nature: drought, war, plague, cattle-diseases. The appearance of a "prophet" always causes excitement in a district; few venture to defy him, and many believe in him and credit him with all sorts of power.

Before attempting to explain the "prophets," let me sketch, as briefly as I can, the inspired doings of a few of these strange people.

At the beginning of last century, Europeans were not inclined to bestow much thought upon what they regarded as "devilish superstition"; but in 1818 a "prophet" named Makana arose in Ndlambe's section of the Amaxosa, and forced himself upon the attention of South African Europeans. "Possessed of great powers of mind," Theal says,[1] this man "had framed a creed for himself by combining what he could learn of Christianity with different native superstitions, and had announced to his countrymen that he was in communication with the spirit world. It was he who taught them to bury their dead, for before his time the corpses of common people were merely dragged away from the kraals and exposed to be devoured by carrion birds and beasts of prey. His bearing was that of a man who claimed superiority even over chiefs, and who knew that his orders would be obeyed." His interests were mainly political. "He aimed at moulding a nation into form, by uniting its fragments under a common head, and giving it nobler aspirations than it had before." After playing a leading and successful part in the internecine disputes of Amaxosa clans, he finally led his people against the British forces in Grahamstown, delivering his attack in three columns and keeping the fourth in reserve. "The heaviest of the three columns, composed of the veterans, was directed against the barracks, and was led by Makana in person. . . . They seemed regardless of death when under Makana's eye, and pressed eagerly on." But the musketry and field-pieces that played upon them were irresistible with such weapons as they had, and after a while "they broke and fled, carrying their leader

[1] *Compendium of South African History*, etc., 2nd Edition. Lovedale, 1876. Chap. xvii.

along with them, and leaving five hundred of their bravest men dead on the spot, while nearly a thousand were so badly wounded that they died before they could reach their own country." Some four months later, knowing that no peace would be possible to his people so long as he remained at large, he voluntarily surrendered, upon condition that his life should be spared. "He was banished to Robben Island, and was drowned on the following Christmas when attempting to make his escape in a boat. But the generation to which he belonged passed away and another took its place before his countrymen could be brought to believe that he was dead. When told that he had been drowned, they would reply that it was false, as Makana could not die." Such was the impression that this man made upon his countrymen, and such was the wonderful faith that they had in his power, that it was not till 1870 that the last shred of hope for his return was abandoned and his mats and ornaments buried. What a pity it is that we are not acquainted with the inner history of this man's claim to be inspired!

The most noteworthy of the Amaxosa "prophets" was, however, Mhlakaza. Mhlakaza was the "medicine-man" of his clan, and at the time when his inspiration began (May, 1856) his daughter was thirteen or fourteen years of age. The story begins with the appearance of unearthly visitants to the girl as she was fetching water from the little stream that flowed past her home. She told her father, and he found the strangers, and recognised his dead brother among them. They announced themselves as eternal enemies of the White-man, having come from battle-fields beyond the sea to aid the Kafirs with their invincible power in driving the English from the country. Theal says: [1] "The revelations communicated through Mhlakaza and Nongquase grew apace. The girl standing in the river in presence of a multitude of deluded people, heard strange unearthly sounds beneath her feet, which her father pronounced to be the voices of spirits, holding high council over the affairs of men. The first order was to slay cattle, but the greedy ghosts seemed insatiable in their demands. More and more were killed, but still never enough. And thus the delusion continued month after month, every day spreading wider and em-

[1] *Op. cit.* Chap. xxvii.

bracing fresh victims in its grasp. By and by Sandile gave way to the urgent applications of his brother Maqoma, who asserted that he had himself seen and conversed with two of his father's dead councillors, and that these commanded Sandile to kill his cattle if he would not perish with the white man. Before this time the last order of Mhlakaza had been given, that order whose fulfilment was to be the final preparation of the Kafirs, after which they would be worthy of the aid of a spirit host. Not an animal out of all their herds must be left living, every grain of corn in their granaries must be destroyed. But what a future of glory and wealth was predicted for the faithful and obedient! On a certain day, myriads of cattle, more beautiful than those they were called upon to kill, should issue from the earth and cover the pastures far and wide. Great fields of waving corn, ripe and ready for eating, should in an instant spring into existence. The ancient heroes of the race, the great and the wise of days gone by, restored to life on that happy day, would appear and take part in the joys of the faithful. Trouble and sickness would be known no more, nor would the frailties of old age oppress them, for youth and beauty were to return alike to the risen dead and the feeble living. Such was the picture of Paradise painted by the Kafir prophet, and held before the eyes of the infatuated people. And dreadful was to be the fate of those who opposed the will of the spirits, or neglected to obey their commands. The day that was to bring so much joy to the loyal would bring nothing but destruction for them. The sky itself would fall and crush them together with the Fingoes and the whites."

It is estimated that some 200,000 head of cattle were slaughtered by the Amaxosa; enormous kraals were prepared to contain the cattle that were soon to rise from the earth, and huge sacks, to hold the milk that was soon to be as plentiful as water. Some of the people were already starving; but the day of resurrection was postponed in mercy to chief Sandili, the laggard in faith, who had not yet finished killing his cattle.

"At length the morning dawned of the day so long and so ardently looked for. All night long the Kafirs had watched with feelings stretched to the utmost tension of excitement, expecting to see two blood-red suns rise over the eastern hills, when the heavens would fall and crush the races they hated. Famished with hunger, half dying as they were, that night was yet a time of fierce, delirious joy. The morn that a few short hours, slowly becoming minutes, would usher in, was to see all their sorrows ended, all their misery past. And so they watched and waited. It came, throwing a silver sheen upon the mountain peaks, and bathing hill-side and valley in a flood of light, as the ruler of day appeared. The hearts of the watchers sank within them: 'what,' said they, 'will become of us if Mhlakaza's predictions turn out untrue?' It was the first time they had asked such a question, the dawn of doubt had never entered their thoughts till the dawn of the fatal day. But perhaps, after all, it might be midday that was meant, and when the shadows began to lengthen towards the east, perhaps, thought they, the setting of the sun is the time. The sun went down behind clouds of crimson and gold, and the Amaxosa awoke to the reality of their dreadful position."

"The horrors that succeeded can only be partly told. There are men living now, intelligent Christian men, then wild naked fugitives, who cannot recount the events of those days. The whole scene comes home to them as a hideous nightmare, or as the remembrance of one in a state of delirium. In many instances all the ties were broken that bind human beings to each other in every condition of society. Brother fought with brother, father with son, for scraps and shreds of those great milk sacks so carefully made in the days when hope was high. The aged, the sick, the feeble were abandoned by the young and vigorous. All kinds of wild plants and even the roots of trees were collected for food. . . . In other instances whole families sat down and died together. From fifteen to twenty skeletons were afterwards often found under a single tree, showing where parents and children met their fate when the last ray of hope had fled. . . . Worse instances of suffering even than these remain to be told. Charred human bones, fragments of skeletons afterwards found in many a pot, revealed the state to which the most desperate had fallen. One instance has been authenticated of a man and woman eating the flesh of their own child. . . . The lowest computation fixes the number of those who perished on both sides the Kei at twenty-five thousand, ordinary calculations double that number. . . . Among those that perished was Mhlakaza himself."

Such is the story as Theal told it while living in the midst of people more likely to know the truth than any others. It ought to be said, however, that no one knows or is ever likely to know how much of Mhlakaza's conduct was due to delusion and how much to political chicanery. A witness before the 1883 Native Affairs Commission of Cape Colony held strongly, and gave some reason for his belief,[1] that the whole thing, from start to finish, was a scheme engineered by some of the Amaxosa chiefs to force all the Amaxosa clans into a great united attack upon the Whites. There is clearly room in the story for much intrigue and some hypnotism; but he who satisfies himself that Mhlakaza was but a trickster, and that his little daughter was either hypnotised or carefully coached for her part, has still to explain how it came about that scores of thousands of not unintelligent people could place such implicit confidence in his prophecy that they were willing to stake all they had upon its fulfilment.

But not all "prophets" are politically minded. About a decade later, there arose among the Barolong of Morokweng, in Bechuanaland, a "prophet" named Marethe, who was mainly interested in reviving ancient forms of worship. He claimed to be in communication with a spirit who forewarned him of the coming of locusts, drought, or an epidemic of sickness. His delight was to gather the children around him; teach them songs which he professed to have learnt from the spirit; and lead them in procession through the town, singing songs and pouring out libations of water from little pots which they carried, after the manner of the ancient rain-rites. But the adults believed in him; heeded his warnings; gave him beads, bracelets, and karosses of tiger-cat, wild-cat and lynx skins when he demanded them; and provided a feast for the children who sang his songs. Although he told the people that what he said and did was by direction of the god who inspired him, they said that he was god, because the things which he foretold came true. It was his habit, so it is said, to retire into the little caves by the Cwaing

[1] R. 1883, pp. 269-70.

lake and there commune with the god; but he was not, apparently, priest of a cave-dwelling spirit.

The Batlhaping of Taung, in Bechuanaland, were excited a few years ago by the arrival in their midst of a "prophet" who claimed, not that he was inspired by an ancestral spirit, but that he was a reincarnation of Jesus Christ. Notwithstanding the originality of his claim, he acted in the traditional manner of Bantu "prophets," commanding the people to leave their gardens untilled for a season, as a mark of obedience, and promising that obedience would be rewarded by the expulsion of the Whites. The excitement was cut short by the intervention of the magistrate, who committed the "prophet" and his henchmen for trial on a charge of sedition.

Smith & Dale give a fine description of some "prophets" whom they have known.[1] In the case of Chilenga the anti-European tendency is evident, and it should be noted, also, that he required the people to slaughter their cattle as a mark of obedience. A story quoted from the Rev. A. Baldwin's diary for August 26, 1895, is, as these authors remark, an admirable illustration of the way in which some "prophets" receive their messages; and so is the next story of Mupumani; but the "prophets" described by a Native informant[2] are really "possessed" people, though it is hard to draw the line between two forms of so-called "spirit-control" which seem to shade off into one another.

Till a century or two ago all nations regarded comets and eclipses as harbingers of calamity, and backward races are still of that opinion.[3] While Halley's comet was in the sky in April, 1910, I was living in Bechuanaland but happened to spend part of that time in Matabeleland, and was assured by many Natives of both countries that that comet presaged the death of some great chief. During my stay at the Victoria Falls, word came

[1] IPNR. ii. 142-152.
[2] IPNR. ii. 140-41.
[3] Before the total eclipse of the sun which was visible in England in 1715, Halley, the astronomer, published a description of the coming event, in order "that the sudden darkness wherein the Stars will be visible about the Sun may give no surprise to the people, who would if unadvertised be apt to look upon it as Ominous, and interpret it as portending evil to our Sovereign Lord King George and his Government, which God preserve."

that King Edward was dead, and for many weeks I had to bear the gentle reproof of my Native friends for the smile of incredulity with which I had greeted their warning. At that time Enoch Mgijima,[1] a middle-aged commoner, who owned a plot of land at Bullhoek, near Queenstown, began holding nocturnal meetings on a neighbouring hill and awaiting the nightly appearance of the comet. Enoch was originally a Wesleyan, who had attained to Standard III in a village school; but he had been swept by the Ethiopian movement into an American sect which called itself "The Church of God and Saints of Christ." He is said to have been deposed from this body because of his visions, one of which was that of a stone rolling down a mountain-side and sweeping away those at the foot, and another was that of two white goats fighting, while a baboon looked on and afterwards gathered the spoil from both combatants—visions which were interpreted as foreshadowing the overthrow of the White race. Enoch declared that the comet was a sign that God was angry with the world; and, as a panacea for the ills that threatened humanity, he urged that the New Testament should be cut out of the Bible, since it was the White-man's fiction, and that Jehovah should be worshipped after the manner of the patriarchs of Israel. Accordingly, he founded a new sect, which he called the *Ama-Sirayeli*, or "Israelites," who regarded themselves as the peculiar people of Jehovah, and were convinced that Jehovah would miraculously deliver them from the Whites as he had delivered their spiritual ancestors from the Egyptians, if only they were obedient to his will as it was shown to the "prophet." The sect was officered by Natives with high-sounding ecclesiastical and military titles, and observed an annual Passover festival, which lasted eight days and was attended by adherents from outlying parts of the country.

At first, it is believed, Enoch was sincere; but he relied upon visions for ascertaining the divine will; came in course of time to adapt his visions to his policy; and was ultimately eaten up with vanity. People who came to the "passover" began to settle alongside the "prophet," selling their cattle, land, and other possessions and putting the proceeds into a common fund from

---

[1] The information about Enoch is culled from South African journals, especially *The Christian Express*, now called *The South African Outlook*.

which the camp was fed, clothed and equipped. By 1920 the camp had become a cave of Adullam for the restless and discontented; deafening blasts on horns took a prominent place in the fanatical excitement; heathen people came in with their assegais; and a speedy interposition of Jehovah was expected. The crowd had overflowed on to adjoining Government land, disregarding the local authorities and forbidding their officials to enter on this "holy" ground. Government dealt very patiently with the deluded people; and, even when all else had failed and a force of a hundred police was sent to overawe them, the police were ordered not to fire. This force was resisted, and accordingly withdrawn; whereupon the "prophet" is said to have claimed that an angel had turned the armed men back.[1] Further efforts were made, through the Native Affairs Department, the police, and influential Natives of the district, to bring them to reason; but without result. Finally, an ultimatum was sent them in May, 1921, and a force of eight hundred police was assembled against them—a force so large that it was expected to overawe opposition and prevent bloodshed. But to men who believe themselves magically invulnerable, the number of guns is of little moment; and the "Israelites" declared that Jehovah had commanded them to resist the dispersion or arrest of any of their people. The police dismounted and were allowed to approach within fifty yards, and then the white-robed crowd charged straight at the bayonets, with assegais and whatever weapons they had. Then came the command to open fire; and the casualties were heavy. The "Israelites" fell back, and, when the police had occupied an eminence overlooking their village and had reopened negotiations, surrendered the "prophet" and his brother, the latter being a man of somewhat superior education who had been in Government service and retired on pension but was now Enoch's second in command.

There was an epidemic of "prophets" on the lower Congo in 1921.[2] Simon Kibangu, who lived in a village a few hours away

[1] It came out at the trial that their "Spy," who was an unsuspected employé in the office of a Queenstown lawyer, had managed to discover that the police were under orders nôt to fire, and had hurried off to inform the "prophet" beforehand.

[2] For the following facts, the writer is indebted to articles by the Rev. W. B. Frames in *The Congo Mission News* and by Dr. Lerrigo in *Missions,* and in *The International Review of Missions.*

from Wathen (Gombe Lutete), on the lower Congo, a man of good character, had been a member of the local church for five or six years. When people were dancing at the funeral of a friend, which he was attending at a distant place, he fell in a fit and remained unconscious for a time. His father and mother took him home, and on the way they met a finely dressed man "who was neither black nor white, nor was he a mulatto," who told them that Kibangu was not ill and would soon be all right. While camped for the night on their homeward journey, Kibangu, going to the stream to quench his thirst, fell into a deep hole, and when his parents came to seek him, his mother fell into the hole beside him. "But suddenly," said Kibangu in telling the story to one of his companions, "we were lifted out of the pit without any effort on our part." After reaching home he fell ill and had sores all over his body. Then came a mysterious stranger, clothed in a rag and asking for water, who told him to rub himself with palm-oil and he would be cured. "That night the stranger came again in a dream. He brought a Bible and said, 'This is a good book; you must study it and preach.' " The stranger told him, also, that there was a sick child in a neighbouring village and that he must go and pray that she might be healed. He refused to do this, upon the ground that nobody would believe him and he would be persecuted. The stranger next came to his mother in a dream, and told her that her son must preach and heal; but he still resisted. Finally the stranger visited him again and told him that he would require his soul of him if he did not obey. So next day he found the sick child, and, pushing the wailing people aside, prayed a long time for her recovery. Then he laid his hands upon the child, and immediately shook with great violence; the child was healed, and, nestling in its mother's bosom, began to suck. Thereupon, sick people were brought to him, and his career commenced. He prayed and touched them, and they were healed. A blind man was brought to him to be cured of his blindness, and he spat and made clay and told the man to go to the river and wash. Lame people were brought to him to be healed, people suffering from sleeping sickness, and even dead people. Thousands came, Protestant and Romanist, and the excitement spread far and wide.

A week or two after Kibangu began his work, he was joined by another, who soon separated from him and practised in his own town. Then "prophets" began to appear all over the country from the river Congo on the north to Portuguese terri-tory on the south; men and women, Protestants and Romanists, people of good character and people notorious for roguery or immorality. Each adopted the same procedure: there was an involuntary (?) shaking of the "prophet's" body; he was not to be touched by any one; he heard the voice of God in his ears; he had to have the requests of suppliants interpreted to him by an intermediary; he told the people to claim healing in spite of appearances, in order to receive the blessing; and he turned aside or entered a house that he might learn God's will, and came back, often enough, to tell the patient that he could not be cured on account of his lack of faith, or because he had fetishes in his house.

Baptist missionaries in the district visited Kibangu's town to see him at work, and investigated many cases of reputed healing; but they failed to find a single patient who had received more benefit than could be accounted for by the excitement of the crowd, the earnest desire and expectation of the patient, and the exercise of will-power. Upon pointing this out to Kibangu and his helpers, they were met with the retort that the cures were as God willed, and that Kibangu did nôt profess to cure all. Their judgment of the work of other "prophets" whom they visited was alike unfavourable; but many of the best people in the churches regarded it as a visitation of God, and joined the "prophets" as singers and helpers; and no man could shake their belief in the wonders which they said they had seen.

Kibangu's sincerity is indicated by the fact that he neither asked nor accepted pay, and insisted that all help given in carry-ing the sick to him should be gratuitous. Prayer and praise, denunciations of fetishes and sin, and exhortations to trust the Saviour, were prominent in his work, and in healing he used the formula, "In the name of Jesus Christ." There were many extravagances in the movement: the Lord was to come imme-diately, and no gardens need be tilled; God would drive the White-man from the Congo and give back the country to the Natives; and Natives ought no longer to work for the White-man or pay taxes to the State. These latter features caused the Belgian State officials to fear a Native uprising, and to arrest the leaders of the movement. But many of those who were punished posed as martyrs, claiming that they suffered joyfully for Jesus' sake.

If we underline one or two facts that have not hitherto been stressed, it may help us to estimate these "prophets" at their true value. A Native Commissioner of wide experience among the Zulus says that they generally belong to the class of hereditary priests; and others have noticed that they are often acquainted with the diviner's art—all of which means that many of them spring from families that are soaked in magico-religious lore. In enquiring about "prophets" of the olden days, I was struck with the fact that most of them arose at a time of stress to the community, though evidence for or against that conclusion was sometimes lacking. The afflatus usually takes its rise, at any rate in the first instance, in a crisis of some sort (often delirium followed by a comatose condition), during which the vision is seen; and when the person regains consciousness he is wont to declare that he died, went to the spirit-world and was sent back with a message to men. The "prophet" often grows comparatively rich through presents which he receives; but it is significant that these presents are given him, not on account of his message, but for subsidiary services that he is supposed to render by reason of his uncanny powers, such as making guns shoot straight, fertilising gardens, protecting cattle from disease, or finding stray animals.

How are we to account for these "prophets"? Are they all mere hypocrites, or is there any reality behind their claim to be "inspired"? Some of them may be consigned at once to the Rogues' Gallery; some may be set down as mental and nervous wrecks; [1] but there is no reason to doubt the subjective truthfulness or mental normality of others. Not a few are astonishingly ready to bear persecution, though they have more than the usual streak of cunning in their character and are as stubborn and easily blown with pride as any of their neighbours. In judging them one must never forget that they belong to a race that is neurotic by nature (in spite of an acquired stolidity of face),

[1] See p. 99.

and were trained from childhood to confuse subjective and objective, habitually mistaking dreams for real visits between spirits of the living and the dead.[1] Any convincing explanation of such instances of primitive contact with the unseen as appear in the stories of Eli, Saul, and Samuel, or the narratives of Isa. vi., Jer. i., and Ezek. i., ii., and iii. would help us to understand them, I think; and the genesis of a "prophet" is more easily understood by students of modern psychology, which recognises the fact that the great crises of life, especially among a neurotic people, may be accompanied by what the subject can only regard as visible and audible experiences.

That uprush of emotion and startling transformation of character which is known in psychology as *religious conversion*—a very different thing from the intellectual operation of scrapping an outgrown creed or institution and choosing another that is better suited to one's present outlook on life—is not peculiar to any one religion or any one branch of the human race.[2] It appears in the most backward families of man, as well as in those that ripened earlier into social development. There is something at the back of personality that eludes the most delicate tests of the scientist, however patient and penetrating his method of investigation; but psychologists throw light on subtle processes that always precede religious conversion, though they cannot reveal its final cause. Each individual is furnished in the plastic years of life with the predominating religious ideas of his parental group, and retains them in the subconscious area of his personality long after intensely interesting pursuits have made him indifferent, or even adverse, to their presence. Although this furniture of the imagination finds place in most, perhaps all, normal individuals, it takes an almost incredible variety of pattern in the many diverse groups that constitute the human race. In Roman communities, it consists of vividly sensualised images of the Madonna, the infant Jesus, the Crucified Redeemer, the Almighty Father, and such like; in Protestant societies of the older pattern it was composed of dogmatic conceptions of the Trinity, of sin, judgment, atonement, forgive-

---

[1] See pp. 4, 92 f.
[2] See *Conversion: Christian and Non-Christian.* By Alfred Clair Underwood, D.D. London: Allen & Unwin, 1925.

ness, heaven and hell—verbal images, it is true, but none the less crudely visualised, while in recent years such pictures as "The Prodigal Son," "The Good Shepherd," and "The Light of the World" have left a more indelible impression upon the minds of millions; in nations long swayed by Mohammedanism, Buddhism, or other systematised religions, the pattern is very different, but the furniture is there; and in Bantu tribes, it is made up of such magico-religious notions as those that we are studying. Under stress of a crisis in life, especially between the ages of fifteen and twenty-five, the floodgates of emotion are opened, there is a conscious surrender of self to the ideal, and the mind finds relief in hitherto unavailing imagery that it accepted without effort and without questioning in its formative years. "The vision of the American Protestant, Finney, was of 'the Lord Jesus Christ,' but the Catholic, Merswin, at the crisis of his career, saw a picture of the crucifix; and the Japanese Buddhist, Nichiren, saw Kokuzo, the god of wisdom." [1] These old images rise in a glorified form from their burial-place in the subconscious; they are sublimated, as the psychologists say; they glow in the high lights of spiritual exaltation with a significance for present difficulties that wears the semblance of a new revelation. And always there is a sense of "otherness" in this experience, as though a divine personality seizes the human and fills it with gladsome peace and power. To illustrate my meaning, reference might be made to that remarkable passage in the *Confessions* where St. Augustine tells of the change that came over his life as he sat in a garden at Milan; or to St. Patrick's experience as he tended sheep on the hillside at Slemish; or to Bunyan's account of how he recovered his better self after being rebuked by a woman of blemished character; but more to the point in our present argument is a quotation from the ideal story of the conversion of Saul Kane,[2] a foul-mouthed roisterer, who, to the dismay of the countryside, was out, after nineteen terms in gaol, to snatch all that he thought the world could give him. Saul bragged that he did not believe in prayer nor the Bible, and flouted his neighbours for what he called their

[1] Underwood's *Conversion: Christian and Non-Christian*, p. 247.
[2] "The Everlasting Mercy," in *The Poems and Plays of John Masefield*, New York: The Macmillan Co., 1918, vol. i., pp. 121-176.

servility and hypocrisy; but he was not without that religious furniture of the mind of which we were speaking, and even when having his fling he could pat a kitten and brother a lonesome little boy who stood crying in the market-place; and, moreover, his bouts of debauchery had, for quite a while, been punctuated by spasms of self-reproach. One night, having gone the limit and been jaded by the pace, he sat in a pot-house with his smutty companions, when a Quaker lady entered, seeking stray sheep from her Master's flock; and in a madcap mood, he so insulted her that even his comrades stood dumb, wondering how she would take it.

> " 'Saul Kane,' she said, 'when next you drink,
> Do me the gentleness to think
> That every drop of drink accursed
> Makes Christ within you die of thirst,
> That every dirty word you say
> Is one more flint upon His way,
> Another thorn about His head,
> Another mock by where He tread,
> Another nail, another cross.
> All that you are is that Christ's loss.' "

And then with one parting remark, "He waits until you knock," the lady left. It was enough; the appeal to the Christ within him had gone home, and Saul Kane wandered forth and on throughout the night, battling with wind and rain. The story that he tells is too long for quotation, but here is the kernel of it:

> "I did not think, I did not strive,
> The deep peace burnt my me alive;
> The bolted door had broken in,
> I knew that I had done with sin.
> I knew that Christ had given me birth
> To brother all the souls on earth,
> And every bird and every beast
> Should share the crumbs broke at the feast.

> "O glory of the lighted mind.
> How dead I'd been, how dumb, how blind.
> The station brook, to my new eyes,
> Was bubbling out of Paradise,

The waters rushing from the rain
Were singing Christ has risen again.
I thought all earthly creatures knelt
From rapture of the joy I felt.
The narrow station-wall's brick ledge,
The wild hop withering in the hedge,
The lights in huntsman's upper storey
Were parts of an eternal glory,
Were God's eternal garden flowers.
I stood in bliss at this for hours.

"O glory of the lighted soul.
The dawn came up on Bradlow Knoll,
The dawn with glittering on the grasses,
The dawn which pass and never passes.

. . . . . .

All earthly things that blessèd morning
Were everlasting joy and warning.
The gate was Jesus' way made plain,
The mole was Satan foiled again,
Black blinded Satan snouting way
Along the red of Adam's clay;
The mist was error and damnation,
The lane the road unto salvation.
Out of the mist into the light,
O blessèd gift of inner sight."

Looked at from the outside, the glutting of a tribe with a dozen oxen at the installation of a new chief is a millennium away from the elegance of a Lord Mayor's Banquet; and, in mode of expression, the upheaval of Bantu personality that results in a "prophet" is as widely sundered from the conversion of Saul Kane. Nevertheless, the difference is in accidentals rather than essentials; and if we greet the one with a sneer and the other with a cheer, is it not because the one is garbed grotesquely, while the other is clad in garments that we already revere? I lean to the opinion that Bantu prophetism, when it is genuine and not due to disease, is as near an approach to *religious conversion* as we could hope to find in people whose minds are stored with the crude furniture of ancestor-worship, and that among our own people this upthrust from the subliminal self sometimes manifests itself in forms that are just as outlandish.[1]

And further. It has been observed that, in a Bantu community, times of stress are likely to produce a "prophet," and that tribal politics are always religious, and religion always political. I remember reading some years ago a speech made by M. Poincaré, the famous Parisian scientist, during his visit to America, of which, I am ashamed to say, I kept no record. He stated, if my memory may be trusted, that there are four stages in all great discoveries: (1) a stage in which one grapples with the problem, collecting data concerning it, and seeking a formula that will solve all difficulties; (2) a stage in which one realises that the problem is too great, and lays it aside; (3) a stage in which it is banished from thought and one is engrossed in other pursuits; and (4) a stage in which the solution of the old problem comes with a flash, and all its baffling elements become clear. He maintained, also, that this process is familiar to all men of genius, and that it throws light on the relation of the conscious and sub-conscious self. His description is so true to fact that all who have grappled with difficult problems in their ordinary work will recognise that the process is not confined to men of genius, or to those who make great discoveries; but it is important to note that the flash comes only to men who have already given their best to the problem, and been baffled by it. What the flash does, apparently, is to fuse what the man has already absorbed; it provides nothing new, except the blending; and the value of the result for the community depends upon the size of the man. The character of the message depends upon his character, and it is phrased in the thought-forms of his race and day, often with a leaning to archaism. This explains the "false prophets," except those of them who were mere hypocrites, as well as Isaiah and Amos; and it explains the "prophets" of Africa.

When measured by our standards, these Bantu "prophets" are not intellectual, moral, or spiritual giants; but, as Professor James says somewhere in his *Varieties of Religious Experience,* when

[1] See *Primitive Traits in Religious Revivals.* By Frederick Morgan Davenport. Macmillan Co. 1905.

speaking of a similar subject, a flood need not rise very high to overwhelm a pigmy, and though one inch above his head is as important for him as a foot would have been, it is not of the same importance to his taller neighbours. The message of "prophets" who arose in bygone days of war, famine, or oppression always bore upon the calamity. There were no trained observers among their neighbours to tell us of significant preceding events, and they were but inconspicuous tribesmen till the afflatus brought them into notice; but I take it that they were men who had passed through a crisis, struggling with the problem before them till they felt themselves utterly baffled, and then the revealing flash came, compelling them to go forth with their message, whether men sneer or approve. The value of their message for them is immense; its value for others must be judged by its contents. We are offended by the whimsical allegories that their utterances wear, and often by the obliquity of their doctrines; but if my explanation is tenable, we are not justified in treating them all as hypocrites, though a prophet's prestige, like the worth of a coin, is a temptation to counterfeiters.

It would be a mistake, I think, to look to them for any light on the spirit-world, though that is what they profess to give; but those of us who sympathetically study the problems of Native life may wisely take their message as a valuable indication of processes that are going on under the surface of tribal behaviour. Take, for instance, the "prophets" who preach an anti-White crusade; they prove that in their districts there is an extensive but unvoiced resentment against the White-man's rule and the break-down of Native institutions and customs that accompanies contact with Europeans.[1] What their neighbours talk of now and then in a hesitating, uncertain and intriguing manner, they have carried as their own special burden, and found it beyond their strength; then the hopelessness of it all has been followed by the supreme crisis of their life, and the inspiration that meant for them vocation. Others have been troubled about the decay of their old religion, rather than what we should call its social and political concomitants, and have become inspired with another message that is more to their pur-

[1] See SRK. 22, 217, 220 f.

pose; but the same explanation holds. We have had "prophets" arising in the Native church, and the explanation is the same—they carried the burden of the Church in their own peculiar manner, and were overwhelmed by it. I remember one such case which gave trouble and inflicted damage upon our work. While among the bushes at his cattle-post, a deacon of more than average intelligence, zeal and activity, had a vision of Christ, which was repeated on three separate occasions. He described it as something very objective. But the point was that Christ had told him to come to us for ordination, and as we could not consider such a proposition in his case, he started a *true Church* in his own name.

Hallucination occasionally attends the conversion of a European or a semi-Europeanised native, but it is not surprising that there are few, if any, authenticated instances of its appearance in the conversion of a heathen African to Christianity. The fact is that the term "conversion" is made to cover two dissimilar processes. Lodged in the minds of people of Protestant upbringing is the idea of sin as an ethical transgression which incurs the wrath of God; and among those who are drawn to revivalistic services there are some whose ineffectual struggle against a sense of sinfulness has caused them to despair. If a chance remark should cause a sublimation of the contents of their consciousness—and a small spark may produce a great conflagration—they may be overwhelmed with a sudden realisation of salvation, and hallucination may supervene upon the relief of mental strain and anxiety, as upon amative and other excitement.[1] The conversion of an African from heathenism to Christianity is a different process. Sin, to a heathen African, however it may be to those of Christian parentage who have lapsed into surrounding heathenism, is a ceremonial transgression, for which ceremonial expiation and purification is available; he is never burdened with a profound sense of personal guilt. That may come to him later, when his idea of sin becomes Christianised; but what he aspires after in the first instance is not salvation from sin, but harmony with the unseen, and his conversion consists in a gradual scrapping of his old belief and a slowly growing conviction that God is accessible to him, and that Christ is the Way,

[1] See p. 98.

the Truth, and the Life. It is an intellectual process, a recantation (if that word may be used without innuendo), rather than what the psychologists call *religious conversion*, in which the emotional element is not prominent.

Two objections are likely to be raised to my explanation of the "prophets." One is the trivial and often absurd contents of their messages; and the other is the cunning with which they enrich themselves.

As to the contents of their messages. It must be remembered that they are small people who live in a small world. Their field of vision is mostly occupied by their own tribe, the largest part of which is invisible in the spirit-world, but not less real and potent. They know something of neighbouring tribes, but regard them as so inferior as to be unworthy of careful study; and distant tribes of which they have heard are mere shadows on the field of vision. Their ethics is all summed up in obedience to the "laws and customs" of the ancestors; and their view of the world is magical through and through. If my explanation is correct, this flash of inspiration would merely focus in the "prophet" what is prevalent around him in a more diffused form—would give life and intensity to what he had been absorbing with every pore of his body for many months before the crisis came. It would not make a small man great, except in the intensity of his conviction, or an ignorant man learned. And I submit that the message of the "prophets" is in keeping with what we should expect.

Similarly, with regard to the cunning and acquisitiveness of the "prophets." These characteristics are common to Bantu, as every trader soon discovers. People wishing to exploit the supernatural power which they believe the "prophet" to possess, bring him presents and requests and will brook no denial. If he disclaims the power with which they credit him, they take his reluctance as a hint that the present is not large enough, and return with a bigger gift. Most doctors are acquainted with witless patients whose demand for some impossible medicine to take the place of their own care and effort is a temptation to administer harmless drugs and render a subsequent account. One may doubt whether many trades or any profession, lay or clerical, is exempt from such temptation. Now the Bantu "prophet" is as avaricious as his neighbours, and, what is more, he sees no inconsistency in being sincere in what he deems to be his vocation and at the same time using it to enrich himself by wilful deception. The burden that he carried was not in our sense an ethical burden; and the inspiration has left his morals as it found them.

One word more before we pass from this topic. What is written on preceding pages makes it abundantly evident that Bantu prophetism may clothe itself in quasi-Christian phrases and invade the Church. Here lies a real danger; and it behooves missionaries to be on the alert for anything that threatens to lead to this disaster; such as Corybantic methods of worship, Koranic interpretations of the Bible, and fanatic doctrines which are impervious to reason. The best preventive is a sane appreciation of the evolution of Old Testament religion and of its relation to Christianity. At a five days' convention, attended by thousands of people, at Ekwendeni in Nyasaland, religious fervour rose to a pitch of great intensity. "Of course," says Donald Fraser, "so great a crowd and so much intensity of feeling required to be carefully guided, lest physical emotions be mistaken for true religion, and fervour waste itself in harmful directions. One morning two of the leading teachers came to me to relate strange experiences they were having. They had been out in the bush at night praying. They felt as if their bodies had been lifted up from the earth, and bright angelic forms had come down to meet them, and they asked me to explain what these visions meant. Instead of doing so, I went through to the dispensary, and getting two big doses of salts, gave them each a dose and sent them off to bed. Next day the visions had disappeared. But the strong piety that burst into bloom at that convention remains with them still, and in increasing beauty."[1] Blessed is the tribe whose missionary is instinct with both spiritual passion and strong common sense, and open-eyed to the psychological peculiarities of his parishioners!

REVELATION BY DIVINATION

When a divine ancestor reveals himself by dream, calamity, or reincarnation, it is often necessary to consult a diviner for the

[1] WPP. 93, AA. 143.

discovery of the spirit's wishes, or sometimes before one can be sure of its identity; but diviners are more frequently consulted when divine guidance is desired but not forthcoming. The diviner discovers what spirit is displeased, or what sacrifice is demanded, or, rarely, where the sacrifice is to be offered, or, much more frequently, what the result of a contemplated transaction or journey will be, what thief has been stealing one's property, what neighbour has been ill-wishing one's dependants, what direction one must take to find stray animals, and a variety of similar matters. If Saul, the son of Kish, had been of the Bantu tribes, he would inevitably have repaired to the seer as soon as he realised that he had lost the spoor of his stray asses. The diviner is the commonest of all Bantu practitioners of the occult; and his mode of procedure is manifold.

The Becwana method is that of throwing "the bones." These "bones" are usually thrown on to a mat from a bag of polecat-skin. The sets are not all alike; two sets in my possession have four bones each, and a third has nine, each piece differentiated from the others by proper conventional signs and shapes, and each set containing four leading pieces which are called, respectively, King, Queen, Jack (or King's servant), and Jill (or the servant's wife).[1] Though the "bones" owe something of their occult power to their conventional signs and patterns, they must be made of bones or hoofs of animals offered in sacrifice, or of those of the wild boar, ant-pig or spring-hare; that is to say, animals associated with the dead.[2] The tusk of a wild boar is regarded as the best material for the purpose. In Bechuanaland wild boars do not now feed on corpses; but I have found them plentiful in parts of Central Africa where exposure of the

[1] Cf. ABN. 153.

[2] In the desert jackal tracks are the best paths to follow, since they avoid impassable ravines and keep to the best gradients; hence at Asyut, the Egyptian end of the Oasis road, the jackal, as Upuaut, was regarded as "the opener of the ways" amid the ravines of the desert to the blessed west of the immortals. It was widely venerated, also, as Anup (Anubis), the god of the cemetery, because of its liking for the cover that tombs provided and the food-gifts that pious mourners placed there for their dead. (RLAE. 14, 80.) Jackals are common enough in many parts of Bantu Africa; they sometimes feast upon corpses (see p. 27 f.), and their cry is imitated by Bagesu mourners who anticipate them at this gruesome feast (see p. 35); but in Bantu thought the jackal does not seem to be very intimately associated with the dead. Ant-pig holes are sometimes utilised for hurried burials.

dead was the general practice. The ant-pig and the spring-
hare are burrowing animals, and therefore in contact with the
underworld. There are stories of people who have reached the
underworld through an ant-pig's hole, and interviewed the
spirits. The bones of the duiker and steinbok are also suitable
for use in divining.[1]

The Bakgalagadi, who occupied Bechuanaland before the
Becwana swarmed into the country and drove them into the
desert, use similar bones; but they insist that the bones must be
cast into a bowl of water, instead of upon a mat.

The Shangaans, who are the most famous diviners in South
Africa, use somewhat similar appliances, though their sets are
much larger. Junod gives a detailed and authoritative description of their practice.[2]

Divining implements of the same general type are in vogue
in widely separated parts of Bantu Africa.[3] Callaway mentions
them among the Amazulu, but thinks they were derived from
the Basuto.[4] A gourd full of sticks, bones, claws and pottery
was used in a similar manner in Macdonald's time,[5] and is still
used in Kenya Colony;[6] though, according to the Routledges,[7]
the Kikuyu interpretation is not nearly so complicated as that
of the south, since the crucial point lies with the odd numbers
left over after the bulk of those thrown from the gourd have
been arranged in groups of tens, five being a good number for
the odd pieces and seven a bad one.

---

[1] I had supposed that these little antelopes were associated with the dead by
reason of their fondness for hiding in such thickets as those in which the graves
lie; but the Bamangwato told me that only horns of the duiker (which is their
totem) or the steinbok, could make divining-tablets for their clan, supporting their
assertion with an old saying, *Lesapo la phuduhudu, ba re, Malope!* ("Bone of the
steinbok, they say, Malope!"). There is something of a puzzle here, which some
more fortunate student may be able to solve. Malope, the common ancestor of a
group of tribes to which the Bamangwato are akin, did not venerate the duiker,
nor does any other tribe of this group; and, also, the duiker (*cephalophus grimini*)
and the steinbok (*nanotragus oreotragus*) are called by different names in the vernacular, and no Native would ever confuse the one with the other.

[2] LSAT. ii. 488-523.
[3] Cf. A. i. 161.
[4] RSZ. 333-337.
[5] A. i. 42-5.
[6] *Africa in the Making.* London: C. M. S. 1922, p. 41, AK. 94.
[7] PP. 264.

Lane says [1] that the gipsies in Cairo, "mostly divine by means of a number of shells, with a few pieces of coloured glass, money, etc., intermixed with them. These they throw down; and from the manner in which they chance to lie, they derive their prognostications: a larger shell than the rest represents the person whose fortune they are to discover; and the other shells, etc., represent different events, evils and blessings, which, by their proximity to, or distance from, the former, they judge to be fated to befall the person early or late or never."

Among the methods used by Kaonde diviners to discover which villager has been practising witchcraft, there is one that seems akin to the foregoing, though it has features peculiar to itself. The witch-doctor "takes a small calabash cup (*chipeshi*) generally ornamented with beads sewn round the lip, or sometimes with a skin (such as a genet skin) attached to it: in this calabash are placed some pieces of pierced wood (*mpingo*) and occasionally pieces of human bone from the leg. The calabash containing the *mpingo* is held in the left hand: in the right hand the doctor holds a rattle. He moves round shaking the *mpingo* about (or, making many incantations, answered in set words by the people gathered together for the trial, names them one by one). When opposite the guilty person (or when naming him), the *mpingo* stands on end in the calabash instead of lying down." [2]

The Yorubas of Southern Nigeria divine by means of sixteen palm-nuts, or by eight pieces of flat wood strung together in two rows of four each; and Sierra Leone tribes use sixteen palm-nuts, sixteen stones from the stomachs of crocodiles, or even sixteen ordinary stones, beans, or cowries.[3]

In Uganda, some diviners pray to the god: "Oh, Mwanga, my master, give the right decision in this matter"; and then blow upon pieces of buffalo-hide or cow-hide and throw them. Others use nine coffee-berries; or throw nine pieces of stick into a pot of water; or cast powdered herbs into a pot of water, rock the pot, and then scrutinise the arrangement of the particles. Others still, take the auspices from the entrails of fowls.[4] Some

[1] MCME. 394.
[2] WBA. 224.
[3] BBMM. 246-252, 270-271.
[4] Bg. 338-340.

Bunyoro diviners shake up seeds in a basket and then scatter them, and others strew powder on a pot of water; but in more important affairs, the throat of a fowl, goat, or bullock is cut, and the divine will is màde out by observing the flow of blood from the carotid arteries and the markings of the liver and intestines.[1]   This old Roman method of haruspication is in vogue, also, in Northern Congoland; and so is the kindred practice of taking the augury from the flight of birds.[2]

Hobley describes a diviner and his son in Kikuyu who detect guilt by means of a lizard.[3]   The diviner, having dabbed white powder on the noses and hands of accused persons and on the head of a lizard which the boys had caught for him, asked each suspect in turn whether he had committed the theft; and upon receiving his denial, held the lizard to the man's nose, whereupon the little beast nipped the nose of the guilty person, and even held on after the diviner released it.   Efforts were made to discover why the lizard bit one man and not another, and the suggestion is put forth that it may have been due to some disturbance of breathing in a man who knew himself guilty and dreaded detection.

Sortilege, that is divination by casting lots, is practised by some Kikuyu diviners;[4] and is one of two methods in use on Likoma Island, in Lake Nyasa; "in the other the diviner pretends to talk with an inane little image, often made up with parts of animals, skin, tail, etc."[5]   The Bushongo, also, divine by means of images; but they use a wooden model of a crocodile, rather conventional in shape, with a flat back and carefully prepared patterns on the sides.   The diviner rubs the flat back of the crocodile with a small wooden disk, repeating at the same time the names of those who are under suspicion; and at the mention of the guilty person's name the disk clings to the image.[6] Fetishes are frequently consulted by tribes of the West Coast, and fetishes often take the form of caricatures of man or beast, or both.

[1] SCA. 189.
[2] GGC. 664.
[3] BBM. 188-190.
[4] AK. 143. See also SRK. 234 f.
[5] NGW. 122.
[6] LPK. 210. See also SRK. 229.

In Central Africa it is a common practice to discover the mind of ancestral spirits by slowly pouring out a little flour so as to form a cone, generally at the head of the inquirer's sleeping-mat, but occasionally on the verandah of the house of the chief's deceased brother, and saying at the same time a prayer to the spirit. If the flour does not fall so as to form a cone it is a bad omen.[1]

Machinga divine with three two-inch lengths of a certain root, each about as thick as a pencil. Having carefully placed two of these on the ground and the third above them, the inquirer puts the question which perplexes him, retires a few paces and returns; and if they have remained as he placed them, he takes it as a good omen. Or, a traveller sticks his knife into the ground at cross-roads, and, having poised two lengths of this root against the blade, points to one of the paths and asks, "Shall I take it?" If the roots remain poised, he takes that road; if they fall, he takes the other.[2]

Baila poise a small spherical pot on the edge of an axe which is fixed firmly in the ground, with an arrow on each side to help in balancing it: if the pot remains rigid when the diviner withdraws his hands, the answer to the question propounded is in the affirmative.[3] They use two pieces of dark root, also, but the answer in this case depends, not upon poise, but upon the adherence of the pieces of root to the divining-rod.[4]

From time immemorial, wonder-working wands, like that of Moses and Aaron, have figured among the paraphernalia of magicians in Egypt,[5] and are still used in Central Africa. The

---

[1] A. i. 76-7. In some parts of Germany, if a person wishes to know whether he will die during the coming year, he makes a little pointed heap of flour upon the table before going to bed on St. Andrew's Eve, and if the heap has fallen asunder by the morning, he knows that he will. St. Andrew's Eve in Germany, like Hallowe'en in Britain, seems to have inherited customs that originated in connection with the old New Year festivals of Northern Europe, when the dead revisited their homes. See p. 215 of *Christmas in Ritual and Tradition*, by Clement A. Miles (T. Fisher Unwin, 1912).

[2] A. i. 214.

[3] The Konde of Lake Nyasa also practise this method of divination (SRK. 231), but the Bakaonde of the Kasempa District, with that contempt for their neighbours which marks most Bantu tribes, regard this as playing at divination (WBA. 230).

[4] IPNR. i. 269-270.

[5] EM. 5.

Baila divining-rod is about an inch and a half thick, bow-shaped, with one end carved into the head of a *shimakoma* snake, the eyes of which are represented by beads. After an invocation of the spirit, accompanied by inevitable byplay, the diviner calls two men to hold the magic wand, and the wand takes them irresistibly towards the thief, or the lost article, as the case may be. They use a smaller divining-rod, also, which reveals the desired information by means of taps.[1] In every Kaonde village "there are elders who are skilled in the cult of the spirits and can locate spiritual troubles by divining with a rod (*ng'ombu*) or other means. They are often called *ayimbuki* or doctors (pl. of *chimbuki*). They are frequently skilled herbalists" and magicians.[2] Rowley witnessed a remarkable instance of divination by means of two rods, about four feet long and as thick as a broom-handle;[3] Macdonald mentions the same method;[4] and Miss Werner says that the method is still in vogue on Lake Nyasa.[5] Such scenes as that described by Rowley suggest the employment of hypnotism by the diviner, and one wants to know more of the four men who were selected to hold the rods, and who, after being thrown almost into convulsions, were rushed off at a killing pace, through thorns and over obstacles, straight to the feet of the supposed thief—who, by the by, proved her innocence to the satisfaction of her neighbours!

In the Northern Territories of the Gold Coast, the diviner's outfit consists mainly of a stick and two or more smoothly rounded stones, little larger than a golf ball. Apart from the byplay, the main features of the operation are an invocation of the spirits by the diviner, while the client tells each stone in a whisper whether it is to stand for a negative or positive reply. The diviner and his client then hold opposite ends of the stick, which, after the diviner has made a few passes, eventually hovers over the stones till the client's end touches a stone which stands either for a positive or a negative reply. Then the spirits are

[1] IPNR. i. 266 *et seq.*
[2] WBA. 176-77.
[3] UMCA. 258-260.
[4] A. i. 161.
[5] NBCA. 92.

asked to return to their abiding-places, and the consultation is over.[1]

Among the various types of Zulu diviners, there is one which uses rods in a manner altogether different from that of the foregoing examples.[2] When such a diviner is consulted, he takes snuff, shudders, yawns, goes to a clump of trees, and, calling the people to him, tells them to cut rods for smiting the ground. They tell him nothing. In an oracular manner, and carefully guarding himself against explicit statement, he makes a series of guesses, after the manner of our parlour game, "A thing and its object"; and if he is "warm" they smite the ground with their rods, or if he is "hot," they strike the ground vehemently. This beating of the ground appears to serve two purposes: it expresses assent or otherwise on the part of the inquirers, thus informing the diviner when he is following the right clue; and it excites the inquirers and throws them off their guard so that they do not pay too much attention to the diviner. It is possible that it may also produce an exalted or mesmeric condition of mind in the diviner. When the diviner has established their faith by telling them definitely what he has cunningly gleaned from their responses to his ambiguous remarks, he clothes himself with a far-away manner and proceeds to deal with the disease. But he attributes all that he says to what "our people," that is "our ancestral spirits," have told him.

Scrying or crystallomancy (that is, divination by means of the slightly hypnotic condition produced by gazing intently into a bright object) is practiced in some parts of Africa. Du Chaillu says[3] that a black earthenware pot filled with water is used in Gaboon for this purpose. Winwood Reade, speaking of Mpongwe "fetishmen" in the Gaboon country, says: "The looking-glass serves them as a magic mirror, in which they exhibit the images of the absent and the dead."[4] One wonders whether "exhibit" is not a mistake for "discern." A few pages later he mentions that the "fetishman" "looks intently in his glass" to

[1] NTG. pp. 30-31.
[2] See RSZ. 281-298, 313 and 324-25 for statements embodied in this paragraph, and much other valuable information on this subject.
[3] *A Journey to Ashango-Land* (London: Murray, 1867), pp. 173-174.
[4] *The African Sketch-Book* (London: Smith, Elder & Co., 1873), p. 45.

discover the cause of a person's death.[1] Smith mentions a diviner who used to look intently into a calabash of whitish "medicine," in which he descried tiny spirits who gave him the guidance he sought; and another who achieved the same result by peering into a mortar filled with a black mixture.[2]

A Kaonde method which differs in detail from the above, is identical in principle. "In a pool in a river—in the open, not in a *jitu* nor under trees—some medicine (*wanga*) is placed, and the person seeking information or guidance peers into the pool. Herein he sees the hitherto unrevealed past, or the secrets of the future. Among the neighbouring Alunda the water is put in a pot with medicine in it, which turns the water black. It is largely used for the interpretation of dreams; in the case of dreams—or merely of suspicions—it enables the person to discover what it is that is troubling him; *e.g.*, if it is an enemy's *mulombe* that is the trouble, he will see the *mulombe* pictured (or reflected) in the water."[3]

Some Boloki (Upper Congo) diviners place a pot of medicated water in a good position, pour by its side some sugar-cane wine (of which spirits are fond), and call the spirits by putting a leaf on the closed fist of the left hand and striking it with the palm of the right. The spirits then appear, one by one, in the pot of water, and show their faces and shake their heads negatively when challenged; but by and by the witch's familiar spirit appears and persistently refuses to show its face, whereupon the medicine-man stabs it with a splinter of bamboo. The witch herself (or himself) soon dies after that, and the medicine-man's client, freed from this malign influence, recovers from his sickness.[4]

Looking into mirrors or basins of still water is a form of

[1] *Op. cit.*, p. 49.
[2] IPNR. i. 270-71. In Europe during the Middle Ages, when everybody's thoughts were soaked in magic and swarming with spirits (cf. my p. 425), scryers often saw diminutive demons in the crystal, the mirror, or whatever speculum they used for the purpose. There was a widespread notion, too, that only virgin boys and girls had power to scry, though a woman quick with child could sometimes do it by virtue of the innocent babe in her womb. See *Crystal-Gazing*, by Theodore Besterman. (London: William Rider & Son, 1924.)
[3] WBA. 225.
[4] ACC. 286.

divination among West Coast Bantu, according to Miss Kingsley.[1] In her description of divination on the Gold Coast,[2] the diviner, having put on the head of every image in his fetish-house a little of the rum which he received as part of his fee, or else poured a small quantity of it as a libation to the whole pantheon, places a brass pan of water between him and his fetishes, and begs them to tell him what he wants to know. The description, which she quotes from a "most excellent native authority," leaves much to be desired, but is apparently a delineation of scrying by one who saw it and could not distinguish between its essentials and non-essentials. On the Bimbia peninsula (north of the Cameroon delta) the diviner consults spirits which appear to him in a bowl of water and look like little fishes.[3]

Crabtree defines *linga madzi*, in his Manual of Luganda, as "to divine by water"; but gives no information concerning the method of divination.

There is a strong family likeness between Arabian and African notions of divination,[4] and where Arabs are influential in Africa, divination by sand, by rods, and by crystal-gazing have become popular. Arabs introduced the practice of divination by sand into the extreme north and east of Congoland.[5] Lyne describes[6] methods of divination by rods and by scrying that are practised, apparently both by Arabs and Africans, at Zanzibar. In using rods for this purpose, two men sit face to face, each holding horizontally in either hand a stick, point to point with that of the man opposite. Each suspect in turn is required to place his hands between the four sticks, while a verse in the Koran is recited by the sheikh, and to call the curse of God down upon himself if he should falsely protest his innocence. The sticks are supposed to be held quite lightly, and if they should incline inwards and catch the arm of the suspected person, he is denounced as the thief. In their method of scrying, it is important that the medium should be a boy without physical blemish, who is acquainted with the people of the neighbourhood. Lyne de-

[1] TWA. 305.
[2] WAS. 145.
[3] GGC. 663.
[4] Cf. also, Isa. viii. 19.
[5] GGC. 664.
[6] *Zanzibar in Contemporary Times*, pp. 226-27.

scribes a séance at which the sheikh, after sitting on a mat facing
the Kaaba, counting his beads and muttering his prayers, washed
a boy from the neighbourhood; clothed him with two pieces of
new calico, one for his loins and the other to envelope his head
and shoulders, leaving only the face exposed; and seated him on
a low stool. Then a fire was placed by the side of the sheikh,
and incense burned upon it; and the sheikh wrote something
with pen and ink on the boy's hands; covered the boy with the
calico, and resumed his prayers. A few minutes later, the boy,
upon being asked whether he could see anybody in his hand,
replied that he saw a man. The sheikh instructed the boy to
tell the man to pitch a tent; sweep up; carry water; set a
chair for the chief; call the chief and his guards; kill a goat
and cook it for the chief; tell the chief to wash his hands, eat,
and drink some coffee; and, finally, to give the chief the sheikh's
salaams and ask him to produce the thieves. The boy then said
that the chief in his hand had produced the figures of Mr.
Lyne's cook and the cook's wife; and Mr. Lyne adds that the
sequel proved that the cook was without doubt the culprit. This
narrative is almost identical with Lane's classical description of
scrying in Egypt;[1] but Lane carefully mentions that his diviner,
after drawing magical squares, poured a little ink into the boy's
hand and told him to look into the ink, whereas Lyne seems not
to have noticed such an incident, though it was probably the
central happening of the whole performance.[2]

In Bunyoro, "the priest made seven pots of unbaked clay,
filling them with water, washed his hands in them with a lump
of clay, stirring the water about till the clay made it quite muddy.
Then he poured a few drops of a certain liquid into each pot.
At once the water began to clear, and the spreading of this clear
spot was anxiously watched. If it was unbroken and assumed
a starlike shape the augury was good; but if it broke up into
irregular clear patches, matters looked threatening."[3]

When chiefs of the Amazulu wish to foresee the results of their

[1] MCME. 274, 281.
[2] Students who are interested in the higher Islamic explanation of the phenomena
of scrying, should refer to Dr. D. B. Macdonald's *The Religious Attitude and Life
in Islam:* The University of Chicago Press, especially pp. 97 and 126 in the Second
Impression, 1912.
[3] SCA. 215.

expeditions a vessel of *ubulawo* is churned, and they see the vision in the froth. Young fellows see their luck with a girl in a similar manner.[1] The Amazulu practise another method of divination by means of two pots of "medicine," one of which stands for the chief and the other for the enemy; and the pot which froths up first upon churning indicates the stronger army of the two. A chief will not allow his army to go forth to battle unless his pot froths up first.[2]

According to Callaway, Zulu diviners must be classed with the "possessed."[3] He describes the genesis of a diviner[4] as marked by failing health, loss of appetite, notions about food, pains of one sort and another, and, eventually, a wandering of mind which tends to insomnia and madness. At an early stage of his disease, the budding diviner becomes "a house of dreams," and maintains that constant converse with spirits which is the Bantu analogue of religious mania. People then see that he is inspired by *amatongo* (ancestral spirits), and consult him; but he is told to consult a "doctor," who brews him a black and a white *ubulawo* mixture to make his visions clear. Another case[5] originated in an attack of *utlhabo*, a disease which the Zulu attribute to *itongo* (an ancestral spirit) and which Callaway (an M.D.) identifies with pleurodynia or pleurisy. When this complaint is constantly recurring, it is said that the *itongo* of one of his ancestors who was an *inyanga* ("doctor") is in him, and wishes him to "have a soft head" and become a diviner. Then the patient sacrifices, again and again, to the *amatongo*, and, in the judgment of some, goes mad, while others, noticing his tendency to dig up well-known "medicines," declare that he is a diviner. People talk about him; and he dreams at night that the *amatongo* have told him what the people have said, and becomes convinced that he is the greatest of all "doctors." Then the "doctor" who is initiating him tells him that neighbouring villagers are going to hide things for him to find; and he succeeds, apparently, in discovering the concealed articles. He is now a full-blown diviner, and people bring him

[1] RSZ. 340-44.
[2] RSZ. 440.
[3] See pp. 109 ff.
[4] RSZ. 259-267.
[5] RSZ. 268-280.

"presents." Callaway mentions [1] that diviners often clarify their inner vision by eating white *impepo* [2]—a "medicine" which folk place in their sleeping-mats so that they may have distinct dreams; but that the mere eating of white *impepo* will not of itself make a diviner. He states, also,[3] that Zulus have no faith in a fat diviner, and that diviners fast frequently and are often worn out with fastings, sometimes of several days' duration.

That Kafir diviners are of the same feather is borne out by Shaw's pages.[4] The predestined diviner is afflicted, often for months, with an unaccountable illness, during which he groans constantly, seeming to be in mental and physical pain. "He allows his finger-nails and hair to grow, until the former are like birds' claws, and the latter assumes the appearance of a huge mop or wig. . . . His whole manner becomes strange and like that of an insane person, and his speech is often incoherent and ambiguous. He frequently goes away for many days and nights together to the mountains or other lonesome places, and lives no one knows how. . . . He is indulging strange ideas and indescribable fancies; and sometimes startles the people by seeming to converse with invisible and unknown beings on some strange and incomprehensible subjects." Then the master-diviners take him in hand, and, if satisfied that it is real *ukutwasa,* admit him to their craft. Shaw wondered why this condition was called *ukutwasa* ("renewal")—a word used of the first appearance of the new moon and the vernal sprouting of grass and buds; and he suggested that it was "probably intended to intimate that the individual undergoes a new birth, or new creation, by which he is elevated to a higher state than others, and in virtue of which

[1] RSZ. 322.
[2] *Impepo* is of two kinds—white and black. "The white is burnt as incense when sacrificing to the *amatongo;* diviners use it as an emetic to prevent the return of dimness of the inner sight after the use of black *impepo;* they also eat it; and place it under their heads at night, that they may have clear, truthful dreams." (RSZ. 261.) Kidd, referring to the procedure at a sacrificial feast, describes it (SC. 27) as a sweet-smelling flower which is made into a cake and then powdered; "the powder is mixed with water, and every one rubs his body with the decoction, which has somewhat the smell of incense."
[3] RSZ. 392.
[4] *Story of My Mission in South-Eastern Africa,* etc. By William Shaw. London: Hamilton, Adams & Co. 1860. pp. 447 ff.

he is qualified to hold intercourse with the *imishologu*, or spirits of the departed."

The business of most Bantu diviners is to discover the mind of some ancestor-spirit [1] by carefully observing and accurately interpreting its control of the instruments of divination; [2] but diviners of the above order are almost independent of instruments, except for stage-business, since they themselves are tenanted by their spirit-guides. They differ but little from the lowest kind of Bantu "prophets"; [3] and they help us to understand the "smelling-out" process with which students of South-east Africa are familiar, and the crazy witch-detectives of the Shire uplands. Macdonald says that in his time most of these Shire specialists were women; [4] and he paints a lurid picture of one of them at work.[5] With patches of blood-red upon her face, breast and arms, snaky tresses hanging from her head, a leopard-skin about her loins, and rattles upon her ankles, she bounded, screaming, into the circle of assembled villagers, wildly waving her scourge of tails to drive off invisible fiends; and, after eating grass and chewing branches for several hours, she asked the hand of each one in the crowd, and started back with a yell when she touched the hand of the bewitcher. Then she took her hoe and a pot of water and went forth to unearth the horns which the witch was supposed to have buried. Such harridans bear no resemblance to the diviners that I have seen at work; or to those which Macdonald must have had in mind when he remarked that diviners were the most intelligent men in the country, who often give good advice and claim high fees.[6] But Callaway's pages help us to place them.

In our eyes the random throw of a diviner's "bones," or the chance poise of a round-bottomed pot or a few bits of stick, look for all the world like a hazard of dice, a turn of the cards, the

[1] Cf. ABN. 152; LSAT. ii. 360.
[2] Cf. SRK. 121.
[3] See pp. 113 ff.
[4] A. i. 206-212.
[5] See, also, Kidd's description (EK. 169-73) of a "smelling-out" dance which he saw on the plain between the Zambesi and the hills that overlook Port Herald, noticing that the witch-doctor "pretended to be in a frenzy and *en rapport* with the ancestral spirits" and that now and then she listened intently for some voice from the denizens of the underworld.
[6] A. i. 45.

tossing of a coin, or the drawing of lots—practices which have long been shorn of such religious significance as they once possessed in Europe; [1] but if we are to judge the Bantu fairly, still more if we are to help them to scale the steep acclivity of human achievement, we must open our eyes to the fact that they see no element of chance in the soothsayer's professional operations. The diviner claims that he arrives at his findings by definite and intricate rules, and that the tools of his trade are mere mechanical devices, like the planchette of European spiritualists, for discovering the mind of the spirits. [2] But divination, a business with an income at its heels, is so smothered with secret lore that it must frequently put a tremendous strain upon the moral integrity of even an honest practitioner; and it cannot be denied that many diviners are great rascals. Bentley mentions [3] one who, having retired from business, told some of her friends that she had denounced two hundred people as witches, of whom only sixty were really indicated as guilty by her method of divination. People who are envied for their success, wealthy people who are slow to gladden the greedy, people of insufferable temper, people who put a spoke in the wheel of a powerful schemer, kinless

[1] The Romans believed that the lots were guided by ancestral spirits as well as by the gods.

[2] Cf. IPNR. i. 270 and RSZ. 348. There is a juvenile variety of divination of which this cannot be said. Zulu herd-boys who fail to find the spoor of their strayed beasts, ask a mantis (Hottentot god) to guide them, and expect to find their cattle where the insect steadily points with its head; or they seek similar guidance from a crested bird of about the size of a crow (RSZ. 339). In all Bantu tribes boys imitate their elders in some such manner, never thinking, of course, of the philosophy of divination; and there are, to be sure, mental evergreens among the grown-ups. Such practices still persist among boys of our race, especially in rural districts. In Pennsylvania, Virginia and Ohio, when the milch cows are not "up" at milking-time, farm boys frequently conjure "Daddy-long-legs" to indicate where the laggards are grazing. Standing in front of the insect, the boy points his finger at it and says in a sing-song tone, "Grand-daddy-long-legs, tell me where the cows are." If he repeats his invocation often enough, the insect will eventually point in some direction, and thither he proceeds to seek his beasts. When children in Northern Virginia have lost a plaything, such as a ball batted into tall grass, one or more of them will spit in the palm of his left hand, and chaunt his rune: "Spit-a-spit-a-spider, tell me where my ball is and I will give you a drink of cider!" At the utterance of the last word, he strikes the saliva with the index-finger of his right hand and expects to find his ball in the direction taken by most of the saliva. Is this a playful imitation of a forgotten rite akin to those that we have been considering?

[3] PC. i. 270.

people from whom Time has filched both charm and utility, are not unlikely to become victims of a collusion between a local clique and an imported diviner.

It must be recognised, however, that the intervention of a professional diviner is not essential to the practice of some methods mentioned above, and that spirits quite often discover their will by controlling the ordinary events of human experience. There is a very curious illustration of this in the Kaonde test for ascertaining whether the heir-designate to a chieftainship is approved by the spirit of his predecessor. "He has to go out hunting and, if he has been in any way responsible for the death of the late chief by killing, witchcraft or any other means, or has slept with his wife, he will kill a male and will be unable to succeed. . . . If the heir kills a female it signifies that he has done no wrong to the deceased chief and is a fit successor. . . . One would feel that he could be sure of killing a female, but the Ba-Kaonde say—and in my opinion they believe—that if he be not a worthy successor the spirit of the deceased is too strong, and even though he aim at a female he will not kill her, but will eventually kill a male." [1] The heir-designate to a Lunda chieftainship has to undergo the same test, except that he sends out a party of hunters to shoot a female animal. [2]

REVELATION BY REINCARNATION

Since the notion that the dead may return to earth in the form of animals is remote from our thought, it may not come amiss to preface our evidence of the Bantu belief in metempsychosis with a reminder that this has been the inveterate opinion of widely sundered sections of the human race.

"The archæologist in Egypt has to deal with continuous written history handed down from an antiquity as remote as 5,000 B.C., while back over that dim chasm of ages there is a further period of about 2,000 years, of which we have indeed no written relics, but which has left numerous traces, which can be consecutively classified, in the shape of pottery, flints and tombs. Fragments of mummies of these far-off ages have come down to us—not

[1] WBA. 96-97.
[2] WBA. 102.

straightly laid and bound as in the dynasties of historic Egypt, but crouched up in their rude tombs in the sides of the rocks. Such mummies had nothing but skins thrown over them, while in one case a little copper band was found, for fastening the skins, and this is the earliest use of metal that is known." [1] After mentioning that from four to five thousand of these pre-historic tombs had been opened, Prof. Flinders Petrie said: "One curious kind of object found is discs of various sizes, carved with the figures of serpents, and perforated at the top, evidently meant for hanging on a person or a wall of a house"; and he reminded his audience that in historic Egyptian times we have the guardian serpent of the Temples, while even at the present day an Egyptian native will not disturb a serpent beside his house. One can only guess at the inner significance of these pre-historic amulets; but when we come down to the period of continuous written history, we are on surer ground.

Dr. E. A. Wallis Budge, Keeper of the Egyptian and Assyrian antiquities in the British Museum, writes: [2] "Both from the religious and profane literature of Egypt we learn that the gods and man in the future life were able at will to assume the form of any animal, or bird, or plant, or living thing, which they pleased, and one of the greatest delights to which a man looked forward was the possession of that power. This is proved by the fact that no less than twelve of the chapters of the Book of the Dead are devoted to providing the deceased with words of power, the recital of which was necessary to enable him to transform himself into a 'hawk of gold,' a 'divine hawk,' 'the governor of the sovereign princes,' 'the god who giveth light in the darkness,' a lotus, the god Ptah, a *bennu* bird (*i.e.*, phœnix), a heron, a 'living soul,' a swallow, the serpent Sata, and a crocodile; and another chapter enabled him to transform himself into 'whatever form he pleaseth.' Armed with this power he could live in the water in the form of a crocodile, in the form of a serpent he could glide over the rocks and ground, in the form of the birds mentioned above he could fly through the air, and soar up and perch himself upon the bow of the boat of Rā, in the form of the lotus

---

[1] Prof. W. M. Flinders Petrie, in a lecture reported in *The Brighton Herald*, Oct. 19, 1901.
[2] EM. 230-33.

he had mastery over the plants of the field, and in the form of Ptah he became 'more powerful than the lord of time, and shall gain the mastery over millions of years.' . . . Now the Egyptians believed that as the souls of the departed could assume the form of any living thing or plant, so the 'gods,' who in many respects closely resembled them, could and did take upon themselves the forms of birds and beasts; this was the fundamental idea of the so-called 'Egyptian animal worship,' which provoked the merriment of the cultured Greek, and drew down upon the Egyptians the ridicule and abuse of the early Christian writers. But if the matter be examined closely its apparent stupidity disappears. . . . The educated Egyptian never worshipped an animal as an animal, but only as an incarnation of a god, and the reverence paid to animals in Egypt was in no way different from that paid to the king who was regarded as 'divine' and as an incarnation of Rā the Sun-god, who was the visible symbol of the Creator. The relation of the king to Rā was identical with that of Rā to God. The Hebrews, Greeks, and Romans never understood the logical conception which underlay the reverence with which the Egyptians regarded certain animals, and as a result they grossly misrepresented their religion. The ignorant people, no doubt, often mistook the symbol for what is symbolised, but it is wrong to say that the Egyptians worshipped animals in the ordinary sense of the word, and this fact cannot be too strongly insisted on. Holding the views he did about transformations there was nothing absurd in the reverence which the Egyptian paid to animals. When a sacred animal died the god whom it represented sought out another animal of the same species in which to renew his incarnation, and the dead body of the animal, inasmuch as it had once been the dwelling-place of a god, was mummified and treated in much the same way as a human body after death, in order that it might enjoy immortality. These views seem strange, no doubt, to us when judged by modern ideas, but they formed an integral part of the religious beliefs of the Egyptians, from the earliest to the latest times."

The same writer states that we learn from the religious books of ancient Egypt that the magician, by pronouncing certain words or names of power in the proper manner and in the proper tone of voice, could enable living people to assume divers forms at will, and to project their souls into animals and other creatures.[1] And Petrie, referring to beliefs of the New Kingdom period, says:[2] "This other belief is that the soul could be taken out of the body at will, and placed in any other position; in this case of Bata it was hidden on the top of a tree. While the soul was thus deposited, the life of the man was independent of what might occur to his body; but he fell down dead if the seat of his soul was destroyed. This belief is spread from the Celts to the Chinese, and is, therefore, a standard piece of psychology."

The doctrine of reincarnation in animals is widely held in China, and so is that of rebirth in descendants.[3] In Japan, at the July "Festival of the Dead" (*Bon Matsuri*), when cemeteries are illuminated and lanterns lit in the doorway of the home to guide and welcome the returning souls of one's kindred, if one of the great black-and-crimson or green-and-silver butterflies come into the house, sugar is set for it, because it is certainly the soul of grandpapa or grandmamma,—a belief which reminds us of the Greek Psyche. The doctrine of the transmigration of souls, which has swayed the thought of the people of India from the time of the Upanishads to the present day and has been carried to the pitch of philosophic refinement, postulates that animals as well as people may be dwelling-places of reborn souls.

"Among the Arabs ghosts and Jinn frequently appeared in the forms of beasts and birds, particularly of serpents and owls. The same was true of Babylonia."[4] "Mohammed would not eat lizards because he fancied them to be the offspring of a metamorphosed clan of Israelites. Macrîzî relates of the Seiᶜar in Hadramaut that in time of drought part of the tribe change themselves into ravening wolves. They have a magical means of assuming and again casting off the wolf shape. Other Hadramites changed themselves into vultures or kites. In the Sinai peninsula the hyrax and the panther are believed to have been originally men."[5]

Although cultured Greeks ridiculed the Egyptian worship of

[1] EM. p. x.
[2] *Religion and Conscience in Ancient Egypt.* (Methuen & Co.) 1898. p. 31.
[3] SCD. 26.
[4] SCD. 203.
[5] RS. 88 and cf. 168.

animals, there were cognate ideas in their own religion.[1] All over Greece, the mighty, strong, noble, venerable dead—heroes, they called them—were worshipped in snake form.[2] "In snake form the hero dwelt in his tomb, and to indicate this fact not uncommonly on vase paintings we have a snake depicted on the very grave mound itself." [3] A Spartan relief of the sixth century B.C. shows two heroised figures side by side on a throne-like chair accepting offerings from diminutive worshippers; and "behind the chair, equal in height to the seated figures, is a great curled snake. . . . The intention is clear; he is a *human* snake, the vehicle, the incarnation of the dead man's ghost." [4] Even when, under the influence of the Olympian gods, decorative altars instead of primitive grave-mounds were erected for the worship of heroes and the ancient supposition that the dead assumed snake-forms had faded from the memory of men, conventional snakes were still sculptured on the top of the altar round the cup which served for libations.[5] Long before Greek literature was born, the divine matriarch, mother of the dead as well as the living, genius of the underworld which is at once the home of the dead and the source of fertility, was worshipped by matrilineal tribesmen. When men lived mainly by hunting, they thought of her as "The Lady of the Wild Things"; and when agriculture came into its own, they thought of her as the "Grain-mother" and modified their rites of approach accordingly. In course of time, mainly in connection with agriculture, it would seem, the Earth-goddess developed her double form, Mother and Maid, Demeter and Kore, two persons but one god. "The Athenians of old called the dead 'Demeter's people,' " according to Plutarch; and a cinerary urn decorated with a scene from Eleusinian initiation rites shows Demeter enthroned with a great snake coiled about her and an initiated mystic caressing its head.[6]

In Italy, where autochthonous religion was less sensitive to the influence of the Olympians, "serpents were regarded as the em-

[1] See also my p. 164.
[2] *Prolegomena to the Study of Greek Religion*, by Jane Ellen Harrison (Cambridge University Press, 1903), p. 21.
[3] *Ibid.*, p. 329.
[4] *Ibid.*, pp. 326-328.
[5] *Ibid.*, p. 331; see also pp. 348-351.
[6] *Ibid.*, pp. 263-275 and 547-49.

bodiment of the spirits of ancestors and the guardian heroes of places. . . . On tomb-reliefs snakes were represented, as in Greece, as embodiments of the dead." [1] "At Litternum in Campania, where Scipio Africanus caused himself to be buried because, as he said, he did not wish to leave even his bones to his ungrateful country, the grotto was shown where he rested and where, so men believed, 'a serpent kept guard over his bones.' " [2] *Larva* is the Latin word for "ghost." [3]

"In Poland it is said that every member of the Herburt family is turned into an eagle after death; and that the eldest daughters of the Pileck line are transformed into doves if they die unmarried, into owls if they die married." [4] "In Celtic mythology Maildun, the Irish Odysseus, comes to an island with trees on it in clusters on which were perched many birds. The aged man of the island tells him, 'These are the souls of all my children and of all my descendants, both men and women, who are sent to this little island to abide with me according as they die in Erin.' " [5] "The bird form of the soul after death is still a current belief in the Hebrides. Butterflies in Ireland, and moths in Cornwall, [6] and in France bats or butterflies, are believed to be souls of the dead. King Arthur is thought by Cornishmen to have died and to have been changed into the form of a raven, and in Mediæval

[1] SCD. 96 ff.
[2] ALRP. 47.
[3] Cf. my p. 8.
[4] CPP. 373.
[5] *Prolegomena*, etc., p. 201.
[6] The following is taken from p. 61 of a little book called *Choice Notes from "Notes and Queries"* (London: Bell & Dalby, 1859): "In Yorkshire the country people used in my youth, and perhaps do still, call night-flying white moths, especially the *Hepialus humuli*, which feeds, while in the grub state, on the roots of docks and other coarse plants, 'souls.' Have we not in all this a remnant of 'Psyche'?" The editor adds: "This paragraph furnishes a remarkable coincidence with the tradition from the neighbourhood of Truro (recorded by Mr. Thoms in his Folk Lore of Shakspeare, *Athenæum*, Oct. 9, 1847), which gives the name of *Piskeys* both to the *Fairies* and to *moths*, which are believed by many to be *departed souls*." In *"The Ring of Nestor": A Glimpse into the Minoan Afterworld* (Macmillan, 1925, pp. 53 ff.), Sir Arthur Evans states that the Minoans figured the divine spirit in bird form, generally as a dove (cf. Mt. iii. 16, Mk. i. 10, Lk. iii. 22, Jno. i. 32), and gives ample evidence that they equated butterflies, especially the Common White, with human souls, and used both butterflies and chrysalises in grave-jewellery as emblems of life after death. He remarks also that the *Hepialus humuli*, or Ghost moth, is often seen flickering about the mounds of grassy churchyards.

Wales souls of the wicked appear as ravens, in Brittany as black dogs, petrels or hares, or serve their term of penitence as cows or bulls, or remain as crows till the day of judgment. Unbaptised infants become birds; drowned sailors appear as beasts or birds; and the souls of girls deceived by lovers haunt them as hares. . . . Kerry peasants will not eat hares because they contain the souls of their grandmothers. . . . In Celtic folk-belief the soul is seen leaving the body in sleep as a bee, butterfly, gnat, or mannikin." [1]

Now among the Bantu we find three closely allied doctrines: (1) that it is possible, by magical means, to hide the souls of living men in external objects for safety, or to project them temporarily into animals when the animal form would best help the soul to execute some cherished design; (2) that the souls of the dead are able at will to assume the form of animals, birds, etc.; [2] and (3) that the souls of the dead are often reborn in the bodies of their descendants. [3] If we confine ourselves strictly to our present theme (Methods of Ancestral Revelation), we shall take cognisance only of the second of these doctrines, since the first and the third are not regarded as methods of revelation; but the coherence of these three dogmas makes it expedient to scan them together.

Since the magical hiding of the souls of the living is not in the direct line of our inquiry, it need not detain us long; it shows, however, that the attribution of similar power to discarnate spirits was not a great leap of the imagination. "An Ashanti stool is supposed to be the repository of its owner's soul, and for this reason the miniature fetters are placed round the central support of the stool—'to chain down the soul to it.' " [4] "The old Ashanti bought cats as repositories of their *okra* or breath." [5] Campbell, referring to Bangweulu, writes: "Lycanthropy is practised round the lake, and a few notorious doctors whom I know have earned a great reputation (Kasoma and Chama), and do a profitable business with their reputed lion packs. The natives have an implicit and unshakeable faith in this form of black magic. (See Goulds-

[1] RAC. 360.
[2] See my pp. 7, 12 f., 17, 25.
[3] See my p. 26.
[4] AS. 298.
[5] AS. 234, and cf. my p. 8.

bury's poem on the Chisanguka)." [1] Gouldsbury says: [2] "The superstition anent the *chisanguka,* or were-lion, is interesting, as having its parallel in most of the primitive systems of folklore. It is implicitly believed that certain lions are not merely animals, but human beings, malevolent and endowed with magical powers, who, for their own evil ends, have assumed the dreaded form of the king of beasts. A native will tell you, confidently, that such-and-such a lion is well known to be So-and-so *sanguka'd*—that is to say, transmogrified. And there is a story, widely believed, of a certain so-called were-lion which, being slain by a boar, was thereupon at once declared to be no chisanguka." His collaborator, Sheane, declares that "even the best-educated natives have a sneaking belief in lycanthropy—in other words, the power of a wizard to change himself into a lion or leopard—and it is simply waste of time to point out to them that an open demonstration by the suspect should precede belief." [3] Arnot mentions that the Garenganze people excused themselves for not killing lions and leopards which carried off sick and solitary people from their towns, by saying that the marauders were really men of other tribes who had been turned into these beasts, by magic power, for the purpose of wreaking vengeance upon those to whom they bore malice; but he seems not to have inquired why the tribesmen failed to punish lycanthropes as pitilessly as they punished witches. [4] Perhaps they were invulnerable to human weapons. Both Bakaonde and Alunda believe that the soul of a living man can be deposited for safety in some external object, such as an antelope's horn or a crab's shell, and then hidden where it is unlikely to be discovered. Such an operation requires occult knowledge, of course, and a specialist is consulted; but there is always the risk that the horn, shell, or other container of the soul may be destroyed or stolen, in which case the man who has thus lost his *chimvule* ("shadow") or *wumi* ("life") will die within the year. [5] The Baila cherish a similar belief, holding, however, that the man dies the moment the hiding-place of his soul is destroyed and, conversely, that when the man dies the container of his soul

[1] IHB. 302.
[2] GPNR. 200.
[3] GPNR. 133.
[4] G. 236.
[5] WBA. 132, 165, cf. my pp. 11 f.

comes to grief [1]—though we are not told why the man should ever die while his soul remains securely hidden. Nassau, who spent forty years in the Gabun district, writes that the soul of a living human being may enter temporarily into the body of any animal, guiding it by his intelligence and will to exercise its strength in fulfilment of his purpose; that murders are said to be committed in this way, after the manner of the mythical German wehr-wolf or the French loup-garou; and that this belief must not be confounded with the equally believed transmigration of souls.[2] May I be permitted to add that the suggestion that the belief is related to totemism is also wide of the mark: the animal in which a magician is supposed to do his nefarious deeds is always one of the more formidable beasts, not, save in a few coincidences, the totem of the magician. The Barotse of the Zambesi, according to Decle,[3] "believe that at times both living and dead persons can change themselves into animals, either to execute some vengeance or to procure something that they wish for: thus a man will change himself into a hyena or a lion in order to steal a sheep and make a good meal off it; into a serpent to avenge himself on some enemy. At other times if they see a serpent it is one of the 'Matotela' or slave-tribe, which has thus transformed himself to take some vengeance on the Barotse."

Evidence in favour of the existence of our second dogma (that the souls of the dead are able at will to assume the forms of animals, etc.), is more abundant, and, being germane to our present theme, deserves closer attention. At the burial of a Zulu, the grave is covered with branches and watched till the rotting of the branches indicates that there has been time for the corpse to decay.[4] Now if a snake is seen among these branches, the beholder informs the relatives that he has seen the deceased basking in the sun on the top of his grave.[5] If the snake does not come home after that, or if the relatives do not dream of the dead, they

---

[1] IPNR. i. 256-57.
[2] FWA. 70, cf. TWA. 301.
[3] *Three Years in Savage Africa*, London: Methuen, 1898, p. 75.
[4] Cf. p. 56.
[5] The serpent was a chthonian god or the emblem of such a god in old European paganism, and serpents with rams' heads occur on monuments of the god of the underworld. (RAC. 34, 166.) Cf. AI. 165.

sacrifice an ox or a goat to bring him back from the wilds to the home; [1] or if the snake does come home and they do not dream of the dead, they are still troubled because "his *itongo* (ancestral spirit) is dark"; and they hire a "doctor" who brews *ubulawo*,[2] and sacrifice a goat.[3] It must not be thought, however, that every kind of snake may be an *idhlozi* ("reincarnate ancestral spirit"). We gather from one of Callaway's informants [4] that the snake which is supposed to come out of the corpse is a large, harmless snake, found in trees; and from another [5] that the *ubulube* or *inkwakwa* and the *umzingandlhu* may be the reincarnation of a commoner, that the *umthlwazi*, which is harmless, may be that of a commoner or of a chieftainess, while either the black or green *imamba*, both of which are deadly, may be that of a chief. Chaka sometimes appears as a large *imamba*, followed by snakes who are the men slain at his funeral; and once he was seen fighting with Undigane after both were dead—probably a fight between two mambas.[6] Ex-King Cetywayo stated [7] that ancestral spirits return only in a certain kind of snake, which he described (probably thinking of commoners) as a harmless, green snake with black spots. But most snakes of these species may be killed without danger of insulting an ancestral spirit; the *idhlozi* is distinguished from wild snakes of the same variety by certain definite characteristics. If the snake is seen on the grave, there can be no doubt of its identity; but there are other traits by which it may be known. In ex-King Cetywayo's evidence, some of which is given in the third person, one passage runs: [8] "As to the belief of the Zulu people in *amahlozi*, the king can only corroborate it by saying that the *ihlozi* is distinguished from any other snake like unto it, in that the *ihlozi* comes to a kraal and does not appear to be timid, and when the same kraal is removed to any other place, the same snake will follow the removing inhabitants, and make its residence

[1] Cf. p. 36 *et seq.*
[2] See p. 96.
[3] RSZ. 143.
[4] RSZ. 12.
[5] RSZ. 196.
[6] RSZ. 215.
[7] R., 1883, p. 522.
[8] R., 1883, p. 532.

at the new kraal. . . . You can recognise them even as you recognise a human acquaintance." Divine snakes enter the home unseen and remain quietly coiled in the upper part of the house, taking no notice of frogs and mice, and never attempting to escape when discovered.[1] If such a snake has a scar, or has lost one eye, or is lame, some one remarks that a late lamented dweller in that kraal had a similar blemish, and that it stands to reason that this is his reincarnated spirit. That night the dead man appears to the chief of the village in a dream, asking whether the chief wants to kill him; and when the owners return to their hut after offering a sacrifice to this ancestral spirit in the morning, the snake has mysteriously disappeared. A snake that is nothing more than a snake behaves in a different manner; it enters a hut apprehensively, glancing from side to side; and it may be killed at sight, even if it is of the variety that ancestral spirits are wont to possess. But great care must be taken that no harm is inflicted upon snakes that are possessed with divine shades; even if they are of a deadly variety, such snakes never harm anybody; they have come to look after their kindred and particularly to warn them of approaching danger, and should be rewarded with a sacrifice. If a divine snake lies on its back with its belly uppermost, it indicates that something of unusual importance is about to happen. If by any mischance a divine snake is killed by some stupid or careless person, it comes to life again, and complains in a dream of the treatment received; then there is nothing for it but to appease the offended spirit with a sin-offering. Occasionally a divine snake is found coiling round a vessel, which it refuses to allow any one to touch, till it has been honoured with a sacrifice; but after that it goes quietly away.

Sometimes the spirits of Zulu men revisit their old homes in the form of wasps and lizards; and people do not approach the poisonous kinds even when these are regarded as ancestral spirits.[2] In many parts of Africa there is a rough, ugly lizard, which the Zulus call *isalakuzana*. Natives say that it takes two persons to see one of these creatures after the first chance glimpse, because it has the habit of dodging round to the other side of a pole much faster than a person can follow it. The Zulus believe

[1] RSZ. 196-200.
[2] RSZ. 201.

that the spirits of old women return occasionally to revisit their former haunts in this guise.[1]

Junod,[2] speaking of the way in which the gods reveal themselves to their descendants, mentions that they sometimes appear in the form of a mantis, often in the form of a harmless little bluish green snake, called *shihundje,* which frequents huts, and sometimes in the form of a large green puff-adder. He quotes a story which he heard from a Thonga priest. This man went with his people to worship his ancestors in the sacred woods where they were buried. Upon approaching the spot, a green puff-adder, about as large as his leg at the ankle, came out to meet them. The women of the party fled in terror; but it was only the spirit of his ancestor, the original master of that forest, who circled round the party, doing them no harm, but thanking his worshipping children for the sacrifice and offerings which they were bringing.

This belief was once potent, and is still existent, among the Becwana. When our son was buried at Serowe, Khama ordered one of his regiments to pile a cairn of stones over the grave, and some weeks later he mentioned in conversation that some of his tribesmen had been saying that they had seen the lad basking on the cairn in the form of a large mamba. A Becwana folktale tells of a devoted daughter who pluckily interviewed a python that she might obtain healing [3] for her sick father, the python being evidently much more than a serpent. It is said that the python is still worshipped by a few Becwana; and it is certain that both the python and ancestral spirits of the dynasty are associated with rain in the thought of these people, and that in their Girls' Puberty Ceremonies, which are essentially fertility rites, the image of the snake always figures among the clay gods which the neophytes have to adore.

In 1901 some Batalaote women began to worship a puff-adder [4] in their gardens outside Phalapye, regarding it as a re-embodied human spirit; but the men of their tribe objected to the reactionary movement and promptly killed the reptile. Although the

[1] RSZ. 215.

[2] LSAT. ii. 358-59.

[3] Among Southern Arabs, medicinal waters are regarded as inhabited by jinn, usually of serpent form. (RS. 168.)

[4] See p. 106.

Batalaote have long been identified with Khama's Becwana, they are allied to Mashona tribes, whose belief in the re-embodiment of human spirits in animal forms cannot be called in question. Some Mashona tribes hold that spirits of great chiefs are reincarnated in maneless lions, which will do no harm at a kraal and must not be killed,[1] and that spirits of ordinary people exist in the form of tailless birds of the hawk species, which they call *chapungo*.[2] While Livingstone was at Tete, on the Zambesi, the son of Monomotapa visited the Commandant, which is indicative of the Mashona lineage of the people; and Livingstone refers to the popular belief in that district that the souls of chiefs enter into lions, and that even living chiefs may metamorphose themselves into lions, kill whom they choose, and then reassume human form, and he states that when the people see a lion they therefore commence clapping their hands—their usual mode of salutation.[3] We have already mentioned that the Mashona, like the Herero and many other Bantu tribes, believe that the soul emerges from the corpse in the form of a maggot.[4]

In Urundi (north-east of Tanganyika), "when the king dies, his body, wrapped in a black ox-hide, is mummified by drying it near a big fire, then exposed in the open air on a platform, where it continues to receive funeral honours until the catafalque crumbles of its own accord. The remains are wrapped in matting and buried on the spot. Then, the first worm that comes from the putrefying body receives a hearty welcome and is fed on cow's milk. Soon, they say, this worm changes into a python or a leopard or a lion or some other beast. It is therein the spirit of the deceased resides: this animal is thenceforth sacred; they feed it and offer sacrifice to it."[5]

"The Baila are firm believers in the doctrine of metempsychosis: that is that at death a person passes into another living creature, man, animal or plant."[6] It appears, however, that a man must secure an appropriate "medicine" if he wishes to become an animal after death. The "medicine" prepared by the magician

[1] MLC. 45, 67.
[2] MLC. 68.
[3] MTR. 615, 642.
[4] See p. 8.
[5] The Rev. J. M. Van der Burgt, cited in RP. 104.
[6] IPNR. ii. 124-26.

for this purpose, consists of maggots that have been bred from a small piece of the hide of such an animal as the postulant wishes to become. The postulant has to swallow the maggots whole and alive; [1] and when he is buried, a reed is inserted in his ear and its other end left protruding above the surface of the ground, the opening being carefully covered with a potsherd. Along this channel a maggot issues from the corpse and grows into the chosen animal. Only dangerous beasts, such as lions, leopards, hyenas, wild dogs, elephants and snakes, are chosen for this purpose. Such animals are sacrosanct to surviving friends, though if they prove too destructive the people may lose patience and kill them. The surprising feature of this belief is that the same spirit may at the same time be in an animal and in a descendant, and still be worshipped at the grave in which its human remains lie.

The Bakaonde believe [2] that the spirit of a deceased person (*mukishi*) "can enter animals of any kind: hippopotamus, bush-pig, hyena, etc.," and that its presence can be ascertained by divination; "but there appears to be no taboo against killing nor against eating such reincarnation, even if it be the hunter's (or feeder's) near relative or chief." "Ordinary *wakishi* do not enter lions; but if a chief be so disposed he can take certain medicines in his life-time so that after death he becomes lions (plural) which are called *mikumbe*. After burial, if maggots are seen to emerge from the chief's grave it is known that he has taken this medicine, and each maggot [3] becomes a *mukumbe* lion, who is the chief, directly reincarnated in a multiple form. (This is considered to be a direct reincarnation and not an emanation [4] from the chief's *mukishi*.)" Lunda belief differs in one or two details, but is substantially the same: [5] "Certain *akishi* appear to reproduce themselves into animals. This does not mean that the whole *mukishi* is reincarnated in the animal, but only that it sends off an emana-

---

[1] Cf. p. 8. Druids boasted of their shape-shifting powers, and Irish sagas tell of one hero or divinity after another who was transformed into a worm, insect, fish, or small animal, and reborn of a woman who had swallowed him in this shape. (RAC. 348-359.)
[2] WBA. 150-51.
[3] Cf. p. 8.
[4] See pp. 174 f.
[5] WBA. 172.

tion [1] from the soul into the beast. It is frequently suspected by villagers that certain animals by signs (perhaps by continually haunting the village precincts or by talking to hunters) are possessed by *wumi* ('life') from their elders. *Ayimbuki* or wise men are consulted, and if the decision be arrived at that the animal is so possessed care must be taken not to kill or hurt it lest the *mukishi* be offended, and visitation on the offenders be made. (The late Paramount chief, Kanongesha, is said to have an emanation from his *mukishi* in a rabbit.)"

Rowley, after remarking that the Nungwi (a tribe which lived round Tete on the Zambesi) believed that their dead "prophets" were often reincarnated in lions, wrote: [2] "So common is the belief among them that the lion has the name Pondora, or prophet, and is held in such estimation in some districts that it is death to the individual who kills a lion." Macdonald mentions [3] that some of the divine shades of Nyasaland return in the form of snakes, while hunters come back as lions or leopards, and witches as hyenas. Miss Werner, writing of the Yao tribe, says: [4] "The dead may manifest themselves in the shape of animals; but this does not happen so often as among the Zulus, who quite expect their deceased relatives to come back, like Cadmus and Harmonia, as 'bright and aged snakes,' and are very glad to see them when they do. The Yao theory seems to be that none of the departed will do this, unless they mean to be nasty." "With regard to the spirits of the dead," writes Archdeacon Johnson, [5] "there is a general belief that the souls of men come back in the bodies of animals"; and he refers to spirits that take up their abode in lions. [6] Fraser writes in a similar strain of the Tumbuka tribe (West of Nyasa): [7] "The spirits live in many creatures, especially in snakes. There are two little harmless ones which they particularly frequent: the blind worm and a snake with a sawlike backbone. Should natives meet one of these on the path, they turn home, and the journey is not resumed, but a 'doctor' is called

[1] See pp. 174 f.
[2] UMCA. 113.
[3] A. i. 62.
[4] NBCA. 64. Cf. SRK. 195 for Konde belief.
[5] NGW. 119.
[6] See pp. 25, 87.
[7] WPP. 127.

to tell what ancestral spirit this was that had warned the traveller of danger ahead and oblations are made. . . . The spirits of chiefs and other great people were believed to have a special affinity to lions." Campbell mentions [1] that many of the people whom Msidi had unjustly killed were believed to have wreaked their vengeance upon him by returning in the form of a lion, leopard, or snake and devastating his country. He says, also, that "the Wemba believe that their chiefs are reincarnated often in the shape of lions and prey upon their people from time to time. Such a lion is called *chisanguka*." [2] Sheane, writing of the same region, says: [3] "The spirits of departed chiefs may become reincarnated in animals. The Mambwe paramount chief or the Sokolo becomes reincarnated in the form of a young lion, and Bisa and Wiwa chiefs become reincarnated in pythons. In one of the rest-houses on the Stevenson road, near Fife, lived a tame python, which waxed fat on the sour beer and fowls offered to it by the Winamwanga, who reverenced in it their ancestral spirit Chief Kachinga. One day, alas! the deity so far forgot himself as to dispute the ownership of the rest-house with a German cattle-dealer who was passing by; whereupon his hiss of disapproval was silenced by a charge of S.S.G., and the worshippers of Kachinga saw him no more!" The same writer describes the curious customs at the burial of the paramount Mambwe chief, who is called the Sokolo. [4] "A deep pit was dug for the grave, in which the body of the chief was placed in a sitting position, his wrists being crossed over his knees. His wrists and ankles, moreover, were tied tightly together. The mourners then lowered into the tomb the bodies of a youth and one of the chief's wives, sacrificed to act as his attendants in the spirit Underworld. The body of the wife was laid on the rigid breast of the sitting corpse, while that of the youth served to prop up the back of the dead chief. A hollow bamboo was inserted in the chief's right ear, lengthy enough to project above the surface of the grave. The mouth of the grave was thereupon roofed with stout poles and mudded over, and a hut was built above. The

---

[1] See p. 24.
[2] IHB. 117, cf. my p. 157.
[3] GPNR. 84, cf. SRK. 101.
[4] GPNR. 188.

people believed that, after two days, came a spider through the orifice of the projecting bamboo, a little later a python, and later again a young lion.[1] The older men went to inspect the grave at intervals. When the python appeared it was fed and solemnly warned, before it glided away into the bush, that it must seize game only, and never molest a man. When the lion cub came forth they placed on one side a mixture of flour and water, and on the other a kind of potage tinged with *nkula*—the red camwood. The young lion was exhorted to lick the flour, to show that it was a good spirit. If, however, it licked the mess of *nkula* instead, it was, manifestly, an evil were-lion, and the old men withdrew in haste and dread, admonishing the evil spirit at a safe distance to beware of molesting them. If, however, the cub licked the flour, it was a good spirit, and was fed regularly. When strong enough to fend for itself, the young lion was taken into the bush and shown the fresh spoor of game, with the strict injunction that, though it was free henceforth to hunt the beasts of the forest, it must abstain from hunting men and women of the tribe."

In 1882, when marching into Mpwapwa, in what afterwards became German East Africa, two or three caravan porters from Zanzibar took me aside to see the grave of Dr. Mullens, former Foreign Secretary of our London Missionary Society. As we passed from the bush into the little clearing, we saw a large snake sunning itself on the loose stones that had been heaped upon the grave to ward off hyenas, wild pigs, and other burrowing beasts. "There he is!" whispered the Zanzibaris in awestruck voices; and the startled snake raised its head for a moment and promptly slipped into its hole between the stones. The Zanzibaris declared that it was the reincarnated spirit of Dr. Mullens, which after greeting me had forthwith retired into its grave.

Tribes of Kenya and Uganda make no doubt of the reincarnation of ancestral spirits. "The Kitui people say that sometimes when a snake, crawling outside a hut, is attacked, it will suddenly vanish, and they then know that it was the *imu* of a deceased

---

[1] Sheane adds in a footnote: "For the myth of the young lion emerging, cf. Speke's *Journal*, p. 221. (Edinburgh, 1863), relating the death of Rohinda VI, as told by his grandson." See p. 181 in Dent's "Everyman" ed. of Speke's *Journal*.

person who had either assumed the form of a snake or entered into the body of a snake.   A few days afterwards a woman will become possessed and fall into a state of semi-trance, and the *imu* will speak through her mouth and say: 'I came into the village the other day, and So-and-so wanted to strike me.'   Whereupon the people think it is just as well to sacrifice a goat to soothe the feelings of the injured spirit." [1]   The Routledges reported that a fat, green caterpillar of about two inches in length was thought by the Akikuyu to be the reincarnation of an *ngoma* (ancestral spirit); but in the instance mentioned the people were desperately anxious to get rid of it. [2]   "If on the occasion of a sacrifice at the sacred tree, the [Kikuyu] elders chance to see a snake, they say it is a *ngoma*, or ancestral spirit, which has taken the form of a snake, and endeavour to pour a little of the blood from the sacrificial ram on its head, back and tail." [3]   "If a certain snake, called *nyamuyathi* by the Kikuyu, enters a hut, it is necessary to pour some milk or fat on the floor for the reptile to drink; it may drink and leave, or it may not.   If it does, well and good; if not, the owner of the village has to kill a sheep, cook some of its fat, and pour it out in the hut, saying at the same time: 'We offer you some fat to drink, we beg of you to leave us.'   It is believed that a *ngoma*, or spirit, has come in the guise of a snake, and on no account must such a snake be killed.   After the sacrifice of the sheep has been made the snake will always go, but it disappears mysteriously and no one sees it leave.   If the snake remained in the hut, the wife who owned the hut, and her children, would be *thahu*" (*i.e.*, taboo). [4]   "If a snake is seen at a sacred place it is customary" among the Akamba "to pour milk, butter and gruel over it; it is supposed to be a 'snake of the *aiimu*.' " [5]   The Heart-clan of Victoria Nyanza worshipped a python, which was fed with fowls and goats, and supplied by a woman who lived in the temple with a daily ration of milk.   Roscoe does not say whether it was a reincarnated ancestral spirit; but it was supposed to be the giver of children, and its priesthood was confined to

[1] BBM. 30.
[2] PP. 242.
[3] BBM. 51, cf. RP. 104.
[4] BBM. 122.
[5] BBM. 64.

members of this one clan,[1] both characteristic of ancestor-worship.

"Up and down the main Congo the Bantu populations consider it possible for the spirits of dead *and* living men to enter the bodies of buffaloes, leopards, or crocodiles, in order that they may inflict injuries on their enemies. The Basoko cannibals of the lower Aruwimi believe in a kind of transmigration of souls."[2] Sometimes a disembodied spirit takes possession of a hippopotamus and visits the towns on the river-banks, so the Boloki of the Upper Congo think, and when that occurs the family to whom the spirit is supposed to belong puts a small pot of sugar-cane wine and a little food for its refreshment on its nightly visit. The spirit may at times enter a crocodile and visit a town, but the hippopotamus is more frequently selected.[3] At Nyodi, in the wilds of Angola, Claridge,[4] advising the Natives to trap or shoot the wild pigs that were ravaging their farms, found them shocked at the suggestion that they should destroy their own dead kith and kin who were revisiting the scenes of their human life in this embodiment. Nassau states, also,[5] that metempsychosis is a common belief among all the Gabun tribes; and he informed Miss Kingsley[6] that a Native whose plantations were devastated by an elephant had declared to him that he dared not shoot the beast because the spirit of his dead father had passed into it.

Similar notions are entertained by Hamites and Negroes, stocks from which the Bantu race sprang. The pastoral Bahuma of Ankole, of Hamitic lineage, believe in the transmigration of souls; the king is thought to become a lion after death, his wives (who are not necessarily of royal blood) to become leopards, while princes and princesses take the form of pythons. These creatures are consequently not killed even when they attack tribesmen, unless the diviner discovers that a special marauder is not a reincarnation, but merely a dangerous beast.[7] Whether the lion and leopard spirits that haunt certain hills in Uganda[8] are

[1] Bg. 169, 321.
[2] GGC. 632.
[3] ACC. 266.
[4] WBT. 59.
[5] FWA. 237.
[6] TWA. 300.
[7] SCA. 80.
[8] Bg. 319.

reincarnations, we do not know; it is not unlikely that they are. Snake-worship is found, also, among the Gallas; and the Abyssinians are said to have adored a large serpent before their conversion to Christianity. The Dinkas (a tribe of Nilotic Negroes), who live on the lower courses of the Bahr-el-Jebel, call snakes their brothers, assigning names to those who come into the house, and treating them as friends.[1] "The stalwart Banza Negroes of the western Mubangi basin believe that their chieftains are reincarnated in chimpanzis."[2]   In the *Life of Gollmer*,[3] the founder of the C.M.S. Lagos Mission in 1845, Idagbe, the national deity of the Popos, a Dahomian tribe which dwelt at Badagry, some forty miles west of Lagos, is described as "a black venomous snake" and as "a species of boa constrictor." Bullocks were sacrificed to it; libations of rum poured out upon the ground; and offerings of blood and other foods placed before the hut in which it abode.

Belief in rebirth, that is, that after death souls return to earth as new-born babes, is widespread in Africa; but evidence is too scant and patchy, at present, to warrant the assertion that it is a common article of Bantu faith.

Natives of the Northern Territories of the Gold Coast, a blend of Berber and Negro stocks, believe that if a child dies soon after birth and the next one is of the same sex, the soul of the former has returned in the body of the latter; hence their custom of marking the corpse [4] of an infant before burial, so that it may be easily identified if it is reborn. Furthermore, if a child resembles his father or grandfather, these people say that he is really his father or grandfather, and honour him as such.[5]

Yorubas affirm "that after a period of time, deceased parents are born again into the family of their surviving children."[6] They inspect a new-born babe with great care, searching for traces of likeness to a paternal forbear; and if they find such a likeness, the child is given the name of this particular ancestor,

[1] HM. ii. 357.
[2] GGC. 632.
[3] *Op. cit.*, pp. 18 and 29.
[4] Cf. p. 16.
[5] NTG. 66 and 67. Cf. also AS. 80.
[6] Johnson: *History of the Yorubas*, p. 26.

and "there is no hesitation in saying that it must be this deceased forbear who is born again in this child." [1]

In the Oil Rivers district, farther south, Miss Kingsley observed that the doctrine of reincarnation is strongly held. A new baby is shown a selection of small articles belonging to deceased members of the family, and if he grasps one of them, he thereby indicates that he is its former owner. She was of opinion that the character of the funeral was deemed to decide the status of the soul at its next birth, and that those who were thrown into the bush came back as slaves. [2]

Nassau gives it as the belief of Gabun tribes that "the dead, some of them, return to be born again, either into their own family or into any other family, or even into a beast." [3]

"Transmigration of souls is a common factor of Congo faith," says Claridge. [4] "Some physical peculiarity, a mannerism, anything which reminds them of some one dead, is taken as a proof that the spirit of that particular person has returned in the individual under notice. A tall thin white man, with a spring in his gait, was always considered to be the father of Ntalu, who, some years before, had fallen from a palm tree and broken his neck."

"On the Upper Congo among the Boloki it appears that every family has what is called a *liboma*, it may be a pool in the bush, or in the forest, or on an island; it may be a creek, or it may be a Bombax cotton tree; [5] but wherever the *liboma* may be it is regarded as the preserve of the unborn children of the family. The disembodied spirits (*mingoli*) of the deceased members of the family performed the duty of supplying these preserves with spirit-children to keep their families strong and numerous. They have very misty ideas as to how these *liboma* are supplied with the spirit-children (or *bingbongbo*), but I have a suspicion that underlying the *liboma* is some idea of reincarnation—some thought there was a rebirth of certain deceased members of the family, and others thought that the disembodied spirits had spirit-children, and these were sent to the *liboma* to be endowed

---

[1] Frobenius: *Voice of Africa*, i. 155.
[2] WAS. 114, 122, 123-25, 344-46.
[3] FWA. 237.
[4] WBT. 58.
[5] These great trees are found here and there along the river's bank.

in due time with bodies. . . . If a man has one child by a wife, and no more, he thinks some one has bewitched his *liboma* by taking the family's stock of children from it and hiding them. . . . Only the family to which the *liboma* belongs can give birth to the unborn infant spirits there."[1] "These spirits of unborn children can make boys and girls thin and weak, but are to be appeased by the proper kind of medicine man preparing a suitable feast for them."[2] The names of the dead are "passed on to children if there is any likeness of the child to the deceased; and some natives have a misty idea of the possibility of the rebirth of the deceased in the child who bears the likeness."[3]

A young man of the Batetela tribe, which dwells on the San-kuru River, in South-central Congoland, told the Rev. C. C. Bush of the Methodist Episcopal Church (South) that a birth-mark on his knee was the scar from a wound which one of his ancestors had received in battle.[4]

In the Mweru-Bangweulu district, diviners often discover in cases of pregnancy that a certain relative is coming to be reborn; and "every difficult case of birth is supposed to be a case of re-incarnation." The reborn individual is given the name that he had before.[5]

The Akamba of Kitui (Kenya Colony) believe that crippled children are reincarnations of deceased people who were similarly affected; and they give such children the names they bore in their previous lifetime.[6] When Krapf was told, at the end of 1848, that "The Wanika believe that the spirit of a dying person goes into a child unborn, and that thus every one is born a second time" (at any rate that is how he phrased the information that he had received), he wrote the following lines in his diary: "This was the first time that I had heard of the transmigration of souls as a belief among the Wanika, and I think that only a few of them are acquainted with the idea, which, perhaps, has been learned from the Banians in Mombaz, or from the Mohamme-dans, who may have heard of it in their intercourse with Hindoos.

[1] ACC. 129-30, 291.
[2] ACC. 273.
[3] ACC. 322.
[4] Cf. pp. 16 f.
[5] IHB. 168, 225-26.
[6] BBM. 159.

As children tolerably resemble their parents the Wanika believe that one of the deceased forefathers of the family has entered into the child, and that, therefore, this child resembles him."[1]

The Baila doctrine of rebirth, which Smith has explored with patience and penetration,[2] is marked by the following characteristics. The great *mizhimo* (gods) of the various communities, such as Shimunenga, are not reborn. A soul which a warlock has magically snatched from a corpse or a living person is not reborn; such a "pressed-one" has utterly perished.[3] Sooner or later all other persons return to earth; a woman sometimes returning as a man, or a man as a woman. "A man cannot be reborn on earth through his daughters, only through his son. The children, sons and daughters, take the mother's clan name, but it is not her people, it is the father's people, that are born in her sons"[4]—an interesting mark of passage, by the by, from the matrilineal to the patrilineal conception of society. Baila have more than one method of discovering the identity of a reincarnated spirit. Sometimes they blow water over the child, addressing it at the same time by the name of a forbear who has been indicated by the diviner's method; if the child cries at the touch of the water, that is unimportant, but if it cries whenever it is called by that name, they know that a mistake has been made and appeal to the diviner again. Sometimes they place the child to the breast and pronounce the names of its grandfather and other forbears; if it begins to suck at the mention of a name, they are satisfied of its identity with that particular ancestor. Once its identity is established, its birth-name is fixed; for "as the ancestor has come back to earth he naturally bears the name he had during his previous sojourn."[5] This name is regarded as very sacred—much too sacred for common use. Curiously enough this ancestor whose name he bears, and whom he is, is also worshipped as his guardian spirit—a mystery which our author seeks to understand. "A man's guardian spirit, his tute-

[1] TRML. 201.
[2] IPNR. ii. 152-163.
[3] IPNR. ii. 93.
[4] IPNR. ii. 2.
[5] IPNR. i. 365.

lary genius," says Smith, "is the reincarnate spirit within him: shall we say, is himself. The genius is not only within him, but, in a sense, external to himself, protecting and guiding him. Now at first sight this appears to be an incongruous conception, resulting from the fusion of two disparate ideas derived from different sources. One might imagine that one set of ancestors believed in reincarnation; that another set believed in a guardian spirit, a father or grandfather who, while not actually reincarnated, constituted himself the genius of his descendant. These two sets of people, we say, might have coalesced and one belief become superimposed upon the other in the minds of the children." [1] Our author is, however, inclined to the opinion that the ancestors of the Baila had a philosophic doctrine of the soul, more in line with Plato's idea of an indwelling demon, which has come down to their degenerate children in an obscure form; and he suggests, further, that the modern doctrine of the subliminal self forms a psychological basis for the Baila belief.[2] To seek an explanation of Bantu dogma in conjectural racial degeneration, is, I am convinced, to look in the wrong direction; but his last suggestion is worth considering, and his first guess is probably correct.

Bakaonde and Alunda, in the north-west corner of Rhodesia, believe just as implicitly and devoutly in reincarnation.[3] It is the entrance of the spirit (*mukishi*) into the womb that causes the first perceptible movement of the foetus, so the people think; and as soon as a woman becomes conscious of "quickening," she devotes herself (we are not told how) to the cult of the (as yet) unidentified spirit, lest the spark of life should be withdrawn. Melland's generalisation—"they believe that every one who dies is born again in the person of some infant of the same family"— was probably not meant to cover the case of witches and other criminals who are denied mortuary rites; but the honoured dead, at any rate, return so regularly in their grandchildren, nephews and nieces (if one may use our terms of relationship) that reincarnation is practically limited to two generations. That spirits

---

[1] IPNR. ii. 157.
[2] IPNR. ii. 157-59.
[3] WBA. 56, 131, 150-51, 166-67, 170-72. The Konde of North Nyasa scoff at this idea. SRK. 195.

are not sexless is shown by the ancient demand that wives should accompany their husbands into the world beyond the grave;[1] nevertheless, spirits of persons of one sex are said to return sometimes in babes of the other. A child may be a reincarnation of either a maternal or paternal relative—probably because the tribe is passing, with slow and hesitating feet, from matrilineal to patrilineal conceptions of relationship;[2] but to the rule that spirits do not reincarnate themselves in children that are not, in this broad sense, of their own lineage, there is but one exception: if, by chance, a man slays an animal in which a spirit of another family or tribe has reincarnated itself, the spirit thus turned adrift is likely to take refuge in the slayer's unborn babe. Upon the birth of a child, a diviner is called to name the spirit that has thus returned to human society, and the correctness of his finding may be easily tested: for instance, place a coin (or beads) in the child's hand and call its name aloud, and if the child drops the coin and cries, the diviner was evidently in error; or if a babe falls ill after the spirit-name has been conferred upon it, it is well to summon a second diviner to correct or confirm the finding of the first. Since a diviner, with all his astuteness, would sometimes be encompassed with difficulties if he had to name a spirit of an alien family or tribe who had passed from a slain animal into the slayer's child, it is customary to call such a child Chiwilo (from *ku wilwa*, "to inherit a quality or disposition"), "because its clan is changed: it is of another totem."

The incongruous Ila conception that puzzled Smith prevails among the Bakaonde and Alunda, also: a discarnate spirit may be reincarnated in several children or animals at the same time. Melland and his collaborators, with an intolerance of logical inconsistencies to which their Native friends are strangers, find relief in the plea that tribesmen believe, not that the discarnate spirit itself enters the womb to be reproduced in full, but that it sends forth a complete, life-giving emanation of its eternal self, and still remains as it was before. This explanation appeals to our European craving for consistency, and smacks, moreover, of ancient Greek and Hindu lore; but if it can be established that the unaided Bantu mind has pondered such ideas as "eternity"

[1] See pp. 50 f. and cf. p. 57.
[2] Cf. WBA. 42, 46.

and "emanation," taking pains to find missing links in its chain of reasoning, we shall have to accredit it with a refinement of thought that most observers have never suspected. We are already under obligation to Melland for many valuable facts and much wise and sympathetic criticism, and our debt would be larger still if he had submitted compelling evidence that this excellent interpretation is really indigenous.

In collecting evidence of Bantu belief on this subject, I am impressed with the fact that it nearly all comes from either West Coast tribes, or tribes tinged with the West Coast variety of Bantu culture, and increases in volume as one approaches the Negro belt.[1] The Akamba may be an exception, though the group to which they belong is not without peculiar linguistic affinities with the North-west Bantu and those of the Western Congo, Gabon, and Cameroons.[2] Among the Eastern Bantu, the doctrine of *reborn* souls appears to be uncommon. I say "appears," partly because absence of evidence does not prove absence of the belief, and partly because some features of the available evidence have a doubtful meaning. Let me illustrate this last point with three examples.

At the Baganda ceremony for testing the legitimacy of a new-born babe and adopting it into the clan, the grandmother slowly repeated the names of its father's deceased ancestors, beginning with the one nearest to the child's father; and if the child smiled at the mention of one of the names, it was taken as a sign that that ancestor-spirit would be its guardian. If the child did not thrive, another guardian spirit would be appointed, because the

---

[1] It is noteworthy that the Bagesu (of the valleys and plateaux on the southern and western heights of Mt. Elgon) and the Basoga (between Mt. Elgon and the Nile), who are thought to be of purely Negro stock, have the idea of guardian-spirits, but not that of reincarnation in descendants. Among the former, "the child was named as soon as possible after its birth, by the father if it was a boy and by the mother if it was a girl. In either case, it was called after some deceased ancestor of the father's clan, whose ghost was then expected to look after it. If the child did not thrive, the parents consulted a medicine-man, who took an augury, and would sometimes advise them to change the child's name, for the ghost whose name it bore was causing the trouble and another ghost had to be called upon to befriend it." (GS. 24.) Among the Basoga, "the ghost of one of its ancestors became the guardian of a child, though it was never supposed to enter into it as its animating spirit." (GS. 106.) The agreement and disagreement of this theory with that of reincarnation is alike meaningful.

[2] CSBSL. ii. 30.

first one did not like it.[1] Belief that a child is under the guardianship of a particular ancestral spirit, is obviously not the same as belief that a particular spirit is reborn in the body of the child; but it is significant that the identity of the guardian spirit, like that of the reborn soul, is thought to be indicated by the babe's recognition of a name.

Kidd says that the Kafirs absolutely deny that they believe in reincarnation in children, but that the fumigation ceremony to which babes are exposed soon after birth is thought to impart to the babe a portion of a corporate ancestral spirit, which he calls "a part of the *itongo* of the same grandfather." [2] This comes perilously near to reincarnation; especially when it is remembered that, while some Baila allege that the spirit reincarnates itself in the child in the womb, others affirm that it enters the child at the naming ceremony.[3]

The Becwana disclaim belief in rebirth; but behind their notion of the "namesake" there is something closely akin to the doctrine which they disavow. Here is the translation of a note which I wrote from the dictation of a Native who was well versed in Bakwena lore; it deals with another subject, and its evidence upon the point at issue is all the more valuable because unintentional. "If a person is ill, it is sometimes said: 'It is the vexation of an ancestor, perhaps your grandfather or your grandmother.' Then a handful of earth is scraped from the grave of that person, and the patient is cleansed with it, mixed with 'medicine.' If it is not known where that person's grave is, then his namesake can come and wash, and with the dirt from his body, mixed with 'medicine,' he can with his own hand cleanse the patient, and say: 'If it is the name of him after whom I am called, I am here. Recover!' That is to rebuke the sickness." The Becwana are evidently of opinion that the namesake of a divine ancestor is possessed of much more than his ancestor's appellation!

Smith has shown [4] that though the Baila belong in the main to the Eastern stream of Bantu migration, there are linguistic indications that they have become modified by West Coast blood and

[1] Bg. 61-64.
[2] SC. 12-13, 281-86.
[3] IPNR. ii. 153.
[4] IPNR. i. 18.

culture; and he has further suggested, as we have seen, that their peculiar doctrine of rebirth, which he has so ably expounded, may be due to the interweaving of two strands of ancestral belief. Although final judgment must await the unveiling of Bantu thought in hundreds of uninvestigated communities, it appears probable, in the light of our present knowledge, that the Eastern Bantu believed in the guardianship of particular ancestor-spirits, especially of those whose names they bore; while the Western Bantu absorbed more of the Negro belief in the return of ancestral souls in the bodies of their descendants.

Whatever our successors may discover the Bantu doctrine of metempsychosis to be, they are unlikely to find that it lays the soul under necessity of passing successively through bird, quadruped, fish, reptile and man; and they are sure to find that it has no moral significance,—no suspicion, for instance, that the soul passes at death into that species of animal that best conforms to its acquired disposition or its debased instincts—no notion that its posthumous adventures will enable it to expiate its misdeeds or attain purity.   Nor shall we find the Bantu saying what the author of *The Wisdom of Solomon* says (viii. 19-20) in his Greek way:

"Now I was a child of parts, and a good soul fell to my lot.
Nay, rather, being good, I came into a body undefiled."

CHAPTER III

ANCESTOR-WORSHIP

NO FESTIVAL OF THE DEAD

WHERE the cult of ancestor-worship holds sway, popular Festivals of the Dead often command respect. Mention has already been made of the Japanese Festival of the Dead,[1] when burial-grounds are illuminated, lanterns lit to guide the returning spirits home, and little trays of egg-plant, fruit, rice and cucumber set for their refreshment. In China Confucius worshipped ancestor-spirits and taught men that it was their duty to do so; and the fifteenth day of the seventh moon is observed as a sort of All Souls' Day, for the benefit of kinless ghosts. On the twenty-fourth of August, the fifth of October and the eighth of November, the Romans celebrated special rites by which the door of hell (*lapis Manalis*) was opened to give the dead free access to the open air. From February the thirteenth to the twenty-first, during the festival of *Parentalia*, in the last month of the old Roman year, the dead emerged from their common dwelling in the nether world without ritual assistance; and pious families gladdened their ancestral shades with banquets, oblations of food, flowers or other gifts, and by placing little lamps upon their tombs. At the *Lemuria*, on the ninth, eleventh and thirteenth of May, when the wandering shades of those who died before their time were thought to be specially meddlesome, the father of a Roman family threw black beans nine times at midnight to keep the *Lemures* from the house.[2] These notions were rooted so deep in the thought of the Latin people that Christianity could do no more than clothe them with chastened customs; and on All Souls' Day you may still see the cemetery of *Pere la Chaise* in Paris thronged with pious folk,

[1] P. 153.
[2] ALRP. 71, 131.

clad in crape, laying tributes of flowers upon the graves of their loved ones and paying other homage to the dead. Departed rulers of Ashanti are cheered with libations and sacrifices on set dates which occur twice in every successive forty-three days, and are known respectively as the Big or Sunday *Adae*, and the Wednesday *Adae*.[1] But Bantu ancestor-worshippers know nothing of a Feast of All Souls, nor of any special days when the deathless dead wend their way from the underworld to the homes in which they loved, and still love, to linger. They evidently feel that the unseen world is all around them,[2] and that those who are lost to sight are never far away; but the clan-spirit colours their religious conceptions, as it does their political philosophy, and, with one or two remarkable exceptions,[3] no one worships the spirits of those who could not command their fealty were they present in the flesh. What Smith says of the Baila[4] is substantially true of all Bantu clans: the gods of a husband do not help his wife, nor do her gods help him, and the gods of their children are those of that side of the house from which property and status are inherited—though it is true the mother's divinities may demand occasional attention from children of patrilineal clans that have not divested themselves of all remnants of ancient matrilineal methods of succession.

TRIBAL AND FAMILY WORSHIP

Bantu ancestor-worship takes two forms: public and private. For such public benefits as victory, rain, fertility of lands and herds, salvation from epidemics and ravaging beasts, and often for successful hunting and fishing, resort is had to the spirits of the ruling dynasty. As occasion demands, great public acts of worship are called for by the paramount chief, who presides over them as priest of his ancestral line. Those which mark the inauguration of the agricultural or the hunting season, or the completion of harvest, recur with the regularity of the seasons; but dynastic spirits are not worshipped as a matter of mere routine

[1] AS. 92.
[2] See p. 71.
[3] See pp. 75, 77, 80.
[4] IPNR. ii. 166.

on fixed dates; they are approached only when the soul of the
community is disturbed by a lively sense of its need of supernatural aid.   These dynastic functions are probably what Ellenberger had in mind when he remarked [1] that almost all the national feasts of the Basuto are in honour of the shades, who are
felt to be present and taking part in them.   They are not marked
by solemn ceremonies which readily suggest worship to the Western mind, appearing rather as politico-religious affirmations of
tribal solidarity, at which each unit in the coalition shows its loyalty by homage and oblations to the dynastic gods—a characteristic which probably accounts for their prominence in larger political federations, such as those of Bechuanaland and Basutoland.
But they are essentially ancient acts of religion, and are observed,
often in time-worn forms, by the broken political groups that
are scattered all over Bantu Africa.

For private boons, and for protection or deliverance from private ills, each ancestor-worshipper relies [2] upon the spirits of his
own forbears.   In some tribes simple offerings are occasionally
made to the ancestor-spirits of a family almost as a matter of
routine.[3]   When Kikuyu elders eat, they "always throw a little
food to the spirits before commencing their meal, and at a beer-
drinking always pour a little beer on the ground to propitiate
the spirits. . . . Women, too, when they are cooking porridge
or gruel, invariably throw some on the ground for the spirits." [4]
Alunda have a similar practice.[5]   At a Konde carousal each
drinker spills a little beer on the ground as an offering to his ancestors.[6]   A Mwila traveller, reaching home, hungry and thirsty,
will not quench his thirst till he has poured out a few drops of
water for the spirits, or eat before throwing a morsel of food
on the ground for his unseen protectors.   "If he does not do
that, but simply eats at once, and a piece falls from his hand,"
a tribesman is quoted as saying, "he knows that the ghosts are
asking for a taste.   That is how all the Baila do.   They pay

[1] HB. 246.
[2] But all Bantu are animists, as well as ancestor-worshippers; and animists look
to magic for a charmed life and the smiles of fortune.
[3] LSAT. ii. 363, and see my pp. 365 f.
[4] BBM. 52.
[5] WBA. 170.
[6] SRK. 128-29.

respect to the ghosts. When they smoke, they first throw a piece of tobacco on the ground for the ghosts. Should a man eat without recognising the ghost, he would vomit and grow sick."[1] So, also, "a person visiting at a relative's will first scatter a little food on the ground as an offering to the family ghosts."[2] When Nika or Giryama people eat rice, they put aside a little ball of it for the spirits.[3] Pious people, and people who pride themselves upon their good breeding, make some simple acknowledgment to their ancestor-spirits for every new day that dawns upon them, every meal they take, every pot of beer they brew, and every batch of snuff they grind,[4] never taking a drink of water without spewing some of it upon the ground as a libation to dwellers in the underworld,[5] and accompanying every sneeze with a pious exclamation.[6] These are but pietistic embellishments, like our "grace before meat," in which the shell of devotion is small and its kernel very much smaller; acts of high homage are husbanded for those times of doubt and danger when the gods overwhelm men with a sense of dependence upon the unseen; for the red-letter days of family life, such as births, marriages, or reunion with members long absent or estranged; and for occasions when the gods call men to attention by dreams, visions, reincarnations, or sickness or other calamity in the family. It is this last fea-

---

[1] IPNR. ii. 123.

[2] IPNR. i. 145.

[3] Krapf & Rebmann's *Nika-English Dictionary*, *Art.* "Koma."

[4] Cf. RLR. 44-45.

[5] Cf. AS. 137.

[6] This custom has prevailed among Aryan nations also for a very long period (CPP. 539-543). I have heard a sneeze turned into "God bless us!" in Devonshire, and into *Modimo o nthuse!* ("God help me!") in Bechuanaland. Kafir mothers teach their children to call upon *Tixo* when they sneeze; Zulus, believing that sneezing is caused by ancestor-spirits, cry "Father!" or "Mother!" if either of these parents has died lately, or "Chiefs!" if they cannot distinguish the particular spirit that is affecting them (RSZ. 221); and Angoni called out the name of an ancestor, Zulu's people crying "Gama!" and Mputa's, "Jere!" (NGW. 104.) When a Mwila sneezes, he says, "*Tsu!* My namesake (or guardian spirit), stand by me always!" (IPNR. ii. 156.) A Boloki man exclaims, *Ngai nya, motu mosusu!* ("It is not I, but some one else!") The background of this exclamation is a belief that the spirit escapes through the nostrils; and he means to say, "I am surprised that you want to call away my spirit; I really am not the person you think I am, but somebody else." (ACC. 108.) If these were ever acts of worship, they have been eviscerated by time and use. Zulus regard sneezing, especially that of an invalid, as a lucky sign; but Becwana induce artificial sneezing when they want to forget a bad dream, and spit when they want to remember a pleasant one.

ture of ancestor-worship which gives point to the Baila proverb: "The god that speaks up is the one that gets the meat." [1]

OCCASIONS FOR THE WORSHIP OF FAMILY-GODS: I. BIRTH

Some ceremony for relating the newly born to the ancestral spirits, or for securing the interest of these spirits in the child, is general in Bantu tribes. Kidd says [2] that at the feast which is held when a mother emerges from her puerperium, the Kafirs slaughter an ox to thank the *amatongo* that the mother did not die in childbirth, and to show gratitude for the child which the ancestral spirits have given to the tribe. Macdonald writes [3] that when the child is about two days old, the mother sways it to and fro in the smoke of a fire of sweet-smelling herbs and tomboti-wood, which is made at the north side of the hut; and when the child cries, she exclaims, "There goes the thief!" supposing that the evil spirits escape from the child during this ceremony. This fumigation is repeated by women in attendance during the month of the puerperium, to ensure mental vigour, wisdom, valour, strategy and eloquence. While it is being performed the last time, a number of cattle are collected outside the hut, and prayer is offered to the spirits. Of these beasts the one that happens to urinate first is sacrificed; its lungs and liver are hung in the hut as an offering to the spirits; and a vessel, filled with its blood, is placed "at the side nearest the north," the bearer saying, as he lays it down, "Eat now, ye gods, and be filled," and the by-standers shouting approval.

After mentioning that the Basuto sacrificed a sheep when a woman became pregnant, Ellenberger says: [4] "At the birth of the child the father offered another sheep, by virtue of which he took formal possession of the child and placed it under the special protection of the family gods. The fat which covered the entrails of the victim was stretched and coiled round the neck of the infant. On the recovery of the mother, he again had to offer a sheep, the skin of which was made into a *thari*, in which

[1] IPNR. ii. 318.
[2] SC. 25. So does William Shaw in his *Story of My Mission*, etc., p. 453.
[3] LA. 154-55.
[4] HB. 256.

the mother would carry the infant on her back." Casalis mentions [1] that "when a young mother is about to return to her husband," from her mother's village, where she has gone for her confinement, "her parents offer a sacrifice for her purification, and place the flesh of the victim upon a draught-ox" (he probably means a pack-ox) "to convey it to her abode"; and that from the skin of this sacrifice they make a *thari*, which serves to hold the child on the mother's back till it is weaned.

After the birth of a child, a Herero father sacrifices an ox, sheep, or goat, the animal being suffocated (the usual Herero method of slaughter) with its face turned to the north. A small piece of the sacrificial flesh is taken out of the cooking-pot before the rest, and brought for the mother to consecrate by breathing on it; after which it is placed on the child's big toe, so that the child also may consecrate it. That piece of flesh is kept in a small vessel till the navel-string has sloughed off, whereupon the mother, emerging from her seclusion, takes her babe to the place of the holy fire, and presents it to the divine ancestor, so that both she and her babe may be free to enter her own house. Upon this occasion the father takes the child into his arms and publicly gives it its name. [2]

An Ndau woman who has been safely delivered of a child, makes a little beer, and at a private family gathering puts up a prayer of thanksgiving for her child, pouring a small cupful of beer upon the ground at the door, as a libation, and asking the spirits of old women, who are said to be specially fond of children, to care for the child. Tribes of this group preserve enough attachment to ancient matrilineal usage to warrant the assumption that the Ndau mother addresses her prayer to the spirits of her ancestors, and that the benign old women in the other world are also of her lineage, though the writer [3] does not refer to these points. The father names his child on the day after the navel-cord has separated, but there is no religious ceremony upon this occasion, unless the pouring of an infusion of wild asparagus over the father contains some sort of religious significance; but when the child is about six months old, the father presents it to the

[1] Bs. 192.
[2] *Journal of the South African Folklore Society*, May, 1870.
[3] Dr. Wilder in the *Hartford Seminary Record*, April, 1907.

family spirits, together with offerings of beer, etc. Among some
tribes of this same Mashona group, there is a striking ceremony
of naming the child: the child is laid on a mat, together with one
of the opposite sex; and the midwife, having asked the parents
to name the child, blows water over it and addresses it by the
given name.[1] Blowing plain or medicated water from the mouth
is a frequent accompaniment of Bantu prayer to ancestral spirits:
the technical term for this rite among the Becwana is *go pashetsa*.[2]
But the practice of lustrating an infant soon after birth prevails
among "primitive" people in many parts of the world, and is
often connected with the giving of a name. The Maori, for instance, repeated a long list of ancestral names and gave the child
the name that was being pronounced when it sneezed; and at the
same time they sprinkled the infant with water.[3]

When a child of the Bawenda is four days old, the "doctor"
comes to give it its name, which has been chosen by the mother,
and to make slight incisions in the child's body and limbs and rub
"medicine" into the cuts to make the child strong. A few days
later the "doctor" comes again to tie a charm around the child's
neck, arm, ankle, or waist, and to offer a sacrifice for it.[4]

Junod mentions the *hondlola* rite,[5] which is practised by the
Thonga, and consists of sacrifice and prayer for a blessing on
the child.

A Konde child is taken, a few weeks after birth, by its paternal
grandfather to the *ikiyinja* ("the family place of prayer"); and
there the grandfather spits into the palm of his hand, and, laying
it in blessing upon the child's head, invokes for him the care of
his ancestor-spirits.[6]

The Baila, having ascertained through a diviner which of its
forbears is reborn in the new baby, return to the hut; offer water
at the door; greet the newcomer by the name it used to bear;
and blow water from the mouth over the child. The name thus

---

[1] MLC. 9.

[2] See Index: "Blowing water from the mouth"; and cf. the Thonga utterance
of the sacramental *Tsu!* to which Junod makes frequent reference in LSAT.

[3] MN. 68.

[4] R. BAAS., 1905, iii. 203.

[5] LSAT. i. 57.

[6] SRK. 45.

given is the baptismal or birth name—the great name which is known only to a few of its most intimate friends.[1]

In the clans of Uganda, where the marriage of a child's parents is not of paramount importance to it, the child was legitimised at the naming ceremony, which took place at the house of the head of the clan and under his presidency. No child could go through the ceremony alone; nor could children of one sex only, whatever their number; but those who went through the ceremony together might vary in age from a few months to four or five years, and might be of different parentage. Various methods of testing the legitimacy of a child by means of its umbilical cord were in vogue in different clans; but the commonest method was to place a piece of its umbilical cord in a pot of water, concluding that it was legitimate if the cord floated, but not if the cord sank. The women sat in a row with their feet extended, and the head of the clan jumped over the legs of each,[2] the mother telling the child that he was its father. The child's paternal grandmother then slowly recited the names of its deceased ancestors, beginning with the one nearest to her son, and the one whose name was being mentioned when the child smiled was regarded as its guardian spirit. After naming the child, the grandmother shaved its head.[3]

Speaking of the customs of the Akamba, in Kenya Colony, the Hon. Charles Dundas says:[4] "There is not much ceremony connected with the birth of a child. A goat is killed and sacrificed with prayers for the welfare of mother and child."

Although the people of Northern Nigeria are not Bantu, they are as near in descent as they are in propinquity, and it is interesting to note that somewhat similar customs prevail among them. Cardinall describes[5] a rite of consecrating a child to a totem or ancestor, which is performed when the little one is about two years old, generally upon the occasion of some unusual happening in the family, such as illness or death. It consists in discovering,

[1] IPNR. ii. 152.
[2] The Baganda regard this as a ceremonial equivalent for conjugal intercourse.
[3] Bg. 61-64.
[4] JRAI., 1913, p. 519.
[5] NTG. 71.

by means of divination, what ancestor or totem [1] desires to take the child under his care; placing a pot of medicated water on the burial-mound built in his honour; sacrificing there a cock for a boy or a guinea-fowl for a girl; and repeating the formula: "I give you this cock and this infant; watch him; take care of him; see that his mother and he be always in good health." While this is being done, the mother prepares food, and the parents, having roasted the liver, the heart, and the lungs of the bird, place them with a small part of the food on the pot of water, and thus address the spirit: "See, I give you food and a bird to eat. I beg you to keep all disease from the mother and the child." Then they tie the bones of the bird around the loins of the child, and in the afternoon wash the child with water from this pot.

It is doubtful whether the offering of sacrifice to ancestral shades is a common feature of Bantu Puberty Rites; but Ellenberger states [2] that the Basuto pursue this course whenever they circumcise a child of either sex, and tells an astonishing story of how, in 1828, Moshesh, Paramount Chief of the Basuto, surmounted the difficulty of offering a sacrifice upon his grandfather's grave before his son and heir, Letsie, could be circumcised. Moshesh's grandfather, Peete, was eaten by a well-known gang of men who had been driven to cannibalism by the turmoil and famine that followed Chaka's raids; and Moshesh decided that, to all intents and purposes, the cannibals were the grave of his ancestor. So he summoned them to his court; and having slaughtered an ox, had the chyme from its stomach rubbed over the cannibals, instead of being placed, according to custom, upon the ancestral grave!

OCCASIONS FOR THE WORSHIP OF FAMILY-GODS: 2. MARRIAGE

"Among the caffres of Natal," Casalis says,[3] "it is usual for the parents of the bride to make a present of three oxen to the family whose alliance they have accepted. One replaces the ornaments which the young wife wore in childhood, and which now belong

---

[1] This writer's use of the term "totem" is somewhat ambiguous, but he seems to use it as equivalent to "totem-clan."

[2] HB. 227-28 and 256.

[3] Bs. 201.

to her sisters. . . . The second is offered to the manes of the bridegroom's ancestors, in order to obtain their consent to the union. The third finds a place among the herd which has furnished the marriage portion." In tribes of this great group the sacrifice of a beast to the ancestral spirits—"the shedding of blood," as they phrase it—is an imperative marriage rite if the bride is to be the head wife of the bridegroom; but it is often omitted in the marriage of secondary wives. Since dancing is a conspicuous feature of this sacrificial feast, the victim is called "the *umdudo* beast."

"At every Basuto marriage an ox had to be sacrificed by the father of the bride, so that the Shades might look favourably on the marriage."[1] "The father of the young man gave to the father of the girl a number of cattle, which had previously been agreed upon. These having been accepted, the father of the bride killed an ox, which after their portion had been duly offered to the Shades, was divided according to rule. . . . The spouses were smeared with the gall of the animal, and in some cases the fat of the entrails was rubbed with a special medicine, and made into a collar, which was hung round the neck of the bride, descending as far as her chest. . . . Wristlets were also made of the fat, and, having been duly medicated, were placed round the wrists of both parties, who were thereby solemnly recommended to the care of the Shades of their ancestors."[2]

The Becwana are practically at one with the Basuto in their rendering of this rite; and, although the slaughtered beast was never called a sacrifice in my hearing, the concomitant ritual involves that interpretation. The pots in which the flesh is cooked, the hearthstones upon which they stand, and the joints of the limbs of both spouses are carefully marked with a "purifying" paste; the flesh and chyme of the victim is lustrated with the local equivalent for "holy water"; a slice of flesh, cut from the udder or the breast of the victim, is roasted and eaten by the married pair before the rest of the meat is served;[3] and the sheet of fat around the intestines, after being spread out into a muslin-like veil and "medicated," is cut into two strips, one of which is

[1] HB. 256.
[2] HB. 275-76. Cf. also Bs. 199.
[3] Cf. p. 183.

draped around the neck of the bride, and the other around the
neck of the bridegroom. In some Secwana tribes it is customary
to cut this sheet of fat into three strips, and to place the third
strip around the neck of the younger sister of the bride's mother.
They say that this curious custom is grounded in the fact that if
the bride's mother had died in her early married life, her younger
sister would have become her substitute (according to their law of
santlo) and therefore mother of the bride; but this explanation
still needs to be explained, for the surviving mother who has
never needed a substitute is not thus adorned.

The Ndau people of Mashonaland and adjacent Portuguese
territory notify their family spirits when they send a bride-price
for a wife for one of their sons, and when they receive a bride-
price for one of their daughters, saying to the spirits, "Look
after your child." [1] If a Mashona father failed to offer (not
sacrifice) to his ancestral spirits the bride-price which he received
for his daughter, he would be blamed for any sickness which
befell her or her children. [2]

A Herero bride participates in many ceremonies at the place
of the holy fire, and in one of them, her father squirts a jet of
water over her from his mouth, which, as we have seen, [3] is a
Bantu prayer-rite. Upon her arrival at the bridegroom's home,
other rites are celebrated at the holy fire there, and, also, the
newly married pair have to consecrate the flesh of the sheep that
is then slaughtered for the feast. [4]

An extempore threshold prayer to the spirits is regarded as
essential to the proper celebration of marriage rites by some
tribes on the Zambesi and farther north.

In the Thonga marriage ceremony, [5] a goat is sacrificed at the
door of the hut of the bride's mother; and the bride's father,
having sacramentally touched his tongue with a pellet of half-
digested grass from the paunch of the victim, stands behind
the wedded pair and offers to his ancestral spirits some such
extempore prayer as this: "My fathers, my grandfathers (men-

[1] Dr. Wilder: *Hartford Seminary Record*, April, 1907.
[2] MLC. 23.
[3] See Index: "Blowing water from the mouth."
[4] Cf. pp. 183, 294.
[5] LSAT. i. 110-12. Cf. also IRM. Oct., 1922.

tioning each by name), look! To-day my child is leaving me. She enters the wedded life. Look at her, accompany her where she will live. May she also found a village, may she have many children, may she be happy, good and just. May she be on good terms with those with whom she will be." Then the astragalus of the right leg of the victim is pouched in one end of a long strip of skin cut from its belly and breast, and with this cestus the father of the bride girdles his daughter.

Wachagga marriage rites, which are unusually protracted, culminate in the sacrifice of two bulls by the bridegroom's father. At ordinary sacrifices it is customary all round Kilimanjaro for worshippers to don what they call *kishongu,* that is, rings cut from the hide of the victim and usually worn on toe or finger; but at this hymeneal sacrifice there is a significant variation. Bride and bridegroom are seated on the ground face to face, and a strip of hide from the sacrificed beast is pierced at both ends and slipped over a wrist of each, thus forming a double *sishongu* ring. While thus linked together, they are instructed and exhorted by their elders, and then the strip of hide is severed, leaving each with half. Next day the bridegroom is told that he may consummate the marriage.[1]

Similar evidence from most Central and Western Bantu tribes is unfortunately lacking. Excessive joviality and display of bride-price divert the attention of observers from the religious features of these wedding ceremonies; but as sympathetic seekers after the better elements in Bantu belief penetrate more deeply into the life of these tribes, they are almost sure to discover ways in which these people, also, bring their ancestors into their marital contracts.

OCCASIONS FOR THE WORSHIP OF FAMILY-GODS: 3. SICKNESS

Ancestor-spirits reveal themselves in personal and public calamities;[2] and sickness is therefore a special occasion for family worship. In his evidence before a Government Commission,[3] ex-King Cetewayo stated that when a Zulu is seriously ill, his rela-

[1] K. 238.
[2] See pp. 96 ff.
[3] R. 1883. P. 532.

tives choose an ox or a cow and offer it to the spirits, saying: "We offer unto you, spirits of our departed relations, this beast, in order that you, who are the chief relations of this patient, may invite all your other spiritual relations to partake of this beast offered unto you, even as you did on earth while alive, in behalf of the patient; satisfy yourselves and show kindness unto this patient, your relation, by giving him good health." Then the beast is slaughtered and eaten by the patriarchal group. When they eat the fetlocks, they offer again a similar prayer to the spirits, and, taking the large gut which they have reserved for the purpose, they scatter its contents in the sick room. Callaway mentions that the gall of the victim is poured over the invalid, so that the *amatongo* (spirits) may come and see him and lick him and make him well; that its tendons, after being charred and medicated, are rubbed into scarifications on his body; [1] that its flesh is allowed to remain all night in the hut, so that the *amatongo* may eat it; and that next morning, after the sacrificial feast has been held, the bones of the victim are burnt, lest some wizard should thwart the recovery of the patient by using them in a magical manner. [2]

An Omuherero (sing. of Ovaherero) who is seriously ill is taken to the holy fire, on which there is a pot containing meat killed for the purpose; and, as the pot boils, the sick man is carried round and round by his friends, who chant something like the following supplication to the divine ancestor (*omukuru*): "See, father, we have come here with this sick man to you, that he may soon recover." [3]

Smith tells us [4] that the divine ancestors of ordinary Baila families are worshipped, not upon set occasions, but only when their help is needed or when they make known their need by bringing trouble upon their kindred. "Such an occasion," he says, "is the illness of a member of the family. The diviner on being consulted may say that the sickness is caused by a divinity who thinks himself neglected. So the head of the family makes an offering in his house and prays. . . . Here is a prayer offered

[1] RSZ. 313.
[2] RSZ. 9.
[3] *Journal of the South African Folklore Society*, May, 1870.
[4] IPNR. ii. 175-76.

by a man on behalf of his child: 'Oh, my father, if it be thou (who art troubling him) leave the child alone that he may go about alone. Tsu! Oh, my father, what is the matter? You divinities who are without, he does not see you (*i.e.*, doesn't recognise you). Tsu! Oh, old man, leave him alone. If thou art crying for something to eat, he shall brew the beer thou criest for and make thee an offering. If it be thou, leave him alone that he may walk this very day. Tsu! Oh, my father, we worship thee!' If it is the head of the house himself who is sick, he makes an offering on his own behalf: 'Tsu! If it be thou, O leave me alone, that I may get well. What is it thou requirest? See, here is tobacco, here is water, here is beer. Leave me alone that I may enjoy myself.'

In contradistinction to simple and regular offerings which a Thonga family brings to its ancestral spirits, Junod mentions [1] what he calls "extraordinary family sacrifices," which are offered in cases of disease. Sometimes a diviner discovers that the disease has been caused by some particular spirit, who can be propitiated only by a specified offering, perhaps at a definite place, or possibly by a designated person. Such offerings are not necessarily living creatures; a bracelet may be offered, for instance, if the bones so ordain, the priest pouring consecrated beer over it and saying his prayer, after which it is fastened to the foot of the sick child. Illness may be caused by the ancestral spirits of either the maternal or the paternal line; but offerings to matrilineal spirits must be made by the maternal uncle (*malume*), and the part of the victim which is usually fastened to the invalid as a religious amulet must be taken from its *left* side and attached to the *left* side of the patient. Junod's example of prayers offered on these occasions is in the same strain as those quoted above, except that it is longer and more reproachful.

Casalis found the Basuto observing a similar practice. "Every disease is attributed to ancestral spirits," [2] he tells us; "thus medicine among these people is almost entirely a religious affair. The first thing is to discover, by means of the *litaola* (divining bones), under the influence of what *molimo* (god) the patient is supposed to be. Is it an ancestor on the father's side or the mother's?

---

[1] LSAT. ii. 362, 367-68.
[2] Bs. 249-250.

According as fate decides, the paternal or maternal uncle will offer the purifying sacrifice, but rarely the father or brother. This sacrifice alone can render efficacious the medicines prescribed by the *ngaka* (doctor). The latter points out the victim to be offered. Large and small animals are used in sacrifice; and sometimes, though not often, a cock. The colour, sex, and age of the animal, are determined by the indications drawn from the bones, a dream, or any other significative incident. As soon, as the victim is dead, they hasten to take the epiploön, or intestinal covering, which is considered the most sacred part, and put it round the patient's neck, after having twisted it to give it the form of a necklace. The gall is then poured upon the head of the patient, accompanied by the following prayer: 'Oh, gods, retire (or rather disperse yourselves); leave our brother in peace, that he may sleep his sleep.' A mixture of gall, liquid from the stomach, and pounded herbs, is then placed upon the hut, and all defiled persons are carefully removed from it."

In all essentials the Becwana usage is at one with that of the Basuto. When a person is ill, the Becwana send for a "doctor," who, according to the custom of these tribes, is a general practitioner rather than a specialist. Let me translate an account of a "doctor's" visit to his patient, which was written for me by one of my native friends. "When the 'doctor' arrives he unties his bones, and throws them upon the ground. Then he tells the sick man to throw them for himself. The sick man throws the bones two or three times. Then the 'doctor' enquires whether they have noticed anything unusual. They may mention what they take to be evidence of witchcraft that they have seen in the courtyard: perhaps the ashes have been strewn in an unwonted pattern—probably by dogs; perhaps a spoon has mysteriously disappeared—probably one of the children lost it: anything unusual, which leads them to suspect witchcraft. The 'doctor' says, 'Yes, that's it; he is bewitched.' Then they ask the 'doctor' to help them. He replies: 'If you like, I'll prepare him a potion; it is for you to say. But, you know, it is a case of witchcraft, and an ox would put him right.' 'You should say what is to be done,' they reply; 'you know your drugs; we don't know them. Of course, we called in a "doctor" the other day and told him to cure this man; and he could not do it. But, of course, they don't all drink out of the same bowl; [1] and it may be that you can.' The 'doctor' will now go and get 'medicine,' for he sees that they are ready with an ox. Then he comes to cure the man. He slaughters the ox and removes one of its legs; and he cuts off little pieces of its flesh, saying, 'These are cooked as "medicine," and this leg will be cooked for him to-morrow morning.' And the 'doctor' will carry all the rest of the carcase to his own home, where it will be eaten. [2] Sometimes the 'doctor' will tell them to produce a goat; and when the goat is slaughtered he mixes its blood with 'medicine' and tells them to wash the sick man with the mixture, or it may be to give it to the sick man to drink. And the 'doctor' takes all the carcase to his own home. Sometimes they cut off the ear of the sheep or goat; put 'medicine' into it; spin a piece of cord; thread it on the cord; and hang it round the sick man's neck. And the 'doctor' says, 'That's our ox; [3] let it stay till I come and take it.' "

The Native who gave me this account was able to sketch in graphic phrases scenes that he had often witnessed, and he had evidently formed an opinion of the "doctor's" motives and methods; but he had not been introduced to the esoteric significance of the "doctor's" doings. If the "doctor" had been describing the scene for us, he would probably have omitted many of these little graphic touches; but he would have shown us that even in this case of presumed witchcraft, the ancestral spirits were taken into the transaction, and that they, too, had their share of the slaughtered beast.

But sickness is not always due to witchcraft. Take a passage from the dictation of another Native, who had not the same power of graphic description, but who had eyes to see a little farther into the happenings. "When a person is being 'doctored,' and they say, 'It is a disease caused by the anger of his father, or mother, or grandfather, who is angry with him because of so-and-so; that is what has caused his sickness,' they at once prepare 'medicines' and call upon the name of the dead person. They say: 'So-and-so, what a heartless person you are! This person, where do you think you are taking him? Do pacify your heart,

---

[1] Equivalent to our phrase "eat off the same trencher."
[2] This is his perquisite, not his pay; his pay will come later.
[3] A eulogistic euphemism for what is really a goat or sheep.

and permit this person to rear the children which you left with him. There is a saying: A person dies, and a person remains. Please pray the spirits to permit him to sleep.' For they say spirits can talk with spirits, because they dwell together. In any emergency the dead are thought of by their living relatives. This comes from the divining-bones."

This last sentence is not the bit of philosophic dogmatism which it appears to be: the narrator merely means that the "bones" have revealed the cause of the disease. He makes no mention of sacrifice; because in the case which he describes the attempt is to mollify the angry spirit by lustration and prayer. But if this fails, the "dice" are cast again, till it is ascertained which animal in the herd will appease the spirit. The blood of this victim, or a bit of its flesh is used for the cure, and often an astragalus from one of its legs is tied with a cord or a strip of hide around the patient's neck or wrist. The same is done to a childless woman to cure her of barrenness; to a woman whose children die in infancy; to a woman whose husbands die soon after marriage; or to a man who has had similar misfortune with his wives. Misfortunes like these are always due to the anger of an offended spirit; [1] generally that of a father, grandfather, uncle, or elder brother. Of female relatives, the mother is the only one that has such power after death, except that the spirit of a deceased wife may show her displeasure by killing her successor. In all such cases sacrifice is offered to the offended spirit; the limbs and body of the unfortunate person are smeared with a

[1] The anger of a living father, grandfather, uncle, or elder brother, as well as that of the dead, is thought to be physically injurious to its object; and immature members of the offender's household are more susceptible to its malign influence. If a child fall ill soon after a family quarrel, the diviner is apt to discover that the cause of the illness is the anger of the father's elders in family or clan. There is no cure for such illness till the anger of the offended elder has been assuaged, and he washes the child with "medicine" and recites the formula over it: "If it was I, let him heal!" The Becwana call such a disease *dikgaba.* Smith mentions that if you rouse the discontent of a person by serving him with too small a portion of eland's flesh, your child may be afflicted with such swellings as wens on the head or goitre, and that a cold in the head is said to be caused by jealousy. (IPNR. i. 241, 235.) "The destructive power of anger is firmly believed in by the Konde. To speak the name of a brother in anger, is strictly forbidden, for it may lead to his death." (SRK. 268.) These people believe also that if the parents or relatives of an absent person, having no news of him for some time, give way to anger, the absent one will become ill. (SRK. 277.)

mixture of "medicine" and chyme from the victim's stomach; and the offended spirit is called by name and asked to leave the afflicted one alone.

The notion which underlies these usages finds credence throughout Bantu Africa, and expresses itself in practices which are marked by a multitude of minor modifications. Prayers for the recovery of the sick are addressed to ancestral spirits in the old Kongo kingdom; [1] and in Kikuyu and Kitui ancestral spirits are invoked when there is sickness among people or cattle. [2] Speaking of the Akamba, who live west of the Akikuyu, the Hon. Charles Dundas states: [3] "One of the commonest duties of the medicine man is the curing of sickness, but of course he has first to discover its nature and causes, and this is very commonly found to be the anger or possession of a spirit. . . . Frequently a sacrifice is offered and the names of many deceased members of the family are called until that of the particular spirit molesting the patient is mentioned, when the trouble will abate. . . . Almost every case of sickness is ascribed to a spirit." "Sickness invariably denotes the anger of a spirit following upon some offence or neglect, and it is then often the medicine man who can detect the cause and prescribe the cure." The same writer expatiates on the multitude of sacrifices and offerings to the spirits of his ancestors that an Mchagga will make when he is ill. [4] The Hon. Kenneth R. Dundas found a similar practice among the Wawanga, who live north-west of the Akamba. He says: [5] "If sickness occurs in a family some years, say two or three perhaps, after the death of any member, the medicine man will sometimes attribute it to the spirit of the deceased person. His relatives and kinsmen accordingly brew beer and kill a bullock; or a cow, if deceased was a woman. A great dance, which lasts till early morning, is then held, at which much drink is consumed. At about 4 A.M. libations are poured out at the Msambue and to Were and at the Mokurru stones under the verandahs of the huts." Msambue and Mokurru, it should be explained, are stones dedicated to the ancestral spirits of the paternal and ma-

[1] WBT. 151.
[2] BBM. 52, 58.
[3] JRAI., 1913, pp. 529, 530, 535.
[4] K. 179.
[5] JRAI., 1913, p. 38.

ternal lines respectively; and Were appears to be a kind of high god, of whose lineage we know nothing, but to whom a single stone is set up.

OCCASIONS FOR THE WORSHIP OF FAMILY-GODS: 4. REUNION OF
THE FAMILY

At first sight the Becwana ceremony for the reconciliation of long-estranged brothers appears to have no relation to the worship of spirits. An ox is killed—a white ox, if obtainable; both brothers dip their right hands in the chyme contained in its stomach; and, each grasping the other's arm just below the elbow, both slide their hands down the forearm of the other till both hands clasp in the steaming chyme. Then the flesh of the slaughtered beast is eaten by all who take part in the ceremony, whether as principals or as witnesses. What makes this rite so very binding? It is often performed far from the ancestral graves; and, so far as I have heard, the ritual makes no mention of ancestral spirits. One knows, of course, that the chyme of a sacrificed beast is always of sacred significance; [1] but to understand this rite of reconciliation one must look at it in the light of a ceremony performed when a child born beyond the borders pays his first visit to the ancestral home. In order that the foreign-born kinsman may be given his place in the family, he is anointed with the chyme of a sacrificed victim; and though the beast may be slaughtered anywhere, as in most Becwana sacrifices, the anointing is done at the grave of an ancestor.

Among the Becwana folk-tales that I have collected, there is one which professes to give the origin of this custom. "Once upon a time there was a woman called *Mmammohake*," so runs my version of the story; "who one day called her children, and,

[1] Cardinall mentions (NTG. 93) an analogous use of chyme in peace-making. When fighting has ceased and peace has been agreed upon, both parties "meet at their frontier and kill a cow, which is divided. The undigested food and intestines are then thrown on the ground and both parties stamp on them. That concludes peace and each returns to his compound crying out that 'Peace has been made; the undigested has been stamped on.'" Cf. also LSAT. ii. 52, and see my p. 357.

taking a white ox out of her herd, drove it to a cave in which a god was worshipped. She killed the ox at the entrance of the cave; took out its stomach; and told her eldest child and the others in order of seniority to smear themselves with the chyme, till she came to the youngest, who smeared himself last of all. Then she bade each grasp his brother's right arm with his right hand full of chyme and slip the hand down the forearm till the hands met. And so they all smeared each other's arms with the contents of the stomach of the sacrifice." Thus ran the story; and the narrator proceeded to expound it for my benefit. "The white ox," said he, "was a sign of peace, and peace can be made by it. The stomach showed that they were children of one woman; the smearing by seniority was a sign of the order in which they were born; and going to the cave confirmed the ceremony, because it was performed before the god. The old Becwana regarded this as a work of confirmation. It was observed especially by sons of chiefs when they left home, as they usually did upon the death of their fathers, each moving away with his retainers. Whenever they met again, the first thing they did was to kill a white ox and smear themselves with the contents of its stomach. This was done especially for the sake of the children who had been born during their separation, to show their relationship and precedence. There was a thought, too, of dwelling peacefully together, instead of in separate places where there was no peace, and of removing that bad spirit of jealousy which had separated them and seeking the spirit of peace from the god. When people spread out and multiplied, this anointing was practised by the sons of chiefs, and the common people threw the contents of the victim's stomach at one another's bodies." The ancient myth associates the rite with ancestral worship; and the commentator's remarks show how the rite is still interpreted by a tribesman who is in close touch with the thought of his own people. He did not explain why the mythical woman was called *Mmammohake*, "Mother-of-one-who-binds-securely" (from the intensive form of *go boha*, "to bind"); nor how it happened that a woman could preside over such a rite and take an ox from the herd for slaughter. Indeed, the latter point was probably beyond him; for the Becwana know nothing of a time when they were not patrilineal and the man was not lord of his house-hold and his herd; although this archaic touch to the narrative authenticates its antiquity.

Ellenberger describes the same ceremony as it is practised by the Basuto,[1] and adds that it was a binding ceremony in reconciliation, and was observed also when two people contracted a close friendship—that is, I suppose, when two people swore to be brothers to one another.

In the Thonga *hondlola* rite, which, according to Junod, aggregates a person afresh to the community after a serious illness,[2] the "doctor" first prays to ancestral spirits "by means of" a piece of each limb of a sacrificed goat, and then the patient rubs his whole body with a mixture of "medicine" and chyme (*psanyi*) from its stomach. Junod mentions a Thonga "Sacrifice of Reconciliation," also;[3] and although he does not describe its ritual, the fact that it is a *sacrifice* shows that ancestral spirits are taken into the transaction. His description of the sacrifice and prayer which a father offers before his long absent son is allowed to enter the village to which he has returned, leaves no doubt that the ancestor-spirits of the family are invoked and thanked for their care of the wanderer.[4]

The Baila regard certain spots in their huts as sacred to their ancestors: one is at the foot of the central pole of the hut; others are on either side of the main doorway—on the right for the husband's ancestors, and on the left for the wife's.[5] When a Mwila makes an offering to his divinities, he does it at the doorway of his hut; and the man's divinities are the divinities of his children.[6] To make an offering to the divinities is *kupaila*, in their tongue; and the offering itself is *chipaizho*.[7] Smith says: "When a man's son returns from a long journey, or after a lengthy residence elsewhere, he takes him into the hut and *paila's* him by sprinkling water on him and giving him beads or other things; they are named *impaizho*, and are intended as an offering

---

[1] HB. 258.
[2] LSAT. i. 57, 101; ii. 427, 428, 435.
[3] LSAT. ii. 370.
[4] LSAT. ii. 369.
[5] IPNR. ii. 173.
[6] IPNR. ii. 166.
[7] IPNR. ii. 174.

to the divinities, who have guarded the man's son and brought him safely home." [1]

When sons of Becwana families return home after prolonged absence, their elders asperse them with "holy water"; and no well-bred man would set out on a journey till his elders had fortified him against the dangers of the road by touching the various parts of his body with "medicated" fingers. Although the magical element is to the fore in both these observances, they are sacerdotal acts which are performed by the priest of the family.

When a man of the Wawanga tribe (Elgon district of Kenya Colony) returns from a long journey, he places his spear in the shrine of his paternal ancestor's (*msambue*), and leaves it there for the next twenty-four hours or so. [2]

OCCASIONS FOR THE WORSHIP OF FAMILY-GODS: 5. CARE OF THE FAMILY CATTLE

Except on rare occasions when a cow dies or is killed, milk is the sole food of both sexes of the Bahuma or Bahima of Ankole, although their serfs (Bahera) raise millet and other vegetables. They are a purely pastoral people who idolise their cattle. "The cowman has one love which surpasses all others," says Roscoe, [3] "and that is for his cows. If a favourite cow falls sick, he will tend it day and night, and, should it die, his grief is extreme, at times even greater than for a wife or a child. Men have been known to become insane and to commit suicide when one of these favourites dies. The skill with which two or three of these herdsmen can manage a large herd, often numbering four or five hundred, is wonderful; they have the animals entirely under their control, and can direct them by word of mouth as easily as though they were rational beings." According to this writer, who is a distinguished authority on the people of Ankole, Bunyoro and Buganda, the aristocrats of Ankole "are undoubtedly of Hamitic stock." [4]

[1] IPNR. ii. 177-78.
[2] JRAI., 1913, p. 47.
[3] SCA. 60.
[4] SCA. 56.

Now the Bantu are thought to be a blend of pastoral Hamites and agricultural Negroes, which streamed forth from the watershed between the Nile and the Congo some two thousand years ago, and have since spread over the southern third of Africa. In the vicissitudes of inter-tribal turmoil, many of these tribes have been jostled into regions where cattle cannot thrive, and have had to become tillers of the soil; but the manner in which others of them combine pastoral pursuits with the cultivation of crops, suggests that the Hamitic strain came into their breed through the men, and the Negro strain through the women. These semi-pastoral tribes think agriculture is peculiarly woman's domain: girls pass into womanhood by rites which centre round the fertility of the soil; women vaunt their devotion to tillage; and men, when they work upon the land, profess to be helping their women-folk. Cattle, on the other hand, are associated with manliness, glory, and political power, as they were among our Aryan progenitors: Boys' Puberty Rites are shot through and through with the care and defence of cattle; cattle-raids upon neighbouring tribes were the winter sport of the young bloods; and even chiefs boast of their skill in herding; while women are debarred from milking cows or even entering a cattle-pen.[1] In their love of cattle and management of the herds, these tribes are inferior to the Bahuma, it is true, but they have evidently inherited some share of a similar tradition. Semi-pastoral Bantu patriarchs gloat over their hoarded herds, like misers over gold, seldom slaughtering a beast, even in time of hunger, except for some great religious, political or social function, and holding them as a trust for which their divine predecessors are sure to call them to account, either in this world or in the world to come—probably in both.

Since each successive patriarch in these tribes is buried in his cattle-kraal, with the hide of one of the finest of his beasts wrapped around him, and that of another laid beneath him as a grave-bed,[2] and since he is supposed to maintain a much keener interest in his herd than in any other form of property which he has left to his successor, it is strange that spirits of former mas-

---

[1] The cattle of Konde tribesmen (North Nyasa) generally sleep in the same house as their owners. (SRK. 27, 85, 109.)

[2] Cf. IPNR. ii. 104, 110.

ters of a private herd are not more frequently invoked to look
after its welfare; but when we come to a clear understanding of
the ritual of ancestor-worship, what we now assume to be mere
herdsman's magic, such as frequent prophylactic and curative
fumigation of the cattle, may turn out to be as intimately connected with the worship of the dead as incense is with the
prayers of some Christian congregations. The Baila usage of
consecrating a new riverside cattle-post by sacrificing an ox in the
gateway, making an offering to the spirits north, south, east and
west, and repeating the ceremony upon return to the village some
months later,[1] has its analogue among most tribes which are wont
to transfer their cattle from village to river when water fails and
the grass becomes poor, and to bring them back home when the
new grass has sprouted.

If, as Junod thinks,[2] cattle never played such an important
part in the life of the Thonga as in that of the Zulu and Suto
stocks, it is likely that the progenitors of that tribe were weaned
from their love of cattle by prolonged residence in districts where
cattle could not live.

OCCASIONS FOR THE WORSHIP OF FAMILY-GODS: 6. OTHER
OCCASIONS

For the sake of completeness, it may be well to repeat here
what was said on a former page:[3] that pious people here and
there acknowledge their family-divinities at the beginning of
every new day and thank them for every meal. Whenever the
spirits make known their need of sacrifice or other offering, in
one of the ways described in Chapter II, their earthly kinsfolk
naturally hasten to obey. The tutelary gods of a family are
appealed to, also, in any emergency, the appeal being always
accompanied by some sort of offering, even though it be but a
little water poured upon the ground or spewed forth in a thin
stream from the mouth; and they are sometimes invoked to
give success in hunting and fishing,—a practice which may be
more appropriately described on a later page.[4]

[1] IPNR. i. 132.
[2] LSAT. ii. 49.
[3] See p. 180.
[4] See pp. 256 ff.

Iron-workers of the Northern Bakaonde form a kind of guild, the secrets of the craft being handed on from father to son. "The worker in iron having been initiated by his father (deceased) would take a *chipanda* of *muwumbu* wood on the day before starting his work; and, after placing a circle of flour at the foot of it, would pray to the *mukishi* of his father: 'Oh! Spirit of my father: who worked iron here of yore, listen to me and hear my prayer. To-morrow I, too, will work at the iron. I pray thee, help me, and guide my work, that it may prosper.' If the *mukishi* be adverse the ore will turn to water and not to iron. Such adverse attitude will follow if the prayer be not offered up properly." [1]

OCCASIONS FOR THE WORSHIP OF TRIBAL-GODS

It is impossible to maintain a scientific distinction between family-gods and tribal-gods, though such terms are artistically convenient. The gods of a tribe (by which I mean a political coalition of matrilineal or patrilineal clans) are the ancestors of its superior family,—a family which, in most cases, attained ascendency, through birth, ability, or good fortune, when its gods were young. If this family maintains its hold upon a tract of territory for many generations, its gods become territorial deities, and it is possible that one of them may have the luck to gather such renown that he preserves his ghostly prestige, and even grows in glory, after his descendants have fallen a prey to invaders. A similar tendency appears, on a smaller scale, in families which have been content to live in the shade and enjoy the same estates for ages; for, owing to an inadequate sense of proportion and a superabundant pride of birth, many such families look upon their eponyms as founders of dynasties. Hence it is that, while most religious rites connected with the prosperity of a tribal domain are related to the old lords of the land—that is, ancestor-spirits either of extant dynasties or of dynasties which they or their precursors reduced to political unimportance—some families, especially in regions where there is no strong tribal rule, supplicate their family-gods for boons that are elsewhere supposed to be the prerogatives of dynastic spirits. So far as we

[1] WBA. 136-37.

can make out, however, all ancestor-spirits are credited with power to grant fertility to their descendants, but a line that has occupied a demesne and buried generation after generation of its patriarchs in it, is the only one whose ancestor-spirits are thought to be concerned with the fertility of its soil and the weather which subserves fertility.

OCCASIONS FOR THE WORSHIP OF TRIBAL-GODS: I. RAIN

The worship of tribal divinities is easier to follow than that of family-gods, notwithstanding the fact that immemorial usage requires some of its rites to be muffled with mystery; because its events are on a larger scale and therefore more conspicuous.

Rain-rites are found all over the world[1] and attain superlative importance in arid regions. To dwellers in the parched wastes of Central Australia, the bull-roarer is sacrosanct; for their faith in sympathetic magic is unalloyed, and their fancy likens the weird wail of this whirling bit of wood to the plaint of an approaching storm. "The desert-dwelling tribes of New Mexico and Arizona need rain above all else," writes a student of Amer-Indian art,[2] "so that their religion, their songs, their art, and their decorations express for the most part a prayer for water. Often on Hopi placques of woven grasses may be seen the pageantry of storm or sunset in the many coloured cloud-forms—harbingers of rain—that circle the basket."

Bechuanaland consists of the Kalahari desert and a fringe of poor pasture-land on its southern and eastern borders. It lies within the belt of the South-east Trade Winds; but its altitude of from 3,000 to 4,000 feet makes it cold in the southern winter, and the consequent high pressure on this plateau checks the South-east Trades before they reach very far inland. Its winter is therefore cold and dry, with a tendency to outflowing winds. In the southern summer, as the vertical rays of the sun migrate southwards, the heat becomes intense and the pressure lower; but even then the great terraced escarpments between these uplands and the south-east ocean tap the South-east Trades of their moisture, so that rain is precarious in Eastern Bechuanaland, springs

[1] Cf. Jer. xiv. 22.
[2] *The Southern Workman*, Aug. 1919.

sparse, and perennial streams few and far between, while the Kalahari has hardly any rainfall at all. On this tableland the rainy season is preceded by a period when, to use the local phrase, "the sun screams." Time after time the clouds gather and are scattered with a rising wind, to the disappointment of everybody; and the sky is as molten brass again. It would be astonishing if the tribes of this territory did not link up their solicitude for rain with the ritual by which they approach their divinities; and one is not surprised to find greater variety in the rain-rites of Bechuanaland than in those of any other Bantu territory.

The minor rain-rites of these tribes cannot be explored apart from the broad question of magic, which must be reserved for a future volume; but, although magic rites mingle with ceremonies of the cult, the major ceremonies are unmistakably connected with the invocation of tribal divinities. We note, first of all, that none but the paramount chief could preside over this ritual, and that he, being the senior surviving representative of his line, is the natural priest of his fathers, who are the tutelary deities of the tribe.[1] As the people became [2] increasingly apprehensive at the lateness of the rains, a subordinate chief of some importance would bring a black ox to the paramount at sunrise one morning, saying, "I have come to beg rain, Chief, with this calf." The paramount, having assented by replying, "May the rain fall!" would call in his expert in the rain-rites, and the ox would be sprinkled with "medicated" water and set free to wander where it would, the ceremony being repeated, perhaps, for two or three days in succession, in the belief that this would "cause the rain to wander about in the country." Then the ox was slaughtered, dressed, cooked and eaten in the Place of Tribal Assembly, some parts of it being taken to the "rain-doctor's hearth." In some of these tribes it was customary to hold an Armed Assembly on the following morning, for the purpose of "discussing the rain." The men assembled by regiments and marched forth from the town to the trysting-place, where the

---

[1] Ancestor-spirits tend all the world over to become gods of growth, who give life, fertility, strength, and victory. In Celtic Ireland there was a prevalent belief that fruitfulness depended upon the king. (See RAC. 4.)

[2] The past tense is used, because many of these tribal rites have been thrown into the shade, if not into the discard, since European influences began to play upon the people.

children of the chieftainship each made a formal speech in order of seniority, addressing the paramount in some such words as these: "We seek rain from you, Chief. Where do you cause us to look, that thus you do not give us rain, Son-of-Kgari" (or whatever distinguished ancestor was invoked for the occasion), "who said so-and-so"—and the speaker glided forthwith into the praise-song of the ancestor mentioned. Whereupon the most important men in the Assembly chanted the refrain: "Give us rain, Son-of-Kgari!" The paramount was expected to reply: "I hear you; and the rain will fall." After this "discussion" the regiments scattered for the big game-hunt that is usual after most Armed Assemblies, the men assuring one another that by these words the rain would come quickly; "and," added one of the informants whose accounts I have combined and condensed, "sometimes it would rain after they reached home from the hunt."

If the rain still failed, however, stronger measures had to be taken. Recourse was had to the divining-tablets at every step in the process, that the guidance of the tutelary deities might be secured; and the next step depended upon the diviner's findings.

At such seasons the "rain-maker," as Europeans mistakenly dubbed him, was much in evidence. The chief sent regiments to cut *mokgaló* [1] ("wait-a-bit thorn") bushes, with which to hedge round a small circular space on one side of his courtyard. Within this fence the ground was carefully cleaned and coated with a paste of clay and cow-dung, and a hearth was built on one side, as in Becwana huts. After this inclosure had been purged of all defilement and consecrated by mystic rites, none but the chief, his expert in the rain-rites, and one or two carefully selected assistants were allowed to enter the holy place, and even they had to guard themselves vigilantly against ceremonial contamination. The esoteric rites performed within this temple were sacred mysteries into which it was thought wrong for profane people to pry; but morning and evening for some days in succession, a cloud of heavy black smoke rolled up over the hedge and away towards the sky; [2] and in this atmosphere of mystery the nerves

[1] The Bangwaketse use *morobe* instead of *mokgaló*.

[2] It is a principle of Mimetic magic that like produces like and that, therefore, the way to produce a result is to imitate it; black clouds of smoke will cause black

of the tribesmen tingled with eager expectation of coming showers.

Less than ten inches of rain fell during Livingstone's second and third years [1] at Kolobeng, and in his fourth year the rainfall was insufficient to bring the grain to maturity. It was a time when "rain-doctors" had to be busy. Livingstone was on terms of friendship with these specialists and was in the confidence of the chief Sechele, who had been a noted "rain-doctor," and who still believed implicitly in the rain-rites, in spite of his leanings toward Christianity.[2] He discovered that the "medicines" used behind the screen consisted of "a variety of preparations, such as charcoal made of burned bats, inspissated renal deposit of the mountain coney (*Hyrax capensis*), the internal parts of different animals—as jackals' livers, baboons' and lions' hearts, and hairy calculi from the bowels of old cows—serpents' skins and vertebræ, and every kind of tuber, bulb, root, and plant to be found in the country." But he does not seem to have heard that such fearsome ingredients as untimely human births, twins, and organs taken from the corpse of a brave foe were also needed to give potency to the Bakwena rain-pots. "The rain-maker selects a particular bulbous root," Livingstone continues,[3] "and administers a cold infusion to a sheep, which in five minutes afterwards expires in convulsions. Part of the same bulb is converted into smoke, and ascends towards the sky; rain follows in a day or two. The inference is obvious." At the time when Livingstone wrote, the Science of Comparative Religion had not emerged from its swaddling clothes; and he, like his contemporaries, regarded the rain-rites as a farrago of inept magic; but he was courteous in his method of approach to the "rain-doctors," and scrupulously fair in reporting what he understood to be their claims. They claimed, he said, that it was God alone who made the rain and that they prayed to God by means of these "medicines."[4] He was misled by their ambiguous use of the term *modimo*, which may be applied to any divinity. Bakwena experts

clouds of rain to gather, as surely as the whistling of a sailor will produce a whistling gale.

[1] He went there in 1847.
[2] MTR. 20-21.
[3] MTR. 22.
[4] MTR. 23.

assured me that none but the Supreme Spirit can send rain; but that their prayers for rain are addressed to spirits of the ruling dynasty, who intercede for them at the court of One too great to be approached by mortals, and that the smoke from the rain-pots is incense which gives efficacy to their prayers.

Underlying these Bakwena practices there is evidently a fundamental notion that drought is a punishment inflicted by the tribal divinities upon a community which permits its members to use ancestral laws and customs despitefully. Let me translate a note which I took down from the dictation of a native who was peculiarly familiar with the Bakwena usage.

"When a woman has had a mis-carriage and the result is twins, the twins are placed in a new pot that has never been used but is still as it was when it came forth from the potter's fire; and the pot and its contents are sent to the chief, who consults with his experts in the rain-rites. These twins are what is called *lemapó*.[1] When it is found that the rain does not fall, it will be said, 'It is held by *lemapó*,' or '*lemapó* of a person who had a mis-carriage in the veld.' And if the clouds gather at midday and scatter in the evening, it is said, 'the rain is in the sleeping-mat.' That means that some one has lain with a widow before the ceremony of the Purification of Widows, or that some one has impregnated a marriageable girl. Now in the old days they would be sent to the chief—he who slept with a widow would be sent with the widow to the chief, and he who had impregnated a marriageable girl, and she who had had a mis-carriage in the veld. And a great Civil Assembly would be convened, with women and girls and boys present. And the 'pot of the rain,' which has the rain-medicine mixed with water, would be brought to the Assembly; and the offenders would be stripped naked before the Assembly, and the urethra of each would be cut so that blood flowed into the pot. They would be cut badly, the razor entering deep, it being said, 'Let the blood flow freely.' These people were so treated in public before the eyes of men, women, girls, and boys so that those who saw it might be warned that there must no longer be any one who could do such a deed as lying

---

[1] *Lemapó* appears to be the common word for "peg," and pegs figure prominently in some varieties of Bantu magic; but what is its significance in this connection? Does the word hark back to some archaic sense in its stem?

with an unpurified widow, or impregnating a marriageable girl, or aborting in the veld and hiding her deed.[1] They would fear the shame of being cut with a razor in public."

These endeavours to discover the unexpiated "sin" which hindered the rain and, by publicly punishing the Achan in the camp, to free the community from complicity, imply that rain-rites appeal to the ancestral guardians of law and custom; and the last shade of doubt is removed when, the commoner conciliatory and cathartic rites having failed, the diviner discovers that the drought can be broken only by a sacrifice at the grave of one of these tutelary divinities.[2]

In 1896 an old man of the Bamangwato tribe described to me the last celebration of such a rite by his people, which took place, he thought, about 1860. The drought was terrible; all the ordinary rites had failed to bring rain; and the divination-test indicated that the one thing lacking was a sacrifice at the grave of Mathibe. It was during Mathibe's chieftainship that the Bamangwato had taken possession of this territory, in the latter half of the eighteenth century; but the glory of his career was eclipsed by his abortive attempt to foist his younger son (Tauane) into the chieftainship and his subsequent flight to Ngami with the foiled usurper. In his chagrin at being cast adrift by the favourite son for whom he had risked everything, and rebuffed by his heir (Khame I) to whom, in his evil plight, he had made advances, this forsaken old man put a suicidal end to his intrigue and turmoil, and found a grave in the Lochotlo gorge, some six or eight miles west of Shoshong. To this grave Mathibe's great-grandson, Sekhome, now led the Bamangwato clans for humiliation and worship, but not the many other clans that had by this time taken shelter under the shield of these "masters of the land." From the tribal herds choice had been made of a black bull,[3] without blemish or trace of colour, which, after being given water to drink, was slaughtered at the grave. Many small fires were lit around the sacred spot, and the flesh of the victim was

---

[1] Cf. ABN. 134.

[2] See p. 26.

[3] Is it a mere coincidence of custom that black oxen were sacrificed to Pluto, god of the infernal regions; that in *The Antiquary* "the black ox has trampled on you" means that "misfortune has come to your house"; and that the adage "the black ox never trod upon his foot" is still sometimes heard in Scotland?

roasted. Of this sacrificial meat the chief was the first to partake, and after him, in strict order of precedence, each man, woman, and child in the throng had a morsel. It was necessary that every scrap of the sacramental food should be consumed upon the spot. The hide, blood, and chyme of the victim were buried in the grave; and its bones, horns, hoofs and other inedible parts were carefully laid upon the grave and consumed with fire, lest some unfriendly magician should use them to nullify the sacrifice with his charms. Then the people stood and worshipped, under the presidency of their chief, intoning the "praise-songs" of their dead chiefs, and saying, "We have come to beg rain by means of this ox, O Chief, our Father!" The rain-songs also were chanted; and the people dispersed with a great shout, "Rain! Rain! Rain! Chief, we are dead—we who are your people! Let the rain fall!" As they wended their homeward way, they continued to make the welkin ring with their rain-songs; "and," added my old friend, "on the evening of that same day there was a drenching rain." Of the rain-songs sung upon this occasion my informant could remember but one:

> "Kololo a éé kaka ea komakoma;
> Kgomo co moroka di letse di sa nwa,
> Megobyane e kgadile."

The first line is somewhat obscure; but I venture the following translation:

> Let the klipspringer go, grappling with the gentle rain;
> The cattle of the rain-doctor's folk lay down thirsty last night,
> The rain-pools having dried up.

The mention of the klipspringer [1] in this rain-song probably harks back to some well-nigh unremembered alliance between the Bamangwato and the Bo-Seleka, which is said to have caused the former to adopt the totem of the latter—the duiker. The Bo-Seleka clan dwelt at Nwapa, an isolated hill between the Cwapong range and the Crocodile River, till 1887, when the Bamangwato drove them forth to find shelter among the Bavenda, to whom

---

[1] "Klipspringer" (lit. "rock-jumper") is the Dutch name for the *oreotragus saltator*, a diminutive antelope which resembles the chamois in appearance and habit.

they are more nearly related. They were noted for their rain-rites; and some twenty-five years ago one of their most intelligent men gave me an account of their usage.

In this clan, and in others of the same stock, one of each pair of human twins used to be killed at birth and sent to the chief; children born with teeth, and those who cut their upper teeth first, were similarly dealt with; and the chief's "rain-doctor" dried these little bodies over a slow fire and ground them to powder, which was mixed with the many occult ingredients that constituted the "rain-medicine."

It was the custom in this clan to build a rain-doctor's enclosure of closely woven branches outside the town; because they held that inasmuch as the rain-rites were for the whole community, it would be wrong to favour any one section of the community by building the temple in its midst. For one of their great rain-rites, the chief used first to send out the clansmen to catch a live klipspringer, and take it to the rain-doctor's temple; and then to send them into the veld to dig an assortment of bulbs, which were pounded up, under the rain-doctor's supervision, and placed in the large pots with which the temple was furnished. When these preparations were completed, the herald ascended the hill one evening and summoned the women of the community, in the chief's name, to fetch water on the following morning and carry it to this sacred enclosure. The water was poured into the pots which contained the pounded bulbs and other ingredients; the pots were marked with those mystic spots of white, red and black which denote ceremonial purity; and the mixture was churned with a porridge-stick. After the klipspringer had been washed in this purifying mixture, it was slaughtered and cooked, and eaten by the expert and children who had not reached puberty; and all who partook of this food were required to wash their mouths and hands carefully after eating.

If this rite failed to bring rain, another was tried: perhaps a black sheep was sacrificed in the rain-doctor's enclosure, or a young brindled gnu (*connochætes taurinus*), or a young impala (*æpyceros melampus*), or if the drought persisted perhaps a victim of each of these kinds would be sacrificed on different days. Whatever animal was offered had to be caught alive, and washed in the purifying mixture before it was slaughtered.

If these ceremonies failed to bring rain, the cause of the persistent drought was looked for in the community. One of the things most likely to cause drought is a human abortion. Such an abomination had to be placed in an old pot and buried in some dark spot, or, better still, hidden in a distant cave, where the clouds could not see it; for if the clouds saw it, there would be a mis-carriage of the rain with which they were in labour. Care was taken, even, to scrape up the earth from every spot whereon the woman could remember that she had micturated during this pregnancy, and to hide that earth in a similar manner. If the clouds gathered for rain and then disappeared in the distance in spite of the above-mentioned rites, any woman in the community who had had a mis-carriage during the year, would be made to stand with her husband, both naked, near the centre-pole of a hut from which the crown had been removed, and a quantity of purifying-mixture from the rain-doctor's pots was poured over them from the apex of the roof; and then they were compelled to wash their bodies in a certain infusion of bulbs which causes intense itching. My informant likened the anguish of the unlucky pair to that of a captive taken in war, saying that the pain they suffered was severe, and the shame still harder to bear. If the drought continued in spite of these potent spells, the chief sacrificed a black sheep at his father's grave, and prayed to him for rain. And if even this failed, they had many other customs upon which they relied. As a last resort, he declared, many of the clans that he knew did not hesitate, before the advent of European control, to commit ritual-murder when the tribal nerves were on the stretch. In such cases he thought it was not usual for the chief or his expert to name any particular victim; that the chief sent forth a party of his trusties with orders to catch a "klipspringer with hair," which means a man, woman or child; or to catch a "bull koodoo" (*strepsiceros kudu*), which means a full-grown man; and that the party were told to catch the first, second or third, as the case may be, that they met at a certain time of day on a specified road, in accordance with whatever the diviner's findings may have been. If they chanced upon three or four together at the specified time and place, they would scatter them and kill one. They always sought a very black person, rather than one of lighter complexion, "so that the clouds might become very black." The slayers took a circular patch of skin from the forehead, the private parts, a strip of skin from between the navel and the breastbone, and some parts of the intestines, and conveyed these to the rain-doctor for use in his rites; and they buried the rest of the corpse.

He remarked, also, that when Kobe died,—Kobe was a chief of the Bo-Seleka who was famed for his knowledge of the rain-rites—they took a circular patch of skin from his forehead and let it dry; and from that time till the chief of the clan became a Christian, at the beginning of the present century, it was customary to immerse this patch of skin in water when they were in need of rain.

Newspaper reports [1] of the trial of seven men at Salisbury, Southern Rhodesia, in May, 1923, prove that Mashona rain-rites still call for occasional murder. Dwelling on the Portuguese border north of Mount Darwin, in a tsetse-belt which is inaccessible to the mounted police and others who depend on animal transport, the Mtawara tribe have not been embarrassed in the pursuit of their old ideals by inconvenient questions from intrusive Europeans. In the preceding January these people saw their crops being destroyed by the scorching sun and starvation staring them in the face; and according to evidence which was not disputed at the trial, Chingango, chief of a section of this tribe, ordered his son, Manduza, to be burnt to death, calming the fears of those who dreaded police interference by reminding them that the authorities had never heard of two similar sacrifices that he had offered in recent years. The son was bound and placed alive upon a heap of firewood; more wood was heaped upon him; and in an hour or two nothing remained but ashes and charred bones. The newspaper report of the trial looks at the case from a judicial view-point, and does not reveal the inner meaning of the sacrifice; but to one who reads between the lines it appears fairly certain that these people regarded the drought as a punishment for a breach of ancestral laws and custom of which the chief's son was thought to be guilty, though the suspicion was apparently unwarranted, and that the chief's motive in ordering him to be executed in this manner was to free

[1] Reported in *The Times Weekly Edition*, London, July 5, 1923. See, also, an article in *South Africa Missionary Advocate*, March-April, 1924.

his people from complicity in this "sin" against the god, Mwari, of whom we shall hear more in a future volume.

The rainfall of Basutoland is more copious than that of Bechuanaland; but it is evident from Ellenberger's account [1] that Basuto rain-rites differ only in minor details from those already described. To show that they are inspired by the same motive, it is enough to quote the rain-songs which he records, premising only that Soloane or Tsuloane was an ancestor who is supposed to hold high rank among the immortals, and that Mohlomi was a chief famed alike for his benevolence and his expert knowledge of the rain-rites.

"O, Soloane! we seek rain!
Oh, where is the rain?
Lord, give us rain.
We remain always thirsty,
The cattle too are thirsty.
Soloane, where is the rain?"

And again:

"We have just seen Mohlomi—
Mohlomi, who sits alone.
Tsuloane, where is the rain?
Rain! we want rain!"

Ellenberger mentions one Basuto rain-rite which seems not to be practised in Bechuanaland. When everything had been tried in vain, the rain-makers and the people used to cut themselves with knives in order to show their misery. They would roll in the ashes and rise up uttering weird cries; and after religious dances, in which all took part, they would sing melancholy airs, and again give vent to cries, groans and lamentations, which they kept up day and night, together with this or a similar prayer:

"I am a child of God,[2] yet I starve.
New god, pray to him of old.
Pray, Nkopane Mathunya!
Pray, Mohlomi Matsie!"

Inasmuch as the Kafirs sacrifice an ox to their ancestral spirits as a part of the purification rites of a community in which one

[1] HB. 249-256.
[2] The word used is *molimo*.

member has been killed by lightning, it is safe to assume that they credit them with ability to influence the weather. That their kinsfolk, the Zulus, are of this way of thinking cannot be doubted. An old Zulu told Callaway [1] that men used to pray to the Lord of Heaven for rain long before Utshaka's time, but that Utshaka made the prayers more important: "He sang a song," said he, "and prayed to the Lord of Heaven; and asked his forefathers to pray for rain to the Lord of Heaven. And it rained." And he went on to tell of a great assembly, at which black oxen and sheep and black rams were sacrificed to the ancestral spirits and eaten by the people. It was no common meal; each received his portion in an orderly manner, and held it in his hands while he joined in the song that burst forth from the throats of the multitude; and then all carried the meat to their mouths together. There was dancing, of course, as well as the singing of praises: "They sang very loud," said the reminiscent old man, "and the ground resounded with the noise of their feet."

Varied as these rain-rites are and saturated with magic, it can scarcely be denied, I think, that they were designed as a ritual of intercession with the spirits of the old chiefs, the tutelary gods of their tribes. Hence the surviving successor of any given line of chiefs, who was born to share their divine prestige, is the only possible officiant. For as much as the rites are intricate and, like enchantments that are purely magical, would be ineffectual unless performed with meticulous conformity to rule, the chief is assisted by his expert hierologist, and often by his uncles, in his dramatic invocation of the favour of his fathers upon his liegemen, herds, fields, pastures, and woodlands; but he is the pontiff, and they are but acolytes. Interpreting drought as divine chastisement for the infringement of ancestral custom,[2] any community which discovers that it is under the ban hastens to purge itself of the sin that lurks in its midst, by visiting the offender with a punishment appropriate to his misdeeds, even to the extent of exacting the extreme penalty of their law from flagrant offenders—a penalty which involves not only death, but such a destruction of the body as shall prevent the sacrilegious soul

[1] RSZ. 93.
[2] Cf. 1 Kings viii. 35 et seq.

from being reborn and again endangering the community by its wrong-doing. Some of the so-called "human sacrifices" that disgrace the rain-rites are defended by this plea; and others are not real *sacrifices:* only certain human organs which are necessary to give supreme potency to the mystic mixture by which rainmongers seek to stimulate, if not compel, the uncomplying gods, are taken from the hapless wight who chanced unconsciously to draw the lot. What the python has to do with rain,[1] or what magical notions lie behind the choice of particular ingredients in the incense-pot, it is hard to say; but bats and pythons are bed-fellows with dead chiefs in the caves, and some other animals in the list have a habit of burrowing down towards the underworld, or of feeding on corpses.

Kindred practices were found on the great plateau that stretches for some three degrees south from Tanganyika. Sheane writes:[2] "Among some tribes agriculture is of such supreme importance that in order to remove any hindrance to its pursuit the natives have been known to resort to human sacrifices. To avert a drought the following rites are described by Dr. Chisholm as having taken place among the Winamwanga: 'The head chief sends special messengers (*mavyondongo,* from *kuvyondongola*—to twist the neck) to capture persons—men, women, or youths to be sacrificed to the spirits of the chief. In the Winamwanga tribe they may want three or four. They prefer persons of the family of the priesthood, or those with a large umbilical hernia, or those who have had twins, also twins themselves, or those who have a squint, mothers who have borne only one child, or pregnant women. These are taken to the shrines and are killed in a special manner by these special messengers. They are known to be killed by twisting of the neck, and are never seen again, but what is really done with the bodies is kept very secret.' Nowadays the spirits of the Winamwanga chiefs have to be content with meaner offerings, such as sheep and pots of beer, which are taken to the shrines with much pomp and beating of drums.

---

[1] See pp. 293 f. In view of the Hamitic strain in the Bantu breed, it should be noted that worship of the serpent was a prominent feature in old Ethiopian paganism: the Abyssinians worshipped a large serpent before their conversion to Christianity, and the Gallas reverence it as the mother of men, and refuse to eat fish because they think them of its species. (TRML. 78, 81.)

[2] GPNR. 291.

Among the Senga a woman was sometimes sacrificed to cause rain. Among the Wemba, in case of drought, the *Shing'anga* was summoned to divine the cause. If the spirits of the chiefs buried at Mwaruli were responsible, a bull was sent to Simwaruli for sacrifice, and—by way of a douceur—a slave woman as well. When the drought was acute, a human victim would be conveyed to Mwaruli, and the high priest would keep him caged in a stoutly woven fish-basket, until his preparations for the sacrifices were made."

That rain-rites in the Nyasa district were inspired by the same motive, is plain from a paragraph in Scott's *Cyclopædic Dictionary of the Mang'anja Language:*[1] "The chief of the village goes out with his younger brethren (*i.e.*, his people) and his wives, who bring 'nsima' and fowls, and perhaps a goat to go to the thicket to the temple-hut there where there is a little house builded long ago; the people stay there and clean away the grass (from the sacred place—lambulira), and the chief answers, saying: 'God give us rain, and harden not thy heart against us,' and makes many prayers, while all those clap their hands 'Wu! wu! wu!' and he prays again and again, they clap their hands; then they eat the 'nsima,' the whole of it, and the meat, some of which they place in the house; the children are all about with the portion of 'nsima' in their hands (lapata!); and as the older people, some of whom eat from the 'nsengwa' baskets, when they have eaten they put the baskets all together and they are carried away: other women sing the hymn and surround the thicket hedge, saying—'May there come sweeping rain,—sweeping down. The rain here has been restricted, Sweeping rain!' (And other prayers.) And the rain comes in truth, and the temple gatherers on their return come back with the rain pouring and garments and bodies dripping. Then the villagers say, 'You see it was true, God was angry with us.' "

Of the Konde, who dwell around the northern end of Lake Nyasa, Mackenzie writes:[2] " 'Why do you ask me for rain?'

[1] Quoted in RP. 203-204. I fear the English has suffered by being retranslated from the French of Le Roy's original edition, but I have been unable to find a copy of Scott's Dictionary.
[2] SRK. 180.

says Chungu, when his impatient people come to him, 'God owns the rain, and only He can give it.' 'But,' reply the people, 'common men cannot pray. Pray you to your ancestors, and let them carry your prayer to God.' " The same writer tells us [1] that the rain-rites "are practically the same all over the Konde country, but many chiefs have special practices of their own. A very picturesque ceremony is that of the chief Mwaisumo. When the early rains have fallen, and the ground has been hoed, chief and people go to the grave of the ancestral chiefs, carrying their shields of ox-hide. The chief and his headmen standing in rows, raise their shields above their heads, and Mwaisumo, taking water into his mouth, squirts it upwards, and prays for a good harvest." From other pages of the same book [2] we learn that it used to be customary for the chiefs in secret conclave to select a boy, make him drink beer until he died, and then burn his body, grind it to powder, and distribute it over the district as a "medicine" to ensure a good crop,—a custom that is said to have been observed in the northern clans till quite lately. The ordinary sacrifice, nowadays, is a black or white ox or cow, preferably the latter. When spirits of the dynasty have been told that this is the gift of all the people, and have been besought to intercede for them with the Supreme Being, the beast is killed with a blow from an axe on the back of the neck, and the flesh is laid in little heaps upon the grave, each ancestor being named as his portion is set down. "The chief and his followers also feast until the ants come out and attack the portions laid down for the spirits, when all flee, for the spirits have come to accept the sacrifice, and it is well not to be too near them. For three days those who took part in the ceremony remain in their houses, for they have been in contact with unseen powers, and are dangerous until the effect has passed off." Minor rain-rites of well-known magical pattern are also in vogue among the Konde; but, unlike most tribes, —if the sequence of Mackenzie's narrative is that of actual events —they perform the minor rites *after* the major.

To Engai, the rain-god of the Akikuyu, a black ram is sacrificed at the sacred fig-tree of the community as a prayer for rain;

[1] SRK. 117.
[2] SRK. 208-210.

and the Akamba, neighbours of the Akikuyu, sacrifice a sheep or
a goat (male or female), or a bull or a steer, but not a cow.[1]

On the border of Bantu Africa, some three or four hundred
miles north-west of the Akamba, the Basoga apply to the chief
when they want rain, and, as a rule, he summons his experts, and
a fire is kindled before his fence, prayers offered for rain, and
a bull slaughtered, its liver and heart being cut up, cooked, and
thrown about for the ghosts, who in return cause the rain to
fall. But sometimes he sends to the temple of the departed
chiefs, and the priests make offerings there and pray for rain.
Minor rain-rites, in which magic plays as large a part as religion,
are also performed by these tribesmen: "People sometimes tried
to make rain for themselves. They made large fires upon which
they threw damp grass and leaves so that dense clouds of smoke
arose, and they beat drums to imitate thunder. They called
upon the ghosts of their fathers and offered them beer which
they drank in communion with them."[2]

Krapf,[3] in accord with the spirit of his age, evidently regarded
Wanika "rain-makers" as charlatans with no religious significance—weather-wise folk, who studied the clouds, used "a kind
of thermometer made of a peculiar wood which they placed
in water," and often snatched a verdict by trickery; but that this
is not the whole of the truth becomes apparent from his further
statements that the hereditary dignity of "rain-making" is vested
in certain families of great importance among the people, and
that on the 27th of April, 1847, a black sheep was sacrificed
and its blood poured on a man's grave, "partly to obtain rain, and
partly for the sake of the man who had died." Unfortunately,
he seems not to have enquired why this particular grave was
selected for the purpose.

There is still much to be discovered concerning the true inwardness of West Coast rain-rites. In 1896 the Zi Nganga, or
priests of the groves of Nyambi and Senze, in Loango, discovered
by divination that the existing drought was caused by breach of
ancestral custom, and three girls who had not yet passed through

[1] BBM. 42, 58.
[2] GS. 107, 131.
[3] TRML. 168, 169-170.

the puberty rites were found to be pregnant. In this case the culprits escaped, with the assistance of their relatives; but Dennett says [1] that the time-honoured punishment that would have been inflicted if the enraged people had caught them, was to put the girls and their defilers to shame by compelling them to dance naked before the people, who pelted them with heated gravel and bits of glass as they ran the gauntlet.

Andrew Battell spent two and a half years in Loango, after escaping from Angola, apparently from 1608-1610. According to him, the king of that country was honoured by the people as if he were god, and was called *Nzambi-ampungu* ("god-most-high"). "They believe that he can give rain when he listeth," says Battell,[2] who states that they assembled by their regiments once a year, bringing gifts to the king, and asking him for rain, and that there was a great assembly with sports and music on a day appointed by the king, at which the king "shooteth an arrow into the sky." Battell asserts that he witnessed this ceremony, and that "it chanced to rain mightily that day." Ravenstein, who edited the Hakluyt Society's reprint of *Purchas His Pilgrimes*, mistrusted Battell's description of this rite; because Dennett had told him that nearly three centuries later the king used to send the people to a great rain-doctor, so as not to commit himself, and because Abbé Proyart says the same in his *Histoire de Loango*, which was published in Paris in 1819. But if Battell had been drawing the long bow, he could hardly have linked on the rain-rites to the priestly prerogatives of the chief in this thoroughly Bantu manner, unless he had seen some such rite elsewhere in the country; and the greater reliance of later kings upon expert rainmongers does not weaken Battell's testimony.

OCCASIONS FOR THE WORSHIP OF TRIBAL GODS: 2. SEEDTIME

Seedtime, fructification, and harvest—the three great events in the cycle of the agricultural year—are all marked with rites of approach to ancestor-spirits.

Although day, month, and year are natural measurements of time, the solar year—the year that plants and animals heed—is

[1] BBMM. 68-70.
[2] SAAB. 47.

not a multiple of the lunar month, and neither year nor month is a multiple of the day. The year consists of 365 days, 5 hours, 48 minutes, and 46 seconds; and the lunar month, of 29 days, 12 hours, 44 minutes, and 2.82 seconds. Of the astronomical lunar month, the Bantu know nothing; for the moon presents the whole of its dark side to the earth when in conjunction with the sun, and remains invisible for from 18 to 40 hours afterwards. Their month is the period between the *coming into view* of two consecutive new moons, a period which varies between 29 and 30 days, any successive twelve taking 354 or 355 days, that is, 10 or 11 days short of the solar year; but their year is measured, in practice by the recurrence of the seasons, and in theory by the rising of the Pleiades [1] after sunset; and, to add to the confusion, they name their months after such annual events as the budding, blooming or fruiting of certain kinds of trees, the calving of a particular species of antelope, or the seasonal tasks of the farmer. People whose calendar is purely lunar (Mohammedans, for example) find the same month occurring in the depth of winter one year and at the height of summer some 16 or 17 years later, the seasons going right round their calendar in about 33 years. From the time of the Exile, Jews have mitigated this inconvenience by inserting an extra lunar month into their calendar about every third year; but Bantu tribesmen, ignorant of the discoveries of Babylonian or other astronomers, cannot make out why their lunar months will not keep step with the Pleiades and the bursting forth of bud and blossom. What Casalis says of the Basuto [2] holds good for the common run of Bantu tribes: "The native year is composed of twelve moons, which derive their names from natural phenomena or from special occupations. Each moon is registered with the most scrupulous exactness, as soon as it appears; but, notwithstanding the shrewdness of the old men and the good memory of the young ones, these moons are always out of order, and, when it is least expected, some phenomenon which ought to appear in September is not seen till October. . . . Some minds of greater penetration assert that there is a moon without a name. After endless debates the moons

---

[1] Seleméla = "something to hoe for," is the Secwana name for this constellation. The astral or sidereal year is 20 minutes and 23 seconds longer than the solar year.

[2] Bs. 164.

are left to get out of order as they please; and recourse is had to the phenomena of the atmosphere and the state of vegetation to know when to put the mattock in the ground."

Although the ascendency of the Pleïades and the state of vegetation proclaim the approach of the season for tillage, the unseen guardians of law and custom would be offended were tribesmen to put the mattock in the ground till their vicegerent, the chief, gave the word. All are free to fell trees and burn undergrowth in any garden-plot that they are entitled to reclaim from the forest, but actual cultivation must wait till orthodox tribal rites have been performed,—rites marked by great diversity of practice, everywhere strangely magical, but always designed to secure fertility for the seed.

The Rev. Noel Roberts writes [1] that most tribes in the Northern Transvaal have a hut which is "at once the focus and the source of all the fertility of the tribe," whether of people, herds, or crops. His opinion that this hut is of phallic design finds confirmation, of which he seems unaware, in its name, "*Ntloa oa koma,*" [2] as he writes it. In this primitive fane [3] the drums which are the shrine of the tutelary spirit of the clan are piously preserved, and safe in the sanctuary beyond them a hollow cylindrical vessel, made of cowdung and beeswax, contains layers of seed, with, in at least one tribe (Moletshie), layers of human skin between. When the ploughing season sets in, the chief mixes a few grains of this seed into the contents of each patriarch's seed-basket; and since that which is in contact with a spirit-tabernacle catches the quality of the indwelling spirit, according to a fundamental principle of contagious magic, a pinch of seed

[1] *South African Journal of Science,* No. 2, vol. xiv.

[2] A friend, Karanga by descent and Mongwato by upbringing, who talked to me concerning "hidden things" with a freedom that his neighbours would have reprehended, asserted that *kóma* is an archaic and now esoteric term for *glans penis;* and he wondered how the phrase *go ya kóma* came to mean "to chant the war-songs." In Krapf and Rebmann's *Nika-English Dictionary,* however, *kóma* is shown to mean "spirit of the dead," among the Nika or Giriama who live a little to the west of Mombasa, and Krapf consistently uses it in this sense in TRML. 171, 176, 186, 198. Johnston quotes it (CSBSL. ii. 34) with the same meaning in the tongue of the Pokomo tribe, between the Tana and Sabaki rivers, and thinks the same root appears in *ekum* ("ghost") among the semi-Bantu Nde of the Cross River basin.

[3] Spirits of Ashanti clan-heads, enshrined in blackened stools and housed in temples of another pattern, are also givers of fertility to people and crops. (AS. 96, 105, 106, 136.)

which has been stored in the penetralia of the temple of fertility fertilises a peck of seed-corn, as surely as a bishop's handful of consecrated ground imparts its own mysterious virtue to an acre of new graveyard.[1] In this manner tribal divinities are acknowledged and their aid secured by the ploughman.

Most tribes of the Northern Transvaal are Bawenda; and Mr. Roberts' phallic shrines are probably what Mr. Gootschling[2] calls little round sheds that stand in the *tondo* of each clan and contain all the fetishes of the clan, together with an image of their totem carved in wood and others of a man and woman about two feet in height, fairly well executed in ebony. This writer makes no mention of any tribal function at seedtime, but says that each family gathers around its family altar in the yard of its own patriarch,[3] displays its ancestral relics, and offers sacrifice and prayer to its ancestor-spirits. From a combination of the two accounts we gather that the Bawenda invoke the spirits of the dynasty and those of the family at the beginning of the planting season.

The Vachopi, in the coastland between the Limpopo on the south and Inharrime on the north, make offerings to ancestor-spirits before beginning to till the soil in August and September. Having brought his diggers into his lands at sunrise, the patriarch throws a handful of mealies upon the ground for each of his deceased parents, using the right hand for his father's portion and the left for his mother's, and beseeches these ministering spirits to secure him the fruit of his labour. About the end of November or beginning of December, the chief receives seeds of maize, monkey-nuts, beans, earth-peas, etc., from his

---

[1] "Lambarde, in his 'Perambulations of Kent' (*written* in 1570) mentions the image of St. Edith, at Kensing, by whose interference blasting, mildew, brand-ear, and other injuries to crops were prevented. The sacrifice was as follows: the husbandman who wished to screen his crops from such evil influences, brought a few pecks of corn to the priest, who, after putting by the chief part for his own use, took a single handful of the grain, sprinkled it with holy water, and, 'by mumbling a fewe wordes of conjuration,' dedicated it to St. Edith. He then delivered it back to the farmer, who departed in the full belief that by his mixing the hallowed handful with the seed-corn, the coming crop would be insured against the deprecated calamities. Lambarde thinks that St. Edith must be regarded as the representative of the Roman god *Robigus*, whose office was to protect cereals from those very annoyances." CPP. 327.

[2] R. BAAS., 1905, iii. 200, 204, 213.

[3] For further information, see p. 277.

people, and invites one of the great "medicine-men" to come to his village. Having sacrificed to his own ancestor-spirits before leaving home, the *anyanga* doctors the seeds with a sooty "medicine" called *kahola*, and, going forth at dead of night, plants samples of them in each tribesman's garden. He returns to the chief's kraal at daybreak, and sends out his helpers to gather "leaves of all kinds of trees and plants," which, after being chopped up, are made into soup. Fowls, also, are cooked, and, when all is ready, the men, women, and children of the community partake of a common and ceremonial feast, at which the leaf-soup is eaten with the fowls. "The doctor begins by eating the liver of the fowls. . . . Women who are expectant mothers must not partake of this meal, but the *anyanga* gives them a little of it mixed with *nsita* (medicine made from charred and pounded roots) and they rub it on their arms and bodies. The Chief buries the leaves from which the *muri wakuhola* was prepared in a hole, and they rot away. The *anyanga* puts aside in a wooden bowl some 'medicine' made from uncooked leaves and water. This is the holy water which he afterwards uses for sprinkling huts to keep the evil spirits and sorcerers away. That day all the fires are extinguished in the huts of the people. If they should keep their fires alight, they would lack food at harvest time; the seeds would not grow in the fields! . . . The only fire left burning in all the country is the large sacred fire kindled by the doctor himself and continually replenished with fuel by the wives of the Chief. At sun-down all the fires in the kraals are re-lighted from the big sacred fire by means of torches carried by the adjutants. The *anyanga* himself re-lights the Chief's fire. He then marches solemnly round the Chief's kraal accompanied by two servers, one carrying the bowl of 'holy water' and the other plucking a fowl and scattering the feathers in all directions. The *anyanga* dips a spray of *nkuhlu* leaves into the holy water, and sprinkles the huts with it outside. He afterwards stands in the doorway and throws some of the water inside the hut. His helpers afterwards go to the other kraals and bless them by asperging the huts with holy water, in order to keep evil spirits and sorcerers away. This day is called the day of *muzilo*, because cohabitation is prohibited during the '*kahola-*

rite' night and on the day of *muzilo.*" [1]   We are not told whether the *anyanga* who sacrifices to his own ancestors on this occasion is the natural priest of some ancient family that held the land before the chief's forefathers came upon the scene, or, possibly, the heir to priestly prerogatives that did not pass to the present line of chiefs; [2] nor whether the *kahola* powder contains some more potent ingredient than the "charred and pounded roots of sacred plants and trees"; nor whether the sacred fire is kindled with friction-sticks after the ancient manner.

All tribes of the Becwana group have a custom of "medicating" the seed-corn before commencing cultivation, [3] and then hoeing up two or three patches of their garden (generally a patch at each of the four corners) and sowing a little of this charmed seed. Obtrusively magical as this practice is, it seems to be somehow connected with loyalty to the ancestral spirits.

Libations, offerings, and prayers are made at the ancestral stones [4] in each of the little Makalaka villages that are scattered over the northern borderland of the Bechuanaland Protectorate, before any villager begins to till the soil; and on an appointed day every woman takes a basketful of seed to her patriarch, so that he may put into it a little consecrated seed, which she carefully mixes with the rest. I failed to get a precise account of the patriarch's method of making his seed sacred, but gathered that the process is essentially similar to that which the Rev. Noel Roberts has described.

Shimunenga, who was probably chief of the Bamala when they first settled in the Kasenga district, is now tutelary deity of that community; and it is not permissible for his worshippers to sow their fields till his priest has planted a few seeds at his sacred grove. [5]

Akamba tribesmen sacrifice a goat and offer milk and grain at the village shrine before commencing to sow the new season's seed, and there is, of course, a sacrificial feast. If any man plants before these ceremonies, the elders fine him a goat, which

---

[1] E. Dora Earthy, in BNT., Dec., 1925, p. 194.
[2] See my pp. 82, 202 f., 227 f., 256 f., 278, 334, 336 note.
[3] Cf. ABN. 132.
[4] See p. 273.
[5] IPNR. ii. 183, 188.

is sacrificed at the shrine as an atonement, and what he has sown must be dug up and returned to the village, lest Engai should be angry with the community.[1]

The Hon. Kenneth R. Dundas writes [2] that among the Wawanga of the Elgon District (Kenya), "before the people may sow *mtama* the king must make medicine. About six months" (weeks?) "before the time has come for sowing, a pure white bullock is killed at the *Msambue*." [3] The following month a black ram is strangled before the hut of the king's mother. Both these are sacrifices. "The next day the common people go and sow millet in the chief's fields. After which they may sow in their own plantations. Any one caught sowing millet before the chief has done so is fined and may very possibly even die."

In the Gabun district, a woman makes "medicine" so that she may have plenty of food in her garden; and when she has cooked her decoction of leaves and bark, and rubbed her breast with white clay from the bed of a stream, she places the pot of "medicine" in the middle of her garden-plot, and lustrates the ground with the mixture, saying, "My forefathers, now in the land of spirits! Give me food! Let me have food more abundant than all other people!" [4] If Nassau had failed to give us the information about the woman's prayer, we should have concluded that she was merely trusting to magic; whereas the prayer shows that her act is essentially religious, though accompanied by ritual that could not have been invented by people who were not steeped in magic.

OCCASIONS FOR THE WORSHIP OF TRIBAL-GODS: 3. FIRST-
FRUITS

Robertson Smith tells us [5] that the oldest extant Hebrew laws require the payment of firstfruits, but know nothing of a tithe due at the sanctuary. It is probable that the nomadic Israelites took over from the dwellers in Canaan, together with their knowledge of agriculture, what came to be known in its natu-

[1] BBM. 76.
[2] JRAI., 1913, p. 48.
[3] Stones sacred to ancestral spirits of the paternal line.
[4] FWA. 189.
[5] RS. 246.

ralised form as the Feast of Unleavened Bread—a husbandman's spring festival which was grounded in the belief that the
new crops were taboo [1] to the people till the local Baalim, or
spirit-lords of the land, had been fittingly acknowledged. Analogous ordinances are observed by other agricultural people,[2] and
in some Bantu tribes they are pre-eminent among annual events.
The motive that inspired these periodic celebrations is within
our reach; but inasmuch as the close association between the conjugal intercourse of cultivators and the fertility of their lands,
which is brought out in strong relief in the African version of
these rites, is likely to baffle the imagination of European students,
it is worth while to quote a concise, luminous and chastely worded
passage from Prof. George Foot Moore's lectures on *The Birth
and Growth of Religion.*[3] "A widely distributed type of fertility magic, which also was eventually taken up in religion, rests
on the primitive assumption of what we might call in Stoic phrase
the sympathy of nature, more exactly, the identity of the reproductive processes in all nature, animal and vegetative. In consequence it was believed that the germination of the seed and abundance of increase could be promoted by the exercise of the
generative function by human beings, originally no doubt by the
cultivators of their own fields. More or less attenuated survivals of these rites have been perpetuated in several parts of
modern Europe. When an agricultural religion developed, this
old fertility magic, which had to begin with nothing to do with
spirits or gods, could attach itself to any deity that was believed
to give the increase to the husbandman's labours [4]—an earth
goddess, for instance, or an astral divinity connected with the
germinating season—without regard to the other associations of
the god. In Western Asia they were frequently, but by no means
exclusively, connected with a goddess of fertility worshipped
under many names."

Becwana tribes call the Ceremony of Firstfruits *Go Loma
Ñwaga* ("The Biting of the Year"), and observe it during the

[1] RS. 241; Lev. xxiii. 9, 14.
[2] In Russia "no man dare touch an apple before the feast of Transfiguration
(Aug. 6)." (CPP. 502.)
[3] New York: Charles Scribner's Sons, 1923, p. 60.
[4] Many, if not all, Bantu tribes attribute the fertility of people, herds, and lands
to the ancestor-spirits.

moon which they call *Herekoñ*,[1] *Filikon* or *Perekon* (a word of
unknown derivation), and *Mokono, Mekono* or *Mekonwe* (because it sees the gardens "brought into subjection"[2]), and *Mol-
omo* (because this festival occurs in it).   That is, the first moon
after the southern summer solstice, roughly our January.   This,
together with an idiomatic use of *go loma* (lit. "to bite") in the
sense of "to begin," has led English speaking tribesmen to call
this festival The Becwana New Year Ceremony,—though every
elder who ran through the Calendar for my instruction always
began with *Phatwe*, the moon which is renewed in August.

In all magico-religious celebrations the Becwana are careful to
range the members of a family, and, when the celebration is
shared by a larger group, the families in a clan, or the clans in a
tribe, according to each one's status; but this is the only religious
rite that an independent tribe in Bechuanaland ought not to celebrate till it has been observed by other independent tribes of
superior status in that group.   For some decades this rule of
tribal precedence has been falling steadily into desuetude, but
fifty years ago it was deemed important.   Subject to this condition, however, each paramount chief was free to fix any day in
Herekoñ for the ceremony of Firstfruits in his tribe.   But two
very interesting exceptions to this rule are worthy of notice.

In this group of tribes the Bafhurutse are regarded as senior
to the other branches of the common stock.   The Bafhurutse are
now a small tribe, broken into independent sections, of which two
live in the Western Transvaal.   At Mankgodi, the town of one
of these sections, there is a clan of no great political importance
which takes precedence in religious rites over all other clans in
that community—over even the ruling clan.   When the paramount chief of the Mankgodi Bafhurutse wishes his people to

[1] "The holding of this ceremony in the month of Herekon," so a Bakwena
expert in tribal lore told me, "is to shun the month Tlhakole. Tlhakole is a month
in which no army may set forth from home, no circumcision camps be formed, no
cattle castrated, and no milk poured into milk-sacks lest a curse rest upon the cattle."
Bantu philosophy is apt to be casual in its conclusions, but my friend's gloss has an
interest of its own.   He maintained also that Tlhakole, which is approximately
our February, takes its name from the little furry, green caterpillars that are then
busy taking toll from the beans; but it is easier to believe that the month is so
called because it is spent in "cleaning" or weeding the gardens, and that the caterpillars took their name from the month in which they appear.

[2] By which they mean that the ploughing is finished and early plants are fruiting.

celebrate the Festival of Firstfruits, he must request the head of this privileged clan to take the lead.   There is a similar pecul- iarity in the tribal economy of the Bakwena of Molepolole, who come close after the Bafhurutse in tribal precedence.   One of their clans, called Ntloedibe, which, owing to a succession of incompetent heads, has sunk into numerical insignificance and poverty, and which now carries no weight in the political coun- cils of the tribe, occupies, nevertheless, a position of peculiar privilege.   If any member of this clan is charged with murder, the court of the paramount chief takes jurisdiction in the case; [1] but the paramount is incompetent to judge any member of this sacrosanct clan for any lesser offence, or to levy distraint upon them.   They can be judged only by their own clan-head, and the utmost the paramount chief can do is to request them to deal with any one of their number who is at fault with another clan. Whatever happens, not a single head of their stock can be seized by the paramount, because their birthright is superior to his: *go twe e se ka ea rothéla mo sakeñ la kgosi, ke maila a magolo* ("the saying is, it must not micturate in the cattle-kraal of the para- mount; it is a major taboo.")   They are liable to military ser- vice like other clans; but if one of them shirks duty, the regi- mental police must not punish him, but may bring his conduct to the notice of his own clan-head.   Now the paramount chief is not competent to begin the celebration of the Feast of Firstfruits till this sacrosanct clan has observed it.

I was never able to visit Mankgodi after hearing of its distin- guished clan; but the Bakwena have no difficulty in explaining the privileged position of the Ntloedibe clan, and it is said that the Mankgodi explanation is similar.   At some unknown date in the past, a weakling who was in the direct line of succession to the paramountcy handed over the chieftainship to an abler but younger brother.   The present paramount chief of the Bakwena is the head of the house that that younger brother founded, and the Ntloedibe clan is of the superior lineage of the weakling who parted with his birthright, or, rather, with the military, political and judicial prerogatives of his birthright; for nothing but death can divest such a man of his priestly prerogatives, and even death

[1] Under British rule, offences punishable with death or outlawry are transferred from the court of the paramount to that of the suzerain.

can but transfer him to the company of the divine Shades below
and clothe the firstborn son of the wife that he first betrothed
with his sacerdotal supremacy.[1]   The head of the Ntloedibe clan
still rejoices, therefore, in the title of *Kgosi ea Leshótse* ("Chief
of the Cucurbitacea")—a dignity which is fastidious of birth and
disdainful of energy, ability, and wisdom.

Soon after assuming the paramountcy, Khama abolished the
ancient rites in the Bamangwato tribe; but he told me that in his
younger days the Bamangwato celebration of the feast was on
this wise.   The ceremony began in the Place of Tribal Assembly,
where a large wooden dish was set, containing "medicated" leaves
of a cucurbitaceous plant (of which more must be said presently).
Each of the chief's children, in order of status, crushed one of
these leaves in his hand and rubbed it over his big toes and
navel; then the chief and his younger brothers followed in strict
order of precedence; and so on in regular succession throughout
the Bamangwato clans; after which they went away to their
homes to observe the rite with their several families.   When the
Bamangwato had complied with custom, the many clans of other
lineage that had taken shelter under their shield (probably two-
thirds of the total population) observed the rite in their own way
at their own centres.   Except for small variations in detail, due
perhaps to individual preference and enthusiasm, the family
ritual was similar to that in the Place of Tribal Assembly.   Men,
women, and children smeared themselves with the juice of cucurbitaceous leaves, and mothers either smeared their small children
or pounded up a few leaves so that the little ones could smear
themselves; but some people, not content with applying the
bruised leaves to big toes and abdomen, rubbed it over their
foreheads also, or even over every joint in the body; and in
some groups it was thought better for the father, or failing him,
the eldest son to apply the leaves to each member of the family.
If a child were absent, his place was taken in the line of strict
precedence by his porridge-platter, and the pulped leaves rubbed
over the centre of the dish.   After all members of the family
had been treated, the leaves left over were pounded up and mixed
with milk in a trough, and the dogs were called to drink it; "for

[1] Parallel instances may be found in the Brehon Laws and in the village communities of India.

of old," as one of my Native helpers phrased it, "dogs were highly esteemed and treated almost like children."

Except in one or two places where the paramount chief has not inherited the sacerdotal headship of the clan, there seems to be no important difference between the usage of the Bamangwato and that of other Becwana tribes. Some tribes anoint only the navel and the big toe of the right foot, while others anoint forehead, joints, toes and navel; but the anointing of the forehead is not general, and the anointing of the joints is confessedly a somewhat modern innovation. Some tribes chew the leaf, and others bruise it in the hand or pound it. Probably the ancient usage was to chew the leaf (whence the technical term *go loma thótse* ("to bite the thótse") and rub the masticated mouthful over the navel and the great toe of the right foot.

Thótse is the Secwana name of that genus of herbaceous climbing-plants which we call Cucurbitaceæ, or rather for such of them as are indigenous or acclimatised in Bechuanaland. It is the name of the plants, whether wild or cultivated, not of their fruits; but for the purpose of specifying a particular variety the name of the fruit is added: e.g., *thótse ea legapu* ("water-melon-vine"), *thótse ea lephutse* ("pumpkin-vine"). Of indigenous kinds some are wild and some cultivated. *Thótse ea mokapana* ("wild water-melon-vine") and *thótse ea mokate* ("wild Kafir-melon-vine") grow abundantly in sandy soil, especially in the Kalahari, where the copious but insipid juices of such of their fruits as are not bitter enable people and cattle to sustain life for months without water. *Thótse ea monyako* is a wild, trailing plant, which bears stumpy cucumbers that are studded with spiky protuberances. Of the cultivated varieties, *thótse ea legapu* ("water-melon-vine"), *thótse ea lerotse* or *leshotse* ("Kafir-melon-vine"), and *thótse ea lephutse* ("pumpkin-vine") are found in most Secwana gardens; and many people grow a few gourd-vines (*thótse ea sego* or *segwana*) for the sake of drinking-cups, ladles and larger calabashes which are made from the shelly rinds of the fruits of one variety or another. *Thótse ea lerotse* ("Kafir-melon-vine") is the orthodox variety for use at the ceremony of Firstfruits; but failing that, *thótse ea legapu* ("water-melon-vine") may be used, or, as a last resort, *thótse ea monyako* ("cucumber-vine"); but *thótse ea lephutse* ("pumpkin-vine") is of no avail for this purpose, though, strange to say, it is an ingredient in the purifying "medicine" which will be mentioned later.[1]

Nothing is more remarkable in the Becwana usage for this festival than its linking of sexual congress between husband and wife with the fruitfulness of the fields which they sow. It is a hard and fast rule that every man should sleep with his chief wife on the night of the festival, and that he should sleep on successive nights with his secondary wives in the order of their standing in his family—for each of these wives sows her own field.

In the old days if a husband, detained in the hunting-veld or at a cattle-post, heard that the feast had been kept at his home, he was greatly disquieted. Hoping against hope, he smeared himself with the juice of one of the wild Cucurbitaceæ, probably the one they call *monyako*, though such a plant lacks the virtue of one taken from his own garden and officially prepared; but when he arrived home, he did not dare to enter his courtyard, lest, if his wife had completed the ceremony without him, his shadow should blight any of his children upon whom it might happen to fall. He sat, all of a twitter, in the men's assembly-place of his village, fearing even to send his wife word of his arrival; but if, unbidden, she brought him a calabash of water[2] and took his weapons into her courtyard, he drank the water with delight and followed her as speedily as the restraints of masculine dignity would allow. Of course, she and her children had smeared themselves with the *thótse* on the day of the local celebration, but if she had completed the rite by having commerce with another man, then her husband was taboo to her and her family, and, though there was no pollution in her person, his touch or his shadow would blight her or the children which she had borne him. What risk a wife ran in delaying the last act in the ritual for a few weeks till her husband returned, I could never dis-

---

[1] See p. 233.

[2] It is customary for a Bantu wife to refresh her homecoming husband with a drink of water; but if a wife of a Baganda warrior fails to observe the taboo which requires her to abstain from sexual intercourse while her husband is at the war, such water will make him ill. (Bg. 362.)

cover; but all my teachers of tribal lore agreed that a husband who failed to be at home for the Feast of Firstfruits put an unwarrantable strain upon the fidelity of his wife, and brought misfortune upon his own head. It was scarcely likely, they said, that he would survive the year, and if he did, his wife would die or else one of her children. Before the spouses could come together again it was necessary to seek the guidance and assistance of an expert who prepared appropriate "medicine" and saw that the ritual acts were properly performed. The "doctor's" first work after reaching the wife's hut was to prepare "medicine" with which a neighbour was sent to anoint the feet of the husband. Thus protected, the husband entered his wife's court-yard, but, being still under the ban, carefully avoided touching his children or allowing his shadow to fall upon them. Then the "doctor" caused the woman to sit upon the floor with her knees drawn up to her chin, and the man to sit facing her in a similar posture with his knees outside hers; and, after covering them both with a kaross (which must be of oxhide) and laying some of his "medicine" on live coals in a potsherd, he placed this incense-bowl between her knees. When they had "drunk the fumes" of this "medicine," the charred residue in the pot was ground to powder, mixed with fat, and smeared over husband, wife and children; and each spouse, having made two skin-deep, perpendicular cuts with a razor just below the other's navel, mixed a little of the powder with blood from his or her own wounds and rubbed it into the cuts upon the abdomen of the other. This averted the worst consequences of the breach of custom, but if they resumed cohabitation before the year had expired, both husband and wife would suffer from a disease of which the symptoms are intense pain, green diarrhœa, and the ejection of green vomitus, and one of the spouses would die or one of their children.

Times have changed. Nowadays, when one spouse has com-pleted the rite in the absence of the other, the sceptics of a younger generation think it enough to chew a piece of charcoal from the woman's hearth, rub their own bellies with the re-sultant saliva, and resume cohabitation without further ceremony or delay. Some divergences in various descriptions which I re-ceived of the ancient ritual are probably due to its recent debase-

ment, but others are more likely to be attributable to those gradual and unperceived changes of detail that creep into the rites
of each separate community.   According to my Bamangwato
friends, the purificatory rite was usually performed as soon as
possible after the return of the husband, so that he might not be
excluded altogether from his wife and children; but my Bakwena
friends assert (and they retained the custom after it had fallen
into disrepute among the Bamangwato) that the rite was observed at the next Feast of Firstfruits, and that the spouses
smeared themselves with the ointment of their purification just
before retiring to their sleeping-mat on the evening of that day;
and the son of a famous Bakwena medicine-man supported this
statement with the remark that the only "medicine" that was effectual in such a case consisted of gourd-seeds and roots of pumpkin, Kafir-melon, and wild-melon vines of the year in which they
separated, together with pieces of green Kafir-melon of the year
in which they came together again.   Instead of two perpendicular incisions on the abdomen, the Bakwena made cuts on the
joints of arms and legs and small circular skin-wounds around
the navel.   Some Bamangwato friends taxed my credulity by as-
severating that wives used to confess all their marital infidelities
of the preceding year, and warn their husbands not to approach
them on the night of the Feast of Firstfruits till they had been
purged after the manner recited above; but the Bakwena affirmed
that such confessions were made only by those who had completed the rite in the absence of their lawful spouse.   A man
who had relations with another woman after hearing that the
rite had been observed at his home, had to abide by the same
rule as his wife.   "And," said one of my old instructors, "if a
woman or a man has a habit of performing the ceremony apart
from the other, they must be separated; people say they will
kill one another.   If it is a woman that he married long ago
and by whom he has four or five children, they must still be separated; or a betrothed woman, whether the bride-price has been
paid up or not yet paid up,[1] they can be separated by this custom; but not a woman who has simply been betrothed and not

[1] Becwana men who are hard up take wives on credit, promising the woman's
family a stipulated bride-price when they are able to pay it—often when they receive
bride-price for their first-born daughter.

yet taken, for she is another person." Then he proceeded to explain, to my surprise, that the taboo would not rest upon a spouse who had connection with another person if the spouse was unaware that the Firstfruits ceremony had been performed at home.

One would like to discover the origin and inner meaning of this festival. It was marked by other observances than those mentioned above. All fires were extinguished throughout the town, all hearths swept, and fresh fuel lit with brands from a new fire which had been kindled by means of the fire-drill at the Place of Public Assembly.[1] Supplications were made to ancestral spirits, also, that the harvest might be abundant and the firstborn of people and cattle vigorous and alert. And, finally, when all the rites had been completed, the clansmen mustered in force at the Place of Tribal Assembly, armed with spears, shields and battle-axes, chanting the war-chants and revelling in songs and dances of rejoicing, while the women trilled forth their peculiar ululation; "the commotion," said a Native narrator, "was as if the army had returned from battle." But the great point of the whole festival was this: all the new season's crops were taboo till consecrated by these ordinances to the use of the people. Wild fruits might be eaten as soon as they could be gathered, and so might Bastard Kafir-corn (*makwakwa* or *macwabudu*), which had sprouted from stalks of last year's reaping; but he who tasted the new crops before the rites were rendered would pay for his audacity or heedlessness with an illness that was likely to be fatal.

Somewhat similar characteristics mark the Feast of Firstfruits in tribes of the Kafir-Zulu group: its motive is the lifting of taboo from the new crops; and among its distinctive features we note the breaking of calabashes, the bespattering of tribesmen with the firstfruits of the garden, the appeal to ancestor-spirits, and the military muster of the tribe.

From Kidd's inconsequent description of the Kafir usage,[2] the following facts loom forth. Tembus, Gaikas and Gcalekas used to regard the new crops as taboo till this feast had been observed, those who set the prohibition at naught being accused of witch-

---

[1] At Samhain, the festival that marked the beginning of the Celtic year, new fire was brought into each house from the sacred bonfire, itself probably kindled from the need-fire. (RAC. 259.)

[2] EK. 269-271.

craft and either killed or outlawed; but this taboo has now fallen into disuse. During the festival, which begins with rites of lavation and lasts four days, the king lays his power and dignity aside and may be insulted with impunity; and on the fourth day he comes forth, clad in a ceremonial garb of grass, leaves, corn-sheaths and herbs, which is burnt at the close of the festival, and dances backward and forward three times at the head of his kraal, attended by boys who whistle like sailors becalmed. Then follows a fight between two bulls. Sometimes the chief drinks the gall of an ox which has to be killed without weapons and cooked over a fire made by friction-sticks that the tribal sacristan jealously guards. The flesh of this ox may be eaten by boys, but not by men, lest the chief should be injured by his enemies. Then follows the slaughter of more cattle and a general feast. "Sometimes," says Kidd, referring apparently in his loose and tantalising way to the ox that is killed without weapons, "the first bull that is slain is burnt entire with its skin on; but sometimes it is eaten by the boys." When the king announces the completion of the feast and resumes his former greatness, he shatters a calabash (sometimes three calabashes) of boiled samples of the new crops, and sprinkles the people with the cooked food, frequently spitting it out upon them. Finally, regimental orders are issued, and after a day's rest at the Great Place the people are free to return home and eat whatever their tillage has brought them.

Kidd asserts [1] that this feast is divided into two portions, a Little Festival which is attended only by the great men of the nation and a Great Festival which all warriors are obliged to attend in full panoply of war, and that in some years or some tribes only the one or the other is observed. As far as one can make out from his sketchy account, the Little Festival is purely agricultural, while a prominent feature of the Great Festival is the sacrifice of a bull. In default of a thorough and authentic description of the usage of the tribes of Natal and Zululand, one has to fall back upon what Shooter,[2] Callaway,[3] and ex-King Cetywayo [4] have said of this Feast; and in attempting the impossible task of

[1] EK. 269.
[2] KNZC. 26-27, 392.
[3] RSZ. 389.
[4] R., 1883, pp. 526 and 532.

piecing together the statements of these three authorities so as
to form a chronological narrative of events, I began to wonder
whether, when Europeans first came upon the scene, these tribes
had not almost amalgamated an agricultural and a pastoral spring
festival, somewhat as the Hebrew nomads did after they settled down to agricultural life in Canaan.[1]   Unfortunately the
history of these tribes prior to their settlement in what is now
known as Natal and Zululand has faded from their memory.
Like other Bantu tribes, their historic sense is undeveloped: tribal
self-complacency is not conducive to interest in other groups with
which they came into contact from time to time, and meagre
family traditions which sacrifice verity to vainglory do not suffice to deliver more than a few generations from oblivion.   Crabtree infers from philological evidence that this group of tribes
are "a distinct type of Bantu, a type so near and yet so peculiar
that it could not have developed side by side with normal Bantu";
and that somewhere they had acquired a social improvement not
obtainable in Africa, copied an ornate style of diction, and developed military instincts quite out of keeping with African Bantu
races, as well as a few markedly barbarous customs, such as skinning the Mombo alive, impaling through the anus, and killing
cattle by rupture of the aorta.   For their origin, he is inclined
to look in North Africa for a black race which had come much
into contact with Phœnician or some related Semitic stock.[2]
Theal's ethnographical studies inclined him to believe that they
were remnants of those hordes of cannibal marauders which
streamed forth from the coast of Guinea south-eastward and
were known in the 16th and 17th centuries, as Jaggas when they
ravaged the old Kongo Kingdom and Angola, and as Ba-zimba
when they raided Kilwa and Mombasa.[3]   If Theal is correct,
they had probably paid little attention to agriculture for a century or two before their arrival in South-east Africa, preferring
to live upon weaker tribes whom they vanquished; but wherever
they came from, they had certainly absorbed fragments of all
the miscellaneous tribes that lay in the path of their unrelenting
march.

[1] See *Ency. Biblica, art.* "Feasts."
[2] BNT., May, 1922.
[3] ECSA. 204-206.

It appears from ex-King Cetywayo's evidence [1] that the Zulus observed a Feast in the month of *Zibandhela* (December), at which very few people were present, and another in *Umasingana* (January), [2] which was attended by all the warriors and many women. At the December Festival the king "gets two *amaselwa* (something in the shape of the pig-melon) and strikes them together. His doctors then give him a mixture of different medicines, in order to strengthen his knees, and stomach, and body, so that he may eat of the new crops without injury to his health." Whether this "medicine" was swallowed, as the interpreter appears to have assumed, or applied externally, is doubtful; but there is no doubt that Zulus refrained from tasting the new crops till they were thus fortified. At the January Festival, "certain young men are set on to a fierce bull to overpower it without any weapon. When the bull has been overpowered, it is finally killed by means of a chopper being plunged behind his skull. It is then cut up and given over to boys, who roast and eat all they can eat. Everything that remains appertaining to the bull is burnt to ashes and then buried. . . . The king's *inyanga yokwelapa, i.e.,* medicine doctor, used to take the gall of the bull, mix it up with different sorts of medicine, and give the king to take a little, in order that the king might be strong and well." Then followed a sort of military assembly, the regiments being drawn up in a semi-circle around the king and his chief councillors, who discussed "changes that are to be made in the laws"; and after the ancestor-spirits had been invoked, these changes were announced to the people, who forthwith burst out in "praise-songs" of the king and his ancestors. Throughout the Festival the people regaled themselves with dances and beef of the king's bounty.

According to information which Shooter [3] had gathered from Zulus in Natal a quarter of a century before Cetywayo gave his evidence, a black bull was thrown by the young men, who twisted its neck in the process; and after the "doctor" had taken the gall-bladder from the groaning beast and squeezed it into a vessel

---

[1] R., 1883, pp. 525-26, 531-32.
[2] They appear to be the twin halves of a spring or early summer festival, the intention of which was to promote fertility, like the Beltane and midsummer festivals of the ancient Celts.
[3] KNZC. 26-27, 392.

containing "medicine," the king dipped his fingers therein and applied them to his mouth. Then he squirted a mouthful of a "medicated" mixture of bruised corn and other garden produce over an assegai, pointing it towards the sun, and the bull was dispatched with an axe. In the evening the flesh of this beast was eaten by soldiers, who were thereby inhibited from drinking till the following morning. Next day a bull of another colour was slaughtered with an assegai in the usual way; and when the men had dipped their fingers into its gall mixed with "medicine," and had washed in the stream, the "doctor" rolled balls of its cooked flesh in pounded "medicine" and threw them singly into the air for the men to catch. He who caught a ball took a bite and tossed it up again for others to catch, and so on till it fell to the ground, when another ball was thrown up. Next day the king came into the fold arrayed in grass, and a dance called *unkosi* took place; and after resuming his former dress, he returned and dashed a calabash to the ground. (Isaacs, a European resident in Zululand, said "three calabashes.") The grass that the king wore and the fragments of the calabash which he broke were burned where the black bull was roasted, and the ashes scattered and trodden into the ground by cattle. At the conclusion of the festival, the king announced that the taboo upon the new crops was lifted.

Although Shooter mentions December as the date of the festival which he describes, he seems to have confused two festivals which Cetywayo regarded as distinct. He states that the Feast of Firstfruits was common to all the Zulu tribes, but that Chaka added the military rites; and he credits Flynn (a European who had lived long among the Zulus) with the opinion that Chaka added the war ceremonies in order that his troops might be ready to march when the rivers were down. As an explication of this latter remark, it may be worth while to point out that the above-mentioned sacrifice of a black bull bears some resemblance to rites with which Becwana and other tribes used to purify an army for battle.

Callaway's brief description of this Festival [1] adds little to what has been already said. "At the period of the year when the new food is ripe, varying with different places, the chief summons

[1] RSZ. 389.

all his people to a festival (which is called *ukudhlala umkosi*); all the people make beer which they take with them to the chief's village; at the chief's village, too, much beer is made. When the people are assembled the chief has oxen killed by his soldiers, and there is a great feast of one day with singing and dancing. This is called *ukushwama*, and the people return to their homes and begin to eat the new produce. If any one is known to eat new food before this festival he is regarded as *umtakati*, and is killed, or has all his cattle taken away."

The Matabele, under Umziligazi, broke away from Chaka's army in 1827, and, after a decade between the Vaal and Limpopo, settled in what we now know as Matebeleland, retaining, of course, their Zulu customs. A missionary who lived among them from 1859 gives a valuable account of the "great annual feast of the nation, which is called *inxwala*, and is celebrated at the time of the firstfruits."[1] "The time for its celebration is when the early maize and calabashes are ready for eating, and it continues for seven days." Umziligazi, the king, offers sacrifices and prayers to his ancestors, and provides a feast of slaughtered oxen for the people of most of the large towns and villages, who dance and sing praises to him and the spirits of his forefathers. "When the shades have thus been propitiated, the king, with the priests present, bite the tenderly cooked calabash and the raw sweet-reed. In this way the whole increase of the current year is said to be sanctified." Then priests are sent out into all the towns of the land to repeat the last-mentioned ceremony, which they call *cinsa* ("spitting"), and which lifts the taboo from the new crops. Our author saw this celebration at the place where he was living. "The priest made a fire and placing the clay-pots on it, one was filled with young calabashes, while a mixture of fresh milk and charcoal was poured into the other. Whilst these were cooking the priests led the men out of the kraal, and arranging them all in a row, uttered in the presence of each a number of incantations, which I could not understand, while he sprinkled over them all, out of a gourd shell, some kind of charmed powder. This over, they returned into the kraal, and began to lap with their hands the mixture of milk

[1] *Eleven Years in Central South Africa*, by Thomas Morgan Thomas. London: John Snow, 1872, pp. 301-03.

and charcoal from the pot which was now boiling on the fire, half scalding their mouths, and then splashing it upon their limbs, crying out '*a wa quine amadolo*' (let the knees be invigourated). The calabash was then eaten, and a small quantity of the sweet reed chewed and spat out, and the ceremony was over. These were only the male portion of the people, and the females being now in their gardens had their portion reserved for them till the evening when they would also observe the same ceremony on their return home."

That no great change of usage had taken place in Lobengula's time, is evident from Carnegie's description [1] of the Festival as he knew it. He draws a clearer distinction between what he takes to be the regimental rites of the first four days and the ceremony of Firstfruits which "takes place immediately after the big dance." Sixty, eighty, or even a hundred oxen, contributed by towns far and near, were speared in the king's cattle-kraal on the second day of the great feast, and their carcases, cut into joints, were piled overnight in huts set apart for the purpose, so that the spirits might come and eat their share first; and when this sacrificial flesh was eaten towards sunset on the third day, the use of knives was carefully eschewed. Carnegie makes no mention of any characteristic Firstfruits Ceremony at the Great Place, though he remarks, parenthetically, that the king "is the first to *luma* the green food of the season"; but he gives a detailed account of the local rites which he witnessed. As a preparation for this ceremony the people washed themselves at early dawn in the river. The priest's first act was to asperse the congregation with water in which "some green leaves of *makomani*—a kind of vegetable marrow" had been immersed, using a giraffe's tail tied on a short stick as aspergillum. Then he chopped off bits from his "miscellaneous collection of snakes' skins and bones, feathers of wild birds, bones of wild animals, twigs and leaves of various trees," and placed them in an open pot over a fire; and the men, in batches of four, sucked up through short reeds a mouthful or two of the black smoke that issued from the charring mixture, and blew it into the air. After the last man had taken his turn, the residue was removed from the pot and ground

[1] *Among the Matabele,* by the Rev. D. Carnegie. London: R. T. S., 1894, pp. 70-79.

into a fine powder, not unlike charcoal. Next they brought a
dishful of warm milk from a white cow and poured it into this
vessel; and when the milk began to boil, the priest threw back
into it all this black powder, together with some white dust
which made a perfume, and stirred them all up with a long stick;
and the men dipped their fingers into this frothy concoction, as
Thomas described. This done, they partook of a mess of sweet-
reeds and vegetable marrow leaves, which had been brought
fresh from their gardens that morning, and had meanwhile been
stewing in a covered pot over another fire; and, as they ate,
they struck themselves on their head, elbows and knees. As a
kind of benediction, the priest aspersed them with the milk and
charcoal mixture, assured them that the ritual had been duly fulfilled, and bade them eat the fruits of their gardens with rejoicing. Whatever remained over of the various substances used
in these rites was carefully destroyed by fire, so that not a shred
was left.

Junod, who defines *luma*[1] as "to remove the injurious character of a given food by a certain ceremony," describes a variety
of *luma* rites which are in vogue among the Thonga; such as
the removal of the taboo from a dead man's food-stuff when his
uterine nephew takes a mouthful of cooked and medicated samples therefrom,[2] the ritual tasting by the hunters of the flesh of
a hippopotamus or an elephant that has fallen to their weapons,[3]
and even the practice of eating at the waterside the first catch
from some kinds of fish-traps. He states, however, that "there
is a stringent taboo directed against the person who precedes his
superiors in the enjoyment of the first fruits; this law being applicable to Kafir corn or bukanye in certain clans, and also to
sorghum, pumpkin leaves and beer, etc., in others."[4] "The
great, the official *luma*, amongst the Thonga clans," he says, "is
the one performed for the Kafir-corn (*mabele*)," the well-known
millet with which we feed caged birds, which he thinks is the first
cereal known to the people.[5] After the first grains of corn have
been ground and cooked, together with a little of the black talis-

[1] Cf. Secwana *go loma*, see p. 227.
[2] LSAT. i. 146.
[3] LSAT. ii. 62.
[4] LSAT. ii. 69.
[5] LSAT. ii. 371-72.

manic powder from the tribal calabashes,[1] by his great wife, the
chief offers some of this food to the spirits of his ancestors, at the
main entrance to the royal kraal, and craves their blessing upon
the new crops; then he ceremonially tastes it, and his juniors
follow his example, but women do not partake of the occult
powder.[2]   Elsewhere, the same writer tells us [3] that when the
chief pours this cooked and "medicated" food into the little pot
which serves as an altar at the entrance to the royal kraal, he
prays: "Here has the new year come!   Precede us you gods, and
eat the first fruits, so that, for us also, Kafir corn shall help our
body, that we become fat, not thin, that the witches may increase
the corn, make it to be plentiful, so that, even if there is only a
small field, big baskets may be filled."   Another prayer quoted
in the same article helps us to see the true inwardness of the
Feast of Firstfruits through Native eyes.   The "chief of the
Lebombo clan, near Rikatla, when he offered the sacrifice of the
first fruits, entered the sacred wood where all his ancestors had
been buried; he poured the offering on the graves and calling
them by their names, beginning with the founder of the dynasty
down to his own father, he said: 'Thou Mombo-wa-ndlopfu,
the Master of this land, thou hast given it to thy son Makundju;
Makundju gave it to his son, Hati; Hati gave it to Makhumbi;
Makhumbi gave it to Kinini; Kinini gave it to Mikhabyana; Mikhabyana gave it to Mawatle; Mawatle gave it to me, his son.
Look upon my offering!   Is it not a beautiful one!   And here
I am, left alone.   If I had not brought this with me, who would
have given you anything?   Is it not just so?   I ask of thee, my
ancestor, I ask for all trees; the palm trees for building, the
trunks which can be hollowed out for canoes, and let it be that
these trunks shall not fall on the people and crush them, when
they go to cut them down, over in the marsh.' "   Then it was
that the spirit of the founder of the dynasty came in the form
of a dangerous snake to thank his worshippers for their offering.[4]
Here the spirits of the dynasty are evidently regarded as controlling all that grows in the land that they subdued, and the

[1] LSAT. i. 40; ii. 10.
[2] LSAT. i. 368-69.
[3] IRM., Oct., 1922.
[4] See p. 161.

beginning of a new harvest is deemed a suitable season for giving them an ovation. In one clan at least the rite is performed with a special pumpkin (*kwembe*). The chief eats a little of this pumpkin, which has been cooked together with the occult powder used in rain-making, and makes the sign of a cross on the big drum, which is forthwith beaten to summon the people.[1] Junod, following Meinhof, thinks the *ranga* is the oldest kind of pumpkin known to the Bantu, and that it was called *tanga* in Ur-Bantu. He notes that there are special taboos connected with this vegetable.[2] The Thonga clans observe a Firstfruits Ceremony in connection with the *nkanye* or *morula* plums, also, the first ripe fruits being made into beer and poured on the graves of the deceased chiefs in the sacred wood, who are invoked to bless the year; and at the ensuing feast the tribe musters in military array, and the carnival extends to every village in the country.[3] These are wild fruits; but the people never fell a female tree (the male trees do not bear fruit) and claim as private property those that happen to grow in their lands. "There is a stringent taboo directed against the person who precedes his superiors in the enjoyment of the firstfruits; this law being applicable to Kafircorn or *bukanye* in certain clans, and also to sorghum, pumpkin leaves and beer, etc., in others."[4] Perhaps it should be stated that pumpkin-leaves are eaten as spinach.

In the Vachopi tribe, "on the third month after the '*muzilo*,'[5] the '*lumela*' or feast of first fruits, takes place. No one must reap or gather the produce of the kind of plants of which sample seeds were sown at the '*kahola*' rite until the public thanksgiving is offered, because the first-fruits have not been destroyed by grubs and worms, etc. The same *anyanga* arrives at the Chief's kraal, where a large congregation has assembled. He has a supply of *nsita*, a 'medicine' which resembles soot, and which is also made from charred and pounded roots. The doctor and his helpers provide a plentiful meal of *matshavu* (cooked green vegetables of all kinds), which is served in ten large carved wooden bowls (*tingelo*) borrowed from the Chief. The doctor

[1] LSAT. i. 376.
[2] LSAT. ii. 13.
[3] LSAT. i. 376.
[4] LSAT. ii. 371-72.
[5] See pp. 222 ff.

takes some red ochre, and draws a magic ring (writes) round each
bowl with it. Each person takes a tiny pinch of the *matshavu*,
mixed with *nsita*. The rules for the women are the same as
those described for the '*muzilo*.' The *anyanga* has offered in
his own home sacrifices to the ancestral spirits. In public he
gives thanks-giving for the first-fruits. Then the people go
home, and may gather *matshavu* and *wsifake* (mealies). But if
any of the people are 'possessed' by *Vahdau* or *Vahgoni* spirits,
they will offer sacrifices to those spirits before they dare to reap
the produce of the fields." [1]

In the Northern Transvaal, the high places of Bavenda worship are the graves of chiefs and other ancestors in the holy
groves; but in every village there is a rude altar at which the
villagers hold communion with their tutelary gods.[2] "At the
beginning of the harvest," Gottschling writes,[3] "the various families gather round their family-altar in the yard of their respective
head. The *modzimo*[4] of the family is put on the altar, and
each member has to throw a little new fruit upon it and to pour
some beer over it. In case the *modzimo* of the family is an ox
or other animal it is forced to swallow some of the beer of the
sacrifice." Every chief clothes himself for the occasion in the
skin-robe that one of his ancestors used to wear. "They pray
somewhat to this effect," continues the same writer: " 'O *Modzimo*, thou art our father. We, thy children, have congregated
here; we humbly beg to inform thee that a new year has commenced. . . . See here we bring from what we have harvested.
Thou art our father, also thou our grandfather, grandfather's
father and his grandfather,' and so on as far as any ancestor is
known. After this or such like prayer every member of the
family offers his sacrifice of the firstfruits and the first beer, and
then all are at liberty to harvest and enjoy the new food and the
new beer. These prayers at the sacrifices are never directed to
Kosane, Ralowimba and Thovela, but always to the ancestors."
No mention is made of cucurbitacea, nor of any connection be-

[1] E. Dora Earthy, in BNT., Dec., 1925, p. 197.
[2] See p. 277.
[3] R. BAAS., 1905, iii. 213.
[4] In his vocabulary *modzimo* denotes an ancestor-spirit, an ancestral relic or an
animal dedicated to an ancestor-spirit.

tween the fertility of the gardens and the reproductive faculties of their owners, nor of any military display; but it is clear that the spirits of old notabilities in the community are thanked for the crops with which they have blessed their children.

Between the Limpopo and the Zambesi, from the eastern fringe of the Kalahari Desert to the western border of Portuguese East Africa, in the many small villages which may be roughly classed as Karañga—a most interesting people, of whose inner life too little is known, I have seen rude altars like those of the Bavenda, at which somewhat similar services of thanksgiving to the ancestor-spirits are held when the firstfruits are gathered. On the eastern border of this area, cognate Ndau clans collect in one of the huts a little of everything ripening in the garden, and the head of the kraal enters and presents it to the spirits, craving their blessing upon the gardens.[1]

When Smith and Dale tell us that the "Baila have no such feast of firstfruits as the Zulus and other southern tribes have," they are evidently comparing the homeliness of the Baila rite with the prominence of the great tribal ceremonies in the south; for the following description of the Baila custom is from their pages.[2] "When the early maize is ready, the people go through the ceremonies of *kusomya*: that is, before they eat any of the grain (*kusoma*) they make an offering to their divinities. The man goes to the field and plucks a few ripe ears of maize and takes them to the village. He strips off the husks and takes the cobs to the grave of a certain ancestor. He sweeps round the grave and then kneeling before the grave, says, 'So-and-so, here is some of the maize which is ripe first and which I offer thee.' Having done this he returns to his home, and at the threshold of his hut makes another offering in the same way: afterwards hanging some of the cobs over the door or in the rafters." Now, however slight the external resemblance between this simple domestic rite and the more pretentious tribal festivals of the south, they are both alike at the core: the divine shades must be the first to partake of the crops which are due to their invisible vigilance; and the remark that "it is bad form to celebrate the

[1] Dr. Wilder, in *Hartford Seminary Record*, April, 1907.
[2] IPNR. i. 139-140; ii. 179-180.

harvest in this way in the absence of your wife," cannot be altogether dissociated from the Becwana way of thinking.[1]

Away to the north-west of the Baila, in the Kasempa district of Northern Rhodesia, the Bakaonde worship the ancestor-spirits (*makishi*) before beginning to reap their Kafir-corn. They grind a little of the firstfruits of this crop; mix some of it with water and lay it by the family-altar (*chipanda*) of the village headman; and place the remainder at the cross-roads near the village. Then follow libations. Some of the unripe corn is made into beer; and next morning at sunrise the people are summoned, by the sounding of a kind of gong which forms part of the hereditary insignia of the village chieftainship, for the ceremonial drinking of this beer, and the dancing that inevitably accompanies such a rite; and powdered red bark is smeared on the right cheeks of men, women and children, and white chalk on the left. All this is preparatory to reaping. When the cultivators begin to reap, each takes two or three heads of corn, and sets one on the headman's family altar, one on his own, and one on that of a friend.[2]

Among the Yombe on this same plateau, "no one is allowed to partake of the first-fruits until the ceremonies are completed. Escorted by a band of drummers, his medicine-men, and the village elders, Chief Njera ascends in state the Kalanga Mountain, until he reaches the hollow fastness . . . where the body of his grandfather lay buried. Before the tomb of the departed chief a bull is slain, and pots of freshly made beer and porridge made from the first-fruits are deposited before the shrine. The ground is then carefully cleaned of weeds, and the blood sprinkled on the freshly turned-up soil and on the rafters of the little hut. After offering the customary prayers in thanksgiving for the harvest and beseeching the spirits to partake of the first fruits, the procession withdraws. On return to the village the carcass is divided, all partake of the fresh porridge and beer awaiting them, and the day closes with beer-drinking and dancing."[3]

Of the group of Konde tribes around the north end of Lake Nyasa, Mackenzie writes:[4] "It is forbidden to common people

[1] See pp. 231 *et seq.*
[2] WBA. 134-35.
[3] GPNR. 294.
[4] SRK. 107.

to eat new season's food until chiefs and village headmen and twins have eaten first; and even they eat only when the first fruits have been mixed with medicine by the doctor. The first fish of the season must not be taken to the village. It is eaten at the river by the boys. It belongs to the spirits." And again on another page:[1] "The first maize cobs are taken to the chief; then each head of a family presents a few cobs to his own ancestors; twins also must be presented with early cobs, and it is only then that common people are safe if they begin to eat the new season's crops. . . . In some districts a perhaps more primitive ceremony is observed. With a following of little children, the doctor goes to the grave of the chief's ancestors, and there roasts a few maize cobs, which he divides among the children; on their return, intimation is made that all may now eat the new crops."

Hobley states that before the Akamba of Kenya Colony can eat of the new crops, an elder and an old woman lay a little maize and beans at the ancestral shrine (*ithembo*); and the chyme from the stomach of a goat, which is sacrificed for the occasion, is mixed with green food and cooked, and a portion distributed to each village.[2] After this the green crops can be safely eaten; but before the harvest proper can commence, the firstfruits of the harvest must be gathered and the ceremony repeated. Elsewhere,[3] the same writer states that before any new crop can be eaten, an offering of firstfruits must be made to the ancestor-spirits; that all the people of the district assemble for the occasion; and that a very old man and woman, selected for the purpose, leave the crowd and approach "the place of praying" in the village, and, crying aloud to the spirits, ask permission to eat their crops. "The people then dance and during the dance one of the women present is sure to be seized with a fit of shaking and cry out aloud—this sign is known to be the answer to the people's prayer to the *Aïïmu*."

In Buganda, also, firstfruits were offered to the family-god: the woman called her eldest son (the natural priest of family-gods) to eat some of the first-ripe beans, or she would fall ill; and after the meal her husband jumped over her—a ceremonial

[1] SRK. 120.
[2] BBM. 74.
[3] AK. 66, 86.

equivalent for sexual intercourse. Then the beans might be eaten by all.[1]

Before we leave this subject, the importance ascribed to cucurbitaceous plants demands further consideration. We have seen that these plants are of such consequence to the Becwana ritual that they give their name to the Festival; that calabashes figure in the Kafir ritual, though seemingly only as containers of the boiled firstfruits; that at the December festival of the Zulus the king struck two "pig-melons" together; that in the Matabele rites both young calabashes and the leaves of a cucurbitaceous plant are essential; and that in one of the Thonga clans the rite is performed with a pumpkin. Although I cannot recall any statement that cucurbitaceous plants are used in the Firstfruits Festivals of northern Bantu tribes, such negative evidence is valueless in the face of the fragmentary nature of our knowledge of the ritual of these communities; and it may not be irrelevant to remark that at the burial of a Baganda chief, it was the custom for a relative to put a few pumpkin-seeds into the dead man's hand, and for the eldest son of deceased (who was never heir to his father's property) to remove them with his lips, chew them up, and blow some over the corpse and the rest over one of the childless widows, who thereupon became his wife.[2] Whether the ritual use of these plants is sufficiently explained by the fact that they are among the earliest of Bantu garden-plants to become productive, may be doubted. Bakaonde and Akamba usage prove that there is a Bantu tradition of two Firstfruits Festivals: one for green crops and another for the main crop of cereals—a fact which throws light on the Little and Great Festivals of the Kafir-Zulu tribes; and it is possible that the Becwana have merged these two festivals in one which retains, for the most part, the ritual of the former, while the Zulus have kept them distinct, but have combined a pastoral spring festival with the latter. Even if this theory is tenable, however, it leaves much unexplained.

Bantu totemism is worn to a shadow:[3] the totem is now little

---

[1] Bg. 428. See, also, AS. 203-212 for the ceremony of firstfruits in Northern Ashanti, where sacrifices, libations and prayers are offered to ancestor-spirits as gods of fertility.

[2] Bg. 117.

[3] See my *Notes on the Totemism of the Becwana*, in JRAI., 1905, pp. 295-314.

more than a clan-name and (in most cases) a taboo, and some
clans have lost all recollection of any totem that they ever had.
A large number of clan-names have, however, nothing to do
with totems; they consist of a prefix for "people" (followed by
a possessive particle while the clan is very new) and the personal
name of the leader that first gave them independent political
existence; but inasmuch as these personal names are often taken
from animals, plants, implements, and the like (the very things
that are totems in other communities), they may easily delude
an investigator. Some clans, which have been patrilineal so long
that they have lost all tradition of any other system of descent,
trace their lineage with great probability to a common ancestor
who ruled less than ten generations ago; and yet they have different totems. He who pieces together the shreds and patches
of Bantu totemism so as to show the pattern of the original
fabric, will prove himself an archæologist of uncommon erudi-
tion and skill. A Bantu totem is usually a species of animal; but
one clan that I know takes the hoe as its totem, another, the
smith's hammer, and another, the dregs of the milksack. Students of worldwide totemism are satisfied that plant-totems are
more primitive than animal-totems. If this belief is as well-
grounded as it appears to be, the chances are that where animal-
totems are tottering with age, plant-totems will have left little
more than traces of their former existence, and that even these
will lie buried in time-honoured religious rites, like fossils in
sedimentary rocks. As a matter of fact, there are scarcely any
Bantu plant-totems; and the few survivals (if they are survivals),
like the mushroom and Kafir-corn totems in Northern Rhodesia,[1]
have dwindled to little more than family-names. But many elements in the prevalent religious rites of these tribes can hardly
be explained apart from the assumption that they originated when
plant-totemism was still strong enough to mould the thought of
the tribesmen. This Becwana Festival of Firstfruits, for example, though now taken up into ancestor-worship, looks, for all the
world, like the renewal of the covenant with a plant-totem; and
this opinion is borne out by the following facts. Bamangwato
usually swear by their totem, the duiker; but Khama and his
elders agreed that to swear by the *thótse* is a much more sacred

[1] WBA. 30, 249; IPNR. i. 294, 310 ff.

and binding oath, and explained it by saying that whereas the duiker is but the totem of one clan, the *thótse* is of sacred significance to very many. Similarly, the Bakwena, whose totem is the crocodile, assured me that the oath on the *thótse* is the most sacred oath they know. It runs: *Kea ikana ka thótse le segwana sa metse* ("I swear by the gourd-vine.[1] and the water-dipper"). There is another and fuller formula of adjuration, which attains the very climax of awe: *Kea ikana ka Tintibane ea ñwana a lehatshe; ka thiba ka lehatshe; ke leléméla segwanyana se se kwa go——.* That is: "I swear by Tintibane,[2] child of the land; I barred the way with the land; I crawl towards the little water-dipper that is in the possession of——(here the personal name of the eldest daughter of the chief is inserted)". Tintibane (sometimes pronounced Thintibane or Thinthibane) is said to be lord of the underworld, though nothing else is known of him. *Segwanyana* is a double diminutive of sego ("a gourd"); but everybody professes complete ignorance of "the little water-dipper which is in the possession of the chief's eldest daughter." This word *sego* ("gourd") is used also as a verb in the sense of "to be blessed"; it is the verb used in translating the Beatitudes. There is no tradition that the *thótse* was ever taboo to the Becwana, except in the sense that all cultivated crops are taboo till the Feast of Firstfruits; and I could discover no reliable tradition that it was once the totem of the people, though a thoughtful member of the Bamangwato tribe, to whom I applied for help in understanding the significance of this oath, told me that his father had explained it to him by saying that in his youth he had been told by a very old man that the *thótse* used to be their *seréto* ("totem"). The words *thótse, go fhorola* (pf. *fhorotse*) "to besmear," especially in a ceremonial sense, as in the sentence *banna ba iphorola ka leshwaló* ("the men besmeared themselves with aromatic herbs of magical virtue"), and *Bafhurutse* (the name of the senior tribe of this group) appear to be derived from the same stem. Perhaps it may be well to mention, also, that *go chwara thótse* ("to seize the *thótse*") and *go loma ñwaga*

---

[1] From the association of *thótse* with *segwana* in the formula, I assume that the particular *thótse* referred to is the *thótse ea segwana* ("gourd-vine").

[2] The possessive particle, which I have omitted in translation, is but a grammatical device for linking the noun with its appositional epithet.

("to bite the year") are other technical terms for the rites of the Feast of Firstfruits among these people.[1]

OCCASIONS FOR THE WORSHIP OF TRIBAL-GODS: 4. HARVEST

Writers on Bantu Africa have surprisingly little to say about religious observances at the completion of harvest. Bakaonde chiefs seem to approach the ancestor-gods with libations and prayers when the Kafir-corn is reaped.[2] Basuto make a little hollow, some twelve or fifteen inches in depth and diameter, at the centre of their threshing-floor. Leaving the threshed and winnowed corn in a heap upon the floor, they bring a new pot, cook a few handfuls of the grain, and throw it upon the heap, saying: "Thank you, gods; give us bread to-morrow also!" After they have garnered the pile, all the grain that fell into the central hole during threshing (*mabele a leoa*, they call it) is made into beer and placed, unstrained, in the most remote corner of the hut, where it remains all night as a drink-offering to the gods, and next morning the worshippers drink this consecrated liquor, after it has been strained by the housewife, and again thank the gods for their bounty.[3]

The Becwana have no religious ceremony immediately after the completion of harvest; but in September there used to be a final harvest-rite, which they called *Dikgahéla*, or, to use the full phrase, *Go ntsha dikgahéla* ("to put forth *dikgahéla*"). *Dikgahéla* is a technical term that is not now used in any other connection, but *gahe*, which appears in its stem, means "bonus," "handsel," "something to the good," "luck-money," "the extra handful which a seller gives a buyer." *Dikgahéla* was defined by a Mokwena who used to pilot me along the devious paths of Native thought, as "things which indicate gratitude to the chief who has nourished the corn with his rain." "It means," he affirmed, "you have had rain; you have had corn; a bonus does not ruin the profits; put forth your tithes as a bonus." "Tithes" seems to be

---

[1] It may not be inappropriate to remark here that among the Negro-Hamitic Batuse of Ruanda, a bridegroom twisted a runner of wild gourd into a wreath and put it on his bride's head as a nuptial symbol. (GS. 196.)

[2] WBA. 156.

[3] Bs. 251-52; HB. 257.

an appropriate translation of *dikgahéla*, because, like that which is glimpsed in the Old Testament before Israel became sufficiently sophisticated to build a temple and levy a stated impost for its maintenance, it is a free-will offering of the crops, large or small according to the glow of the giver, which is consumed by the worshippers before the divine benefactors who have first given them the increase of the lands. The ceremony is worth description; it is essentially religious, although an uninitiated European observer might well be excused if he failed to discern a hint of religion in it.

Proclamation is made by the chief's crier: "Produce your tithes!" And every woman in every village [1] takes Kafir-corn to her village assembly-place. No stated proportion of her harvest is demanded: one contributes much and another little, according to wealth and inclination. If the contribution from the village amounts to four baskets of grain, the village-head retains one for himself and sends the other three to the tribal chief. The taking of this grain to the chief's place is a ceremonial affair: women march in procession, carrying the corn upon their heads, raising the ululation-cry [2] as they go, and interspersing it with shouts of "Rain! Rain! Rain!" On reaching the chief's place they pass into the yard at the back of his premises, where the corn-bins are and the threshing-floor. There they meet similar detachments from every village within reach; and the chief's handmaids show each group where to pour their grain on skins laid upon the ground to receive it. If the delegates from a village bring three baskets, as we have supposed for illustration, they pour out two of these upon the heap and take back the third to be mixed with the one which the village-head retained. Then comes the second public announcement: "Let the tithes be immersed!" This is hardly the place for a detailed description of the process of beer-making; suffice it to say that the grain is carefully sorted while malting, so that none shall sprout too little and none too much; that the malt is dried, ground, and divided into two portions, one

---

[1] Becwana towns, from the largest to the least, are organised as compact groups of patriarchal villages.

[2] Becwana women produce this weird sound by uttering a shrill cry while rapidly vibrating the tip of the tongue in the open mouth.

of which is cooked as thin gruel and the other added to the gruel which has been cooked; and that the whole process takes about two weeks. When every village has had time to prepare its allotment of Kafir-beer, the chief's crier makes his third announcement: "Let the tithes come!" And in the morning another procession from each village wends its way to the chief's place; at its head walks a man specially commissioned to represent the village, who is followed by a file of women, each with a waterpot of beer upon her head, and last of all, two women who take turns at carrying the big brew-pot, which is empty on account of its weight. As before, the air is rent with the ululation-cry and interjacent shouts of "Rain! Rain!" At the chief's place, his maid-servants show them where to stand the brew-pot, into which they pour the beer from their waterpots, and then take home the empty vessels. Now each village has kept back about three times as much beer as it has sent to the chief; and in the evening the stentorian voice of the chief's mouthpiece is heard a fourth time: "Think of your beer-pots, all of you!" And at daybreak on the following morning, men and women all wend their way towards the chief's place; and the chief appoints one of his people to serve out the beer, giving each group a brew-pot full, though not necessarily the one they brought. The drinking of this beer is accompanied with a great din: dancing, ululation, and constant shouts of "Rain! Rain! Rain!" It is a very frolicsome party, without a touch of solemnity in any of its proceedings. But we must not be misled by externalities: it is none the less a service of thanksgiving to the chief and his ancestors for the rain with which they have enriched the earth. The particular celebration that is uppermost in my thought as I write was held at Molepolole in 1915. It was a renewal of a custom that had fallen into desuetude for several decades, and its rehabilitation was due to the political, rather than religious, motives of a reactionary chief. Upon this occasion the brew-pots were taken into the cattle-pen, where the chief's father and grandfather were buried; and at this shrine the people ate the flesh of an ox which was slaughtered for the occasion, and drank the beer, and held high festival. In their merriment they poured beer over the chief's body and clothes, which seems to have been part of the ancient ceremonial, and he protested, "No: not me. You ought to worship and thank the originators of these deeds in their graves." This remark goes to the heart of the whole business. One can never understand tribalism by studying its secular features alone; for it is essentially religious. Its roots are in the past, and with the Bantu the past is present. The assumption here is that the land owes its fertility to the spirits of the dynasty, and that this is a proper way of expressing gratitude for their gifts.

To correctly appreciate a type of religion whose ritual culminates in a jovial feast, one must temporarily divest oneself of the comparatively modern idea that religion is concerned, not with material boons, but with spiritual and ethical vigour, and get back to the childhood of society when the god and his worshippers were united in happy fellowship upon terms that came nearer to equality; when people took all the pleasant things of life as direct gifts from the gods, and showed their appreciation by eating and drinking before the gods, dancing, clapping their hands, shouting for joy, singing aloud, and being glad in the Lord—if one may appropriate phrases that most readers of the Psalms take as metaphors because alien to our modern sense of fitness. The "feast of the Lord in Shiloh" [1] and the vintage feast in Shechem [2] are so much after this pattern that one cannot possibly make the mistake of thinking it peculiar to the Bantu. [3] The Hebrew feasts, [4] especially in the earlier ages, were occasions of joyful merry-making, when the festive throng expressed itself in a type of jubilant exultation that would scandalise a Christian community. It is a far cry from the Bantu idea of worship to the nobler conception set forth in the *Gospel According to St. John*; but the path that man has travelled is being travelled still by man.

Each Thonga village sends its chief a basket of mealies at

[1] Judg. xxi. 19.
[2] Judg. ix. 27.
[3] Speaking of the banquets for the dead which Roman families held at a funeral or on certain consecrated days, beside the grave or in a room within the tomb or in the garden around this "eternal house," Cumont remarks that men were convinced that the spirit of the dead man took its place beside its kin, and shared their meal and rejoiced with them. He adds: "Moreover the guests themselves ate copiously and drank deeply, convinced that the noisy conviviality of the feast was a source of joy and refreshment to the shade in the gloom of its sepulchral existence." (ALRP. 200.)
[4] They are often called "solemn assemblies"; but see Lam. ii. 7.

harvest time; but Junod regards this as a tax, not as a tithe, nor as associated with tribal worship.[1]

The Festival of Shimunenga,[2] the communal god of the Bamala, in the Ila country, comes closer to the Becwana procedure. Shimunenga's grave is probably hidden in the almost impenetrable recesses of his sacred grove. In September his "priest" enters this grove and holds conversation with him; and then goes round to all the villages calling upon the people to gather firewood and prepare for the brewing of beer. A few days later, when the moistened grain has had time to malt, he directs them to brew, and for four or five days after the people are busy with their brew-pots. On the fifth day, all the cattle are collected to sleep at Mala and the drums begin to sound throughout the commune. On the sixth day, all the men plaster themselves with white clay; and men and women, adorned in their finery, call upon Shimunenga, the Gatherer of men, the Giver of virility to males, and drink beer, dance, sing lewd songs, and give rein to their passions. It should be noted, however, that Shimunenga's Festival is not connected with the completion of harvest, but with the shooting of new grass and budding of trees, which the Bamala regard as marking the beginning of a new year, and that the sexual processes of the villagers are as closely associated with the fertility of their lands and herds as in the New Year Ceremonies of southern tribes, though manifested in another manner.

Ceremonies cast in the same mould and dominated by the same idea are performed beyond the Bantu border. At the end of May, 1922, in the Brong country of Northern Ashanti, where the seasons are antithetic to those south of the equator, the spirits of dead rulers were gladdened with rice, ground-nut soup and thanksgiving for the rice reaped at the previous harvest, and besought to bless the next season's crop. Attendants at the burial-places of these notabilities presided over the rites; but Rattray was told that a similar ceremony would be performed at every house in the village.[3]

[1] LSAT. i. 378.
[2] IPNR. ii. 189.
[3] AS. 136-37.

Fishing and hunting are often (not always) connected with the worship of family-gods, or tribal-gods, or the gods of tribes that long ago lost political control of the water or hunting-veld.

Fish are taboo to Becwana and some other Bantu; but tribes dwelling near lakes or great rivers signalise the beginning of the fishing season with a definite act of worship, and some of them offer to the gods the "firstfruits" of the season's fishing before any of the first catch is eaten.[1] That this worship is often rendered to the spirits of the old lords of the river or lake is evident and meaningful.

Junod, describing the communal fishing in lakes all over Thongaland, says:[2] "Before the throng enters the lake, some one must make an offering: it must be a descendant of the inhabitants of the country, not necessarily a member of the reigning family. He does not perform the full sacramental *tsu;* he merely spits without having put anything into his mouth, and says: 'Let fish abound! Let them not hide in the mud! Let there be enough of them to satisfy every one.'" "Should there be crocodiles in the pond, the religious act is more important on account of the danger incurred. Then the bones are thrown and designate who must make the offering in order to secure adequate protection from the gods. . . . Amongst the Maluleke, it is a man of the Banyai tribe who must perform the religious act, as the Banyai were in the country before the Thonga."

Strangers who wish to fish or hunt on another community's land in the Ila country, not only obtain permission from what may be called the lay proprietor, and acknowledge the privilege with a gift of some portion of their take, but arrange also to have sacrifices offered to the *mizhimo,* so as to ensure success. To illustrate this "spiritual ownership" of water which is vested in the heads of certain families, Smith & Dale mention a pool in a tract of country that one community wrested from another in an unforgotten war. Although the family which formerly owned this pool came to grief in the fighting, a few of its members sur-

[1] SRK. 132, 142.
[2] LSAT. ii. 70 and 72.

vived; and since the "spiritual ownership" is inalienable and no other mediator could approach the ghostly guardians of the pool, the conquerors induced Nalunkwamba, a scion of that ill-treated stock, to come and live with them and act as priest of the pool. So, at the communal fishing in October, Nalunkwamba, taking his station at a sacred spot where an ant-hill and a tree stand together, offers his ancestors a potful of beer and a prayer for their blessing, and forthwith inaugurates the fishing by entering the pool with his fish-spears. The same writers state that the "spiritual ownership" of the fishing in the river at Nanzela is still vested in a leper woman, one of few survivors of a family which used to own the place, and that she sacrifices to her ancestors for those who wish to fish in that water.[1]

At the beginning of a fishing expedition, the tribes around Lambarene, on the Ogowe River, West Africa, spend the first day securing the aid of the spirits, by throwing rum and tobacco leaves into the water. "The ceremonies were once omitted several years ago," says Schweitzer, "but the following year an old woman wrapped herself in a net and let herself be drowned."[2] It would be interesting to discover the motive that inspired such a heroic act of self-sacrifice.

There are spirits to which Lunda fishermen appeal;[3] and in Uganda each river has its particular deity who must be propitiated and afterwards rewarded with some of the fish caught.[4]

The people of North-east Angola will not fish in the deep side-water of rivers, because of a tradition that *simbi* habitually cook their fish in these still pools. Claridge translates *simbi* into "fairies" and thinks they are a distinct class of supernatural beings who are the real owners of all wild animals; but he knows that hunters pray to the dead for meat; and he tries to reconcile these two ideas by naïvely suggesting that "apparently the dead are agents of the 'fairies' who attend to the distribution of live stock to the people."[5]

Hunting is held in high esteem throughout Bantu Africa, save in a few districts where game is almost extinct. A prolonged

[1] IPNR. i. 388-89.
[2] EPF. 49.
[3] WBA. 173.
[4] Bg. 398.
[5] WBT. 275-77.

and unbalanced vegetarian diet begets a lust for flesh-food, which makes it easy for a skilful hunter to find henchmen in almost any tribe where his reputation is established; and here and there, celebrities of the chase have built up kingdoms for themselves out of the welter of broken clans that faced starvation in the economic aftermath of widespread war. Most Bantu men can look danger in the face; but something more than daring is needed to find the elusive creatures of the woods and marshes, or to come within range of alert animals that roam with seeming unconcern over the open veld; and the cunning and ferocity of some of the bigger beasts is sometimes more than a match for the skill and courage of man. Big-game hunters of our ancestry often mention their "luck"; those of Bantu breed attribute their success or failure to unseen attendants who are never far away and but rarely forgotten.[1]

Since Becwana hunters disdain to take food into the hunting-veld when they make their way thither with their dogs, they are famished unless they find game soon. When pinched with hunger, they look out a fine tree, and in its ample shade they plead with their ancestors: "Oh, my god! why do you kill me, your person! Am I just to perish completely while you are here! Of course, you see that I am dead, my chief! Please bestow your boon, Chief!" And then if the dogs put up game, the hunter says: "The hand of my father has found it for me." If he has lost his quarry through bad marksmanship, he casts about for some *mosimama* bush, which he bruises with stones and immerses in water; and, standing under any large tree, he squirts a mouthful of water in a thin stream over his weapons and washes them with the infusion of *mosimama*, and prays: "O, god! What is it you mean, my chief? I am not a man: I am a boy; and a boy is eluded by things." Upon securing his game, he invokes the spirits once more: "Tarry with me, Chief, and look upon me!" But if he still fails to kill anything, he says: "Our ancestors held my weapons." From another hunter I received practically the same account, except that he washed his face, instead of his weapons, with the infusion of *mosimama*, and bowed to the ground as he uttered his prayer: "God, why do you deny us food! We are your children." "After such

---

[1] They have the idea of "luck"; but see my next volume.

a prayer," said an exponent of the customs of his people, "they are sure to kill an antelope, or find one lying dead,"—which, let me tell you, saves trouble and provides venison of a gamier flavour! "Sometimes," said one of my Native friends, "a hunter, sauntering inadvertently along with his gun upon his shoulder and lost in thought of his father and mother who have gone to their last home, stubs his toe against a stump; that is his father calling to him: 'Be alert! Look, there is game yonder!'"

Sunrise is the great time for prayer in the hunting-veld; and a hunter's prayer at sunrise contains so much of symbol and so little of verbiage that it seems at first sight to be a prayer to the sun; but all Native authorities that I have consulted agree that the prayer is addressed to discarnate spirits, some say the spirits of the suppliant's ancestors, some, the spirits of the old masters of the veld.

When an aged Karanga chief was showing me the ancestral chapel of his village [1] and depicting the worship, he mentioned that the first buck killed each hunting season is laid upon the roof of the chapel and left there all day if killed in the morning, or all night if killed in the evening, and then flayed, disembowelled and jointed upon the ancestral stones. As a further acknowledgment that the spear that did the deed was guided by an unseen hand, the weapon is stuck into the thatch of the chapel and stays there till the rites are accomplished.

In 1856 Livingstone was above Tete on the Zambesi, on his way from Loanda to Quilimane, and his men had just killed a bull elephant. He writes: [2] "Some Banyai elephant-hunters happened to be present when my men were fighting with him. One of them took out his snuff-box, and poured out all its contents at the root of a tree, as an offering to the Barimo for success. As soon as the animal fell, the whole of our party engaged in a wild savage dance round the body, which quite frightened the Banyai, and he who made the offering said to me, 'I see you are travelling with people who don't know how to pray: I therefore offered the only thing I had in their behalf, and the elephant soon fell.' One of Nyamounge's men who re-

[1] See pp. 273 f.
[2] MTR. 607-08.

mained with me, ran a little forward, when an opening in the
trees gave us a view of the chase, and uttered loud prayers for
success in the combat. . . . My own people, who are rather a
degraded lot, remarked to me as I came up, 'God gave it to us.' "
He does not say what word he has translated "God," but it is
more than probable that they thought of an ancestral spirit, as
the Banyai mentioned evidently did.

A Mwila hunter prays and makes offerings especially to the
spirit of the ancestor whose name-child he happens to be, whom
he regards as his tutelary divinity, but pays homage also to his
many other forbears in the spirit-world. Before setting off upon
the chase, he places a gourdful of water and a little tobacco
(and hemp if he uses it) upon the sacred spot by the centre-pole
of his hut; and, spirting forth a jet of water from his mouth
after the manner of many tribes, breaks forth into supplication:
"*Tsu!* So-and-so, see here is tobacco and hemp that I give
thee; when I go to the veld, let us all go together; let there be
none who looks back, let us go on all together. Let the sharp
stick sleep! May the fierce snake be far away! . . . Let there
be good fortune!" At the village altar he offers fine meal to
his guardian spirit, and addresses him in similar phrases. Then
he sallies forth in pursuit of game; and when the prey is at his
feet, he throws bits of its liver, heart, foreleg and rump to the
four winds, calling upon his divinities to accept this acknowledgment of their aid. "When he has done this, he lies on his
back, does obeisance, and claps his hand, saying, 'To-morrow
and to-morrow give me meat!' Having finished, he makes an
offering to his namesake of liver, roasted or boiled, heart and
liver, and says, 'Here is meat, O my namesake. *Pambala, pambala* ("Pray, pray"), a spirit does not refuse his own anything.
To-morrow and to-morrow may I kill even more than this
animal! Be thou around me, O hunter!' He claps his hands.
And at the village when he returns, he does the same, he makes
an offering at the Lwanga ('village altar') to his namesake.
Then also he claps his hands." [1]

Beyond the Ila country northwards, Bakaonde hunters take
home the heart and cheeks of an elephant that has fallen to their
guns, and, having cooked them after the manner prescribed by

[1] IPNR. ii. 156, 165, 176, 177 and cf. i. 262.

a precise ritual, place a small piece of the meat upon the village altar and pour the soup into holes dug for the *wakishi* ("ancestor-spirits"), with this invocation: "Help us again in the future as ye have done this time." [1]

Among the Konde of North Nyasa, hunters are subject to many taboos; [2] but if, in spite of all precautions, they had an unsuccessful hunting season, the diviner discovered what spirits had thwarted their enterprise, and then the hunters repaired again to the hunting-veld, and sought to propitiate the offended spirits with libations of beer and offerings of small pieces of game and porridge sweetened with honey. "Each ancestor was named, as his portion was laid out, and prayer was offered." [3]

Near most Lunda villages, says Mr. J. L. Keith, [4] "may be seen a small pathway cleared up to the base of an anthill and terminating in a forked stick on which are often hung shreds of cloth or bits of animals' entrails. The sticks are often placed in the centre of the village, and the bark trays used for carrying in the killed game are piled round the base. These are the shrines of the hunting spirits who have different names in nearly every village, and are often more family than tribal. A celebrated hunter dies and his spirit is supposed to have certain influence in the local hunting grounds. In time the hunter is forgotten but his name lives as that of a *mukishi* to be propitiated if bad luck is to be avoided." It seems to be the propitiation of one of these hunter-spirits that Mr. F. V. Bruce Miller describes: [5] "*Karombo* or *Ntambo*. The hunting spirit. If a man who is a good hunter suddenly has a run of bad luck and wounds or misses game without killing he has lots cast, and if the man who presides over the lots attributes the failure to the influence of this spirit, the hunter goes to the 'Karombo' doctor. The doctor and he then proceed to an anthill in the vicinity, and they make clay into a heap and hoe a little path up to the side of the ant heap. A pot is placed on the heap of clay inside which is put a certain medicine. The doctor makes the hunter wash in this concoction, after doing which he returns to the

[1] WBA. 260.
[2] SRK. 133-34.
[3] SRK. 139.
[4] WBA. 175. See also my p. 56.
[5] WBA. 179.

hunt. If he kills game he returns and paints the pot with the blood of the slain animal. In this manner is the spirit appeased and ill luck warded off." Ravenstein states,[1] upon the authority of Bentley, that in the Congo region the blood of a beast killed in the chase is poured on the grave of a good hunter, to ensure future success.

The Hon. Charles Dundas states[2] that among the Akamba, in Kenya Colony, "where a hunter had failed to find elephants, he declared that this was due to the fact that he had omitted to offer a sacrifice before starting, and before going out again a sheep was offered. The animal was killed at about sunset, a few pieces of flesh from the throat was laid on the bare earth, next some of the blood was poured on the ground beside the meat, and finally a little water was poured next to the blood. Upon each of these acts the hunter offered a prayer for success coupled with other wishes. From a small patch of dry earth left by the water he divined that shortly he would find two cow elephants."

In North-east Angolaland, "the inauguration of the hunting season is a somewhat picturesque scene. As the spirits of the dead, together with the fairies,[3] control the disposal of the game, the hunters repair to them for communion. The meeting-place is the spot where the dead body of a great hunter was ceremonially washed; where his hair and the clippings of his fingernails were buried. Sometimes they gather at the hunter's grave itself. It is called 'the bloody grave' because the first antelope killed in a season is there offered to the dead. The animal's bladder is taken out and filled with its blood, which, together with a first draught of wine, is poured on the grave. The priest mixes the oblation with the soil, making a mud with which he anoints the face of every hunter present. . . . During the ceremony all kneel, clapping their hands to express their unity in the ritual. The dead are summoned by the priest shaking a rattle. . . . Then follows a remarkable prayer, too long to record here, in which the principal item is a request for meat."[4]

[1] SAAB. 73.
[2] JRAI., 1913, p. 535.
[3] What Claridge calls "fairies" are probably kinless spirits of the wilderness.
[4] WBT. 87.

OCCASIONS FOR THE WORSHIP OF TRIBAL GODS: 6. WAR

Very little has been written concerning the worship of ancestor-spirits in connection with inter-tribal warfare. The rites with which an army is set apart for battle and aggregated afresh to the civil community upon its return home, are predominantly magical, but that portion of the tribe that dwells in the spirit-world is, of course, concerned with every such venture, and consulted and propitiated beforehand.[1] The palladium which is carried before a Becwana host on the war-path, and which is too sacred to be approached save by its specially consecrated guard, consists of certain virile portions of the black bull that, with its eyes sewn up, was driven bellowing from the town on the night before the army left and slaughtered with extraordinary ceremonies as soon as the army overtook it in the morning.[2] Whether this bull is sacrificed to ancestor-spirits, none of my informants could tell me; but the colour of the beast and much of the attendant ritual warrants that presumption.

Junod describes a similar rite that precedes the setting forth of a Thonga army,[3] and, without hazarding an opinion as to whether this animal is regarded as a sacrifice to ancestor-spirits, mentions that the warriors in eating morsels of its flesh are forbidden to touch them with their hands—owing to the sacredness of the morsels, one would suppose, though who can distinguish between magical and religious sacredness even in the case of wafers which priests place upon the tongues of communicants?

Callaway remarks that all Zulus look for the help of the *amatongo* when about to attack with arms and attribute success or failure to these ghostly guardians.[4] Kidd is more explicit in his account of Kafir practice:[5] "The ancestral spirits are interceded with, and begged to help in the war; indeed many natives seem to think that there is far more real warfare among the ancestral spirits of the rival armies than among the actual warriors. It has been pointed out previously that these ancestral

[1] See pp. 145 f.
[2] Cf. p. 294.
[3] LSAT. i. 457 ff.
[4] RSZ. 131-34.
[5] EK. 307.

spirits are sometimes supposed to be fighting in the air just above the heads of the people." He also notes [1] the slaughter of a black ox and the eating of its flesh by the army, and, though he does not say whether this is a sacrificial rite, the fact that its bones are burnt indicates solicitude to prevent them from being desecrated by profane magicians, which is manifest in some other major sacrifices to ancestor-spirits.[2]

The Abangoni, of kindred ancestry, though settled in Central Africa for nearly a century, retain the same custom. In their eager preparations for an attack on the Atonga of Lake Nyasa, when the regiment had assembled, ready for the war-path, "the great witch-doctor was summoned and, after consulting his bones, prophesied that the expedition would be prosperous, but warned them not to pass Chipatula's grave, which lay on their route, without making a sacrifice there, for his spirit must be propitiated so that he might bless his children in the fight. They marched forth with loud boastings, came to the lonely grave in the midst of the deserted village site and there made sacrifice." [3] So, too, upon a later occasion, when the army was making for the stockade of Chipembere, which they intended to raid, a great herd of elephants met them, and the witch-doctors who accompanied the army were called to interpret this omen. " 'As great as has been the number of elephants which passed through the army,' they said, 'so great will be the band of captives that you will take. But let us sacrifice first to the spirit of our father, Zungwendaba, that he may lead to victory the army of his child.' That evening all the men gathered to worship." [4]

Before attacking the Mashukulumbwe (an appellation which the Barotse derisively bestowed upon the Baila), Lewanika sent offerings of beadwork, water, milk, or honey to each of the royal tombs in the country, "and at the same time a sheaf of spears, which remained lying there for forty-eight hours, to give these dignitaries of the other world time to bless them,"—which means, I suppose, to give the spears time to absorb the sacredness of the ancestral shrines. These spears were carried by the bodyguard

[1] EK. 306.
[2] See p. 209.
[3] AA. 32.
[4] AA. 65.

of a young girl who had been designated by the divining bones to precede the troops on the march, bearing a horn full of war-charms. No one was permitted to pass her. When a halt was called, she laid down her horn, her escort stuck their sacred spears in the ground, and the whole army remained at a respect-ful distance. She fired the first shot when the attack was launched, and had to refrain from sleeping, sitting, eating, and drinking as long as the battle lasted.[1]

In Konde warfare, one of the old men behind the fighting-line carried a basket of powerful "medicines," very sacred, which he shook from time to time and carried forward or backward as the enemy retreated or advanced. If the enemy took this sacred basket, it was raised aloft for all to see; and if it were not recap-tured, the dynasty to which it originally belonged would die out.[2]

We are not told what the "medicine" in the horn or in the basket was made of, nor by what magico-religious rites it was consecrated, though these are important points.

So, too, with the Baila.[3] "Before the actual fighting certain ceremonial observances took place, the principal being a solemn sacrifice to the *muzhimo* of the district, with prayers for victory and a safe return." On arriving home from a successful fight, "each warrior bathed his face with a brew of 'medicine,' and each father sacrificed individually to his ancestral spirit. The first sacrifice was made to the demi-god of the district; the heads of the slain enemies were placed before him with a prayer of thanks-giving: 'Thou hast stood by us. We are not dead but alive, and have slain our enemies by thy help. See here are the heads of our foes.' " Similar customs were in vogue among the Balumbu, where the chief distributed among his bravest warriors some of the heads which were laid at his feet and placed others in the manes' hut.[4]

[1] TCA. 303-05.
[2] SRK. 172.
[3] IPNR. i. 176-78.
[4] IPNR. i. 178-79.

CHAPTER IV

MODES OF ANCESTOR-WORSHIP

SHRINES, ALTARS, CHAPELS, TEMPLES

VILLAGE shrines are very common throughout Bantu Africa, and it is not hard to imagine how they originated. Although an ancestor-spirit is not confined to the grave and may be worshipped wheresoever a descendant becomes aware of its presence, the grave is the antechamber of the nether world and the natural place of resort for those who seek intercourse with the dead. At one time, when burial was given only to persons of status, the grave was dug in the dead man's house, as it still is in some tribes,[1] and the house, either intact or ruined like most grave-goods, was allowed to remain over the tomb.[2] Some chiefs in the Ila country are buried in their huts, which are kept in repair for some time and then replaced by smaller and flimsier structures; and in these grave-shrines are preserved various articles that belonged to him whose bones lie beneath.[3] In Macdonald's time, some of the Nyasa tribes demolished the house in which a man died, but if it covered the grave they allowed it to remain, and if he was buried elsewhere in the village they built a new house over his remains.[4] "Great Wind's" grave was "dug in a thick tangle of bush," and libations of beer trickled down to

---

[1] See pp. 28, 35, 42, 70, 71.

[2] Cf. the resemblance of Chinese and other graves to the dwellings of the living (SCD. 40, 129-31). Speaking of Italy, Cumont says (ALRP. 48): "The prehistoric cemeteries of the first iron age have yielded a number of cinerary urns exactly reproducing the various types of huts which sheltered the tribes who then peopled the peninsula. The burial places of the Etruscans are often on the plan of their dwellings." Petrie makes a similar remark about Egypt: "The large tombs of the Ist dynasty were built of brick, with panelled sides copied from the form of the wooden house. The idea was to repeat, in permanent brick for a tomb, the form of the dwelling-house of the chief, where he had slept with his followers around him. The tomb pits were in the midst of the structure." (RLAE. 124.)

[3] IPNR. ii. 171.

[4] A. i. 108-110.

the mouth of the corpse through a reed that came to the surface; [1]
nevertheless beer was placed for his use in the hut where he had
drawn his last breath.[2] The Konde, around the north end of
Lake Nyasa, erect a little spirit hut on the grave of a chief, and
believe that if it is allowed to decay, the dead chief will visit his
resentment upon both his neglectful successor and his tribal
lands.[3] The Bahuma of the Kwilu River district erect a small hut
over the grave; and, indeed, throughout much of Central and
Northern Congoland the graves of persons of importance are thus
furnished.[4] "A very noticeable feature in the villages of the
Okale" (on the Upper Lukenye) "are the neat models of houses
which are erected over their tombs." [5] "Among the Baila proper,
as well as among the Balumbu and Bambala, a tiny temple, consisting of a small conical grass roof supported on sticks, is built
over the grave. Within the temple one usually finds an earthenware pot, sunk into the grave, as a receptacle for beer offerings." [6]
Near the graves of most Baganda, small shrines for ghosts were
built, wherein pious relatives placed offerings of beer and clothing.[7] On the borders of Bantu Africa, the Mañbettu of North-
east Congoland, a mixed race with a Bahima aristocracy, bury
warriors in the place where they fell, and erect a kind of hut over
the tomb, to which relatives repair occasionally with baskets of
provisions and jars of water; [8] and the Basoga, whose country lies
east of the Nile and north of Lake Victoria, bury ordinary men in
their gardens or fields and build at the head of the grave a miniature hut, some three feet high, in which offerings are made at
times to the spirit.[9] "In the open country of tropical Africa,"

[1] AI. 163-64.
[2] AI. 165.
[3] SRK. 197.
[4] GGC. 653-54.
[5] LPK. 176.
[6] IPNR. ii. 171.
[7] Bg. 315, 126.
[8] GGC. 649.
[9] GS. 106, 128, 131. "In some parts of Upper Egypt there was the same belief
as now in Central Africa, that the soul wandered about and needed shelter and
food, which were provided in a model hut. These huts of pottery were placed at
the sides of the grave, on the surface. The simpler form copies the Bedawy tent,
and there is every stage up to a two-storeyed house, with furniture, and food, and
a servant to prepare it. The tent type suggests that these soul-houses were the
product of a nomadic people who were settling in Egypt, and the period—IXth

writes Le Roy,[1] "the Blacks are content to build for the manes of their ancestors, either in the village or outside it, little huts under which they come to make their offerings. These huts, called 'of the *mzimu*' (*i.e.*, of the disembodied soul), are to be seen everywhere. In Uganda they assume more ample proportions: they are veritable sanctuaries, called *masabo*, in which a sort of altar or platform (*mwa-liro*) accommodates the bananas and the beer offered there. . . . In Urundi every village contains these minute huts."

As the conventions of society became a little more refined and hut-burial gave place in most of these communities to burial in the fields or in the waste, the home of deceased still retained its sacredness.[2] The Baluba bury a man in the scrub and burn his house next day at sunrise, but near the site of the destroyed dwelling they build a tiny hut for his spirit. "Before the entrance of this little temple of the dead is dug a ditch which is filled with water mingled with flour; another ditch is dug close beside it, and in it is placed a pot pierced at the bottom, into which palm wine is poured. This is the dead man's meal."[3] Customs of similar significance were in vogue in the Nyasa region; and methods were devised for bringing the spirit home to the village shrine from its grave in the wilds.[4]

The establishment of fanes for the dead at spots remote from their places of sepulture was further facilitated by the instability of Bantu villages. Owing to ignorance of hygiene, improvident methods of agriculture, and the perishability of huts, Bantu communities are obliged to flit after a few years to new and sometimes distant localities, whence it is impracticable to pay frequent visits to the graves of their ancestors. Filial piety prompts them to

to XIth dynasty—points to the Libyan invasion of that age. The custom must have been due to the southern tribes, as these soul-houses are found from Rifeh to Gebelyn, but scarcely ever at the IXth dynasty capital, Sedment." (RLAE. 167.)

[1] RP. 190, 103; see also my p. 17.

[2] See p. 70. Miss Werner says: "The old custom of the Yaos (at any rate in the case of a chief) is to bury the dead man inside his hut (or where he has several, in that of his principal wife), which is then closed and allowed to decay. Lengths of calico (the quantity being proportioned to the wealth of deceased) are draped over the roof and left there. Perhaps the building of a house over the grave, which appears to be done sometimes near Lake Nyasa, is a later modification of this custom." (NLEA. 194, footnote.)

[3] GGC. 645-46.

[4] See p. 38.

take the revered spirits to the new sites, and magical notions of the attachment of a spirit to its personal possessions and the soil in which its mortal remains rest, make the transportation easy. The old shrines need not be removed; [1] that which gave them sanctity may be transferred to the new sanctuaries—a little earth [2] or a few stones from the grave, or something that deceased regarded as his very own, or some nail-parings, hair-clippings or other fragments of his body, or even an image that by words of power has been made an embodiment of the divine spirit; or, according to Akamba beliefs, [3] the spirit may be lured thither with an abundant provision of sacrificial food. The grave never loses its sacredness; but thousands of Bantu villages have shrines of the dead in the midst of the abodes of the living which, being more accessible to worshippers than the distant graves, have become, if I may steal a metaphor from Anglican usage, chapels-of-ease to the tombs.

Externally, these domestic places of worship exhibit considerable variety.

"Most African tribes bury the dead in the heart of the forest," says one writer, "but at the same time near the village a memorial ground is set apart on which are erected tiny memorial huts, which the restless spirits of the departed may inhabit if they so choose. There, when the spirit pays such visits—as all good spirits do nightly—he finds his loin cloth ready, the spoon with which he ate his food, the bottle from which he drank, his battle-axe and cross-bow which played havoc in many an affray; there is generally too a spread of Indian corn or other food, which the thoughtful and sorrowing wives have placed in readiness for his return visit to earth. How safe these memorial tombs are from desecration may be gathered from the fact that very frequently considerable sums of native currency are strewn upon the floor. These little tombs are also surrounded with numerous carved images erected on poles." [4]

---

[1] See, however, my p. 69.
[2] See pp. 272, 287.
[3] JRAI., 1913, pp. 537-38.
[4] DDA. 25. This statement, though made of "most African tribes," occurs in a description of the Baketi on the upper reaches of the Kasai; hence its strong West Coast colouring. Sir Harry Johnston, whose opinion on such subjects is always weighty, states (GGC. 766) that the cross-bow is not indigenous to Africa;

At the back of the cattle-pen and to the right of it as one enters a Thonga village by the main gate, there is a tree which Junod calls "the mystical stem of the village." When the headman was casting about for a new site, this tree was indicated by the diviner's method [1] as the one round which the village should be built; hence he must never cut it, and when he is dead and his hut is crushed down, one branch of it will be put on the place where the threshold was and another used to close the main entrance to the village till the period of mourning is ended. On this tree offerings to the gods are hung, and at its base there is a broken pot which serves as the village altar; but if the "bones" so order, the altar may be removed from this tree and placed among the poles at the main entrance to the village. [2]

"In all the villages of interior Gabon, of Loango, and of Congo, we see in the centre of the public square a little tree at the foot of which the natives place offerings and pour out libations. The passing traveller who has read authors treating the matter *ex professo*, will write in his notebook: 'Dendrolatry, the religion of the Blacks of such a village.' Or else: 'Naturism (see Réville).' But if this traveller had witnessed the foundation of the village, he would have seen the chief or the sorcerer plant this little tree as a sign that they were taking possession of the place, offer a sacrifice, sprinkle the roots with the blood of the victim, and mix some ashes from the bones of the ancestors with the earth that is to nourish the tree. This is why the tree is *sacred*, why they pay a sort of worship to it, why these people appear to be 'dendrolaters' to those who see only the surface." [3] On another page the same writer states that everything placed under the tree in a Bavili (of Loango) marketplace is sacred because this tree is intended to shelter the body of the deceased king before his removal to the grave. [4]

Trees are often associated with graves, shrines, and even with

that some tribes in South-west Congoland appear to have copied it from the weapons which fifteenth-century Portuguese soldiers wielded; and that it seems to have penetrated Africa through Egypt, reaching as far as the North-eastern Cameroons, from the days when the Crusaders included it in their armament.

[1] See pp. 148 ff.
[2] LSAT. i. 283, 290, 293.
[3] RP. 176.
[4] RP. 160.

the worship of ancestor-spirits in the hunting-veld. Dr. Frazer, writing of the Tumbuka, says: "In the villages, and especially beneath the *msoro* tree, the people build diminutive huts, about eight inches in circumference and eighteen inches high. Sometimes these temples are much larger, and so valuable an offering as a tusk of ivory might be placed in them, and it was not taken out to be sold till it was replaced by another. Offerings of beer and meal were also put in them. . . . Though no watch is set upon these gifts to the spirits, no hungry man will dare to steal them, for it is a most dangerous offence to cheat [1] the shades of the dead. Beneath the *msoro* or the wild fig-tree, was the usual place for these little temples. One can imagine a simple reason for the reverence of the fig-tree, but it is a little hard to discover why the *msoro* tree is the peculiarly sacred tree of the Nyasaland people. It has no edible fruit, and is usually scarcely bigger than a well-developed bush. But around it there are many legends." [2] Near most of the older Kamba villages there are sacred trees, often (but not always) wild fig-trees, where sacrifice is offered to ancestor-spirits.[3] "The offerings may be laid on the bare ground, or they may be placed in a hut built on the spot, which is sometimes similarly constructed to the living huts, other times it is scarcely two feet high, though always of the same shape as the living huts. When goats are sacrificed the skin is usually laid over the roof of the hut; in one of them I saw a bowl of grain, a little tobacco, a green gourd, and honey beer, which seems to be the most necessary part of the offering." [4] Hobley writes:[5] "The way in which a particular tree is chosen as a sacred place was explained to me unhesitatingly in the following manner: In a particular locality, long ago, there would be a woman, noted as a prophetess or seer, whose prophecies always came true, and at her death she would be buried in her village. After a time a woman of that village became possessed by the *imu*, or spirit, of the deceased, and, in a state of exaltation, would speak in the name of the prophetess, saying: 'I cannot stay here, I am called by *Engai*,

[1] It is a breach of taboo to take anything from a grave, but spirits may be cheated, and often are, with impunity; see pp. 78 ff.

[2] WPP. 128.

[3] BBM. 53.

[4] JRAI., 1913, pp. 537-38.

[5] BBM. 58, 61.

and I go to live at a certain tree' (which would be specified). The tree thus designated then acquired sanctity. Four elders and four old women would then be selected; taking some earth from her grave, and one (a blood relation of deceased) taking a goat, they would all proceed to the tree. The earth was deposited at its foot, the goat led thrice round the tree and then sacrificed. The delegates then prayed: 'We have brought you to the tree you desire,' and a small hut was built on the spot."

In some Bantu tribes a branch of a tree, or even a forked stick (provided it is of the right sort) is sufficient. The altars for family spirits of the Bakaonde consist of a stick which is planted outside the verandah of the hut, on the side near the door, or instead of the stick there may be an inconspicuous branch, or an erection surmounted by horns, etc.[1] Lunda practice is similar. "Before nearly every Lunda hut one or more sticks may be seen fixed in the ground (usually of the sacred *muyombo* tree). They are usually erected for the family spirits, though sometimes for special spirits. Game heads and rags sometimes decorate the top. Frequently the base is made like a human face, at other times a plain circle is the distinctive mark. Each separate stick represents a separate *mukishi*. These sticks are the family altars, and form a convenient point of communication between the living and the dead."[2]

As an example of shrines of another pattern, it may be well to mention those of the Banyankole and Bakitara.[3] These people pay little attention to the spirits of people who are of no consequence while in the flesh, assuming that a nonentity in this world cannot but be a nonentity in the land of shades; but when a man of property dies, his heir moves the village to another site and builds in his new house,[4] at the side of the bed farthest from the door, a mound or platform of beaten earth, some two feet high, four feet long, and two wide, on which milk is placed daily, in a special wooden pot, for the dead man's spirit. A shrine for the spirit is also built near the kraal-gate, and there offerings are made when the medicine-man discovers that they are required.

---

[1] WBA. 133.
[2] WBA. 169.
[3] SCA. 89, 198; NYN. 25, 149; KT. 41, 296.
[4] Cf. p. 287.

The pastoral people of these countries are not Bantu; but there is a Hamitic strain in Bantu culture, especially in the semi-pastoral tribes, and altars upon which offerings of food are made to ancestor-spirits are to be found near the back wall in many of their dwellings.[1] The *umsamo* in a Kafir hut is a small portion of the floor at the back of the hut marked off by a ridge of earth, and is supposed to be the special haunt of the grandfather's spirit. "It is the spot whereon are placed all meat and beer offered to the *amatongo*," says Kidd.[2] Among the Ila-speaking people, "each family has private altars in the house. We say 'altars,' but in reality they are sacred spots without anything to mark them off. One is at the foot of the central pole of the hut; the others are on either side of the doorway—on the right the husband's, on the left the wife's."[3] A combination of indoor altar and forked stick appears among the Thonga.[4] Some Thonga medicine-men are supposed to be inspired by Angoni or Zulu spirits, possibly because they trace their medical lore to this source. A forked branch, duly cut from a particular kind of tree, is planted, after the manner prescribed by a precise ritual, in the floor of the hut of such a practitioner; around this stick a circle of raised clay is carefully kept up and regularly smeared; and upon it the doctor hangs his baskets of drugs and calabashes of powder. This is an altar at which he worships daily, maintaining amicable relations with the spirit that "possesses" him and acknowledging its continual assistance in his professional practice.

On the Bamangwato-Matebele border, not far from the sources of the Shashi River, I visited the home of a little Karanga clan whose forbears were people of importance in the country long before Matebele or even Bamangwato had invaded it. The village is known as Mhasha, though that is really the dynastic title of the clan-head. The Mhasha of that period, a very old man whose natural kindliness glowed at my charitableness toward the religion of his fathers, had his ancestral temple arranged as if for worship, and explained as well as he could the meaning of it all. Eight forked posts supported a flat, square[5] roof of poles

[1] See p. 70.
[2] SC. 26.
[3] IPNR. ii. 173 and cf. 166.
[4] LSAT. ii. 442, 450, 454-55, 518.
[5] It was the only *square* structure that I saw in these villages.

and grass, which sheltered a floor of beaten earth, carefully finished off with clay and cow-dung mixture. In the centre of this floor, a raised ring, about four inches high and deftly moulded of the same material, enclosed three smooth, black pebbles from the river-bed, each as large as a child's head, and a branch of *mosimama* bush so fixed in the ground that it "overhung"[1] the stones. The old man spoke of the stones as *batatigulu* ("ancestors"), naming each of them after one of the first three chiefs of his clan; but he explained, in answer to my enquiry, that though the clan would grieve if one of the stones which their fathers had used age after age for this purpose were stolen or lost, they could replace it with another pebble from the river-bed, because their idea was that the ancestors did not dwell in the stones, but met their children there and received such offerings as were laid upon them—that, in short, they were trysting-places rather than habitations of the gods. At these stones the villagers craved the aid of their divinities before commencing the three great undertakings of the year—planting, reaping, and hunting,[2] and, also, whenever sickness was epidemic among them. Women of the village prepared the shrine beforehand by renewing the plaster and planting a fresh branch of *mosimama,* but those of them who were not born into the clan still worship their own ancestors and pay no homage to the ancestors of their husbands, though they usually stand at a distance and raise their "ululation" at the right moment. Before sunrise the call to worship is uttered in any phrase that may flash on the mind of the herald, perhaps in the form of the old proverb, "He who gives to god does not go to bed hungry"; and then the descendants of these divinities proceed to the shrine, each carrying a little of the innermost kernel of Kafir-corn grains—the tiny heart of each grain, which will not yield to the pounding that converts the outer laminæ into meal but makes delicious porridge when carefully ground. It is important that these cereal offerings should be carried with both hands, one crossed over the other with palms open and upward. At the head of the procession the village chief carries a pot of Kafir-beer, and when he has poured this as a libation upon the stones each worshipper in turn casts down his little gift of

[1] See below.
[2] See p. 259.

corn-kernels so that they mingle with the beer; and a simple prayer is offered to the ancestors, who are invoked by name, beseeching a blessing on the seed to be sown, the harvest to be reaped, or whatever the festival of the day may denote. And when the offering is made the women raise their peculiar cry as a greeting to the gods. Little variations of symbol are introduced at appropriate seasons; in time of drought each "child of the clan" approaches the shrine carrying a stalk of Kafir-corn, with which they all strike the ground in unison, crying: "O god! Give us rain, that we may have grain in the gardens"; and when the corn-kernels are thrown upon the stones in time of epidemic, a great cry is raised. "This cry," said a younger man in the group, who was probably clothing the thoughts of his fathers in phrases that he had learnt in another school, "this cry is a prayer to God; it is uttered because it is the people who have died and are with God who cause God to kill us."

Shrines of this type are not without variety of pattern. At Shakashugwe's, the next village that I visited, the shrine was roofless, stood clear of all buildings, had two black pebbles instead of three, and a stick of *mogonono* [1] was substituted for the sprig of *mosimama*. Shakashugwe explained, however, that, having recently moved to this site he had not yet built what he had planned, but had placed the shrine in what he intended to become the courtyard of his new dwelling. When I returned home and told the Chief Khama of the Karanga chapels that I had seen, he remarked that in his younger days some of the Bamangwato practised this form of worship, having copied it, he thought, from the older inhabitants of the district; but that they used to "overhang" the stones with a stalk of *motlhatlha oa noka,* that is, *cyperus sexangulus.* [2] Some Bakhurutse of the Northern Protectorate, with whom I discussed the Karanga shrines, informed me that their fathers brought from the river-bed a stone

---

[1] This tree is described in MTR. 167.

[2] Cyperus, like papyrus, is an aquatic plant of the sedge family, and in Egypt there was a popular belief that papyrus was protective against crocodiles (cf. Plut. *Is. et Os.* 358). Now the crocodile was a very ancient totem of dominant tribes in the group from which the Bamangwato and Bakhurutse cut loose, though both these tribes now venerate antelopes of one variety or another. Is it possible that the choice of a plant to "overhang" the tribal stones was influenced by an odour of ancient sanctity that clung to certain plants long after they lost their totemic value?

in the cleft of which a cyperus plant had taken root, and placed this in their shrine when preparing it for worship. A number of natives told me at various times that shrines in some of the more aboriginal villages which are scattered through what has long been Bamangwata territory, are furnished with ancestral stones which are "overhung" with an axe-handle, either with or without a sprig of *mosimama;* but I was never able to verify the statements by visiting such shrines. A colleague who lived in the midst of the Karanga villages of Bulilima, informed me that some sections of the Karanga people place a snake skin (of the *Umhlati* species) beside the stones when they pray, but that he had failed to discover what it symbolised. Aged Becwana often told me that in their youth they had been familiar with shrines in the Northern Protectorate at which ancestor-spirits were symbolised by an axe-handle, or more frequently the helve of a small adze, planted in a circle of smeared ground, often the threshing-floor in the backyard, without stones or other appointments; and that the assembled family worshipped by filling their mouths with beer and spewing it in a thin stream upon the adze-handle. An old mentor of mine, chief of a small section of the Bobididi who lived in what has since become known as the North-western Transvaal, dictated a statement of which the following is a translation. "When my grandfather was dead, the stump that he used as a seat was given to his eldest son. Ground was made ready in the middle of the courtyard, and this stump and a *legoma* bulb were placed in it, a little circle of beaten and smeared earth being prepared around them. Early in the spring of the year, Kafir-beer was cooked and poured as a libation on this circle; and all the children, both boys and girls, being gathered together, each one sucked up a mouthful of beer from the circle and, holding it in the mouth, went outside the village and squirted it upon the ground.[1] This completed the ritual: its name is *Go thebola dithota gonwe medimo* ('To make an offering to the graves, or to the spirits of the dead'). And his praise song may be sung." In the sacred huts of "most tribes in the Northern Transvaal" to which reference was made on a previous page,[2] "drums are regarded as the earthly shrine of the tutelary spirits of the clan."

[1] See Index: "Blowing water from the mouth."
[2] See p. 222.

Mr. Gottschling, writing also of tribes in the Northern Transvaal, refers definitely to the Bawenda, and states that though these people worship at the graves of the old chiefs and ancestors in the sacred groves, they have altars for prayer and sacrifice in their villages, and that these "consist of three stones placed in the ground, in the centre of which a shrub, flower or rush has been planted." He states, further, that at the two annual sacrifices at the time of ploughing and at the great festivity at the beginning of the harvest, the various families gather round their family-altar in the yard of their respective heads, each chief wearing only the kaross of his ancestor, and each member of the family has to throw a little new fruit upon the altar and to pour some beer over it.[1]

It would be a mistake, I think, to pass from shrines of this type without bestowing thought upon their notable peculiarities. All Native exponents, in describing their worship and its paraphernalia, stressed two curious phrases. For one thing, they always used the verb *go okama* to set forth the function of the branch, pole, or axe-handle which is erected beside the stones. This is an untranslatable verb: I have rendered it "to overhang"; but it looks out from this English dress with a reproachful face, protesting that the garb, though fitting enough for most of its commonplace tasks, is much too drab for its professional functions; for it often carries the sense of "to defend" or of "to overlook" (in the sense of bewitching with the evil eye), and in the sentence under consideration it sighs for the dignity and mystery of the terminology of religion. But what can I do! Among the words with which our fathers used to clothe their thoughts, there was probably a term that would befit this old-world notion, but it has either disappeared with the passing of the years or escaped my notice as I rummaged the chests in our linguistic attic. Another point is this: the phrase which came naturally to their lips as they described their worship in time of epidemic, was *go omanya bashwi* ("to scold the dead"), but they sometimes said *go cosa bashwi* ("to rouse the dead"). Both phrases were apparently due to the recollection that prayers offered upon such occasions are protests, rather than petitions; the worshippers con-

[1] See pp. 221, 244.

tend that they do not neglect the ancestor-spirits and demand therefore that the latter should cease sending them trouble and death.[1]

We observe, also, that, however rudimentary as compared with that of Egyptian, Greek, Babylonian, and Indian temples, the apparatus of worship is in its way very complete. As in the High Places of Semitic religion, there is the sacred stone (or stones) and the sacred pole, the former being at once idol and altar; Baetylia, Bethels, or god-boxes;[2] resorts, if not residences, of the gods; where the worshippers greet their divinities with words of prayer, gestures of homage, and material oblations. The Bobididi practice of sucking up a mouthful of beer that has been poured as a libation over their shrine is manifestly an embryonic sacrament of communion with their gods. In Arabia, where the libation of blood that was common to Semitic clans had great prominence, the blood poured over the stones was all that fell to the lot of the gods, the flesh being consumed by the worshippers and their guests.[3] This is not quite true of Bantu sacrifices, as we shall see later; but it is well to take note of the fact that the Mhasha villagers were at least approximating to a libation of blood when they so placed the first kill of the hunting season that its blood would drip on the stones for the satisfaction of the gods, and actually flayed and dressed the carcase upon these same symbols some twelve hours later.[4] Another point of similarity is this: Semites worshipped Baalim, or lords of the land, at their sacred stones and poles; and at shrines of the same type Bantu tribesmen pay court to old chiefs who, by conquering the country and leaving their bones in it, have become "masters of the land" (*Beñ ba lehatshe*), to use the Secwana phrase, and therefore givers of fertility to the soil and all wild things, flocks, herds, and people that live upon it. We shall have to pay a little more attention to these Bantu sacred stones, but for the present it is well to keep our attention fixed on the shrines of various patterns.

In that maze of lagoons, spillways and marshes which is known

[1] See Index: "Scolding the Spirits."
[2] See KM. 59.
[3] RS. 229-231.
[4] See p. 259.

as the Okavango Swamps—the remains of a mighty lake that once filled this great basin—the Bayei (called Makuba by their Becwana neighbours) have sheltered themselves for generations from the ruthlessness of adjacent tribes. They live in separate families, scattered over a multitude of almost inaccessible islets, some no larger than a full-grown ant-hill; and the difficulty of threading their watery labyrinth has daunted their foes and also debarred us from studying their social, political and religious institutions. Lake Ngami, the southernmost extension of their sanctuary, was discovered by Livingstone in 1849; and the following year Mr. Edwards, son of Livingstone's missionary colleague at Mabotsa and himself a hunter and trader of renown among tribesmen of the South-central plateau, visited that district. The greater part of a paper that Mr. Edwards wrote was lost in a fire on board the *Windsor Castle* in 1874, but a fragment was published under the title of "Tradition of the Bayeye." [1] We gather from this fragment that there is an altar or place of sacrifice in the centre of every Bayei chief's village, and that it is generally a circular enclosure, from which women (though matrilineal succession still prevails among these chiefs) and young men are excluded, and in which certain parts of each animal killed in the chase are first exposed for the benefit of the *batotee*,[2] or departed spirits, and then eaten by priests and certain old men who have been initiated into the mysteries of their religion. Although I lived five hundred miles away and was never able to visit the district, the missionary work in this area was under my supervision for two or three years; and one of my Native evangelists who travelled extensively through these swamps described the temples of these villages as large, well-built sheds, with flat roofs upon which some part of every animal that fell to the hunters was placed. In one shrine that he examined, the gods were symbolised by a pair of very large turtle shells, each filled with a compound of powdered roots and the fat of all sorts of game, and called by the name of one of the ancestors of the people. As soon as a young man succeeded in killing his first hippopotamus, he took

---

[1] See vol. ii., pt. 2 of the *Folk-lore Journal* (Cape Town) for March, 1880.

[2] Mr. Edwards was familiar with Secwana, but not with Sekuba; and his *batotee* is evidently the Secwana word *dithota*. See p. 276.

up his lodgings in the temple, bringing hither whatever game
the gods gave him on his daily hunting-trips; but as soon as
he killed his second hippopotamus, or, failing this, when the
first rain fell, the priest performed certain incantations over
him, thus setting him free to return to his own home. Although
the ancestors appear to be always symbolised in these temples
by vessels of occult mixture that the people call "medicine," the
containers vary both in kind and number.

Defunct rulers of distinguished dynasties are glorified, as
might be expected, in more pretentious temples. The Portuguese, desirous of discovering an overland route that would link
together their East and West Coast possessions, sent two expeditions to the court of Mwata Cazembe, who was regarded as a
great African potentate, though feudatory, in theory at least, to
Mwata ya Nvo. In 1799, before the expedition of Governor
Lacerda had left the country, Cazembe IV, surnamed Lekeza,
had removed his court to a new capital, eight or ten miles away;
and in 1831 Monteiro and Gamitto were forbidden to proceed
to the new capital till they had paid tribute to the spirits of the
dynasty at the royal tombs, which were apparently in the neighbourhood of the old site. Gamitto calls them tombs of the
deceased Muatas Mashamos, but Lacerda had called them
Massangos. Of the four tombs which they visited, Gamitto
described two, and as these were much alike it is probable that
all four were of the same pattern. The first to be visited was
the sepulchre of Muata Canyembo III. "It consisted of a large
quadrangular enclosure, about a hundred paces on each side, constructed of branches of trees and stakes, forming an impenetrable
barrier. Near the entrance stood a heap of human skulls, and
outside the door, seated cross-legged on a lion skin, was the
Muine-Mashamo (grave-keeper or minister), smeared over with
impemba (white earth) from the head to the waist." Having
made their offerings, the soldiers were invited to enter. "They
found the whole space inside in a state of the utmost cleanliness,
and in the centre they saw a large circular house, thatched with
straw, in front of the door of which stood another heap of skulls.
In the centre of this large house was a smaller one, of a cylindrical form, made of plaited cane-work, perfectly empty, and
without any decoration, except two painted pillars at the entrance.

This was the tomb of the Muata, and here they found the minister seated cross-legged, with the presents before him." Gamitto tells how the minister remained for some time in apparent meditation, occasionally muttering a few words, and then cried with a loud voice "Averie!" (Hail!);[1] after which he told the soldiers that the spirits thanked them for their gifts. The second sepulchre was much the same as the first, except that some thirty gun-barrels were stood near the chief's grave, and the only skulls visible were those of two powerful Mambos who had been vanquished and slain by Cazembe Lekeza. These skulls were attached to a tree.[2]

In Buganda, although the ruling dynasty has been upon the throne for a millennium, there was till lately, if not now, a separate temple for each king in the long line, from Kintu, the conqueror, to Mutesa, who saw the dawning of Christianity; and every fane still had its own relics. Pursuant to the custom of his fathers, Mutesa built, within the precincts of his court, a temple for his own umbilical cord,[3] and placed an official of very high rank in charge of it and the royal fetishes. The navel-string figures prominently in rites by which the legitimacy of Baganda children is established, and, moreover, the ghost of the afterbirth is thought to cling to it—hence its name, "the Twin"; but, inasmuch as ghosts are credited with a more inveterate attachment to the jaw-bone than to any other fragment of their outworn bodies,[4] custom demanded that the jaw-bone of a deceased ruler should be decorated with beads and placed in the temple of his umbilical cord, a new building being erected for these sacred objects. Once these relics were lodged in their final resting-place, the king's spirit would be sure to take possession of some man, who would thereupon be installed in the temple as the medium of communication between the canonised king and his royal successor.[5]

At the head of a great chief's grave in Busoga, there is erected

[1] It seems that the Cazembe people had learnt from the Portuguese to cry "Ave Maria!" as a sort of greeting, and that upon their lips the foreign phrase became "Averie!"

[2] LC. 249-50.

[3] See p. 185.

[4] See p. 34.

[5] Bg. 110, 236, 283-85.

quite a large building, where the widows lodge during the time of mourning, and where the one selected to guard the grave dwells for a much longer period. Instead of completely filling the grave, it is customary to attach a bell to the head of the corpse, place a basket underneath it, and leave a shaft open to the surface; when the ringing of the bell warns the watchers that the skull has dropped into the basket, the jaw-bone (or the skull in some tribes) is cleaned, decorated with beads, wrapped in a goatskin, put into a bag and a wooden vessel, and exposed in a shrine with that of his predecessor. Each shrine is served, in addition to the widow who guards the relic of her late husband, by a priest who obtains from the dead such guidance as the reigning chief desires. The final disposal of these sacred bones is hardly what we should have expected. Where the skull is preserved and venerated, the installation of a new skull involves the displacement of its predecessor, which is then taken away to the customary repository for such antiques, and left without further attention. Obsolete jaw-bones have a still greater comedown. When a fresh jaw-bone is enshrined, the widow who guards the one already there is given a sheep or a goat and sent away with her relic; after passing the night at some house on her way, she slips off in the morning without it, and·her host, realising the nature of the luggage that she has left behind, puts it where it is unlikely to be disturbed again.[1]

In Bunyoro, "when a king died, his body had to be interred in a particular part of the country which was reserved for the tombs of kings. A large pit was dug for the grave, and over it a hut was built. The body of the king was arranged with the knees bent up towards the chin in a squatting attitude, and was stitched in a cowskin. The whole of the grave was lined first with cowskins and then with bark-cloths, and the body was laid on a bed of bark-cloth. Two of the king's wives were selected to go with him into the other world, and they went into the grave, laid the body on the bed as though sleeping, and covered it with bark-cloths. Then they lay down, one on either side of the body, and the grave was filled with innumerable bark-cloths, some of which were spread over the body, while others were thrown in until the grave was full and they were heaped

[1] GS. 106-107, 131.

above the level of the floor. No earth was put into the grave, which was filled with bark-cloths only. In this large shrine or temple [meaning evidently the hut which was built over the grave] some of the widows kept watch, guarding it constantly, and a priest and medium were in attendance. People came to the tomb to visit the king as if it were his court, and they made requests of him and brought him offerings, which became the property of the widows. At times the reigning king would send gifts of cows to his predecessor, and the priest and medium held communication with the dead and informed the king of anything that came to their knowledge which concerned him or his country." [1]

Roscoe seems to place his Kitara shrine of the "rain-makers" in another category, but there are reasons, I think, why we should deal with it here. He was privileged to visit the shrine and witness its rites, after promising not to reveal its locality nor the identity of its ministrants; and his description [2] is worthy of notice. The sacred place "lay in the forest some distance from any path where people passed. A glade some ten yards wide and four hundred yards long, lay between tall trees whose branches met above, making a sombre shade over the quiet place. No grass grew, but lemon grass was spread in the glade and a path led through it to the end where there were two pits, dug, so the people affirmed, not by the hand of man but by Ruhanga (God) himself. One was about four feet in diameter and four to five feet deep, and the other two feet in diameter and eighteen inches deep; both were lined with lemon grass, and when specially solemn and important offerings and prayers were to be made, shrines were built over them. All the preparations were made by the priest and his attendants on their arrival. At the back of the larger pit an altar was erected consisting of three spears and a long cow's horn, which were stuck in the ground in a row. The horn was filled with herbs and decorated with cowry-shells, and the thick end, which was uppermost, was closed by an immense stopper or bung; by its side stood a short iron spear. In front of these, on a leopard-skin spread on the ground, was placed a stool covered with a second leopard-skin

[1] SCA. 199-200.
[2] KT. 29-31; SCA. 155-56.

and on this lay the rain fetish, a large buffalo-horn. Near this fetish were placed a bow and arrows which always accompanied it." That which throws all else into the shade in his delineation of the ceremony, runs as follows: "The priest killed a fowl, or sometimes one of the animals, either the black goat or the sheep, and smeared some of the blood on the fetishes. The bottoms of both pits were smeared with fat, some of the blood was poured into each, and the body cast into one. The priest knelt while doing this and, after the animal had been sacrificed, he sprinkled millet, dwarf beans, and semsen into the pits. A vessel of water was next brought from the spring near and the rain-maker raised his hands and prayed thus to Ruhanga: 'Ruhanga, bless us. Thou king of all the earth, hear us. The people are dying from hunger.' With much ceremony the water was then poured into some of the pots and left exposed in order to draw down rain by sympathetic magic. The meat of the offering was then taken from the pit, cooked, and eaten in the presence of the god. The bones were burned and the skin was used by the rain-maker for sacred purposes. The ceremony lasted in all some two hours or a little longer, and the procession then returned home." Now, waiving all question of the identity of Ruhanga, the first salient feature of this picture is the sacred pits, which are the very things that would be left when time had done its work on such a king's grave as that portrayed by the same author and quoted in our preceding paragraph; and the second is the striking likeness of the ceremonies to the major rain-rites at a great chief's grave.[1] Like all rain-rites, they are shot through and through with magic; but the stool, the leopard-skins, the spears, and the bow and arrows, are the insignia of royalty, not the tools of the magician, and the black goat, the libation of blood, the sacrificial meal, and the burning of the victim's bones, all whisper that the pit is sacred because it was the grave of some chief who achieved fame for his dynasty. Who was he? Does the lineage of his priesthood indicate his clan? And what was his relation to Ruhanga, the god to whom the prayer of invocation was addressed?

[1] Cf. p. 208.

ANCESTRAL STONES

It would be worth while to discover why black pebbles from the river-bed became symbols for divine ancestors. To ascribe the pattern of these shrines to poverty of mind and imagination in Bantu artists, is pathetically inconclusive. Three black pebbles in a circle with raised rim, describes the hearth in every woman's courtyard on the South-central plateau; and the hearth, if not sacred, is regarded as symbolical of the community that gathers round it. Throughout Bechuanaland, whether in clan or tribe, the hearth in a Place of Public Assembly is without hearthstones, but it was always fortified with special magical devices. On the death of a husband or wife, it used to be customary in Khama's tribe for the surviving spouse to take one of the hearthstones, deposit it in a broken pot, place the pot in an old winnowing-basket, and send it to be laid at the cross-roads outside the town. The custom had been abandoned before I arrived in the country, and I hesitated to believe that it applied to the death of a man; but the people assured me that the break-down of the home, whether caused by the death of husband or wife, was always symbolised in this manner. However that may be, it is undoubtedly true that when a Becwana wife scatters her hearthstones in the bush, she gives out in unmistakable terms that, for good and all, she has broken with her husband. Among the Batuse of Ruanda, bride and bridegroom place their hands on the stones of the fireplace, as one of the symbols of marriage.[1] The Akikuyu regard it as important that the mother of a bride should take her daughter to the river-side to select the hearthstones for her new home.[2] The sacred fire, also, of which we shall speak presently, seems to link the religious life of the community with the hearth of the clan.[3] If all shrines were of this design, it might be permissible to surmise that the ancestral

---

[1] GS. 196.

[2] P. 131. See also my p. 57.

[3] Seebohm states (TCASL. 34) that Cymric tribesmen carried their hearthstones with them from one locality to another; and I have read somewhere, though I cannot lay my finger upon the passage, that they regarded fire-back stones not only as symbols but as proofs of descent. The Celtic "cult of the dead culminated at the family hearth, around which the dead were even buried . . . the belief in the presence of ancestral ghosts around the hearth was widespread." (RAC. 165.)

hearth was deemed the natural rallying-place for the descendants
of the divinity; but many shrines consist of two pebbles, or one,
or four, and the hearth idea is intolerant of the upright stick
or whatever is erected to "overhang" the stones. Two black
pebbles and a short stick, or a bulb and a native axe-handle,[1]
look for all the world like a crude phallic symbol, which is
not inappropriate to gods of fertility; but when the shrine consists of three or four pebbles, the phallic symbolism disappears
or is conventionalised beyond recognition; and when a sprig of
mosimama or a *cyperus sexangulus* plant is substituted for the
short stick or the axe-helve, one pricks up one's ears for a whisper
of plant-totemism. If I had suggested hearth-stones, phallic
symbols, or plant-totems, some of my Native friends would, no
doubt, have been ready to humour me, for the imagination of
these affable people is readily kindled with a spark, and they are
strangers to scientific accuracy; but when I asked how the stones
came to represent ancestors, no Native ever suggested such symbolism; they knew that the stones did represent ancestors and
always had done so, and there was an end of the matter.
Genetics is not in my line: I leave flight into the abstract and
remote to men of stronger pinion: but no theory of the origin
and significance of these symbols can be convincing unless it
comprehends the following facts.

Cardinall, writing of spirit-haunted stones in the Northern
Territories of the Gold Coast, says:[2] "The neolithic implements
and the old grindstones have a semi-religious status, and to these
must be added the stones used as anvils by the blacksmiths.
These are called *nari* (Kassena), *nia* (Builsa), and are generally
fallen from heaven. Indeed, some are, I believe, meteorites,
and such are of great value, costing sometimes as much as three
cows. The ordinary *nari*, however, is found in river-beds, is
extremely hard. . . . Sacrifices are made to them, since their
spirit is a beneficial one to the blacksmith. . . . This deference

---

[1] Budge, writing of Egyptian magic, states: "It is probable that even the use of
the sign which represents an axe, and which stands as the hieroglyphic character both
for God and 'god,' indicates that this weapon and tool was employed in the performance of some ceremony connected with religious magic in prehistoric, or at any
rate in predynastic times, when it in some mysterious way symbolised the presence
of a supreme Power." (EM. p. x.)

[2] NTG. 35.

to a stone necessary to one's trade is common to most tools of a like importance. The wandering troubadour sacrifices to his violin or pipe; the iron-maker to his furnace; the hunter to his bow or gun." Cardinall evidently regards these stones as abodes of earth-spirits; the identity of the spirits is open to question, but we must take his facts into account. Again: "The worship of ancestors is by far the most important cult for the individual, just as the worship of the Earth-gods is for the community. A religious man—or an over-superstitious one, according to how one chooses to regard the matter—will do nothing without a sacrifice of some sort, generally a fowl, to his ancestors. In every compound is the mound representative of the founder's grave, and outside are the small pyramids representative of other deceased members of the household. Each of these is capped with a stone, and thereon are placed blood and feathers from the sacrifices. And when a family migrates, earth from them is taken to the new abode, and the sacrifices continue." [1] Dennet states [2] that Ela is the divinity to which Yoruba tribesmen present harvest offerings, especially in the yam season, before partaking of the new crops; and on another page [3] he informs us that Ela is one of the principal attributes of Ifa, according to Bishop Johnson, a native bishop who wrote *Yoruba Heathenism*, and is sometimes described in praise-songs as the offspring of a stone, that is, the hard stone from the bed of a spring of water (an emblem of great strength). In an article on "West African Religion" [4] he writes: "As to sacred stones, they are generally found in three representing Fatherhood, Motherhood and Sonship. I traced such phallic symbols from Benin City to a place called Ifa, which is the Canterbury of Yorubaland. In one case, in this place, instead of three, I only found one complete figure and the parts of another. I was told that there had been three but that during the war with Abeokuta one had been taken away by the conquerors." Here again, the writer's theory may be meritorious or meretricious, but his facts cannot be ignored. Mr. F. W. H. Migeod, who has been interested for years in

---

[1] *Op. cit.*, p. 45.
[2] BBMM. 256.
[3] BBMM. 254-55.
[4] *Church Quarterly Review*, Jan., 1921, p. 270.

West African Social Anthropology and has recently travelled extensively among some tribes of the Cameroons, said: [1] "There was also a custom at the time of burial of placing a round stone in the house of the bereaved, and over this every year, the eldest son would ceremoniously pour palm-oil."

There is evidence, also, from the eastern side of the continent. The Hon. Kenneth R. Dundas reports [2] that the Wawanga, in the Elgon district of Kenya Colony, have little shrines which seem to fall into three classes: *Msambue, Mukurru*, and *Were*. *Msambue* consists usually of three stones put up to the male ancestors, with a miniature hut erected over them. The place for this shrine is facing the door of the chief wife's hut—the hut which will be the burial-place of the head of the house. On the death of the father, the eldest son inherits these stones, and generally retains one for his own use and gives the others to his younger brothers, who supplement them with stones taken from the bed of a river. If there be not sufficient stones for all a man's sons, the elder sons will add a few extra ones to those of their father, and, as their younger brothers grow up, they give them one of these. *Mukurru* is the stone erected to the maternal spirits; it is usually to be found under the verandah of the chief wife's hut—that is, where women, children and unmarried males are buried. When a man dies, his son puts up this stone to his own mother, if she be dead; and women also erect stones to their ancestors. *Were* is a high god, of whom more must be said in a future volume. The place selected for his stone is usually just off the pathway leading to the village. As a rule, only one is put up; but when a Kavirondo crosses the Malaba River for the first time, he takes a stone from the bed of that stream and deposits it alongside *Were's* stone. It appears that the sacred stones in all these shrines are oblong in shape, but it is not clear whether they are set up like little pillars or laid flat like the pebbles in Karanga shrines.

When the people of Kikuyu [3] found a new village, the elder of the family collects three stones, weighing from thirty to forty pounds, two being usually brought from the bed of a river in the north, the direction from which the tribe migrated, and one

[1] In an interview with *The Worthing Herald*, Dec. 15, 1923.
[2] JRAI., 1913, p. 31.
[3] BBM. 69-72.

from a river to the south. It is laid down that the stones must not be taken from a river which supplies the villagers with water for domestic use, and must be taken from a river with perennial flow. Having obtained the stones, the head of the village, another elder of the same clan and the two senior wives of the village head, take a black ram, sew up its left eye, bury it in the middle of the village, and plant around its burial-place the three stones and branches from trees of three specified varieties, the latter being periodically replaced if they fail to take root.[1] Whenever a sacrifice is made in the village, the ram is killed near this spot, blood and fat are poured into the ground between the stones, and meat for the spirits is put out in two heaps, one for the male and one for the female spirits; and in a service of morning prayer at one of these shrines, the head of the village poured libations of sugar-cane beer upon the trees and prayed to the spirits "for wealth in live stock, abundance of children, safety in journeying, and so forth." If the village is moved, the stones are moved with it; but before they can be disturbed with impunity, the head of the village and his senior wife pour honey-beer and sugar-cane beer on the space between them; and before they are placed in position in the new village, another ram is buried on the site for the new shrine. These stones are associated particularly with the *ngoma* ("ancestor-spirits") and have no connection with the high god, Engai; they are not supposed to possess spirits, but they must never be used as seats, and if one of them is stolen, it is looked upon as a terrible crime, for he who possesses it has power to inflict a serious curse upon the village. "The same idea," he says, referring to the shrines, not the stolen stone, "occurs in Bantu Kavirondo, where these stones are found in each village. Mumia pointed out such a shrine, decked round with white feathers, where a fowl was periodically killed and the blood poured between the stones. The stones were said to have come from the Nzoia River, from a place whence the Wanga clan were supposed to have migrated."

[1] Mr. Hobley's description is not foolproof, but if it be interpreted in the light of his remark (on p. 72) that the trees grow *between* the stones, it would appear that the three trees are planted around the burial-place of the ram, and the stones around the group of trees.

Another writer[1] tells us that near the door of a Chaga hut (Kilima-njaro district) there is placed a broad stone, called "stone of preservation," which is consecrated with libations and prayers to the ancestor-spirits of the owner of the hut. It is not stated that the stone is used as an altar after it has been consecrated with libations and prayers; but it is the seat of honour for the owner of the hut, and none but he may sit upon it. Perhaps I should state that before chairs and stools became common, there used to be a somewhat similar stone in every Becwana courtyard; they called it the "grindstone," because the head of the household sharpened his tools and weapons upon it; but he used it as his seat, and it was a grave offence for any son to sit upon it, such an act being interpreted as a dramatic suggestion to the spirits that they should remove the present head of the house and place the intruder upon the seat of honour.

In Basutoland, "if it was intended to purify a sick person of any enchantment which might, perchance, have been put upon him by his enemies, and which was preventing his recovery, an ox had to be sacrificed at the grave of the ancestor it was desired to invoke; or, if that was too far off, a stone was fetched from it for the occasion."[2]

That these sacred stones are associated with ancestor-spirits, seems fairly clear—most of them certainly are; but in the dim light of the few facts that have yet been reported, it is hard to make out what the connection is. I cannot pass on to other subjects without expressing my hope that some of the many students now interested in the field-work of Bantu Social Anthropology will be able to discover new facts which will lead to a solution of the problem that baffles me.

SACRED FIRE

To waft the sacrifice skyward on wings of flame, is foreign to the conceptions of Bantu ancestor-worship;[3] but fire is used in rites of ceremonial cleansing, and, like the flame on altars of ancient Roman households, in rendering homage to tutelary

[1] K. 257.
[2] HB. 258. Cf. Bs. 256.
[3] See pp. 57 ff.

divinities of family and clan. It figures also in Bantu magic; but that is another subject.

In Bechuanaland, the lighting of the first fire in a new township was a very important ceremony. The first act in the ritual was to fell a *modumela* tree and decorate the trunk, bark and all, from one end to the other, with alternate zones of black and red "medicated" paste. Since the pastes were laid on with the open hand, each band was about a handbreadth. Then the chief, either with his own hand or by his explicit instructions, kindled a fire by means of the friction-sticks (*go hétlha moleló ka dithole*) on the spot marked off as the site of the official hearth in the Place of Assembly; and, after incense (*mashwaló*) had been thrown upon the fire, the decorated log was drawn up to it. When this log had been burning for a little while, the chief's subordinate headmen, carefully observing their proper order of precedence, carried some of its embers to their own courtyards, whence the fire was again distributed among the several families in their wards of the town. It was not necessary to take embers; the important thing was that all fires in the town should be lit from this sacred fire; some took a live coal in a potsherd, while others lit a wisp of straw or a bundle of twigs, and ran home with the sacred flame. It is to this fire, which was kept perpetually burning, that tribesmen alluded when addressing their chief as *Moñ-a-moleló* ("Master-of-fire"). If an epidemic prevailed in the town, it was usual for the chief to order all fires to be extinguished, all hearths swept, and all ashes taken out of the town; and when each woman had laid a stick of *moñololo* and another of *mokompatla* (both of which are bushes) across the threshold of her courtyard, as a sign that she had completed her task, the chief lit and distributed new fire as if founding a new town.[1] The same ritual was observed at the Feast of Firstfruits.[2]

[1] "In Shaw's 'History of the Province of Moray,' in Scotland, he mentions that 'when a contagious disease enters among the cattle, the fire is extinguished in some village around; then they force fire with a wheel, or by rubbing a piece of dry wood upon another, and therewith burn juniper in the stalls of the cattle, that the smoke may purify the air about them. They likewise boil juniper in water, which they sprinkle upon the cattle; this done, the fires in the houses are re-kindled from the forced fire.' He describes it as a Druid custom." (CPP. 328.)

[2] See p. 234. Theal mentions (ECSA. 230) that the Karanga when first visited by Europeans, had a custom of extinguishing all fires on a day named by the chief,

In Bakaonde villages a similar extinction of fires and sweeping of hearths takes place when sickness invades a settlement. If diviners discover, as they occasionally do, that a case of sickness is due to the spirit of some dead person, it is customary in this tribe to exhume the corpse of the malignant individual; and when the exhumation party has returned to the village, all fires are extinguished, all ashes thrown away, and new fires kindled.[1]

When a Konde chief (of north Nyasa) founded a new village at his installation, all old fires were extinguished and ashes removed, and brands from a new fire, which the young chief kindled with friction-sticks, were given out to all householders in the district. Before Konde warriors go forth to battle, also, old fires are extinguished and a new one lit in this ancient manner.[2]

The Baila put out the fire in a widower's hut before bringing him the substitute-wife with which his conjugal relatives replace his loss. The fire in his courtyard remains burning; and when he has performed the ritual acts on the substitute-wife who has been given him, the friends gathered around the door take a red-hot potsherd from the courtyard fire, place it on some grass, and, carrying it quickly into the hut, light a new fire therefrom. "That fire is thus a new one," adds the Native narrator, "and the woman becomes new."[3]

On the death of a Kitara king, all fires in the royal enclosure are extinguished, and so is the centre fire in each royal cow-kraal.[4] In each kraal of the pastoral Bahuma of Ankole, a people who have kept their Hamitic breed comparatively pure, a large fire of dried cowdung is guarded by the inmates and never allowed to die out. This fire is too sacred to be used for cooking purposes.[5] The sacred fire at the main entrance to the king of Buganda's enclosure was always kept burning when the king was at the capital, and carried with him when he went on a journey, being sheltered on wet nights with a broken cooking-

and relighting them with the aid of friction-sticks; but he does not say when this was done, nor why.

[1] WBA. 229, 146.
[2] SRK. 76, 171.
[3] IPNR. ii. 60.
[4] KT. 48.
[5] SCA. 59.

pot. It is said to have been kept alight from the time of Kintu,—perhaps a thousand years! A general appointed to the command of an expedition, was privileged, as he passed out from the king's presence, to rub his chest and forehead with ashes from this sacred fire, but all other commoners were forbidden to touch it; and if a warrior was condemned for cowardice in war, or a prince or princess for treason, it was from this holy fire that the pyre was lit, by means of a burning fuse made of barkcloth, which the guardian of the fire always carried with him.[1]

"The Mucelis" (who live in the hinterland of Novo Redondo in Angola) "have a curious custom which I have not heard of as existing in any other tribe, namely, that on the death of the great 'sobas' of Ambuin and Sanga, all fires in the kingdom must be put out, and relighted by the succeeding 'soba' from fire struck by rubbing two sticks together."[2] A missionary to the Bailundu (a little farther east), having witnessed the obsequies of a chief and the installation of his successor (some time later than 1892), mentions particularly that the new chief covenanted with the corpse of his predecessor "to rekindle new fires in the Ombala" (i.e., the head village) "when the fires of the dead chief shall be put out, and to keep them going all his lifetime."[3]

It is the duty of the first wife of the chief of a Thonga clan[4] to keep a perpetual fire burning in the sacred hut where the Great Tribal Talisman is stored; so sacred is this fire that its embers are tabooed, and its priestess forbidden to have conjugal intercourse with her husband. If it should die out by any mischance, it would have to be relit with the aid of two friction-sticks of ntjopfa, a shrub which is taboo for common fires.

"The Ushi tribe in N. Rhodesia have two great Ju-Jus or oracles, called Makumba and Ngasa, male and female. . . . They are kept in a small temple about ten feet in diameter, where a priestess resides to keep the fire burning. . . . On examination," says Dugald Campbell,[5] "I was surprised to find that they were both meteorites of several ounces' weight." These "oracular

[1] Bg. 202, 349.
[2] ARC. ii. 167.
[3] "The Story of Chisamba." Toronto: Canada Congregational Foreign Missionary Society, p. 38.
[4] LSAT. i. 364.
[5] IHB. 236-37.

fetishes" were both wrapped in python skins, and the male [1] was "surrounded by large Mpande shells, which used to be the native insignia of chieftainship." They were consulted as oracles by Msidi, Kanyanta and other powerful chiefs, and "in the old days when they were carried before the armies, victory was always sure." One would be glad to hear how these meteorites came by their names and sacred powers; but at the moment we are mainly concerned with the fact that a priestess keeps a sacred fire burning in their temple.

In the social life of Herero tribes, the holy fire (*omurangere*) plays a very important part. A Herero chief dwells on the eastern side of his village, and next his residence, westward, follow one after another, the holy house (*otyizero*), the place of holy fire (*okuruo*), and the cattle-fold. The prime duty of the eldest daughter of the chief's great wife is to keep the holy fire perpetually burning; and if it should accidentally become extinct, the community offers an expiatory sacrifice of cattle, and then the fire is relit by means of two friction-sticks, which the chief has inherited from his forefathers and treasures up in the holy house.[2] The fire kindled by means of these fire-sticks, which are called *ondume* and *otyiza* and represent respectively the divine ancestor and his wife, is said to be obtained from the ancestors, and is removed with many formalities by the priestess when the site of the village is changed. Should the community remove to a site that it occupied in the time of a former chief, the holy fire is extinguished at the place they are leaving; and in the town they are rebuilding, a new fire is kindled with the fire-sticks on the spot where the consecrated flame used to burn, a sheep [3] being sacrificed near it and its flesh eaten by persons of both sexes and all ages. A further sacrifice of an ox or a sheep must be offered for each son of the man whose bones lie in the old cattle-kraal, and the flesh of the victims consecrated by being laid upon the grave.[4]

[1] Bantu are accustomed to speak of two adjacent hills or other related objects as "male" and "female," the larger being always "male."

[2] Mr. Hammond Tooke, writing on this subject, in *The African Monthly* (Dec., 1907), remarks: "This recurrence to an obsolete practice, it will be remembered, is equally insisted on when the virgin daughter of a Latin king or chief rekindles the flame sacred to Vesta."

[3] This sheep is called "that of the fire."

[4] *Folk-Lore Journal.* Cape Town, May, 1879, p. 62. The Hottentots—southern neighbours of the Herero, but not Bantu—fire a little faggot with the friction-

Until our knowledge is fuller and better organised, it will not be possible to determine the precise significance of fire in the ritual of Bantu religion. In the old Iranian religion, the care of the sacred fire was deemed so important that Zoroaster preserved it when he founded Mazdaism, though he swept away almost every other feature of the ancient cultus; but ancient Persians probably regarded fire as a symbol of the sun, whose beneficent aid was invoked for their crops. Bantu magic has a few practices that are capable of a similar interpretation; but in Bantu ancestor-worship there is nothing that provides a link with that theory. The use of fire in rites of ceremonial purification, to which reference is made on another page,[1] may be explained by the idea that it consumes noxious things; hence the quenching of all fires in a village and the removal of ashes when great ritual purity is desired. One of the noticeable peculiarities of Bantu travellers is their reluctance to utilise a fire that some unknown precursor has left by the path. I have often asked them why they shunned such embers, and they have always replied, either that it was their custom—a remark which contents most of them—or that such fire may have been used for unholy rites and gathered contamination thereby.

Mr. Hobley found the same notion among the Akamba of Kibwezi. "The fire required for sacrificial purposes was formerly always made anew by friction," he says, "as fire so produced could carry no evil with it, whereas if firebrands were brought from a hut some *thahu* or curse which rested on the family owning the hut might inadvertently be brought with it, and the wood might in fact be infected. Nowadays, however, it is curious to note that a sacrificial fire is lighted with matches; for they consider that these, being of foreign origin, can bring no infection derived from Kamba spirit influence."[2] The custom of renewing the fire in a ceremonial manner upon certain occasions is not found among the Akamba;[3] but they have another custom which requires explanation. When a party of travellers

---

sticks when a child is born, and keep the fire burning till the umbilical cord drops; and when a Hottentot goes forth to hunt, his wife lights a special fire, and carefully tends it till his return, knowing that if it goes out he will bring back no game. (Quatrefages: *The Pygmies*. New York: Appleton, 1895, p. 232.)

[1] See pp. 223, 234.
[2] BBM. 68.
[3] AK. 29.

leaves a spot where they have camped, the headman throws a
firebrand on their path and prays that they may reach their
destination in safety and amity; and the next man in the Indian
file throws a few leaves on the firebrand and steps on it.[1]

That there is some occult connection between fire and the
spirits of the dead is indicated, I think, by the custom which
prevails in some tribes of lighting a fire on a new grave. The
Wawanga of Elgon district, Kenya Colony, bury their dead
either in the hut or under the verandah. "After the burial all
present proceed to the river to bathe," says the Hon. Kenneth
R. Dundas;[2] "until they have done so they may not enter any
hut but that of deceased. On their return a fire is lit on the
grave over the feet. This fire is kept burning for one whole
month. Should it go out it must be relit from the fire in the
hut;[3] should this also be extinct, it must be lit again by means
of a fire drill."

Sir Harry Johnston states[4] that widows, daughters, or sisters
of the dead chiefs of great importance among the non-Bantu
Nsakara (Mbomu) people, who live north of the Mubangi,
"have to spend their lives maintaining a perpetual fire on the
dwelling-tomb of the deceased potentate"; and then, without a
touch of tenderness for readers who are more shy of belief than
he is, he adds in a footnote that "the Nsakara Sultan, Bangasa
of Mbomu, has or had fifteen hundred wives." One wonders
how many sisters and daughters helped this potentate's regiment
of widows to keep one fire perpetually burning upon his tomb,
and how they all managed to find some share in the task.

IMAGES

It is doubtful whether any tribe south of the Zambesi made
common use of images in worship, though the idea was not alto-

[1] BBM. 24.
[2] JRAI., 1913, p. 35.
[3] He states on p. 37 that "the dead man's chief wife remains in the hut, where
the body is buried, during the following two months for the purpose of tending the
fire. After this the hut is broken down and the timber is used as firewood." This
means, I suppose, that for two months the usual domestic fire in the hut is kept
burning, and for the first of these months the special fire on the grave, which
would also be in the hut if deceased was the head of the household.
[4] GGC. 674.

gether foreign to their sense of fitness.   Junod holds that the
Thonga people worship spirits and spirits alone, and that there
is neither idolatry nor fetishism among them.[1]   Certain images,
which usually repose in the holy house [2] at a Bavenda chief's
village are exhibited to neophytes in the Boys' Puberty Rites; and
the boys are apprised of their meaning and use, but forbidden,
upon heavy penalty, to disclose this secret lore.   Although Mr.
Gottschling did not state whether these images are actually used
in worship, he did say that they are placed as central objects
of the dance of both sexes that forms the second part of Bavenda
Puberty Rites; and, from what Theal says [3] upon the authority
of a Dutch book written by Mr. Hofmeyer (missionary among
the Bavenda for twenty years), it would seem that they function
much in the same way as sticks and axe-helves do in certain other
shrines.   This use of images to represent ancestors is exceptional
in Eastern Bantu tribes, but common in Western; and it is
interesting to note here that the Rev. C. Benster, who lived for
thirty years as missionary among the Bavenda, found reason to
believe that the tribe came originally from the Lower Congo.[4]
Mr. Gottschling, relying more upon philological arguments,
thought they came from the Great Lakes—a region, be it remarked, that has been influenced considerably by the distinctive
culture of Western tribes.   Theal seems to have thought that
the Bavenda use of images established the kinship of this tribe
with the Bakwena—an inference which it is not easy to follow.
During the quarter of a century that I spent in the midst of the
Bakwena group of tribes, the use of images in worship was conspicuous by its absence.   Realistic figures of animals and very
crude manikins were carved for the decoration of articles of
utility, or as expressions of the instinct for artistic creation which
were of no earthly use, and, since the railway came, as devices
for extracting shillings from the pockets of curio-hunters; but
these objects were not invested with either magical or religious
value.   In all tribes of this group, magicians use images in casting spells, and there is little room for doubt that images once
figured in their worship.   In some of these tribes it was cus-

[1] LSAT. ii. 388.
[2] See p. 222.
[3] ECSA. 188-89.
[4] R. BAAS., 1905, iii. 195.

tomary, once a year, to set up in the Place of Tribal Assembly a (*kgomoeamothu*) wax figure of a cow with a boy milking her, and to offer prayers that their cattle-lifting bands might come home unscathed and with much booty.   It is said, also, that little gods of clay, called "shepherds of the people," were kept by an old woman in some villages and occasionally exposed in the Place of Assembly, and that people not only had these images in their houses but carried them about in little bags that did duty as pockets.[1]   Both these customs perished long ago, and in my time nothing remained but a vague tradition of their former existence; I sought in vain for some hint of the nature of these images.   Every afternoon during the last week of their Puberty Rites, the girls were escorted to the Place of Tribal Assembly by a crowd of initiates who screened them carefully from profane eyes; and each day the crowd parted asunder for one brief moment to reveal the neophytes kneeling in adoration around a clay image.   The image was made anew for each day's worship; one day it was the image of a snake, another day it was that of a person, but most days it was the image of some kind of animal, the choice depending, so the men said, upon the fancy of the Mistress of the Mysteries.   The neophytes, as in all these mystery-cults, were forbidden to divulge what they were taught about these images; but since the fertility of woman is the central theme of these rites, it is likely that the images are related in some occult manner to those ancestor-spirits to whom the women frequently pray for the power to conceive.   Basuto women—and the reigning family of the Basuto nation is Bakwena—who wish to be cured of barrenness, make a rude image, call it by the name of some tutelary deity,[2] and get up dances in its honour, in order that the deity may give them the power of conception.[3]   The most conspicuous feature of the *Bogwera yoa Secho*, or Men's Circumcision Rites of the Second Degree, which but few tribes practised, was a sacred symbol at the centre of a labyrinth.   It was called *Modimako* ("Thy-god"), and neophytes were re-

[1] The teraphim of Gen. xxxi. 30-34 were probably images symbolic of family ancestors.

[2] According to the notions of Bantu magic an image need not resemble the person whom it represents; it is enough if it be called by the esoteric name of the person.

[3] Bs. 251.

quired to reverence it; but it was not an image; it was a tall pole, painted black, white and red in horizontal bands of a handsbreadth and crowned with ostrich feathers or the tails of wild animals. No interpretation of its meaning can be obtained from the Becwana. A somewhat similar symbol stood at the High Places of ancient Semitic religion.

That the use of images in Becwana worship was either infrequent or inconspicuous during the second quarter of last century, may be gleaned from Moffat's statement that the missionary among these people had "no idolatry to arrest his progress." Probably some critic will retort that Moffat also stated that "the missionary could make no appeals to legends, or to an unknown God, or to kindred ideas to those he wished to impart," that "he seeks in vain to find a temple, an altar, or a single emblem of heathen worship," and that he himself, during years of apparently fruitless labour, "often wished to find something by which I could lay hold on the minds of the natives,—an altar to an unknown God, the faith of their ancestors, the immortality of the soul, or, any religious associations; but nothing of the kind ever floated in their minds." [1] To this rejoinder I am content to reply that the statements are not of equal value. Moffat failed to discover such things as appeared in "the letters and journals of missionaries in India," and had not been trained to recognise the much more primitive religion around him; but if he had found sacred images used in worship, he would have recognised them as akin to the idols of which he had read. Moffat stands forth as an exemplification of the truth that if an able and zealous missionary is not trained in Comparative Religion and Social Anthropology, he may labour long among African tribesmen without being able to discern those indigenous religious ideas that lie ready to his hand and would help him immensely in his work. In this criticism of an honoured predecessor there is no undertone of reproach. These sciences had not come into their own till Moffat's work was well-nigh done; no such training as that now offered to students was within his

[1] *Missionary Labours and Scenes in South Africa.* London, 1842, pp. 243-45. Other remarks concerning "the entire absence of theological ideas, or religion" appear on pp. 257 *et seq.*

reach; [1] but as one reads these pathetic pages from his pen it is vain to suppress commiseration for pioneer mariners who cried for water when they lay becalmed in the mouth of the Amazon.

Livingstone, too, had spent his years in Bechuanaland and travelled far enough up the Zambesi to come within the orbit of Lunda influence before he saw what he recorded as "the first evidence of the existence of idolatry, in the remains of an old idol at a deserted village. It was simply a human head carved on a block of wood," he wrote. "Certain charms mixed with red ochre and white pipe-clay are dotted over them when they are in use, and a crooked stick is used in the same way for an idol, when they have no professional carver." [2] From that time he became increasingly familiar with the use of images in Bantu worship. A little farther on his westward way, he writes again in his journal: "We passed two small hamlets . . . and near each of these I observed, for the first time, an ugly idol common in Lunda—the figure of an animal resembling an alligator, made of clay. It is formed of grass plastered over with clay; two cowrie-shells are inserted as eyes, and numbers of bristles from the tail of an elephant are stuck in about the neck. It is called a lion, though, if one were not told, he would conclude it to be an alligator. It stood in a shed, and the Balonda pray and beat drums before it all night in cases of sickness." [3] Again, a day or two later: "We found that every village had its idols near it. This is the case all through the country of the Balonda, so that, when we came to an idol in the woods, we always knew that we were within a quarter of an hour of human habitations. One very ugly idol we passed, rested on a horizontal beam placed on two upright posts. This beam was furnished with two loops of cord, as of a chain, to suspend offerings before it." And yet again, while in the same district, "In the deep dark forests near each village, as already mentioned, you see idols intended to represent a human head or a lion, or a crooked stick smeared with medicine, or simply a pot of medicine in a little shed, or

---

[1] "Whatever gifts may have been bestowed upon Robert Moffat to fit him for his work as a missionary," writes his son and biographer (*Lives of Robert & Mary Moffat*, p. 23), "it certainly could not be said that they came in the form of collegiate opportunities."

[2] MTR. 275.

[3] MTR. 282.

miniature huts with little mounds of earth in them. But in the darker recesses we meet with human faces cut out in the bark of trees, the outlines of which, with the beards, closely resemble those seen on Egyptian monuments." [1]

If Livingstone had struck into the north-east trail from Sekhosi, instead of going up the Zambesi towards the north-west, he would still have had to wait for his first glimpse of "idols" till he reached some community that had been influenced by Luba-Lunda civilisation. Smith & Dale tell us that the Baila proper neither make images of their divinities, nor portray them in any way whatever. "It is only on the north-eastern border of Bwila and under the influence of Baluba, that one finds graven images. Chibaluma, chief of the Lusaka commune, who is of mixed Baila and Baluba blood, took us into his sanctum—an ordinary hut surrounded by trees, entry to which is forbidden to ordinary people—in the centre of the village. . . . In the hut there are two figures about ten inches high, roughly carved in wood. . . . In the heads of these images there are holes into which 'medicine' is poured. The hut is sacred to Chinenga, an ancestor of Chibaluma. . . . He is reincarnate in Chibaluma and is his genius. It is believed by some of his people, and some of his sons, that Chibaluma's life is hid in these images. . . . The 'medicine' is poured in at times to renew their power. On occasions, such as departure for a trading or hunting expedition, or before going to war, and when he is sick, he makes an offering before these images and implores the help of his divinity." The hut was not built over a grave.[2]

When the Mwata Cazembe (the fifth of a dynasty of Lunda origin which long professed allegiance to the Mwata-ya-Mvo) received the Portuguese envoys, Monteiro and Gamitto, with much barbarous ceremony and ostentation (Nov., 1831), roughly carved images with negro features and horns of animals on their heads were arranged in two curved lines extending for four or five yards in front of his seat, and at the end of the lines two men burnt aromatic leaves in a small earthen vessel filled with live coals.[3] In all likelihood these images were sacred emblems,

[1] MTR. 304.
[2] IPNR. ii. 169.
[3] LC. 252-56.

and the burning of aromatic leaves, a fumigation rite to ward off evil influences; but one regrets that the envoys took no pains to find out what they meant.

When Livingstone was in the Bemba country, on Nov. 24, 1868, he wrote in his *Journal:* [1] "A sort of idol is found in every village in this part; it is of wood, and represents the features, markings, and fashion of the hair of the inhabitants; some have little huts built for them, others are in common houses. The Babemba call them Nkisi ('Sancan' of the Arabs): the people of Rua name one *Kalubi,* the plural *Tulubi;* and they present pombe, flour, bhang, tobacco, and light a fire for them to smoke by. They represent the departed father or mother, and it is supposed that they are pleased with the offerings made to their representatives, but all deny that they pray to them. Casembe has very many of these nkisi: one with long hair, and named Motombo, is carried in front when he takes the field; names of dead chiefs are sometimes given to them." And again, when he was at Kitette, which is shown by his map to be about midway between 4° and 5° S., a little west of 27° E., and a few miles north of the Lualaba where it bends westward, he wrote under date, Aug. 3, 1871: "I have often observed effigies of men made of wood in Manyuema; some, of clay, are simply cones, with a small hole in the top: on asking about them here, I for the first time obtained reliable information. They are called 'Bathata' (fathers or ancients), and the name of each is carefully preserved. Those here at Kitette were evidently the names of chiefs, Molenda being the most ancient. . . . The old men told me that on certain occasions they offer goat's flesh to them: men eat it, and allow no young person or woman to partake."

A friend and colleague of my Central African days, who resided in Uguha, mentioned in one of his reports [2] that the first thing that struck a traveller who crossed Lake Tanganyika from east to west, was an image at the entrance of every village, and almost every native hut, especially that of the chief,—images carved after the shape of the human figure. He heard that images of lions were kept in the cornfields. These images, carved by the Waguha, and in still greater perfection by the Warua to

[1] See LLJ. *in loco* for both quotations.
[2] *Chronicle of the London Missionary Society,* Dec., 1880.

the west, were called *mkissi*—a word which he equated with the Swahili *mzimu* and the English "spirit." Most of those that were deemed efficient were housed in small huts and honoured with food, *pombe* (beer) and prayers in time of trouble or war, or before starting on a journey; but in the larger villages more spacious and imposing huts were built for them.

Another old friend and colleague writes [1] that while exploring the north-west corner of Lake Tanganyika, he saw a group of images placed in a circle in a grove of banana trees. "They were beautiful specimens of carving, but represented most hideous faces of men and beasts. Bead work of pretty design adorned the necks, and by the side of one lay a broken spear. Near was a miniature hut, most beautifully fashioned and thatched with grass. It was just a toy house about a foot high, such as any lad might make to play with. A small mat lay spread on the verandah; a stool stood near the door, at which had been placed a pot of maize flour." This hut was for the spirit of their dead chief to sleep in, so the people said, and it was their custom to place gifts of food there when they sought the good offices of their ancestor-spirits with the god Leza.[2]

These quotations indicate what may be roughly regarded as the eastern limit of the *common* use of sacred images at ancestor-shrines; but, as we have seen, they are not unknown among tribes of the southern line of migration. Miss Werner writes: [3] "It is generally believed that the Eastern Bantu have no 'idols' properly so called. . . . But the Tonga chiefs used to carry about with them little wooden images called *angoza*—representing men, women, or animals. Sometimes they were only sticks with a little head carved at one end. The Rev. A. G. MacAlpine, who seems puzzled what to make of them, does not state whether any are now in existence. 'Long ago they used to be owned by chiefs only, and were lodged in the house of the head-wife. . . . They were not displayed except on special occasions. In the talking of important cases, they are said to have been brought out and planted in the ground at some little distance from the

[1] *Fighting the Slave-hunters in Central Africa*, by Alfred J. Swann, London: Seeley, 1910, p. 208.

[2] One is surprised to find Leza so far north, and wonders whether it was their word or one that they accepted from his lips.

[3] NBCA. 68-69.

chief, and when he went on a journey they might be carried along with him. . . . Often people came asking to see them, when they would be brought out covered up and not exposed till some gift had been made.' We find that the Achewa have articles described as 'fetiches' and consisting 'of a few short pieces of wood the size of one's forefinger, bound together with a scrap of calico into the figure of a child's doll. Inside the calico is concealed a tiny box made of the handle of a gourd-cup . . . and supposed to contain the spirit of some dead ancestor.' Spirits wandering homeless in the bush are apt to annoy the living in various ways, till captured by a 'doctor' and confined in one of these receptacles." Swann, also, mentions [1] that medicine-men on Lake Nyasa (he does not say what tribe) "generally possess wooden images, many of which are beautifully carved, representing human beings; some are hideous in appearance, and are used on occasions to strike terror into the hearts of those over whom they desire to exert some influence. The images are sometimes given names, e.g., the god of water, or of grain fields, or of game. Others have special functions allotted to them, e.g., to watch over women during child-birth, or to protect the graves from desecration by midnight cannibals, who are said to dig up the corpse and eat it. Groups of these images may at times be seen placed near crossroads, for the purpose of preventing evil approaching the village; as, for instance, smallpox may be raging in an adjacent district, and to stop it creeping along their roads these images will be posted."

Mackenzie described the use of an image by a Konde diviner at the north end of Lake Nyasa.[2] "The diviner took a small image of a man, about two feet in height, made from a block of wood. In the head was a cavity, into which medicine was put, and the cavity closed. The party went to the garden from which the food had been stolen, and, the image being laid on the ground, the diviner prayed to it to lead them to the thief. It was then taken up in the right hand of a strong man, and presently began to shake violently, so that it could with difficulty be held. In a little it swayed in one direction, and the holder moved thither, the whole party following, until the shaking of

[1] *Fighting the Slave-hunters in Central Africa*, p. 127.
[2] SRK. 231-32.

the image ceased in a garden. Digging at that spot the stolen food was discovered; and the image, being asked now to find the thief, led them to a certain house, the owner of which at once confessed the theft, and paid a cow as fine." One would much like to know what "medicine" was placed in the head of the image; [1] but since the diviner, whose business is to discover the mind of the spirits,[2] prayed to the image, it is fairly safe to assume that the image was ancestral.

Most tribes west of the great lakes are addicted to the use of images. The Kaonde people of North-west Rhodesia do not worship idols;[3] but among their western neighbours, the Lunda, "graven images are made for the hunting spirits, often like a pair of lions, one male and one female." Mr. J. L. Keith came to the conclusion that these images are not intended to represent the spirit, but are conventional symbols from which the spirit is pleased to receive such offerings of blood and intestines as are laid thereon. He states, also, that "when diseases are attributed to some local spirit a clay image of a snake is made, but the Alunda do not believe that the spirit itself has this form. In no case do the Alunda worship idols." [4] "According to some notes of Grenfell concerning fetishes in use on the Zombo plateau (west of lower Kwango), a certain amount of phallic worship exists or existed among the eastern Bakongo; not that the representations of the generative powers—male or female— were worshipped, but that these rude images were the abiding place of a spirit force which, if rightly propitiated, would promote fruitful intercourse between men and women. Torday reported a somewhat elaborate ritual amongst the eastern Bayanzi (Kwilu-Kasai). *Vide* 'The Ethnology of the Congo Free State,' *R. Anthrop. Inst. 1907.* He noted among the fetishes of the eastern Bayanzi the male emblem in various forms (called in fact, *Mulume*, or 'Male'). Usually the male fetish consisted

[1] See p. 336.
[2] See p. 149.
[3] WBA. 154.
[4] WBA. 175. Mr. Keith is evidently assuming that idolaters believe their idols to be likenesses of their gods—a conceit that undoubtedly satisfied crowds of unthinking idolaters; but people who are steeped in the magical conception of the world and unacquainted with portraiture, see no need for such likenesses, and thoughtful idolaters regard idols as symbols of divine powers rather than portraits of their gods.

of a shallow basket in which were set from one to four phalli made of clay. These were anointed with kola juice when being prayed to. Another fetish represented the female principle. Either or both received 'worship' with the idea of propitiating the forces they symbolised, and thus promoting fertility amongst the women, or even the crops. According to Lord Mountmorres, in many parts of the Mubangi phallic worship is common, probably of the same character as that described by Torday in connection with the Bayanzi of the Kasai." [1] "The commonest type of spirit-indwelt object or fetish (as apart from a mere charm or amulet)," says the same writer, "is a head, a mask, or a large or small figure. For the most part it is humanity that is mimicked; but the demon may be associated with the model of a dog, leopard, buffalo or snake." [2] "The Buaka and the Banza of the left bank of the lower Mubangi show their care for the dead in a touching manner. When they lose one who is dear to them, they make a wooden statuette, to which they give the name of the departed child or relative. They carefully preserve this in their home, surrounding it with loving care." [3]

Sacred images were in vogue among West Coast Bantu tribes long before the Portuguese visited these regions. Early in the sixteenth century, King Affonso, the seventh Ntotela of the Kongo Kingdom, an ardent son of the Roman Church, "ruthlessly ordered all fetishes to be destroyed throughout his dominions, but supplied their place with images of saints, crosses, agni dei, and other ecclesiastical paraphernalia, which he held to be more effectual." [4] The effect of this edict was, however, neither far-reaching nor enduring—except that images of the new pattern secured such standing among those that had been long revered that even at the present day, so Ravenstein writes,[5] images of St. Francis and other saints may be seen in the collection of royal fetishes at S. Salvador, and a cross called *santu* (Santa Cruz) is the common fetish which confers skill in hunting.

The earliest record of travel in the *interior* of Angola and

[1] GGC. 638.
[2] GGC. 637.
[3] GGC. 652.
[4] SAAB. 113-14.
[5] SAAB. 24-25.

the adjoining regions is that of Andrew Battell, which was edited by the Rev. Samuel Purchas in 1613, and in a completer form in 1625. When Battell was at Kasila (10.8° S., 14.3° E.) in 1602 or thereabouts, there stood in the centre of the town an image "which is as big as a man and standeth twelve feet high," with a circle of elephants' teeth planted in the ground at its feet, and skulls of slain foes stuck upon the tusks. Battell wrote the name of the image *Quesango*, and Ravenstein identifies the word with the Kimbunda *kizangu* ("fetish"), noting the fact that Burton (*Two Trips in Gorilla Land*, vol. ii., p. 120) saw a similar image with the same name in a village above Boma. Battell states that in the worship paid to this image, palm oil and the blood of goats was poured at its feet; and that there were little images in many parts of the town and great stores of elephants' teeth piled over them.[1] When Battell, having finally escaped from slavery, took refuge in Loango, north of the Congo estuary (probably 1608-1610), there were two idols at Mani Longo, the capital of that province, the one called *Mukishi a Loango*, and the other, a little black image, called *Checoke* (which Ravenstein identifies with Dapper's *Kikoko*);[2] and at Mani Mayombe (*i.e.*, Yumbe Bay, 3° 19′ S.) there was a "fetish called Maramba, and it standeth in a high basket made like a hive, and over it a great House." A person accused of witchcraft had to prove his innocence by clasping this "fetish" in his arms, whereupon, if guilty, "he presently dieth." Battell was at this place for a year, and "saw many die after this sort." As one of the final rites in their Circumcision Ceremonies, neophytes "are brought before Maramba, and have two marks cut upon their shoulders before, like a half moon, and are sworn by the blood that falleth from them that they shall be true to him." The people "all carry a relique of Maramba in a little box, and hang it about their necks, under their left arms," said Battell, and "the Lord of this province of Mayombe has the ensign or shape of Maramba carried before him, and whithersoever he goeth; and when he sitteth down it is set before him; and when he drinketh his palm wine the first cup is poured at the foot of the Mokiso or idol, and when he eateth anything,

[1] SAAB. 19-24.
[2] SAAB. 48.

he throweth towards his left hand with enchanting words." [1] Purchas, his editor, removes all doubt as to the shape of this "fetish" by stating definitely that the basket "proportioned like a hive" contained an image. [2]

Father Merolla (1682-89), speaking of Loango, says: "I saw likewise at a distance an oath administered, which that it might be done with the greater efficacy, it was proposed to be taken in the presence of their idol: this hobgobbling resembled in some measure a mountebank's merry-andrew, having a divers coloured vest on, and a red cap on its head, and standing on a little table. . . . Before the gates of their houses almost all have one of these idols, whereof I have seen some five or six foot high; others are smaller, but both are clouterly carved: they place them likewise in the fields where they are never worshipped, but on account of finding out some theft, for which the thief when discovered must die. They that keep idols in their houses, every first day of the moon are obliged to anoint them with a sort of red wood powder'd." [3]

In Barbot's *Description of the Lower Æthiopia*, [4] published in 1746, but dealing with the period between 1682 and 1700, we have the following testimony concerning the natives of Loango, Cakongo and Goy. "All acts of devotion they perform to the field and house-devils, represented under the shape of idols, of which they have great numbers, to each of which they give a particular name, according as they attribute to them power, having their distinct jurisdiction. To some they ascribe the power of lightning and the wind; and also to serve as scarecrows, to preserve their corn from fowl and other vermin; to one they give the command over the fishes of the sea; to another over the fishes in the rivers; to a third over the cattle, &c. Some they make protectors of their health and safety; others, to avert evils and misfortunes: to another again they command the charge of their fight; of some they beg to be instructed in the mysteries of hidden arts, or magick, and to be able even to forejudge of destiny; neither do they believe them at large, but circumscribe them

[1] SAAB. 56-58.
[2] SAAB. 82-83.
[3] C. i. 583.
[4] C. v. 477.

to limited places, and shew their figures in several shapes; some like men; others only poles with small irons on the top, or else a little carv'd image; some of which shapes and representations they carry commonly with them, wherever they travel to and fro. Their greater idols are stuck with hens or pheasants feathers on their heads, and with all sorts of tassels about their bodies: some make them in the fashion of long slips, which they wear about their necks and arms; others of cords, trimmed with small feathers, and two or three Simbos, or little horns with which they adorn their middle, neck and arms; some are nothing but pots filled with white earth; others buffaloes horns stuffed with the same matter, and at the small end some iron rings. Another sort yet more ridiculous, is to fill an ordinary round pot without feet, with red and white earth kneaded together with water, pretty high above the edges; which they mark on the outside quite round with white streaks, and stripe it on the top with variety of colours." He mentions, also, that experts in idol-making are called *Enganga* or *Janga Mokisie*, and gives the same name to all their priests or conjurors, "that is, their prophets or divines." And on the next page we have the following: "To instance in one of their idols, *Likokoo Mokisie* is the chiefest of them, being a wooden image, carv'd in the shape of a man, sitting, at Kinga, a town near the sea-coast, where they have a common burial-place."

Monteiro wrote of Angola in much more recent years (1875), but claims that his is "the first detailed account" of that territory. "In almost every large town there is a 'fetish house,'" he says, "generally in the form of a diminutive square hut, with mud walls, painted white, and these covered with figures of men and beasts in red and black colours." [1] "Hung in the huts, and out-side over the doors are all kinds of 'fetishes,' and in the towns and about the huts are various figures, generally roughly carved in wood, and sometimes made of clay, but always coloured red, black and white. The finest 'fetishes' are made by the Mus-surongos on the Congo River. Some of these large 'fetishes' have a widespread reputation, and the 'fetish men' to whom they belong are often sent for from long distances to work some charm or cure with them. I have constantly met them carrying these

[1] ARC. i. 248.

great ugly figures," etc.[1]   He speaks also of "one or two large
figures made either of clay or straw, or smaller ones roughly
carved of wood, and always of a very indecent character," which
were placed at the point where the temporary track to a Puberty
Camp diverged from the main path.[2]   But the largest "fetish
houses" that he saw in Angola were in a district between Ambriz
and Loanda, from which Europeans were excluded till it was
forcibly traversed by a Portuguese military expedition of which
he was guest.   "One was a large hut built of mud, the walls
plastered with white, and painted all over inside and out with
grotesque drawings, in black and red, of men and animals.   Inside were three life-sized figures very roughly modelled in
clay, and of the most indecent description.   Behind this hut was
a long court the width of the length of the hut, enclosed with
walls about six feet high.   A number of figures similar in character to those in the hut were standing in this court, which was
kept quite clean and bare of grass."[3]   Monteiro, who was not a
sympathetic student of Bantu religion, knew nothing of the
motive that inspired the creation of these images, nor of the use
to which they were put.   He thought, however, that the "fetish
houses" were the abode of spirits, and that he meant discarnate
human spirits may, perhaps, be inferred from his next remark:
"At one of the towns we saw a number of the natives running
away into the bush in the distance, carrying on their backs several
of the dead dry bodies of their relatives.   I hunted in all the
huts to find a dry corpse to take away as a specimen, but without
success; they had all been removed."

In *Seven Years Among the Fjort*[4] (1887), Dennett mentions[5]
"a wooden image of a woman with a tremendous stomach," which
is supposed to punish with death those who eat food that has
been forbidden to them as unclean; and in his second book
(1906), he refers[6] to Bavili figures of a man and a woman,

---

[1] ARC. i. 251-52.
[2] ARC. i. 278.
[3] ARC. ii. 7.
[4] The Bafiote are the dominant race between the lower Kwilu and the Congo
estuary, the Cabindas of Portuguese writers, the northern branch of the Kongo
nation.
[5] Pp. 47-48.
[6] BBMM. 85-9.   The Bavili are a tribe of Bafiote.

about eighteen inches in height, which are first carved and then charged with occult power by means of certain "medicine," as well as another class of images (*zinkisi*), called *zinkisi mobowu*, which are made out of a large tree (*muamba*) with soft wood. Before felling this tree, the name of some spirited person is called out, and when the *nganga* cuts the tree and its "blood" gushes out, the blood of a fowl, killed for the purpose, is mixed with that of the tree. The *kulu* ("spirit"?) of the person thus named will enter into the tree and preside over the image that is made of its wood; but the individual who has thus been robbed of his vitality will die within ten days. Men drive nails into these images and call upon them to kill them if they are lying, or, it may be, to kill their foes. Each of the many images of this kind has a name that is all its own; [1] Dennett thinks they are connected with *ndongo*, which he takes to be an evil spirit, the spirit of witchcraft [2]—something very different from the *nkisi* spirit which is connected with the groves and the kingly office. [3] Le Roy mentions another image of repute in Loango. [4] "The fetich, Bwiti, which is very well known in the region of Gabon and Loango and is the centre of a secret association, materially consists of a stick rudely carved in the shape of a human figure. Pieces of glass form the eyes; a bit of mirror takes the place of the navel; therein the sorcerer will look for the truth. Beneath are a tiger skin, some little bells, grass, strips of leather, etc. The bag from which this sculptured stick emerges contains a skull filled with various powders, corrupt matter from a corpse, and a bone from a snake. The fetich is placed in a decorated niche in the interior of a little hut that has no other opening than a door. A fire which, they say, must never go out, is fed by three big logs renewed by the sorcerer. A little path leads from this hut to a clearing in the neighbouring forest where the initiated assemble. As in all similar ceremonies, the mildest, simplest, and most approachable Blacks are unrecognisable at this time; for whole nights they will beat the tam-tam,

[1] BBMM. 93, 94.
[2] BBMM. 92, 103.
[3] BBMM. 96.
[4] RP. 229.

sing, dance, and perform fantastic sarabands. To approach them
at such a period is impossible."

In what is probably the most recent book on the district around
San Salvador, Claridge mentions a variety of images: male and
female figures, with prominent phallic characteristics, that stand
in ancestral shrines;[1] images called *nkenge* ("caretaker"), which
are placed at the entrances of circumcision lodges; others called
sole, which defend the town and promote conjugal prosperity;
others, bearded images, called *sansa,* that are concerned solely
with trade; and yet others, called *nzanzi* ("lightning") which
control lightning. He describes, also, a very large image (the
one in his possession stood nearly five feet high), called *ekunfu,*
"partly medical but chiefly phallic."[2]

Of the Gabun country (from 3° S. to 1° N.), Nassau wrote in
1904:[3] "Idols are rare among most of the coast tribes, but
are common among all the interior tribes. That they are not
now frequently seen on the coast is, I think, not due to a lack
of faith in them, but perhaps to a slight sense of civilised shame.
The idol has been the material object most denounced by missionaries in their sermons against heathenism. The half-awak-
ened native hides it, or he manufactures it for sale to curio-
hunters. A really valuable idol, supposed to contain a spirit,
he will not sell. He does not always hide his fetich charm worn
on his person; for it passes muster in his explanation of its use
as 'medicine.' That idol, charm, or plant, as the case may be,
is believed for the time to be the residence of a spirit which is
to be placated by offerings of some kind of food." On another
page[4] he quotes a paragraph written of the Mpongwe tribe by
the pioneer of his Mission some forty years before: "Images are
used in the worship of ancestors, but they are seldom exposed to
public view. They are kept in some secret corner, and the man
who has them in charge, especially if they are intended to represent a father or predecessor in office, takes food and drink to
them, and a very small portion of almost anything that is gained
in trade."

[1] WBT. 150.
[2] WBT., chap. x.
[3] FWA. 92.
[4] FWA. 158, quoting WA. 393.

Le Roy states[1] that in many Bantu districts of the West Coast—he instances Loango and the great forests of Gabun—it is customary to clean the whole or part of the skull of a deceased person, paint it red, put it in a bark-box, set it in a niche in the dwelling or in the community house, surmount it with a statuette of wood or clay, and erect a sort of altar before it. Those statuettes that are made of clay contain hair, eyelashes, finger-nails, bones, or other relics of the defunct; and, whether of wood or clay, they derive all their value from the relics which they enclose or surmount.

If the scope of our study warranted us in going beyond the northern border of Bantu territory, we should find sacred images in pagan communities throughout the Sudan; but of this two quotations must suffice, both of which are selected for the light they throw upon the working of the image-worshipper's mind. Dennett, writing in *The Church Quarterly Review*[2] on West African Religion, says: "In the environment of Benin city, as well as in the Congo, during the funeral ceremony an effigy of the king is made in wood or clay, and people make obeisance to it as if it were the still living king. Then you will find what we should call temples dedicated to the spirit of the departed in which figures in clay are dressed up as a king and his courtiers, and these figures are arranged in much the same order as courtiers appear in native courts to-day." And Cardinall mentions[3] that a man in the Northern Territories of the Gold Coast who discovered through the diviner that the leopard was his totem, made two clay leopards (they looked more like elephants) and placed them outside the gate of his compound and sacrificed to them.

"FETISH"

"Fetish" is an altogether unsatisfactory term. When Portuguese navigators and traders first visited West Africa, they saw every Native wearing a shell, a small horn, a bit of twisted root, or some trinket that had been charged with spirit-power, which was trusted to protect and aid them in all sorts of emergencies and

[1] RP. 102, 179, 191, 192.
[2] January, 1921.
[3] NTG. 40.

treated with proportionate respect.   Now the Portuguese themselves donned medallions, agnus deis, crucifixes, images of saints,
and other sacred symbols that had been duly blessed by their
priests and were credited with similar virtue; and, rightly concluding that the West Coast knick-knacks were poor relations of
their own charms, amulets, talismans, mascots—call them what
you will—they called these gimcracks by the same name, "feitiço"
—a word which had come, by long years of special use in a world
enthralled by magical notions, to carry a peculiar meaning, though
of the same parentage as our "feat" and "factitious."   When
other European nations followed in the wake of the Portuguese
mariners, they adopted the name which the latter had bestowed
upon these outlandish articles, and it is likely that English sailors
have used the term "fetish" ever since they first sailed along the
Guiné Coast, as it was then called.   The term crept into English
literature, however, through an epoch-making book by a Parisian
savant [1] in 1760; which accounts for the fact that our spelling
wavers between Anglicised "fetish" and Gallicised "fetich" or
"fetiche," and lapses occasionally into the bastard form "fetisch."

The subsequent history of the word may be gathered from Dr.
Haddon's compact criticism of the misuse of "fetishism" as a
designation.   "De Brosses introduced Fetichisme as a general descriptive term," he says,[2] "supposing the word to be connected
with *chose fée, fatum*.   Comte employed it to describe the universal religious tendency to which Dr. Tylor has given the name
of Animism.   Bastholm claimed everything produced by nature
or art, which receives divine honour, including the sun, moon,
earth, air, fire, water, with rivers, trees, stones, images and animals, considered as objects of divine worship, as Fetishism;
and Lippert defines Fetishism as 'a belief in the souls of the departed coming to dwell in any thing that is tangible or visible
in heaven or earth.'   Although Miss Kingsley expresses regret
that the word Fetish 'is getting very loosely used in England,'
she scarcely helps forward the work of distinction and arrangement when a few lines further on she announces 'When I say

[1] *Du Culte des Dieux fétiches* by Charles de Brosses.
[2] *Magic and Fetishism* by Alfred C. Haddon, Sc.D., F.R.S., University Lecturer in
Ethnology, Cambridge.   London: Constable, 1906, p. 65.

Fetish, or Ju Ju,[1] I mean the religion of the natives of West Africa.'[2] Subsequently she overstepped her own definition, describing the secret societies as 'pure Fetish' although they 'are not essentially religious,' but 'are mainly judicial.' The Rev. R. H. Nassau perpetuates this vague use of the word, grouping under the name of Fetichism all native customs even remotely connected, as everything is in West Africa, with religious or magical beliefs, until the ejaculation uttered when one sneezes or stumbles received the sounding title, 'fetish prayer.' These lumpings are all the more to be regretted since Miss Kingsley and the Rev. R. H. Nassau are among the chief authorities on West African Fetishism in its most characteristic forms, and a clear definition of the use of the word, with a rigid adherence to its proper meaning, would have done great service in preventing many misconceptions."

This criticism is both just and gentle. When a doctor of medicine and of sacred theology, who has had forty years of intimate intercourse with West Coast natives, entitles his book *Fetichism in West Africa*, he practically pledges himself to tell his readers what "fetich" and "fetichism" really mean; and on page 62, speaking of the native doctor (*nganga*), he says: "By his magic arts any spirit may be localised in any object whatever, however small or insignificant; and, while thus limited, is under the control of the doctor and subservient to the wishes of the possessor or wearer of the material object in which it is thus confined. This constitutes a 'fetich.'" "Any spirit?" Students who have dug deep in the magico-religious practices of the Bantu, are, of course, familiar with the notion that the magician can localise and control any one of a legion of spirits, but "any spirit" includes spirits of ancestors and high gods. Now, although spirits of ancestors and high gods may be propitiated by those who have the right to approach them, the assertion that they can be dominated by magicians needs vindication; and one searches this book in vain for facts that substantiate the theory. "Subservient to the wishes

[1] "Ju Ju," in spite of its disguise, is nothing more than the French word *joujou*, a "toy" or "doll."

[2] Dr. Haddon is referring to Miss Kingsley's article on "The Fetish View of the Human Soul" in *Folk-Lore* (viii., 1897); but in WAS. 96-102, also, she wants to use "fetish" of the whole of West African religion, and complains that she cannot do so in face of the prior use of the term by Tylor and other ethnologists.

of the possessor," etc.?   According to Bantu belief, he who possesses the tabernacle of a spirit that can ward off disease, must
obtain another if he wishes for success in trade, and yet another
if he craves luck in his lovemaking, and so on.   Spirits that are
controlled by magicians are not omnipotent; their activities are
highly specialised; no one of them can do every sort of thing
that the possessor of its habitation may happen to desire.   But
we are seeking a definition of "fetish" and "fetishism"; so we
ponder the phrase, "This constitutes a 'fetich.'"   Whether "this"
refers to the process, the object, the imprisoned spirit, or, possibly, the combination of object and spirit, we are not sure; but
since there is abundant evidence that our author, perhaps from
long use of African vernaculars, is hardly a master of precise
and lucid English, we read on, hoping that some future page will
dissipate the fog.   On page 75 we are told that "The fetich
worshipper makes a clear distinction between the reverence with
which he regards a certain material object and the worship he
renders to the spirit for the time being inhabiting it."   If there
are "fetish worshippers," then it must be that fetishes are worshipped, and since the spirit alone is worshipped, the material object being merely reverenced, it seems to follow that the former,
not the latter, is the "fetish."   But according to page 81, there
is a flaw in our reasoning; for there we read: "A fetich, then, is
any material object consecrated by the 'oganga,' or magic doctor,.
with a variety of ceremonies and processes, by virtue of which
some spirit becomes localised in that object, and subject to the
will of the possessor."   So the "fetish" after all is the shrine in
which the spirit is constrained to sojourn,—a conclusion that is
confirmed by the title and contents of Division III of the next
Chapter (VII), "the Use of Charms or 'Fetiches.'"   But then
how is it possible to write: "The manner of practising the white
art by the magic doctor may be purely ritual without his making
or the patient's wearing any material amulet, but the performance
is none the less fetich in its character"? [1]   And how can the term
"fetishism" be made to include all the processes of witchcraft
or black magic, of white magic (in which our author includes the
Matebele rain-rites [2]), and of the interdicts of the Ukuku secret

[1] FWA. 107.
[2] FWA. 117 (footnote).

society. The only thing that keeps me from saying that the term "fetish" has become a fetish to our author, is the fact that I am still unable to discover what "fetish" means.

Let it not be supposed, however, that Miss Kingsley and Dr. Nassau are sinners above all others. The excellence of their reports of West Coast magico-religious practices, makes one regret that, by yielding to the spell of a word that defies definition, they became so fascinated and bewildered that they lost the power to look with understanding eyes upon facts with which they were peculiarly familiar; but the worst that can be said of them is that they moved in the rut that their predecessors had made.

From the beginning, writers on West Coast customs have allowed the term "fetish" to obscure their vision and baffle their understanding; they have used it in so many different senses that it has come to conceal what it pretends to reveal. Battell (1590-1610) speaks of a "fetish called Maramba," [1] and Purchas, his editor, uses "fetish" as an equivalent of "gods." Father Merolla (1682-89) speaks of "idols," "enchanted bracelets," "divers other magick charms," "certain superstitious cords made by the wizards," and "religious relicks" that he had enjoined the people to substitute for "wizard mats"; but he never uses the term "fetish." [2] John Barbot (1682-1700), on the other hand, has much to say of "grigris" and "fetiches." "Grigri are little square leather bags, in which are inclos'd some folded pieces of written paper, . . . being in the nature of spells." [3] He thinks [4] the inscriptions are passages from the Koran and related to the phylacteries of the Jews. Some "grigris"—meaning the containers, I suppose—are made of a horse's tail or of the horns of deer, rams, or bullocks, covered with red serge or cloth. He seems to limit this term to the Islamic area of what he calls North Guinea or Nigritia. The following quotations give Barbot's opinion of the term "fetish," and show at the same time that it stood for many things. Of a fish about seven feet long, he says: "The Blacks call it Fetisso, but for what reason I cannot determine, unless it be to express, that it is too rare and sweet for mortals to eat, and

[1] See p. 307.
[2] C. i. 521 *et seq.*
[3] C. v. 35.
[4] C. v. 60.

only fit for a deity: the word Fetisso, which in Portuguese signifies sorcery, being by the Blacks applied to all things they reckon
sacred, because the Portuguese gave the name of sorcery to all
their superstitions." [1]   Speaking of the dexterity of the Blacks
in "sophisticating their gold": "The first sort of false gold is
mixed with silver or copper, and cast into sundry shapes and sizes,
which some there call Fetissos, signifying in Portuguese, charms,
because that nation gave the said name to whatsoever belonged to
the superstitions of the Blacks.   You may see them represented
in the cut.   These are generally some sort of toys commonly used
there by the women for ornament, as also by young men, and
worn in their hair, or by way of necklaces and bracelets." [2]   "The
word Feitisso is Portuguese, as has been observed before, and
signifies a spell or charm, the Portuguese looking upon their practices as no other, and from them the Blacks borrowed it: . . .
this word is chiefly taken in a religious sense, and they are so far
fallen into the Portuguese trap, that they call whatever is consecrated to the honour of their god, Feitisso, or a charm; and so
the name is given to those artificial bits of gold they wear as
ornaments. . . . We don't find any nation in the universe besides the Blacks of Guinea, and the northern people above Nova
Zembla that use this word Feitisso in a religious sense; and the
latter give that name to their idols, which are half figures of men
cut in the trunks or stumps of trees." [3]   "When they have a mind
to make offerings to their idols, or desire to know anything of
them, they cry, let us make Feitisso, that is, as has been before
observed, according to the Portuguese, whence they have the
word, let us conjure, or make our charms; but according to their
meaning is, let us perform our religious worship, and see or hear,
what our god will say to us. . . . When they drink the oath-
draught, they commonly add the imprecation, Let the Feitisso,
that is, the idol kill me, if I do not perform the contents of the
obligation." [4]   "Some authors have endeavoured to persuade the
world that the Blacks worship the devil, which I have shown to
be a mistake; as also that their priests are sorcerers or magicians,

[1] C. v. 223.
[2] C. v. 230.
[3] C. v. 308.
[4] C. v. 313.

who converse with evil spirits, by whose means they pretend to foretell future events, and perform other extraordinary matters, which is as false as the other. This notion came from the Portuguese, who gave those priests the name of Feitisseros, which they still retain, and signifies sorcerers; and this they did because these people being idolaters, and worshipping very deformed figures, they concluded them to be devils; and the extravagant ceremonies performed by the priests, they looked upon as witchcraft."[1] John Barbot's brother James gives information concerning the idols of Calabar, saying that people of that country call their idols "Jou-Jou, being in the nature of tutelar gods"; but he never uses the word "fetish" or any of its derivatives.[2] Bosman (1705) says: "They cry out, Let us make Fetiche; by which they express as much, as let us perform our religious worship"; he speaks also of "Gold . . . mixed with Fetiche's, which are a sort of artificial gold composed of several ingredients."[3] Snelgrave (1734) remarks: "The Lord of the Place had taken his Fetiche or Oath": and "They have all their particular Fetiches. . . . Some are to eat no Sheep, others no Goats."[4] Atkins (1735) often falls back upon this word: "At Accra they have Fetish-Women . . . who pretend divination." "The women fetish with a coarse paint of Earth on their Faces." "She being always fetished with chains and gobbets of gold at her ancles." "The women are fondest for what they call Fetishing, setting themselves out to attract the good graces of the men." He also applies the term to the rock, Tabra.[5]

Such was the undiscriminating use of this word that prevailed on the West Coast in bygone days; but in 1856 Wilson tried to unravel the tangle. "*Fetichism* and *Demonolatry*," he writes, "are undoubtedly the leading and prominent forms of religion among the pagan tribes of Africa. They are entirely distinct from each other, but they run together at so many points, and have been so much mixed up by those who have attempted to write on the subject, that it is no easy matter to keep them separated. A fetich,

[1] C. v. 316.
[2] C. v. 462.
[3] *New Oxford Dictionary, in loc.*
[4] *Ibid.*
[5] *Ibid.*

strictly speaking, is little else than a charm or amulet, worn about the person or set up at some convenient place, for the purpose of guarding against some apprehended evil or securing some coveted good. . . . A fetich may be made of a piece of wood, the horn of a goat, the hoof of an antelope, a piece of metal or ivory, and needs only to pass through the consecrating hands of a native priest to receive all the supernatural powers which it is supposed to possess. It is not always certain that they possess extraordinary powers. They must be tried, and give proof of their efficiency before they can be implicitly trusted. If a man, while wearing one of them, has some wonderful escape from danger, or has good luck in trade, it is ascribed to the agency of his fetich, and it is cherished henceforward as a very dear friend, and valued beyond price. On the other hand if he had been disappointed in some of his speculations, or been overtaken by some sad calamity, his fetich is thrown away as a worthless thing, without, however, impairing his confidence in the efficacy of fetiches in general. He has simply been unfortunate in having trusted to a bad one, and with unimpaired confidence he seeks another that will bring him better luck. Where a person has experienced a series of good luck, through the agency of a fetich, he contracts a feeling of attachment and gratitude to it; begins to imagine that its efficiency proceeds from some kind of intelligence in the fetich itself, and ultimately regards it with idolatrous veneration. Hence it becomes a common practice to talk familiarly with it as a dear and faithful friend, pour rum over it as a kind of oblation, and in times of danger call loudly and earnestly upon it, as if to wake up its spirit and energy."

Wilson was sagacious in judgment and piquant in expression. One wishes that he had discarded that word "fetich," which was already frayed beyond repair; and that he had written "to be exposed to the spell of a native magician," instead of "to pass through the consecrating hands of a native priest"; but, living as he did before the scientific method could be applied to the study of Bantu thought, he is noteworthy for his discrimination between the magical and the worshipful, and for the penetration of his perception that a mascot may become almost, if not altogether, an idol. And yet, somehow, his influence upon subsequent investigators of West Coast thought is often imperceptible. Monteiro,

writing twenty years later, makes the much-abused term a synonym for "witchery" in one passage,[1] for "taboo" in another,
while in others he applies it to ancestor-images.[2] When he says
that the only reason that Natives of Angola have for practising
circumcision is "that it would be 'fetish' not to perform it,"[3] he
seems to use the term as equivalent to "disregard of tribal custom"; but when he writes: "I filled a tumbler with wine, and
after drinking a portion (to show that there was no 'fetish' in it)
I handed him the rest,"[4] he was thinking, surely, of harmful
substances. To "undergo fetish" means, on another page,[5] to
"take oath." Sometimes the term serves as a smoke-screen behind
which the author hides his inability to interpret what he saw, as
in the statement quoted a few pages back,[6] and in the sentence:
"A singular custom of the kings of Congo is that of never expec-
torating on the ground in public, it being 'fetish' to do so, and
foretelling some calamity."[7] I leave the International Champion
of Missing-word Competitions to discover what word should be
substituted for "fetish" in the following criticism of Bantu beliefs: "His whole belief is in evil spirits, and in charms or 'fetishes': these 'fetishes' can be employed for evil as well as to
counteract the bad effect of other malign 'fetishes' or spirits."[8]

"A fetish," says Bentley,[9] "is something which has the power of
exercising an occult influence. The fetish itself may be very
various. The power may be contained in a rag, stone, water, pipe-
clay, or rubbish of all kinds; the more singular and uncanny the
better." Then he gives us a long list of fetish-forms, with more
detailed description of some fetishes that he has examined, and
concludes with the following remark: "Those fetishes which are
shaped as images, rudely carved, hideous, and often most indecent, are but vehicles of fetishes. Charm-powder is somewhere
secreted in them. . . . The image shape is an accident. . . .

[1] ARC. i. 61.
[2] See pp. 309 f.
[3] ARC. i. 278.
[4] ARC. ii. 174.
[5] ARC. ii. 117.
[6] See pp. 309 f.
[7] ARC. i. 220.
[8] ARC. i. 247.
[9] PC. i. 256-59.

When some mystery powder has been put into it, it becomes a charm; not an idol or god of any kind."

Weeks [1] is in substantial agreement with Bentley: whatever the fetish-vehicle may be, whether an image (as on the Lower Congo) or any other convenient article (as among the Boloki), its efficacy depends upon the occult mixture with which it is charged. The mixture varies according to the variety of power with which the fetish is to be endowed: fragments of strong beasts give it strength, collops of cunning creatures confer craftiness, bits of swift birds that sail on tireless wings furnish flight, the head of a snake or some poisonous plant or bean makes it deadly, and curative herbs endow it with the quality of healing." We shall find in a future volume, that all this is in strict accord with a principle of Bantu magic, and that Weeks was on the verge of the truth when he wrote: "It is quite probable that the medicine men and the more intelligent natives believe that by mixing the skins, plants, chalk, etc., in different ways they induce different spirits to take up their abode in the various fetishes, because they like the mixture prepared for them, and in thus taking up their residence in them, or being influenced by them, the medicine-men gain power over them." Upon this principle it is easy to understand, also, that the mixture "put into the fetish is after a time played out, . . . so the owner takes it to a medicine-man to have it refreshed by renewing the charms." But when we are told that sacrifices, ranging from an occasional drop of blood from a frog's foot to a goat every new moon, are offered to the spirits in these fetishes, we confess to a longing for some esoteric interpretation. We can understand that a sprinkling of fresh blood may be deemed to impart fresh vigour, but a sacrifice implies worship, and Weeks states definitely that though "the native offers periodic sacrifices to his fetish," yet "he never worships it, nor does he ever pay homage to it." There is some confusion. On one page we are told: "No native thinks the fetish he uses is possessed of divine power, nor does it represent a deity to him, and he uses no language about it that would lead us to suppose that for a moment he in his own mind invests it with divinity"; and on another page: "They try to appease them by frequent sacrifices; and they have dances about some of the fetishes, during which

[1] ACC. 252-260.

they call upon them, or the spirits they influence, to protect their fighting-men and destroy their enemies." How are we to reconcile these statements unless we import unwonted definitions into some of the terms used, or else assume, as in all probability we should, that there are "fetishes" and "fetishes," and that the fallacy of the double middle lies in wait for any writer who clings to the use of this term?

Hilton-Simpson writes: [1] "As is usually the case with the people of Kasai, the Batetela do not worship their fetishes, but merely regard them as charms which have been endowed by the 'medicine-man' with powers to ward off some evil or to produce some good effect. Small fetishes are worn on the person everywhere in the Congo, and Jadi wears some in his hair, which are supposed to warn his head [2] against any plot that may be hatched against it."

Claridge, in his chapter on "Fetishes & Fetishism," [3] makes the following statements: "An image set in a garden to keep the thieves off or the demons out; mysterious articles to mark off land boundaries or to regulate the affairs of man with man, clan with clan; magic things by which to swear a witness or to sway a sceptre, is fetishism in the realm of ethics. Roots, claws, bones, skin, hairs, etc., fastened on the person to cure or mitigate a malady, is fetishism in the realm of medicine. The blood of a goat in sacrifice for guilt, its flesh as the medium of communion with the dead, its skin as the mystic element in spirit charming, is fetishism in the realm of theology. Congo fetishism is a double-barrelled arrangement of charms (*mwangu*) and images (*teke*). An image is a charm, but a charm is not always an image. . . . Images among the Ba-Congolese are not idols to be deified, but effigies to ward off aggressive spirits, or to win the favour of friendly spirits. They are more often instruments of revenge to incite the spirits to murder, to maim, or to inflict a malady. A charm may be anything dedicated by a priest for a fetish purpose." "There is a significant moral element in the fetishism of the

[1] LPK. 58.
[2] If Jadi had not been influenced by European ideas, it is unlikely that he regarded his head as the seat of intelligence; see my footnote on p. 34 f. Weeks makes a similar mistake when he suggests that powdered chalk in the occult mixture is symbolical of brain matter "that gives intelligence to the whole mass." ACC. 256.
[3] WBT., chap. x.

Congolese. . . . 'Fetishes will never work for a guilty party,' says the creed. The Congo phrase is, *'Nkisi kuma kadilanga,'* literally; fetishes never justify wrong. That is a fetish will never injure, or in any way operate against an innocent person." He illustrates this last remark by pointing out that innocent persons may safely tread on leaves which have been invested with a fetish element that is guaranteed to destroy thieves. "Before an article becomes a fetish it must be consecrated by a native priest. An image is simply a marketable article until officially ordained. Any one with skill enough can make an image, but no one except a 'wise one' can turn it into a fetish." "There is a fetish for almost every conceivable object within the compass of a Negro's mind—for hunting, fishing, trapping," etc., etc. In his chapter on "Comparative Religion" the following passage occurs: "When a Congo man is disgusted with the favours or generosity of his fetish, he will throw it on to the rubbish heap outside his house and leave it there until he thinks it is ashamed of itself. But the Congo native has an instinct which prompts him to something more than a fanaticism of self-preservation. He offers to his patron spirits the flesh of fowl, of venison, and of other game for meat. For drink he gives the best beverage known to the Congo tapster. The Congo woman shuts herself up for months in close association with her fetishes to pacify any anger on their part or to gratefully acknowledge some benefit, such as freedom from disease, gifts of skill, divination, and so forth, even to the gift of a child she dearly loves." [1] And on the next page: "Fetishism is an improvement on Hindu idolatry because it is not idolatrous. It may be infantile, but it is not adoration of infantile things. A Congo witch can pass into a lion, a boar, or a crocodile as easily and completely as the Indian Vishnu can do it, but the Congolese seek to kill her, not to honour her with the gory offering of a Juggernath." In a chapter entitled "The Man from Below," Campbell says: [2] "There are various kinds of doctors, with twelve of which I am personally acquainted, and there are higher and lower grades in the profession, but the chief significance of the African fetish doctor is seen in the above name which indicates the leading characteristic of his professional duties. He is

[1] WBT. 264.
[2] IHB. 75.

a man of the underworld and has to do with the dead, and 'dead man's land,' from whence come all trouble and disease. . . . As a qualified practitioner he claims to be, and is, called 'the father of fetishcraft,' and the initiate he agrees to take along with him, and teach the secret of smelling out witches, and making charms, poisons, and medicines, . . . is called 'the son of fetishcraft.' " On page 81 he catalogues the twelve kinds of doctors: "Doctor of the boiling-pot ordeal"; "Diviner about sickness and trouble"; "Witch doctor who uses crystal gazing"; "Seed-gourd-rattling doctor and diviner"; "Doctor who divines with axe on a skin"; "Rain doctor"; "Pot and basket diviner"; "Clairvoyant, who professes to see in a gourd of oil sickness and trouble, etc."; "Doctor who does not divine, but treats those who have already been diagnosed"; "Smeller-out of witches and wizards"; "Doctor who is supposed to be able to give a man power to speak—only during demon-possession—tongues he never knew before"; and "Poison-cup doctor." The same comprehensive term, "fetish," is applied, in the chapter on "Fetishism & Medicine," [1] to charms; "the large *mantis* called in South Africa the Kaffir God" (*sic*); two meteorites wrapped in python-skins; [2] a basket of occult mixture containing a piece of the skull of a famous warrior; and magical things that farmers tie to the fences of their fields to catch thieves. He avers that *"Fetishism and medicine are two distinct systems,* and are used for the following specified purposes and reasons: *Fetish* comes from the Portuguese word *Feitiço*, meaning a superstitious charm or magic medicine. For this the Bantu word *Bwanga* is used, and these charms are used exclusively in the practice of the black and white art of magic by qualified doctors, or by wizards and impostors. A man who employs fetishes for his own personal ends, or to injure or kill an enemy, is guilty of sorcery, *buloshi*, and is punished by death. A qualified fetish doctor or wise man, who employs the same system of charms and magic medicines for the tribal good, is a public benefactor, and is so recognised and treated among his tribe." [3] But this does not prevent him from writing: "The fetish doctor goes to the bush regularly to replenish his supplies of leaves, barks, roots, etc.,

[1] IHB. 234.
[2] See p. 294.
[3] IHB. 240.

from which he makes up his stock-in-trade of medicines for use. Aperients, astringents, aromatics, soporifics, etc., are well known, and many other medicines whose name and action and locality are kept secret from laymen." [1]   Schweitzer writes: [2] "What is fetishism?   It is something born of the fears of primitive man. Primitive man wants to possess some charm to protect him from the evil spirits in nature and from those of the dead, as well as from the power for evil of his fellow-men, and this protecting power he attributes to certain objects which he carries about with him.   He does not worship his fetish, but regards it as a little bit of property which cannot but be of service to him through its supernatural powers.   What makes a fetish?   That which is unknown is supposed to have magical power.   A fetish is composed of a number of little objects which fill a small bag, a buffalo horn, or a box; the things most commonly used are red feathers, small parcels of red earth, leopard's claws and teeth, and . . . bells from Europe!   Bells of an old-fashioned shape which date from the barter transactions of the eighteenth century!   Opposite the mission station a negro has laid out a small cocoa plantation, and the fetish which is expected to protect it hangs on a tree in a corked bottle. . . . There are big fetishes and little ones.   A big one usually includes a piece of human skull, but it must be from the skull of some one who was killed expressly to provide the fetish."

In these many quotations I have striven to provide a just exemplification of the use of "fetish" and "fetishism" by West Coast writers; [3] but it is easier to extract sunbeams from cucumbers than to elicit a precise definition of the term from these utterances.   A vague appellation, first applied by aliens who had not begun to understand the Native and his ways, quickly captured European imagination; and ever since, unfortunately, it has been

[1] IHB. 243.
[2] EPF. 30-31.
[3] Writers in other Bantu areas seldom flirt with this term.   Roscoe is fond of using it to denote god-boxes, or at least emblems of the gods (*e.g.*, Bg. 166, 352; SCA. 79, 95; KT. 46; NYN. 24, 30); but he applies it, also, to concoctions that are apparently in another category, such as a ball made of herbs, cowdung, and a little hair from each cow in the herd (NYN. 66), a swallow which has been dried and stuffed with herbs (NYN. 40), and a "fetish of herbs" that is placed in the path of an army going forth to battle (NYN. 158).

distracting the attention of careful observers, and enabling hasty writers to screen their aloofness from Native thought behind its dazzling atmosphere of mystery. Most of the writers whom I have quoted would have materially modified their interpretation of what they saw and heard if they had rigidly adhered to terms that they were able to define, instead of translating now one Native notion and then another into a word that has no equivalent in the vernaculars of the tribesmen whose possessions and practices it presumes to denote.

"There is one term," says Rattray,[1] "the indiscriminate use of which, I believe has done infinite harm, the word 'fetish.' . . . This term will befog the enquirer who is ignorant of the vernacular, at every turn. . . . Broadly speaking, all these objects which we ourselves would loosely call charms, amulets, talismans, mascots or fetishes, he [the Ashanti] calls *suman*, and I think that the word 'fetish' should be rigidly confined to designate such only. His other category of non-human spirits, which he himself calls *abosom*, which he clearly distinguishes from the *suman*, we should never call 'fetishes,' for it is a totally misleading term. The only correct word to use for the Ashanti word *obosom* is 'god' or, when speaking of the brass pan itself, which is the potential resting-place of this non-human spirit, 'a shrine.' "

Bantu tribes draw a similar line between what is purely magical and what is mainly concerned with worshipful spirits. Even when practices of the latter kind bear external evidence of long and intimate contact with those of the former variety, expert practitioners (however it may be with the uninstructed crowd) are wont to designate each by separate vernacular terms. As for the correct use of the word "fetish," a word that has been so blurred and disfigured that it may stand for almost anything in West Coast magic or religion, and even for the captivating embellishments of Native philanderers, is surely past redemption. Why retain it at all? The objects for which Rattray himself uses four other words in the same sentence, can be described without impressing this misleading term into our service. It would be better to relegate it to the terminological scrap-heap, and sort out, into groups that correspond much more nearly with Native notions, the

[1] AS. 90.

various rites that it has been allowed too long to distort. These, I think—waiving the claim that the high gods (the "non-human spirits," as Rattray calls those of Ashanti) may prove upon analysis to have originated in defunct dynasties—would fall into three classes: (1) Charms which have been quickened with non-human spirits and are consequently never worshipped; (2) God-boxes that are the haunts of discarnate human spirits; and (3) Emblems of high gods whose worshippers are unaware that they were ever human.

Before we can understand the amulets in Class (1), we must explore the principles that underlie the practice of magic; and our interpretation of the emblems in Class (3) will depend upon our opinion of the nature of these high gods: themes which demand each a separate chapter.[1]   Many of the god-boxes in Class (2) have been sufficiently described in preceding pages; but one variety of them—relics of the dead—claims more consideration than we have hitherto given it.

RELICS OF THE DEAD

The custom of preserving the skull, the jaw-bone, or some other portion of the corpse of a patriarch whose good offices in the spirit-world may be of service to his children, is evidently born of the belief that these relics ensure the presence of the spirit; [2] a notion that clothes itself with a variety of practices and is probably coextensive with Bantu culture.

Wilson, after mentioning images that are used by Western Bantu in the worship of ancestors, continues: [3] "But a yet more prominent feature of this ancestral worship is to be found in the preservation and adoration of the bones of the dead, which may fairly be regarded as a species of relic worship. The skulls of distinguished persons are preserved with the utmost care, but always kept out of sight. I have known the head of a distinguished man to be dissevered from the body when it was but partially decomposed, and suspended so as to drip upon a mass of chalk provided for the purpose. The brain is supposed to be the seat of

---

[1] In a future volume that I hope to publish.
[2] See Index: Relics of the dead and cf. RAC. 34, 102, 165, 241, 242.
[3] WA. 394.

wisdom,[1] and the chalk absorbs this by being placed under the head during the process of decomposition. By applying this to the foreheads of the living, it is supposed they will imbibe the wisdom of the person whose brain has dripped upon the chalk. In some cases all the bones of a beloved father or a mother are, after being dried, kept in a wooden chest, for which a small house is provided, where the son or daughter goes statedly to hold communication with their spirits. They do not pretend to have any audible responses from them, but it is a relief to their minds in their more serious moods to go and pour out all the sorrows of their hearts in the ear of a revered parent."

But pious relatives are not the only ones who preserve skulls. "In 1890 I saw in Bonjoko—a town just below Monsembe—" writes Weeks,[2] "the entrance, six feet by eight feet, to a house paved with skulls; and it was customary not only to use skulls in this way, but also to put the skulls of enemies at the base of palm trees and to use them as foot-stools. The desire was, by these indignities, to insult the fallen enemy and to maintain some hold on the spirits of those slain in war that they might attend their conqueror in the spirit land." Here the motive is very different, but the underlying theory is the same.

What some Thonga clans call the "great *mhamba*," reposes in its own proper hut, over which a specially appointed guardian keeps watch and ward. Clansmen hold this mysterious bundle in such veneration that they shrink from pronouncing its name; and the fact that they allude to it, when they must, as "riches," is proof positive that they regard it as the treasure of the clan. "It consists of the nails and hair of the deceased chiefs. When a chief dies, the more or less imperishable portions of his body, such as the nails and the hair of his head and beard, are carefully cut, kneaded together with the dung of the oxen which have been killed at his death, and a kind of pellet is thus made. This is bound round with thongs of hide. When another chief dies a second pellet is made and added to the first one, and so on down through the centuries. The *mhamba* of the Tembe clan is at the present time about one foot in length."[3] Junod defines the term

---

[1] It is risky to assume that one's own fundamental conceptions are, as a matter of course, shared by the Bantu. See footnote on p. 34.

[2] ACC. 323.

[3] LSAT. ii. 373 f. Cf. RP. 191.

"*mhamba*," after examining various objects to which it is applied, as "any object by means of which men enter into relation with the spirits of the ancestors." [1] That he is correct in his indication of the function of these venerable relics is borne out by the fact that the brandishing of the bundle at a sacrifice does away with the need for the sacramental "*Tsu!*" which invokes the spirits upon other occasions.

The home of the Thonga is in the south-east of Bantu Africa, while that of the people of whom Miss Kingsley wrote is at the extreme north-west of this area; but the bundles that she saw in the sleeping-apartments of Fan and Adooma tribesmen, and those which Nassau found among the Mpongwe,[2] were undoubtedly relics of similar character and significance. They belonged to the family, apparently, instead of to the clan; but they were much more than heirlooms held in honour of the dead: they were links between the worshipful dead and their pious descendants. Nassau was aware that a medicine-man "selects substances such as he deems appropriate to the end in view"; [3] but in the false light of his synthetic term "fetish" he could not perceive that the end which the manufacturer of amulets has in view is the occult appropriation of some coveted quality with which his quickening material is thought to be highly charged, while that of the preparer of relics is to ensure the real presence of a spirit to whom petition is to be made.

But, it may be argued, if the function of a relic is to secure the presence of the spirit that once animated it, it would surely be kept so separate from others that those who wished to approach that particular ancestor could select it and use it; whereas here we have fragments of successive chiefs of a Thonga clan, or successive generations of a Mpongwe family, so combined that they cannot be used apart. The Secwana phrase *go ya nkabo* ("to eat a lonely portion") is a common idiomatic expression for "sheep-stealing," because the only conceivable folk who would want to eat their food unshared are those who have stolen it. This dominant communistic feeling is taken over into the spirit-world. Individual shrines are common enough, like individual graves;

[1] LSAT. i. 142; ii. 383.
[2] See p. 34.
[3] FWA. 82.

but when the head of a family or clan approaches his discarnate elders with the nutriment that they require, he often refuses to name any one of them to the exclusion of the rest; [1] or if he names one whom the diviner has discovered to be specially resentful, he asks him to call the other spirits of their kindred to the feast. Miss Werner quotes Duff Macdonald as saying that the chief of a Yao village worships his immediate predecessor as the representative of all the people who have lived in his village in past times, and the whole line of his ancestors. "In presenting his offering he will say, 'Oh, father, I do not know all your relatives, you know them all, invite them to feast with you.' The offering is not simply for himself, but for himself and all his relatives." [2]

In a hut built for an ancestor's spirit, one usually finds his pipe, axe, porridge-bowl,[3] stool, or other personal belongings. These are more than mere mementos of the precious dead; they are real religious relics; things to which deceased had become particularly attached, not by sentiment alone, but by the exudations from his body with which they are coated. The secretions from a person's body are a part of himself, and there is no essential difference between sweat and saliva, or clippings of hair, or parings of toe-nails. If you can provide your magician with a little sweat scraped from your enemy's sandals or wooden pillow, he can blast him almost as effectually as if you brought the victim in chains and compelled him to see and hear the enacted and enchanted curse; and if you can also supply the magician with the victim's real name—the name that is known only to his intimates—there is no "almost" about it.

The stool of a dead Ashanti chief is a great religious relic. "After the death of a wise ruler, if it be desired to perpetuate his or her name and memory, the late owner's 'white' stool is 'smoked' or blackened by being smeared all over with soot, mixed with yolk of egg. It then becomes a black stool and is deposited in the stool house, and becomes a treasured heirloom of the clan. The stool, which during the lifetime of its possessor was so intimately bound (literally and metaphorically speaking) with its owner's *sunsum* or soul, thus becomes after death a shrine into

[1] See p. 399.
[2] NBCA. 49.
[3] Cf. p. 229.

which the departed spirit may again be called to enter on certain special occasions, that it may receive the adulation and those gifts that were dear to it in life, and so be induced to continue to use its new and greater spiritual influence in the interest of those over whom it formerly ruled upon earth." [1]

In Bantu tribes the stool is as symbolic of the chieftainship as it is in Ashanti; but a Bantu chief's stool passes, with other insignia of office, to his successor. The Ashanti practice is based upon a belief that a chief's "white stool" of office is the repository of his soul; and the fact that these stools are subjected to an occasional ceremonial scrubbing with unboiled water and sand, suggests that the connection between soul and stool does not depend upon any bodily secretions with which the latter may be coated; it probably depends upon some process akin to that mentioned on another page.[2] There are, however, indications in Ashanti lore of some mysterious connection between the soul and the secretions of the body. Everybody has heard of the Golden Stool of Ashanti. No king ever sat upon that stool, although it was the great symbol of Ashanti kingship. The legend is that it fell from the sky, in a black cloud and with a rumbling noise, and rested gently on the knees of Osai Tutu, the fourth known king of the Ashanti nation. Now it was to the supernatural power of a priest named Anotchi that this mysterious event was due: and Anotchi told the king that the Golden Stool contained the *sunsum* ("soul") of the Ashanti nation: their power, their health, their bravery, and their welfare. "To emphasise the fact," says Rattray,[3] "he caused the king and every Ashanti chief and all the Queen Mothers to take a few hairs from the head and pubes, and a piece of the nail from the forefinger.[4] These were made into powder and mixed with 'medicine,' and some was drunk and some poured or smeared on the stool." Rattray gives, of course, the Ashanti version of this mythical happening; but if an accurate and chronological account could be obtained, we should probably find that the smearing of the stool with secretions from the bodies of all the rulers of the nation was an essential part of the ritual by which the "soul of the nation" was hid in it.

[1] AS. 92.
[2] See p. 156.
[3] AS. 289.
[4] Cf. p. 31.

As our knowledge of Bantu practice deepens and extends, we are likely to discover that some relic of an ancestor is always necessary for the consecration of a shrine to his spirit: some fragment of his body or the grave in which it lies,[1] some article that he often used and left coated with the secretions of his body, or, at least, some material from a properly constituted shrine at which he has hitherto manifested his presence; though it is possible that the name alone contains enough of the personality to link the spirit closely to the shrine. Whether ancestral stones will demand another explanation, it is not yet possible to say; but it is conceivable that grave-earth is moulded up with the clay of which some images are made, and it is certain that wooden images and a variety of other ancestral emblems are nothing more than specimens of a craftsman's handiwork till they are quickened. What we have to discover is whether the quickening material that the expert conceals in a cavity of the emblem, or beneath some ornamental adjunct, is of the nature of a relic of the dead; whether, in fact, the image or other emblem is really a reliquary. Other elements in Bantu thought are sure to figure in the making of these sacred objects: the esoteric name of the individual is a part of his personality, and "words of power" are certainly employed.

THE PRIEST IN ANCESTOR-WORSHIP

Mention has been made of "priests," "doctors," "fetish-doctors," or "medicine-men," as they are variously styled by translators of local appellations. The vernacular titles behind these terms pertain also to specialists in other occult arts, but for the nonce we concern ourselves only with those who function as adepts in ancestor-worship.

Pride of birth plays a prominent part in Bantu social intercourse: seniority is defined in terms of status without regard to

---

[1] When Edward the Confessor was canonised and his body enshrined by Archbishop Thomas à Becket in 1163, it was a traditional custom that the Archbishop of Canterbury, when he translated a saint, should carry home with him a portion of the body for the relic-chests at Christ Church. But St. Edward was a recent king as well as a saint, and so Archbishop Thomas contented himself with taking the gravestone which had hitherto covered these sacred remains. That gravestone stood for many years beside the martyr-shrine of St. Thomas à Becket at Canterbury, and when King Henry IV set up an altar for St. Edward he made it the altar-slab. (From an article in *The Observer*, London, July 29, 1923.) Cf. my pp. 287, 290.

age, but the legend *seniores priores* is written large upon the life of the people. The senior member of any Bantu coterie is its natural leader; it would be bad form, for instance, for a traveller to slaughter a goat which his friend might give him on the road, without first carrying the consent of the senior member of his company. In family activities, whether secular or religious (if I may use a distinction that Bantu thought would disavow), the senior is attorney for the group; and the fact that he is the greatest surviving son of the family gods makes him the proper officiant in all important rites of approach to these divinities, though minor acts of worship are the birthright of every member of the family. For the same reason, the patriarch of patriarchs in a clan is the only possible high priest at shrines of the clan-gods. He need not despatch the victim or offer the gifts with his own hands; [1] but he orders every act in the ritual, and personally invokes the gods, offers the gifts, and presents the petitions. Tribal worship, if we ignore for the present the High Gods and Nature Spirits, is rendered only to ancestors of the ruling clan, of which the paramount chief is the natural patriarch; or, in some districts, to old gods of the land, that is, ancestors of ancient paramount clans which have become politically effete, whose greatest living descendants are alone competent to serve as their priests. To sum up in a single sentence: Any Bantu family or clan has free access to gods of its own lineage without the intervention of an outside priest, but the heritor and successor of a deified patriarch is the only high priest of that divinity. With grains of allowance for tribes that have passed less completely or more completely from matrilineal to patrilineal modes of inheritance, Junod's statement of Thonga practice accords with all we know of Bantu procedure. "The Thonga have no sacerdotal caste," he says,[2] "but the right of officiating in religious ceremonies is strictly confined to *the eldest brother*. All the offerings must pass through him. To supplant him is a great taboo, and would entail the malediction of the gods, and even the death of the trespasser. There are, however, some minor offerings which any one is allowed to bring to his gods." But Kidd writes:[3] "The headman of a kraal or vil-

---

[1] Cf. RSZ. 158, 173-77.
[2] LSAT. ii. 376.
[3] EK. 169.

lage may occasionally act as priest, though the doctor more frequently exercises the function.   The national witch-doctor is the national priest, and ought to conduct all tribal ceremonies, such as doctoring the soldiers before war.   When an ox is sacrificed to the spirits, the doctor, or in his absence, the headman of the village, decides which beast shall be killed."   These are discrepant statements, but the explanation is not far to seek.   Kidd, the impressionist, depicts in artistic phrases the panorama that passes before his eyes; but Junod, the careful student, preferring the fluoroscope to the camera obscura, looks through the trappings of the rite to its inner structure.   The truth is that the worship of these spirits, though often a complicated affair, must be rendered with such meticulous conformity to rule that an untrained man who was born to be priest of his father's spirit is often obliged to seek the guidance of an expert.[1]   If, for instance, the patriarch or one of his "children" is disturbed by dream or calamity—a common occurrence—it generally takes an expert to identify the importunate spirit, or else to discover what the spirit wants or what warning it wishes to utter; and there are experts everywhere who make it their business to guide patriarchs in properly propitiating the spirits of their fathers.   Adepts in the higher reaches of this ritual are rare; there is seldom more than one man in a tribe who has mastered the rain-rites and the ritual of war, and he cuts a very big figure in the community.   Whether we dub these people "priests," will depend, of course, upon our conception of priesthood.   They have no standing before the gods of the family or the clan that calls them to its assistance; the only sense in which they can be said to be "in orders" is that they are authoritatively appointed on each several occasion as agents and assistants of the only person whose birthright it is to minister to his gods for himself and his retainers.   It is true that they perform much of the ritual in which their guidance is sought; but the heritor and successor of the family gods, who is vested with an inalienable right to approach the spirits of his lineage, is surely the "priest," while his coadjutor, who lacks spiritual authority but has much greater professional knowledge and skill, is merely an adept.[2]

Now, it should be noted, I think, that these skilled coadjutors

[1] See p. 214.
[2] Cf. RP. 182, 187 and SRK. 98-99, 196, 202.

of the patriarch of patriarchs are trained magicians, who rely for the bulk of their income upon purely magical practices, and that the meticulous accuracy demanded in the performance of the higher rites of ancestor-worship is indispensable in the efficacious utterance of a magical incantation. The spirits which the magician controls are clearly differentiated from those to which the ancestor-worshipper pays homage; but the ritual of ancestor-worship borrows so much from that of magic that in its rendering the magician and the sacerdotalist must unite. In this interesting combination we have a real but rudimentary professional priest-hood, in which the sacerdotal prerogative of the king [1] is fortified and turned to account by the masters of esoteric learning. Is it possible that we are here looking at the seed-bed in which the great royal priesthoods of ancient organised religions sprouted?

Writers from the lower Congo and some other Western terri-tories, seem to imply that the intervention of an adept or *official* (in contradistinction to *natural*) priest is needed even for simple acts of ancestor-worship. If this is correct, one wonders whether it is due to greater shattering of social solidarity in the west, with consequent loss of clan and family traditions, or whether it comes from the popular use of ancestral images. By esoteric rites of which the adept holds the key, a mere sample of a craftsman's skill is transformed into a haunt or a habitation of some one who is lost to sight; and it would not be surprising if the "quickener" of the image should come to be deemed the safest guide in all that pertains to the worship that gathers around it, especially if the sacerdotal authority of the heir has been shattered by cen-turies of political turbulence.

SACRIFICIAL VICTIMS

In summarising the observances of ancestor-worship, the first place must be given to sacrifices; [2] for, although simpler methods

[1] Of the four fundamental functions of hereditary Bantu chieftainship (I speak not of despots who cleared their path to power with spear points), a weak chief may be deprived of the civil, the judicial, and the military, but no power on earth can rob him of his sacerdotal prerogative; even death does but transfer him to the abode of his gods and pass the prerogative unimpaired to his heir.

[2] For the sake of precision, I consistently use the word "sacrifices" in its common English sense of "slain victims," though it would be etymologically correct to use it of all offerings to the gods.

of intercourse with the divinities are preferred upon ordinary occasions, resort is always had to sacrifice, the supreme expression of longing souls, upon the red-letter days of life.

Before European suzerains compelled dynastic divinities to be content with less precious gifts, some tribes offered human sacrifices upon great occasions. Andrew Battell describes what he calls a sacrifice to the Devil at the camp of the great Jaga, where he found refuge upon his escape from slavery. The rites, designed apparently to propitiate the spirit of Kinguri, the founder of the Jaga dynasty, lasted all day; and after sun-down the medicine-man handed the Jaga chief his *casengula*, "which is a weapon like a hatchet," bidding him be strong against his enemies, "for his *mokiso* is with him." "And presently," continues Battell, "there is a man-child brought which forthwith he killeth. Then are four men brought before him; two whereof, as it happeneth, he presently striketh and killeth; the other two he commandeth to be killed without the fort." At this juncture Battell was commanded to leave, for the medicine-man feared that his presence would mar the rites; but he heard that five cows were also killed within the fort and five without, and the same number of goats and dogs, and that their blood was sprinkled in the fire and their bodies eaten.[1] It is possible that this was ritual-murder rather than human sacrifice;[2] for Battell was neither competent to discover the true inwardness of the rites that he witnessed nor permitted to see the culmination of the ceremony.

While Grenfell and Comber were at Bolobo (on the Congo) in 1884, four slaves, bought for the purpose, were sacrificed as part of the funeral rites for a chief's wife.[3] Weeks, writing of his experiences at Monsembe after 1890, says: "If a family were troubled with much sickness, and a witch-doctor said it was due to the dissatisfaction of So-and-so's spirit (mentioning the name of an important and recently deceased member of the family), because no offering had lately been made to him, then the family would kill a slave and send him with a message to their troublesome deceased relative, requesting that he would not cause them any further misfortune. If the deceased belonged to a 'bush' or

[1] SAAB. 33.
[2] For ritual-murders that are not human sacrifices, see pp. 211, 215, 217.
[3] GGC. 111.

inland tribe, the slave would be killed and buried; but if the departed one was a member of a riverine tribe, then the slave was tied up and thrown into the river. We induced them to stop this custom, but the more timorous ones for a time compromised the matter either by burying brass rods, equal to the price of a slave, in the grave, or scattering them in the river." [1] So strong was the attachment of some Congo tribes to these customs, that they stealthily observed them awhile in spite of all that the Belgian authorities could do to suppress them; but Melland's statement [2] that the human sacrifices mentioned by Pereira and Livingstone continued with the Machiamvos and Musokatandas till the reign of Kanembu, but not later, indicates that they ceased on the Congo-Zambesi watershed in the "seventies" or "eighties" of last century—before the advent of European rule in that territory.

When Gottschling remarks [3] that "in olden times even mankind 'could' be used" as sacrifice among the Bawenda of the Northern Transvaal, he may be thinking of such ritual-murder as that which the Boseleka practised.[4] But Junod mentions [5] that in many sacred woods a living human victim was abandoned to the gods when the people were in need of rain.

From the earliest times, the gods of Uganda were wont to demand, through their medium, a sacrifice of from two to five hundred people. Most of these victims were offenders, or people marked by some peculiarity of person or attire, or by their passing given points on main roads at a specified time: but sometimes the gods ordered the inclusion of a number of princes or other selected individuals for the sake of obviating rebellion. Roscoe avers that men and women victims scarcely ever protested or appealed, but went to their death without a murmur, thinking they were saving their country from some calamity.[6] He is of opinion, however, that women were seldom slaughtered as sacrificial victims.[7]

It cannot be disputed, I think, that some Bantu tribes sacrificed

[1] ACC. 97.
[2] WBA. 38, 47.
[3] R. BAAS., 1905, iii. 213.
[4] See p. 211.
[5] LSAT. ii. 357, 373, 378.
[6] Bg. 284, 331-39.
[7] Bg. 98.

human beings to the spirits of their dynasties;[1] nor that paramount chiefs and people of much lower status were escorted into the lower world by a befitting retinue of wives and other retainers;[2] nor that ritual-murder was committed for the sake of providing the hierologist or the magician with such human organs as he needed to give potency to his occult mixtures;[3] nor that people were killed because it was considered that their infraction of tribal morality had roused the ire of the gods and brought calamity upon the clan;[4] but I know of no convincing evidence that human sacrifices were offered to ancestors of *ordinary* families, or even to the dynastic spirits of most Bantu tribes, though life was undoubtedly held cheap from one end of Africa to the other.

Furthermore, no investigator has yet discovered a Bantu clan that sacrifices its totem; nor even a clan with a tradition that their forbears had such a usage. The nearest approach to that is a myth which feigns to explain how the Fans[5] came to have the crocodile for their totem: the spirit of their common ancestor, they say, was incarnated in a wonderful crocodile, which, after its many adventures, the first Fans sacrificed and ate. A definite tradition that the Fans used occasionally to sacrifice their totem, even if the custom has now perished, would command greater deference than this wonder-tale; for ontological myths are but naïve attempts to account for puzzling rites or customs that none of the first narrator's neighbours were able to elucidate. In view of the practices of totemistic people in other parts of the world,[6] the fact that the Bantu do not sacrifice their totem is remarkable—the more remarkable in that they do sometimes offer other wild animals to their gods. If the idea of sacrifice does not lurk behind such transactions as killing an animal whose organs are needed to give the final touch of efficacy to the rain-pot mixture,[7]

[1] See p. 215.
[2] See Index: Servitors of the dead.
[3] See pp. 211, 217.
[4] See pp. 212 f.
[5] The Fan, Faṅg, Pañwe, Paamwe, or (French) Pahouin tribes live in the hinterland of the Cameroons-Gaboon coast-line; the myth is twice mentioned by Le Roy, who in RP. 75 cites BBMM. 154 as his authority, and in RP. 208 falls back upon Trilles, *Proverbs, etc.*, without quoting the page.
[6] Cf. *e.g.*, RLAE. 79.
[7] See pp. 206, 211 ff.

placing trophies of the chase in the temple or grove of a god,[1] or smearing ancestral emblems with the blood and chyme of game that has fallen to the clansmen's spears,[2] it is surely explicit in the worship of famous hunter-spirits,[3] and in the rewarding of benevolent divinities with portions of the prey.[4] But though apparently incorrect to say of all Bantu tribes what Junod says of the Thonga,[5] that game is not accepted for their altars, it is beyond all dispute that domestic animals are usually selected for this purpose.

Almost any variety of domestic animal may be offered in sacrifice. The maxim that the gods eat whatever their worshippers eat, contains truth enough to keep it afloat, but must not be interpreted too strictly; for the ritual of magic and religion is intolerant of new-fangled notions, whether of food or anything else, and some tribes fancy that some animals which have long figured among their food-stuffs are, nevertheless, ineligible for sacrifice.

The wild bush pig is said to have been domesticated in North-central and North-west Africa; [6] but these brutes were so intimate with corpses that most Bantu tribes tabooed them, instead of taming them. European pigs, introduced in the sixteenth century by Portuguese and later by other Europeans, have so far failed to find favour with the majority of Bantu communities; the Bateke of French Congo treat them as pets [6] and they are bred in many parts of Western and South-western Congoland, and in some other Bantu districts that have been long exposed to European influence; but I know of no clan that has come to think the pig a fit animal for sacrifice to ancestor-spirits.[7]

Blue rock pigeons have found their way into some tribes, through contact, direct or indirect, with Arabs, Sudanese and Portuguese; but they, too, are a modern innovation and not yet used in sacrifice.

[1] See p. 280 and IPNR. ii. 171, 188.
[2] See pp. 278, 305.
[3] See p. 261 and cf. IPNR. ii. 210.
[4] See pp. 256, 257, 260.
[5] LSAT. ii. 377.
[6] GGC. 192, 197, 616.
[7] Cf. LSAT. ii. 52. Claridge, who was not a careful observer, included pigs among Kongo sacrifices. WBT. 286.

Johnston finds philological evidence that the proto-Bantu had received the domestic fowl (probably from Egypt or Abyssinia) and given it a well-marked generic name, before setting forth from what is now the south-western part of the Anglo-Egyptian Sudan to embark upon their great career of conquering and colonising the southern third of Africa.[1] This would explain the general distribution of the fowl throughout Bantu Africa and its extensive use as a sacrificial victim. It is true that some semi-pastoral tribes, such as the Becwana and Basuto, seldom sacrifice a fowl; but then it is true, too, that all but the indigent among them would disdain to set a fowl before an honoured guest, lest parsimony should imply disparagement.

In North Congoland, peace-making ceremonies "are often accompanied by the sacrifice of a dog (as in Eastern Equatorial Africa)."[2] A friend who lives among the Ndau section of the Mashona informs me that the Changabiyas, to the east of his district, sometimes sacrifice dogs.[3] About every fourth year, at the time of planting their fields, that section of the Manyika which lives under Chihota in the Marandellas district of Mashonaland, used to sacrifice an ox and a dog to the spirit of an ancestor named Muroro, and a heifer to an ancestress called Banyemba. The dog (called Muroro) "was always a black dog, kept in a hut and not permitted to wander about, and specially fattened for the sacrifice." The legend with which the people account for this and attendant ceremonies [4] is evidently of the reinterpretation type; but it is noteworthy that a dog was sacrificed, that it was always black, that it was named after the ancestor to whom it was destined to be sacrificed, and that it was specially fattened for the occasion.

The dog appears to have been the first animal to enter the service of man; its remains have been found in Danish kitchen-middens of the Neolithic phase of culture, and at the antipodes with those of extinct marsupials and the first known human inhabitants of Australia. Perhaps it was first domesticated in Asia; but the fact that the forerunners of the Mediterranean race

---

[1] CSBSL. 22.
[2] GGC. 776.
[3] Dogs are offered to a lake-dwelling spirit in Ashanti. AS. 61.
[4] *Nada: The Southern Rhodesia Native Affairs Dept. Annual*, December, 1924, pp. 11-13.

crossed from Africa to Europe, bringing their dogs with them, shows that it was the friend of Africans at a very early period. Many amulets representing tribal animals, the dog among the rest, are found in the prehistoric remains of Egypt; a tablet in the brick pyramid of Uah·ankh (about 2902-2852 B.C.) represented the king standing with four dogs that bore Libyan names; and in the catacombs of Dendereh, dating from the XVIIIth dynasty (say 1500 B.C.), the preserved carcases of many dogs were found.[1] Strabo (died A.D. 21) mentions the small but fierce dogs that the Ethiopians kept when he visited their city, near the first cataract of the Nile.[2] In the legends of Uganda and Unyoro, the cattle-breeding, civilising, Bahima demigods who came out of the mist, a thousand years ago, and founded dynasties that have not all perished, are pictured, like the Tyrian Heracles (or Melkart), as each companioned by his dog; and the careful rites with which their descendants in Kitara still protect dogs,[3] lend colour to these traditions. It is more than possible, therefore, that the Bantu had discovered the value of the dog before they dispersed from the cradle of their race, not much more than two thousand years ago, and that this accounts for the fawn-coloured dogs of pariah type that are found in every Bantu village, and for the fact that most Bantu describe them by a word of which the root is -bwa. Perhaps it goes far to account, also, for the high value that many of these people attach to dogs. Wealthy men of the Kafir-Zulu tribes were fond of keeping race-oxen and dogs.[4] We have already observed that the Becwana set store by dogs,[5] and shall see later that they have an elaborate magical ritual for training dogs to hunt. Bullock tells us that "dogs were, until recently, considered to be of great value" in Mashonaland; "if one were killed even accidentally—say, by a grass fire—the owner could claim *annual* compensation from the man responsible for the dog's death"; and "a slaughter of dogs is supposed to have a bad effect upon the rainfall." [6] But all this still leaves us won-

[1] RLAE. 169, 185, and Petrie's *History of Egypt*, i. 133-34.
[2] ECSA. 159-61.
[3] KT. 211; see also NYN. 41, 74, 162.
[4] ECSA. 241.
[5] See pp. 229 f.
[6] MLC. 84.

dering why dogs should be offered in sacrifice.[1] Dogs were sacrificed to Hecate, as swine were to Demeter, and one can understand
that a dog might be deemed an appropriate offering to the spirit
of a mighty hunter, since all ancestor-spirits are thought to be
gladdened by things that used to give them pleasure when they
were in the flesh; but we probably verge upon the truth when we
discover that the Wasambara (Pangani R.) used dogs for food,[2]
and that dogs appeal to the Congo palate almost as much as
human flesh.[3]

Cattle and goats, if not sheep, were bred by the proto-Bantu
before they left the Congo-Nile watershed,[4] and still rank as
prime sacrifices to ancestor-spirits. Cattle are not everywhere
available. Dense forests, and tsetse-flies and other pests, render
huge areas unfit for cattle-breeding; and tribes located in such
districts have neither cattle nor the traditions of a cattle-loving
community;[5] but in semi-pastoral tribes, cattle and wealth are
synonymous terms, as they were to Greeks who stamped their
first coins with the head of an ox, and the herdsman is honoured
for his skill. Much of the actual herding is done by the sons and
servants of the family, but even paramount chiefs boast of the
proficiency which they attained by years of apprenticeship to this
craft. Goats and sheep are much more frequently sacrificed to
ancestors of private families; but in these tribes cattle are regarded as the correct offering to spirits of status.

After fowls, goats are the commonest sacrificial victims;[6] but
tribal theories about the relative value of goats and sheep as
piacular offerings are incomprehensibly discordant. "If the ox
plays an important part in the *social life* of the Thonga," says
Junod, "the goat seems to be specially reserved for the sacrifices,
that is to say for *religious usages*";[7] and he proceeds to argue that

[1] See p. 54.
[2] TRML. 277.
[3] GGC. 614. Crawford, *Thinking Black*, 52, 94.
[4] CSBSL. i. 22.
[5] See p. 200.
[6] Cf. Gen. xv. 9, Lev. iii. 12.
[7] Bantu often belittle the gift they bestow upon gods or men, calling an ox a
calf or a goat a kid, probably from a sense of modesty, but the reverse is so
uncommon that it raises a question. When the officiant in LSAT. ii. 368 sacrifices
a hen and calls it an ox in his address to the gods, does he not suggest that the
ox is (or was) the correct victim and that the hen is its surrogate?

"this ritual use authorises us to suppose that, as millet seems to be the oldest cereal, the goat is the most ancient domestic animal amongst the Thonga, and no doubt, amongst all South African Bantu." [1] But he states on the same page that though sheep are scarce among the Thonga, "this animal is connected in a special manner with the chiefs. Its astragalus designates royal personages in the set of divinatory bones. [2] It is used in the national sacrifices, those offered to the chief's ancestors at the capital." That is tantamount to saying that sheep are preferred in the very sacrifices that we should expect to be most conservative in the choice of victim. Ellenberger's editor, whose long residence and official duties among the Basuto have made him familiar with their usages, remarks in a footnote [3] that the Basuto never sacrifice goats, except when specially ordered by the doctor (diviner?), always preferring sheep; while the Zulus, on the contrary, always sacrifice goats and never sheep. Callaway is in accord with this last remark. "The doctor comes and mixes ubulawo," says a Zulu in describing a sacrifice for bringing home the *itongo* of a relative, [4] "and a goat is killed, it being an animal which makes a great noise and cries; but a sheep is not killed, because it is said it will cause the Itongo to be dark; for a sheep is foolish and makes no noise, and therefore it is not usual to sacrifice a sheep to the Itongo. The Itongo has a goat sacrificed to it; when a man pricks it with a needle, it at once makes a great noise; and so they rejoice greatly and say, 'Cry, beast of So-and-so, who did such and such things' (mentioning the things that he did)." [5] Kidd, referring to the slaughter of a sheep in Western Pondoland, writes: [6] "Not a sound had betrayed the suffering of the sheep, and this is why natives usually choose a goat or an ox for a sacrifice to the spirits of their ancestors. Goats and oxen make a noise when they are being killed, and thus attract the notice of the ancestral spirit. A sheep is dumb before her slayers." Although the Becwana are near of kin to the Basuto, their usage in this

---

[1] LSAT. ii. 52.

[2] See also LSAT. ii. 496.

[3] HB. 248.

[4] RSZ. 143.

[5] This is the Bantu way of saying that they break forth into the "praise-song" of the man who is being worshipped.

[6] EK. 42.

matter is that of the Kafir-Zulu tribes. The fount of Native preferences in ritual procedure lies farther back than any native is able to look; but the best guide that ever piloted me along the tortuous trail of Becwana learning, once remarked that although his people explained their disinclination to sacrifice sheep by saying that the sheep is dumb and the groans of a stricken beast indicate its acceptance by the gods, their explanation lacks cogency,[1] because when at times the victim is drenched with a purifying mixture before being slain, its shivers then have the same significance. It has been remarked, however, that the Secwana word for the bellowing of a slaughtered animal is an intensive form of their verb for "to chant a praise-song." The Herero, who live on the other side of the Kalahari Desert, sacrifice sheep, as well as oxen.[2]

A similar discordance of practice is found at the other extremity of Bantu territory. The Wawanga of the Elgon district (Kenya Colony) hold that "sheep may not be offered as a sacrifice;"[3] but the Bakyiga of Kigezi (a Bantu tribe living on the southern part of the Ruwenzori range) sacrificed a sheep when the family of a murdered man consented to accept the weregild.[4] In Kikuyu the victim is always a ram, but it is called *mburi*, a word which (though loosely used in this district as a general term for small stock) really means "goat"; and a he-goat was offered in former times before going to war.[5] In Ukamba, on the other hand, a black bullock is the ideal sacrifice, and a white sheep is next best, but goats are much more commonly used for this purpose.[6] This contrast in custom is conspicuous in the sacrifice for rain: the Kikuyu victim is a ram, preferably black; that of the Akamba is a black goat.[7]

There is something in the Bantu estimation of the sheep that I have never been able to define. I need not repeat Junod's remarks concerning its function in the social economy of the Thonga

[1] If the outcry of the victim were the only determinative factor in the choice, the pig would be an ideal victim; but Zulus, Kafirs and Becwana alike would be shocked at such a suggestion.
[2] See p. 294.
[3] JRAI., 1913, p. 32.
[4] GS. 181.
[5] BBM. 42, 43, 44, 46, 48. It is said that the Akikuyu never sacrifice oxen—an astonishing departure from the general practice of the semi-pastoral tribes.
[6] BBM. 54, 58.
[7] BBM. 60.

tribes. Sheep are not scarce among the Becwana, though goats are much more common; but these tribes have strange notions concerning them. A man or boy must remove all his clothes except the *tshega* (adult's perineal band and boy's equivalent apparel) before entering a sheep-pen;[1] mutton must not be grilled or fried, but cooked with water in a pot; sheep's milk may not be drunk by people who are living the sexual life, but only by boys and girls who have not reached puberty; a woman (between puberty and the menopause) must not enter a sheep-pen or pass through a flock of sheep. Tribesmen who were immersed in the lore of their people assured me that sheep were highly valued in the old days and were constantly "doctored," and that the above prohibitions were born of a fear that the charms of the magician would be counteracted. Sacred sheep were kept by some Becwana tribes in the eighteenth century; one of the various legends concerning the separation of the Bamangwato from the Bakwena, turns upon the straying of some sacred sheep that the Bamangwato erroneously believed the Bakwena to have stolen; but no one that I ever met could explain the sacredness of these sheep, beyond saying that they were a few (less than a dozen, apparently) that were in some way connected with spirits of the dynasty. Similar notions are found in other tribes. Some Kaffir tribes forbid women to use paths by which sheep are wont to pass. The Bakitara hold sheep in high esteem and keep them with the cows.[2] In Uganda "a large sheep was frequently herded with cows, for it was thought that the sheep gave health to the herd, and also kept them from being struck by lightning"; both women and men who stayed at home when the army was in the field, were forbidden to eat mutton; and he who butchered a sheep at any time first stunned it with a blow from behind, when it was not looking, lest it should see him in the act and its ghost should haunt him and afflict him with fatal illness.[3] Mutton is taboo to women of the Bakonjo tribe (eastern slopes of Ruwenzori).[4] Women of the

---

[1] The *tshega* is the most primitive garment worn by Becwana men; they continue to wear it long after adopting European trousers. They have a notion, shared by Makalaka and Mashona (cf. MLC. 86), that if a man wears any other garment while milking the cows, the cows will withhold much of their milk.
[2] KT. 198.
[3] Bg. 288-89, 363, 421, 423.
[4] GS. 140.

Bakyiga of Kigezi (southern part of the same range) must not eat mutton or goat's flesh.[1] Busoga women are forbidden to eat mutton, but not goat's flesh.[2] Each herd of cattle in Ankole is accompanied by a single large sheep, which prevents the cattle from being struck by lightning.[3] Before a man can be accepted as priest among the Batuse of Ruanda, he must accomplish the dangerous exploit of taking a sheep to their god, who keeps a flock of sacred sheep in his mountain fastness.[4]

How can these facts be explained? "In contradistinction to the words for 'goat' (which in the main continue faithful to the original Bantu root *buzi* or *budi*), the terms applied to sheep are legion," writes Johnston. "It would seem as though the sheep—popular and widespread as it is now throughout the Congo basin—came to the Bantu peoples in this region at a later date than the goat, and from several different directions. The goat they obviously possessed before commencing their invasion of the southern half of Africa."[5] This holds good, apparently, of other Bantu regions. The Tumbuka never saw a sheep till the Ngoni brought some from the north;[6] but there was a sheep-clan in Uganda before Kintu came—a thousand years ago.[7] The bringing of sheep from diverse quarters goes far to explain the fact that Bantu sheep are not all of the same breed,[8] nor Bantu words for "sheep" all from the same root.[9]

The sheep played an important part in the religion of many communities. In Carthage, as in Cyprus, Astarte, in one of her types, had originally the form of a sheep, and was herself a sheep.[10] In Egypt the ram was worshipped before any of the human gods. It was associated with Osiris at Mendes, with Atmu at Heliopolis, with Hershefi at Herakleopolis, with Khnumu at Elephantine, and with Amen at Thebes. Amen, the ram-god, came into Egypt from the Oasis of Amon, and became famous at

[1] GS. 165.
[2] GS. 113.
[3] *Handbook of the Uganda Protectorate* (I.D. 1217), pp. 204 and 254.
[4] GS. 188.
[5] GGC. 878.
[6] WPP. 186.
[7] Bg. 154.
[8] GGC. 617-19. See also art. "Sheep" in *Encyclopædia Britannica*.
[9] CSBSL. ii. 373.
[10] RS. 477.

Thebes and in the Negro territory of Cush or Ethiopia.   In the XIIth dynasty his name and worship were extended; and in the course of the next thousand years his priesthood outrivalled the king in wealth and political importance, established dynasties of their own, and made Amen so secure in the regard of his worshippers that even when Osiris regained his former supremacy in Egypt, under Greek influence, the priests of Amen were still able to dominate Ethiopia.   Women performed important functions in the service of Amen, King of the Gods and Lord of the Thrones, especially after the daughter of Ramessu VI became high priestess and divine wife of the god.   In the XXIInd dynasty, the ceremony at the consecration of Egypt to Amen was also "the consecrating of the harem of Amen, and consecrating all the women who are in his city (Thebes), and who act as priestesses since the days of his fathers"; and the queens of Ethiopia were his high priestesses for many centuries.[1]   That mutton was taboo to those who bent the knee to Amen, goes without saying; worshippers of theriomorphic deities were everywhere forbidden to partake of the flesh of the sacrosanct animal, except where the purified and devout ate of the piacular victim as an act of communion.

If Ethiopian sheep stole along, step by step, they would surely bring their Bantu owners some confused glimmer of the nimbus that they wore in their old home.   Philosophy and sacerdotal lore are less easily exported, but purveyors of talismanic articles always advertise their virtues; and legends that had gathered round the sheep in Ethiopia, even though worn threadbare in tardy travel from tribe to tribe, would leave tatters enough to indicate that sheep were somehow royal, soterial, and sacrosanct creatures.   On the other hand, Bantu tribes that received sheep from other regions, where they were nothing more than an economic venture, might well hesitate to offer such timid and helpless newcomers to the spirits of their conservative fathers.

SELECTION OF THE VICTIM

Except when the diviner discovers that some exasperated spirit can be placated only by the slaughter of a specified animal [2]—a

---

[1] RLAE. 12, 52, 98, 99; RS. 302, 431.
[2] See p. 136 and Bs. 249.

discovery often hit upon when previous sacrifices have proved futile, tribal tradition determines the kind, sex, and colour of the sacrificial victim that is proper to each particular occasion; but these traditions vary greatly from tribe to tribe, and we must be content with a few illustrative examples of their diversity.

In some tribes sex is of importance in the selection of a victim; that is to say, there is a demand for some relation between the sex of the victim and that of the divinity, or that of the person to be benefited by the sacrifice; but it is undeniably difficult to discern the principle that underlies these preferences. Thonga sacrificial ritual lays it down that "as a rule there must be opposition between the sex of the victim and that of the one for whom, or to whom, the sacrifice is made. A woman is prayed for by means of a he-goat or cock, and a man by a she-goat or hen. Another course, which is considered still more praiseworthy, is, when sacrificing on behalf of a man, to add a second offering of a cock." [1] What the sex of the victim should be when sacrifice is offered to the spirit of a man for the cure of a sick woman, we are not told. The Wawanga (Elgon district) forbid the offering of female stock at the ancestral stones.[2] Kamba people sacrifice both male and female sheep and goats, and also bulls and bullocks, but never a cow.[3] Zulus offer barren cows as well as oxen to the spirits of their fathers.[4] Wachagga deem it correct to offer any animal of their large or small stock, except a castrated ram,[5] but when ancestors are unresponsive to appeals for the cure of a very sick man, they offer a pregnant cow to Ruwa.[6]

Colour counts in the selection of a victim, as well as sex; and, according to the Bantu characterisation of live stock, colour comprises pattern. In ancient Egyptian religions, "the selection of a sacred individual for worship," from a sacrosanct species, "was fenced round with minute examination. The Apis bull had a white spot of crescent form on the side, or a white triangle on the forehead, a flying vulture patch on the back, a black lump under the tongue. Of course these signs and others were never

[1] LSAT. ii. 381.
[2] JRAI., 1913, p. 32.
[3] BBM. 58.
[4] RSZ. 147, 157, 158.
[5] K. 149-50.
[6] K. 180.

exactly found, but marks approaching them were sought."[1]
Something of the same sort appears in the choice of an animal for
sacrifice to Bantu spirits.   The Wachagga believe that animals
with certain colours and markings are sent into the world by
certain spirits; sheep and goats that are entirely black, white, or
red (which are called *kisuku*) are derived from the first chief who
reigned in the country, and epidemic, famine, drought, or other
general calamity, may be attributed to the anger of dynastic
spirits at having their animals withheld.   Such animals may be
appropriated at any time by the reigning chief, wherever he finds
them in his country, and when the tribe is scourged by widespread
disaster, he ferrets out those that have been negligently or wil-
fully withheld, and seeks to mollify his ancestors by giving them
their due.[2]   Among the Kamba a black goat should be sacrificed
for rain; a red one, however, is occasionally used.   But whatever
the colour of the animal sacrificed, it is very important that it
should be entirely of one colour, and not spotted or parti-
coloured."[3]   "A black bullock is thought to be the most acceptable
and a white sheep comes next, whilst many of the Kamba people
consider a red animal bad for the purpose of sacrifice."[4]   In
Kikuyu, "if the elders go to the sacred fig tree for rain they
sacrifice the usual ram, preferably a black one.   If on the other
hand they pray for rain to cease, the sacrificial ram is preferably a
white one, although a red one may be used."[5]   The Bavenda of
the Northern Transvaal sacrifice black sheep, goats and oxen, but
Mr. Gottschling does not state that they sacrifice no others.[6]
Some Thonga clans sacrifice a black ram without any white spot,
when much in need of rain.[7]   The Becwana are not fastidious
about the colour of victims for ordinary sacrifices, but a black ox
with white belly and flanks (*phachwa*) is a very choice gift to
the dead or the living, and for some offerings to ancestors of the
paramount chief the victim must be wholly black.[8]   In Konde

[1] RLAE. 10.
[2] K. 150, 181.
[3] BBM. 60.
[4] BBM. 58.
[5] BBM. 60.
[6] R. BAAS., 1905, iii. 213.
[7] LSAT. ii. 372.
[8] See pp. 204, 208 f., 263.

tribes (around the north end of Lake Nyasa), when the foretellers
of coming events are apprehensive of an epidemic of smallpox, a
much dreaded disease, "the chief and his subordinates go to the
grave of the ancestors, and there, by night, a black ram is killed.
The lungs and liver are roasted and laid in little heaps on the
grave, each ancestor being named as his portion is laid down, and
prayer is offered." [1] The offering of a black animal at prayers for
rain is widespread; [2] and so is the sacrifice of a white one as a
token that the worshipper's heart is "white" or blameless. An
incident mentioned by Ellenberger may be cited to illustrate this
last remark. [3] The Thoyane debauch is the final fling of the Girls'
Puberty Rites in Basuto and Becwana tribes; under cover of keeping the initiates awake for their last test of endurance, it assumes
the form of an all-night frolic, famed for unflagging revelry and
abundant beef and beer. It is, however, one of those time-
honoured institutions over which the unseen custodians of immemorial custom keep watch and ward; and he who trespasses upon
their preserves must walk with wary feet. Now it was after such
a night, while every man, and most women, of the Boramokhele
clan of Bataung lay wrapped in drunken slumber, that their
Bakwena foes swooped down upon the village and looted its cattle. The loss of these beloved beasts filled the clan with sorrow,
and while they were still chafed with chagrin, Leqhaqha, chief
and therefore priest of the clan, convoked an assembly; saluted
his fathers with a white ox to show that his heart was unstained
by guile, arrogance, or neglect; [4] and decreed that this hapless
but ancient Thoyane function should never again be fulfilled by
his people. The ox was forthwith slaughtered for a commensal
meal, and the clan, visible and invisible, ate together.

That it is thought possible to discover which particular animal
will be acceptable to the gods, apart altogether from its sex or
colour, is shown by the occasional practice of some Kafir tribes. [5]
Before calling an expert in a case of sickness, a relative [6] takes

[1] SRK. 204.
[2] Cf. pp. 208 f., 210, 211 f., 214.
[3] HB. 66.
[4] See pp. 196 f.
[5] LA. 229.
[6] The relative is obviously the sick man's patriarch, for no other person would
take such liberties with the village cattle.

his stand at the door of the patient's hut and invokes his ancestors; and then all the cattle of the village are driven to the door, and the one that urinates first receives a deep prod from an assegai. If the beast bellows with pain, the people know at once that it is the victim which the ancestors need, and it is immediately sacrificed. This rough and ready method of divination is probably grounded in some such notion as that which underlies the omens.

OFFERING THE SACRIFICE

Ritual regulations for the slaughter and disposal of the sacrifice prevail in most tribes, probably in all. In some tribes the victim is consecrated to the spirits before it is slain. Becwana pour a purifying mixture over it.[1] While the beast is standing in the cattle-pen, the head of a Zulu kraal rubs incense again and again over its back as he cries, "All hail, spirits of our tribe," and after remonstrating with the spirits for sending sickness to one of the villagers, lauds them by recounting the mighty deeds they did whilst living.[2] At a communal sacrifice to Engai, a Kikuyu elder lifts up the ram into a standing position on its hind legs, facing the sacred tree,[3] or if the sacrifice is offered for the cessation of drought or epidemic, "an important magician pours medicine into its mouth, and also squirts beer from his own mouth into that of the ram."[4] Akamba lead the sacrificial goat up to the sacred tree, and "stand it on its hind legs before the tree, or, as they say, 'Show' it.[5] But the commoner practice is to consecrate the flesh by laying it (or part of it) upon the grave,[6] or some other place, indoors or outdoors, that is sacred to the spirit.[7] In Thonga tribes, "the priest takes a little of the psanyi mixed with the blood of the victim, puts it to his lips, emits a little saliva, and spits out the whole in making *tsu*, this being the means of consecrating the offering, or, so to say, of forwarding it to the gods."[8]

[1] See pp. 204, 345.
[2] RSZ. 174-75.
[3] BBM. 43, 52.
[4] BBM. 46.
[5] BBM. 55.
[6] See p. 294.
[7] See pp. 97, 274, 279 f.
[8] LSAT. ii. 376.

Most victims are slaughtered as if intended for food. The Akikuyu suffocate a sheep offered to Engai or to ancestors by clasping its muzzle till it becomes insensible, though not quite dead, when they slit its throat with a sacrificial knife and catch its blood in a gourd. They say they do this that its life breath shall not escape, but they choke sheep for the pot also, though oxen intended for food (they never sacrifice them) are stabbed at the back of the neck.[1] Suffocation is the method of sacrificial slaughter that prevails in some Kamba clans,[2] but the Akamba of Kitui cut the throats of sacrificial goats, without previous suffocation.[3] Of sacrifices made by a Chaga family, the Simai[4] is the greatest, "because it appertains to the remotest ancestor, the great-grandfather's grandfather, who is only remembered at rare intervals"; this bull is first stunned, and then its mouth tied and its nose plugged; but a sheep offered at the same time is first stabbed to the heart, and then throttled.[5] We are not told whether this differs from the ordinary Chaga method of butchering. Suffocation is the usual Herero method of butchering, whether for food or for sacrifice, except that beasts despatched to *yondyoza* a departed spirit[6] are stabbed with assegais. Thrusting a spear into the heart of an ox is a common method of butchering for culinary purposes among the semi-pastoral Bantu; and Zulu,[7] Kafir, Thonga, and Becwana tribesmen use it for sacrificial cattle. Kafirs sacrifice goats in the same way, and Thonga, both goats and sheep;[8] but Becwana cut the throats of goats that are offered in sacrifice, and of both goats and sheep that are killed for food. Thonga people often sacrifice fowls by cutting their throats; Kafirs, Zulus and Becwana look askance at such trifling offerings. Kafirs perform gruesome rites at the slaughtering of some of their sacrifices: in certain cases of illness, after a beast offered for the invalid's recovery has received its fatal thrust, a man puts his hand through the gash in its side and tears away

[1] BBM. 43-44, 50.
[2] BBM. 57.
[3] BBM. 55.
[4] The Simai is described as a bull with only one testicle.
[5] K. 141, 145.
[6] See p. 36.
[7] But see pp. 235, 237.
[8] LSAT. ii. 376.

the abdominal aorta and as much fat as he can grasp, the fat being immediately burned on a fire previously prepared in the sick man's hut; and animals slaughtered at some of their tribal gatherings have the front leg and shoulder sliced off, and are then allowed to limp about till they bleed to death, the shoulder being often roasted and eaten and its bones burning among the embers before the victim is quite dead.[1] The only reason that I can suggest for this last-mentioned cruelty is that it would increase the groans of the victim, which are said by some people to call the spirits, and by others to indicate that the spirits are pleased with their gift.[2]

Le Roy's vague and vagrant description of the ritual of sacrifice,[3] erroneously supposes identical procedure in sacrifices for rain, for the cure of the sick, or for the satisfaction of a spirit who has appeared in a dream. According to him, "an animal is slaughtered in the middle of the cattle field in the evening." The word "field," although it occurs nine times in this brief passage, is probably the slip of a translator who knew nothing of Bantu life, but assuming (as we must if we are to make anything of the account) that "field" should be "fold," "pen," "kraal," or some other synonym, one at once begins to wonder whether the tribes that he had in mind used to bury their patriarchs in this enclosure. A black ox was slaughtered in the Place of Assembly at Becwana rain-rites,[4] but then paramount chiefs were buried in the tribal cattle-kraal which was attached to this arena; and if drought persisted after that and the diviner found that it was necessary to approach some former paramount who was buried where the tribe then dwelt, tradition demanded that the bull offered to him should be slaughtered at his grave.[5] This is the prescriptive practice of many tribes.[6] It is probably safe to assert, however, that the majority of Bantu sacrifices are not slaughtered at the grave or at the shrine of the person whose spirit is invoked: that is subject, like much else in sacrificial procedure, to the finding of the diviner. "The bones are first con-

[1] LA. 229.
[2] See pp. 334 f.
[3] RP. 204.
[4] See p. 204.
[5] See pp. 26, 208, 356.
[6] See pp. 216, 217, 246, 247.

.sulted," as Junod says,[1] "and give many indications, *e.g.*, what must be the nature of the offering; to which god it must be consecrated; in which place the act of worship must be performed, (in the hut, behind it, at the door, in the square, in the sacred wood, or in the bush?). When the ceremony takes place over the grave the bones reveal whether the officiant must stand at the head or at the feet."

The disposal of the carcase, though dependent to some extent upon the object which the sacrificer has in view, is largely determined by two regulative principles: the evoked spirit and his ghostly kinsmen [2] feed upon the victim, and the sacrificer and his living relatives share the feast with their unseen guests. From the time when, either before slaughter or after, the victim is consecrated to the gods, every part of it is sacred; but there is no instance that I can discover in which the whole of it is abandoned to the divinities; always the idea of communion between worshipper and divinity seems to pervade the transaction. When a member of a semi-pastoral patriarchal family slaughters a beast for domestic consumption, each of his near relatives has a prescriptive right to some specific portion of the carcase. Tribes differ in their allocation of the several joints; some of my Becwana friends held, for example, that the owner's mother was entitled to the breast of the beast, "because she suckled him at her breast," while others maintained that the animal's loins were the mother's rightful share, "because she carried its owner upon her loins when he was an infant in the carrying-skin." So, also, every tribe has its own fixed rules for apportioning the carcase of a sacrificial victim, nothing being left to chance or the passing whim of a sacrificer. All agree that the gods must have their proper portions before their earthly children presume to taste of the banquet; but there is much variety in the rules of apportionment to divinity and worshippers, as the following citations show.

In a Kikuyu communal sacrifice to Engai, the left half of the carcase, wrapped in its skin, is laid at the foot of the sacred fig-tree, and an elder climbs into the tree and pours the boiled-down fat of the sacrifice over its trunk. The right half of the carcase

[1] LSAT. ii. 364.
[2] See pp. 330 f.

is eaten by the sacrificing elders, but the bones of their portion, with the marrow still in them, are broken and placed at the foot of the tree. If Engai does not send a hyena or a wild cat to eat his half during the night, they know that their sacrifice has been rejected, and there is nothing for it but a fresh attempt to please the divinity with a fatter ram. At the communal sacrifice offered when the maize is just coming up, the bones of the victim are burnt in the fire on which the flesh is roasted, "so that the smoke may ascend into the tree and be pleasing to the deity"; and half the blood is poured at the foot of the tree, while the other half, mixed with tiny pieces of intestinal fat, is placed in the large intestine of the ram, roasted over the sacrificial fire, and eaten by the senior elders. At the communal sacrifice when the crops are ripe, the blood is poured at the foot of the tree, and the contents of the victim's stomach are sprinkled over the ripe crops and the grain receptacles in the granaries.[1] At a sacrifice to Engai witnessed by the author to whom we are indebted for the above information—whether communal or private, he does not say—before the ram was dismembered, "a strip of skin and fat running from the throat of the carcase down to its belly, and including the genitals, was cut off and hung up on a small branch projecting from the tree."[2] At private sacrifices to Engai, the fat of the victim is smeared over the sacrificer's family, flocks and herds, and its skin is presented to the head wife of the elder of the village.[3] A pious son sacrificing a ram at his father's grave, pours its blood and fat upon the grave, and leaves its skin there.[4] It is customary among the Akamba to place at the foot of the sacred tree the ram's blood, one of its kidneys, one testicle, and small pieces of its tongue, ribs, left flank, liver, heart, and every internal organ; and those of Kitui also bury the upper part of its skull, with horns attached, at the foot of this tree.[5]

To the Herero people, "the holiest portion is the left hind-quarter (because the cows are milked on this side), and of this a small piece, which, when appointed for this purpose, is called

[1] BBM. 44-47.
[2] BBM. 52.
[3] BBM. 48-49.
[4] BBM. 50.
[5] BBM. 55, 57. See also my p. 271.

ehango. This *ehango* is not eaten with the rest of the meat, but is taken into the holy house (otyizero), and there kept for several weeks. It is eaten by preference when the Chief is visited by one of his fellow Chiefs." [1]

Thonga tribesmen put aside one limb, or small pieces of each limb, for the gods. [2]

"When the skinning is completed," said one of Callaway's informants, "the owner takes a little blood, and cuts off a portion of the caul, and burns it in a secret place with the blood, which also he places in a secret place; and he takes incense and burns it, having placed the caul on the incense, thinking he is giving the spirits of their people a sweet savour. After that they eat the flesh." [3]

If a sacrifice is offered on behalf of a particular individual, care is taken to link him in some way with the victim. In commending his new-born babe to the care of his family gods, by sacrificing a sheep on its behalf, a Basuto father used to take the fat that covered the victim's entrails and coil it round the child's neck; [4] and when he sacrificed an ox at his daughter's wedding, its gall was sprinkled upon bride and bridegroom, and the fat about its intestines wrapped round their necks and wrists. [5] Or if the sacrifice was for the recovery of a sick man, the victim's epiploön was draped about the patient's neck, some of its gall poured upon his head, and a mixture of its gall and chyme and pounded herbs placed upon the hut in which he was lying. [6]

"The sacrifice of reconciliation," writes Brown of the southern Becwana tribes, [7] "requires two different coloured animals—a black to be sacrificed for the sin, and a white for the purification of the sinner. Whatever animal, ox, goat or sheep is offered, it is the contents of the stomach and the entrails of the slaughtered animal that are used for the purification—the flesh being, of course, the perquisite of the priest-doctor. In the case of an individual the sacrifice is slain while the penitent is on bended

---

[1] *Folk-lore Journal.* Cape Town, May, 1879, p. 43.
[2] LSAT. ii. 376.
[3] RSZ. 141.
[4] HB. 256.
[5] HB. 256.
[6] Bs. 250.
[7] ABN. 155.

knee, having previously made a full confession of all his fault.
Then the priest-doctor takes the blood of the heart and the contents of the paunch, both of which have been taken out of the
sacrifice before the animal is quite dead.   The blood is drunk
by the person on whose behalf the sacrifice is being made while it
is still fresh, then on him is placed the fatty membranes of its
bowels.   When this is done, or while it is being done, the priest-
doctor, or the chief, or the parents, if it is for a child, cries out
that this is a sacrifice of reconciliation, and call upon the name of
the supposed estranged ancestor or god."   Kafirs take the right
forequarter of the victim into the invalid's hut, broil a slice of
it, and give that to the invalid to eat.[1]   Or, to quote Kidd's description,[2] "the blood of the beast has to be carefully caught in a
calabash, and none of it is allowed to fall on the ground.   Then
the fat and bones are burnt, and as the smoke ascends into the
air the doctor addresses the spirits," asking them to remove the
sickness.   "The doctor cuts the animal down the spine, and one
half has to be eaten by the people in public, while the other half
is the portion of the diviner and his relations.   None of the
meat is allowed to be eaten in private, or a charge of sorcery
against the culprit will be sure to follow."   Among the Zulus,
when the bullock is skinned and laid open, "a small piece of the
caul is taken and a sherd, and a live coal, and incense, and they
go with it into the house of the sick man; or into the chief house
of the village where it is said the Amatongo dwell; for it is said
the Itongo lives in the great house.   And the smoke arises in
the house, and there is the odour of the burnt caul.   Then the
sick man pours gall on his body."[3]   In Thonga tribes, "should
the offering have been made on behalf of a particular individual,
the astragalus of the goat, or some parts of the hen are tied to
him and worn for a time on the left or right side of the body; left
if the offering was made to the maternal ancestors, right if it was
made to the paternal gods."[4]   If the maternal uncle of a sick

[1] LA. 229.
[2] EK. 168-69.   His narrative is wanting in logical sequence; the bones could
hardly be burnt before the carcase is quartered, unless he means the bones of the
hoofs; and he omits to mention what is done with the blood that is so carefully
caught in a calabash.
[3] RSZ. 178.
[4] LSAT. ii. 376.

child sacrifices a hen for the youngster's recovery, for example, he "takes a feather from one of the wings, a claw of the left foot and the beak, and after tying them together, attaches them to the left wrist or left ankle of the child, or to his neck, passing the string over the shoulder and under the left arm." [1]   In the sacrifice which Le Roy describes, "the blood is brought in a basket to the house of the person who dreamed of the ancestors or who is sick; it is placed in the hut behind the door. While carrying it they tip it so as to spill a few drops on the ground. [2] All the bones and flesh of the animal are brought into the same hut and placed on little branches." [3]

Every part of a sacrificial victim is supposed to possess occult protective power. The skin of the sheep which is sacrificed when a Mosuto woman becomes pregnant, is made into an apron for her protection against witchcraft; and that of the sacrifice offered when she emerges from her puerperium, is made into a *thari* ("carrying-skin") for the baby. [4] When a Kafir mother leaves her lying-in hut, [5] an ox is sacrificed; and the father pours part of its blood on that portion of the floor of his hut which is marked off as sacred to the *amatongo,* and gives the rest of the blood to be cooked and eaten by his people. At the sacrificial feast, "the father takes the gall-bladder of the slaughtered ox and allows a little of the bile to trickle from it as he touches with it a spot on the baby's right foot; he then raises the gall-bladder up along the right side of the baby's leg and trunk, allowing the gall to trickle on to the child's skin. A little bile is placed on the baby's head and a few drops are inserted into its mouth. The father then puts a few drops of bile on his own right foot, and, if any of his brothers are present, he calls them up and places a few drops of bile also on to their right feet. After this the father cuts the gall-bladder into a long strip and winds it around his right

---

[1] LSAT. ii. 368. The senior maternal uncle is sacrificing priest to the gods of his lineage (the mother's family), and everything is therefore on the left side; if the sacrifice were to the gods of the father's family, the senior paternal uncle would officiate, and everything would be on the right side.

[2] From this we infer that the beast was slaughtered at the grave, or at the shrine, and the blood spilt here and there to lure the spirits thence to the hut where their services were needed.

[3] RP. 204.

[4] HB. 256.

[5] Zulus observe this custom only on the birth of the eldest son.

wrist. All this is done in praise of the *itongo,* and to ensure its good will." "The skin of the sacrificial ox is dried and made into a kaross in which the mother has to carry her baby." A month or so later, "the father cuts off the dried gall-bladder which he had bound round his wrist on the day of the feast, and burns it in the fire. Beer is made and the father throws a little on the ground for the *itongo,* giving the rest to his friends. He then says to the *itongo* and people present, 'To-day I am dedicating the baby to the *itongo.*'"[1] The many gall-bladders that a budding diviner wears in his hair in Zululand are from goats that were sacrificed on his behalf at the onset of the illness that ushered in his uncanny powers.[2] Claridge says:[3] "A sacrifice is offered to take away guilt. It is literally offered in place of the guilty. The blood is the propitiation. It is dripped on the fetishes, smeared on everything of importance used in the ceremony, and put on the lips, temples, and forehead of the principal party as a symbol of mediation. The priest cannot act without blood." Campbell speaks in the same strain:[4] "The Bantu people are very strong in their views about blood sanctification, and I have seen this carried out on many occasions. . . . I remember being present at the inheriting and coronation of Msidi's elder brother. The throats of several goats were cut, and the blood as it spurted warm was caught on a switch of animal tails, and everything animate and inanimate was sprinkled. Not only guns, furniture, stock, etc., but all slaves and wives were duly sanctified by the sprinkling of blood." This use of blood comes home to these writers because it consorts with their peculiar theology; but, as a matter of fact, the fat, gall, and chyme of the victim are credited with like mystic virtue, and hence are sprinkled over people and things whose interests are to be subserved by the sacrifice.[5] The belief that every fragment is so charged with occult power that an unfriendly

---

[1] SC. 26-29.
[2] RSZ. 299.
[3] WBT. 286.
[4] IHB. 249.
[5] See pp. 194, 196, 198, 235, 237 f. and LSAT. ii. 380-81. In sacrifices to departed rulers of Ashanti clans, "the omentum or covering of fat on the lower intestines" is placed on the centre supports of their stools, and allowed to remain after other offerings have been removed. (AS. 97-98.)

magician could make immeasurable mischief by means of it, is the reason given me by my Becwana friends for destroying inedible portions of important sacrifices; [1] and, in all likelihood, it explains the charge of sorcery that would lie against any one who took away the sacrificial flesh for private consumption in the case quoted on a preceding page.

Junod's judgment concerning the use of blood and chyme in the prayer of consecration at Thonga sacrifices, is sound, I think. After inquiring whether these people share the old Jewish notion that the blood contains the life of the animal and may be used "to cover the soul" or the sins of the worshipper, he gives it as his opinion that "there is no sign of there having been a similar conception among the Thonga." "It is true," he adds, "that they prefer to resort to sacrifices with blood in case of misfortune, disease and death, when some idea of guilt may be entertained. The moral element, if it ever existed, has, however, entirely disappeared from the actual horizon of ancestrolatry. On the other hand the use of the *psanyi*, the half digested grass found in the shihlakahla stomach, is easier to explain. It is evidently a means of purification for the family, if not exactly from sin, at least from misfortune: hence their custom of washing their bodies with the green liquid extracted from it, a religious act which to us seems very disgusting, but to the Natives quite clean, their ideas about dung being very different from ours. A large ball of *psanyi* is put on the head of the bride after the dlaya shilongo ceremony in order to remove the dangers of consanguineous marriage, and so help her to have children." [2]

DOMESTIC ANIMALS CONSECRATED TO THE GODS

Before passing from the subject of sacrifice, cognisance should be taken of the fact that living domestic animals may be consecrated or devoted to the divinities. When a Kafir girl is married, her father gives her a special cow, "which is said to belong to the ancestral spirits that preside over the fortunes of her house. In some tribes this cow is called 'The Doer of Good.' The animal is sacred, and its calves are neither killed nor sold so long as the

[1] See pp. 37, 209, 238, and cf. K. 145, HB. 256 and RP. 204.
[2] LSAT. ii. 380-81.

cow is alive. In case of great family trouble, or when the woman is barren, the sacrifice of the cow is said to be specially acceptable to the ancestral spirits. As soon as the child is born, a few hairs are pulled out of the tail of the cow and are made into a small necklace charm, which has to be worn by the baby, to ensure good luck. The baby is then 'washed' in cowdung, a practice supposed to be of great advantage to the child." Over and around the grave in which Dhlambi, chief of a section of the Amaxosa was buried in 1828, a circular cattle-fold was built and stocked with ten oxen and some cows, which, by trampling out all traces of the grave, foiled any alien sorcerers who might plan to work magic with some portion of the chief's corpse. These beasts remained there for about a year, and then mingled with the tribal herds; but, having been devoted to the spirit of the dead chief, they could never be slaughtered, unless, in time of calamity, their invisible owner intimated through the diviner that he required one of them as a sacrifice; and the watchman of the grave, whose person was as sacrosanct as the corpse that he guarded, had the privilege of milking, for his own use, the cows of this little herd.[2]

Junod, speaking of the offering of domestic animals, says:[3] "The victim is generally killed, but there are cases of its being consecrated *living*. If a hen or a goat is given living to the gods (a ring sometimes being attached to the leg of the fowl), it is taboo henceforth to kill it; if it dies, it must not be eaten, and it must also be replaced by another. . . . Another kind of living offering is the *human sacrifice* made in certain sacred woods to obtain rain, but they rarely resort to this. 'The victim wanders about in the forest till he dies,' says Mboza; 'the gods take him.' " In Bechuanaland, "occasionally, though very rarely, in these modern days, one hears of a sacred animal of the bovine species, called *kupe*. This is an animal that has been dedicated to divine honours and, because of that, it is on no account to be killed, but permitted to roam about until natural death claims it. Any ox or cow may thus be set apart, and to him who sets it apart and

---

[1] EK. 201, 216 and SC. 28.

[2] *The Story of My Mission in South-Eastern Africa.* By William Shaw. London: Hamilton, Adams & Co., 1860, pp. 429-30.

[3] LSAT. ii. 377-78.

to those of his family and clan it is looked upon as a god or as belonging to the spirits." [1] It is not unlikely that the few sacred sheep which the Bamangwato kept in the eighteenth century [2] had been devoted to one of their former chiefs. Among the Bahuma of Ankole, "after the purificatory rites are ended the heir usually gives a few cows to the ghost of the deceased, and these cannot be taken away or used for any purpose without the sanction of the ghost, which must be obtained through the priest, who ascertains its wishes by oracle. The milk from the cows is placed daily before the shrine and by the heir near his bed." [3] Similar customs prevail among the Banyoro; and "if a ghost's herd of cattle increases, and the heir wishes to dispose of some of them or to kill any of the bulls, he cannot do so without first summoning the priest, and through him obtaining permission from the ghost to take animals from its herd." [4] In Uganda animals devoted to the ghost roam near the shrine and must not be killed. [5] The Wawanga of Elgon District, Kenya Colony, select a young bull, cut off its ears, and place them at the ancestral stones, or sometimes at Were's stones. "This bull is now a kind of sacred beast, and should any member of the family fall sick, it is brought to him and its urine sprinkled over him, [6] whilst at the same time the ancestral spirits are called upon to cure him. It would be a dire calamity were this beast to be lost or stolen; and the least that could be expected would be that one of the family should fall sick. When the bull is full grown (not

[1] ABN. 92.
[2] See p. 346.
[3] SCA. 88.
[4] SCA. 198-99.
[5] Bg. 286-87.
[6] Does this throw light upon that puzzling prayer that Becwana offer for a man who is dangerously ill? They say, insisting that it is an urgent prayer, though it takes the form of direct statement: *Modimo o rara o tla rothéla mo seatleñ, o tla mhodisa.* Accepting *go rotha* in the dictionary sense of "to rain in occasional large drops," I wanted to translate it, "The father-god will rain in large drops into the hand, and will heal him"—a not unnatural metaphor to be used by people who constantly speak of rain as a symbol of the greatest blessing, and whose word for "heal" in this very sentence is "cool." But *go rotha* is a common word for the micturition of cattle, though it would be indelicate to use it of people, and the many tribesmen whose help I sought would have it that in this sentence it means "micturate," though not one of them could, or would, unravel the tangle for me. The Baila call the first rain of the season Leza's urine.

necessarily immediately it is full grown; sometimes it is not sacrificed till old age), the members of the family assemble and sacrifice it to the ancestral spirits. Its blood is poured out at the Msambue (ancestral stones); the lungs, tongue, hoof of the right foreleg, stomach, liver, windpipe, etc., are boiled together in a pot inside the hut and then cut up. Some of this is placed at the foot of the Msambue and at Were's, and some is thrown out in different directions in the kraal to the ancestral spirits, each of whom is called by name. The remainder" (of the mixture? or of the carcase?) "is given to the women and children to eat." [1] Among the Akamba of Kitui, it sometimes happens that when a man consults a magician about a contemplated marriage, or some other matter, the magician informs him that in his village a cow is in calf and that this cow will bear a bull calf which will be of a certain colour . . . that the calf must not be killed or sold in the ordinary way, as it will be the property of the ancestral spirits (*aiimu*)." If for any special reason this beast has to be killed or disposed of, it and its substitute are thrown and placed touching each other; some hair is taken from the forehead, chest and tail of the original beast and placed upon its substitute; and, after a libation has been offered to the spirits, they are informed of the need for disposing of the original beast and of the provision of a suitable substitute.[2] At the north end of Lake Nyasa, after the body of a Konde cattle-owner has been laid in the grave, "a cow is brought, and made to look into the grave where her late owner lies, her head being forcibly bent if necessary. The cow is now the property of the spirits, and must never be given away or sold out of the family." [3]

LIBATIONS AND OFFERINGS

Libations and offerings are common concomitants of sacrifice. If Engai signifies his acceptance of a communal sacrifice, in the manner set forth on a preceding page,[4] the wife of each elder goes out next morning and puts uncooked bananas and various kinds

[1] JRAI., 1913, p. 32.
[2] BBM. 140-41.
[3] SRK. 294. Cf. 212.
[4] See p. 356.

of grain at the foot of the sacred tree;[1] and dutiful Akamba sons[2] add half a gourd of beer to those portions of the sacrifice that are proper to the spirits of their fathers.[3]

Much more frequently, however, libations and other small gifts are offered to the spirits as a separate act of worship.[4] "Sometimes," says Smith,[5] "people gather round the grave of a departed relation or chief. The chief takes a calabash-cup of beer or water, pours a little upon the grave, and passes it to the next person to him, who does the same. So the cup circulates and each person pours out in turn a little of the contents. This is *kulazha muzhimo* ('to greet the divinity')." In Giryama, at the harvest, "when *pombe* (beer made from sorghum) is brewed, they pour a little liquid at the village gate, at the foot of the consecrated trees, and on the graves, praying that those who will drink may go quietly to sleep after becoming conscientiously intoxicated, without stirring up a quarrel or beating their wives."[6] The Thonga often pour libations to their divinities into the utensil that serves as altar,—"beer, when a beer feast is to take place, wine, when it has been bought at the neighbouring store: palmwine when the big pot . . . has been filled, and the precious drink has been brought to the village."[7] Rum is often used for this purpose on the West Coast; Dr. Bastian (*Loango Expedition*, i. 70) saw them pouring libations of rum on the royal graves at Loangiri, and Capello and Ivens state (*Benguella*, i. 26) that the Bandombe, before drinking spirits, pour a portion on the ground as a libation to Nzambi.[8] As a libation to his divinities, a Chaga chief spits out a little of the liquor he drinks, or a mouthful of specially mixed milk and honey.[9] Pious Becwana perform a rite which they call *go phasha*, or *go phashetsa modimo*, upon rising in the morning and before retiring at night, and ultra-religious folk repeat it at intervals during the day, saying

[1] BBM. 45.
[2] See p. 356.
[3] BBM. 57.
[4] Cf. pp. 180 f, 251 f, 274 and see LSAT. ii. 362 f. and SRK. 196.
[5] IPNR. ii. 178.
[6] RP. 203, citing W. F. Taylor's Giryama Vocabulary, p. 81.
[7] LSAT. ii. 364.
[8] SAAB. 73.
[9] K. 282, 311.

that all times are suitable for prayer; it consists in rinsing the mouth with a mouthful of water and then squirting the water out in a small stream and offering some such prayer as, "My god! Father-god! I am poor though you are here! Have compassion upon me and let me be like other people." *Go phasha* is sometimes tried as a cure for sickness, but in that case an infusion of *mosimama* is used instead of plain water. At the more formal gatherings for worship, described on a preceding page,[1] when the little circular altar that contained the sacred stones was almost filled with beer, which had been poured as a libation to the god, each worshipper sucked up a mouthful of this liquor, blew it out in a thin stream upon the ground around the altar, and forthwith prayed for whatever he wanted.[2] Callaway states that the Zulus make similar use of an infusion of *intelezi*, believing it capable of warding off inimical magic and of sending evil to others.[3] In Mackenzie's account of Konde customs, the squirting of water from the mouth is often mentioned, as either a prelude [4] or supplement [5] to prayer. A somewhat similar ceremonial is reported from Kikuyu.[6]

"None shall appear before me empty" was a precept which Hebrews applied at first to the Feast of Unleavened Bread (Ex. xxiii. 15, and xxxiv. 20) and extended later to their three national feasts (Deut. xvi. 16). The approach of Bantu worshippers to their divinities is governed by the same rule of conduct. To gain the ear of the god, something must be given, even though it be but a little water, or a gentle expectoration of saliva.[7] Grain, milk, porridge, or other food is most frequently offered, liquid nourishment (Kafir-beer, palm-wine, etc.) being always

---

[1] See pp. 274 f.
[2] See, also, pp. 276 f.
[3] RSZ. 434-37.
[4] SRK. 24, 74.
[5] SRK. 43, 117, 202.
[6] The pouring of water as a libation to gods was an ancient Semitic practice (cf. 1 Sam. vii. 6; 2 Sam. xxiii. 16), but modern Islamic rites of ablution preparatory to prayer come nearer to those of the Bantu. After a Muslim has washed his hands three times, with an appropriate invocation, "he rinses his mouth three times, throwing the water into it with his right hand," and repeats another invocation. "Next, with his right hand, he throws water up his nostrils (snuffing it up at the same time), and then blows it out," repeating yet another invocation. (MCME. 70.)
[7] IPNR. ii. 174.

in order; but cloths, beads, hoes, tobacco, hemp, or almost anything that a person used in his earthly life may be offered as an
act of worship to his spirit.[1]   The colour of the offering is often
important: white cloths are unacceptable to certain Mashona
spirits,[2] and the cloth offered to spirits of the Chungu dynasty
(Karonga, Lake Nyasa) at the rain-rites must be black.[3]   What
Claridge says of the Ba-congo,[4] squares with general Bantu behaviour: the worshipper brings "offerings of various kinds—pud-
dings, roots, nuts, wine, and so forth.   It must, however small,
be the best of the farm, the chase, the rivers, or their culinary
art.   If liquid, a little is poured on the ground. If food, portions are thrown to the four quarters."

This custom of throwing food-stuffs for the gods to the four
cardinal points of the compass, is both widespread [5] and perplex-
ing.   "The four children of Horus . . . originally represented
the four supports of heaven, but very soon each was regarded as
the god of one of the four quarters of the earth, and also of that
quarter of the heavens which was above it." [6]   They were called
Mestha, Hāpi, Tuamutef, and Qebhsennuf.   "Mestha was man-

<hr>

[1] A writer to the *Cleveland Leader* (U.S.A.), strolling a little way outside the
city limits, near the head of 18th Street, happened upon the funeral of a Negro
baby, and noticed that the bereaved mother laid two or three infant toys upon the
mound.   "Looking about among the large number of graves of children," he continues, "I observed this practice to be very general.   Some were literally covered
with play-things.   There were nursing-bottles, rattle-boxes, tin horses and wagons,
'Noah's arks,' sets of dishes, marbles, tops, china cups and saucers, slates, picture-
books, in endless number and variety. . . . On many of the larger graves were
pretty vases, statuettes, and other articles suitable to more adult years. . . . Upon
fully half of the small graves, lying or standing, partly buried in the earth, were
medicine-bottles of every size and shape.   Some were nearly full and all contained
more or less of the medicine which had no doubt been used to ward off the visit
of death. . . . One old woman who was loitering about the cemetery said, in
answer to my question: 'I kain't tell ye why, mister, but' dey allers does it.   When
I was a chile, I libed down in ole Virginny, an' it was jes de same dar.   I d'no,
but mebbe dey t'inks de medisun'll he'p de chil'en arter dey's buried, but I don't
see no good in it nohow.' "   Another illustration, surely, of how ritual outlives
belief!   But before pointing the finger of scorn at such survivals, it would be well
to inquire into the origin of our custom of placing wreaths and flowers on the
graves of our loved ones.
[2] MLC. 69.
[3] SRK. 211-12.
[4] WBT. 286.
[5] Cf. RP. 205.
[6] EM. 91.

headed, and represented the south, and protected the stomach and large intestines; Hāpi was dog-headed, and represented the north, and protected the small intestines; Tuamutef was jackal-headed, and represented the east, and protected the lungs and heart; and Qebhsennuf was hawk-headed, and represented the west, and protected the liver and gall-bladder." [1]   In the ceremony of opening the mouth in the Ritual of Embalmment, one of the first acts was the sprinkling of water round about the statue or mummy from four vessels, one for each quarter of the earth; and this was followed by the purification by means of incense, also contained in four vases, one for each of the four quarters of the earth. [2]   After the use of his mouth had been restored to deceased, "four touches of the *ur hekau* instrument on the lips endowed the deceased with the power of uttering the proper words in the proper manner in each of the four quarters of the world." [3]   In the ritual enjoined in the XXXIXth Chapter of the Book of the Dead for the overthrowing of Apep, the words of power that were to be uttered when the figure of Apep was given to the flame had to be said "four times, that is to say, one for each of the gods of the cardinal points." [4]   Did the Bantu practice take its rise in the theogony of Horus, or in some cruder antecedent conceit that the Egyptian hierophants turned to account?

PRAISE AND PRAYER

No Bantu community allows praise to lie idle till the tombstone is ready: it is the key that unlocks the heart of a giver, and the ointment that mollifies the soreness of an affronted elder. Praise-names are in everybody's mouth, and praise-songs, which make up in glory for all they lack in veracity, are chanted upon occasion by the men whom they extol, and by people who curry favour with these heroes.   Tribesmen beg, too, as unblushingly as they flatter, esteeming mendicancy as in strict accord with the manners of polite society, a credit to the beggar and a compliment to the potential almsgiver.   To lavish praise and prayer upon

[1] EM. 89.
[2] EM. 193.
[3] EM. 197.
[4] EM. 80.

the dead falls in with good manners towards the living. I have said "praise *and* prayer"; but the Bantu would say that praise *is* prayer. That constant reiteration of praise-names for God which makes the prayers of Christian converts so uncouth in our ears, is not the mere thoughtless habit that some Europeans fallaciously suppose; it is grounded in the conviction that the utterance of a person's praise-names is enough of itself to win his favourable consideration. If an old chief's praise-song is chanted at the Zulu feast of first-fruits, the continued drought is likely to be broken, or if sung by an army on the march, an unwelcome downpour is likely to cease.[1]

Prayers are dramatised as well as spoken. To a primitive people, action is as natural as speech, and gives vent to overcharged emotions as nothing else can do. Dancing and singing go together. "Songs of war and other sad occasions," said a Mosuto to me, "are the only ones not *sung with the feet*." Like living chiefs, discarnate spirits are often greeted with the clapping of hands and that shrill ululating cry that African women know so well how to utter.[2] People of the old Kongo kingdom chant the virtues of the spirits, to the accompaniment of drum, harp, and trumpet, always concluding their praise with the clapping of hands—an indispensable "Amen."[3] Not only is this practice found in all Bantu communities, but the dramatic element is sometimes much more prominent in prayer. If the drought was severe in Bechuanaland, a man would take his wooden milk-pail, the thong used for tying his cows' legs before milking, his shepherd's crook (*mogolaséló*), and an ox-bone, and cry aloud as he held these over his ancestor's grave: "Have compassion upon us, and let these things still be of use!" Junod defines *mhamba* as a means of entering into communication with the gods. "Hear!" cried Mankhelu, "I will show you the mhamba I made when the enemy rushed on us. I took a bundle of grass[4]

---

[1] RSZ. 409, 413.

[2] The same "quavering cry of joy" that Egyptian women call *zaghâreet*, and which Lane describes (MCME. 168) as a sharp utterance of the voice, accompanied by a quick, tremulous motion of the tongue.

[3] WBT. 281.

[4] It appears from IRM., Oct., 1922, that what Mankhelu used was a rope of twisted grass, which a woman had used for tying up her bundle of firewood, and which happened to be lying on the ground.

like those which women use for binding their sticks, and fever-
ishly separated the blades, saying: 'Let them fail to surround us,
or to entice us!' Then I scattered them in all directions and
said: 'Let them be so dispersed, carried off and destroyed!' And
this is exactly what happened. On my return from the battle I
showed all the army how I had prayed." The old general's
spontaneous appeal to the gods on behalf of his country in its
hour of supreme danger, was, as Junod remarks,[1] a prayer in
action; for it was addressed to the gods of the community; but
its dramatic expression is that which magicians employ in casting
spells with thistledown, images of the victim, etc. That mimetic
magic is not thought incompatible with prayer, appears clearly
in an instance described by Smith.[2] At the bidding of a
"prophet," Baila build one or two prayer-huts and requisition
the services of an expert performer of rain-rites, who puts roots
of the *mutimbavhula* tree into a pot containing water. "Then
holding a small forked stick between the palms of his two hands
he twirls it round in the liquid, producing froth. Some of this
froth he throws in all directions, the idea being that it will collect the clouds. Then another kind of medicine is burnt, and
throws up a dense smoke which is supposed to have some connection with clouds. The ashes are put into a pot of water, so
that the water becomes very black—another reference to black
clouds. Then he once again twirls his stick in this mixture—
to gather the clouds. As the wind brings up clouds, so will the
movement of his *lupusho*. All the time this is going on the
people are singing and invoking the praise-names of Leza."

Verbal prayers are sometimes indirect, often extempore, never
concerned with other than material blessings, and usually chanted
or intoned. Indirect prayers are characteristic of Bantu mentality. After compliments, the suppliant contents himself with
a statement, as if meditating upon his necessities, losses, or embarrassment; or, in prayers for rain, he calls the attention of the
spirits to the perishing cattle, the empty food-bins, the parched
gardens, and the cries of hungry children, and leaves it at that.
It is a subtle form of flattery that tells upon his tribal superiors,
and is therefore carried over into the spiritual domain: there is

[1] LSAT. ii. 382.
[2] IPNR. ii. 209.

no need for a definite request; if the attention of his friends is
called to his distress, they may be trusted to do what they can
to relieve it. He deals with the dead as he deals with the living.
This explains his habit of belittling his sacrificial offering in his
prayer to the spirits—a very different practice from that of tribes
who offer a fowl and call it an ox! No well-bred person in the
tribes that I lived with would receive a pinch of snuff with one
hand, as if the proffered boon were a very little thing; if he
did not stretch out both hands for the snuff, he would support
the extended hand with the other, as though one hand could never
carry such a favour. But if he were the giver, he would politely
disparage the gift that he bestowed; and he does not forget his
manners when approaching the spirits. He underrates the offering which he asks the spirits to accept, calling his ox a goat, or
possibly even a kid, and bemoaning the fact that it is all that he
in his poverty can bestow.

Junod writes of Bantu heathen prayers [1] that "as a rule they
are not a spontaneous expression of religious feeling, but a ritual
act performed only by certain official agents in relation to family
or national circumstances. . . . The more one studies the customs of these semi-primitive and so-called savage tribes, the
more one is struck by the fact that their whole life is conducted
according to fixed laws, leaving very little scope for individual
thought or individual feeling." I concur with the general sense
of this finding as far as it refers to the more ceremonial acts of
devotion; but all my Native friends insisted that their prayers
were extempore, and that they had never heard of set forms of
prayer that people memorised and recited. It must be owned,
however, that extempore prayers made by people of limited vocabulary and slender imagination, whether Christians or heathens,
are mostly mosaics of well-worn phrases, often secondhand,
which vary with the passing mood and predilection of the speaker.
Le Roy was acquainted with prayers of both kinds, he writes: [2]
"With them prayer is essentially a request. Not only do they
pray for favours which are in no way spiritual—to keep away a
present or dreaded evil—but also to satisfy their revenge, to seize
the goods of another without being caught, or to kill an enemy.

[1] IRM., Oct., 1922.
[2] RP. 196.

There are prayers that issue spontaneously from the inspiration of the moment, according to the circumstances and favours asked; and there are prayers consecrated by usage, formulas that the ministers of worship must recite on certain occasions. . . . In the course of the ceremonies, offerings, and sacrifices, there are always prayers indicating the purpose thereof. These prayers are generally cabalistic utterances, obscure words or phrases, allusions difficult for the European mind to grasp, archaisms that come from distant ages whose meaning has been lost but which have been faithfully preserved and are considered the more efficacious the less they are understood." Perhaps it ought to be said, also, that though Bantu prayers are occasionally high-flown utterances, they seldom or never attain to rhapsody or a rhythmic flow of words, except when praise-songs are recited as prayers.

The fact that Bantu prayers are intoned, like Bantu spells, is no warrant for assuming that they are essentially magical. Bantu prayer is a free utterance; but the virtue of a Bantu spell *depends upon* the correct rendering of the syllabic and tone values of the formula. Intonation is not equivalent to magic. "Incantation" and "enchantment" have unfortunately been English synonyms for "magic" ever since Gaelic priests of the early British Church dubbed their pagan opponents *incantatores* and *magi;* but that labour-saving device in theological disputation seems all awry to modern students of Bede's *Ecclesiastical History,* and was never a sign of mental ability, Christian charity, or even just judgment. Surely we have moved a century or two away from that mental attitude! Since the intonation of speeches to unseen powers occurs in primitive tribes, in cultured churches, and in the ugly, unnatural voice that some uncultured speakers reserve for the prayer-meeting and the pulpit, it is safe to assert that it is a universal and persistent tendency from which men everywhere find it hard to break away.

Due decorum must be observed in approaching the spirits, and whatever posture a tribe enjoins on those who pay homage to its living chief is usually required of suppliants at its ancestor-shrines, a more servile bearing being characteristic of those which have long been the sport of tyrants. Some tribes think it becoming for a worshipper to prostrate himself in the dust;[1]

[1] RP. 195.

others show deference by kneeling and touching the temples with earth,[1] or clapping the hands softly; and some sit upon their heels, or pray standing.[2] "When you exult, Leza sees you." So runs the Ila proverb;[3] and tribes that never heard of Leza or this identical adage, whatever their posture when they pray, all agree that humility, not exultancy, beseems the man who reverences the gods.[4]

CONFESSION, MEDITATION, AND FAITH

Le Roy has a page or two on what he regards as the Bantu usage of confession and absolution.[5] Upon the authority of Father Cayzac, missionary at Nairobi, he asserts that the Akikuyu have recourse to remission of sins by confession, followed by absolution and penance. "The ceremony is called *Ko-tahikio* (literally, *to vomit*, sc. sin)." He explains what he means by "sin." "Among the Wa-Kikuyu, the *megiro* (taboos) are countless and the transgression of the least of them constitutes a *sahu*[6] or *sin*." From this we conclude that the "sins" are breaches of taboo; but in the half-dozen examples that he cites five are not breaches of taboo, but unlucky omens that have disquieted the "penitent." As "confessor and penitent" squat in the open air at some deserted corner of the village, the "penitent" mentions, item by item, the things that are preying on his mind, "and at each of the *sahu* which he thus spits out, the patient expectorates." So far, Le Roy's remarks are evidently based upon Father Cay-

---

[1] WBT. 280.

[2] Cf. 258; and notice that in the instance cited it was not thought irreverent to introduce a pun into the prayer. My rendering, "a boy is eluded by things," is a somewhat free translation of *Mosimane o simamélwa ke diló* (lit. "boy is-gone-in-a-straight-course-from by things"). There is no ambiguity in the phrase, but another verb would almost certainly have been chosen were it not for the desire to pun on the word *mosimane*, and the pun is heightened by the use of the archaic form *simamélwa* instead of the usual *siamélwa*. It is still more interesting to note the feeling of a pervasive presence that can be appealed to anywhere in an emergency.

[3] IPNR. ii. 322.

[4] Junod quotes from a Thonga prayer: "Death does not come to him for whom prayer is made; death only comes to him who trusts in his own strength!" (LSAT. ii. 366.) Cf. my pp. 258 f.

[5] RP. 163-65.

[6] Cf. *thahu*, pp. 167, 295.

zac's unquoted testimony; but he continues: " 'These are the sins of the Kikuyus,' adds Father Cayzac, 'or rather some of their sins, for they have hundreds of them, without counting the others, the real ones, which they must also confess at times. They are so persuaded of the evil influence of sin that they even believe a child may suffer for the faults of his parents: thus, two or three days after its birth, every little Kikuyu is the object of a ceremony designed to free it from all moral stains it may have. Should it later on fall sick, its father and mother will go and make confession to obtain its cure. As a preliminary necessity the penitent must be accompanied by a fine sheep that he presents to the "confessor," as a visible sign of his interior repentance. As to this offering there is no compromise, but they are more accommodating on the question of the avowal of sins. When any one finds himself embarrassed in confessing such or such fault, the confessor hands him a little stick: the penitent retires, tells his sin to the stick, which he then hands back to the sorcerer. The latter gladly accepts the avowal as though made to himself. The absolution follows. Turning his eyes successively to the four directions, the confessor pronounces the formula: "God who art in front, remove his sins; God who art behind, God who art to the right, God who art to the left, remove his sins." Then he says in these very words: "I free thee from thy sins, all, those which thou knowest and those which thou knowest not." After this he leans over the penitent, makes a sign of taking the stains out of his heart, and throws them far, far away. When this is done, the good Kikuyu goes away, relieved of his faults . . . and of his sheep.' "

From Father Cayzac's quoted statement we glean three other important particulars: (1) Some of the sins are such as cause embarrassment to the man who has to confess them—which implies that they are moral or ceremonial transgressions rather than unlucky omens; (2) The confession is made to the "sorcerer"— which indicates that the man who is at fault needs either magical protection from impending evil or magical relief from the contamination of taboo-contact; and (3) The sins are removed by gods who are summoned from all directions, as ancestor-spirits often are. It is impossible to understand the inner nature of this rite without putting a dozen other questions to the Akikuyu.

Relying on a note from Father Briault, a missionary in Gabon, Le Roy goes on to say that "a sort of confession exists among the Fans" of the Como estuary of the Gabon. "A Fan who is sick is invited by the feticher to avow his sins so as to obtain his cure. The confession takes place before the men of the village, in the midst of a scene specially prepared. The sins that are to be revealed are usually ritualistic faults, violations of things forbidden or sacred, taboo or 'eki,' sometimes even acts that are insignificant in themselves and that imply no idea of fault. However, grave faults and even crimes have been made known under such circumstances, although this is not generally the case. 'Tell thy sin,' cries the feticher to the sick man. And as soon as the latter has uttered a new accusation, the feticher, in his capacity of penitentiary, cries: *'Kan oshu nki!'* literally, 'May thy fault fly abroad, toward the sea.' And the others present repeat: *'Kan oshu nki!'* 'May it fly abroad!' The ceremony is complicated by purifications, aspersions, and the sacrifice of a hen or goat on which the feticher and the rest of the gathering make a meal at the expense of the sick man. If he does not get better, it is because his confession was not complete." Here again it looks as if the rite were intended to appease ancestor-spirits whose laws have been broken.

Both the husband and the father of a Konde woman (Lake Nyasa) who is in labour will pray, without ceremony, that the child may be born safely; but if labour is protracted, in spite of the usual medicines and prayers, "it is clear that the woman has sinned; and her only hope of life for herself and her child lies in confession. The midwife takes a number of small sticks which she throws on the ground one by one, inviting the suffering woman to name the men with whom she has consorted. Natives assert emphatically that birth becomes easier after confession." [1] The Konde people confess other misdeeds, also. If one of them has smallpox, prayer and confession of sins must be made before medicine is administered. "Any matters against the sick man are now enquired into. It may be a debt or a quarrel, or a charge of impudence in the case of a boy. The sick man is also questioned, and makes his confession, usually of misconduct with girls, who

---

[1] SRK. 43. The Vachopi of Gazaland have a similar belief (see IRM., Oct., 1926, p. 665); so have the Mashona (see MLC. 10-11).

are forbidden to approach the house. If married women are involved, neither they nor their husbands may come near. A prayer for the removal of the disease is now offered by the family representative, at the door of the house in which the patient lies, and the prayer is accompanied by the usual squirting of water from the mouth, which is never omitted." [1]

When sickness occurs in a Becwana tribe, "sacrifice by itself is not considered sufficient. It must be accompanied by confession, and the confession usually, if not always, precedes the sacrifice. In the case of an adult, confession of faults against the dead, of dereliction of duties, of failure to live 'according to custom,' or some other probable cause of calling down the curse of the insulted one, must be made unto the priest-doctor, who has been called upon to find out the cause of the sickness and remove it, or to discover the reason for the sad condition that has befallen the stricken one, and have it changed. In the case of a child on whose behalf the doctor has been called in, confession of possible strife between the parents, or of their failure in any respect towards the recognised customs of their tribe, is required. But if it is a case of prolonged drought, or a murrain among the cattle of the tribe, or an epidemic of sickness that is carrying off the people in large numbers, then public confession on the part of the tribe must be made, confession of all their evil ways which may be hindering the coming of the rain or bringing about the death of cattle and people." [2]

Weeks tells us that the Boloki believe smallpox to be due to witchcraft,[3] and that when it is in the district, apprehensive people go to a witch-doctor and have the witchcraft sucked out. If the person thus operated on gets smallpox, it is due to his own witchcraft, and the only way to ensure recovery is to confess his guilt. If a person not thus operated on gets smallpox, it is because he has bewitched others, and here again his chance of recovery lies in confessing his misdeed. Similar notions of confession have been reported from other Bantu communities, but observers have too often failed to discover what unseen powers are affronted, what deeds these powers resent, and what the

[1] SRK. 283.
[2] ABN. 151.
[3] ACC. 288.

confessant must do to repair his fault and find relief from the consequences of his sin.

We should understand Bantu character better if we could discover why they believe that the confession of some varieties of sin is good for the body and the soul. If Petrie may be trusted in this matter, the ancient Egyptians had no such convictions. "The weakness of the Egyptian in all ages," he writes,[1] "has been his conceit, the very human leaning to exonerate himself, and deny his own faults. This produced the moral code of repudiation of sins. . . . The same self-laudation is familiar in the biographical inscriptions. Every sort of assistance and protection to inferiors is habitually asserted in the tomb-biographies. 'It is my virtue which justifies the honours bestowed on me, and which is clear in the sight of all; has any one ever been seen who is supplicated as I am, on account of the vastness of the property that has come to me, which testifies that I am just in my old age?' So says the great Amenhetep, son of Hepu. It does not seem that the ethics of the priesthood included any idea of humility. The modern Egyptian never acknowledges that he has done wrong; if he suffers for it, that is fate. He always feels that by asserting his innocence he justifies himself. The sense of wrong-doing, of sin, is foreign to his nature, as it is to all Mediterranean folk; it belongs to the Semite and the Indian. The Egyptian realises and approves righteousness in every age; but he thinks little of its omission, that is merely a negative and not a positive evil."

I have often wondered whether meditation plays any part in a tribesman's worship. Aged Becwana, finding it pleasant to admonish their juniors without straining after originality, are wont to fall back on the following trite remarks: "Keep a firm grip upon yourselves! The hills to which I am bound have come into view; I can see the verdure along the watercourse, and even the overhanging branches of the *modubu* trees." It is a metaphor of approach to the home of a tribe, with its stream for household supply and its hills for refuge in sudden attack. Time after time, jaded with their journey and drawing near to such a settlement, they have seen first the adjacent hills, then the ver-

[1] RLAE. 66.

dure of the riverside, and at last the trees that overhang the watercourse, and have hailed with satisfaction the long-looked-for abode of men, where friends would greet them or loved ones welcome them back to their habitations.   Such a metaphor for death and the beyond could hardly have become hackneyed among people who did not look upon impending death with some complacency.   I should protest against the proposition that contemplation and introspection are characteristic of Bantu mentality, and if there are tribesmen who practise habitual, confidential intercourse with the unseen, or who regard meditation as an act of worship, I have failed to meet them in the flesh or in literature; but many of my Bantu friends assured me that the future life is often in the quiet thought of people who are no longer young, and that those who are stricken in years think much of the divine forbears with whom, ere long, they will foregather.

Faith stands in another category: faith is insisted on.   All Bantu would accept St. Paul's definition of faith as "the confidence of what we hope for, the conviction of what we do not see," and would affirm, moreover, that without faith it is impossible to please the gods.   "Absolute faith in the virtue of the fetish is indispensable to the receiving of its aid," says Rowley; [1] "to doubt its potency is to lose the benefit of its power.   So say the fetish-men.   For instance,—on one occasion a party of natives, before crossing a river on a stormy day, bought of a wizard a fetish against accidents.   The canoe was upset, nevertheless, and some of the party were drowned.   The survivors went to the wizard and upbraided him with being the cause of the death of their friends, inasmuch as without the protection of the fetish they would not have attempted to cross the river, and he had encouraged them to make the passage by selling them a charm which was valueless.   He listened patiently to their reproaches, then questioned them as to their doings, and having gained from their accounts what he sought for, informed them that the misfortune was caused by the incredulity of the steersman, who tried to sound the river with his paddle in order to discover whether they were in shallow water.   This action indicated mistrust of the gregree, and so the power of the spell was

[1] RA. 173.

broken." Rowley's use of the terms "wizard," "fetish," "gre-gree" and "spell," would seem to indicate that he has taken his illustration from the sphere of magic, pure and simple; but these loose terms came readily to the pen in the days when Rowley wrote, and it is just possible that the "wizard" was really priest of a spirit that dwelt in the river, and that the fetish was some sacred object, though the probability is that the wizard was wriggling out of his quandary by throwing dust in the eyes of his ignorant clients. It is doubtful whether faith is essential to the potency of a "charm" or a "spell," properly so-called; and much clearer exemplifications of its necessity in the worship of ancestor-spirits are obtainable. For instance, in intercession for the recovery of the sick, no good ensues and no medicine avails till the invalid definitely makes the sacrifice an act of his own will. Were anxious friends to sacrifice one of his animals, omitting no detail pertaining to the rite, anointing his body even with the sacrificial bile and fat, it would profit him nothing, unless it were done at his desire. This principle pervades all their acts of worship.

CHAPTER V

ANCESTOR-WORSHIP AND CHRISTIANITY

BEFORE proceeding to study other phases of Bantu religion, it is convenient to inquire into the influence of ancestor-worship upon its votaries and the extent to which it may be interpreted as a preparation for Christianity—subjects which deserve more attention than they have hitherto received. Here let me interpose two remarks: (1) The grip of a religion upon its devotees can never be measured by what we deem its reasonableness: no people are more devoted to cult than those of the Stone Age were, and no cults cruder than theirs, but man's pathetic willingness to sacrifice reason to distorted images of the divine is not peculiar to any age or race. (2) Our higher interpretation of the more primitive religions needs no justification, for everybody knows that blossoms have a deeper meaning for botanists than for children who love them.

INFLUENCE OF ANCESTOR-WORSHIP UPON ITS VOTARIES

Smith is of opinion [1] that, "while perhaps the direct influence over the individual may be small, it is certain that ancestor-worship has considerable effect socially, especially as a binding force, and therefore indirectly it must have considerable influence over the individual, in ways difficult to define, perhaps, but none the less real." Wilson is more explicit. "This belief," he writes, after describing the veneration of relics of parents in West Coast tribes [2]—"This belief, however much of superstition it involves, exerts a very powerful influence upon the social character of the people. It establishes a bond of affection between the parent and child much stronger than could be expected among a people wholly given up to heathenism. It teaches the child to look up

[1] RLR. 48.
[2] WA. 394.

to the parent not only as its earthly protector, but as a friend in the spirit-land. It strengthens the bonds of filial affection, and keeps up a lively impression of a future state of being. The living prize the aid of the dead, and it is not uncommon to send messages to them by some one who is on the point of dying; and so greatly is this kind of aid prized by the living, that I have known an aged mother to avoid the presence of her sons, lest she should, by some secret means, be despatched prematurely to the spirit world, for the double purpose of easing them of the burden of taking care of her, and securing for themselves more effective aid than she could render in this world."

ANCESTOR-WORSHIP, THE SOURCE OF BANTU ETHICS

The first thing to be noticed in studying the influence of ancestor-worship upon its votaries, is that this religion is the basis of Bantu ethics. Wilson's last remark about the aged mother is not at all at variance with this assertion. Although the moral code of the Bantu is so unlike ours that we often fail to treat it with justice, we are all agreed that these people have a fundamental idea of right and wrong. Of course, there are individuals among them in whom this sense of obligation seems to have greatly deteriorated. "Sometimes," as Le Roy says,[1] "a lack of moral sense is met with that quite disconcerts us: it may be a calm and ferocious egoism, or deep conceit, perfect treachery, real and deliberate cruelty, or a shameless want of pity for the weak, the sick, the useless, the abandoned." No one disputes that fact; but though we have all met bandy-legged individuals, none of us have ever come upon a bandy-legged tribe, and Le Roy's judgment of the moral sense of the race is trustworthy. "Beyond any doubt," says this writer,[2] "our Blacks have a morality whose basis is fundamentally just the same as that acknowledged by the conscience of the whole human species, whatever race, country, or period of development may be considered. The soul of the primitive is made like our soul: between the two types there is not the slightest essential difference. Only the applications of morality differ." That Arbousset's Basuto were acquainted with

[1] RP. 160.
[2] RP. 168.

upbraidings of conscience and associated it with the diaphragm appears clearly in Makoniane's interpretation of the rites by which he had been purified from taboo-contact.[1]

Not only do Bantu and European applications of morality differ, but those of one Bantu clan differ from those of another. For example, all clans condemn incest and destroy its fruit as an abomination; but incest depends on relationship, which is traced through mothers alone in matrilineal clans, and through fathers alone in clans that have passed on to the patrilineal system, the other parent being practically ignored in each case. It follows, therefore, that those whom one clan considers too closely related to marry would be thought eligible, perhaps desirable, spouses if they belonged to another. There is even a further complication: some clans are in process of passing from mother-right to father-right, and those that have well-nigh completed the process retain vestiges of more antiquated matrilineal method. Let me illustrate what I have in mind by quoting a tag that I often heard among patrilineal Bakwena: *"Ñwana oa ga rrañwané, ntsaea, kgomo di boele sakeñ!"* ("Marry me, son of my father's younger brother, that the bride-price cattle may return to their kraal.") Exogamous, matrilineal clans do not regard these two people as relatives, save in the unlikely case of their mothers happening to be of the same lineage; under father-right they are what we should call first-cousins, but the patrilineal Bakwena retain enough of the old matrilineal conception of life to make such a union desirable. What is moral in one clan may be immoral in another, for morality is the discipline of custom.

It is not uncommon to hear natives assert that the Ten Commandments were known to their tribes before Christianity came to them, and if they are allowed to define the terms used, they can make a good case for this claim. Where the moral sanctions of tribal life have not broken down under stress of superficial contact with European civilisation, the danger of taking the name of a god in vain is generally acknowledged; reverence for parents and those in authority is commonly inculcated, and disobedience punished; self-control is cultivated; men of probity are respected; brotherliness, courtesy, and hospitality are common

[1] NET. 396-99.

virtues; a high respect for property prevails; mercy is highly esteemed and justice praised; murder, witchcraft, stealing, adultery, bearing false witness against one's neighbour, hatred, and arrogance are all condemned; and there is such a sense of family responsibility that orphans and destitute people are provided for. All this may be truly said; but it would mislead an English reader who interpreted the terms in the only sense with which he was familiar; for the Bantu idea of the relation of the individual to the community is radically different from ours. Nothing is easier than to traverse each of the above admissions with scathing criticism. Dread of the magical consequences of uttering a divine name has far more to do with the prohibition than what we should call reverence for the divine; brotherliness is not incompatible with the conviction that there is no such thing as social equality among men, and that the heir to a family headship is vastly superior to all other sons of his father, even those born before him and those of greater probity and ability. It is true that, unless disaster befalls the community, the orphan and the destitute are kept from starvation; but then they are always worth their keep and add greatly to the glory of the head of the establishment. Bearing false witness against one's neighbour is regarded as very wrong; but "neighbour" is defined in terms of political propinquity and members of alien tribes may be traduced, deceived and exploited without compunction, so far as is consonant with the safety of one's own social group. Adultery is reprehensible; but adultery means sexual relation with another man's wife without the other man's consent; if the woman's husband has consented, there is nothing more to be said. That the Bantu have a keen sense of justice, however peculiar its exemplification may be, is evidenced by their submission, without rancour or recrimination, to punishment for faults which they have been shown to have committed, and their lively resentment against what they deem unjust treatment; [1] and yet justice is overlaid with venality and favouritism in many a chief's court and outsiders are fair game for loyal tribesmen. To sum it all up in a sentence, African ethics is as thoroughly African as is African language: there are elements in both that one admires, and

[1] Cf. RP. 138.

neither of them can satisfy the requirements of Europe. The basal sense of right and wrong which is found in every Bantu tribe is the same as ours, being evidently universal and innate; but the application of morality depends upon local conceptions of life, and theirs are very different from ours. What I want to emphasise, however, is the fact that there is an African morality; and that this morality, such as it is, has saved the people from greater degradation than that which has been their lot, and is all grounded in ancestor-worship.

The readiness with which good people jump at a wrong conclusion on this question is regrettable. One of my missionary correspondents cited many instances of the care with which Kafirs remove what they consider defilement, and yet he asserted, when criticising the native idea of sin, that sin with the "red Kafir" is only greediness and witchcraft! Another, after affirming that adultery was punished by death in Zulu and Kafir tribes, declared that the native feels sin only as the conviction is begotten of the Holy Ghost, meaning, apparently, not that the conviction of sin is begotten, in heathens and Christians alike, by a divine spirit of wholesomeness which broods over humanity, but that among natives of Africa it is found only as a post-conversion experience of those who have accepted Christianity. Missionaries know that the Bantu conception of sin is largely ceremonial and most curiously juristic, and some of them forget that holiness in its rudimentary form is an external and negative thing, that sin, among backward races, is always first legal, ceremonial, and fearfully entangled with its strange antecedents of taboo, and that a true ethical sense is gradually developed through the social bearings of wrong-doing. In Europe morality is related consciously or unconsciously to the brotherhood of man, even by those who are unfaithful to it; but the earnestness that expends itself so lavishly on pilgrimage and sacrifice everywhere in India is for the most part a desire to escape the penalty of ceremonial offences, not a moral sense of guilt, and much of the morality demanded from Hebrews when the nineteenth chapter of Leviticus was written was what we should call regard for custom rather than ethical integrity. Primitive morality consisted in conformity to custom, and the connection of "morals" with *mores* and "ethics" with *ethos* is an abiding testimony to the fact that our more highly developed ethical theories have grown out of this germ.[1]

It is not surprising, therefore, that the only path to an understanding of Bantu moral sanctions traverses at the outset that great phrase, "law and custom." In Bantu tribes which have not yielded to military despotism, there is no equivalent of statutory law, unless it be occasional orders on comparatively important subjects, issued by a chief in the name of his tribe after discussion in Civil Assembly. "Law" is customary law: the regulative idea which is supposed to have been transmitted unchanged from the founders of the community. "Customs" are practical embodiments of "law," which emanated from the same source and have been endowed with peculiar validity by centuries of effectual use. Every phase of an individual's activity is controlled by a common sense of obligation to "law and custom"— a notion so embryonic that it has not yet been differentiated into legal, ceremonial, and ethical vetoes. Indeed, "individual" is hardly the right word; for what we term an individual is regarded by the Bantu as a kind of political zoöid, or unit of the tribal organism, whose functions must all be subordinated to the normative idea of tribal life. It follows, therefore, that wrongdoing, whether trivial or enormous, whether what we should call legal, ceremonial, or ethical, is always, upon last analysis, sin; because it is an offence against divinities who are thought to be dispensers of fertility, victory, and all the blessings of tribal life, and vigilant vindicators of the rules of conduct which they ordained.

Le Roy asserts [2] that the natives of Loango regard incest, marriage between near relatives, adultery with the wife of the king, moral disorders between young people who have not yet passed through the ceremonies of initiation, and like misdeeds, as "offences against God," for which not only the guilty person but the whole community is considered responsible and held to reparation; and that they regard other offences as offences against man, for which the guilty person alone is responsible, or, in his default, all members, though they are free to turn against him.

[1] See Moore's *Birth of Religion*, p. 64.
[2] RP. 162-63.

This writer's record of Bantu life is too valuable to be neglected, though his cavalier manner of castigating philosophic round-heads for daring to look on life through their own eyes is likely to offend a student's good taste and cause him to lose patience with the book; but some of his conclusions are vitiated by a Garden of Eden theory that the religion of the primitives, as he miscalls them, consists of fragments of a primitive revelation that suffered, I suppose, as all such mechanical devices must suffer, for want of an infallible record and an infallible interpreter,—a theory which blinds him to the fact that God builds the thoughts and aspirations of men, as well as their bodies, by an evolutionary process, and which causes him to credit the Bantu with more knowledge of the Supreme Being than can be justly deduced from the evidence of his pages or those of other writers. The Bantu do believe that certain breaches of ancestral law and custom expose the whole community to the wrath of spirits of the dynasty, who are both gods of fertility and unsleeping guardians of "law and custom," and that certain other offences are visited mainly, if not exclusively, upon the offender and his accomplices; but they do not distinguish between offences against God (or the gods) and offences against man.

The truth is that Bantu ancestor-worshippers do not bring God into the problem of morality at all, for they think he stands aloof from that section of humanity which is still in the flesh.[1] Pindar's phrase, "one is the race of gods and men," goes to the heart of their belief, though they never heard of Pindar or his well-turned phrases. Their gods are the mighty spirits of their fathers, and they know them well. As during their earthly career, so now, these divine persons are neither puritans nor martinets, do not bother about peccadilloes, and can occasionally be hoodwinked over little things; but there is a limit to their good nature, and they are always severe upon any violation of laws and customs which were established "in the beginning" for the well-being of the community, whether it be killing a neighbour, eating of the new crops before the Ceremony of Firstfruits, or contact with that which is ceremonially unclean. Although

---

[1] See chaps. vii and viii (Volume II) for a review of the evidence concerning Bantu belief in a Supreme Being and confusion of certain High Gods with the Supreme.

among clansmen no act that a man can perform is ever referred to any principle of ethics as such, it is demanded that every deed shall be in conformity with religious usage, for their gods are rewarders of righteousness and avengers of iniquity, and seldom slow in executing judgment. If by "divinity" you mean God, then you may say correctly that among the Bantu duty is not related to divinity; but if by "divinity" you mean that which they regard as divine, nothing could be farther from the truth. If you find your moral sanctions in the attributes of a transcendent God, you may truthfully state that the religion of the Bantu is non-moral; but if you mean that their every-day deeds are not related to their worship, then your statement cannot be justified. It is true that they look upon morality as the discipline of custom —conformity to the ideal if not the conduct of the majority, and upon sin as fundamentally the self-assertion of the individual against the community; but then it is true, too, that they think of custom as emanating from the gods and always vindicated by its divine authors and custodians.

The relation of morality to religion in the early stages of human history is an interesting subject for speculative enquiry. Nothing in the world, neither the eternal hills, as we call them, nor the mental outlook of a vegetative people, is proof against change. However slow the process, subtle modifications of thought are inevitable even in the most conservative societies. If a clan does not move forward or backward, it still moves in some direction or other; and Le Roy's unfortunate phrase, "Religion of the Primitives," must not tempt us to assume that the dominant notions of Bantu society are unchanged survivals of a primitive stage that communities now in the van of civilisation once passed through. But in so far as the historic connection between morality and religion can be inferred from existing Bantu practice and belief, the probability is that morality and religion were twin-sisters from the time of ancestor-worship, and that the passion for morality ran *pari passu* with the depth of the religious experience.

BANTU WORDS FOR "SIN"

Inasmuch as words for "sin" imply valuation, it is reasonable to suppose that a complete and accurate exposition of the essential meaning of all such Bantu terms would reveal the fundamental idea that lies behind the expression; and if experts in some two hundred Bantu vernaculars would investigate and make known the common terms for "sin" in their respective localities, comparative philologists could compare and correct their separate statements, and furnish students of Bantu theology with valuable guidance. Although the usage of a single language-area can never warrant a final judgment on this question, it is permissible, I think, to illustrate my point by quoting the Secwana words for "sin," with which I have long been familiar.

In Secwana, *sebe* is often used as the equivalent of "sin," though some of these tribesmen insisted that *sebe* is specially suggestive of adultery—perhaps because that is the commonest of all their sins.[1] The stem of the word is *-be,* and other words from this stem indicate that its essential meaning is "bad." *Bobe* means "badly." *Metse mabe* is not "dirty water," but "bad water"; and *eo o bopelompe* is not a man of filthy imagination, but a man who sets himself up above everybody else,—the most objectionable man in a native community. This idea can be traced, I think, through all words from this stem, and if the stem is to be translated, it must be by some term denoting that which is "objectionable" or "offensive." *Go leoha,* the common verb for "to sin," appears to be a fair equivalent for "to transgress"; but it does not of necessity carry a moral content, for "to sing out of tune" is *go leoha.* It denotes the introduction of a disorderly, discordant, disturbing element into the community. *Go senya* means "to spoil," and, strange to say, it carries the same ambiguity as the English verb. *Molato,* generally translated "fault," is related to the verb *go lata;* but it is hard to say whether the noun comes from the active or passive form of the verb, and, therefore, whether it suggests something that has to be fol-

[1] Ellenberger, referring to the Basuto, who are closely related to the Becwana, says (HB. 291): "The word *sebe* (sin) was seldom used except in connection with sexual irregularities; and if these could be hidden or successfully denied, they were not considered sin." The latter remark will receive more attention presently; the former is sufficiently characteristic of Bantu morality to attract the attention of observers in far distant parts of the country. Mackenzie, for instance, using the capital "G" in God to indicate his belief that the Konde of North Nyasa pray to the Supreme Being, pens the following sentence (SRK. 182): "Of the many sins which bring the wrath of God and the spirits on the community, the most important are widespread sexual sin, and neglect of sacrifices."

lowed up or something that dogs one's steps. Nowadays it is the common word for "debt," but natives say that that use of the word came in with the European trader and his credit system. Now, all these words suggest offences against "law and custom," breaks in the harmony of communal life, objectionable elements introduced by the individual, acts which have to be corrected. And *mokgwa*, "custom," is the ultimate standard of judgment for all who are charged with such offences.

FUTURE PUNISHMENT

Those who believe that the dread of future punishment evokes the great moral imperatives sometimes argue that the *practical* effect of Bantu religion upon the worshipper is doubtful, because he lacks this dread and is concerned only with what happens in this present life. Whether this dread does really impart much moral fibre to character, we cannot stay to consider, being here concerned only with Bantu beliefs; but, notwithstanding the undoubted and common opinion of tribesmen that material rewards and punishments are meted out from the spirit-world with but little delay, piety making the crop heavier and the calves lustier, and impiety meeting with speedy vengeance, it is nevertheless true, so they think, that those who sin grievously in this life are greatly punished hereafter. "When men who have lived selfish and cruel lives die," writes Fraser of the Tumbuka,[1] "their spirits get a poor welcome in the nether world. The others meet them with scorn, slap their faces, and dance about them in derision. But beyond this lack of welcome I have never heard of any belief in rewards or punishments in the hereafter life." Bantu eschatology is not without this belief, however, although Fraser does not happen to have found it among the Tumbuka. We have already had evidence of its existence among tribes of the Upper and Lower Congo,[2] and when we study Bantu demonology [3] we shall find that spirits of witches, suicides, and all malefactors who are denied full mortuary rites, are doomed to become earthbound spirits, wandering in waste

[1] WPP. 126.
[2] See pp. 57 f., 62.
[3] See Volume II.

places, cold, hungry, and outlawed from the society of men and gods. Tribesmen are not given to theorising about the experience that awaits them beyond the grave; but it is not unusual to hear a chief say, in objecting to some course of action that is proposed to him, "How shall I meet my father (or grandfather) if I do that!" Such a phrase presupposes an unpleasant experience in the spirit-world for one who has wasted his patrimony, broken up his tribe, or sacrificed the domain that his ancestors won. I have heard natives declare, indeed, that the thought of meeting their ancestors in the other world keeps them from committing what they think the grosser sins of murder and witchcraft.

WEAKNESS OF BANTU ETHICS

It is unreasonable to complain, as travellers and residents in Bantu Africa sometimes do, that the habit of mind which induces us to make good a promise is imperfectly developed among these people, and that, in traditional tale and historic narrative alike, acts of flagrant perfidy are mentioned without blame and sometimes with approbation. That criticism applies with equal pertinence to every section of humanity in the earlier stages of its civilisation. Nor can we justly censure their failure to discover a universal and fundamental righteousness that ought to be the basis of every transaction. Our own communities, which ripened much earlier into civilisation, so far from recognising the existence of absolute right and wrong, still call that right in war which is wrong in peace, and justify themselves by asserting that self-preservation is the first law of a nation's life—an undemonstrable hypothesis which has consecrated innumerable barbarities besides that on Calvary. In Europe this axiom of a tribalism which we have not quite outgrown, has fortunately been modified for centuries past, by altruistic considerations; but when we find it dominating a Bantu society, without check or compensation, we take it amiss and charge them with having a double standard of morality—one for their dealings with each other, and another for their dealings with the rest of the world. This charge, however regrettable the Pharisaic spirit with which it is sometimes laid, can be substantiated without difficulty. Tribesmen who are not kindly and helpful in their dealings with their own folk are held in derision; but undiluted Bantu morality cares little for the character of a tribesman's treatment of outsiders, unless it is likely to involve him or his group in trouble, and nothing but inability prevents a group from securing ease, opulence, or glory, either in this world or the next, at the expense of other communities. Looking upon disease as an inimical spirit that invades any one with whom it comes in contact, tribesmen never scruple to conjure their ailments into some suitable article and then place the article where a passing stranger is likely to pick up both it and its unseen guest. The Konde sacrifice a black ram to their ancestors and beseech them to ward off a threatened epidemic of smallpox: "Ye fathers, look upon us in mercy," they pray. "Drive away from us this plague, lest our children die, and none be left in the land. Send it to the Basango or the Basafwa, but save us. Pray to God for us. Hear, O God, the words of those we have named. And go to the west, O God, or to the Basango." [1] That is the sentiment of tribalism, "Save us; to hell with all the rest!" However terribly the history of Africa has been disfigured by cattle-lifting, slave-raiding, and the slaughter of servitors for the dead, it is still more terrible that such deeds have been done, time out of mind, in the name of the highest loyalties that the doers knew. This ambiguous morality, so callous to the suffering of people outside the group, is attributable to the lack of divine examples of moral excellence to whom tribesmen can turn for spiritual help in the mending of life. It is not that the people are deaf or disobedient to the imperative call for man's recognition of the divine: it is that their divinities are men whose earthly careers were stained with passions and defects that they never discovered the secret of mastering, and with intense clannishness of interest and sympathy. They who worship little tin gods always grow little tin souls.

To this same cause most of the weaknesses of Bantu ethics may be traced. Personality and morality are interdependent ideas, and the Bantu conception of personality is poor. In worship, appeal is made to the pity, the kinship, the sense of fitness,

---

[1] SRK. 204. Is "God" in the last two sentences a mistranslation for "god"? It is difficult to harmonise such petitions to the Supreme Being with the sacrifice of a black ram to ancestors, with the first four sentences in the prayer, and with the practice of many other Bantu tribes. See also my footnote on p. 388.

and the self-interest of divine forbears, but never to their affection for their offspring; and love is the most personal quality of personality. So, also, in civil relationships; that which has done most to retard the advancement of Bantu communities in civilisation is their persistent preference for people of standard pattern, without inconvenient angles, and their resultant readiness to hound down all who show capacity, initiative, enterprise, or other characteristic of strong personality. It is the same in morality; since the family is the unit of society and the individual has scarcely emerged, some attention is paid to the cultivation of domestic and civil virtues upon which family and clan depend, but private and personal virtues are neglected. Morality, according to Bantu thinking, is a matter of conduct, not of inward purity and integrity. It winks at character, and is content with external conformity to ancestral demands. Its exemplars never failed to insist upon the complete subservience of individuals to the group, and the duty of each to protect the community from the sacrilege of those who would improve upon the ancient and perfect pattern of life to which their fathers clung; but they never caught a glimpse of what we should call personal righteousness. Although fortified with spirit-sanctions, Bantu morality has never become aware of a Spirit who reads the heart and cares most for what is found in the sacred and secret recesses of the human soul.

Now, the notion that morality is a matter of conduct rather than character leads to queer conclusions. Ellenberger, writing of Basuto manners before the tides of European life swept over them, acknowledges that the people had good qualities, but goes on to say: [1] "They stole without scruple, and their morals were very lax; they were also jealous and would cheat, lie, and slander without shame. Such crimes were punishable, so they knew quite well, when they committed them, that they were doing evil; but when once convicted and punished for any offence, the memory of it ceased to trouble the offender. It was paid for, wiped out, and his character cleaned. . . . Falsehood and deception were very common, one may say that they were the rule, among the old Basuto; and, to judge by the following prayer of one of

[1] HB. 291.

them, an old man who became a Christian, they were quite alive
to the fact: 'O Lord, we are such liars that even if the tail of
a fish was sticking out of our mouth, we would swear we had not
eaten it.' " In this picture of moral decrepitude, the most striking
feature is not that they who did bad things knew all the while
that they ought to do better (we are too familiar with that), but
the cherished notion that punishment wipes out offence. And
yet, if morality be a matter of conduct and not of character, the
wrongdoer who has paid the just penalty of his misdeed has a
right to claim that he is quits with the world!

Akin to this fundamental feebleness is that strange juristic
sense of sin which marks Bantu mentality, to the amazement of
Europeans. "What they blame," we cry, with some truth and
little discrimination, "is not lying, cheating, nor stealing, but a
clumsiness of operation that leads to detection." Junod has some
wise words on this subject.[1] He suggests that the Bantu idea of
wrong is not that of wrong against God, but of wrong against
society, and that consequently if society does not discover your
fault (i.e., does not feel wronged), you have no fault.[2] If his
word "society" includes the disembodied members of the clan, I
agree with his interpretation; but it is important to remember that
vigilant spirits of the mighty dead may discover and punish transgression of which the sinner's contemporaries are unaware. It is
this latter fact which explains those remarkable confessions that
sometimes supervene upon a public attempt to discover the Achan
in a tribe. Students of ethical theories are sure to be interested
in this juristic conception of sin, but it is very important that
missionaries should understand it. Dissatisfied with the sincerity
of a man who professed penitence and claimed restoration, I was
questioning him rather closely: "Were you penitent at such-and-
such a time?" I asked, mentioning an incident that had come up
in the evidence against him. "No," he replied; "it had not been
found out then." I used the Secwana word for "to be penitent,"
which means, literally, "to whip oneself." Why should he
whip himself for an offence that neither gods nor men had yet
resented!

Missionaries, knowing that converts are sure to take over into

[1] LSAT. ii. 532.
[2] Cf. footnote on my p. 388.

the Christian Church much of the old ethical notion in which they have been nurtured, should be on the alert for external and legalistic conceptions of sin, but if they can look at life from the Native's standpoint, they will not be dismayed when they discover some convert contending obstinately for rigid adherence to the laws of the Church, and, at the same time and without conscious hypocrisy, giving no great care to the purity of his own heart.

To us, the ethical development of the Old Testament is intelligible only in the light of its outcome in the New, just as blossoms find their explanation in ripe fruits that seem to be formed after another pattern; and yet Hebrew prophets who tried to lift the tribalistic morality of their people a little nearer to the ideal that Jesus eventually embodied and expressed, had to pay the price that is always exacted from those who insist upon something truer than the thought of the common herd; and even the teaching of Jesus, despite the preparatory work which the prophets had done and the winsomeness of his temper and method, was a grievous offence to his contemporaries. Now, the Bantu have been accustomed for ages to regard aliens as lawful prey, mendacity and deception as cunning and desirable weapons of defence against designing strangers, revenge as a sacred duty of kinship, and chastity as unmanly weakness. That high appreciation of moral qualities, hatred of wrong-doing, and profound sense of sin which mark the utterances of some Hebrew prophets, belongs to an ethical altitude that the Bantu have not yet reached; and the Master's demand—that "neighbour" shall be interpreted in terms of human need, the law of the second mile substituted for the *lex talionis,* and every thought, even those that never find visible or audible expression, swayed by truthfulness, disinterestedness, singleness of purpose, and sexual purity—rises above their conception of duty like an alpine peak, clad in glittering, unclimbable ice. Nevertheless Bantu conceptions and applications of morality are allied to those of Early Israel.

This latter point deserves to be emphasised. It is not only in the conception of conscience, with its appeal to a fundamental sense of right and wrong, truth and falsehood, that the tokens of kinship appear: there is the same confusion between ceremonial and moral transgression; the same demand that the relationship of fellow-tribesmen shall be marked by justice, honest dealing, neighbourly regard, respect for the rights of others, refusal to injure another by word or deed, and sympathy with the unfortunate and oppressed; the same exclusion of aliens from all such privileges; and the same inability to measure up to the accepted standard. Probably the Bantu have something of this sort in mind when they assert that their fathers always knew the Ten Commandments.[1]

Stress must be laid, also, upon the fact that in both systems there is a sense of obligation to the unseen. In Bantu ethics, as in that of Early Israel, a man's duties towards his fellows are never referred to any principle of ethics as such, but are justified by religious sanctions; and if it be urged that the religion of the Bantu is related to a multitude of intermediate and intercessory divinities rather than to one great tribal god, it must also be conceded that the tribal god of Early Israel was very human in his characteristics, and that it was out of a care for his "laws and statutes," not very different from that of the Bantu, that there grew a lofty conception of a personal and righteous God who cares for all mankind and reads every heart, and an enthusiasm for personal righteousness which differentiates the best Old Testament saints from those of every other ancient nation. Many centuries passed over the tribes of Israel while the hard old root of legal and ceremonial righteousness was slowly producing growths that were to blossom into personal purity of heart, and missionaries, although they bring to the tribes of Africa a much more magnificent conception of God than ever gladdened the vision of an Old Testament saint, must not be impatient for ideal ethical results. Such growths cannot be hurried; but they may be retarded by a clumsy presentation of our message, unless we link its ethical contents to those moral obligations that the Bantu readily recognise.

[1] See p. 382.

SIGNIFICANCE OF BANTU RELIGIOUS RITES

So much for Bantu ethics; now let us turn to the religious rites of these people and see what points of attachment for the Christian message may be discovered there. It must be confessed that the ritualist is no more likely than the tailor to capture Europe by copying Bantu patterns, and that few of these rites are worth preserving even for Bantu use; but we shall find in them, I think, a permanent element, an underlying idea that prepares the way for Christianity and is too valuable to be wasted.

What is the meaning of the sacrifices, offerings and libations that are so conspicuous in Bantu worship? Precision in the ritual with which these gifts are offered to divinities, is everywhere insisted on, notwithstanding differences of detail in different communities; but no precise Bantu theory of sacrifice is anywhere to be found, and no authoritative interpretation of the rites. Every clan has its Master of Ceremonies, who insists on meticulous accuracy in the performance of ritual; but no clan has a professional hierophant to expound the sacred mysteries, or even a zealous amateur who has bestowed coherent thinking upon the meaning of them. It is essential that the rites should be correctly rendered, not that they should win the allegiance of the worshippers' reasoning powers. That rites have a much longer life than the theories that give them birth, is abundantly shown in the history of human behaviour; and this magical conception of the function of ritual helps us to understand the secret of their superior longevity. But what we have to notice particularly here, is the fact that for want of authoritative explanation of the ritual, European observers tend to read it in the light of their own preconceptions of what sacrifice and offering ought to mean, and therefore to confuse the issue.

It is questionable, for instance, whether the piacular idea bulks so large in Bantu sacrifices, offerings and libations as some Europeans would have us believe. Tribesmen who are conscious of having wronged a friend, often seek reconciliation, not by apologising for what they have done, but by offering the offended person a present; and no one disputes the fact that they sometimes carry over this practice into their religious life, seeking the restoration of relations with an offended divinity by means of a gift. When impending or actual disaster indicates that they have failed in obedience or been remiss in their offerings, feverish efforts are made to discover what the offence is and who is the individual offender, and in all probability the sacrifice which follows upon these discoveries is intended to expiate the sin. There are certainly individuals, too, more niggardly or more procrastinating than their fellows, who seldom bring gifts to the gods till they feel the sting of the divine whips. In the sacrifice offered at the wedding of a daughter, on the other hand, there is no apparent thought of transgression; that ritual is designed to commend the girl to the protection of her family gods as she goes forth from her old home into a new life that is fraught, as all new things are, with possibilities of disaster. So, also, no hint of transgression is found in the sacrifice that precedes the despatch of an army for battle, which is designed to secure the help of the gods in the coming fight. Upon the whole, the gods are not difficult to get on with, and the worshippers are not greatly troubled with a sense of sinfulness, even in their acceptation of the term. It is probably true to say that most sacrifices and nearly all offerings and libations are brought by people who are not aware that they have sinned, and that we err in reading our motives into their actions.

Ancestor-spirits need food, which it is the duty of their heirs to provide. The liquid nourishment that they were never known to refuse when dwelling as elders in this drouthy upper world, always pleases them; but any food which they relished in the days of their flesh is acceptable still, and, although a small quantity is enough for a ghost,[1] they like to receive their portions frequently and with customary marks of respect. They need clothing, too, and ornaments, and other things. Any gift that would have gladdened them when they moved as men among men, gladdens them now, and they are affronted if their little personal belongings are not set apart for their exclusive use. The gods need the worshippers, and the worshippers need the gods. When their children are neglectful, the gods call by dream, divination or calamity for beef and beer; and when the gods are remiss in providing for the safety and prosperity of their de-

[1] Cf. SCD. 137-38.

scendants, they are warned that to let their children perish is to lack worshippers and the sustenance which worshippers alone bring.[1]

That the *quid pro quo* consideration should enter to some extent into such transactions, appears inevitable; but, it must be remembered that although Bantu delight in driving a hard bargain with others, they do not import the commercial spirit into their dealings with their own elders. So long as their old social and economic notions are not riddled with ideas from Europe, every member of a family or a clan deems it his simple duty to lay the proceeds of labour, trade or chase at his elder's feet, not as a tax which must be paid, but as a contribution which he is proud to make to the welfare of his group. Those of us who were brought up in poor homes and have not forgotten the joy with which we laid our boyish earnings in our mothers' laps, know quite well how they feel. Now, it is with that same feeling that Bantu worshippers bring offerings to elders who have passed over into the world of shades. Call it homage if you like, only do not eliminate the personal element from the term; but you mislead yourself and others when you liken it to a tax levied by some power that is too strong to be resisted and too impersonal to be revered. What such worshippers want is not to expiate an offence, nor to bribe their gods, but to maintain filial relations with forbears who are less palpable than they used to be, but none the less real.

Another notion attributed to Bantu worshippers by European observers, is that of the substitution of a sacrificial victim for a sinner who has forfeited his life by his transgression. As far as I can ascertain, this notion is absolutely foreign to Bantu thought. Indeed, it is extremely doubtful whether they intend to offer the life of the victim at all, notwithstanding the significance of "the sprinkled blood" to those of them who have been inoculated with another theology: the animal is slaughtered to provide a feast for gods and men, and its death seems to carry no other significance.

The best clue to the Bantu meaning of sacrifice is provided by the regulative principles of their practice. With them, sacrifice

[1] Cf. RSZ. 144-46, and see my p. 242.

is never an individual affair. If a single worshipper were to offer a sacrifice on his own behalf, or if a group of worshippers were to sacrifice to a single ancestor without inviting his divine associates to come with him to the feast, it would be abhorrent to the Bantu sense of fitness.[1] Neither gods nor men eat lonely morsels; the gods come to the feast in kindred groups, and the worshippers do likewise. This rule holds even when the sacrifice is intended to placate some particular divinity, or to secure the good offices of the gods for some afflicted person. In the former case the offended divinity is specially invoked, and in the latter, the invalid is specially associated with the gift; but the feast is always a family affair for the living and the dead. For the proper offering of a sacrifice, the offerers must invite the gods by name, show them by some act that the victim is given with a good grace, and share the flesh with their divine guests,[2] all of which goes to show that sacrifice aims at renewing and strengthening, or, in some cases, restoring, the bond between worshippers and divinities by means of a common meal; not an ordinary meal, but one in which you honour your guests by slaughtering for them the best animal in your herds. That is to say, the fundamental meaning of sacrifice, according to Bantu thinking, is that of sacramental communion with the gods.

Between sacrifice, offering and libation there is no essential difference; they all express desire for good relations with the gods. Most piously minded people salute the gods frequently by giving them a little of the food or drink of which they are about to partake, by squirting out the water with which they have rinsed their mouths in the morning, or by spitting upon the ground.[3] Such petty gifts cost the worshipper nothing, and are probably of no intrinsic value to the spirits (though these diminutive shades are popularly supposed to be refreshed with very small quantities of nourishment): they are but customary marks of attention, good feeling, and respect. Rich and learned men have been known to hoard trifles that their little children gave them with a like intent, and it is conceivable that even gods may thus be gladdened with worthless things. Saliva, interpreted as the Bantu interpret it,

[1] See pp. 330 f.
[2] See, e.g., pp. 352, 355, 357, 359.
[3] See pp. 184, 373 f.

is the most significant of all these offerings; for, since personality inheres in secretions,[1] spitting is almost like giving a part of oneself, and is accordingly used in conferring a blessing[2] and in consecrating a sacrifice.[3]

Similar points of contact for the Christian message may be found in other Bantu religious rites. Their ceremonies for the consecration of an army before battle, barbarous, though they be, and steeped in a magical conception of life, are due to the conviction that morale counts as well as machinery—that victory depends upon being right with the unseen world as well as upon big battalions. Their wedding ceremony, though as crude as their conception of sex, is nevertheless an acknowledgment that marriage ought to be carefully and formally arranged, and contracted in the presence of the gods. Their custom of rinsing the mouth before uttering the morning invocation, though rooted in an archaic notion of personality, is nevertheless a rudimentary suggestion that prayer, to be worth while, must issue from clean lips. And their ceremony for relating the newly born to the clan and its divinities, is in reality an embryonic baptismal rite.

CHRISTIANITY AND THE TRAPPINGS OF PAGANISM

When Christianity was grappling with the paganism of Europe, its attitude towards the dominant deities was unmistakable: it fought them tooth and nail; called upon its converts to break with the gods; and, as that call woke the hero that slumbers in most souls till the trumpet sounds, applauded thousands who preferred torture and death to the disloyalty of worshipping discredited divinities. This was a clear-cut issue. But for untold centuries before these arrogant gods were born—from the Stone Age, if not before—our forefathers had been accustomed to an animistic religion, whose ritual aimed at the magical reproduction of things that contribute to bodily comfort; and every seasonal festivity that came like a burst of sunshine into the cheerless routine of their daily drudgery, seeded their imagination afresh with this notion of life. Now that which is oldest in the affec-

[1] See chap. ix. in Volume II.
[2] See p. 185.
[3] Cf. LSAT. ii. 380 and RLR. 44.

tions of a people is as hard to eradicate as weeds from a cornfield or brushwood from a cocoa-plantation. None but the thoughtful and the learned—always a small minority—ever dreamed that these familiar, and sometimes pretty, customs contained elements that clashed with the Christian conception of life. The maypole dance, the bonfire at midsummer or at the Anglo-Saxon New Year (now called Martinmas), the yule-log, the Christmas-tree, the decoration of the home with evergreens, the mistletoe-bough, the wassail-bowl of hot spiced ale and toasted apples, the drinking of healths, the lighting of ceremonial candles, the yule-tide mummers, the soul-cakes or hallow-buns, the taboo on May marriages, the sprinkling of a bride with wheat (now rice), the telling of the bees, the spitting upon a handsel coin, the lucky stones and crooked sixpences, the throwing back of luck-money to a vendor, the rowan-tree to ward off witches, the first-foots who are still welcomed in countries as far apart as Scotland and Macedonia—these, and scores of other extant folk-customs, are animistic survivals; many of them, indeed, are bits of wreckage from vegetation-sacraments and the worship of the dead, that came, after the storm had done its work, to adorn the ritual of neighbourly intercourse and jollity, as figure-heads of old ships garnish a beachcomber's garden. People unaccustomed to research are not quick to investigate the pedigree of customs which they accepted without question in the plastic period of youth; such customs are cherished for old sake's sake by thousands of guileless Christians.

Furthermore, from the time of Constantine, though the Church grew more and more comprehensive, its relation to pagan notions, rites, symbols, conventions, and edifices, was not consistently governed by a clear-cut policy. Then as now, the Church vacillated between two ideals. Some of its propagandists looked askance at this world, being persuaded that it is at best a place of discipline for the life to come, and were concerned only in preparing for another and a better. Others, of kindlier temper, finding their fellowship with man and nature deepened and sweetened by their religion, never thought shame to mingle delight in earthly things with joy in the eternal. Appurtenances of paganism were judged with severity or with leniency according as they could be made subservient to the ideal that happened to prevail. Some were ruthlessly repressed; some were judiciously ignored; and some were arrayed in white garments, given new names, and often new meanings, and taken over into institutional Christianity. To repress is, however, not the same thing as to destroy: the only sure way of destroying an objectionable custom is to put something better in its place. Some of the rites that were driven into holes and corners gathered the glamour of illicitness, instead of loosening their hold upon the imagination of credulous and conservative peasants, and emerged centuries after in the ghastly ritual of mediæval witchcraft; while some of those that were ignored lost their religious significance and could linger only among the diversions of frolicsome folk.

Soon after his consecration as Archbishop of the English nation, Augustine sent messengers to Pope Gregory requesting guidance on certain points of procedure, some of which are of interest to modern missionaries. The messengers set out from Rome on their return journey in June, 601, accompanied by reinforcements for the new mission to the English, and bearing letters from the Pope, one of which was addressed to Ædilberct, king of Kent, commending him for his reception of the Christian faith, and urging him to be zealous for the conversion of his people, to "suppress the worship of idols" and "overthrow the buildings of their temples." While the deputation was on its way home, Gregory thought better of his advice to Ædilberct, and sent another letter after the Abbot Mellitus, one of the new appointees, in which the following passage occurs: "When the omnipotent God shall have brought you to that most reverend man, our brother Bishop Augustine, tell him what I have a long time thought over with myself, concerning the case of the English— to wit, that the temples of the idols in that nation ought not to be destroyed; but let the idols themselves that are in them be destroyed. Let water be consecrated and sprinkled in the same temples; let altars be constructed, relics deposited: because if these temples are well built, they ought of necessity to be converted from the worship of devils to the service of the true God, that whilst this nation sees that its temples are not destroyed, it may put away error from its heart, and acknowledging and adoring the true God, may the more familiarly meet at its accustomed places. And because they are wont to kill many oxen in sacrifice to devils, some solemnity ought to be specially appointed for them on this account, as, that on the day of the dedication, or on the birthdays of holy martyrs whose relics are there deposited, they may make for themselves huts of the boughs of trees, around the same churches which have been altered from temples, and celebrate a solemnity with religious feasting, and no longer immolate animals to the devil, but kill them for their own eating, to the praise of God, and return thanks for their satiety to the Giver of all things; to the end that, whilst some outward joys are reserved for them, they may more easily be able to consent to inward joys. For, without doubt, it is impossible to cut off all things at once from their rough minds, because also he who endeavours to ascend to the highest place, is elevated by steps or paces and not by leaps. So, indeed, the Lord made Himself known to the Israelitish people, in Egypt, but reserved to them in His own service, the use of the sacrifices which they were wont to offer to the devil, and charged them to immolate animals in His sacrifice, to the end that, changing their hearts, they might let go one thing with respect to the sacrifice and retain another; so that although they were the same animals as they were wont to offer, yet being immolated to God and not to idols, they were no longer the same sacrifices. These things therefore it is necessary that you, well-beloved, should yourself say to the aforesaid brother, that he at present being there placed, may consider how he ought to order all things." [1]

The method of approach which Gregory enjoined upon his missionaries to pagan England is not without interest to those who now face the same problems in other lands. The temples mentioned are obviously those of gods that came with the Romans; for the courts of the more ancient gods of the land were held at megalithic tombs that could not be converted into Christian churches. Many pagan temples had been ruined in spite of their beauty and durability; but a few had been consecrated for Christian worship, that of Isis at Philæ, for instance, in A.D. 577.[2] On the first of May, A.D. 610, less than ten years after Gregory wrote to Mellitus, the Pantheon in Rome was dedicated to all Christian martyrs. The Church had always held martyrs

[1] Bede's *Ecclesiastical History*, bk. i., chap. xxx. (Gidley's trans.).
[2] RLAE. 33, 60.

in high honour, and often worshipped round their tombs, feeling, in the old pagan way, nearer to the dead when closer to their bones—the heart is a hiding-place for exiles from the brain. Worth shades off easily into worship, as history and etymology show: when the Church began in A.D. 549 to dedicate churches to martyrs as patron saints of altars in which their relics were enshrined, she took no great leap from her prescriptive practice to reach a notion with which people accustomed to tutelary divinities were quite at home. Holy water, to which Gregory alludes, had long played a great part in the magico-religious rites of paganism all over the world. At the entrance to an Egyptian temple in Roman times, there was a supply of purifying water, a portion of which was released on putting a coin into a box; [1] and holy water stoups (without the penny-in-the-slot attachment) found their way into the vestibules of Christian churches at an early date. The burning of incense, too, a common feature of worship in Babylonia, Assyria, Egypt, and other pagan lands, passed readily into Christian worship, because converts associated its fragrance with their devoutest hours and inferred from the Old Testament that it was acceptable to God. In the same spirit, objects of devotion were interpreted afresh and brought into relation with Christianity: images of the Virgin and Child appealed to parental instinct as strongly as they used to do, only now they were regarded as images of Mary and the Child Jesus, instead of Isis and Horus, Venus and Cupid, Rhea and Zagreus, Semele and Iachhos, Brimo and Brimos, or some other pagan embodiment of the glory of motherhood.

Perhaps the most noteworthy part of Gregory's letter is that which reveals his willingness to have the sacrificial feasts of paganism transformed into parochial picnics to the praise of God and the honour of patron saints who were to oust the faded tutelary divinities. Since pagan festivities were frank and gleeful expressions of bodily enjoyment that lent themselves readily to the unbridling of passions, the Church had formerly met them with uncompromising hostility. In Rome, at the Calends of January, men gave themselves to gluttony and debauchery, tricked out with women's clothes, or animal masks and the hides of cattle—the latter custom, though inherited from magically-

[1] RLAE. 26.

minded worshippers who hallowed their doings by covering themselves with the skins of their sacrifices, having probably lost its ancient meaning and passed into the ritual of revelry. From this particular debauch, the Church had tried to turn away the faithful by going to the other extreme, prescribing the solemn fast and litanies of the Vigil of the Nativity on the first three days of the Roman year. Popular festivities of a like character were common in other parts of Europe, too; and in A.D. 567, only a few years before Gregory wrote to Mellitus, the Council of Tours had decreed that the Roman Church in Gaul should observe the solemn fast of the Circumcision on the first of January. "Our holy fathers of old," said a preacher of this century,[1] "considering that the majority of men on those days became slaves to gluttony and riotous living and raved in drunkenness and impious dancing, determined for the whole world that throughout the Churches a public fast should be proclaimed"; and he admonished his hearers that "he who on the Kalends shows any civility to foolish men who are wantonly sporting, is undoubtedly a partaker of their sin." Gregory had evidently come to the conclusion that something more than prohibition of friskiness is needed for taming a herd of wild horses; and, whatever we may think of his holy water, altars, relics, patron saints, identification of pagan gods with devils, and fantastic exegesis, we gladly confess that he struck a true note of sympathy with rough minds that resist refinement and climbers who can reach higher places only by taking one rung at a time, and that he was right in his contention that an old symbol may be transformed into something new by changing the motive behind it. Whether a particular pagan symbol is worth transforming for Christian use is, of course, another question; to pass upon that, one needs the spirit of Jesus and intimate knowledge of what the symbol stands for in both the mind and the emotions of its pagan users.

The origin of many of the red-letter days of institutional Christianity is shrouded in obscurity. Instead of being deliberately devised, they seem to have grown up spontaneously in local Christian communities and then spread to other centres,

[1] The sermon, often ascribed to St. Augustine of Hippo, is thought to have been composed in the sixth century. See p. 170 of *Christmas in Ritual and Tradition* by Clement A. Miles (Fisher Unwin, 1912).

never being authoritatively approved by ecclesiastical authorities till they had won their way into the favour of many. History has a trick of presenting us with an accomplished fact and leaving us to bring our theories and sanctions into line with actual experience.

From the outset, the first day of the week was regarded by the Church, not as a substitute for the Jewish sabbath or tabooday (that notion came into vogue at the beginning of the fourth century), but as *the* day for joyful worship and the "breaking of bread"—"the Lord's Day," as it was christened. For at least a century or two before Christ was born, Sunday (we give pagan names to all the days in the week) had been sacred to Mithra, a Persian light-god, who, in his triumphal progress through Babylonia, Armenia, Asia Minor, and the Roman world, had been identified successively with Shamash, Helios, and Bel; but, though our name for the day came from Mithraism, the day itself was marked off for Christian worship before the Church was affected by that cult—the most powerful rival that it ever had in the Roman Empire.

Next to nothing is known of the history of the Church for the last thirty years of the first century; but, so far as we can make out, the Church then had no anniversaries that were distinctively its own. Jewish Christians seem to have continued to observe the three great festivals of their nation—Passover, Pentecost, and Tabernacles, each recurring Passover reminding them afresh, we may be sure, of the last scenes in our Lord's earthly life; and so it is likely that Easter was the first anniversary to be Christianised. It was observed in Rome about A.D. 120, and in Asia Minor still earlier if Polycarp traced his observance of it to the Apostle John, as Irenæus seems to say. It was called Pascha before it took from the Saxon Goddess of Dawn the name of her Spring-feast; but even the prolix second-century debate between those who wished it to follow the day of the week and those who preferred a fixed day of the lunar month, leaves us wondering whether it was intended to commemorate the crucifixion, or the resurrection, or the whole group of events that occurred at that Passover.

The Feast of Epiphany appears first, early in the second century, as an unorthodox commemoration of the baptism of Jesus.

Clement of Alexandria, one of the first writers to mention this feast, states that it was observed by the followers of Basilides, who expounded a Gnostic variety of Christianity in that city about A.D. 130. Some of these heretical sects held that God entered into the human Jesus at his baptism, when the Holy Spirit descended upon him, like a dove from the cloven skies, and the voice of the Eternal proclaimed from the heavens, "Thou art my beloved Son; this day have I begotten thee!" That was the day of the incarnation, according to their thinking, the real birthday of the divine in humanity. But their reason for fixing the sixth of January as the date of this event is a riddle that no man can read. Reason seldom takes the lead in such adventures: inclination generally has its fling before reason is called in to justify its doings. In that same city, some two centuries later, the worshippers of Kore the Maiden (an old Greek personification of the fertility of the earth) were wont to celebrate with ancient mystic rites the birth of the World or Æon from their goddess on the night of January 5-6.[1] If Alexandrian sentiment favoured this date for the birthday of the divine, one may conjecture with some serenity of confidence that whimsical arguments, compounded of bold assumptions and childlike faith in symbolical systems of numbers, which were then in vogue, would be enough to satisfy willing minds. Be that as it may, it is fairly clear that the Feast of Epiphany was fixed for the sixth of January by unorthodox Christians; crept gradually into favour with those of more regular belief; and finally won its way into the West. By the end of the fourth century it was firmly established in both East and West, the East regarding it as the anniversary of the baptism of Jesus (as the Armenian Church still does), and the West as that of the adoration of Jesus by the Magi, to accord with their date for celebrating the birth in Bethlehem.

There is less room for doubt about the pagan pedigree of our Christmas. The twenty-fifth of December, the day of the winter solstice according to the Julian Calendar, was kept by the Romans as the birthday of Sol Invictus, the Unconquered Sun. In the first centuries of our era the cult of Mithra had spread

[1] *Christmas in Ritual and Tradition* by Clement A. Miles (London: Fisher Unwin, 1912), p. 20.

like wildfire through the Roman world.   Mithra was a masculine deity who attracted virile and venturesome men.   Numerous
inscriptions and votive offerings "to the Sun, Invincible Mithra"
from officers and soldiers, which have been found where Roman
camps once stood, testify that Mithra was popular with the troops
and absolutely identified with Sol.   So it goes without saying
that the twenty-fifth of December was his birthday.   But though
the cult of Mithra was frankly syncretistic, early Christianity,
with which it had much in common, was exclusive.   Converts
from paganism to Christianity, confident that they alone had the
whole truth, were intolerant of everything that smacked of their
old faith.   Their children and grandchildren, however, like
Christians of the second and third generation in the modern mission field, were not so bitter; they thought it enough to avoid
what was in open conflict with Christianity, and saw no inconsistency in celebrating the birth of the Sun of Righteousness, the
Light of the World, on a day when their pagan neighbours kept
holiday to mark the birth of the Unconquered Sun.   It was a
spontaneous movement, apparently, rather than a deliberate decision of the Church; but by the fourth century Roman Christians
had come to regard the twenty-fifth of December as their festival of the birth in Bethlehem.

Sun-worship was prominent in the Roman Empire during the
second, third and fourth centuries because it was introduced
afresh from the Orient when the old gods were tottering and
men were spiritually forlorn, and because it was patronized by
the Emperors Commodus, Elagabalus, Aurelian, and Julian; but
in Europe it was shorn of its beams at other periods.   It was not
an indigenous religion, like the cult of the dead.   From time immemorial Celtic and Teutonic families had been wont to regale
their home-coming dead with warmth, welcome and food on
New Year's Day, or, as we should say, on New Year's Eve.[1]
These tribes began their year with the advent of winter, but had
the same difficulty that the Bantu have with their lunar calen-

---

[1] Everybody knows that ghosts shun the daylight, and our forefathers with their
old lunar reckoning counted time by nights (witness "sennight," "fortnight,"
"Twelfth Night") and considered that "the evening and the morning were the first
day."   The ecclesiastical day still begins at sundown in the Eastern Church and in
Islam.

dar.[1] The likeliest date for the feast of Samhain, as the Celts called their New Year festival, is the evening preceding our first of November;[2] and the Teutonic year began about the same time.[3] It was a season of feasting and revelry; for flocks and herds had to be reduced to such numbers as could be fed during the winter, and there was an abundance of flesh-food and much salting of beef, mutton and pork. When the family forgathered for this great annual jollification and talked wistfully of those who used to grace the board, unseen presences seemed to hover over the vacant places, and it was easy to give credence to the common belief that this was the one night in the year when the dead revisited their old homes, expecting to find a good fire burning, candles lit, and the table laid for a meal. Filial piety demanded that those who had been loved and lost should not be forgotten; so institutional Christianity provided Lauds for the Dead on the evening of November the first and a solemn requiem mass for the following day, as a more excellent way of caring for departed souls; and even in the present year of grace those who adhere to the Roman usage regard the Feasts of All Souls and All Saints as auspicious opportunities for mitigating, by prayers and alms, the sufferings of souls in purgatory.

Greece and Rome also kept festivals of the dead, though not at this season of the year. *Anthesteria*, important enough to give its name to the Attic month (Feb.-Mar.) in which it occurred, was a festival of All Souls before Dionysos, the wine-god, came south to Athens and draped it with his garlands. *Parentalia* and *Lemuria*, Roman festivals, are mentioned on a previous page.[4] Rites of purification (*februa*) were so lavish at *Parentalia* that the month in which it took place was called *Februarius;* and

[1] See pp. 219 ff.

[2] RAC. 256-58.

[3] Whether it was due to the incompatibility of the lunar year with the solar, or to improvements in agriculture that made it possible to fodder the livestock a little longer, or to the fact that Anglo-Saxons found winter beginning a little later in Britain than in their old German home, our experts cannot discover; but the Anglo-Saxon year seems to have begun a few days later. The English municipal year still begins on the 9th of November; Martinmas (Nov. 11th) is still a Scottish quarter-day; and it is hard to understand the phrase "Martinmas beef" and the rancorous old maxim, "His Martinmas will come as it does to every hog" except upon the assumption that this was the proper time for killing cattle and pigs.

[4] P. 178.

Roman Christians fixed the second of this month as the most suitable date for the anniversary of the Purification of the Virgin Mary. A creed can be intellectually superseded as knowledge expands and reason extends its sway; but paganism is not a creed: it is a habit of mind which is bred (not born) in pagan society, and which insidiously modifies the thinking of people of pagan upbringing long after they have repudiated the religion of their youth. No sacred edifice of paganism was complete without its altar, so altars were introduced into churches, and candles set upon them as ostensible symbols of the Light of the World. Candles were conspicuous at the *Parentalia;* for feasts of the dead all over Europe were coupled with vegetation-sacraments, the lighting of fires and candles, and other magical rites that were thought likely to help the powers of life and growth.[1] In pagan temples everything had to be ceremonially cleansed and consecrated to sacred uses; and the intimate association of Christianity with Judaism made it easy for those who were imbued with formalism to transfer this notion to churches; so candles needed for the service of the altar during the year were purged of secularity at the Feast of the Purification of the Virgin. From the fact that Anglo-Saxons, a thousand years ago, commonly called this day Candle-mass Day, it may be inferred that the purification of the candles touched their imagination more effectively than the purification of the Virgin.

Another word should be said about the Feast of All Saints, or, to give it its Anglo-Saxon name, All Hallows. This feast was · instituted on the first of May, A.D. 610, when the heathen pantheon in Rome was converted into a Christian church and dedicated to All Martyrs, and was not transferred to the first of November till A.D. 834. Now in Rome May was the month of *Lemuria,* and one wonders whether it was a mere coincidence that the Feast of All Martyrs was assigned to the month in which the shades of those who had died before their time were thought to be specially meddlesome.

Much that was heathen before found work in the Church after Christianity came. Even some of the old gods of Northern Europe survived as jailers and myrmidons under the new régime.

---

[1] This implies that the dead had to do with fertility in Europe as well as in Africa. See chap. iii. from p. 202.

The realm of Hel was transformed into a terrible prison-house for unchristian souls, and Odin, slightly changing the name he bore as ruler of tempestuous skies and lashing seas, became "Old Nick," with sinister significance.

Perhaps the influence of paganism is more obvious in public worship than in any other activity. Sacred rites are not mere frills of religion, designed to catch the fancy of the voluptuously minded, as some of us are nothing loth to think. Whether they strike strangers as æsthetic, or uncouth, or natural, or artificial, or magical, to people who habitually use them as means of spiritual exaltation they become winding stairways of imagination up to God. As Prof. George Foot Moore pithily puts it,[1] "There is no religion where man does not do something about it, even if that something be, as in the more advanced Oriental religions, the most concentrated doing nothing"; and people who often do the same "something" or "nothing" must be uncommonly fertile of invention if they do not fall into a habit of doing it in the same way or saying it in the same phrases. I attended a Methodist Class-meeting on one occasion; it was a simple affair, and a means of grace to its members, I am sure; but of ritual there was enough and to spare, albeit of a home-made variety: clothes and faces plainly consecrated to Sunday use; pulpit voices; "experiences" and prayers, all different, but all set in moulds into which they had been poured when they were warm and fluid, and all sprinkled with fine old crusted phrases of eighteenth century vintage; and applause uttered in the tongues of Holy Writ. A stereotyped expression of emotion or belief, that is, ritual, bald, chaste or ornate, becomes second nature to most worshippers, however earnest and sincere; and symbols, postures and phrases that converts from paganism had always associated with their devoutest hours were soon at home in Christian assemblies. No thoughtful and observant student of classical paganism can come with fresh eyes to a Greek, Roman, or Anglican cathedral when some high act of homage is being celebrated without noticing rites and symbols that came from Mithraic, Greek, and Roman shrines, and phrases that are reminiscent of Greek philosophy, Oriental mysticism, or Roman law. Church Fathers in

[1] *Birth and Growth of Religion*, p. 17.

the second century and Roman Catholic priests who went to China, Mexico and Peru in the sixteenth, were bewildered by the similarity between heathen rites and Christian sacraments, and tried to escape through the assumption that the former were counterfeits devised by the Devil for the snaring of souls. It is but fair to remember that in their day the historical method was unknown and the Devil was a very present help in such intellectual troubles; but the clue, or what remains of it, leads in another direction. People who have lived all their lives in the swamps of animistic practice and belief, feel that there is something lacking in the rarefied air of spiritual uplands where God is worshipped without the intervention of hierophant, altar, sacred vestments, or mystic rites. Early in the history of the Church, the Lord's last supper with his disciples, touching and simple in the setting that he gave it, came to be interpreted in the light of the sacrificial worship of Judaism and regarded as the central act of Christian worship; and when the Church became predominantly Gentile this memorial of the great sacrifice was shrouded with cryptic altar-rites, fashioned after the pattern of those sacramental guarantees for this life and the next which were provided by secret guilds attached to most of the pagan religions of the period. To these guilds many who were in search of salvation eagerly resorted, and some found their way afterwards into the Christian Church, bringing with them a tender regard for the elaborate liturgy in which they had found comfort. Old pagan rites and symbols were therefore reinterpreted in accordance with Christianity as it was then understood, and quietly naturalised in the Church. The change was gradual, and so thoroughly in accord with the current tendencies of the time that it provoked no controversy and called forth no ecclesiastical decree.

Our spiritual ancestors appear to have acted on the principle that the world could be made Christian without being painted drab, and that some of the trappings of paganism were too lovely to throw away and good enough to be turned to Christian uses, while others were intrinsically out of harmony with Christianity and had to be discarded. The principle is good enough; though they, with their magical conception of nature, applied it in ways that appal us whose creeds are shorn of excrescences and squared with what is now known of God's method in nature. It is the bounden duty of African missionaries, whose training should have made them familiar with the facts of my last few pages, to consider how much of the accretion that Christianity gathered in its progress through pagan Europe ought to be commended to their converts; and whether these converts, also, may rightly retain some of their own pre-Christian formalities and predilections.

"If in teaching the Africans," says Smith in his valuable chapter on the contribution that Christianity has to make toward the solution of our problems in Africa,[1] "we demand that they shall surrender all that they have hitherto cherished, we are asking them to do what we Europeans have never done. For Christianity of to-day is other than essential Christianity—it is an amalgam of elements drawn from many sources. . . . As Christianity adopted the vocabulary of paganism and spiritualised it, so in consecrating them it also transformed many pagan institutions. If then we insist upon the African taking our institutional Christianity as it stands, and surrendering all his past, what we are really requiring of him is that, in addition to the pure essence of our religion he should take over what it has absorbed from its European environment."

I agree. It should be remembered, however, that the "pure essence of our religion" is never found without some sort of container; or, to put it differently, the incarnation is much more than a historic event: it is a perpetual process. "The pure essence of our religion," as I see it, is the attitude of Jesus towards God, man, and nature, and the consequent sublime temper that made him pre-eminent among men and gives distinction to all who persistently make him their director of spiritual endeavour. But this soul of Christianity must shine forth from ordinary human activities if men are to see the glory of its grace and truth—must embody itself in beliefs, rites, and ecclesiastical, political and commercial institutions. I know how sorely we are tempted to flout institutional Christianity when it flaunts its institutionalism and slurs its Christianity; but, decry it as we may, the fact remains that but for it we should never have had "the essence of our religion" to cheer us, nor even the books that tell us the story of Jesus. I fail to see how Christianity can do much for Africa

[1] GLD. 262.

unless it works through some human institution. The point that we unfortunately overlook, however, is that "the essence of our religion" can dwell, as history abundantly shows, in forms of very varied pattern. Europeans were not obliged to become Asiatics in order that they might become Christian, and Africans can take Christ as the Lord of their lives and institutions without recasting them in a European mould. When Christianity is naturalised in Africa, as it certainly will be, it will be found wearing African bodies as different from European Christian bodies as Black men are from White. To borrow a happy metaphor, "the mollusc must secrete its own shell if it is to live in the midst of a given environment."

Jesus never organised the little fellowship that came under the spell of his spiritual insight and serenity. He treated his followers as friends, taught them to work amicably together in spreading his evangel through the world, and checked their fitful longing for administrative authority and posts of honour. They called him "Master," acknowledging the proficiency of his spiritual leadership, and he accepted the description, little as he cared for titles; but he was careful to explain that his mastership was one, not of dominion and glory, but of service untrammelled by self-regard. He had not the type of mind that invents machinery, or conceives corporations, with executive officials, rank upon rank, each rising in power and prestige according to his nearness to the chief; and when he went to his Father he left neither archetype nor canon for the formation of a universal society of quickened and redeemed souls. So the Church has taken various forms in diverse communities, and will continue to do so. It derived its most distinctive name, ecclesia, from the political assemblies of self-governing Greek cities, and shaped its framework after the pattern of social, religious, and political institutions that were already functioning in lands where it found a home. Even Roman institutions, with that hierarchy of officials that always sprang to life at a touch of the Roman mind, though poles asunder from the Galilean fellowship, profoundly affected the organisation of the Church. It may be said of history, as of nature, that she never copies her own handiwork, but there are certain principles of procedure from which she never seems to depart. When the Church becomes naturalised in the southern third of Africa, it will respond to the change of intellectual climate and modify its organisation according to the genius of Bantu life, in spite of all our plans.

What form that Church will take, no man can tell. Inchoate Bantu political institutions, like those that peep out when a corner of the veil that covers the early history of Europe is lifted for a moment, include rudiments which develop into democracy, oligarchy, or despotism according to conditions. The community always dwarfs the individual, if it does not extinguish him. In clans that have taken despotic pattern, a common clansman risks his head by loosing his tongue; in clans that cling to ancient liberties, he is granted great freedom of speech, especially in their formal assemblies; but he is everywhere deemed a wicked man if he persists in differing from his group. Political groups of every pattern are dominated by local loyalties, but inclined to fissiparous multiplication whenever foiled ambition provokes some blue-blooded child of vanity to figure as queen-bee for a new swarm. The Bantu have no difficulty with the doctrine that religion means service, but, like Hebrew tribesmen, are not at home with the Hindu theory that a man should take the lone trail in search of his own salvation. This saves them from the danger of the self-centred life, but does not lead to tolerance; for tolerance (not supineness) is born of the conviction that each man, being directly responsible to God for his own behaviour, ought to make out the meaning of life for himself and scrap any pet theory, however hoary and respectable, which he finds defective. The Bantu mind, if we read it aright, is not given to speculation; defers readily to what it recognises as law; often fails to distinguish between fact and phantasy; pays homage to negative precepts that curb the human instincts; and cares less for motives than for the scrupulous rendering of religious duties and rites. It assumes that a man's relation to his gods is involved in his relation to the community; that he can no more choose his gods than his parents, though he may enter into amicable relations with others without being disloyal to his own, or supplement their providential care with charms, spells, and other magical contrivances; that secular and religious authority are generally vested by the gods in the same person; and that, though every man should perform minor acts of obeisance for himself, the great rites of religion are profaned if performed by those who are not in the direct line of succession.

Brief descriptions of foreign mentality are a snare; but if all this is correct, and if the Church in Bantu Africa shapes its framework, as the Church in Europe did, according to the political and religious preconceptions of the people, one is tempted to infer that, though its structure may be as democratic as Congregationalism, or as oligarchic as Presbyterianism, or as despotic as the Papacy itself, it is likely to prefer parochial loyalties to catholicity of spirit; to care more for the group than for the individual; to be slow in discovering toleration; to show more zeal for regulations and correctness of behaviour than for the continuous moral development of its members; to confound religion with politics; and to suffer from epidemics of wild exuberant fancy, but not from a tendency to dissipate its energies in wrangling over philosophic formulas. Such an inference would, however, ignore two moral certainties: before the Church has had time to become naturalised in Bantu Africa, the spirit of Christ will have fashioned afresh the ideals which determine the thought and action of many tribesmen; and the surging currents of Western civilisation that are now rousing the tribes from the mental lethargy of age-long seclusion will have changed them and their institutions, as the Roman occupation did the British— probably much more, for modern methods of political control touch every phase of Native life. That the Bantu will carry over into the Church many relics of their pagan practices and institutions which we should not choose for it, is a foregone conclusion; but, as I said, no one can predict just what these will be.

Some Bantu rites are innocent enough; some, being incompatible with the moral demands of Christianity, can be condemned without hesitation; some, though offensive to our sense of fitness or beauty, are not incapable of being sublimated and retained by Bantu Christians. What can be more repugnant to our way of thinking than the Bantu custom of preserving and venerating skulls, jaw-bones, fingers, nail-parings, hair-clippings, and other gruesome fragments of corpses that have long since decayed! And yet Buddhists and Romanists revere such relics as incentives to faith and piety, and a lock of hair may be treasured for sentimental reasons by people of refinement.

Even when some rites have perished, the occasions that called for them will still remain. In Khama's country, where I lived for many years, it had been customary to hold tribal assemblies for the celebration of pagan religious ceremonies at the beginning of the ploughing season and of the new year, and at the completion of harvest. Khama thought these particular ceremonies unworthy of perpetuation, but continued to summon his people to worship in the Great Place of Tribal Assembly upon these several occasions, substituting Christian observances for heathen rites. These gatherings continued to be true communal assemblies, convoked and presided over by the Chief in his official capacity, after the ancient manner, and attended by thousands of tribesmen. The Church had no responsibility for them; but former Chiefs had called for the assistance of experts in tribal rites, and Khama always invited the resident missionary to lead the devotions of his people. Whatever else may be said of the ritual that formerly marked these assemblies, it was avowedly intended to express the thanks of the people, and to implore the blessing of the gods. Ploughing and Harvest Ceremonies acknowledge that something more than human effort and skill is needed for the growing of crops, and that man's labour comes better when there is no discord between the human and the divine. The New Year Ceremony was a ritual of new beginnings. I found no difficulty in giving an appropriate Christian setting to these acts of worship, or in finding a suitable topic for the homily that was always expected on such occasions; and I welcomed these festivals as opportunities for exhibiting the comeliness and significance of ideas that had loomed up grotesquely in the morning twilight of the tribesmen's spiritual day.

THEOLOGICAL AFFINITIES WITH CHRISTIANITY

The Bantu are interested in eating, but not in any theory of digestion, nutrition, or food values: delight in their mothers' love and find joy in the faces of friends, but never analyse and rationalise these emotions. Philosophy is a stream of thought that flows forth from the grotto of wonder; but the intellectual curiosity of the Bantu is seldom piqued by the wonder of their religious experience. Nevertheless, being human, they have had to relate that part of their experience to the whole of it; which is but another way of saying that they have had to find some sort of reasoned exposition of their traffic with the unseen. Consequently they have a theology, though it is neither systematic nor authoritative.

Some missionaries act upon the unwarrantable assumption that the theology of crude people must be too crude to repay investigation. That is a mistake. In his book, *Raymond*,[1] Sir Oliver Lodge quotes Plotinus (205-262 A.D.) without the least touch of unkind criticism: "Souls which once were men, when they leave the body, need not cease from benefiting mankind. Some indeed in addition to other service, give occult messages (oracular replies), thus proving in their own case that souls survive." He affirms, also,[2] upon the authority of Prof. J. H. Muirhead, that "roughly speaking, Plotinus teaches that things there are on the same plane as things here; each having its counterpart or corresponding existence there, though glorified and fuller of reality."

Now these are fundamental ideas of Bantu theology, and we are on the horns of a dilemma: either Plotinus, whose powerful mysticism opened up the path that Greek philosophy thenceforth travelled till the world of antiquity reached its end, must have entertained crude notions, or else Bantu theology must be absolved from the charge of crudity—at any rate as far as its central tenets are concerned.

The truth is that man began at an early period of his history to rationalise the mystery of his own self-consciousness, and was driven, not by the logical conclusion of a chain of reasoning, but by his own simple and direct experience, to believe that the soul outlives the body and retains its old interest in human affairs. Hence it is that this conviction is as widespread as the human race, dominating the incoherent beliefs of barbarous tribesmen and the intellectual fabrics that philosophers built, and appearing to be more firmly and generally grasped the farther back we go in our study of human behaviour. Unsophisticated humanity has always stolidly refused to believe in the finality of death, or to part with its fond trust in the posthumous activities of those lost to sight, and ancestor-worship has been the staple of most religions.

[1] *Op. cit.*, 324-25.
[2] *Ibid.*, 337.

Nor can it be maintained, as some who are influenced mainly by the literary prophets would have us believe, that the Hebrews were a remarkable exception. In the earlier narrative literature of the Hebrew people, it is recorded that Samuel was evoked from the underworld of the dead by the magical rites of a necromancer; came up as a god, wearing the characteristic mantle of his prophetic calling; and threatened the God-forsaken king with disaster as the penalty of his misdeeds.[1] Immigrant tribes of Israel took over High Places at which autochthonous lords of the soil had long been worshipped, instead of regarding them as Canaanitish foibles and absurdities, and sought to win the favour of these old gods of growth, much as Bantu tribes have been wont to do in territories that they have conquered and occupied.[2] An old song embedded in the Book of Deuteronomy charges the contemporaries of Moses with an unholy proclivity for offering sacrifices to the dead,[3] and the condemnation of this practice in later literature shows that it continued for many centuries in the backwaters, if not in the main currents, of the religious life of Israel.

When institutional Christianity was superseding the paganism of Europe, common people, aware of the risk and futility of personally presenting petitions to great potentates, hesitated to make direct approach to the Mighty Monarch who presided over the destinies of mankind, and longed for intermediaries who were touched with a feeling of their infirmity and yet welcome at the court of the Great King. So the old notion of tutelary divinities was re-interpreted, and patron saints have ever since been dear to those Christians who think more of the Majesty of God than of his Fatherhood. In a letter to me, an Anglican priest, struck with the resemblance between some of the religious beliefs of his Bantu parishioners and some of his own, wrote thus: "Their belief in the prayers of their dead ancestors to God for them, is practically what we believe, that our dead relations (like Dives) [4] are praying to God for us, and that so they can help us. But their belief in what their ancestors do for them is really much

---

[1] 1 Sam. xxviii.
[2] See p. 278.
[3] Deut. xxxii. 17.
[4] He seems not to have noticed that the Rich Man in the parable prayed to his great ancestor, Abraham, not to God, and failed to obtain the help that he sought for his five brothers.

the same as our belief in what angels do for us, though they of course have no knowledge of angels, only of spirits departed."

Soon after receiving this letter, I went to Australia, and there chanced upon a copy of *Freeman's Journal*,[2] in which it was stated that "numbers of Catholic wounded are now praying to the little nun of Lisieux, who throughout the war has seemed to have a deep affection for the soldiers in the trenches, many instances of her intervention in moments of danger being on record." I wonder whether Christianity will provide hospitality, in like manner, for the mediatorial divinities of its Bantu converts; or whether it will set forth such a noble conception of the character of God that converts, even when conscious of unfilial behaviour, will find it easier to cast themselves upon his care than to trust to the best of their forbears?

That the Bantu should find their saints in the progenitors of their tribes, seems to me quite natural, and not altogether lacking in beauty when looked at with human sympathy. Were they not feeling after the truth that the great persons of the world are the great facts of the world, and that the light that we have upon the divine has come to us through them? Who has not cried in moments of anguish or bewilderment for the comforting touch of a dead mother's hand or the steadying counsel of a dead father's voice! I am not pleading that Bantu converts should continue to pray to ancestor-spirits, nor that they should substitute guardian angels or mediatorial saints for these ancient divinities: I am content, as Jesus was, with the immediate access of every one of God's children to their Father in Heaven; but I maintain that we ought to regard this old Bantu worship with benevolence, not "scout it as the Devil's lie," as a zealous missionary with undisciplined mind once advised me to do. I thank God that the lives of African tribesmen, left for many centuries without that revelation of God with which Jesus illumined the thoughts of men, were nevertheless redeemed from gross materialism by this glimmering of the light that never shone on land or sea. If they had not worshipped at all during these long centuries of neglect, their faculty of devotion would have atrophied ere the Church, in its lethargy, found them. Besides, is our theology not spacious enough for the entertainment of a suspi-

[1] Dated, Sydney, Dec. 20, 1917, p. 5.

cion that God is too big a soul to turn down the prayers of his little children merely because they ask in baby talk for the spiritual nourishment and protection that they need?

It is human, rather than denominational, to "compound for sins we are inclined to by damning those we have no mind to"; but Christians of some denominations, though shocked by the worship of saints, especially saints of outlandish morality, have been slow to jettison another of the doctrines of ancestor-worship. Edmund Gosse affirms [1] that fifty years ago fatalistic views of disease prevailed among deeply religious people, and that if a person was ill it showed that "the Lord's hand was extended in chastisement," and much prayer was poured forth that it might be explained to the sufferer, or to his relations, in what way he had sinned. He remarks [2] that his father, who was minister of a Plymouth Brethren Church, "retained the singular superstition, amazing in a man of scientific knowledge and human experience, that all pains and ailments were directly sent by the Lord in chastisement for some definite fault, and not in relation to any physical cause." And he points out [3] that it was not moral turpitude that his father credited with these pains and ailments, but such spiritual sins as uncertainties of doctrine, lukewarmness, intellectual pride, or in the case of gentle Mrs. Goodyer, making an idol of her husband. Substitute "discarnate lords" for "the Lord," and compare this with what I have said concerning *Revelation by Calamity*,[4] and you have something closer than a parallel.

As a pathfinder for the evangel of Jesus, Bantu ancestor-worship is not without merit. We are not talking in an unknown tongue when we speak to its adherents of inspiration, communion, sacrifice, offerings, prayer, praise, faith, or incarnation. Taboo contains the germ of the idea of holiness, as we see in the Bible— that wonderful record of the evolution of religious ideas! And an ancestor-worshipper's awe for people, places, things, and days which worshipful spirits claim as "peculiar possessions" (their "very own," to translate the archaic word), may be used to in-

[1] *Father and Son*, p. 41.
[2] *Op. cit.*, p. 83.
[3] *Op. cit.*, p. 295.
[4] See my pp. 96-98.

culcate the sacredness of personality, which is God's "peculiar possession." To people nurtured in the worship of the spirits of their fathers, who crave something more human than an impersonal deity, the Christian doctrine of the Fatherhood of God, "from whom every fatherhood on earth and in heaven is named," is the satisfying revelation of a truth that has hitherto flitted elusively before them; and their theory of the potential divinity of humanity prepares them to believe that there is a divine person at the heart of Christianity who carries in himself the promise and potency of spiritual aid in the mending of life. If they write a new life of Jesus, interpreting his manifold character afresh according to their own genius, as every age in the last two thousand years has done, it will be devoid of philosophic speculation concerning the nature of his person and work; but if they look out on life through his eyes and see the New Jerusalem coming down out of heaven, they will fashion their own tribal habitations after the pattern of the City of God, where hatred, suspicion, and antagonism give place to love, forbearance, and peace.

The easiest way to a mother's heart is through her child, even though he be not the prince of perfection that she thinks; and when our message comes to the Bantu through ideas which they regard as true, sacred, and their very own, it finds favour with them. No doubt the data of their religious experience are couched in terms that are geocentric, tribal, temporary, and sometimes flatulent; but a teacher of dietetics does not increase his efficiency by pedantic and ill-natured criticism of school-boy slang for all that pertains to nourishment. In talking of spiritual things to children, we use their words and imagery, instead of the more adequate terms that we prefer with our peers; and if they jump occasionally to a wrong conclusion,[1] we greet their misinterpretation with a smile, and steadily lead them on as they are able to bear it, filling out what is positive in their knowledge with a fuller meaning. Demolition is speedier work than building, and needs less skill, especially when the house-breaker sets no great store by the material; but there are wreckers enough in

---

[1] When our daughter was a little girl, she had learnt something about "Our Father who art in heaven," and one day she surprised us with a paraphrase on heaven as a place where God would carve the joint and her mother would pour the tea!

Africa. The missionary builds up Native thought and character; and when at times he has to take down parts of the old temple, so that the new may be without defect, he handles it respectfully, mindful that what is mere lumber to him is hallowed to people who have always associated it with whatever visions of reality have gladdened their eyes.

THE EXPERIENCE BEHIND CEREMONY AND THEOLOGY

Man, if we may judge from legacies left in prehistoric caves and the behaviour of existing breeds that have dawdled on the way of advance, has always taken spiritual values into account. Backward races hug the belief that man is at the mercy of a crowd of supernatural beings who stand upon ceremony and are touchy about trifles, and that life without ritual would therefore be sure to go wrong. Whether their ritual belongs to the domain of religion or to that of magic, is often open to question; because rudimentary forms of religion and magic, both grounded in a sense of awe in the presence of the unseen, are easily fused, and the blend is always a mode of behaviour, not a reasoned reflection on the nature of things.

Bantu life, though not nearly so primitive as that of some races, is built after this pattern. They never think of the world of practical activities apart from sacred but intangible things that lie deep in their hearts. Their agriculture, animal husbandry, and craftsmanship are based upon experience and fashioned by reason, but steeped in a sense of the unseen and set with cult and ritual. They work in a time-honoured way for the production of crops and artifacts, always sure that their efforts may be aided or thwarted by veiled beings of great capability. Bantu medicine-men have discovered useful remedies and potent poisons by the method of trial and error, but have attributed the virtue of the drugs to indwelling spirits that are stronger than the spirits of disease and witchcraft, and their own discoveries to the guidance of friends in the unseen; hence they are more punctilious than their neighbours in committing their ways to the spirits of their ancestors and preceptors, fortifying themselves with invocations, supplications, and customary charms before embarking on any pursuit.

It is a mistake, however, to infer that the Bantu do not reason from cause to effect, or that they are unaware of the difference between certainty and probability. They are keen observers of all that is of interest to them in their ordinary surroundings, and they reason from what they see to what they expect to find. They notice the freshness, direction, and peculiarity of a buck's spoor, the time of day, and the nature of the surrounding veld; apply a process of inductive reasoning to what they have perceived; set out upon its track; and return with venison for their larder. They draw rude maps in the sand to show the way they have gone or the path which they advise you to take, and lay out bits of stick and stone to demonstrate their plan for concerted attack upon an alien village or wild things of the wilderness. They infer from the rising and setting of certain stars and the sprouting of specific trees that the time is propitious for planting one kind of seed and too early or too late for another. In their judicial assemblies, they display much forensic ability in pleading for a friend or attacking an offender, citing parallel cases, and trying to establish the main fact by arguing, with empiric logic, from circumstantial evidence. Criticism, reconstruction, initiation, and improvement are not cultivated; but doubt of their ability to discriminate between absolute and comparative certitude is soon dissolved by a careful study of any one of their vernaculars, with its fine shades of verbal meaning and its equivalents for such phrases as "of course," "certainly," "perhaps," "it seems," "can it be that," "whereas," and "therefore."

In the primary sense of the terms, the Bantu have a science and a logic of their own. If we call them "unscientific," we mean that their knowledge of nature is not organised in conformity with the fundamental principles of modern science, and it is better to say "pre-scientific"; because, before the rise of modern science, men everywhere regarded nature in some such way as they do. Similarly, if we call them "illogical," we do not mean that there is an inherent defect in their understanding, or that they have no ability in argument, but that their thought is controlled by assumptions which we exclude, but which were once common among men; and "pre-logical" is a better term. Both "pre-scientific" and "pre-logical" denote stages in the evolution of human thought; neither passes judgment upon inborn mental qualities. Our trouble with Bantu mentality is, not that it differs innately from our own, but that, being entangled in the generalisations of an antiquated and effete science that lacked reliable rules for testing the soundness of its conclusions, and hampered with an unenlightened and desultory method of dialectics, it often bewilders us with perverse deductions from unuttered assumptions.[1] It is these unspoken postulates that matter most. The structure of a man's thought may be seen in his utterances, but the bed-rock of his conclusions, being composed of assumptions so self-evident to him that to mention them would be to cast a slur upon his interlocutor's intelligence, is seldom exposed. Men of archaic and up-to-date civilisation alike, get into the way of taking for granted whatever is generally regarded as ultimate fact by the community in which they are reared; for, though what the neighbours designedly teach is open to scrutiny, the faith that they live by is catching. People bred in European society, even those who do not dabble in science and are puzzled by such phrases, base their judgments upon the assumption that phenomena are subject to uniform laws and free from the interference of capricious spirits; and their intercourse with their neighbours subjects them to logical discipline which is more potent than apparent. If they never hear of the "law of contradictories," they fall nevertheless into the prevalent habit of assuming that contradictory propositions cannot both be true—that a man cannot be his own grandfather, for example, and that the fact that a person was here is proof enough that he was not elsewhere at the same moment; and they learn in the first decade of life to distinguish between the flummery of a dream and the substantial facts of objective experience. They live in a world of reason and order. True, an older stratum of thought crops out here and there in their conversation, but such terms as "luck" are little more than verbiage or badinage, save to the callow-minded. People bred in Bantu society, on the other hand, base their judgments upon the assumption that phenomena are caused by spirits of several sorts; that things, people and events are magically related to one another; and that the symbol or semblance is identical with—not merely suggestive of—that which it

[1] Cf. *The Evolution of Man* by G. Elliot Smith (Oxford Univ. Press, 1924), p. 133.

suggests or represents. Terms which we regard as mutually exclusive are not so regarded by them; and their dream-experiences
are as real to them as their waking experiences. To their thinking, the fact that a woman was seen sleeping in her hut is no dis-
proof of the charge that she was at that very moment riding a
hyena, miles away, in infamous pursuit of her victim. Nor is the
woman herself sure that the charge is false, especially if it is
confirmed by the divination test and the sufferer was one to whom
she bore malice. The multipresence of the individual is axio-
matic to her judgments; she cannot doubt what she sees with her
own eyes, waking or sleeping; [1] she has always understood that
a person may be possessed by a spirit of witchcraft without being
aware of anything more than spitefulness; and she has often fluttered back to her body from a dream-jaunt, flushed with weird
adventures that she could not recall or emotions that slipped the
leash of her waking hours. She is not impervious to experience,
as we allege in our haughty and unimaginative manner, but to
the foreign presuppositions that underlie our interpretation of it.

Students of Bantu life should be on their guard lest they be
led off on a false scent by the theories of Bantu illogicality and
impermeability to experience that I have alluded to. Both these
slanders, plausible enough to satisfy those who have but a nodding acquaintance with the Bantu habit of mind, call for scrutiny.
People with a turn for unkind quips declare that a Bantu chain
of reasoning is made up mostly of missing links; but the links are
there, though hidden from eyes that cannot see far into Bantu
convictions. Bantu findings, as I said before, are controlled by
silent suppositions, soaked in magic, and at odds with the settled
principles of our rational and regulated world; but their mental
processes, however untrimmed, are so near akin to ours that we
should often fall in with their verdict if we had enough imag-

---

[1] Some African tribes hold a man responsible for what he does in a dream (cf.
RAA. 93), and even for what another dreams that he sees him doing. The latter
is common among the Bantu, and is traceable to the belief that dreams are warnings
from one's spirit-friends. Monitions from *dead relatives who appear in dreams*
are everywhere heeded; and when the friendly monitor is not visible, the diviner's
help is sought. "If Casembe dreams of any man twice or three times," wrote
Livingstone (LLJ. 222), "he puts the man to death, as one who is practising
secret arts against his life." (See my pp. 94 ff., and cf. RSZ. 228, 230, 234 and
240, and *Forty Years Among the Zulus* by Rev. Josiah Tyler: Boston Congregational Publishing Society, pp. 95 and 108.)

ination and intellectual sympathy to discard our own view of the world for a moment and take theirs instead. The theory that the Bantu never trouble to examine conditions that bring about a phenomenon and learn nothing from experience, must be set down to the theorist's want of insight and imagination or to his imperfect apprehension of the evidence. It is a hasty generalisation that does not fit the fact that they have learnt many things about agriculture, animal husbandry, craftsmanship, and political association; and however poor their advance in these arts may appear when set side by side with that of many other races, it becomes significant when compared with that of the aborigines of Australia or the Bushmen of Africa. Even this small measure of progress would have been impossible if they had been impervious to the experiences, thoughts, and emotions of which life is made. The real ground of our quarrel with Bantu thinking, is that it does not interpret what we call the objective data of their experience in the way that we should interpret them; but then the objective data are but a part of their experience. Formidable beings from the unseen world always mingle with these data, the one as real as the other to the Bantu, and the former much more important. Our judgment of an endeavour to fathom the mystery of a steam engine by examining its mechanism without taking steam into account, is pretty much the same as the Bantu estimate of attempts to deal with the objective data apart from the subjective. (I use our terms; they make no such philosophic distinction.) In studying Bantu life we come back again and again to those authoritative preconceptions that the individual gets as part of his social inheritance,[1]—preconceptions which affect his experience as well as his interpretation of it. It is this orientation of thought that must be changed before the Bantu can rise into the intellectual liberty of the children of God. They know that every event must have an efficient cause, though they do not

[1] Many of my Bantu friends are sticklers for the correct use of their mother-tongue, and can tell in a moment whether an expression is right or wrong, and often whether its use marks the speaker as well-bred or uncultured; but I never met a tribesman who could give a reason for the faith that was in him—unless he had had foreign tuition. They get their vernacular as part of their social inheritance, and speak it with precision, fluency, and certainty, but never worry out the *why* of anything that is in it: masters of diction, and yet ignorant of every formal rule of grammar or syntax; men with a *feeling* for the felicitous in their own speech who *know* very little about it.

formulate their belief in such phrases; they rule their search for causes, as we rule ours, by what are taken to be fundamental facts; and they seldom, if ever, regard second causes as of first importance. They may be absolutely sure, for example, that death supervened upon lightning-stroke, or a wound inflicted by a snake, a leopard, a fall, or a foe; but since they know offhand, or think they do, that the ultimate cause must have been the activity of a spirit, they set themselves without further ado to discover what spirit used this lethal weapon and what (or who) induced the spirit to strike the blow. Perhaps it was provoked by the doings or neglect of the deceased or his group, or stirred to action by the occult knavery of a neighbour; and something must be done to prevent recurrence of the mischief.

Let us try to get at the religious experience of these people; for it is the experience that matters most. If there were no religious experience, there would be neither theology nor religious rites; for, whether cultured or crude, theology is the philosophy of religious experience and ritual is a dramatic endeavour to express religious emotion in a more colourful medium than speech. If we were peering into genetics, we should have to bestow thought upon the fact that art is older than literature, that pictography had to run to seed before an alphabet could be grown, and that in the religion of the backward races (whatever may be said of the others) theology often attempts to explain rites that retain their odour of sanctity after they have lost their original meaning, while rites never originate as dramatic expressions of dogmas; but at present we are concerned only with the certainty that the existing theology and religious ritual of a tribe are both efforts to shadow forth the tribesman's experience. Two difficulties lie in the way of our clear understanding of the real import of these utterances: in the first place, we find it hard to escape, for the sake of experiment, from a universe in which everything is linked up with everything in a chain of causation, and to move freely in a magical multiverse where existences and events are the sport of spirits and may be hobbled, let loose, or deflected by spells whose efficacy depends upon unerring symbolism, pronunciation, intonation, and dramatic rendering; and, in the second place, we are haunted by a suspicion that the Bantu are as likely as we are to confuse the conventionalities and realities of religion, and cling to rites and phrases, consecrated by age-long use and reminiscent of unforgettable hours of religious exaltation, but not genuine expressions of the speaker's present experience. There is more husk than kernel in every religion, and the husk shows how precious the kernel is. Nevertheless, if we take a compassionate view of the typical ancestor-worshipper who comes to light in the preceding pages, we can hardly avoid the following inferences about his experience.

The deepest thing in his soul is an instinct for God, though he has not yet discerned the drift of his inward urging. Unsatisfied with himself, he craves for divine aid in the mending of life. He has a sense of mystery; a feeling that he is somehow related to the unseen and dependent upon it. Sometimes he feels that he is in touch with it; and then he is conscious of hope and vigour. At other times he feels out of harmony with it, and makes no doubt that the break must be due to himself or the social group of which he is but a fragment: that self-centredness has caused alienation, and that peace can be found only in the sacrifice of self-will. Even then, he makes no doubt that his beatified ancestors are as reasonable as he himself is: that the divine are still human, and that if he shows his penitence by purging himself of his misdeeds in the only way he knows, they will not be too hard upon him. In emergencies, he throws himself upon their care, confident that if he keeps their laws and complies with their demands his times are in their hands. He feels that they have a right to his allegiance, and, to his gratitude for whatever help they give. Moreover, he is satisfied that it is possible to discover their will. He cannot resist the feeling that death is not the end of life: that those to whom he owed so much did not cease to care for him after they entered the spirit-world, nor cancel their claim upon his service; that they are near him still, often willing and able to lend him their aid, which is mighty but not omnipotent.[1] His experience of his fellows is that some of them are

---

[1] I am speaking of ancestor-worshippers and their gods. It must be borne in mind, however, that these gods do not fill the whole horizon of Bantu experience. The common opinion that fear of spirits is a dominant motive in Bantu life, contains truth enough to keep it alive; but the ancestor-spirits of a man's own family, clan, and tribe are as friendly as they would be if they were still in the flesh. Some of them were never much good while they were alive: selfish, jealous, revengeful people; and death has not changed their characters, though it has enhanced

sometimes endowed with power and knowledge so vast that it can
be attributed only to an unearthly source.   That is to say, his
experience includes a feeling that the human soul may be stimu-
lated by the divine.

WEAKNESS OF ANCESTOR-WORSHIP

The frequent use of "feel" in the above paragraph is not due
to slackness of phrasing.   Feeling and thought grow together in
Bantu experience, as in our own; but feeling is prolific in that
rank soil and thought tends to rot at the roots.   Dancing out their
religious experience relieves their surcharged feelings and brings
them peace, but thinking it out would be unwonted and wearisome
work.   Religion to them is a corporate affair, which demands
from the individual no more thought than is necessary to enable
each participant to conform to rule.   No rule could have been
devised without thinking, of course; but the thinking was group-
thinking.   The opinion of a tribe, like the paths that wind hither
and thither throughout its domain, has been slowly beaten out by
wayfarers whose easiest and safest course was to tread as near as
they could upon the tracks of their predecessors.

I do not know whether there was a period in the evolution of
man when individualisation had not yet taken place and a diffused
principle capable of penetrating everywhere was thought to animate persons and things.[1]   This notion, so far as I can see, is
more likely to have had its rise in minds that moved easily in
the sphere of abstract ideas; but my old Bantu neighbours, I am
sure, never interpreted themselves or the external world after
that fashion.   They attributed their own activity and resistance,
and that of every other person and thing, to the sway of an indwelling soul.   When, talking with one of them about another,

their power.   But most of them were kind to people of their own lineage, except
when they were flouted, and are regarded as helpful still.   (Cf. pp. 158 f., 160;
RSZ. 146; IPNR. ii. 168; A. i. 74.)   Unfortunately, however, many other spirits are
prowling round: spirits of murderers, suicides, witches—god-forsaken people who
had to be denied the mortuary rites that open the gates of the nether-world; spirits
of former dwellers in the land, also, whose foreign mentality makes them take
harmless deeds amiss; spirits of animals, too, and very many spirits of things.   Ancestor-spirits of unblemished reputation are terrible when neglected or disobeyed; but
these other spirits are a haunting terror.   One never knows what they may do!

[1] See HNT. 365.

I often asked what his next step would be, the reply was usually prefaced with the remark, "We don't know what he will do, because he is another person, but we think," &c. Every individual in the group is self-conscious—many are self-conceited; but the individual counts for little in that old-world society: the proper thing for him to do, if he cares for his own comfort and reputation, is to put on the emotional and intellectual uniform of the tribe. Independent thinking about religion, politics, war, hunting, agriculture, craftsmanship, or any other social activity, is a costly eccentricity. Not that ancestor-spirits know or care what any one of their descendants *thinks;* his thoughts are not heard in spirit-land, and he may think what he likes so long as his conduct is correct; but nothing that he does or says escapes the attention of his gods, and they are great sticklers for the old ways. Thought languishes when forbidden to modify behaviour, and orthodox usage is a snug blanket that smothers individual initiative and enterprise. "Among the Alunda," writes Melland,[1] "iron work is much more intertwined with spirit worship, and every part of the apparatus is sacred, and being ordained by divine custom cannot be changed. We tried to introduce a simple but much more effective bellows among Alunda iron workers, the special merit of which was that it saved a great waste of time and energy. Several of these bellows were made at Mwinilunga by a native (under supervision) from a model made at Kalene Hill Mission, and Mr. Bruce Miller had hopes that they would be of great assistance to the smiths. They indeed admitted the superiority of the new model and its simplicity, but they would not use it, as the innovation would have aroused the spirits to anger. In another case a Kalunda smith who was making a regular income from his smithy stopped work for a year because the spirit of his deceased wife was adverse." That is a faithful picture of the ultra-conservative sway of ancestor-worship in every Bantu tribe, and this rigid grip of the dead hand goes far to account for the backwardness of their civilisation.

Ancestor-worship has a rudimentary appreciation of truth, justice, and self-forgetfulness in the service of the community; but, blind to the need for harmonious development of the whole man, it insists that all deeds shall be cast in the old moulds. By taking

[1] WBA. 137.

the men that were for its ideal, instead of the men that are to be, it forswears power for the betterment of life. It cannot elevate marriage or womanhood; nor abolish ancient forms of cruelty, violence, or oppression; nor give manners a finer polish than they had "in the beginning"; nor help clansmen to adapt themselves to the rapidly changing conditions of modern African life. It is true that ancestor-worshippers have felt the upward urge which makes for the evolution of morality and the restraint of passion, and which must be attributed, I think, to the unwearied play of the spirit of God upon the souls of men; and that a process of amelioration, however fitful and lethargic, is discernible by those who apply the comparative method to the study of Bantu law and custom: savage rites have certainly been softened; manners, sweetened; and feeling, refined. But—and this is the point of immediate interest—the people have had no help from their religion in the mending of life; on the contrary, they have found it an insurmountable obstacle and have worked their way round it by means of shifty devices. Ancestor-worship, with its fundamental doctrine that everything should be kept as the ancestors left it, has provided cement for the social structure; every enduring religion has done that; but the cohesion of the community is merely a by-product of religion. The true business of religion is to give life, and give it more abundantly; and life maintains continuity by sloughing off superficial and outworn stuff and repairing the tissue with fresh and healthy material.

Sacerdotalism is another weakness of this religion. Although, as I explained before,[1] its priests are born, not made, and do not belong to a priestly caste or a sacred college, yet ancestor-worship is sacerdotal to the core; for it invests the head of a family or a clan with sole sacrificial functions and concomitant power with the gods, however defective he may be in moral excellence or spiritual insight, and holds that its great acts of worship would be invalidated and even profaned if performed without his authority. All religions that have centred round this notion have been inevitably ritualistic: I mean, not that they have clung to their own religious rites, nor that they have set a high value upon order, seemliness and beauty in worship, but that they have depended more upon what the officiant did and how he did it than

[1] See pp. 333-336.

upon the inner disposition of the worshipper. Ancestor-worship, sacerdotalism and magic all lay in the same cradle when humanity was young, and nobody could tell them apart; and from that day to this ancestor-worship has been touched with the conceit that it can rouse gods to action by meticulously pronouncing, intoning, and dramatising time-honoured spells, and make the spells compelling by adding the god's true name. Its adherents have never tried to purge themselves from this taint; and upon conversion they take it naturally into the Church if they are not carefully taught the true relation of man to God.

These things may be said by an impartial critic; but it is not fair to assert that ancestor-worship is destitute of adoration, as some have done in their haste, flaring up at outlandish dances and dramas of devotion that were in conspicuous contrast with all that they deemed devout; and it must be maintained, in spite of people who cavil about Confucianism, that ancestor-worship is religion—religion reinforced by magic, if you like, and often woven round with a strange web of which the warp is credulity and the woof chicanery, but still religion. Notwithstanding the fact that it is made up largely of rites and traditions and has neither a system of metaphysics nor an authoritative body of doctrines, it renders the theme of man's forebodings less poignant to its adherents, does much to satisfy their thirst for religious emotion and restore spiritual calm, and gives them fresh courage to do the right and eschew the wrong. A definition of religion that is too narrow to cover that ground, cannot stand the test.

If we may wander into a little glade, just off the path of sequence, I should like to suggest that ancestor-worship was the seedbed in which the notion of a deified sovereign germinated. The opinion that that conception was the monstrous figment of Oriental imagination, is at times buttressed with a reminder that living potentates of Egypt were invested with divinity for thirty centuries before Augustus claimed it for himself; but that is not the whole truth. Egyptian potentates would never have built cities in the clouds if they had not been accustomed to clouds and cities. Every Bantu chief whose status is not based on force or fraud is credited with divine power. His tribesmen look to him and his ancestors for fertility of fields and flocks; and in their eyes he is more than a priest, or even a hierarch: he is a peer of the gods. Where the doctrine of rebirth in descendants prevails, he is held to have come from the gods; and everywhere it is assumed that he will one day take a high place among the gods and be worshipped. The time factor is of subordinate importance to pre-logical mentality, and I have heard tribesmen, still immersed in a superannuated past, salute their living chief as "my god." Now, if in process of time a line of such chiefs blossomed forth as territorial lords (as they tend to do) and ultimately opened out as full-blown sovereigns, they would surely be deified sovereigns, unless something happened meanwhile to change the pattern of their thinking.

To return to the path from which we strayed, ancestor-worship undoubtedly makes for polytheism. Its theory is that these lesser divinities, like patron saints of Christendom, are mediators with the Great Chief of the spirit-world; but a bridge where there is no gap to be crossed is a whimsical obstruction on the king's highway. God, impressive though it be to speak of him as too exalted for common men to approach, has had to pay the penalty of remoteness from common tribesmen and their affairs. The Bantu idea of a Supreme Being must be reserved for examination in a future volume; nothing more can be said here than that ancestor-worshippers have no direct dealings with God—a bald assertion that is sure to be challenged by Africanists who have not scrutinised all available evidence on this intricate question.

There is also something akin to fatalism in this faith. Accidents don't happen; congenial circumstances come from the favour of spirits, and unwelcome events from their wrath. Every occurrence is specifically ordained by unseen beings of some grade or other: spirits of the home and clan, earthbound spirits of wicked people, kinless spirits of more aboriginal races than one's own, spirits of the newly dead that have been enslaved by knavish neighbours, and spirits of things that may be called into play by anybody who knows how. Sagacity or fatuity, forethought or thriftlessness, idleness or industry, skill or clumsiness, is but as the small dust of the balance; the world is full of spirits, and the spirits send what they will to men. What they send depends more upon their character than upon that of the recipients. This is not quite the same thing as fatalism; for spirits can be influenced, according to their order, by punctilious conformity to custom, or by religious rites, or by redoubtable magic; but when piety is equated with prosperity and defined in terms of conventionality, fatalism draws perilously near. Fortunately, nobody quite conforms to this view of life; men are everywhere a bit bigger than their beliefs; but there is the belief.

Divination is another defect of ancestor-worship. Its aim is to provide mortals with the guidance of the gods.[1] That is brought out in strong relief by those diviners who say they can see or hear the spirits, and is equally true of the common herd of diviners who lack this sixth sense and depend upon signals that spirits send through instruments of divination. Diviners who have a nodding acquaintance with the mechanical notion of inspiration that was common among missionaries fifty years ago, have been known to explain that divination was their Bible; that they find divine guidance in the mystic movements of their inspired kit just as Christians find it in mystic signs on the printed page; that it contains no element of chance and brings reliable guidance from divine forbears whose senses are not now hampered with trammels of flesh. Any criticism of divination as a gambling device that casts its glamour over greenhorns, is sure to miss the mark; but, accepting it at the diviner's valuation and saying nothing about the validity of his belief, I remark that cribs save laggard brains at the expense of scholarship. Junod's remarks on this point are pithy and correct.[2] This kind of divine guidance is so fatally accessible that the Bantu turn to it upon every occasion, instead of working out their own problems in practical life or probing their own conduct for faults that cause trouble.

THE FATE OF BANTU ANCESTOR-WORSHIP

Till a few decades ago it had never dawned upon the Bantu mind that a man has any right to choose his own religion. A tribesman's proper gods were those of the family and clan into which he happened to be born; but if his group came to grief and found refuge with a friendly clan whose ancestors had had time to become territorial deities,[3] he looked to the latter for rain

---

[1] See pp. 146-150.
[2] LSAT. ii. 522.
[3] See p. 202.

and fertility; and, lest he should toil in vain or meet with disaster, he paid court to the old spirit-lords of any land in which he went hunting or fishing, taking care to be introduced or represented, if he could, by some one who stood in the good graces of these divinities. His gods were not exclusive: so long as he did his duty by them, they were not felt to be challenged by his flirtations with other deities, nor by his use of magic as a valuable adjuvant to their providential vigilance. But they were all marked out for him by force of circumstances, not by his own choice or conviction.

The right of private judgment in the selection of one's gods—a theory imported into Greek thought some six centuries before our era—has long been such a commonplace of European belief that it is bandied about in Bantu Africa by thousands of Europeans whose religion sits loosely upon them. This theory, simple as it looks to us, acts like a ferment upon Bantu society; because it has far-reaching implications. It eliminates notions of pedigree and locality from the idea of god; makes religion a personal obligation instead of a civic duty; and takes for granted that an individual ought to do his own thinking about religion and let it tell upon behaviour. Neither ancestor-worship nor tribalism can persist in a community of individuals who assume the right to scrap their family gods and set knowledge and judgment above tradition as controller of worship and conduct.[1] Missionaries teach tribesmen that each individual soul is of infinite value and directly responsible to God, and that the traditions of the elders should be subjected to the ethical test, quoting the example of Jesus;[2] and the sanctions of ancestor-worship crumble in that atmosphere. But missionaries of religion are few in Africa and missionaries of Western civilisation many; and my point is that the tide of Western civilisation now flooding that continent is enough of itself to seal the doom of ancestor-worship as a living religion, apart from the work that the missionaries are doing; for every precinct of Bantu institutions, as well as its sanctuary, is being undermined by some doctrine or other of our civilisation.

The religion of a backward race cannot hold its own against

[1] Cf. pp. 5, 90, 385, 391 f., 415, 430 f.
[2] Mt. v. 17-48; xii. 1-14; xv. 1-20; Mk. ii. 23 to iii. 6; vii. 1-23; Lk. vi. 1-11; xiii. 10-16.

the thought and faith of a much more progressive people; but it always makes terms with its conqueror. Tacit assumptions of monotheism are at first overlooked by polytheists, the heart clinging to what the head has abjured. A new god or two does not matter to them, and they try to combine the old worship with the new. Bede says[1] that Redwald, king of the East Angles, was made acquainted in Kent with the sacraments of the Christian faith, but seemed on his return home to serve both Christ and the old gods, having in the same temple "an altar for the sacrifice of Christ, and a small altar for the victims offered to demons"; and even Bede did not see that the same practice was enshrined in his own vocabulary. Some oddments of traditional belief or fragmentary rites of the old faith are always embedded in the new, like fossils in sedimentary rocks; and others linger in secluded nooks as folk-lore, secret rites, or private magic, leaving work for reformers of a future age that is immune from the glamour of the ancient cult. So it was that Hindu gods became Buddhas and Bodhisats; that the country faiths of Siam were embalmed in the new ritual of Buddhism; that Persian polytheism crept into the monotheistic faith of Zoroaster, the ancient prophet of Iran; that Canaanitish shrines and festivals were reconsecrated to the service of Yahwe and relics of ancestor-worship tolerated till attacked by the literary prophets; that the Lady of the Wild Things, who ruled the worship of matrilineal tribes in Thrace, Macedonia and Greece during the hunting period, maintained her sway as Demeter throughout the age of civic culture, and even survived till A.D. 1801 as Saint Demetra of the Greek Church; that many beliefs of heathen Arabia were caught up into Islam; and that old Slavic gods became angels and saints after the Church conquered Slavonia.[2]

The force of tradition is never greater than when it touches rites and beliefs that centre in the grave. In spite of a millennium of Islam and well-nigh two of Christianity, the fellahin of Egypt still place funeral offerings in the tombs for the sustenance of the dead, just as the custom was thousands of years ago. Centuries of intellectual discipline have not sufficed to lay the ghosts in European graveyards, or in the imagination of wayfarers who

[1] *Eccles. Histy*, Bk. II, Chap. xv.
[2] See also pp. 400 f., 402, 403 f., 407 ff., 411 f.

pass that way at the witching time of night, nor even to exclude them from the drawing-rooms of society; and it is still a prejudice among the vulgar, though not a dogma of the thoughtful, that he whose corpse is torn from the tomb can have no part in the resurrection of the flesh.   Rites, notions, and phrases of Bantu ancestor-worship, and some of its hopes and apprehensions, are likely to loiter for a long time yet; but that system of faith, worship, and morals is sure to be overthrown.   What is to become of the fifty million tribesmen whose political and social institutions are built on this doomed religion?   Are they to be left derelict amidst the ruins of their dismantled dwellings, or can they be helped to build fairer habitations for the human spirit? That is the problem that missionaries are out to solve.   But they are too few and too poorly equipped to solve it.

GENERAL INDEX
INDEX TO AFRICAN CLANS, TRIBES AND
LOCALITIES MENTIONED
LIST OF BOOKS REFERRED TO IN THIS VOLUME

GENERAL INDEX

(The numbers refer to pages. A lower-case "n." after the number draws attention to footnote on that page.)

INDEX TO AFRICAN CLANS, TRIBES AND LOCALITIES MENTIONED

LIST OF BOOKS REFERRED TO IN THIS VOLUME

The symbols used in the text are here arranged in alphabetic order.
Other books are arranged in the alphabetic order of their authors' surnames.
A few books not included in the following list are cited on pp. 142, 143, 155, 209, 314, 319, 333, 403 and 437.

A. AFRICANA. By the Rev. Duff Macdonald. Vols. 2. (London: Simpkin, Marshall & Co. 1882.)
Cited on pp. 14, 18, 25, 49, 56, 69, 96, 137, 140, 141, 148, 164, 266, 429.

AA. AUTOBIOGRAPHY OF AN AFRICAN: Retold in Biographical Form & in Wild African Setting of the Life of Daniel Mtusu. By Donald Fraser, D.D. (London: Seeley, Service & Co., Limited. 1925.)
Cited on pp. 70, 135, 264.

ABN. AMONG THE BANTU NOMADS: A Record of Forty Years Spent Among the Bechuana, a Numerous and Famous Branch of the Central South African Bantu, with the First Full Description of Their Ancient Customs, Manners & Beliefs. By J. Tom Brown. (London: Seeley, Service & Co., Ltd. 1926.)
Cited on pp. 3, 136, 148, 208, 224, 358, 363, 376.

ACC. AMONG CONGO CANNIBALS: Experiences, Impressions, and Adventures During Thirty Years' Sojourn Amongst the Boloki and Other Congo Tribes, with a Description of Their Curious Habits, Customs, Religion, & Laws. By John H. Weeks, Correspondent to the Royal Anthropological Institute and to the Folk-lore Society, etc., etc. (London: Seeley, Service & Co., Ltd. 1913.)
Cited on pp. 11, 16, 22, 25, 28, 39, 52, 54, 58, 62, 66, 79, 80, 143, 168, 171, 181, 321, 323, 329, 338, 376.

African Monthly, The.
Cited on p. 294.

AI. AFRICAN IDYLLS: Portraits & Impressions of Life on a Central African Mission Station. By Donald Fraser, D.D. Third Edition. (London: Seeley, Service & Co., Limited. 1923.)
Cited on pp. 33, 49, 158, 267.

AK. ETHNOLOGY OF THE A-KAMBA AND OTHER EAST AFRICAN TRIBES. By C. W. Hobley, C. M. G., A. M. Inst. C. E., East African Protectorate Service. (Cambridge: University Press. 1910.)
Cited on pp. 3, 7, 20, 25, 28, 109, 137, 139, 247, 295.

ALRP. AFTER LIFE IN ROMAN PAGANISM: Lectures Delivered at Yale University on the Silliman Foundation. By Franz Cumont. (New Haven: Yale University Press. London: Humphrey Milford. 1922.)
Cited on pp. 15, 24, 30, 33, 59, 73, 74, 155, 178, 254, 266.

Arbousset (Rev. T.). See NET.

ARC.   ANGOLA AND THE RIVER CONGO. By Joachim John Monteiro, Associate of the Royal School of Mines, and Corresponding Member of the Zoological Society. Vols. 2. (London: Macmillan & Co., Ltd. 1875.) Cited on pp. 22, 293, 309, 310, 321.

Arnot (Fred S.). See G.

AS.   ASHANTI. By Capt. R. S. Rattray, M.B.E., of the Gold Coast Political Service; of Gray's Inn, Barrister-at-Law; Diplomé in Anthropology (Oxon.), etc. (Oxford: Clarendon Press. 1923.) Cited on pp. 8, 14, 74, 156, 169, 179, 181, 221, 248, 255, 327, 332, 341, 360.

Battell (Andrew). See SAAB.

BBM.   BANTU BELIEFS AND MAGIC: With Particular Reference to the Kikuyu and Kamba Tribes of Kenya Colony, etc. By C. W. Hobley, C.M.G.; M. R. Anthropological Institute; Assoc. M. Inst. C. E.; late Senior Provincial Commissioner, Kenya Colony. (London: H. F. & G. Witherby. 1922.) Cited on pp. 2, 57, 75, 78, 86, 103, 109, 139, 167, 171, 180, 195, 218, 225, 247, 271, 288, 295, 296, 345, 349, 350, 352, 353, 356, 364, 365.

Bentley (Rev. W. Holman). See PC.

BBMM.   AT THE BACK OF THE BLACK MAN'S MIND: Or Notes on the Kingly Office in West Africa. By Richard Edward Dennett. (London and New York: Macmillan & Co. 1906.) Cited on pp. 138, 219, 287, 310, 311, 339.

Bg.   THE BAGANDA: An Account of Their Native Customs and Beliefs. By the Rev. John Roscoe, Hon. M.A. (Cantab). (London: Macmillan & Co., Ltd. 1911.) Cited on pp. 16, 20, 27, 34, 43, 83, 94, 138, 168, 176, 185, 231, 248, 257, 267, 281, 293, 326, 338, 346, 347, 363.

Bleek (Dr. W. H. I.). A COMPARATIVE GRAMMAR OF SOUTH AFRICAN LANGUAGES. By W. H. I. Bleek, Ph.D. (Cape Town: J. C. Juta. London: Trübner & Co. Part I, 1862; Part II, 1869.) Cited on p. 66.

BNT.   BANTU STUDIES: A Journal Devoted to the Scientific Study of Bantu, Hottentot, and Bushman. (Johannesburg: University of the Witwatersrand Press.) Cited on pp. 24, 224, 236, 244.

Brown (J. Tom). See ABN.

Bs.   THE BASUTOS: Or Twenty-three Years in South Africa. By the Rev. E. Casalis. (London: James Nisbet & Co. 1861.) Cited on pp. 14, 17, 19, 27, 36, 60, 66, 68, 79, 80, 113, 183, 186, 187, 191, 220, 251, 290, 298, 348, 357.

Budge (Dr. E. A. Wallis). THE BOOK OF THE DEAD. (London: British Museum monograph. 1922.) Cited on pp. 44, 65, 73. See also EM.

Bullock (Charles). See MLC.

C. A COLLECTION OF VOYAGES AND TRAVELS. Some now first printed from Original Manuscripts, Others now first Published in English. In Six Volumes. To which is prefixed, An Introductory Discourse (supposed to have been written by the Celebrated Mr. Locke) entitled, The Whole History of Navigation from its Original to this Time. Illustrated with near Three Hundred Maps and Cuts, curiously Engraved on Copper. The third edition. (London: Printed by Assignment from Messrs. Churchill, for Henry Lintot and John Osburn, at the Golden-Ball in Paternoster Row. MDCCXLIV.) Cited on pp. 34, 46, 47, 308, 317, 318, 319.

Callaway (Rev. Canon). See RSZ.

Campbell (Dugald). See IHB.

Cardinall (A. W.). See NTG.

Carnegie (Rev. D.). AMONG THE MATABELE. By the Rev. D. Carnegie. Second edition. (London: Religious Tract Society. 1894.) Cited on p. 240.

Casalis (Rev. E.). See Bs.

Claridge (G. Cyril). See WBT.

Clodd (Edward). See MN.

Coillard (François). See TCA.

CPP. CREDULITIES PAST AND PRESENT: Including the Sea and Seamen, Miners, Amulets and Talismans, Rings, Word and Letter Divination, Numbers, Trials, Exorcising and Blessing of Animals, Birds, Eggs, and Luck. By William Jones, F.S.A. (London: Chatto and Windus. 1880.) Cited on pp. 155, 181, 222, 226, 291.

Crawford (D.). THINKING BLACK: 22 Years Without a Break in the Long Grass of Central Africa. By D. Crawford, F.R.G.S. (London: Morgan and Scott, Ltd. MCMXII.) Cited on p. 343.

Crawford (O. G. S.). Article in the *Journal of the Royal Geographical Society*. (London: May, 1923.) Cited on p. 70.

Cumont (Franz). See ALRP.

CSBSL. A COMPARATIVE STUDY OF THE BANTU AND SEMI-BANTU LANGUAGES. By Sir Harry Johnston. (Oxford: Clarendon Press. Vol. I, 1919; Vol. II, 1922.) Cited on pp. 43, 175, 221, 341, 343, 347.

Davenport (Frederick). PRIMITIVE TRAITS IN RELIGIOUS REVIVALS. By Frederick Morgan Davenport. (The Macmillan Company. 1905.) Cited on p. 131.

DDA. DAWN IN DARKEST AFRICA. By John H. Harris. (London: Smith, Elder & Co. 1912.) Cited on pp. 22, 269.

Decle (Lionel). THREE YEARS IN SAVAGE AFRICA. By Lionel Decle. Second edition. (London: Methuen & Co. 1898.) Cited on p. 158.

Dennett (Richard Edward). Article in *Church Quarterly Review.* (London: January, 1921.)
Cited on pp. 287, 313.
SEVEN YEARS AMONG THE FJORT (FRENCH CONGO): Being an English Trader's Experiences in the Congo District. By R. E. Dennett. (London: S. Low, Marston, Searle & Rivington. 1887.)
Cited on p. 310. See also BBMM.

Doré (Henry). RESEARCHES INTO CHINESE SUPERSTITION. By Henry Doré, S.J. (Shanghai: Tusevei Printing Press. 1914.)
Cited on p. 79.

Driberg (J. H.). THE LANGO: A Nilotic Tribe of Uganda. By J. H. Driberg. (London: T. Fisher Unwin. 1923.)
Cited on p. 20.

Dundas (Hon. Charles). See K.

ECSA. ETHNOGRAPHY AND CONDITION OF SOUTH AFRICA BEFORE A.D. 1505. By George McAll Theal, Litt.D., LL.D. Second edition of the present form (illustrated), enlarged and improved. (London: George Allen and Unwin, Ltd. 1919.)
Cited on pp. 19, 27, 236, 291, 297, 342.

Edwards (Sam.). Article in *Journal of the South African Folk-lore Society.* (Cape Town: March, 1880.)
Cited on p. 279.

EK. THE ESSENTIAL KAFIR. By Dudley Kidd. (London: Adam and Charles Black. 1904.)
Cited on pp. 61, 148, 234, 235, 263, 264, 334, 344, 358, 362.

Ellenberger (Rev. D. F.). See HB.

Ellis (George W.). NEGRO CULTURE IN WEST AFRICA, etc., etc. By George W. Ellis, K.C., F.R.G.S. (New York: The Neale Publishing Company. 1914.)
Cited on p. 70.

EM. EGYPTIAN MAGIC. By E. A. Wallis Budge, M.A., Litt.D., D.Lit. Keeper of the Egyptian and Assyrian Antiquities in the British Museum. Second impression. (London: Kegan Paul, Trench, Trübner & Co., Ltd. 1901.)
Cited on pp. 2, 17, 23, 34, 92, 140, 151, 153, 285, 367, 368.

Encyclopædia Biblica.
Cited on p. 236.

Encyclopædia Britannica.
Cited on p. 347.

EPF. ON THE EDGE OF THE PRIMEVAL FOREST: Experiences and Observations of a Doctor in Equatorial Africa. By Prof. Albert Schweitzer, Dr. Theol., Dr. Med., Dr. Phil. (Strassburg). (London: A. & C. Black, Ltd. 1922.)
Cited on pp. 257, 326.

Evans (Sir Arthur). THE RING OF NESTOR: A Glimpse into the Minoan After-world. By Sir Arthur Evans. (London: Macmillan & Co. 1925.) Cited on p. 155.

HANDBOOK OF THE UGANDA PROTECTORATE: Prepared by the Geographical Section of the Naval Intelligence Division, Naval Staff, Admiralty. (London: H. M. Stationery Office. I. D. 1217. Undated.) Cited on p. 347.

Harris (John H.). See DDA.

Harrison (Jane Ellen). PROLEGOMENA TO THE STUDY OF GREEK RELIGION. By Jane Ellen Harrison. (Cambridge: University Press. 1903.) Cited on pp. 154, 155.

Hobley (C. W.). See AK., BBM.

Hooper (H. D.). AFRICA IN THE MAKING. By H. D. Hooper. (London: Church Missionary Society. 1922.) Cited on p. 137.

HB. HISTORY OF THE BASUTO, ANCIENT AND MODERN. Compiled by the Rev. D. F. Ellenberger, and written in English by J. C. Macgregor. (London: Caxton Publishing Company. 1913.) Cited on pp. 3, 14, 73, 94, 180, 182, 186, 187, 198, 213, 251, 290, 344, 351, 357, 359, 361, 388, 392.

Hilton-Simpson (L. W.). See LPK.

HISTORY OF THE YORUBAS: From the Earliest Times to the Beginning of the British Protectorate. By the Rev. Samuel Johnson, Pastor of Oyọ. (London: George Routledge & Sons, Ltd. 1921.) Cited on pp. 31, 70, 169.

HM. THE HISTORY OF MANKIND. By Professor Friedrich Ratzel. Vols. 3. (London: Macmillan & Co. 1896.) Cited on p. 169.

HNT. HOW NATIVES THINK (Les Fonctions Mentales Dans Les Sociétés Inferieures). By Prof. Lucien Lévy-Bruhl of the Sorbonne. Authorised Translation by Lilian A. Clare. (London: George Allen & Unwin, Ltd. 1926.) Cited on p. 430.

IHB. IN THE HEART OF BANTULAND. By Dugald Campbell. (London: Seeley, Service & Co., Ltd. 1921.) Cited on pp. 24, 63, 68, 86, 157, 165, 171, 293, 324, 325, 326, 360.

IPNR. THE ILA-SPEAKING PEOPLES OF NORTHERN RHODESIA. By Edwin W. Smith and A. Murray Dale. Vols. 2. (London: Macmillan & Co., Ltd. 1920.) Cited on pp. 3, 9, 13, 15, 19, 20, 24, 30, 33, 40, 53, 57, 68, 69, 77, 84, 93, 95, 107, 110, 113, 114, 121, 140, 141, 143, 149, 158, 162, 172, 173, 176, 179, 181, 182, 185, 190, 194, 198, 199, 200, 201, 224, 245, 249, 255, 257, 260, 265, 266, 267, 273, 292, 301, 340, 365, 366, 370, 373, 429.

IRM. INTERNATIONAL REVIEW OF MISSIONS. (London and New York: Humphrey Milford.) Cited on pp. 85, 123, 188, 242, 269, 371, 375.

Johnson (Ven. William Percival). See NGW.

Johnson (Rev. Samuel). See HISTORY OF THE YORUBAS.

Johnston (Sir Harry H.). THE RIVER CONGO, FROM ITS MOUTH TO BÓLÓBÓ: With a General Description of the Natural History and Anthropology of Its Western Basin. By H. H. Johnston, F.Z.S., F.R.G.S. Third edition. (London: Sampson Low, Marston, Searle & Rivington. 1884.)
Cited on p. 21. See also CSBSL., GGC.

JRAI. *Journal of the Royal Anthropological Institute of Great Britain and Ireland.* (London: Published by the Institute in January and July.)
Cited on pp. 11, 15, 34, 41, 56, 70, 72, 185, 195, 199, 225, 262, 269, 271, 288, 296, 345, 349, 364.

Journal of the South African Folk-lore Society. (Cape Town. Last issue dated July, 1880.)
Cited on pp. 18, 36, 183, 190, 279, 294, 357.

Junod (Henri A.). See LSAT.

K. KILIMANJARO AND ITS PEOPLE: A History of the Wachagga, Their Laws, Customs and Legends, Together with Some Account of the Highest Mountain in Africa. By the Honourable Charles Dundas, F.R.A.I., O.B.E. (Senior Commissioner, Tanganyika Territory). (London: H. F. & G. Witherby. 1924.)
Cited on pp. 28, 41, 43, 57, 80, 81, 83, 84, 96, 189, 195, 290, 349, 350, 353, 361, 365.

Kidd (Dudley). See EK., SC.

Kingsley (Mary H.). Article in *Folk-lore.*
Cited on p. 315. See also TWA., WAS.

KM. KINSHIP AND MARRIAGE IN EARLY ARABIA. By W. Robertson Smith, M.A., LL.D. (London: A. & C. Black. 1903.)
Cited on p. 278.

KNZC. THE KAFIRS OF NATAL AND THE ZULU COUNTRY. By the Rev. Joseph Shooter. (London: E. Stanford. 1857.)
Cited on pp. 18, 47, 56, 235, 237.

Krapf (Rev. Dr. J. Lewis). See TRML.

Krapf and Rebmann. A NIKA-ENGLISH DICTIONARY: Compiled by the late Dr. L. Krapf and the late Rev. J. Rebmann, Missionaries of the Church Missionary Society in East Africa. Edited by the Rev. T. H. Sparshott, formerly Missionary of the Church Missionary Society in East Africa. (London: S.P.C.K. 1887.)
Cited on pp. 181, 221.

KT. THE BAKITARA OR BANYORO: The First Part of the Report of the Mackie Ethnological Expedition to Central Africa. By John Roscoe, M.A. (Cambridge: University Press. 1923.)
Cited on pp. 272, 283, 292, 326, 342, 346.

LA. LIGHT IN AFRICA. By the Rev. James Macdonald. (London: Hodder and Stoughton. 1890.)
Cited on pp. 24, 27, 97, 182, 351, 354, 358.

Lane (Edward William). See MCME.

LC. THE LANDS OF CAZEMBE: Lacerda's Journey to Cazembe in 1798, Translated and Annotated by Capt. R. F. Burton; Also Journey of the Pombeiros, P. J. Baptista and Amaro Jose, Across Africa from Angola to Tette on the Zambese, Translated by B. A. Beadle; And a Résumé of the Journey of MM. Monteiro and Gamitto by Dr. C. T. Beke. (Published by the Royal Geographical Society.) (London: John Murray. 1873.)
Cited on pp. 281, 301.

LeRoy (Most Rev. Alexander). See RP.

Lerrigo (Dr. P. H. J.). Articles in *Mission News* and in IRM.
Cited on p. 123.

Lévy-Bruhl (Prof. Lucien). See HNT.

Livingstone (Dr. David). See MTR., LLJ.

LLJ. LIVINGSTONE'S LAST JOURNALS.
Cited on pp. 302, 426.

Lodge (Sir Oliver J.). RAYMOND: Life and Death, With Examples of the Evidence for Survival of Memory and Affection After Death. By Sir Oliver J. Lodge. (New York: George H. Doran Company. 1916.)
Cited on pp. 75, 418.

LPK. THE LAND AND PEOPLES OF THE KASAI. By L. W. Hilton-Simpson, F.R.G.S., F.R.A.I. (London: Constable and Company, Ltd. 1911.)
Cited on pp. 139, 267, 323.

LSAT. THE LIFE OF A SOUTH AFRICAN TRIBE. By Henri A. Junod. Vols. 2. (Neuchatel: Imprimerie Attinger Freres. 1912.)
Cited on pp. 3, 10, 13, 19, 30, 58, 61, 66, 80, 95, 107, 111, 137, 148, 161, 180, 184, 188, 191, 196, 198, 201, 241, 242, 243, 255, 256, 263, 270, 273, 293, 297, 329, 330, 334, 338, 340, 343, 344, 349, 350, 352, 353, 355, 357, 358, 359, 360, 361, 362, 365, 370, 373, 393, 400, 435.

Lyne (Robert Nunez). ZANZIBAR IN CONTEMPORARY TIMES: A Short History of the Southern East in the Nineteenth Century. By Robert Nunez Lyne. (London: Hurst & Blackett, Ltd. 1905.)
Cited on p. 144.

Mabille (A.). SE-SUTO—ENGLISH AND ENGLISH—SE-SUTO VOCABULARY. By A. Mabille. (Khatiso ea Morija. 1893.)
Cited on p. 110.

Macdonald (Rev. Duff). See A.

Macdonald (Dr. Duncan Black). THE RELIGIOUS ATTITUDE AND LIFE IN ISLAM: Being the Haskell Lectures on Comparative Religion Delivered Before the University of Chicago in 1906. By Duncan Black Macdonald, M.A., B.D. (The University of Chicago Press. Second impression. 1912.)
Cited on pp. 92, 145.

Macdonald (Rev. James). See LA.

MacKenzie (D. R.). See SRK.

Marett (Dr. R. R.). Psychology and Folk-lore. By R. R. Marett, M.A., D.Sc., Fellow and Tutor of Exeter College, Oxford; University Reader in Social Anthropology. (London: Methuen & Co., Ltd. 1920.)
Cited on p. xxiv.
The Threshold of Religion. By R. R. Marett, etc., etc. Second edition. (London: Methuen & Co., Ltd. 1914.)
Cited on p. xxv.

Masefield (John). The Poems and Plays of John Masefield. (New York: The Macmillan Company. 1918.)
Cited on p. 129.

Masters (Henry and Dr. Walter). See WR.

MCME. The Manners and Customs of the Modern Egyptians. By Edward William Lane. No. 315 of Dent's Everyman's Library.
Cited on pp. 32, 42, 92, 95, 110, 138, 145, 366, 369.

Melland (Frank H.). See WBA.

Merolla (Father Jerom). A Voyage to Congo and Several Other Countries Chiefly in Southern Africa. By Father Jerom Merolla da Sorrento, a Capuchin and Apostolick Missioner in the Year 1682. Made English from the Italian. [Included in C.]
Cited on p. 46.

Methuen (Henry H.). Life in the Wilderness: Or Wanderings in South Africa. By Henry H. Methuen. Second edition. (London: Richard Bentley. 1848.)
Cited on p. 114.

Migeod (F. W. H.). Interviewed by The Worthing Herald.
Cited on p. 288.

Miles (Clement A.). Christmas in Ritual and Tradition, Christian and Pagan. By Clement A. Miles. (London: T. Fisher Unwin. 1912.)
Cited on pp. 140, 405, 407.

MLC. Mashona Laws and Customs. By Charles Bullock, Acting Native Commissioner and Special Justice of the Peace, Darwin District, Southern Rhodesia. (Salisbury, Rhodesia: Argus Printing and Publishing Co., Ltd. 1913.)
Cited on pp. 8, 21, 30, 37, 162, 184, 188, 342, 346, 367, 375.

MN. Magic in Names and in Other Things. By Edward Clood. (London: Chapman and Hall, Ltd. 1920.)
Cited on p. 184.

Moffat (John Smith). Lives of Robert and Mary Moffat. By John S. Moffat. Third edition. (London: T. Fisher Unwin. 1885.)
Cited on p. 300.

Moffat (Dr. Robert). Missionary Labours and Scenes in Southern Africa. By Robert Moffat. Ninth thousand. (London: John Snow. 1842.)
Cited on p. 299.

Monteiro (Joachim John). See ARC.

Moore (George Foot). THE BIRTH AND GROWTH OF RELIGION: Being the Morse Lectures of 1922. By George Foot Moore, Professor of the History of Religion in Harvard University. (New York: Charles Scribner's Sons. 1923.)
Cited on pp. 226, 385, 411.

Moss (Rosalind). LIFE AFTER DEATH IN OCEANIA AND THE MALAY ARCHIPELAGO. By Rosalind Moss, B.Sc. (Oxon.). (Oxford: Clarendon Press. 1925.)
Cited on p. 43.

MTR. MISSIONARY TRAVELS AND RESEARCHES IN SOUTH AFRICA. By David Livingstone, LL.D., D.C.L. (London: John Murray. 1857.)
Cited on pp. 25, 49, 162, 206, 259, 275, 300, 301.

NADA: The Southern Rhodesia Native Affairs Department Annual. (Salisbury, Southern Rhodesia.)
Cited on p. 341.

Nassau (Rev. W. Hammill). See FWA.

NATIVE TRIBES OF SOUTH AUSTRALIA. (Adelaide: E. S. Wigg & Son. 1879.)
Cited on p. 55.

NBCA. THE NATIVES OF BRITISH CENTRAL AFRICA. By A. Werner. (London: Archibald Constable and Company, Ltd. 1906.)
Cited on pp. 14, 17, 21, 49, 61, 98, 141, 164, 303, 331.

NET. NARRATIVE OF AN EXPLORATORY TOUR TO THE NORTH-EAST OF THE COLONY OF THE CAPE OF GOOD HOPE. By the Revs. T. Arbousset and F. Daumas of the Paris Missionary Society. Translated from the French of the Rev. T. Arbousset by John Croumbie Brown. (London: John C. Bishop. 1852.)
Cited on pp. 58, 382.

NGW. NYASA THE GREAT WATER: Being a Description of the Lake and the Life of the People. By the Ven. William Percival Johnson, D.D., Archdeacon of Nyasa. (Oxford: Humphrey Milford, Oxford University Press. 1922.)
Cited on pp. 25, 139, 164, 181.

NLEA. NATIVE LIFE IN EAST AFRICA: The Results of an Ethnological Research Expedition. By Dr. Karl Weule, Director of the Leipzig Ethnographical Museum and Professor at the University of Leipzig. Translated by Alice Werner. (New York: D. Appleton and Company. 1909.)
Cited on p. 268.

NTG. THE NATIVES OF THE NORTHERN TERRITORIES OF THE GOLD COAST: Their Customs, Religion and Folklore. By A. W. Cardinall. (London: George Routledge & Sons, Ltd. New York: E. P. Dutton & Co. Undated, but probably 1920.)
Cited on pp. 32, 142, 169, 185, 196, 286, 287, 313.

NYN. THE BANYANKOLE: The Second Part of the Report of the Mackie Ethnological Expedition to Central Africa. By John Roscoe, M.A. (Cambridge: University Press. 1923.)
Cited on pp. 272, 326, 342.

O'Neil (Owen Rowe). ADVENTURES IN SWAZILAND: The Story of a South African Boer. By Owen Rowe O'Neil. (London: George Allen and Unwin, Ltd. Undated, but copyright 1921.)
Cited on p. 53.

Oxenham (John). BEES IN AMBER.
Cited on p. xxv.

Paton (Dr. Lewis Bayles). See SCD.

PC. PIONEERING ON THE CONGO. By the Rev. W. Holman Bentley. Vols. 2. (London: Religious Tract Society. New York: The Fleming H. Revell Company. 1900.)
Cited on pp. 23, 28, 33, 52, 149, 321.

Petrie (Dr. W. M. Flinders). A Lecture delivered in Brighton, England.
Cited on p. 151.
A HISTORY OF EGYPT FROM THE EARLIEST TIMES TO THE XVITH DYNASTY. By W. M. Flinders Petrie, D.C.L., LL.D. Third edition. (London: Methuen & Co. 1897.)
Cited on p. 342.
RELIGION AND CONSCIENCE IN ANCIENT EGYPT. Lectures delivered at University College, London. By W. M. Flinders Petrie, D.C.L., LL.D., Ph.D. (London: Methuen & Co. 1898.)
Cited on p. 153. See also RLAE.

Pliny the Younger.
Cited on p. 36.

PP. WITH A PREHISTORIC PEOPLE: The Akikuyu of British East Africa; Being Some Account of the Method of Life and Mode of Thought Found Existent Amongst a Nation on its First Contact with European Civilization. By W. Scoresby Routledge, M.A. (Oxon.) and Katherine Routledge, Som. Coll. (Oxon.); M.A. (Trin. Coll., Dublin. (London: Edward Arnold. 1910.)
Cited on pp. 114, 137, 167, 285.

Quatrefages (Prof. A. De). THE PYGMIES. By A. D. Quatrefages, late Professor of Anthropology at the Museum of Natural History, Paris. Translated by Frederick Starr. (New York: D. Appleton and Company. 1895.)
Cited on pp. 3, 294.

R., 1883. REPORT AND PROCEEDINGS, WITH APPENDICES, OF THE GOVERNMENT COMMISSION ON NATIVE LAWS AND CUSTOMS. (Cape Town: W. A. Richards and Sons, Government Printers. 1883.)
Cited on pp. 120, 159, 189, 235, 237.

RA. THE RELIGION OF THE AFRICANS. By the Rev. Henry Rowley. (London: W. Wells Gardiner. Undated.)
Cited on pp. 6, 22, 25, 378.

RAA. RELIGION AND ART IN ASHANTI. By Capt. R. S. Rattray, M.B.E., B.Sc. (Oxon.). (Oxford: Clarendon Press. 1927.)
Cited on pp. 93, 426.

RAC. THE RELIGION OF THE ANCIENT CELTS. By J. A. MacCulloch, Hon. D.D. (St. Andrews); Hon. Canon of Cumbrae Cathedral. (Edinburgh: T. & T. Clark. 1911.)
Cited on pp. 16, 29, 45, 72, 92, 106, 156, 158, 163, 204, 234, 285, 328, 409.

Rattray (Capt. R. S.). See AS., RAA.

Ratzel (Prof. Frederich). See HM., EM.

R.BAAS. REPORT OF THE BRITISH ASSOCIATION FOR THE ADVANCEMENT OF SCIENCE, SOUTH AFRICA, 1905. (Published by the South African Association for the Advancement of Science, Johannesburg.) Vols. 4.
Cited on pp. 57, 184, 222, 244, 297, 338, 350.

Rebmann (Rev. J.). See Krapf.

RLAE. RELIGIOUS LIFE IN ANCIENT EGYPT. By Sir Flinders Petrie, F.R.S., F.B.A. (London: Constable & Company. 1924.)
Cited on pp. 26, 33, 41, 44, 92, 136, 266, 267, 339, 342, 348, 350, 377, 404.

RLR. THE RELIGION OF THE LOWER RACES: As Illustrated by the African Bantu. By Edwin W. Smith. (New York: The Macmillan Co. 1923.)
Cited on pp. 181, 380, 400.

Ravenstein (E. G.). See SAAB.

Roberts (Rev. Noel). Article in the *South African Journal of Science.*
Cited on p. 221.

Roscoe (Rev. John). See Bg., GS., KT., NYN., SCA.

Routledge (W. Scoresby and Katherine). See PP.

Rowley (Rev. Henry). See RA., UMCA.

RP. THE RELIGION OF THE PRIMITIVES. By Most Rev. Alexander LeRoy, Superior General of the Fathers of the Holy Ghost. (New York: The Macmillan Company. 1922.)
Cited on pp. 9, 10, 14, 20, 26, 51, 112, 162, 167, 216, 268, 270, 311, 313, 329, 335, 339, 354, 359, 361, 365, 367, 371, 372, 373, 381, 383, 385.

RS. LECTURES ON THE RELIGION OF THE SEMITES. By the late W. Robertson Smith, M.A., LL.D. (London: Adam and Charles Black. 1901.)
Cited on pp. xviii, 153, 161, 225, 226, 278, 347, 348.

RSZ. THE RELIGIOUS SYSTEM OF THE AMAZULU: Izinyanga Zokubula: Or, Divination as Existing Among the Amazulu in Their Own Words with a Translation into English and Notes. By the Rev. Canon Callaway, M.D., Loc. Sec. A.S.L. (Natal: John A. Blair, Springvale; Davis and Sons, Pietermaritzburg; Adams & Co., Durban. Cape Town: J. C. Juta. London: Trübner and Co. 1870.)
Cited on pp. 45, 47, 64, 83, 93, 94, 96, 102, 113, 114, 137, 142, 146, 147, 149, 159, 160, 161, 181, 190, 214, 235, 238, 263, 334, 344, 349, 352, 357, 358, 360, 366, 369, 398, 426, 429.

SAAB. THE STRANGE ADVENTURES OF ANDREW BATTELL OF LEIGH IN ANGOLA AND THE ADJOINING REGIONS. Reprinted from "Purchas His Pilgrimes." Edited with Notes and a Concise History of Kongo and Angola, by E. G. Ravenstein. (London: Printed for the Hakluyt Society. 1901.)
Cited on pp. 46, 219, 262, 306, 307, 308, 337, 365.

SC. SAVAGE CHILDHOOD. By Dudley Kidd. (London: Adam and Charles Black. 1906.)
Cited on pp. 15, 147, 176, 182, 273, 360, 362.

SCA. THE SOUL OF CENTRAL AFRICA. By the Rev. John Roscoe, Hon. M.A. (Camb.). (London: Cassell and Company, Ltd. 1922.)
Cited on pp. 87, 139, 145, 168, 199, 272, 283, 292, 326, 363.

SCD. SPIRITISM AND THE CULT OF THE DEAD IN ANTIQUITY. By Lewis Bayles Paton, Ph.D., D.D. (New York: Macmillan. 1921.)
Cited on pp. 17, 23, 27, 31, 35, 39, 41, 44, 72, 75, 92, 107, 153, 155, 266, 397.

Schweitzer (Prof. Albert). See EPF.

Scott (Rev. D. C.). CYCLOPÆDIC DICTIONARY OF MANG'ANJA. (London: Blackwood. 1892.)
Cited on p. 216.

Seebohm (Dr. Frederic). See TCASL.

Shaw (Mabel). Article in *The Chronicle of the London Missionary Society.*
Cited on p. 14.

Shaw (William). THE STORY OF MY MISSION IN SOUTH EASTERN AFRICA, comprising Some Account of the European Colonists; with Extended Notices of the Kaffir and Other Native Tribes. By William Shaw, late Wesleyan General Superintendent in that country. (London: Hamilton, Adams & Co. 1860.)
Cited on pp. 48, 147, 182, 362.

Sheane (Hubert). See GPNR.

Shooter (Rev. Joseph). See KNZC.

Smith (Edwin W.). See IPNR., RLR., GLD.

Smith (G. Elliot). THE EVOLUTION OF MAN: ESSAYS. By G. Elliot Smith, M.A., M.D., Litt.D., D.Sc., F.R.C.P., F.R.S. (Oxford: Humphrey Milford. Reprinted November, 1924.)
Cited on pp. 34, 425.

Smith (W. Robertson). See KM., RS.

South African Journal of Science.
Cited on p. 221.

Southern Workman, The.
Cited on p. 203.

Speke (John Hanning). *Journal of the Discovery of the Source of the Nile.* By John Hanning Speke. (No. 50 in Dent's EVERYMAN'S LIBRARY.)
Cited on p. 166.

SRK. The Spirit-ridden Konde: A Record of the Interesting but Steadily Vanishing Customs & Ideas Gathered During Twenty-four Years' Residence Amongst These Shy Inhabitants of the Lake Nyasa Region, from Witch-doctors, Diviners, Hunters, Fishers & Every Native Source. By D. R. MacKenzie, F.R.G.S. (London: Seeley, Service & Co., Ltd. 1925.)
Cited on pp. 25, 32, 34, 38, 56, 62, 63, 69, 85, 108, 109, 113, 132, 139, 140, 148, 164, 165, 173, 180, 184, 194, 200, 216, 246, 247, 256, 261, 265, 267, 292, 304, 335, 351, 364, 365, 366, 367, 375, 376, 388, 391.

Story of Chisamba. By Herbert W. Baker. (Toronto: Canada Foreign Missionary Society. 1904.)
Cited on pp. 54, 293.

Swann (Alfred J.). Fighting the Slave-hunters in Central Africa: A Record of Twenty-six Years of Travel and Adventure Round the Great Lakes and of the Overthrow of Tip-pu-tib, Rumaliza and Other Great Slave-traders. By Alfred J. Swann, Late Senior Resident Magistrate of the Nyasaland Protectorate. (London: Seeley, Service & Co., Ltd. 1910.)
Cited on pp. 303, 304.

TCA. On the Threshold of Central Africa: A Record of Twenty Years Pioneering Among the Barotsi of the Upper Zambesi. By François Coillard. (London: Hodder and Stoughton. 1897.)
Cited on p. 265.

TCASL. Tribal Custom in Anglo-Saxon Law: Being an Essay Supplemental to (1) "The English Village Community," (2) "The Tribal System in Wales." By Frederic Seebohm, LL.D., F.S.A. (London, New York and Bombay: Longmans, Green & Co. 1902.)
Cited on p. 285.

Theal (George M.). Compendium of South African History and Geography. By George M. Theal. Second edition. Vols. 2. (Lovedale, South Africa: The Institution Press. 1876.)
Cited on pp. 116, 117. See also ECSA.

Thomas (Thomas Morgan). Eleven Years in Central South Africa: A Journey into the Interior—Sketch of Recently Discovered Diamond and Gold Fields—Umzilikazi, His Country and People—A Brief History of the Zambesi Missions. By Thomas Morgan Thomas of the London Missionary Society. (London: John Snow and Co. 1872.)
Cited on p. 239.

Tooke (Hammond). Article in *The African Monthly.*
Cited on p. 294.

Transactions of the Asiatic Society of Japan. (Yokohama: Meiklejohn & Co.)
Cited on pp. 17, 45.

TRML. Travels, Researches, and Missionary Labours, During an Eighteen Years' Residence in Eastern Africa: Together with Journeys to Jagga, Usambara, Shoa, Abessinia, and Khartum; and a Coasting

Voyage from Mombaz to Cape Delgado. By the Rev. Dr. J. Lewis Krapf, etc., etc. (London: Trübner & Co. 1860.)
Cited on pp. 172, 215, 218, 221, 343.

TWA. TRAVELS IN WEST AFRICA, CONGO FRANCAIS, CORISCO AND CAMEROONS. By Mary H. Kingsley. Second edition. (London: Macmillan and Co., Ltd. 1904.)
Cited on pp. 7, 14, 26, 33, 34, 39, 74, 144, 158, 168.

Tyler (Rev. Josiah). FORTY YEARS AMONG THE ZULUS. By the Rev. Josiah Tyler. (Boston: Congregational Publishing Society.)
Cited on pp. 48, 426.

Tylor (Dr. Edward B.). RESEARCHES INTO THE EARLY HISTORY OF MANKIND AND THE DEVELOPMENT OF CIVILIZATION. By Edward B. Tylor, D.C.L., LL.D., F.R.S. Third edition. (London: John Murray. 1878.)
Cited on p. 3.
ANTHROPOLOGY: An Introduction to the Study of Man and Civilization. By Edward B. Tylor, D.C.L., F.R.S. (London: Macmillan & Co., Ltd. 1881.)
Cited on pp. 3, 46.

UMCA. THE STORY OF THE UNIVERSITIES' MISSION TO CENTRAL AFRICA. By the Rev. Henry Rowley. (London: Saunders, Otley and Co. 1866.)
Cited on pp. 49, 114, 141, 164.

Underwood (Dr. Alfred Clair). CONVERSION: CHRISTIAN AND NON-CHRISTIAN. By Alfred Clair Underwood, D.D. (London: Allen and Unwin. 1925.)
Cited on pp. 104, 127, 128.

Viehe (Rev. G.). Article in the *Journal of the South African Folk-lore Society.*
Cited on pp. 18, 36.

WA. WESTERN AFRICA: Its History, Condition and Prospects. By the Rev. J. Leighton Wilson, eighteen years a Missionary in Africa, and now one of the Secretaries of the Presbyterian Board of Foreign Missions. (New York: Harper & Brothers. 1856.)
Cited on pp. 93, 312, 328, 380.

WAS. WEST AFRICAN STUDIES. By Mary H. Kingsley. Second edition. (London: Macmillan & Co., Ltd. 1901.)
Cited on pp. 144, 170, 314.

WBA. IN WITCH-BOUND AFRICA: An Account of the Primitive Kaonde Tribe and Their Beliefs. By Frank H. Melland, B.A. (Oxon.), Magistrate for the Kasempa District, Northern Rhodesia, 1911-1922. (London: Seeley, Service & Co., Ltd. 1921.)
Cited on pp. 11, 12, 21, 25, 40, 56, 68, 80, 87, 94, 138, 140, 141, 143, 150, 157, 163, 173, 174, 180, 202, 246, 249, 251, 257, 261, 272, 292, 305, 338, 431.

WBT. WILD BUSH TRIBES OF CENTRAL AFRICA. By G. Cyril Claridge. (London: Seeley, Service & Co., Ltd. 1921.)
Cited on pp. 2, 4, 23, 39, 41, 62, 78, 168, 170, 195, 257, 262, 312, 323, 324, 340, 360, 367, 369, 373.

Weeks (John H.). CONGO LIFE AND FOLKLORE. By the Rev. John H. Weeks. (London: Religious Tract Society. 1911.)
Cited on p. 63. See also ACC.

Werner (A.). See NBCA.

Weston (Jessie L.). THE QUEST OF THE HOLY GRAIL. By Jessie L. Weston. (London: G. Bell & Sons, Ltd. 1913.)
Cited on p. 59.

Weule (Dr. Karl). See NLEA.

Wiedemann (Dr. Alfred). RELIGION OF THE ANCIENT EGYPTIANS. By Alfred Wiedemann, Ph.D., Professor in the University of Bonn. (London: H. Grevel & Co. 1897.)
Cited on p. 64.

Wilder (Dr. George Albert). Articles in the *Hartford Seminary Record*.
Cited on pp. 13, 37, 64, 69, 183, 188, 245.

Willoughby (Rev. W. C.). "Notes on the Totemism of the Becwana" in JRAI.
Cited on p. 248.
RACE PROBLEMS IN THE NEW AFRICA. By the Rev. W. C. Willoughby, F.R.A.I., F.R.G.S. (Oxford: Clarendon Press. 1923.)
Cited on p. 65.

Wilson (Rev. J. Leighton). See WA.

WN. THE WORSHIP OF NATURE. By Sir James George Frazer, O.M., F.R.S., F.B.A., Fellow of Trinity College, Cambridge. (London: Macmillan & Co., Ltd. 1926.)
Cited on pp. 3, 61.

WPP. WINNING A PRIMITIVE PEOPLE: Sixteen Years' Work Among the Primitive Tribes of the Ngoni and the Senga and Tambuka Peoples of Central Africa. By Donald Fraser, with introduction by John R. Mott, LL.B., F.R.G.S. (London: Seeley, Service & Co., Ltd. 1914.)
Cited on pp. 21, 27, 38, 57, 69, 72, 73, 94, 135, 164, 271, 347, 389.

WR. IN WILD RHODESIA. By Henry Masters and Walter Masters, M.D., D.D., M.R.C.S. (London: Francis Griffiths. 1920.)
Cited on p. 50.

Yorubas. See HISTORY OF THE YORUBAS.

Lightning Source UK Ltd.
Milton Keynes UK
UKHW041549190420
361941UK00017B/446